HR Analytics in an Era of Rapid Automation

Radha Yadav
CHRIST University, India

Mudita Sinha
CHRIST University, India

Joseph Varghese Kureethara
CHRIST University, India

A volume in the Advances in Human Resources Management and Organizational Development (AHRMOD) Book Series

IGI Global
PUBLISHER of TIMELY KNOWLEDGE

Published in the United States of America by
IGI Global
Business Science Reference (an imprint of IGI Global)
701 E. Chocolate Avenue
Hershey PA, USA 17033
Tel: 717-533-8845
Fax: 717-533-8661
E-mail: cust@igi-global.com
Web site: http://www.igi-global.com

Library of Congress Cataloging-in-Publication Data

Names: Yadav, Radha, 1989- editor. | Sinha, Mudita, 1982- editor. | Kureethara, Joseph Varghese, editor.
Title: HR analytics in an era of rapid automation / edited by: Radha Yadav, Mudita Sinha, and Joseph Varghese Kureethara.
Description: Hershey PA : Business Science Reference, [2023] | Includes bibliographical references. | Summary: "HR Analytics in an Era of Rapid Automation is a valuable guide for academics, researchers, and practitioners interested in the latest developments in HR analytics. It covers relevant theories and conceptual models based on quantitative and qualitative findings, and emphasizes the importance of utilizing HR analytics for sustainable decision-making. With a focus on recruitment analytics, talent acquisition, employee performance analytics, and more, this book provides practical solutions to the challenges facing HR professionals in the rapidly changing business world. By highlighting the value of people and HR analytics for business success, this book offers several solutions for the analysis of challenges facing HR professionals today"-- Provided by publisher.
Identifiers: LCCN 2023021231 (print) | LCCN 2023021232 (ebook) | ISBN 9781668489420 (hardcover) | ISBN 9781668489437 (paperback) | ISBN 9781668489444 (ebook)
Subjects: LCSH: Personnel management--Data processing. | Personnel management--Statistical methods. | Personnel management--Decision making.
Classification: LCC HF5549.5.D37 H84 2023 (print) | LCC HF5549.5.D37 (ebook) | DDC 658.300285--dc23/eng/20230615
LC record available at https://lccn.loc.gov/2023021231
LC ebook record available at https://lccn.loc.gov/2023021232

This book is published in the IGI Global book series Advances in Human Resources Management and Organizational Development (AHRMOD) (ISSN: 2327-3372; eISSN: 2327-3380)

British Cataloguing in Publication Data
A Cataloguing in Publication record for this book is available from the British Library.

Advances in Human Resources Management and Organizational Development (AHRMOD) Book Series

Patricia Ordóñez de Pablos
Universidad de Oviedo, Spain

ISSN:2327-3372
EISSN:2327-3380

Mission

A solid foundation is essential to the development and success of any organization and can be accomplished through the effective and careful management of an organization's human capital. Research in human resources management and organizational development is necessary in providing business leaders with the tools and methodologies which will assist in the development and maintenance of their organizational structure.

The **Advances in Human Resources Management and Organizational Development (AHRMOD) Book Series** aims to publish the latest research on all aspects of human resources as well as the latest methodologies, tools, and theories regarding organizational development and sustainability. The **AHRMOD Book Series** intends to provide business professionals, managers, researchers, and students with the necessary resources to effectively develop and implement organizational strategies.

Coverage

- Organizational Learning
- Outsourcing HR
- Employee Benefits
- Succession Planning
- Workplace Culture
- Collaborative Method
- Skills Management
- Corporate Governance
- Employee Evaluation
- Job Enrichment

IGI Global is currently accepting manuscripts for publication within this series. To submit a proposal for a volume in this series, please contact our Acquisition Editors at Acquisitions@igi-global.com or visit: http://www.igi-global.com/publish/.

The Advances in Human Resources Management and Organizational Development (AHRMOD) Book Series (ISSN 2327-3372) is published by IGI Global, 701 E. Chocolate Avenue, Hershey, PA 17033-1240, USA, www.igi-global.com. This series is composed of titles available for purchase individually; each title is edited to be contextually exclusive from any other title within the series. For pricing and ordering information please visit http://www.igi-global.com/book-series/advances-human-resources-management-organizational/73670. Postmaster: Send all address changes to above address.

Titles in this Series

For a list of additional titles in this series, please visit:
www.igi-global.com/book-series/advances-human-resources-management-organizational/73670

Policies, Protocols, and Standards for Professionalism in a Diverse Work Environment
Christiana Bevier (Purdue University Global, USA) Barry Regan (Purdue University Global, USA) and Carolyn N. Stevenson (Purdue University Global, USA)
Business Science Reference • copyright 2023 • 324pp • H/C (ISBN: 9781668473085) • US $225.00 (our price)

Measuring the Effectiveness of Organizational Development Strategies During Unprecedented Times
Kyla Latrice Tennin (College of Doctoral Studies, University of Phoenix, USA & Forbes School of Business, USA & World Business Angels Investment Forum (WBAF)-G20, USA & Lady Mirage Global, Inc., USA)
Business Science Reference • copyright 2023 • 345pp • H/C (ISBN: 9781668483923) • US $250.00 (our price)

Role of Human Resources for Inclusive Leadership, Workplace Diversity, and Equity in Organizations
Caglar Dogru (Ufuk University, Turkey)
Business Science Reference • copyright 2023 • 421pp • H/C (ISBN: 9781668466025) • US $240.00 (our price)

Global Citizenship and Its Impact on Multiculturalism in the Workplace
Randa Diab-Bahman (Kuwait College of Science and Technology, Kuwait) and Abrar Al-Enzi (Gulf University for Science and Technology, Kuwait)
Business Science Reference • copyright 2023 • 300pp • H/C (ISBN: 9781668454367) • US $240.00 (our price)

Talent Acquisition and Retention Strategies in Global Startups
Neetima Agarwal (Symbiosis International University, India) Leo Paul Dana (Kingston University, UK) and Sujata Khandai (Amity University, India)
Business Science Reference • copyright 2023 • 305pp • H/C (ISBN: 9781668475140) • US $250.00 (our price)

Addressing Corporate Scandals and Transgressions Through Governance and Social Responsibility
Carlos Flórido Lopes (Center for Research in Accounting and Taxation (CICF), Portugal) Augusta Ferreira (Center for Research in Accounting and Taxation (CICF), Portugal) Carlos Ferreira (DEGEIT/LASI/IEETA - University of Aveiro, Portugal) Helena Inácio (GOVCOPP, University of Aveiro, Portugal) and Carlos Santos (Center for Research in Accounting and Taxation (CICF), Portugal)
Business Science Reference • copyright 2023 • 300pp • H/C (ISBN: 9781668478851) • US $250.00 (our price)

IGI Global
PUBLISHER of TIMELY KNOWLEDGE

701 East Chocolate Avenue, Hershey, PA 17033, USA
Tel: 717-533-8845 x100 • Fax: 717-533-8661
E-Mail: cust@igi-global.com • www.igi-global.com

Table of Contents

Detailed Table of Contents

This chapter explores the impact of job insecurity on psychological well-being in the context of the COVID-19 pandemic. This chapter is based on empirical study measuring the six elements of job insecurity on psychological wellbeing, i.e., perceived threats to job features, role insecurity, role conflict, powerfulness, meaningfulness, and perceived threats to total job. Further, this chapter the role of HR analytics in ensuring psychological wellbeing and job security, with a focus on the lessons learned during the COVID-19 pandemic. highlights the importance of HR analytics in identifying and addressing employee needs related to psychological wellbeing and job security, and explores the ways in which HR analytics can be used to improve organizational decision-making and drive business outcomes. This chapter also briefly highlights the emerging practices, and the ways modern digital technologies can be harnessed for the betterment of the employees.

The volume and nature of work undertaken by the tech employees is humongous, tech employees are known to manage those high tides because of attractive salary packages, perks, and other incentive options, which turn out to be a catastrophic collapse when such layoffs are levied, giving little or no room for a quick transfer to another job from the viewpoint of the affected employees. User-generated unstructured data content in the forms of either tweets, reviews, or comments from around seven major social media platforms were collected to understand the various expressions and discussions linked to layoffs. The collected data is further segregated into – employee expressions, social media reviewers, news critiques views, etc., and their perspectives were further analysed. The overall analysis of sentiments on various stakeholders are formulated using Python (Juypter Notebook) package. The authors attempt to model out the viewpoints of various expressors and suggests various measures to be taken by the tech majors to better handle the phenomenon of layoffs.

HR analytics is becoming increasingly important for organizations to manage their workforce effectively and make data-driven decisions. Several studies have explored the current state of HR analytics in organizations, their challenges, and the emerging trends in the field. In fact, 71% of companies see people analytics as a high priority in their organizations. In this chapter, initially, the authors will focus

HR analytics has been envisaged as recent research trend for providing a comprehensive decision support system to the top level management in terms of employee's performance, recruitment and behaviour analysis. Globally, organizations are using technology to support and ease HR processes. Every organization should give maximum value to every available human resource, and they should minimize the attrition and absenteeism rate and ensure what are the factors that contribute towards employee attrition as well as the causes for workmen absenteeism. The ultimate objective is to correctly identify attrition and absenteeism in order to assist the company to improve retention tactics for key personnel and increase employee satisfaction. Through this chapter, a machine learning-based model is proposed to get quick results for such employee attrition and workmen absenteeism. The model is trained and tested for its accuracy. The result shows that the proposed model has high sensitivity. The managerial implications are also discussed for taking informed decisions.

The main emphasis of this chapter is to identify the effect of motivation on variables of employee job performance in people analytics, which is seen as one of the major initiatives in human resources. The secondary sources have been utilised to identify the sources of the thematic approach. Considering this, the study explains how to determine the moderating factors in people analytics. The chapter offers an introduction to problem identification and focuses on detailed literature that helps in finding factors relevant according to the theme that has been elaborated in a thematic approach. A part of the Prisma model has been used to explain the four stages of literature identification. The moderating factors have been better explained through the case studies, and one case study has been explained in the context of an Indian scenario. While explaining the moderating factors, thematic methods have been used using manual screening. The major highlights have been reviewed, discussed, and summarised.

This study synthesizes the various studies on the construct of employee engagement and HR analytics. This is a theoretical and methodological study substantiating the factors identified from the literature causing employee engagement and its effect on organizational performance indicators. This chapter is descriptive at first as it defines the employee engagement and HR analytics construct. Secondly, this study has the feature of being diagnostic to identify the cause and effect of employee engagement. Lastly, the study has the characteristic of being a prescriptive study to suggest solutions based on data derived through HR analytics to enhance the engagement level of employees. Thus, this three-fold study (descriptive, diagnostic, and prescriptive) is a readymade solution kit for management to investigate the low level of employee engagement through the lens of HR Analytics.

Preface

Welcome to *HR Analytics in an Era of Rapid Automation*, an edited reference book that delves into the transformative world of HR analytics and its significance in the face of rapid automation. As editors, we, Radha Yadav, Mudita Sinha, and Joseph Varghese Kureethara, are honored to present this comprehensive collection of research and insights, which aims to provide a deeper understanding of contemporary issues and challenges within the HR domain.

In today's data-driven landscape, the power of analytics has become increasingly vital in unlocking the potential of human resources and enhancing workforce performance. HR analytics goes beyond the surface-level examination of employee data, offering a deeper understanding of the intricacies of human resources and its impact on organizational success. By supporting, tracking, and monitoring employee performance, culture, turnover rate, and absenteeism, HR analytics provides a holistic perspective through its four levels: descriptive, diagnostic, predictive, and perspective.

The rapid advancement of technology has ushered in a period of significant transformation within the business world, necessitating the need for insightful decision-making based on data and facts. This book aims to attract academicians, researchers, and practitioners seeking guidance amid this dynamic landscape. By exploring relevant theories and conceptual models backed by quantitative and qualitative findings, it sheds light on the inseparable value of people and HR analytics, emphasizing their importance for achieving sustainable business success.

Within these pages, readers will gain insight into the strategic decision-making process and the deployment of human capital, utilizing various techniques and methods to understand the complexity of the business environment. Through an evidence-based approach, this book underscores the crucial role HR analytics plays in interpreting data, identifying patterns, drawing analogies, and implementing analysis for informed decision-making in an ever-changing world.

Human resource analytics not only streamlines operational tasks but also nurtures strategic approaches, creating job opportunities while decreasing repetitive work. As the HR department increasingly automates its functions, it can focus on more strategic initiatives that maximize human potential. Acknowledging the HR department's pivotal role in the employee lifecycle, from onboarding to off-boarding, businesses across industries are embracing automation to enhance HR proficiency. This edited collection of research serves as a crucial knowledge resource for understanding the future of HR analytics in this technology-driven era.

Our book covers a wide range of topics, including capability analytics, competency analytics, recruitment analytics, employee performance analytics, and employee attrition analytics. By exploring areas such as HR metrics, HR agility, workplace analytics, talent retention practices, and employee happiness index, readers will gain a comprehensive understanding of the diverse applications of HR analytics. We also delve into the role of HR analytics in compensation and pay management, employee engagement and turnover, talent acquisition, layoff procedures, employee involvement, organizational culture, and business development.

Integrating DEI metrics into recruitment analytics provides insights to organizations to build more diverse and inclusive teams, leading to better decision-making and increased productivity. Another aspect of the recruitment process is to explore the skill gap efficiently. The Skill gap employability model addresses this.

HR analytics identifies and addresses employee psychological well-being and job security needs. Once deployed carefully, this helps improve organizational decision-making and drive business outcomes. In one of the chapters, the authors present a model using the viewpoints of various expressers using social media and suggest various measures to be taken by the tech majors to handle the phenomenon of layoffs better. This has an impact on societal well-being. Further, data-driven layoff decisions can be the best basis for layoffs. Random layoffs affect current and laid-off workers' levels of trust.

There are challenges in the implementation of HR Analytics in diverse businesses. A comprehensive understanding of the challenges faced in implementing HR Analytics is covered, and the authors suggest ways to overcome these challenges.

By measuring and improving employee engagement and turnover, employee engagement analytics uses data in the decision-making process by integrating employee engagement with other HR and non-HR data. A shift to a more rigorous and process-oriented perspective on HR analytics is proposed in one of the models presented in this book. The descriptive, diagnostic and prescriptive study is a readymade solution kit for management to investigate the low level of employee engagement through the lens of HR Analytics.

A machine learning-based model proposed in this book can be used to get quick results for understanding and addressing employee attrition and workers' absenteeism. Artificial intelligence-based methods have a symbiotic relationship with human resources management. A chapter probes into factors contributing to employee happiness, such as company culture, job satisfaction, and mental health. It also highlights the significance of artificial intelligence and machine learning in collecting and analyzing employee feedback.

One of the chapters introduces the problem of identifying the effect of motivation on employee performance in people analytics. Talent retention practice will serve as a base for employer branding and will influence IT companies to reach the pinnacle of success. This would allow for establishing the employer branding concept, which would pay off handsomely.

The target audience for this book includes professionals and researchers working in the field of HR, HR analytics, talent analytics, and business analytics across various functions. Whether you specialize in recruitment, performance management, employee engagement, talent acquisition, or training and development, this book offers insights and sustenance in managing expertise, knowledge, information, business success, HR development, and decision-making within the realm of HR analytics.

We extend our gratitude to all the contributors who have shared their expertise and research, making this book a valuable resource for both beginners and industry professionals. We hope that *HR Analytics in an Era of Rapid Automation* enriches your understanding of the latest developments and advancements in HR analytics, fostering excellence in this transformative field.

Radha Yadav
CHRIST University, India

Mudita Sinha
CHRIST University, India

Joseph Varghese Kureethara
CHRIST University, India

Chapter 1
Integrating Diversity, Equity, and Inclusion (DEI) Effectiveness Metrics Into Recruitment Analytics

K. V. Arunima
https://orcid.org/0000-0001-5259-6131
T A Pai Management Institute, Manipal Academy of Higher Education, Manipal, India

Kartikeya Bolar
https://orcid.org/0000-0003-2277-3357
T A Pai Management Institute, Manipal Academy of Higher Education, Manipal, India

ABSTRACT

The proposed book chapter aims to integrate diversity, equity, and inclusion (DEI) metrics into recruitment analytics of the hiring process of a data science start-up company. A CRISP-DM (cross-industry standard process for data mining) methodology is used to develop a predictive model that can accurately predict whether a candidate will be hired based on the available data to identify the best features highly correlated to hiring. HR metrics focusing on DEI would be integrated into the model to help build a more diverse and inclusive team. The proposed chapter contributes to the growing research on integrating DEI metrics into recruitment analytics. It provides a practical example of achieving this in a real-world setting. Integrating DEI metrics into recruitment analytics provides insights to organizations to build more diverse and inclusive teams, leading to better decision-making, and increased productivity.

INTRODUCTION

Quality recruitment is crucial for organizations because it leads to better job performance, lower turnover rates, improved workplace culture, and cost savings (Breaugh, 2008). Hiring the right people with the necessary skills, knowledge, and experience can increase employee engagement, productivity, and

DOI: 10.4018/978-1-6684-8942-0.ch001

teamwork, ultimately contributing to the organization's success (Huselid, 1995). In today's competitive business environment, organizations increasingly leverage recruitment analytics to optimize their hiring processes and make data-driven decisions (Cascio & Boudreau, 2011).

Recruitment analytics involves collecting, analyzing, and interpreting data related to the recruitment process (Ployhart & Ryan, 1998). It enables organizations to gain insights into various aspects of their recruitment strategies, such as the efficiency of hiring channels, the effectiveness of their employer branding efforts, and the quality of candidates they attract (Sullivan, 2004). Descriptive analytics, measuring candidate fit, reducing bias, and predictive analytics are advantages of using analytics in recruitment (Hausknecht & Holwerda, 2013). Descriptive analytics can help organizations understand historical hiring patterns and identify areas for improvement (Ployhart & Ryan, 1998). On the other hand, predictive analytics can identify potential high-performing candidates based on data analysis of past successful candidates and using algorithms to identify patterns in candidate data (Boudreau & Ramstad, 2005). This data-driven approach can enhance the overall effectiveness of the recruitment process and contribute to better hiring decisions.

Recruitment metrics are the specific data points used in recruitment analytics to measure and analyze the recruitment process (Hausknecht & Holwerda, 2013). These metrics are quantitative measurements of recruitment activities, such as the number of applications received, time to fill positions, cost per hire, and applicant-to-hire ratio. Recruitment analytics uses data visualization tools and statistical methods to analyze the metrics and identify trends and patterns that can inform recruitment decisions (Ployhart & Ryan, 1998). By tracking and analyzing these metrics, organizations can make more informed decisions about their recruitment strategies and better allocate resources to maximize return on investment (Cascio & Boudreau, 2011).

The advent of the 21st century has brought a paradigm shift in how organizations approach recruitment. A vital aspect of this transformation has been the increasing recognition of Diversity, Equity, and Inclusion (DEI) as indispensable components of a successful recruitment strategy. DEI initiatives prioritize creating a diverse workforce that mirrors the rich tapestry of society, implementing equitable policies and practices that ensure all employees, irrespective of their background, have equal access to opportunities, and fostering an inclusive environment where all individuals feel valued and accepted (Herring, 2009; El-Amin, 2022). A solid commitment to DEI helps organizations adhere to ethical standards and legal requirements and drives business performance and innovation (Cox & Blake, 1991). Research has shown that diverse and inclusive teams are more innovative, productive, and better at problem-solving (Page, 2007). These teams bring a more comprehensive range of perspectives, ideas, and experiences to the table, fueling creativity and enhancing decision-making capabilities.

Furthermore, organizations that embrace DEI are more likely to attract and retain top talent from diverse backgrounds, leading to greater workforce satisfaction, reduced turnover rates, and improved overall performance (Itam & Bagali, 2019). In an era characterized by rapid globalization and increasing demographic diversity, integrating DEI into recruitment strategies has become a business imperative for organizations seeking to remain competitive and sustainable.DEI metrics are used to track and measure the diversity of applicants and hires and identify any disparities or gaps in representation (Herring, 2009). DEI metrics can include a variety of data points such as gender, race, ethnicity, disability status, and veteran status. In today's increasingly diverse and globalized workforce, fostering a culture of diversity, equity, and inclusion is a moral imperative and a strategic advantage (Cox & Blake, 1991). Research has shown that diverse and inclusive teams are more innovative, productive, and better at problem-solving (Page, 2007).

This research aims to integrate DEI metrics into the recruitment analytics of a data science start-up company by utilizing the CRISP-DM methodology to develop a predictive model for hiring decisions. The CRISP-DM (Cross-Industry Standard Process for Data Mining) methodology is widely adopted for data mining projects, offering a structured approach to model development, evaluation, and deployment (Wirth & Hipp, 2000). The study will use data analysis tools to track and measure the diversity of applicants and hires, identify disparities or gaps in representation, and help companies build more diverse and inclusive teams which are more innovative and productive (Page, 2007).

By developing a predictive model using the CRISP-DM methodology, the research seeks to provide practical insights for organizations to enhance their recruitment analytics, fostering more diverse and inclusive workforces (Herring, 2009). The proposed model is expected to offer a scalable and adaptable solution for organizations seeking to integrate DEI metrics into their recruitment strategies, ultimately contributing to a more equitable and diverse workplace (Cox & Blake, 1991). The findings from this research will add to the growing body of literature on the importance of DEI in recruitment analytics (Hausknecht & Holwerda, 2013) and provide a practical example for organizations seeking to implement these principles in real-world settings.

REVIEW OF LITERATURE

Recruitment Metrics and Analytics

Recruitment metrics are used to measure the effectiveness of the recruitment process, including the quality of hire, time to fill, cost per hire, and retention rate (Indeed, 2019; Prasad, Rao & Vaidya, 2019). Recruitment analytics involves using data to make informed decisions about the recruitment process, including identifying the most effective sourcing channels, predicting a candidate's success, and optimizing the recruitment process (Krause, 2018). Vlastelica and Holmstrom (2019) found that organizations that use recruitment analytics tend to have more diverse candidate pools and make more diverse hires. The study also found that organizations that used analytics to track diversity metrics, such as the percentage of female and minority applicants and hires, tended to have more diverse candidate pools and make more diverse hires. The recruitment metrics should provide a benchmark for internal performance; they should be actionable, predictive, and consistent and help in the best quality of hire and return on investment (Prasad, Rao & Vaidya, 2019).

Integration of DEI Metrics to Recruitment

Diversity, equity, and inclusion (DEI) have become increasingly important in modern workplaces. Managing diversity in organizations involves embracing and celebrating unique traits and characteristics such as gender, race, ethnicity, geographic origin, religion, or sexual orientation of employees (WISE, 2020). Diverse companies are more likely to attract top talent and show improvements in customer orientation, employee satisfaction, and decision-making (McKinsey, 2015 and 2018). Gender, ethnic, and cultural diversity, especially in executive teams, is also linked to better financial performance (Hunt et al., 2018). Organizations need to prioritize inclusivity and treat employees with equity and respect to manage diversity effectively. Furthermore, implementing diversity management practices and offering flexible scheduling can help increase the proportion of women in management positions (Schoen and Rost, 2020).

Therefore, integrating DEI metrics into recruitment processes is crucial to creating a more diverse and inclusive workplace, resulting in effectiveness from multiple perspectives. Firstly, measuring DEI metrics during the recruitment process can help organizations identify any biases within their hiring practices. Biases can be unconscious, and without metrics, it can be challenging to identify where biases may be present (Knight, 2017; Tursunbayeva et al., 2022). Collecting data on the demographics of applicants, interviewees, and hires can help organizations to analyze their hiring practices and identify areas where changes need to be made (Bogen, Rieke and Ahmed, 2020). For example, if an organization consistently hires more men than women, it may need to adjust its recruitment strategies to attract more female applicants.

Secondly, measuring DEI metrics during the recruitment process can help organizations to create a more diverse and inclusive workforce (Romansky et al., 2021; Avery et al., 2022). By tracking the demographics of their applicants, organizations can identify which groups are underrepresented and develop strategies to attract more diverse candidates (Karakhan et al., 2021). Additionally, by measuring the demographics of their hires, organizations can track their progress toward creating a more diverse workforce.

Thirdly, measuring DEI metrics during the recruitment process can help organizations to improve their employer brand (Matuska and Sałek-Iminska, 2014; Davenport, Harris and Shapiro, 2010). In today's world, candidates are increasingly seeking companies prioritizing diversity and inclusion. Organizations can attract more diverse candidates and improve their reputation as inclusive employers by demonstrating a commitment to DEI through the metrics they collect and report (Dixon-Fyle, Mckinsey, 2020).

There are various DEI metrics that organizations can measure during the recruitment process. Some of the most commonly tracked metrics include the demographics of applicants, interviewees, and hires, the source of hires, the diversity of interview panels, and the percentage of underrepresented groups in the talent pipeline (Formanek and Formanek, 2021). Organizations must have a robust data collection and reporting system to track DEI metrics during recruitment effectively, which involves investing in technology to help automate data collection or hiring DEI specialists to oversee the recruitment process (Pinkett, 2023).

In conclusion, measuring DEI metrics during recruitment is critical for organizations that want to create a more diverse and inclusive workforce. Organizations can reap the benefits of DEI by identifying biases, attracting more diverse candidates, and improving their employer brand. To effectively track DEI metrics, organizations must have a robust data collection and reporting system in place. Ultimately, by prioritizing DEI in recruitment, organizations can create a more welcoming and inclusive workplace culture for all employees.

DEI metrics can include measures such as the representation of underrepresented groups in the candidate pool, the diversity of the interview panel, and the use of unbiased language in job descriptions (Enders et al., 2021).

Previous research on DEI metrics integration in recruitment metrics and analytics: Several studies have examined the integration of DEI metrics into recruitment processes. For example, a study by Aguinis and O'Boyle (2014) found that diversity-oriented recruitment practices lead to higher job performance and satisfaction levels. Another study by Jackson et al. (2019) found that using diverse recruitment panels led to more diverse hires. In a review of the literature on DEI metrics in recruitment, Bilimoria and Liang (2017) found that although there is an increasing emphasis on DEI in the workplace, integrating DEI metrics into recruitment processes is still limited. Recruitment metrics such as time to fill and cost per hire do not provide a complete picture of recruitment effectiveness, and DEI metrics such as diversity of applicant pools and hiring rates for underrepresented groups should also be considered; therefore, integrating DEI metrics into recruitment analytics can help organizations to identify and address disparities in hiring practices and improve diversity and inclusion outcomes (Ruyle et al., 2021). Organizations should develop a comprehensive set of DEI metrics that can be tracked and analyzed over time, and these metrics should be integrated into recruitment analytics and other talent management metrics (Aguirre, Pinder, & Roebuck, 2020)

Critical analysis of the gaps and limitations of previous research: Although there is evidence to support the integration of DEI metrics into recruitment processes, there are several limitations to the previous research. First, much of the research has focused on the benefits of DEI rather than the practicalities of integrating DEI metrics into recruitment processes. Second, there is a lack of consistency in the definitions and measurement of DEI metrics, which makes it difficult to compare studies. Finally, there is a lack of research on the effectiveness of different DEI metrics and how they can improve recruitment outcomes. In conclusion, integrating DEI metrics into recruitment metrics and analytics is crucial to creating a more diverse and inclusive workplace. While previous research has provided evidence of the benefits of DEI, there are limitations in the practical application of DEI metrics in recruitment processes. Future research should focus on the practicalities of integrating DEI metrics, the standardization of DEI metric definitions and measurements, and the effectiveness of different DEI metrics.

PURPOSE AND OBJECTIVES OF THE RESEARCH

The purpose of this research is to apply the CRISP-DM (Cross-Industry Standard Process for Data Mining) methodology to the hiring process of *Klaymatrix*, a data science start-up, to develop a predictive model that can accurately predict whether a candidate will be hired or not based on the available data. The objective is to identify the best features that are highly correlated to hiring or not hiring and to integrate DEI metrics into the model to help build a more diverse and inclusive team. The final output will be a user-friendly *RMarkdownShiny* Application that the Klaymatrix hiring team can use for future recruitment processes. By doing so, we hope to contribute to the growing body of research on integrating DEI metrics into recruitment analytics and provide a practical example of how this can be achieved in a real-world setting.

DATA AND METHODOLOGY

Forming DEI Metrics

It is important to track these metrics over time to understand the organization's progress toward its DEI goals and identify areas for improvement.

Methodology

CRISP-DM (Cross-Industry Standard Process for Data Mining) is a popular methodology for data mining and machine learning projects. It is a six-phase process designed to guide a team through a data mining project from start to finish. We will apply the CRISP-DM methodology to the Klaymatrix data science start-up's hiring process in this case.

1. ***Business Understanding***: We must understand this phase's project objectives and requirements. In this case, the aim is to predict whether a candidate would be hired based on the given dataset. To achieve this, we must develop a predictive model that uses the available candidate data to make this prediction.
2. ***Data Understanding***: In this phase, we need to perform exploratory data analysis and visualization on the data to understand its structure, quality, and any patterns that may exist. We need to analyse the Meta Data in the dataset, which includes the candidate's identification number, qualification, age, gender, type of industry experience, academic score, years of work, training or certification, number of live projects, publications, and whether they were hired or not.

Data is regarding the hiring process of *Klaymatrix* data science hiring process. Table 1 illustrates the Meta data of data.

3. ***Analysis and predictions using the DEI metrics***. We analyzed the data *to* determine the best features highly correlated to hiring or not hiring and checked for any data quality issues. We will also need to split the data into training and test sets. The DEI metrics are identified at this phase
4. ***Evaluate the predictions using the DEI metrics***. When the predictors are Years of Experience, Qualification, Certification/Training Credits, Research Publication, Industry background experience, Age, Gender, and Academic Score, one can follow these steps:
   a. *Determine the relevant DEI metrics*: Based on the context and goals of the hiring process, determine which DEI metrics are most appropriate. For example, if the goal is to ensure fairness in hiring, the adverse impact ratio and hiring parity ratio may be helpful for metrics to evaluate.
   b. *Collect and label data*: Collect data on the relevant predictors and outcomes of interest, such as whether a candidate was hired. Ensure the data is labeled with relevant demographic information such as gender, age, and race.
   c. *Train and test the predictive model*: Develop a predictive model using the available data, such as logistic Regression or a decision tree. Use cross-validation or holdout samples to test the accuracy of the model.
   d. *Evaluate the DEI metrics:* Once the model has been developed and tested, evaluate the DEI metrics of interest. For example, calculate the adverse impact ratio by dividing the Percentage of hired candidates in one demographic group by the Percentage of hired candidates in another demographic group. Calculate the hiring parity ratio by dividing the Percentage of hired candidates in one demographic group by the overall hiring rate.
   e. *Interpret the results and make adjustments*: Interpret the evaluation results and adjust the hiring process or model to improve DEI metrics.

Table 1. Metadata

Headers	Variable	Label	Remarks
Candidate ID			Identification number for each candidate
Qualification	0	no bachelors	
	1	Bachelors	
	2	Masters	
	3	Ph.D.	
Age			in years
Gender	0	Female	
	1	Male	
Type of Industry Experience	0	Miscellaneous	Industry the candidate has worked in or has experience of. These include experience during a job, internships, academic projects etc.
	1	Entertainment	
	2	Services	
	3	Automobiles	
	4	Healthcare	
	5	Telecommunication	
	6	Insurance	
	7	Banking	
	8	Retail and CPG	
Academic Score			marks scored in highest academic qualification
Years of Work			in years
Have training or certification?	0	No	Whether the candidate has undergone any training or certification course. The courses include both online as well as classroom.
	1	Yes	
Live Projects			Number of live projects that the candidate has worked upon
Have Publications?	0	No	
	1	Yes	
No of Publications	0 to 20		
Hired	0	not hired	
	1	Hired	

Relevant DEI Metrics

To design Diversity, Equity, and Inclusion (DEI) metrics using the above-provided variables, we can focus on different aspects such as educational background, gender, age, industry experience, and other relevant factors.

Table 2 illustrates possible DEI metrics calculated based on the dataset:

Table 2. The DEI metrics

Sl no	Metrics	Formula	Value
1	Gender Diversity Ratio:	(Number of female candidates) / (Total number of candidates)	0.508
		(Number of male candidates) / (Total number of candidates)	0.492
2	Age Diversity:	Average age of candidates	23.26
		Age distribution (percentage of candidates in different age groups):	
		18-29	23.02%
		30-39	24.20%
		40-49	27.95%
		50 +	24.83%
3	Educational Background Diversity:	Percentage of candidates with no bachelor's degree	23.40%
		Percentage of candidates with a bachelor's degree	25.40%
		Percentage of candidates with a master's degree	23.30%
		Percentage of candidates with a PhD	27.90%
4	Industry Experience Diversity:	Percentage of candidates from each industry	
		Miscellaneous	10.90%
		Entertainmen	10.30%
		Services	13.30%
		Automobile	10.80%
		Healthcare	11.10%
		Telecommunication	10.90%
		Insurance	10.70%
		Banking	11.70%
		Retail and CPG	10.30%
5	Training/Certification Diversity:	Percentage of candidates with training or certification	51.50%
6	Academic achievement diversity:	Average academic score (CGPA ranging from 1-5)	2.89
		Distribution of academic scores (e.g., percentage of candidates in different score ranges)	CGPA 1-2: 3.6% 2-3: 54% 3-4: 41% 4 & above: 41%
7	Work Experience Diversity:	Average years of work experience	10.815
		Distribution of work experience (e.g., percentage of candidates in different experience ranges)	0-10 yrs.: 58.7% 11-20 yrs.: 22.7% 21-30 yrs.: 14.5% Above 30 yrs.: 4.1%
8	Publication diversity	Percentage of candidates with publications	51.80%
		Average number of publications per candidate	10.33
		Distribution of the number of publications (e.g., percentage of candidates with different publication counts)	Less than 10: 47% 10-20: 48% 20 and above: 6%
9	Live Project Diversity	Average number of live projects per candidate	10.21
		Distribution of live projects (e.g., percentage of candidates with different live project counts)	No projects: 6% 1- 10 proj: 51% 11-20 proj: 44%

continues on following page

Table 2. Continued

Sl no	Metrics	Formula	Value
10	Hiring ratios	Hired	35.50%
		Not Hired	64.50%
		No of Females hired	182
		No of males hired	173
		Age diversity in Hiring(in percentage)	
		18-29	34.17%
		30-39	24.51%
		40-49	23.38%
		50 +	17.75%

The hiring parity ratio is a metric used to measure the equality of hiring practices within an organization. It is calculated by dividing the Percentage of job offers made to a particular demographic group (such as gender or race) by the Percentage of job applicants from that same demographic group.

Percentage of Female applicants = 50.8; Percentage of Females hired = 51.26
Hiring parity ratio for females: Percentage of Females hired/ Percentage of Female applicants
= 51.26/50.8= 1.009
Percentage of male applicants = 49.2; Percentage of males hired = 48.73
Hiring parity ratio for males: Percentage of males hired/Percentage of male applicants
= 49.2/48.73= 1.009

The hiring parity ratio is 1.009 for males and females, indicating that the company has achieved gender parity in its hiring practices. A hiring parity ratio of 1.00 means that the job offer rate for a particular demographic group equals the applicant rate for that same group. A ratio less than 1.00 would indicate under-representation.

Adverse Impact Ratio (AIR) is another commonly used metric in hiring practices to identify potential discrimination against a particular group of candidates. It measures the difference between the selection rates of two groups, typically the majority group and a minority group. The AIR is also known as the impact or selection rate ratio.

To calculate the Adverse Impact Ratio, we first need to determine the selection rate of each group. The selection rate is the number of candidates selected from a group divided by the total number of candidates.

Selection rate = number of candidates selected / Total number of candidates
Selection rate of females = 182/1000*100 = 18.2
Selection rate of males = 173/1000*100 = 17.3
Adverse Impact Ratio = Selection rate of the minority group / Selection rate of the majority group
= Selection rate of females/ Selection rate of males = 18.2/17.3=1.052

An AIR value of 1 indicates no adverse impact, as both groups have the same selection rate. If the Adverse Impact Ratio is less than 1, the minority group has a higher selection rate than the majority group, which could indicate reverse discrimination. On the other hand, an AIR value greater than 1 indicates an adverse impact against the minority group, which could indicate potential discrimination.

5. ***Model Development and Evaluation*** In this phase, we develop a predictive model that can accurately predict whether a candidate will be hired based on the available data. The model is based on the following hypotheses developed considering the Business and Data Understanding Phase.

1. Hypothesis 1: Candidates with higher qualifications are more likely to be hired.
    - H0: There is no relationship between a candidate's qualification and their likelihood of being hired.
    - Ha: Candidates with higher qualifications (Master, Ph.D.) are more likely to be hired than those with lower qualifications (Bachelor, no degree).
2. Hypothesis 2: Candidates with more work experience are more likely to be hired.
    - H0: There is no relationship between years of work experience and the likelihood of being hired.
    - Ha: Candidates with more work experience are more likely to be hired than those with fewer years of experience.
3. Hypothesis 3: Candidates with training or certification are more likely to be hired.
    - H0: There is no relationship between having training or certification and the likelihood of being hired.
    - Ha: Candidates with training or certification are more likely to be hired than those without.
4. Hypothesis 4: Candidates with a higher number of live projects are more likely to be hired.
    - H0: There is no relationship between the number of live projects a candidate has worked on and their likelihood of being hired.
    - Ha: Candidates with more live projects are more likely to be hired than those with fewer live projects.
5. Hypothesis 5: Candidates with publications are more likely to be hired.
    - H0: No relationship exists between having publications and the likelihood of being hired.
    - Ha: Candidates with publications are more likely to be hired than those without.
6. Hypothesis 6: Candidates with experience in specific industries are more likely to be hired.
    - H0: There is no relationship between the type of industry experience and the likelihood of being hired.
    - Ha: Candidates with experience in specific industries (e.g., Healthcare, Telecommunication, Banking) are more likely to be hired than those with experience in other industries.

We have tried machine learning algorithms such as Logistic Regression, decision trees, random forests, etc. We will use techniques such as cross-validation to improve the performance of our models. In ***Model Evaluation***, we evaluate the performance of our model using a confusion matrix and metrics such as accuracy and precision.

The results of the predictive modelling using the hiring data are shown in the table 3 as follows:

This table presents the AUC, Classification Accuracy (CA), F1 Score, Precision, and Recall for each model, making comparing their performance in the hiring context easier.

Table 3. Evaluation of different prediction models

Model	AUC	CA	F1	Precision	Recall
Support Vector Machine (SVM)	0.552	0.548	0.446	0.41	0.49
Decision Tree (Tree)	0.573	0.592	0.479	0.455	0.505
AdaBoost	0.572	0.597	0.468	0.459	0.476
k-Nearest Neighbours (kNN)	0.624	0.637	0.385	0.52	0.306
Random Forest	0.647	0.644	0.458	0.528	0.405
Neural Network	0.653	0.651	0.482	0.538	0.436
Naive Bayes	0.691	0.665	0.449	0.579	0.366
Logistic Regression	0.681	0.67	0.437	0.596	0.346

1. *Support Vector Machine* (SVM): Merits: SVM is effective in high-dimensional spaces and can handle linear and non-linear relationships between features. Demerits: In the hiring context, SVM has relatively low performance across most metrics and may require more computational resources for large datasets.
2. *Decision Tree* (Tree): Merits: Decision Trees are easy to understand, interpret, and visualize, making it simple to comprehend the decision-making process behind each hiring prediction. Demerits: They are prone to overfitting, particularly with complex trees, and may have moderate performance compared to other models.
3. *AdaBoost*: Merits: AdaBoost is an ensemble method that can improve the performance of weak classifiers, resulting in a more accurate and robust hiring prediction model. Demerits: It may be sensitive to noise and outliers in the data, which can affect its performance.
4. *k-Nearest Neighbors (kNN)*: Merits: kNN is a simple, non-parametric method that can work well for specific problems without requiring extensive tuning. Demerits: In the hiring context, kNN imbalances precision and recall. It is also computationally expensive for large datasets and sensitive to the choice of the number of neighbors and distance metric.
5. *Random Forest*: Merits: Random Forest is more robust and accurate than single Decision Trees, reducing overfitting and improving generalization. Demerits: It may be less interpretable than a single Decision Tree, and training multiple trees can be computationally intensive.
6. *Neural Network*: Merits: Neural Networks are robust, flexible models that can learn complex relationships between features, potentially improving hiring predictions. Demerits: They can be more difficult to interpret than other models, require significant tuning of hyperparameters, and may need larger datasets to perform well.
7. *Naive Bayes*: Merits: Naive Bayes is a simple, fast, and computationally efficient model that can work well for specific problems with limited data. Demerits: Its performance may be affected by the assumption of feature independence, and it may have less balanced precision and recall in the hiring context.
8. *Logistic Regression*: Merits: Logistic Regression is a simple, interpretable model that can work well for binary classification problems, such as hiring. Demerits: Without feature engineering or transformation, it may struggle to capture complex, non-linear relationships between features.

In hiring, where "hired" is a positive class, choosing a model that balances performance metrics, interpretability, and computational efficiency is essential. The specific priorities and objectives of the organization, such as minimizing false positives or negatives, should also be considered when selecting the most suitable model.

The performance metrics considered in the above table are essential for evaluating the performance of classification models in the hiring context. Here is a brief description of each metric:

1. Area Under the Curve (AUC): AUC represents the area under the Receiver Operating Characteristic (ROC) curve. It measures the classifier's ability to distinguish between the positive and negative classes, with values ranging from 0 to 1. Higher AUC values indicate better performance.
2. Classification Accuracy (CA): Classification Accuracy is the ratio of correctly classified instances to the total number of instances. It is a standard metric for evaluating the overall performance of a classifier. However, it may not be suitable for imbalanced datasets, as it can be misleading when the class distribution is skewed.
3. F1 Score: F1 Score is the harmonic mean of precision and recall, providing a metric that balances both values. It benefits imbalanced datasets, where one class is more prevalent than the other. Higher F1 scores indicate better performance.
4. Precision: Precision measures the proportion of true positive instances among the instances classified as positive. In the hiring context, it reflects the model's ability to identify candidates who should be hired correctly. Higher precision values indicate better performance but can sometimes come at the cost of lower recall.
5. Recall: Recall, also known as sensitivity or true positive rate, measures the proportion of true positive instances among the actual positive instances. In the hiring context, it reflects the model's ability to identify all suitable candidates for hiring. Higher recall values indicate better performance but can sometimes come at the cost of lower precision.

These metrics help us understand the strengths and weaknesses of different classification models in various scenarios. Depending on the specific priorities and objectives of the organization, one may choose to prioritize specific metrics over others when selecting the most suitable model.

The choice between precision and recall as a better measure in a hiring context depends on the specific goals and priorities of the organization. If the positive class is "hired" and the negative class is "not hired," let us consider the implications of false positives and false negatives.

A false positive occurs when the model incorrectly predicts that a candidate will be hired (i.e., the candidate is not hired, but the model predicts they will be), which could lead to an inefficient hiring process, as more time and resources may be spent on interviewing and evaluating candidates who are not ultimately selected.

A false negative occurs when the model incorrectly predicts that a candidate will not be hired (i.e., the candidate is hired, but the model predicts they will not be). It could result in potentially suitable candidates being overlooked, which might negatively impact the organization's ability to build a diverse and skilled workforce.

Precision is the ratio of true positives to the sum of true and false positives. It measures the model's accuracy by predicting the positive class (hired). High precision indicates that when the model predicts a candidate will be hired, it is more likely to be correct. It helps minimize false positives, ensuring that resources are better allocated during hiring.

Recall is the ratio of true positives to the sum of true positives and false negatives. It measures the ability of the model to identify all relevant instances (i.e., all candidates who should be hired). High recall indicates that the model is less likely to overlook suitable candidates, reducing the occurrence of false negatives.

From the analysis of various predictive models used to aid hiring decisions, it is clear that each model offers a unique combination of benefits and trade-offs. These models vary in complexity, interpretability, computational efficiency, and performance in various metrics such as AUC, Classification Accuracy (CA), F1 Score, Precision, and Recall. Logistic Regression emerges as a promising option for a startup hiring context, mainly due to its balance of simplicity, interpretability, and relatively strong performance across the board.

In comparison, while models like Neural Networks may offer higher potential performance, they also require significant tuning, more computational resources, and larger datasets to realize their full potential. These constraints may not be optimal for a startup context where resources are limited and quick; robust decisions are often required. On the other hand, simpler models like k-Nearest Neighbors or Naive Bayes may not capture the complexity and nuances in the hiring data, resulting in suboptimal performance.

The Logistic Regression model demonstrates relatively high precision, indicating its effectiveness in correctly identifying suitable candidates, which is vital to optimizing resource allocation during hiring. This model also shows good recall, suggesting it can capture a reasonable proportion of suitable candidates from the pool. Such a balance of precision and recall can be crucial in a startup environment where resource optimization and sourcing the best talent are vital.

Deploying the Logistic Regression model via a web-based application in *RMarkdown* allows for real-time, interactive, and user-friendly access to predictive hiring analytics. This ease of use can benefit a dynamic startup environment, allowing for efficient, data-driven decision-making.

Model Deployment

Precision and recall are essential in a hiring context, as they address different aspects of the hiring process. The choice between them depends on the organization's priorities:

- If the organization is more concerned about the efficient allocation of resources during the hiring process, precision may be a better measure.
- If the organization prioritizes identifying all suitable candidates and minimizing the risk of overlooking qualified individuals, the recall may be more critical.

Organizations may often choose to balance precision and recall by considering the F1 score, which is the harmonic mean of precision and recall and allows for a more comprehensive evaluation of the model's performance in the context of hiring.

Based on the provided metrics, Logistic Regression appears to be the best-performing classifier for this hiring problem. However, the best model choice also depends on the specific priorities and objectives of the organization, such as minimizing false positives or negatives. It is essential to consider these priorities when selecting the most suitable model.

Hence, we go ahead to deploy a logistic regression model for predictions in a web-based application in *RMarkdown*.

In the given scenarios, we have two situations that could potentially impact the hiring process fairness, equity, and inclusiveness, which are essential components of DEI metrics. In the first scenario, a female candidate is selected while an otherwise identical male candidate is not. In the revised scenario, a male candidate must have one more live project than a female candidate with the same profile in all other aspects to get selected.

To conclude the overall DEI metrics in these situations, it is crucial to consider the broader context, such as the organization's hiring practices, historical trends, and workforce composition. A single hiring decision may not necessarily indicate a trend or systematic bias in the hiring process. However, if an organization consistently demonstrates a pattern of favoring one gender over the other, even when candidates have similar qualifications and experience, this would be a cause for concern regarding the DEI metrics.

To ensure that the hiring process is fair, equitable, and inclusive, organizations should:

1. Establish clear and consistent selection criteria for all candidates, regardless of their gender or any other demographic factors.
2. Regularly review and update the selection criteria to ensure they align with the organization's DEI goals and do not inadvertently perpetuate biases.
3. Implement hiring analytics and predictive models to minimize the influence of conscious or unconscious biases in the decision-making process.
4. Continuously monitor and evaluate the organization's hiring practices and DEI metrics to identify potential areas for improvement and ensure that the hiring process is fair and equitable for all candidates.

By implementing these strategies, organizations can foster a diverse, equitable, and inclusive workforce, promoting a positive work environment and driving innovation, creativity, and decision-making. Careful consideration of these factors in the context of the organization's broader practices is essential for determining the impact of these scenarios on DEI metrics.

DISCUSSION

Hiring analytics have revolutionized the recruitment process by offering organizations the means to make data-informed decisions and optimize their hiring strategies (Fernandez-Araoz, Groysberg, & Nohria, 2009) in a world that is progressively acknowledging the value of diversity, equity, and inclusion (DEI), such analytics play a crucial role. Companies today focus on fostering a diverse and inclusive workforce, understanding that this drives innovation, nurtures creativity, and enriches decision-making (Herring, 2009). Given this significant shift in the corporate landscape, hiring analytics have proven to be an indispensable tool to secure unbiased, equitable, and effective hiring processes (Dobbin & Kalev, 2016; Uma, Velchamy & Upadhyay, 2023).

In driving DEI initiatives, accurate hiring analytics act as our compass, measuring and tracking DEI metrics, thereby contributing to the holistic success of an organization's diversity goals. Candidate profiles, spanning aspects like education, experience, skills, and demographics, provide a treasure trove of information. Analyzing these profiles allows us to unearth potential biases and barriers obstructing a diverse and inclusive hiring process (Bogen & Rieke, 2018). A close examination of the applicant pool's demographics, for instance, can provide insights into whether a company is successfully attracting a broad spectrum of candidates. Similarly, a comparative study of diversity metrics between hired and non-hired candidates can throw light on the fairness of an organization's hiring practices, revealing areas that might require enhancement.

Moving deeper into hiring analytics, we encounter predictive models – the backbone of contemporary recruitment practices. Leveraging the power of machine learning algorithms and statistical techniques, these models sift through enormous amounts of data to discern patterns. Doing so helps identify candidates most likely to succeed in a given role based on past performance, skills, and experience (Isson & Harriott, 2016).

In the context of DEI, the accuracy of predictive models is of utmost importance. High-accuracy models ensure the hiring process remains merit-based, selecting the most suitable candidates irrespective of their demographic backgrounds. This approach reduces the scope for conscious or unconscious biases, contributing to a diverse and inclusive workforce. Nonetheless, it is essential to acknowledge that even accurate predictive models can unintentionally perpetuate existing biases or introduce new ones. Organizations, therefore, must commit to a cycle of continuous evaluation and refinement of these models (Raghavan, Barocas, Kleinberg, & Levy, 2020).

Our analysis employed several predictive models, comparing their performance in the hiring context. We evaluated these models based on crucial metrics such as Area Under the Curve (AUC), Classification Accuracy (CA), F1 Score, Precision, and Recall. The goal was to identify a model that balanced performance, interpretability, and computational efficiency. After thorough consideration, Logistic Regression emerged as the suitable model, demonstrating a compelling performance across all metrics.

Despite the promising results, it is essential to consider that our approach, like any other, is not foolproof. In deploying this model, organizations must carefully consider their priorities, such as minimizing false positives or negatives.

While predictive models and hiring analytics provide powerful tools for optimizing recruitment strategies, organizations must continuously scrutinize and adjust these models to meet their evolving DEI objectives. Only through continuous refinement can we ensure that these tools effectively contribute to building a fair, diverse, and inclusive workplace (Raghavan, Barocas, Kleinberg, & Levy, 2020).

The research findings provide substantial insight into how data analysis and predictive modeling can enhance hiring processes, particularly in promoting Diversity, Equity, and Inclusion (DEI). Here are some practical implications of these findings:

1. Streamlined Decision-making: Using predictive modeling in hiring allows organizations to make more informed, data-driven decisions. By using models such as logistic Regression to predict hiring outcomes, companies can efficiently identify the most suitable candidates, streamlining their recruitment process (Isson & Harriott, 2016).
2. Efficient Resource Allocation: The application of these models also has the potential to save significant time and resources. For example, high-precision models help minimize false positives, ensuring that resources are not wasted on unsuitable candidates. On the other hand, high recall models ensure that all potentially suitable candidates are considered, reducing the risk of missing out on qualified applicants.
3. Promotion of DEI: The findings underscore the role predictive modeling can play in promoting DEI. Predictive models can help create a more diverse and inclusive workforce by minimizing bias in hiring decisions. Notably, the data reveals that while predictive models can help reduce bias, it

is crucial for organizations to regularly evaluate their models to ensure they are not inadvertently introducing or perpetuating biases (Bogen & Rieke, 2018; Raghavan, Barocas, Kleinberg, & Levy, 2020).

4. Targeted Improvement of Hiring Practices: By providing insights into hiring performance metrics (such as precision, recall, and F1 scores), the research assists organizations in identifying areas for improvement in their hiring practices. If, for instance, an organization's model has high precision but low recall, it might indicate a need to broaden the scope of their candidate search to avoid missing suitable applicants.
5. Increased Transparency: By leveraging data-driven approaches in hiring, organizations can increase transparency in their recruitment processes. Clear, statistical measures can provide a quantifiable basis for hiring decisions, which can be communicated to all stakeholders, including applicants. This openness can enhance an organization's reputation and make it more attractive to potential candidates.
6. Continuous Learning and Improvement: The research emphasizes the dynamic nature of predictive modelling. It is crucial that organizations continually monitor, evaluate, and refine their models, adapting to changing realities and objectives. This iterative process fosters a culture of continuous learning and improvement, which is beneficial beyond just the hiring process (Raghavan, Barocas, Kleinberg, & Levy, 2020).

Hence, the research findings strongly endorse predictive models in hiring while highlighting the importance of continuous evaluation and adaptation in response to changing objectives and potential biases. As more organizations incorporate data-driven methods into their hiring practices, it is hoped that the benefits of increased efficiency, transparency, and promotion of DEI will be widely realized.

CONCLUSION

Accurate hiring analytics are vital for ensuring the accuracy of DEI metrics in the hiring process. Organizations can make informed decisions and optimize recruitment strategies by utilizing data-driven insights and predictive models to attract and retain a diverse and inclusive workforce. To maintain the integrity of DEI metrics, organizations must continually evaluate and refine their hiring analytics, ensuring that their models and processes are unbiased and equitable. By doing so, companies can foster a more inclusive work environment that drives innovation, creativity, and success.

REFERENCES

Abdullayev, M. M., & Aldulaimi, S. H. (2020). Trends and opportunities of artificial intelligence in human resource management: Aspirations for public sector in Bahrain. *International Journal of Scientific and Technology Research*, *9*(1), 3867–3871.

Aguirre, D., Pinder, J., & Roebuck, D. (2020). Talent Analytics for D&I: Moving Beyond Diversity Metrics. *People + Strategy, 43*(3), 20-29.

Avery, D. R., Ruggs, E. N., Garcia, L. R., Traylor, H. D., & London, N. (2022). Improve Your Diversity Measurement for Better Outcomes. *MIT Sloan Management Review*, *64*(1), 1–6.

Bassett-Jones, N. (2005). The paradox of diversity management, creativity and innovation. *Creativity and Innovation Management*, *14*(2), 169–175. doi:10.1111/j.1467-8691.00337.x

Bogen, M., & Rieke, A. (2018). Help Wanted: An Examination of Hiring Algorithms, Equity, and Bias. *Upturn*. https://www.upturn.org/reports/2018/hiring-algorithms/

Bogen, M., Rieke, A., & Ahmed, S. (2020, January). Awareness in practice: tensions in access to sensitive attribute data for antidiscrimination. In *Proceedings of the 2020 conference on fairness, accountability, and transparency* (pp. 492-500). ACM.10.1145/3351095.3372877

Boudreau, J. W., & Ramstad, P. M. (2005). Talentship, talent segmentation, and sustainability: A new HR decision science paradigm for a new strategy definition. *Human Resource Management*, *44*(2), 129–136. doi:10.1002/hrm.20054

Breaugh, J. A. (2008). Employee recruitment: Current knowledge and important areas for future research. *Human Resource Management Review*, *18*(3), 103–118. doi:10.1016/j.hrmr.2008.07.003

Cascio, W. F., & Boudreau, J. W. (2011). Investing in people: Financial impact of human resource initiatives. Upper Saddle River, NJ: FT press.

Cox, T. H., & Blake, S. (1991). Managing cultural diversity: Implications for organizational competitiveness. *The Academy of Management Perspectives*, *5*(3), 45–56. doi:10.5465/ame.1991.4274465

Davenport, T. H., Harris, J., & Shapiro, J. (2010). Competing on talent analytics. *Harvard Business Review*, *88*(10), 52–58. PMID:20929194

Dixon-Fyle, S., Dolan, K., Hunt, V., & Prince, S. (2020). *How diversity, equity, and inclusion (DE&I) matter*. McKinsey. https://www.mckinsey.com/featured-insights/diversity-and-inclusion/diversity-wins-how-inclusion-matters

Dobbin, F., & Kalev, A. (2016). Why diversity programs fail. *Harvard Business Review*, *94*(7), 14.

El-Amin, A. (2022). Organizational climate change: diversity, equity, inclusion, and belonging. In Implementing Diversity, Equity, Inclusion, and Belonging Management in Organizational Change Initiatives (pp. 1-23). IGI Global. doi:10.4018/978-1-6684-4023-0.ch001

Enders, F. T., Golembiewski, E. H., Pacheco-Spann, L. M., Allyse, M., Mielke, M. M., & Balls-Berry, J. E. (2021). Building a framework for inclusion in health services research: Development of and pre-implementation faculty and staff attitudes toward the Diversity, Equity, and Inclusion (DEI) plan at Mayo Clinic. *Journal of Clinical and Translational Science*, *5*(1), e88. doi:10.1017/cts.2020.575 PMID:34007470

Formanek, K., & Formanek, K. (2021). Measuring and Monitoring the Vital Signs of Diversity. *Beyond D&I: Leading Diversity with Purpose and Inclusiveness*, 239-260.

Groysberg, B., Nohria, N., & Fernández-Araoz, C. (2009). The definitive guide to recruiting in good times and bad. *Harvard Business Review*, 74–84.

Hausknecht, J. P., & Holwerda, J. A. (2013). When does employee turnover matter? Dynamic member configurations, productive capacity, and collective performance. *Organization Science*, *24*(1), 210–225. doi:10.1287/orsc.1110.0720

Herring, C. (2009). Does diversity pay? Race, gender, and the business case for diversity. *American Sociological Review*, *74*(2), 208–224. doi:10.1177/000312240907400203

Hunt, V., Layton, D., & Prince, S. (2018). *Why diversity matters*. McKinsey & Company. https://www.mckinsey.com/business-functions/organization/our-insights/why-diversity-matters

Huselid, M. A. (1995). The impact of human resource management practices on turnover, productivity, and corporate financial performance. *Academy of Management Journal*, *38*(3), 635–672. doi:10.2307/256741

Indeed. (2019). The 10 Recruitment Metrics You Need to Know in 2019. *Indeed Blog*. https://www.indeed.com/hire/c/info/recruitment-metrics-you-need-to-know

Isson, J. P., & Harriott, J. S. (2016). *People analytics in the era of big data: Changing the way you attract, acquire, develop, and retain talent*. John Wiley & Sons. doi:10.1002/9781119083856

Itam, U., & Bagali, M. M. (2019). Diversity and inclusion management: a focus on employee engagement. In Gender and Diversity: Concepts, Methodologies, Tools, and Applications (pp. 1771-1788). IGI Global. doi:10.4018/978-1-5225-6912-1.ch093

Johnson, M. P., & Chichirau, G. R. (2020). Diversity, equity, and inclusion in operations research and analytics: A research agenda for scholarship, practice, and service. *Pushing the boundaries: Frontiers in impactful OR/OM research*, 1-38.

Karakhan, A. A., Gambatese, J. A., Simmons, D. R., & Al-Bayati, A. J. (2021). Identifying pertinent indicators for assessing and fostering diversity, equity, and inclusion of the construction workforce. *Journal of Management Engineering*, *37*(2), 04020114. doi:10.1061/(ASCE)ME.1943-5479.0000885

Knight, R. (2017). *7 Practical ways to reduce bias in your hiring process*. Harvard Business Review.

Kollen, T. (2019). Diversity management: A comprehensive review of the field. *Journal of Business Research*, *98*, 319–330.

Matuska, E., & Sałek-Iminska, A. (2014). Diversity Management as Employer Branding Strategy-Theory and Practice. *Human Resources Management & Ergonomics*, *8*(2), 72–87.

Page, S. E. (2007). *The difference: How the power of diversity creates better groups, firms, schools, and societies*. Princeton University Press.

Pinkett, R. (2023). *Data-driven DEI: The Tools and Metrics You Need to Measure, Analyse, and Improve Diversity, Equity, and Inclusion*. John Wiley & Sons.

Ployhart, R. E., & Ryan, A. M. (1998). Toward an explanation of applicant reactions: An examination of organizational justice and attribution frameworks. *Organizational Behavior and Human Decision Processes*, *74*(3), 199–214. doi:10.1006/obhd.1998.2777 PMID:9606169

Prasad, K. D. V., Rao, M., & Vaidya, R. (2019). Recruitment metrics and accomplishments: A study with reference to information technology sector. *Journal of Management Research and Analysis*, *6*(2), 106–111. doi:10.18231/j.jmra.2019.020

Raghavan, M., Barocas, S., Kleinberg, J., & Levy, K. (2020, January). Mitigating bias in algorithmic hiring: Evaluating claims and practices. In *Proceedings of the 2020 conference on fairness, accountability, and transparency* (pp. 469-481). 10.1145/3351095.3372828

Romansky, L., Garrod, M., Brown, K., & Deo, K. (2021). How to measure inclusion in the workplace. *Harvard Business Review*, 27.

Ruyle, K., Peterson, S., & Rassi, R. (2021). The Business Case for Diversity, Equity, and Inclusion Metrics in Recruitment Analytics. *Journal of Corporate Recruiting Leadership*, *5*(2), 31–39.

Schoen, J., & Rost, K. (2020). Organizational diversity management: A systematic review integrating two decades of research. *Journal of Business Research*, *117*, 182–195.

Sullivan, J. (2004). Rethinking strategic HR: A change in approach to delivering results. *Strategic HR Review*, *3*(2), 20–23.

Tursunbayeva, A., Pagliari, C., Di Lauro, S., & Antonelli, G. (2022). The ethics of people analytics: Risks, opportunities and recommendations. *Personnel Review*, *51*(3), 900–921. doi:10.1108/PR-12-2019-0680

Uma, V. R., Velchamy, I., & Upadhyay, D. (2023). Recruitment Analytics: Hiring in the Era of Artificial Intelligence. In The Adoption and Effect of Artificial Intelligence on Human Resources Management, Part A (pp. 155-174). Emerald Publishing Limited.

Vlastelica, R., & Holmstrom, A. (2019). Diversity, Inclusion, and the Use of Analytics in Recruiting. *Harvard Business Review*. https://hbr.org/2019/03/diversity-inclusion-and-the-use-of-analytics-in-recruiting

Wirth, R., & Hipp, J. (2000). CRISP-DM: Towards a standard process model for data mining. *Proceedings of the 4th international conference on the practical applications of knowledge discovery and data mining*, (pp. 29-39). ACM.

WISE. (2020). *Diversity management in the workplace*. WISE. https://www.wise-qatar.org/diversity-management-workplace/

Yarger, L., Cobb Payton, F., & Neupane, B. (2020). Algorithmic equity in the hiring of underrepresented IT job candidates. *Online Information Review*, *44*(2), 383–395. doi:10.1108/OIR-10-2018-0334

Chapter 2
Predictive Analytics in Recruitment:
Unveiling Through Skill Gap Employability Model

Kamaladevi Baskaran
Amity Business School, Amity University, Dubai, UAE

ABSTRACT

This study aims to identify the competencies and skills possessed by the job seekers to secure jobs in the field of business administration, analyses the impact of soft skills, technical skills, and social networking sites on their employment using predictive analytical tool and proposes skill gap employability model to streamline recruitment process. Primary data of 172 samples were obtained from the UAE residents using simple random sampling. The employability skills are extracted from the secondary sources like job search portals. The regression analysis reveals that soft skills have significant impact on employment and the results state that it is statistically significant at 5% level. The author derives the skill gap employability model to bridge the skill gap to ensure job demand meets the supply of right candidates. This research provides insights to the business administration professionals who are searching for employment in the areas of human resources, finance, accounting, marketing, sales, operations, logistics, supply chain management, and business analytics in UAE.

INTRODUCTION

Social networking sites have transformed the way how people interact, communicate, and work. The use of social media in recruitment and career advancement has been growing popular. Companies and prospective employees now have a vibrant social media platforms platform to connect, network, and establish a professional identity. Social media platforms have become incredibly powerful networking and marketing tools, and workplace usage of social networking sites has grown significantly. (Choudhary and Baskaran 2022) Social networking sites are significantly influencing employment opportunities, and

DOI: 10.4018/978-1-6684-8942-0.ch002

the hiring and recruiting process. Job seekers can use social networking sites to interact with possible employers and research employment opportunities. According to a survey by the Society for HRM, job applicants who utilize social networking sites are more likely to secure a position than those who do not. (Rockwood 2021) Furthermore, social networking sites can give job applicants valuable knowledge about potential employers and the labor market, enabling them to make smart decisions about their job search. Social networking sites, however, can sometimes be detrimental to job seekers. Companies frequently utilize social networking sites to assess potential employees, and those who project a negative or unprofessional image on these networks might be less likely to get hired. (Rockwood 2021)

According to a LinkedIn survey, in 2021, employers are likely to be most interested in individuals with the top skill set of innovation, adaptability, cooperation, and leadership. The study also discovered that HR professionals are becoming interested in applicants who possess a growth mindset and are eager to learn and acquire new skills. According to the survey by Society for Human Resource Management, HR professionals are also focusing more on diversity, equality, and inclusion (DEI) during the recruitment process. This entails seeking out applicants with multicultural competency, experience working with diverse teams, and a dedication to DEI. Overall, there is an increasing emphasis on soft skills, a growth mindset, and diversity and inclusion in the hiring process, even though the abilities and attributes that HR professionals seek during recruitment may vary depending on the industry and job function. According to CareerBuilder study, the qualifications, experience, and cultural fit of candidates are the most crucial elements that HR professionals take into account. The study also revealed that HR professionals place a high value on interpersonal and problem-solving skills, as well as an optimistic mindset and work ethic. (Choudhary and Baskaran 2022) Social media sites can be an effective tool for companies to identify and hire new professionals. Employers who use social networking sites are more likely to find competent candidates than those who do not. (Cyriac and Baskaran 2021) Social networking sites can also give companies useful data about prospective employees, enabling them to make wise recruiting decisions. Social networking sites, however, can sometimes provide complications for employers. For instance, it may be challenging for employers to determine which content is accurate and pertinent from social networking sites, which could raise legal and ethical concerns.

Employers' Use of Social Media for Career Development/Recruitment

91% of companies use social media to recruit new employees. 45% of companies use social media to post content to engage with job seekers. 21% of companies reject the job applicants after looking at their social media posts. LinkedIn (91%) is the social media platform that businesses use most frequently for recruitment, followed by Facebook and Twitter. Employers advertise job openings on social media, reach out to potential applicants, and even conduct background checks on applicants. Social networking sites have significantly impacted employment, from job applicants' professional networking to businesses' recruitment and selection procedures. (Fennell 2022) Employers would also evaluate a candidate's personal brand and online presence on social media. Employers look for proof of the applicant's effective oral and written communication abilities as well as their ability to engage with others in a professional manner. This can give employers a better understanding of a candidate's personality and fit with the company's culture, which can be difficult to determine from a traditional resume or cover letter. (Papacharissi 2010)

The job search process is now quicker and more effective thanks to social media. Nowadays, job seekers have several options for how to look for employment, including using social networking platforms to explore for job vacancies, network with connections and prospective employers, and follow companies that interest them. Job seekers can connect with potential employers and find job posts on social media sites like LinkedIn, Twitter, and Facebook that may not be accessible through traditional job search methods. Additionally, a large number of companies now promote job openings on social networking sites, making it easier for job seekers to seek them. As a result, the job search process is expedited and made more effective, as job seekers can quickly identify the relevant job postings.

Employer Assessment

Social media changed the way, employers evaluate potential employees. Employers increasingly evaluate candidates on social media, assess their qualifications, and gain insight into their skills, employment history, and interests. Social media can also be used by recruiters to validate a candidate's references, review their online profile, and get a clear understanding of their identity as a person. Employers can find potential applicants on social media and contact them. (Baskaran and Rajavelu 2020) For instance, if a hiring manager is seeking for a candidate with a particular set of skills, they can use social networking sites to look for people who meet their job requirements. This helps companies to identify suitable employees more easily without having to rely on traditional job search methods. The workplace has been strongly influenced by social networking sites, from employee engagement to employer governance. (Ashok and Baskaran 2022) Employers may now engage with and monitor the progress of their employees much more efficiently due to social networking platforms. Employers can leverage social networking sites to easily address employee questions, post job announcements and vacancies, and keep employees updated on corporate news. Additionally, social media has altered how employees interact with each other. Employees can collaborate on projects and interact with one another in real-time using social media tools like Slack, Zoom, and WebEx. (Baskaran and et al 2020) Employee collaboration and connectivity are facilitated as a result, regardless of location.

In addition to the social media verification, technical skills, generally referred to technical or job-specific skills, are the specialized talents and knowledge needed to complete a particular job. Technical skills are essential for success in many professions since they usually determine a people's ability to perform a task efficiently. (Majji and Baskaran 2021) An assessment plays a crucial role in the hiring process, as it is essential for many jobs. Technical skills helps in determining the suitability of candidate for a particular job and are frequently used to screen job applications. Furthermore, studies have shown that those with strong technical skills have higher earning potential and are more likely to obtain jobs than people without these skills. Additionally, technical skills can improve a person's chances of career growth and job promotions. (Fajaryati, et al. 2020) Factors workers are trained in standardized technical skills but they found formal education less valuable, and became less literate. (Carada, et al. 2022) In many industries, technical skills are necessary for an employee to perform their job effectively. A software developer must have a strong understanding of programming languages in order to develop and maintain software systems. (Baskaran 2019) Similarly, a financial analyst must have a deep understanding of financial analysis techniques and tools in order to make informed investment decisions. (Ashok and Baskaran 2019) (Mohan and Baskaran 2021)Employees can provide evidence of their technical abilities by showcasing their portfolio or demonstrating their expertise in using specific tools or software. (Ahmed and Baskaran 2020) This can make it easier for employers to assess an individual's skills and qualifications for a job. Technical skills are no longer adequate to sustain in the dynamic job market.

Finally, communication, teamwork, problem-solving, time management, leadership, adaptability, and emotional intelligence are some of the most widely acknowledged soft skills, sometimes known as "people skills" or "interpersonal skills," have grown in significance in the field of employment. (Baskaran 2019) Soft skills are a combination of personality traits, interpersonal behaviors, and communication abilities that help people collaborate successfully and harmoniously with others. (Bruce, et al. 2022). This study aims to analyze the impact of soft skills, technical skills, and social networking sites on the employment of job seekers and identifies the competencies and skills required to obtain positions in the field of business administration.

REVIEW OF LITERATURE

Computer systems enhance human lives in all domains. The recruitment sector is one of the most significant sectors supported by the latest technology. Recruiters previously wasted important time, energy, and resources to reach the right candidates. Neither the needs of the recruiter nor the goals of the job seeker are met by the conventional hiring procedure. Companies now post job openings on their websites or social media, while job seekers typically showcase their qualifications and skills through job portals. To make the hiring process better for both sides, all of these might be combined on one webpage. The online E-recruitment system will enable them to communicate and meet the expectations of recruiters and job seekers (Malki and Atlam 2021).

Soft Skills on Hiring Decisions

Despite the fact that employers need skilled human resources with high competitiveness to deal with the modern era of technological disruption, they frequently encounter job seekers who lack these skills. The problem of poor education quality is connected to a lack of skills. The study findings revealed that employers will recruit candidates with the skillset of problem-solving, communication, teamwork, and technological proficiency in order to meet future job expectations (Fajaryati, et al. 2020). Soft skills are crucial for professional success. Soft Skills are the most desired qualities among job seekers. Candidates with excellent soft skills are more likely to be promoted and experience higher levels of job satisfaction. Soft skills are crucial for improving employee performance as they help employees interact well with others, solve problems, and manage their time. (Lokaj, Miftari and Hajdari 2021) The significance of soft skills in recruiting decisions is still emphasized by recent research.

The recent study conducted by Burning Glass Technologies about the labor market found that employers are increasingly looking for applicants with a combination of technical and soft skills. The study found that among the most commonly stated abilities in job ads across several industries were soft skills like communication, problem-solving, and teamwork. 80% of hiring managers believe that soft skills are important than technical skills when making hiring decisions. Soft skills can increase employee engagement, productivity, and job satisfaction, according to a recent Deloitte study, which also revealed that they are essential for both employee success and retention. The study also discovered that investing money on soft skill development could significantly influence employee retention rates and company performance as a whole. These studies emphasize the continuous value of soft skills in recruiting processes and the necessity for job seekers to give these abilities priority. In today's dynamic environment, employers are not only looking for technical skills, but also communication, team work and handle conflict management in a professional manner. (Fadhil, Ismail and Alnoor 2021) Also, soft skills boost the chances of selection as it is more difficult to teach and develop compared to technical skills. They can provide a competitive edge to job seekers and increase their probability of success in the selection process.

Strong communication skills influence the people in the workplace. It is essential for building connections, collaboration, and effectively communication of ideas and thoughts. Employees must be able to communicate efficiently in the dynamic world to accomplish their objectives. Effective communication skill of an employee can influence, inspire, and manage teams easily. According to a National Association of Colleges and Employers (NACE) survey, 91% of employers said that communication skills are the most crucial factor to take into account when recruiting new employees. (Fadhil, Ismail and Alnoor 2021) Teams enable people to pool their knowledge and skills to accomplish common goals. In order to succeed at work, employees need strong teamwork abilities for collaboration, share ideas, and problem solving. Individuals who have strong teamwork skills are more likely to be motivated and engaged, which boosts job satisfaction and increases productivity. (Fadhil, Ismail and Alnoor 2021) Critical thinking and problem solving are soft skills that are crucial for employees to identify the problem, analyze situations and propose solutions. Employers give weightage to the potential employees who possess critical thinking and problem-solving skills, as they are more likely to make effective decisions, improve processes, and drive innovation. (Fajaryati, et al. 2020) Crucial soft skill that can significantly affect employment is time management. It requires the ability to set priorities, manage deadlines, and utilize time effectively. Employees who have effective time management skills are more likely to be productive, experience less stress, and stay healthy. Employees can effectively meet the requirements of their jobs and accomplish their goals by learning efficient time management skills. (Cyriac and Baskaran 2020) Another soft skill that strongly impacts employment is adaptability. Employees must be able to quickly adapt to new scenarios and changes in the workplace considering the continually evolving nature of the job market today. Employees who possess this ability are adaptable, open-minded, and eager to acquire new knowledge. Adaptability is one of the most crucial soft skills that employers look for in new hires, according to a Manpower Group study, since it enables workers to be more productive in their roles and contribute to the success of the company. (Fajaryati, et al. 2020) Leading others is an important soft skill that strongly influences employment. In organizations, leaders are vital because they plan, prepare, inspire and motivate their teams, and promote innovation. Being a successful leader in the workplace requires the ability to influence, inspire, and manage teams. Strong leadership abilities increase an employee's chances of promotion and career success.

Technical Skills on Hiring Decisions

Technical skills play a significant role in determining an individual's eligibility for a job and are a crucial determinant in hiring decisions. Technical skills are usually applied as a screening technique in the hiring process. Employees who have strong technical skills are more likely to result in a job offer than candidates who lack these skills. In addition, technical skills give job applicants an advantage over their competitors. Strong technical skill holders are more likely to be given consideration for employment opportunities and have a higher earning potential than individuals without these talents. (Fajaryati, et al. 2020) Technical skills continue to be considered highly when making recruiting selections, especially in sectors like technology, engineering, and healthcare. According to a survey by the Indeed Hiring Lab, technical skill sets, such as proficiency in Microsoft Office, data analysis, and coding languages, were among the top five skills stated in job advertisements across all industries. Technical skills turned out to be the most frequently cited talent in job advertisements for IT roles in another study conducted by

CompTIA, an information technology trade organization. The most in-demand technical skills include those related to coding languages, network administration, and cybersecurity. In addition, a LinkedIn survey revealed that technical skills like cloud computing, AI, and blockchain will be in high demand among employers in 2021. (Choudhary and Baskaran 2022) According to these research, employers continue to place a high value on technical skills, especially in fields where using technology is a crucial component of the job. However, as previously mentioned, soft skills are also playing a bigger role in the workplace and can be used in combination with technical abilities to succeed in a wide range of professions.

Social Networking Sites on Hiring Decisions

The use of social networking sites (SNS) in hiring decisions has become a topic of growing interest. Job seekers are attentive to messages coming from Social Networking Sites (SNS). Job seekers may have a negative impact due to information inconsistency provided in both SNS and corporate websites. Job seekers should apply for jobs at companies they find more appealing. The majority of US businesses use their websites to promote carefully designed pictures and descriptions of themselves, with many doing so specifically to highlight workforce diversity as a core value. Recent research has studied the impact of SNS on hiring decisions and job candidate evaluations. According to survey by Statista, 70% of employers in the USA screen job applicants using social media during the hiring process. The study also found that, LinkedIn was the most used social media site for recruiting followed by Facebook and Twitter. According to research done by CareerBuilder, 57% of employers who use social media to screen job applicants have come across content that induced them to decline an application, such as inappropriate photos or posts, negative comments about previous employers, or evidence of drug use. Furthermore, a North Carolina State University study revealed that hiring managers who look at the Facebook profiles of job seekers were more likely to have a negative impression of those individuals if they had posted material about using drugs or alcohol, or using profanity. According to these research, social media can significantly influence hiring decisions, thus prospective employees should be aware of the potential consequences of their social media usage. (Brouer, Badawy and Stefanone 2022)

Recruiters' hiring practices may be tainted by social media platforms as well as their content. In the present scenario, hiring managers have access to candidates' social media like Facebook, LinkedIn to capture job relevant and irrelevant information. Even though the hiring managers find job related information from social media, they may view irrelevant content like marital status, political affiliation, nationality or religion of the candidate which has strong influence on selection decision. Hiring managers may exhibit a range of cognitive and emotive reactions to material provided by social media assessments that is both job-relevant and job-irrelevant. Affective responses are frequently rapid and emotional, but cognitive responses suggest deliberate and controlled evaluations of a candidate's social media content. Traditional selection process evaluates the candidate based on cognitive & rational assessment criteria. In addition, they considered suitability and job relevant information. Due to lack of social media information assessing policies, most of the organizations convert the data from social media to candidates' assessment in an unstructured manner. It confirms that social media information has impact on business decision making. (Wade, et al. 2020)

Professional networks facilitates the connections of powerful individuals, explore new resources and opportunities (such as employment leads), and gain new information and skills to promote career growth. However, studies show that women frequently experience challenges in engaging these networks. This research used a randomized field experiment and discovered that networking results for women were lower than those for men. (Bapna and Funk 2021) In comparison to men, women made 42% fewer new connections, spent 48% less time interacting, and created 25% fewer connection on LinkedIn. Also this research hypothesizes two networking barriers—social and search—affect men and women differently in industries (such as IT) where women are underrepresented. The goal of the search intervention was to make it easier to find a new connections and information. The objectives of the social intervention were to promote prosocial conduct and cross-social interactions. The research shows how simple interventions might help women to build networks and find employment opportunities. (Bapna and Funk 2021)

The potential issues faced during the process of recruitment should be identified. Such challenges must be examined from the perspectives of recruiters, job seekers, and the system. If one of the issues being faced is finding the suitable candidate, a talent pool development strategy is required. Brand messaging be carefully considered to ensure that it is in line with the desired talent. (Moncey and Baskaran 2020) Consider strategies to connect with more socially enabled employment seekers in light of current technological advancements by designing a social media strategy to build and maintain a suitable talented community portfolio. (Lima, et al. 2015) Based on the literature, it is understood that soft skills, technical skills and candidate presence in the social networking sites influences employment. This study aims to identify the competencies and skills possessed by the job seekers to secure jobs in the field of business administration, analyses the impact of soft skills, technical skills and social networking sites on their employment and proposes skill gap employability model to streamline recruitment process as mentioned in Figure 1.

Figure 1. Theoretical model

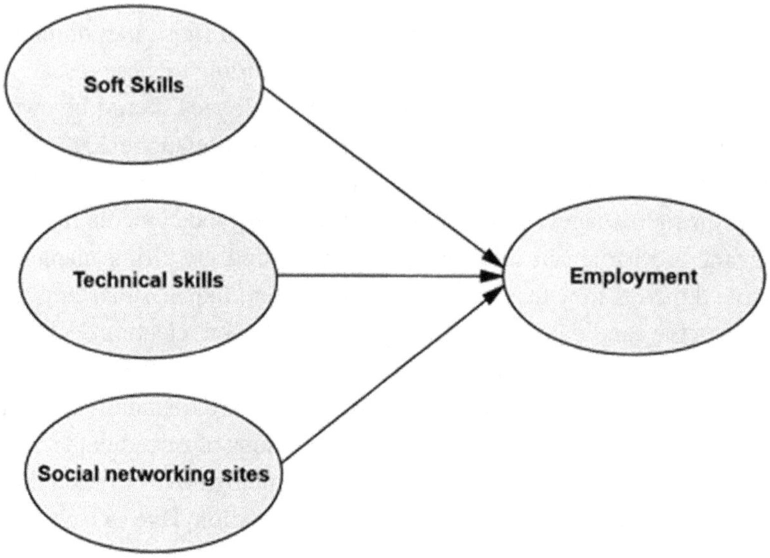

RESEARCH METHODOLOGY

This research aims to identify the competencies and skills possessed by the job seekers to secure jobs in the field of business administration, analyses the impact of soft skills, technical skills and social networking sites on their employment and proposes skill gap employability model to streamline recruitment process. Such Descriptive research design suits this research as it captures the characteristics of the population. (Baskaran 2022) The questionnaire has been developed through Microsoft forms to obtain primary data from job seekers. Specific soft skills and technical skills have been captured from the various business administration related job advertisements. Data analysis has been done using SPSS and Amos. Using Simple Random Sampling, 172 samples obtained from the respondents who reside in UAE. The questionnaire covers the demographic factors followed by self-evaluation and rating of soft skills like communication skills, leadership, teamwork, critical thinking, creativity, problem solving, valuing ethics, positive attitude, self-awareness, emotional intelligence, self-learning, multi-tasking, empathy, agility and readiness in Likert scale. The next segment covers the self-evaluation of technical skills such as research skills, technical writing, data management and analytics, accounting tools, project management software, marketing analytics tools, SPSS and simulation followed by questions related to the accessibility to social networking sites, presence in social media and its impact on employment in the last segment. Such skills have been extracted from the social media like Linkedin, Bayut, Indeed, NaukriGulf and MonsterGulf. The hypothesis have been framed to identify the significant impact of soft skills, technical skills and social networking sites on employment.

Hypothesis One:

$H_0 1$: There is no significant impact of soft skills on employment.

$H_a 1$: There is a significant impact of soft skills on employment.

Hypothesis Two:

$H_0 2$: There is no significant impact of technical skills on employment.

$H_a 2$: There is a significant impact of technical skills on employment.

Hypothesis Three:

$H_0 3$: There is no significant impact of social networking sites on employment.

$H_a 3$: There is a significant impact of social networking sites on employment.

Regression analysis is the statistical technique used as a predictive analytical tool to forecast the dependent variable with independent variables. The testing of hypothesis has been done using regression analysis through Statistical Package for Social Science (SPSS) version 29 and AMOS. Finally, the author seek to derive the Skill gap employability model to bridge the skill gap and ensure demand meets the supply.

DATA ANALYSIS AND INTERPRETATION

Table 1 highlights the Reliability Statistics that provides the actual value for Cronbach's alpha of 0.846 for this set of measures, indicating good reliability and suggesting that the measures are consistently measuring the intended construct. It indicates a high level of internal consistency for the scale with the given set of sample.

Table 1. Reliability statistics

Cronbach's Alpha	Cronbach's Alpha Based on Standardized Items	N of Items
.846	.862	4

Table 2 presents the Item-Total Statistics highlighting the "Cronbach's Alpha if Item Deleted" and "Corrected Item-Total Correlation". The Corrected Item-Total Correlation values for this measure ranges from 0.552 to 0.854 and Cronbach's Alpha if Item Delete is between 0.751 and 0.877 indicating adequate item discrimination for most items and suggesting that the items are contributing meaningfully to the overall measure score. Hence, elimination of any question would affect the Cronbach's alpha by ending up to further lower value.

Table 2. Item-total statistics

	Scale Mean if Item Deleted	Scale Variance if Item Deleted	Corrected Item-Total Correlation	Squared Multiple Correlation	Cronbach's Alpha if Item Deleted
Soft skills	11.909	3.812	.854	.748	.751
Technical skills	12.347	3.733	.683	.563	.805
Social networking sites	11.834	3.625	.552	.364	.877
Employment	12.039	3.670	.717	.604	.791

Table 3 descriptive statistics presents the values of mean, standard deviation and variance. The mean value ranging between 3.7 and 4.2 indicating that, on average, participants tended to respond positively to the measure. Similarly, the standard deviation for this measure is ranging between 0.622 and 0.887, indicating that there was a lower level of variability in the responses.

Table 4 provides the summary of ANOVA. The model used to analyze the data had a simple correlation of 0.777 and R^2 value of 0.604 indicating that 60% of the variance in the outcome variable can be accounted for by the predictor variables included in the model ie., Employment is explained by the independent variables, ie., soft skills, technical skills and social networking sites.

Table 3. Descriptive statistics

	N	Mean	Std. Deviation	Variance
Soft skills	172	4.134	.622	.387
Technical skills	172	3.700	.750	.562
Social networking sites	172	4.210	.887	.786
Employment	172	4.003	.746	.556
Valid N (list wise)	172			

Table 4. Model summary table for ANOVA

Model	R	R Square	Adjusted R Square	Std. Error of the Estimate
1	.777[a]	.604	.597	.474

a. Predictors: (Constant), Social networking sites, Technical skills, Soft skills.
b. Dependent Variable: Employment

ANOVA in table 5 presents how well the regression equation fits the data that predicts the employment significantly. This indicates P<.001, which is less than 0.05 at F value of 85.291, here the regression model statistically significantly predicts the outcome variable.

Table 5. ANOVA

Model		Sum of Squares	df	Mean Square	F	Sig.
1	Regression	57.413	3	19.138	85.291	<.001[b]
	Residual	37.696	168	.224		
	Total	95.109	171			
a. Dependent Variable: Employment						
b. Predictors: (Constant), Social networking sites, Technical skills, Soft skills.						

Coefficients in table 6 provides information to predict employment from soft skills, technical skills and social networking sites as well as to understand whether soft skills, technical skills and social networking sites contribute to the model and the regression equation is:

Table 6. Coefficients

Model		Unstandardized Coefficients		Standardized Coefficients	t	Sig.
		B	Std. Error	Beta		
1	(Constant)	0.176	0.246		0.717	0.474
	Soft skills	0.794	0.098	0.662	8.061	<0.001
	Technical skills	0.137	0.072	0.138	1.893	0.060
	Social networking sites	0.010	0.051	0.012	0.193	0.848
a. Dependent Variable: Employment						

Employment = 0.176 + 0.794 (Soft skills) + 0.137 (Technical skills) + 0.010 (Social networking sites)

The results of regression analysis reveals that soft skills have significant impact on Employment and the results states that it is statistically significant at 5% level, which emphasizes that soft skills such as communication skills, leadership, teamwork, critical thinking, creativity, problem solving, valuing ethics, positive attitude, self-awareness, emotional intelligence, self-learning, multi-tasking, empathy, agility and readiness are crucial for employment in the field of business administration sectors in UAE.

Table 6 demonstrated the hypotheses formulated and tested using regression analysis. H1 predicts that soft skills have strong positive relationship with Employment and the results states that it is statistically significant at 5% level, hence it is supported. H2 results revealed that technical skills does not have significant impact on Employment at 5% level, which makes H2 not supported. Similarly, H3 states that social networking sites does not have significant impact on employment, and H3 was not supported.

Table 7. Results of hypothesis testing

Hypothesis	T Statistics	P Values	Result
H1: Soft skills › Employment	8.061	<0.001	**Supported**
H2: Technical skills › Employment	1.893	0.060	Unsupported
H3: Social networking sites › Employment	0.193	0.848	Unsupported

Figure 2. Skill gap employability model

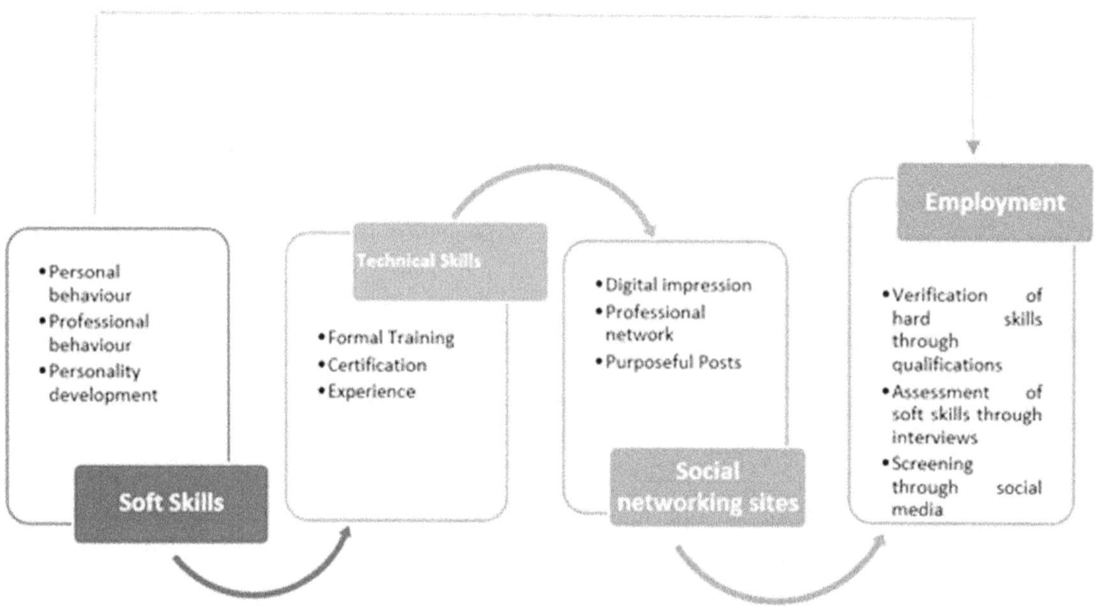

Skill gap employability model shown in figure 2 has been proposed based on the given results. The Skill Gap Employability Model is a framework for evaluating an individual's employability in relation to the skills required for a particular position. The model depends on the claim that there is a gap between the skills that companies seek from job seekers and the skills they actually possess. This gap can lead to decreased employment rates, job dissatisfaction, and other negative outcomes. The main process of the Skill Gap Employability Model are as follows. Initially, soft skills are personal cum professional behavior enhanced through personality development programme have been assessed by the employer through tests, discussions and interviews. Secondly, technical skills obtained from formal education, training, certification and experience should been verified by the employer through their credentials. At the later stage, employers assess the Social networking sites of the job seekers to screen the applicants based on their professional digital impression. As per this model, failing to achieve soft skill or technical skill or presence in social networking site may adverse impact on the prospective employment opportunity. As per the hypothesis testing results, soft skills such as communication skills, leadership, teamwork, critical thinking, creativity, problem solving, valuing ethics, positive attitude, self-awareness, emotional intelligence, self-learning, multi-tasking, empathy, agility and readiness have statistically significant impact on employment and it cannot be eliminated or ignored.

Skill Gap Employability Model captures the skills required by the company, skills possessed by the job seekers and bridging the gap between both. The company should share the job requirement for the specific job which showcases the specific knowledge and skills needed for a given job which includes given soft skills, technical skills and active presence in social networking sites. Furthermore, the job seekers should do the self-assessment of their skills and competencies meeting the requirement of employer. These skills may be acquired through education, training, work experience, or other sources. Finally, skill gap assessment done by the employee to find the difference between the required skills and the available skills. If the required skills exceed the available skills, there is a skill gap, which can lead to challenges in finding and continuing employment. The job seeker can identify the solution to overcome such challenges through trainings, hands on workshops, certifications, and professional development activities.

The Skill Gap Employability Model recommends that prospective job seekers can improve their employability by identifying the gaps between the skills required by employers and the skills they possess and fulfill those gaps by acquiring new skills through trainings, education, relevant work experience or improving communication and interpersonal skills or through their active presence on social networking sites. Employers can also use the Skill Gap Employability Model to identify areas where their employees may have lack of skills, and develop strategies to address these gaps for continuous improvement through on the job training and development opportunities, offering incentives for employees to acquire new skills, or adjusting job requirements to better match the available skills of the employees. Overall, the Skill Gap Employability Model act as a valuable tool to identify, assess and address the skills gap that impact the employability of job seekers and the productivity of organizations. By identifying and addressing these gaps, job seekers and organizations can improve their probability of success in identifying the right candidate for the right to achieve their goals.

CONCLUSION

Soft skills have a substantial and inevitable impact on one's job. Employers place a higher value on employees who have strong interpersonal skills and the ability to collaborate smoothly, therefore soft skills have become more crucial in the employment landscape. It is necessary for job seekers to focus exclusively on enhancing and demonstrating their soft skills in the workplace because those with strong soft skills have a higher chance of being hired and excelling in their jobs. Employees can better contribute to the success of their company, foster positive relationships with their coworkers, and accomplish their professional goals by having excellent soft skills. (Fadhil, Ismail and Alnoor 2021)

The impact of technical skills on employment is significant and cannot be overlooked. Technical skills play a crucial role in the hiring process and determine an individual's ability to perform a job effectively.

Individuals with strong technical skills are more likely to secure employment and have higher earning potential, making it essential for job seekers to focus on developing and showcasing their technical skills in the workplace. (Baskaran 2023) Technical skills are essential for success in many jobs and industries, and they play a crucial role in determining an individual's competitiveness in the job market. As the job market continues to evolve and demand for skilled professionals continues to increase, it is increasingly important for job seekers and employees to develop and demonstrate their technical skills in order to remain competitive and achieve their professional goals. (Fajaryati, et al. 2020) Technical skills are crucial in the hiring process since they determine a person's ability to do a job efficiently. Job seekers must concentrate on enhancing and showcasing their technical skills in the workplace because it helps not only to find employment but also to have higher earning potential. Technical skills are critical for professional success in almost, all the industries, and a key factor to establish an individual's brand value for employment. As the job market continues to evolve and demand for skilled professionals continues to increase, it is increasingly important for job seekers and employees to develop and demonstrate their technical skills in order to remain competitive and achieve their professional goals.

Social networking sites have significantly transformed employee hiring process and the job market. It has altered how job applicants look for employment, how businesses evaluate prospective employees, and how employees interact with others. Social networking sites have expedited and improved the job search process while allowing employers to search and reach out to potential candidates. Social networking sites have significantly changed the business, facilitating both employee and employer communication and collaboration. The impact of social networking sites on employment is multifaceted. Though these platforms has numerous opportunities to connect both job seekers and employers, it has its own challenges in the hiring process. To fully understand the impact of social networking sites on employment, it is important to consider both the potential benefits and challenges of these platforms. Social media is a platform that job searchers use to search for openings, connect with prospective employers, and showcase their talents and accomplishments. Social media sites like LinkedIn give job seekers the opportunity to interact with recruiters and companies and stay updated about available positions and the job market. Additionally, job seekers can use social media to enhance their personal brand and demonstrate their competencies to prospective employers. Individuals who use social media sites like LinkedIn have the opportunity to establish a professional profile that highlights their qualifications, education, and previous employment. Job seekers may use this to effectively present their skills and qualifications to prospective companies. (Brouer, Badawy and Stefanone 2022)

HR experts always check for a wide range of skills, qualifications, and traits in candidates during the recruitment process to make sure they are choosing the best applicant for the role. Among the most important things HR considers, job-related skills and experience with the qualifications needed to do the job well. This could include technical know-how, professional experience, and other credentials. Also they look for soft skills, including leadership potential, teamwork, communication, and problem-solving abilities crucial for creating a healthy working environment and for fostering relationships with clients and coworkers. Employers seek applicants who value and adhere to the company's culture and align with the company's mission, vision, and goals. During the hiring process, HR experts evaluate applicants' personalities and attitudes to see if they would fit perfectly with their peers and the company's culture. This could involve elements like a strong work ethic, enthusiasm, and a positive attitude. Also, they take into account applicants' educational backgrounds and any professional certificates or licenses they may hold. To confirm a candidate's employment history and guarantee they have no criminal record, HR experts frequently perform reference and background checks. In order to choose the candidates who are the best fit for the role and the corporate culture, HR experts take a variety of criteria into account when conducting recruitment. By emphasizing the abilities, knowledge, and traits that are most important to demonstrate the job and contribute positively to the organization.

In the recent years, there is a sharp increase in the usage of social media for career development and recruitment, with both companies and job seekers taking advantage of the platform. While job seekers use social media to identify possibilities, network with possible employers, and market their talents and qualifications, employers utilize it to source and recruit candidates. It is evident that social media has grown as a significant instrument for career development and the hiring process for both employers and job seekers. Having a significant social media presence is crucial for anyone searching for job, whether they are an employer looking for the best candidates or a job seeker looking for their next career opportunity. This research provides insights to the business administration professionals who are searching for employment in the areas of human resources, finance, accounting, marketing, sales, operations, logistics, supply chain management, and business analytics in UAE. This research focuses significantly to the skills required to secure business administrative jobs in UAE. Firstly, the study explores the various skill requirement from the employers based on job postings. Secondly, the skills were grouped into soft skills and technical skills. Based on the literature review, this study attempts to analyze the impact of social networking sites on employment. Finally, the skill gap employability model has been proposed with its impact on employment.

REFERENCES

Ahmed, S. H., & Baskaran, K. (2020). Blue-collar Workers behind the Success Story of UAE. *International Journal of Scientific & Technology Research*, *9*(2), 5221–5224.

Ashok, S., & Baskaran, K. (2019). Audit and Accounting Procedures in Organizations (with reference to Petty Cash). *Audit and Accounting Procedures in Organizations.*, *8*(4), 8759–8768. doi:10.35940/ijrte.D9165.118419

Ashok, S., & Baskaran, K. (2022). The Prominence of Corporate Governance in Banking Sector with Reference to UAE. In *Pervasive Computing and Social Networking. Lecture Notes in Networks and Systems* (Vol. 317). Springer. doi:10.1007/978-981-16-5640-8_33

Bapna, S., & Funk, R. (2021). Interventions for Improving Professional Networking for Women: Experimental Evidence from the IT Sector. *Management Information Systems Quarterly*, *45*(2), 593–636. doi:10.25300/MISQ/2021/15620

Baskaran, K. (2019). An Interpretive Study of Customer Experience Management towards Online Shopping in UAE. *International Journal of Mechanical Engineering and Technology*, *10*(2), 1071–1077.

Baskaran, K. (2019). The Impact of Digital Transformation in Singapore e-Tail Market. *International Journal of Innovative Technology and Exploring Engineering*, *8*(11), 2320–2324. doi:10.35940/ijitee.I8046.0981119

Baskaran, K. (2022). E-Consumer Behavioral Analytics: Paradigm Shift in Online Purchase Decision Making. In *Handbook of Research on Consumer Behavior Change and Data Analytics in the Socio-Digital Era* (pp. 192–209). IGI Global. doi:10.4018/978-1-6684-4168-8.ch009

Baskaran, K. (2023). Customer Experience in E-Commerce Market through virtual world of Metaverse. In *Consumer Behavioral Analytics in Metaverse and the Adoption of a Virtual World*. IGI Global. doi:10.4018/978-1-6684-7029-9.ch008

Baskaran, K. (2020). *Journey of Education Technology towards Innovation. Innovations in Engineering Education Conference - Advances in Science and Engineering Technology Conferences*. ASET. doi:10.1109/ASET48392.2020.9118334

Baskaran, K., & Rajavelu, S. (2020). Digital Innovation in Industry 4.0 Era – Rebooting UAE's Retail. *International Conference on Communication and Signal Processing*. IEEE. 10.1109/ICCSP48568.2020.9182301

Brouer, R., Badawy, R., & Stefanone, M. (2022). Social media and recruitment: Examining (counter) productive diversity messages. *Organizational Management Journal, 19*(1), 34–43. doi:10.1108/OMJ-09-2020-1029

Brouer, R., Badawy, R., & Stefanone, M. (2022). Social media and recruitment: Examining (counter) productive diversity messages. *Organizational Management Journal, 19*(1), 34–43. doi:10.1108/OMJ-09-2020-1029

Bruce, L., Bellesini, K., Aisbett, B., Drinkwater, E. J., & Kremer, P. (2022). A profile of the skills, attributes, development, and employment opportunities for sport scientists in Australia. *Journal of Science and Medicine in Sport, 25*(5), 419–424. doi:10.1016/j.jsams.2021.12.009 PMID:35190264

Carada, I. G., Aliazas, J., Palacio, L., & Palacio, C. (2022). Perceived Skills and Employability of Senior High School Graduates: Basis for Youth Employment Policy. *International Journal of Social Sciences and Humanities Invention,* 6759-6766. . doi:10.18535/ijsshi/v9i01.05

Choudhary, P., & Baskaran, K. (2022). The impact of Social Networking Sites among Modern Youth. *Interdisciplinary Research in Technology and Management, 2022*, 1–6. doi:10.1109/IRTM54583.2022.9791522

Cyriac, N. T., & Baskaran, K. (2020). A Study on the Effectiveness of Non-Monetary Retention Strategies in UAE. *International Conference on Reliability, Infocom Technologies and Optimization 2020,* IEEE. 10.1109/ICRITO48877.2020.9197867

Cyriac, N. T., & Baskaran, K. (2021). Predictive Analytics in a Post Covid-19 World: India's Travel and Tourism Industry. *International Conference on Advances in Technology, Management and Education 2021*. IEEE. 10.1109/ICATME50232.2021.9732706

Fadhil, S. S., Ismail, R., & Alnoor, A. (2021). The influence of soft skills on employability: A Case study on technology industry sector in Malaysia. *Interdisciplinary Journal of Information, Knowledge, and Management, 16*, 255–283. doi:10.28945/4807

Fajaryati, N., Budiyono, M. A., Akhyar, M., & Wiranto. (2020). The Employability Skills Needed To Face the Demands of Work in the Future: Systematic Literature Reviews. *Open Engineering, 10*(1), 595–603. doi:10.1515/eng-2020-0072

Fennell, A. (2022). *StandOut CV.* Standout DV. https://standout-cv.com/social-media-recruitment-statistics

Jiang, H., & Chen, C. (2021). Data Science Skills and Graduate Certificates: A Quantitative Text Analysis. *Journal of Computer Information Systems*, 1–17. doi:10.1080/08874417.2020.1852628

Lima, L., Wangb, Y., Hoshinoc, Y., & Islamd, M. N. (2015). Unveiling the mysteries of the "black hole" in recruiting systems: Connecting recruiters and job seekers like a jigsaw puzzle. *Procedia Manufacturing*, *3*, 3470–3477. doi:10.1016/j.promfg.2015.07.652

Lokaj, A., Miftari, V., & Hajdari. V. (2021). Leading students toward a new soft-skills perspective: development. *Journal of Education Culture and Society,* 283-296. . doi:10.15503/jecs2021.1.283.296

Majji, K. C., & Baskaran, K. (2021). Artificial Intelligence Analytics—Virtual Assistant in UAE Automotive Industry. In *Inventive Systems and Control - Lecture Notes in Networks and Systems* (Vol. 204, pp. 309–322). Springer. doi:10.1007/978-981-16-1395-1_24

Malki, Z., & Atlam, E. (2021). Graduate Students and Companies Web Based E-Recruitment System. *Journal of Computer and Communications*, *9*(9), 71–84. doi:10.4236/jcc.2021.99005

Mohan, M., & Baskaran, K. (2021). Financial Analytics: Investment Behavior of Middle Income Group In South India. *International Conference on Cloud Computing, Data Science & Engineering.* IEEE. 10.1109/Confluence51648.2021.9377029

Moncey, A. A., & Baskaran, K. (2020). Digital Marketing Analytics: Building Brand Awareness and Loyalty in UAE. *International Conference on Technology Management, Operations and Decisions.* IEEE. 10.1109/ICTMOD49425.2020.9380579

Papacharissi, Z. (2010). *A Networked Self: Identity, Community, and Culture on Social Network Sites.* Routledge. doi:10.4324/9780203876527

Rockwood, K. (2021). The Hard Facts About Soft Skills. *HR Magazine Summer 2021.* https://www.shrm.org/hr-today/news/hr-magazine/summer2021/pages/why-soft-skills-are-important.aspx

Wade, J. T., Roth, P. L., Thatcher, J. B., & Dinger, M. (2020). Social Media and Selection: Political Issue Similarity, Liking, and the Moderating Effect of Social Media Platform. *Management Information Systems Quarterly*, *44*(3), 1301–1357. doi:10.25300/MISQ/2020/14119

KEY TERMS AND DEFINITIONS

Recruitment: Systematic process of choosing right person for the right job by identifying, interviewing, hiring, and onboarding candidates.

Skill Gap: Difference between the skills required by employers and skills possessed by the job seekers. If the required skills exceed the available skills, there is a skill gap.

Social Networking Sites: Online platform that allows users to create a public profile, connect, communicate, and share information with other users.

Soft Skills: Personal traits which enable a person to communicate effectively and harmoniously with others.

Technical Skills: Specialized knowledge to perform the task proficiently using specific tools and programs.

Chapter 3
Role of HR Analytics in Ensuring Psychological Wellbeing and Job Security:
Learnings From COVID-19

Bhanupriya Khatri
Chandigarh University, India

Harshita Shrimali
Geetanjali Institute of Technical Studies, India

Shad Ahmad Khan
University of Buraimi, Oman

Arshi Naim
King Khalid University, Saudi Arabia

ABSTRACT

This chapter explores the impact of job insecurity on psychological well-being in the context of the COVID-19 pandemic. This chapter is based on empirical study measuring the six elements of job insecurity on psychological wellbeing, i.e., perceived threats to job features, role insecurity, role conflict, powerfulness, meaningfulness, and perceived threats to total job. Further, this chapter the role of HR analytics in ensuring psychological wellbeing and job security, with a focus on the lessons learned during the COVID-19 pandemic. highlights the importance of HR analytics in identifying and addressing employee needs related to psychological wellbeing and job security, and explores the ways in which HR analytics can be used to improve organizational decision-making and drive business outcomes. This chapter also briefly highlights the emerging practices, and the ways modern digital technologies can be harnessed for the betterment of the employees.

DOI: 10.4018/978-1-6684-8942-0.ch003

1. INTRODUCTION

Human resources (HR) analytics is a rapidly growing field that has become increasingly important in the contemporary world. With the explosion of data and the increasing demand for evidence-based decision-making, HR analytics has become a critical tool for organizations to improve their human resource management practices and drive business outcomes (Marler & Boudreau, 2017; Zareen & Khan, 2023). HR analytics is the process of collecting, analyzing, and interpreting data related to HR practices and processes (Arora et al., 2021). The goal of HR analytics is to identify patterns and trends in HR data and use this information to make data-driven decisions about HR practices and processes. HR analytics can be used to measure employee performance, identify talent gaps, evaluate the effectiveness of training programs, and more (Mohammed & Quddus, 2019). With the use of Artificial Intelligence and digital technologies, modern organizations can become more sustainable and active (Naim, 2022; Yadav et al., 2022; Magd et al., 2023; Khan & Rena, 2023). In the modern times if the organizations are healthy from inside (internal environment), they are expected to have a better outlook to the world (Brand Image), thus it is not only important for an organization to ensure customer satisfaction and loyalty, but also to ensure the loyalty and satisfaction among its employees (Saleem et al., 2022; Kamal et al., 2022; Khan et al., 2021; Ligori et al., 2022; Khan et al., 2020; Ligori et al., 2019). The modern analytics is incomplete if the online and digital technologies are not harnessed to the optimum level (Khan, 2023; Khan & Magd, 2023; Magd & Khan, 2022; Sharma et al., 2023; Magd et al., 2023). This also includes the utilization of efficient database management, E-HRM, S-service Quality etc. (Berber et al., 2018; Kamal et al., 2022; Khan et al., 2022). It becomes even more relevant for HR in modern times as the culture of Work from Home (WFH), online working, remote working, hybrid working etc. is on the rise and is expected to grow further.

One of the major challenges in front of the managers today is to deal with adversities. Adversities do not similarly disturb and distress all persons. Covid 19 brought on surface many learnings. Covid 19 has disturbed the global economy, amplifying established hazards to its viewpoint. Corona originated during the period when nation's economic condition was by this time slackening due to insistent monetary sector flaws. The influence of tragedies depends on the susceptibility of pretentious people, which habitually diverges steadily across financial status, civilization, and other factors. Mahmud & Islam (2021) concluded that Covid 19 is responsible for not only a community's well-being disaster but also a monetary one. With demands for social distancing, service sector jobs that are to be subject to on customer-provider connections or include the crowd of people are to take a massive smash (Bocar at al., 2022; Khan et al., 2021; Khan & Magd, 2021). The government had ordered the people to remain inside and isolated to discontinue the blow-out of the coronavirus. Businesses requested their personnel to work from home (Magd & Khan, 2022; Bocar et al., 2022; Sinha et al., 2023). Big congregations of people were not allowable. Some traces of the practices initiated during Covid 19 are expected to continue in the post pandemic era (Magd et al., 2023). Like Corona Virus Disease and its effects on health, unemployment and psychological wellbeing are a malignant delinquent. Job security means liberty from disturbing over the work's constancy and the deserted sensation that conveys it. Well-being is a constructive consequence that is significant for people and numerous subdivisions of humanity since it expresses that people observe that everything is going fine. Many of the articles are claiming that a big recession is on the way which will have a very bad impact on the scarcity of the resources and may create a situation like World War.

Covid 19 also emerged as a lubricant for digital and online practices (Khan & Magd, 2021; Khan et al., 2023; Saleem), whereby a fast adoption of technology was observed among the users. This includes various industries representing different industries and all the sections of an organization including HR. This chapter considers the impact of six elements of Job insecurity on psychological wellbeing of the employees during the outbreak of Covid 19 and discusses the ways HR analytics can help to ensure the psychological wellbeing in times to come, taking Covid 19 as a precedence.

2. LITERATURE REVIEW

Job instability is usually perceived as a stress factor that affects a precise group of workforces and leads to undesirable effects. We disagree with this viewpoint, which is founded on novel occupation pomposity that assumes that job uncertainty is ubiquitous but not detrimental; somewhat, job insecurity can foster professional growth and development (De Cuyper et al., 2019; Ansari & Khan, 2023). Because of numerous factors such as high demand for jobs and the government's incapacity to meet such a high demand in a short period of time, job insecurity is becoming a major risk to the careers of aspiring, meritorious, and industrious employees in our country (Ansari & Talan, 2017).

The study of Cheung et al. (2019), incorporated emotional state into consideration the influence of work insecurity and offered experiential indication on the importance of individual resources in reducing job insecurity's impact. The findings have ramifications for creating effective management strategies and practices to deal with employment instability. Cappa et al. (2020) conducted a study that revealed that women face job uncertainty and underemployment due to time constraints, as well as workplace discrimination.

Perceived job instability is a major source of workplace stress, resulting in negative health and performance results for employees and higher health-care expenses for businesses. Sleep eminence, a significant indicator of well-being, has received little attention regarding the influence of job uncertainty (Kim et al., 2021). Breevaart et al. (2020), conducted a study with a goal to look at how job uncertainty affects employee voice and quiet on a weekly basis. The authors specifically suggest that because employment satisfies important wants, employees' needs are less satisfied when they believe their job is in jeopardy (i.e., high job insecurity).

Excessive stress causes enormous financial losses for individuals, employers, and taxpayers. While many occurrences of stress are linked to loss of control and exhaustion because of shift work, others are linked to incidents of occupational violence, work overload, job insecurity, and precarious employment (Mayhew, 2018). Mayhew (2018) felt job instability is frequently viewed as a source of stress for a specific group of employees, with negative consequences for all. We disagree with this viewpoint, which is founded on novel job rhetoric that accepts that job uncertainty is ubiquitous, but not inevitably negative; somewhat, job insecurity can foster professional growth and development.

Yeves et al. (2019) Felt job instability is frequently viewed as a source of stress for an exact group of employees, implying unfavorable effects in general. The service industry has grown in importance in the post-industrial age, and specialized activities have been changed into service-oriented information labor, such as the commercial accessing occupation. With the deregulation of the labor market, the variety of employment patterns has risen, and the service design of specialists employed in the service segment has been characterized by immediate projects and service agreements (Haapakorpi, 2021).

The findings of Koen et al. (2020) can help guide future study into the specific scenarios in which job insecurity may prompt job preservation efforts, as well as research into the mechanisms that underpin employees' negative and positive reactions to job insecurity. Several studies have found that job uncertainty, work-family conflict, research funding applications, and a heavy workload are all contributing to increased psychosocial stress in academia (Bolliger et al. 2020).

While work uncertainty often hinders performance, there are times when it might encourage it. The goal of this paper is to look at how job insecurity can affect task and contextual performance in each setting (reorganization). The writers specified that the act can be used as a work conservation policy, with workforces using it only when administrator delivered performance ratings are critical to keeping their jobs (Goslinga, 2017). Blázquez et al. (2021) showed concerns about employment insecurity should not be separated from concerns about rising domestic debt, and policies aimed at improving individual welfare should take both factors into account.

As per Pentón Herrera, et al. (2021), students typically feel emotional and psychological hardship while earning a degree, which can interfere with their ability to equilibrium their individual, monetary, and professional existence. Talent in advanced instruction also endure negative sentiments and feelings related to their work, such as exhaustion, stress, worry, insecurity, anxiety, despair, and burnout.

Redundancy has a negative influence on individuals, as well as its spillover effects on couples (Inanc, 2018). Though, when it originates to the same repercussions of provisional employment, we have a knowledge gap. This is problematic because, while provisional occupations are often thought to be a better substitute to joblessness in relationships of if revenue and prospects to system with companies, they are also associated with stress factors such as high stages of job uncertainty and bad superiority effort, which can disturb partners.

Service-connected pressure had a negative association with welfare for persons who existed in sections with additional optimistic population healthiness factors (Probst et al., 2018). The undesirable influence of joblessness on persons and its spillover to partners is extensively recognized. However, we have a gap in our knowledge when it comes to the similar consequences of temporary employment (Veronese et al., 2021). Organizations must determine which characteristics relate to this mental state to build a workplace environment that promotes employee well-being. The hope is that by doing so, social resources will be replenished, and member presentation will progress (Parent-Lamarche et al., 2021).

Study of McKeown et al. (2011), the findings showed the importance of focusing on unique work organization conditions. Having an adequate number of employees on hand to alleviate mental pressures, allowing employees to work fewer hours, and creating job security through greater organizational communication are all options. There is considerable epidemiological and clinical evidence that joblessness has an undesirable impact on mental well-being, although the processes by which this happens are still being disputed. Furthermore, the impact of underemployment on mental health is even less well-documented.

The rising usage of provisional contracts has sparked discussions about the potential consequences on employees' attitudes, well-being, and behavior. From a theoretical, empirical, and conceptual standpoint, the complex issues surrounding this argument are examined (De Cuyper et al., 2008). As per Briody et al, (2020) the Covid 19 pandemic, which has been followed by an economic downturn and a slew of restrictions on our lives, has reignited interest in the topic of loneliness and its causes.

Bocar et al., (2022), conducted a study on WFH stressors and emphasized the fact that the employer will only act when the employee has given his reaction on the WFH related stress. The study emphasized on the fact that the employer must become pro-active and take measures by way of observation and adoption of technologies.

The findings of the study by Chambel and Farina (2015), emphasize the relevance of HRM practices in establishing positive psychological states among Temporary Agency Workers, not only at work but also outside of it. In two distinct countries, this observation was confirmed. The Covid 19 pandemic, which has been followed by an economic downturn and a slew of restrictions on our lives, has reignited interest in the topic of loneliness and its causes (Angel and Angel, 2014). Specific modifications in emotional intelligence and political skill, according to the concept, alleviate the pressure practiced by subordinates because of their supervisors' use of intimidation and pressure (Meisler et al., 2017).

As conclusion to the literature review, it has been found evident that the work related stress and job security are two major concerns for the employees, and with the changing trends, it needs to be addressed as the work culture is going to reduce the physical contact between the HR department in the employees in the time to come.

3. RESEARCH GAP

A lot of studies are available on Job insecurity and psychological wellbeing, but no research paper is available by considering these two parameters during the Covid 19 pandemic. The association of Job security with psychological well-being has also been increased after Covid 19 since well-being assimilates psychological health (mind) and bodily health ensuing in additional all-inclusive methods to illness prevention and health advancement. Covid 19 aroused the fear among people not only for outbreak of the disease but also for unemployment and ultimately, the fear of losing the job may impact the well-being of the people as well-being is a binding populace result extent further than ill health, impermanence, and financial position that expresses us in what way persons recognize that they are enjoying from their own their own perspective. Also limited studies were found where HR analytics has been studied in context of the pandemic, stress and job security among employees.

4. CONCEPTUAL FRAMEWORK, OBJECTIVES, AND HYPOTHESES GENERATION

It is evident from the literature that psychological wellbeing and job security are important considerations for any organization (Alcover et al., 2020). To check this element, an empirical study was warranted, thus, the researchers explored various literature to find reliable models that could provide antecedents to psychological wellbeing in the context of this study. One of the aspects of this research is job insecurity. De Witte et al. (2010) & Shoss (2017) explored this element and found that Job insecurity is not only the threat of losing job, but also, includes the threat of losing position and responsibilities leading to dissatisfaction from the job role in total referred as perceived threats to the total job. On the similar lines, Park & Ono (2017), considered job insecurity as a combination of perception of threat and powerlessness. This threat not only means losing of job, but also losing some important job features having a significant impact on the mental health (Park & Ono, 2017). Long et al. (2021) explored the psychological wellbeing from the perspective of employee motivation, where they identified meaningfulness as a positive contributor to the psychological wellbeing. As meaningfulness is the justification to an individual's physical, cognitive, or emotional energy. If an employee doesn't find a job meaningful to his physical, cognitive, or emotional energy, he becomes insecure and suffers on the account of psychological wellbeing. Role conflict was also identified as a significant contributor to the stress level of employees (Baillien & De Witte, 2009). De Witte (1999) conducted a study on job insecurity and psychological wellbeing and explored the elements like skill utilisation, workload demand, job insecurity, autonomy, responsibility as stressors to the individual. Bocar et al. (2022), conducted a study on the employees during the Covid 19 pandemic, and highlighted the growing expectations from the employers on the embracing of digital technology among employees. Thus, as a compilation of these studies, six dimensions of the job insecurity are identified i.e., Perceived threats to Job features, Role Insecurity, Role Conflict, Powerfulness, meaningfulness and Perceived threats to total job. To evaluate psychological wellbeing six items were identified i.e., autonomy, environmental mastery, personal growth, positive relations, purpose in life and self-acceptance. (De Witte 1999; Sun et al., 2016; Akin, 2008; Akhtar et al., 2023).

The main objective of the study is to find out the impact of six elements of Job insecurity on psychological wellbeing of the employees during the outbreak of Covid 19. The second objective of the study is to discuss the possible role HR analytics can play in ensuring psychological wellbeing. To accomplish the first objective empirical study has been conducted by establishing the following six hypotheses:

H1 There is significant relationship between Perceived threats to Job features and Psychological Wellbeing.
H2 There is a significant relationship between Role Insecurity and Psychological Wellbeing.
H3 There is a significant relationship between Role Conflict and Psychological Wellbeing.
H4 There is a significant relationship between Powerfulness and Psychological Wellbeing.
H5 There is a significant relationship between Meaninglessness and Psychological Wellbeing.
H6 There is significance relationship between Perceived threats to total job and Psychological Wellbeing.

5. RESEARCH METHODOLOGY AND TOOLS

To address the first objective, two questionnaires are designed by the researchers. The first tool that is used to measure Job Insecurity is comprised of six dimensions: Perceived threats to Job features, Role Insecurity, Role Conflict, Powerfulness, meaningfulness and Perceived threats to total job. Second tool is based on Psychological Wellbeing which comprised of six elements are autonomy, environmental mastery, personal growth, positive relations, purpose in life and self-acceptance. The conceptual model for the same is presented in Figure 1 along with the sampling technique and measures are discussed in point 5.1 and 5.2.

To address the second objective, review of key studies was adopted (secondary data) using the key words as "HR analytics"; "Psychological wellbeing"; "HR analytics AND Employee Stress" etc., from in google scholar to get a brief idea on the role HR analytics can play in ensuring the psychological wellbeing, the same has been discussed in the discussion section of this chapter.

5.1. Sampling Technique

Convenience sampling is used to collect data from working professionals. The sample of the research was taken from public sector, private sector, non-profit and others. Sample size was 424 out of which were 233 males and 199 were females.

Figure 1. Conceptual framework

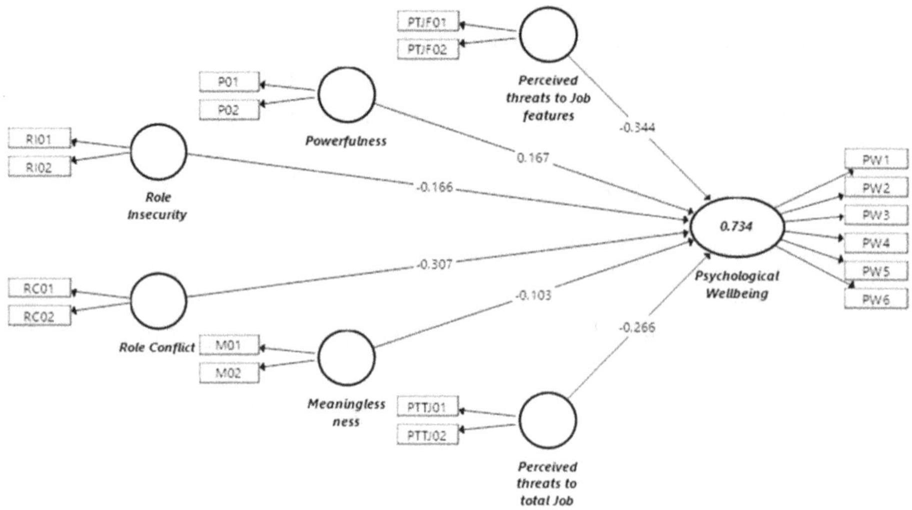

5.2. Measures

Measurements for Cronbach alpha of Perceived threats to Job features, Role Insecurity, Role Conflict, Powerfulness, meaninglessness and Perceived threats to total job are 0.78, 0.78, 0.74, 0.71. 0.78 and 0.84 respectively. Cronbach alpha for Psychological Wellbeing is 0. 91. Five-point Likert Scale has been used to measure all the constructs of Job Insecurity and Psychological Wellbeing.

6. DATA ANALYSIS

6.1. Common Method Variance

Due to the object that data collected in this research were self-reported through a questionnaire directed throughout an alike period, common method bias was inspected using Harman's single-factor test (Podsakoff et al., 2003). The outcomes showed that the largest variance described by the first factor was 44.48% of the total variance, less than the 50% threshold recommended (Podsakoff et al., 2003). Therefore, common method bias is not concerned in this data set.

6.2. Measurement Model

To build the measurement model, SmartPLS 3.2.6 software was applied as the central purpose of this research analysis is to envisage the fundamental constructs. For estimating the measurement model, convergent validity was examined by noticing into indicator loadings, average variance extracted (AVE), composite reliability (CR) and Dillion-Goldstein's rho (rho_A).

Statistics have presented perfect loadings as all numbers are more than the standard of 0.7 which is shown in Table 1. rho_A and Composite reliability are more than the threshold value of 0.7 and hence, the internal reliability has been succeeded. Convergent Validity is also accomplished as Average Variance Extracted is above than threshold value of 0.50.

Table 1 shows that all HTMT numbers are less than the threshold value of 0.90 and hence, it is achieved as per the standards. Hence, the research measurement model has completely validated the convergent validity and discriminant validity.

Table 1. Result of measurement model

Construct	Indicator	Loading	rho_A	CR	AVE
Meaninglessness	M01	0.885	0.794	0.899	0.816
	M02	0.921			
Powerfulness	P01	0.814	0.813	0.866	0.765
	P02	0.931			
Perceived threats to Job features	PTJF01	0.894	0.781	0.899	0.817
	PTJF02	0.913			
Perceived threats to total Job	PTTJ01	0.917	0.851	0.925	0.861
	PTTJ02	0.938			
	PW1	0.848			
Role Conflict	RC01	0.869	0.755	0.884	0.792
	RC02	0.910			
Role Insecurity	RI01	0.896	0.779	0.899	0.817
	RI02	0.911			
Psychological Wellbeing	PW1	0.848	0.915	0.932	0.694
	PW2	0.843			
	PW3	0.799			
	PW4	0.867			
	PW5	0.870			
	PW6	0.768			

Table 2. HTMT criterion

	1	2	3	4	5	6	7
1. Meaninglessness							
2. Perceived threats to Job features	0.458						
3. Perceived threats to total Job	0.315	0.613					
4. Powerfulness	0.673	0.422	0.716				
5. Psychological Wellbeing	0.388	0.862	0.746	0.384			
6. Role Conflict	0.307	0.702	0.865	0.563	**0.869**		
7. Role Insecurity	0.361	0.772	0.598	0.453	**0.770**	0.745	

6.3. Structural Model

The VIF values need to be below the threshold value of 3.33 and our values are under the threshold values which range from 1.42 to 2.99. For consequence of projected hypothesis, bootstrapping re-sampling technique has been assessed. Table 3 shows that all the five hypotheses are accepted.

Analysis demonstrated that Perceived threats to Job features, Role Insecurity, Role Conflict, meaningfulness and Perceived threats to total job negatively influence the psychological well-being as (β= - 0.34, t=6.50 , $p<0.05$), (β= -0.17 , t= 4.67, $p<0.05$), (β= -0.31 , t= 5.79, $p<0.05$), (β= -0.10, t= 2.59, $p<0.05$) and (β= -0.27, t= 3.55, $p<0.05$) respectively and Powerfulness positively influence Psychological Well-being as (β= 0.17 , t= 3.59, $p<0.05$).

Table 3. Hypothesis testing of direct relationships

Hypothesis	Relationship	Std Beta	Std Error	t- value	P Values	Decision
H1	Perceived threats to Job features -> Psychological Wellbeing	-0.344	0.053	6.504	0	Supported
H2	Role Insecurity -> Psychological Wellbeing	-0.166	0.036	4.672	0	Supported
H3	Role Conflict -> Psychological Wellbeing	-0.307	0.053	5.792	0	Supported
H4	Powerfulness -> Psychological Wellbeing	0.167	0.047	3.587	0	Supported
H5	Meaninglessness -> Psychological Wellbeing	-0.103	0.04	2.586	0.01	Supported
H6	Perceived threats to total Job -> Psychological Wellbeing	-0.266	0.075	3.552	0	Supported

Co-efficient of Determination was calculated and 73.4% of variance of psychological wellbeing was conjointly explained by Perceived threats to Job features, Role Insecurity, Role Conflict, Powerfulness, meaninglessness, and Perceived threats to total job.

To scrutinize the effect size, Cohen's f^2 is inspected to recognize large, medium and small size with importance of 0.35, 0.15, and 0.02 respectively. To illuminate the psychological wellbeing, Perceived threats to Job features (0.24), Role Conflict (0.16), indicates medium effect size and Role Insecurity (0.06), Powerfulness (0.06), Meaninglessness (0.3) and Perceived threats to total job (0.11) indicate small effect size.

To assess the predictive relevance, Stone Geisser's Q2 has been calculated. The Q^2 value for Psychological Wellbeing was 0.50 which is above 0. Therefore, it produces suitable predictive relevance.

6.4. Key Findings

6.4.1. Impact of Perceived Threats to Job Features on Psychological Well-Being

Correlation between Perceived threats to Job features and Psychological Well-being is -0.344. So, we may say that if there is an increase in Perceived threats to Job features, Psychological Wellbeing is decreased.

6.4.2. Impact of Role Insecurity on Psychological Wellbeing

Correlation between Role Insecurity and Psychological Wellbeing is -0.166. So, we may say that if there is an increase in Role Insecurity, Psychological Wellbeing is decreased.

6.4.3. Impact of Role Conflict on Psychological Wellbeing

Correlation between Role Conflict and Psychological Wellbeing is -0.307. So, we may say that if there is an increase in Role Conflict, Psychological Wellbeing is decreased.

6.4.4. Impact of Powerfulness on Psychological Wellbeing

Correlation between Powerfulness on Psychological Wellbeing is 0.167. So, we may say that if there is an increase in Powerfulness, Psychological Wellbeing also increases.

6.4.5. Impact of Meaninglessness on Psychological Wellbeing

Correlation between Meaninglessness on Psychological Wellbeing is -0.103. So, we may say that if there is an increase in Meaninglessness, Psychological Wellbeing is decreased.

6.4.6. Impact of Perceived threats to total job on Psychological Wellbeing

Correlation between Perceived threats to total job and Psychological Wellbeing is -0.266. So, we may say that if there is an increase in Role Conflict, Psychological Wellbeing is decreased.

7. IMPACT OF JOB SECURITY ON PSYCHOLOGICAL WELL-BEING

A job is a significant part of anybody's life and life with significance and determination is a basis to develop psychological well-being. The general primary consequence of COVID 19 is bad impact on immunity and even deaths and overall terror of corona virus may influence the psychological aspects on communities at large. Those people who are doing the job, it's tough for them to retain it in near future. Think about the fresher students who have just completed their degrees. The scenario is so tough that companies are preparing for layoffs, the new recruitment of especially fresher students is far behind to even think in near future. Assessing, following and encouraging safety measures can be valuable for numerous participants convoluted in sickness inhibition and well-being up gradation.

Well-being is more than the non-appearance of virus infection; it is a means that permits persons to understand their ambitions, content their necessities and to accomplish with the surroundings to conscious an elongated, creative, and rewarding life. In this logic, healthiness lets societal, financial and individual improvement be fundamental to well-being. Well-being advancement is the procedure of permitting individuals to upsurge control over, and to progress their strength. Ecological and communal means for wellbeing can comprise harmony, financial safety and harmless accommodation.

In places with a great occurrence of COVID 19, movement of people was restricted, lockdown decreasing customer expenses? COVID 19 mostly affected financial development by plummeting demand.

Services linking face-to-face interaction had been dispensed a severe setback by the extensive terror of contamination over such connections. Travel, transportation (particularly air companies), and trading had been the toughest knockout segments as customers are avoiding going out for purchasing, dining out, entertainment etc. Each sector is adversely affected by this epidemic.

Work from home can be a basis for the employees to sense loneliness, creating it further significant to regularly tie up with the people, not only about their efforts, but also to know how they are. Isolation can be prime to sadness and psychological wellbeing issues. Be mindful of noteworthy fluctuations, one can realize in their pears' performance because it might be a symbol that an individual is stressed. As the psychological well-being's element is health and employment, therefore, COVID 19 pandemic plays a crucial role to affect psychological well-being. Till now, the major focus of Government has been to force and motivate the people to stay at home only. When this pandemic and lock down will be over, the people's expectations will be increased that the Government will frame certain measures to eradicate employment and raise the standard of the people. After the lockdown, the role of the Government will increase to uplift the economy at large.

8. HR ANALYTICS AND PSYCHOLOGICAL WELLBEING

HR analytics refers to the use of data and analytics to understand and improve HR practices and outcomes (Huselid, 2018). In the context of job insecurity and psychological well-being, HR analytics can play a critical role in understanding the factors that contribute to job insecurity and developing strategies to mitigate its negative effects (Darvishmotevali & Ali, 2020; Chatterjee et al., 2022; Orben & Przybylski, 2019). One approach to HR analytics is to conduct surveys to measure the level of job insecurity and its impact on employee well-being. These surveys can help identify the specific factors that contribute to job insecurity, such as organizational restructuring, changes in job duties or expectations, or concerns about job security. By understanding these factors, HR can develop targeted interventions to address them and reduce job insecurity (Fernandez & Gallardo-Gallardo, 2021; Chatterjee et al., 2022).

Another approach is to use data analytics to identify patterns and trends in employee behavior and well-being. For example, HR can use data on employee absenteeism, turnover, and job performance to identify employees who may be at risk of experiencing job insecurity and negative mental health outcomes (Lawrance et al., 2022; Hastuti & Timming, 2022). By identifying these employees early, HR can provide support and resources to help them cope with job insecurity and maintain their mental health and well-being (Darvishmotevali & Ali, 2020; Bocar et al., 2022).

HR analytics can also be used to develop and evaluate interventions to address job insecurity and its impact on employee well-being (Greasley & Thomas, 2020). For instance, HR can use data to identify the most effective strategies for reducing job insecurity, such as providing clear communication about job expectations and security or offering career development opportunities. HR can also use data to evaluate the impact of these interventions on employee well-being, job satisfaction, and job performance. The emerging technologies, like wearable bands, smart watches etc. if synchronized with HR analytics, can provide real time data by way of measuring blood pressure, heart rate, sleep time etc. This can also help the HR department to take proactive measures on their part (Bandari, 2019).

9. CONCLUSION

Job insecurity can have more damaging consequences for one's well-being than unemployment. A positive approach with high determination and smart work may lead to good psychological health and well-being. Businesses are expected to suffer damage to revenues, which would lead to unemployment. So, as job security vestiges on everyone's attention. This is an impeccable period for all organizations to show that all employees are assets for the organization by providing wisdom of Job security and for maintaining the psychological wellbeing of the employees. The COVID 19 pandemic has brought about significant changes in the world of work, with many employees experiencing job insecurity and its negative impact on psychological well-being. HR analytics can play a critical role in understanding the factors that contribute to job insecurity and developing strategies to mitigate its negative effects. By using data and analytics to measure, analyze, and intervene in the context of job insecurity and psychological well-being, HR can support employees in maintaining their mental health and well-being, even in times of uncertainty and change.

10. MANAGERIAL IMPLICATIONS

The thoughtful of the relationship between Job Insecurity and Psychological wellbeing may aid to control the noteworthy potential for humanizing the situations, during the bad times of COVID 19. This study endows the organizations to suggest functioning of methods and essentials to improve the psychological well-being of the employees. It's a great period to provide job security for illuminating the optimism in the workforce to develop the psychological well-being of the employees. The present exploration is a genuine effort to realize the highlights and importance of job security and psychological wellbeing of the employees.

11. LIMITATIONS

1. The sampling method which is convenient sampling is devising some limits like it does not signify normalize distribution as liken to different sampling techniques.
2. The data was collected from the working employees, but an industry-wise comparison is not made.
3. Sample size is too minor which does not signify the whole population among working professionals.
4. Additionally, other factors such as stress, quality of work life, commitment and job satisfaction can be considered for future research related to Corona Virus Disease.
5. The role of HR analytics is not empirically tested.

REFERENCES

Akhtar, N., Francis, L. J., Sailer, A. B., Hasan, S. S., & McKenna, U. (2023). Introducing the Psychological Wellbeing Scale for Muslim Societies (PWS-MS): A study among young adults in Pakistan. *Mental Health, Religion & Culture*, 1–12. doi:10.1080/13674676.2022.2139364

Akin, A. (2008). The scales of psychological well-being: A study of validity and reliability. *Educational Sciences: Theory & Practice*, *8*(3), 741–750.

Alcover, C. M., Salgado, S., Nazar, G., Ramírez-Vielma, R., & González-Suhr, C. (2020). Job insecurity, financial threat and mental health in the COVID-19 context: The buffer role of perceived social support. MedRxiv, 2020-07. doi:10.1101/2020.07.31.20165910

Angel, R. J., & Angel, J. L. (2014). *Latinos in an aging world: Social, psychological, and economic perspectives*. Routledge. doi:10.4324/9781315814582

Ansari, A. H., & Talan, A. (2017). Antecedents and Organizational Commitment Related Consequences of Job Insecurity among Teachers. *International Journal of Applied Business and Economic Research*, *15*(18), 321–333.

Ansari, M. S. A., & Khan, S. A. (2023). FDI, disinvestment and growth: An appraisal of Bhutanese economy. *Journal of Chinese Economic and Foreign Trade Studies*, *16*(1), 64–82. doi:10.1108/JCEFTS-05-2022-0031

Arora, M., Prakash, A., Mittal, A., & Singh, S. (2021, December). HR analytics and artificial intelligence-transforming human resource management. In *2021 International Conference on Decision Aid Sciences and Application (DASA)* (pp. 288-293). IEEE. 10.1109/DASA53625.2021.9682325

Baillien, E., & De Witte, H. (2009). Why is organizational change related to workplace bullying? Role conflict and job insecurity as mediators. *Economic and Industrial Democracy*, *30*(3), 348–371. doi:10.1177/0143831X09336557

Bandari, V. (2019). Exploring the Transformational Potential of Emerging Technologies in Human Resource Analytics: A Comparative Study of the Applications of IoT, AI, and Cloud Computing. *Journal of Humanities and Applied Science Research*, *2*(1), 15–27.

Berber, N., Đorđević, B., & Milanović, S. (2018). Electronic human resource management (e-HRM): A new concept for digital age. *Strategic Management-International Journal of Strategic Management and Decision Support Systems in Strategic Management, 23*(2).

Blázquez, M., Budría, S., & Moro-Egido, A. I. (2021). Job insecurity, debt burdens, and individual health. *Review of Income and Wealth*, *67*(4), 872–899. doi:10.1111/roiw.12506

Bocar, A. C., Khan, S. A., & Epoc, F. (2022). COVID-19 Work from Home Stressors and the Degree of its Impact: Employers and Employees Actions. *International Journal of Technology Transfer and Commercialisation. Inderscience*, *19*(2), 270–291.

Bolliger, L., Lukan, J., Luštrek, M., De Bacquer, D., & Clays, E. (2020). Protocol of the STRess At Work (STRAW) project: How to disentangle day-to-day occupational stress among academics based on EMA, physiological data, and smartphone sensor and usage data. *International Journal of Environmental Research and Public Health*, *17*(23), 8835. doi:10.3390/ijerph17238835 PMID:33561061

Breevaart, K., Lopez Bohle, S., Pletzer, J. L., & Munoz Medina, F. (2020). Voice and silence as immediate consequences of job insecurity. *Career Development International*, *25*(2), 204–220. doi:10.1108/CDI-09-2018-0226

Briody, J., Doyle, O., & Kelleher, C. (2020). The effect of local unemployment on health: A longitudinal study of Irish mothers 2001-2011. *Economics and Human Biology*, *37*, 100859. doi:10.1016/j.ehb.2020.100859 PMID:32114328

Chambel, M. J., & Farina, A. (2015). HRM and temporary workers' well-being: A study in Portugal and Brazil. *Cross Cultural Management*, *22*(3), 447–463. doi:10.1108/CCM-07-2013-0105

Chatterjee, S., Chaudhuri, R., Vrontis, D., & Siachou, E. (2022). Examining the dark side of human resource analytics: An empirical investigation using the privacy calculus approach. *International Journal of Manpower*, *43*(1), 52–74. doi:10.1108/IJM-02-2021-0087

Cheung, F. Y. L., Wu, A. M., & Ching Chi, L. (2019). Effect of job insecurity, anxiety and personal resources on job satisfaction among casino employees in macau: A moderated mediation analysis. *Journal of Hospitality Marketing & Management*, *28*(3), 379–396. doi:10.1080/19368623.2019.1525332

Crowe, L., & Butterworth, P. (2016). The role of financial hardship, mastery and social support in the association between employment status and depression: Results from an Australian longitudinal cohort study. *BMJ Open*, *6*(5), e009834. doi:10.1136/bmjopen-2015-009834 PMID:27235296

Darvishmotevali, M., & Ali, F. (2020). Job insecurity, subjective well-being and job performance: The moderating role of psychological capital. *International Journal of Hospitality Management*, *87*, 102462. doi:10.1016/j.ijhm.2020.102462

De Cuyper, N., De Jong, J., De Witte, H., Isaksson, K., Rigotti, T., & Schalk, R. (2008). Literature review of theory and research on the psychological impact of temporary employment: Towards a conceptual model. *International Journal of Management Reviews*, *10*(1), 25–51. doi:10.1111/j.1468-2370.2007.00221.x

De Cuyper, N., Van Hootegem, A., Smet, K., Houben, E., & De Witte, H. (2019). All insecure, all good? Job insecurity profiles in relation to career correlates. *International Journal of Environmental Research and Public Health*, *16*(15), 2640. doi:10.3390/ijerph16152640 PMID:31344856

De Witte, H., De Cuyper, N., Handaja, Y., Sverke, M., Näswall, K., & Hellgren, J. (2010). Associations between quantitative and qualitative job insecurity and well-being: A test in Belgian banks. *International Studies of Management & Organization*, *40*(1), 40–56. doi:10.2753/IMO0020-8825400103

Fernandez, V., & Gallardo-Gallardo, E. (2021). Tackling the HR digitalization challenge: Key factors and barriers to HR analytics adoption. *Competitiveness Review*, *31*(1), 162–187. doi:10.1108/CR-12-2019-0163

Goslinga, S. (2017). Job insecurity, union participation and the need for (new) union services. In *Job insecurity, union involvement and union activism* (pp. 81–96). Routledge. doi:10.4324/9781351154925-5

Greasley, K., & Thomas, P. (2020). HR analytics: The onto-epistemology and politics of metricised HRM. *Human Resource Management Journal*, *30*(4), 494–507. doi:10.1111/1748-8583.12283

Haapakorpi, A. (2020). Freedom but insecurity: The business consulting profession in the post-industrial service society. *Nordic Journal of Working Life Studies*, *11*(1), 45–62. doi:10.18291/njwls.122225

Hastuti, R., & Timming, A. R. (2022). Can HRM predict mental health crises? Using HR analytics to unpack the link between employment and suicidal thoughts and behaviors. *Personnel Review*.

Huselid, M. A. (2018). The science and practice of workforce analytics: Introduction to the HRM special issue. *Human Resource Management*, *57*(3), 679–684. doi:10.1002/hrm.21916

Inanc, H. (2018). Unemployment, temporary work, and subjective well-being: The gendered effect of spousal labor market insecurity. *American Sociological Review*, *83*(3), 536–566. doi:10.1177/0003122418772061

Kamal, S., Naim, A., Magd, H., Khan, S. A., & Khan, F. M. (2022). The Relationship Between E-Service Quality, Ease of Use, and E-CRM Performance Referred by Brand Image. In *Building a Brand Image Through Electronic Customer Relationship Management* (pp. 84–108). IGI Global. doi:10.4018/978-1-6684-5386-5.ch005

Khan, S. A. (2023). E-Marketing, E-Commerce, E-Business, and Internet of Things: An Overview of Terms in the Context of Small and Medium Enterprises (SMEs). In A. Naim & V. Devi (Eds.), *Global Applications of the Internet of Things in Digital Marketing* (pp. 332–348). IGI Global. doi:10.4018/978-1-6684-8166-0.ch017

Khan, S. A., Devi, T. P., Ligori, T. A. A., & Saleem, M. (2020). Customer Satisfaction and Customer Loyalty in Online Shopping: A Study on University Students of Bhutan. *Delhi Business Review.*, *21*(2), 11–22. doi:10.51768/dbr.v21i2.212202002

Khan, S.A, Epoc, F., Gangwar, V.P., Ligori T.A.A, & Ansari, Z.A. (2021). Will Online banking sustain in Bhutan post Covid – 19? A quantitative analysis of the customer e-satisfaction and e-loyalty in the Kingdom of Bhutan, *Transnational Marketing Journal*, *9*(3), 607-624. doi:10.33182/tmj.v9i3.1288

Khan. S.A. & Magd. H. (2021). Empirical Examination of MS Teams in Conducting Webinar: Evidence from International Online Program conducted in Oman. *Journal of Content, Community and Communication, 14.* doi:10.31620/JCCC.12.21/13

Khan, S. A., & Magd, H. (2023). New Technology Anxiety and Acceptance of Technology: An Appraisal of MS Teams. In *Advances in Distance Learning in Times of Pandemic* (pp. 105–134). CRC Press, Taylor and Francis. doi:10.1201/9781003322252-5

Khan, S. A., Magd, H., & Epoc, F. (2022). Application of Data Management System in Business to Business Electronic Commerce. In A. Naim & P. K. Malik (Eds.), *Competitive Trends and Technologies in Business Management* (pp. 109–124). Nova Science Publishers. [REMOVED HYPERLINK FIELD]

Khan, S. A., Magd, H., Khatri, B., Arora, S., & Sharma, N. (2023). Critical Success Factors of Internet of Things and Digital Marketing. In A. Naim & V. Devi (Eds.), *Global Applications of the Internet of Things in Digital Marketing* (pp. 233–253). IGI Global. doi:10.4018/978-1-6684-8166-0.ch012

Khan, S. A., & Rena, R. (2023). Emerging Green Practices, Internet of Things, and Digital Marketing: A Response to the Global Economic and Climate Crises. In A. Naim & V. Devi (Eds.), *Global Applications of the Internet of Things in Digital Marketing* (pp. 1–16). IGI Global. doi:10.4018/978-1-6684-8166-0.ch001

Kim, Y. K., Kramer, A., & Pak, S. (2021). Job insecurity and subjective sleep quality: The role of spillover and gender. *Stress and Health*, *37*(1), 72–92. doi:10.1002mi.2974 PMID:32790912

Koen, J., Low, J. T., & Van Vianen, A. (2019). Job preservation efforts: When does job insecurity prompt performance? *Career Development International*, *25*(3), 287–305. doi:10.1108/CDI-04-2018-0099

Lawrance, N., Petrides, G., & Guerry, M. A. (2021). Predicting employee absenteeism for cost effective interventions. *Decision Support Systems*, *147*, 113539. doi:10.1016/j.dss.2021.113539

Ligori, T. A. A., Suresh, N., & Khan, S. A. (2019). Measuring Student Satisfaction Index using Structural Equation Modeling. [Special Issue]. *International Journal of Research in Social Sciences*, *9*(6), 15–24.

Ligori, T. A. A., Suresh, N., Khan, S. A., Rabgay, T., & Yezer, K. (2022). The mediating effect of university image on the relationship between curriculum and student satisfaction: An empirical study of the Royal University of Bhutan. *International Journal of Pluralism and Economics Education. Inderscience*, *13*(2), 192–208.

Long, L. R., Tu, Y., Wang, H. J., & Jiang, L. (2021). The content of the threat matters: The differential effects of quantitative and qualitative job insecurity on different types of employee motivation. *Journal of Business and Psychology*, 1–14.

Magd, H., Jonathan, H., & Khan, S. A. (2023). Education Situation in Online Education before the Pandemic and in the Time of Pandemic. In Advances in Distance Learning in Times of Pandemic, 53-72. CRC Press, Taylor and Francis. doi:10.1201/9781003322252-3

Magd, H., Jonathan, H., Khan, S. A., & El Geddawy, M. (2023). *Artificial Intelligence—The Driving Force of Industry 4.0. A Roadmap for Enabling Industry 4.0 by Artificial Intelligence*. Wiley.

Magd, H., & Khan, S. A. (2022). Strategic Framework for Entrepreneurship Education in Promoting Social Entrepreneurship in GCC Countries During and Post COVID-19. In Magd. H., Syed, R.T., Spicer, D. (Eds). International Perspectives on Value Creation and Sustainability Through Social Entrepreneurship (pp. 61-75). IGI Global.

Magd. H., & Khan. S.A. (2022). Effectiveness of using online teaching platforms as communication tools in higher education institutions in Oman: Stakeholders perspectives. *Journal of Content, Community and Communication, 16*, 148- 160. DOI: doi:10.31620/JCCC.12.22/13

Mahmud, A., & Islam, M. R. (2021). Social stigma as a barrier to Covid-19 responses to community well-being in Bangladesh. *International Journal of Community Well-being*, *4*(3), 315–321. doi:10.100742413-020-00071-w PMID:34723103

Marler, J. H., & Boudreau, J. W. (2017). An evidence-based review of HR Analytics. *International Journal of Human Resource Management*, *28*(1), 3–26. doi:10.1080/09585192.2016.1244699

Mayhew, C. (2018). Exploration of the links between workplace stress and precarious employment. In *Work Stress* (pp. 203–219). Routledge. doi:10.4324/9781315223339-10

McKeown, T., Bryant, M., & Cochrane, R. (2011). The role of emotions in supporting independent professionals. In What Have We Learned? Ten Years On (Vol. 7, pp. 133-147). Emerald Group Publishing Limited. doi:10.1108/S1746-9791(2011)0000007010

Meisler, G., Vigoda-Gadot, E., & Drory, A. (2017). Stress, psychological strain, and reduced organizational effectiveness: the destructive consequences of the use of intimidation and pressure by supervisors. In *Power, politics, and political skill in job stress* (Vol. 15, pp. 51–80). Emerald Publishing Limited. doi:10.1108/S1479-355520170000015005

Mohammed, D., & Quddus, A. (2019). HR analytics: A modern tool in HR for predictive decision making. *Journal of Management*, *6*(3). doi:10.34218/JOM.6.3.2019.007

Naim, A. (2022). Application of Digital Technologies for the Students with Diverse Skills During COVID: 19. *American Journal of Research in Humanities and Social Sciences*, *1*, 46–53.

Ons Cappa, M., Sánchez Ollero, J. L., & García Pozo, A. (2020). Gender differences in the returns on human capital in the Spanish hospitality sector. *Investigaciones Turísticas*, (19), 28–49. doi:10.14198/INTURI2020.19.02

Orben, A., & Przybylski, A. K. (2019). Screens, teens, and psychological well-being: Evidence from three time-use-diary studies. *Psychological Science*, *30*(5), 682–696. doi:10.1177/0956797619830329 PMID:30939250

Parent-Lamarche, A., Marchand, A., & Saade, S. (2021). How do work organization conditions affect job performance? The mediating role of workers' well-being. *Journal of Workplace Behavioral Health*, *36*(1), 48–76. doi:10.1080/15555240.2021.1872382

Park, J. H., & Ono, M. (2017). Effects of workplace bullying on work engagement and health: The mediating role of job insecurity. *International Journal of Human Resource Management*, *28*(22), 3202–3225. doi:10.1080/09585192.2016.1155164

Pentón Herrera, L. J., Trinh, E. T., & Gómez Portillo, M. D. J. (2022). Cultivating calm and stillness at the doctoral level: A collaborative autoethnography. *Educational Studies (Ames)*, *58*(2), 121–140. doi:10.1080/00131946.2021.1947817

Probst, T. M., Sinclair, R. R., Sears, L. E., Gailey, N. J., Black, K. J., & Cheung, J. H. (2018). Economic stress and well-being: Does population health context matter? *The Journal of Applied Psychology*, *103*(9), 959–979. doi:10.1037/apl0000309 PMID:29733623

Saleem, M., Khan, S. A., Al Shamsi, I. R., & Magd, H. (2023). Digital Marketing Through Social Media Best Practices: A Case Study of HEIs in the GCC Region. In A. Naim & V. Devi (Eds.), *Global Applications of the Internet of Things in Digital Marketing* (pp. 17–30). IGI Global. doi:10.4018/978-1-6684-8166-0.ch002

Saleem, M., Khan, S. A., & Magd, H. (2022). Content Marketing Framework for Building Brand Image: A Case Study of Sohar International School, Oman. In Building a Brand Image Through Electronic Customer Relationship Management (pp. 64-83). IGI Global.

Sharma, N., Khatri, B., Khan, S. A., & Shamsi, M. S. (2023). Extending the UTAUT Model to Examine the Influence of social media on Tourists' Destination Selection. *Indian Journal of Marketing*, *53*(4), 47–64. doi:10.17010/ijom/2023/v53/i4/172689

Shoss, M. K. (2017). Job insecurity: An integrative review and agenda for future research. *Journal of Management*, *43*(6), 1911–1939. doi:10.1177/0149206317691574

Sinha, M., Yadav, R., & Kishore, M. (2023). How E-Working Is Effective in Education: Observable Determinants and Challenges. In Managing Technology Integration for Human Resources in Industry 5.0 (pp. 214-233). IGI Global.

Sun, X., Chan, D. W., & Chan, L. K. (2016). Self-compassion and psychological well-being among adolescents in Hong Kong: Exploring gender differences. *Personality and Individual Differences*, *101*, 288–292. doi:10.1016/j.paid.2016.06.011

Veronese, G., Pepe, A., & Vigliaroni, M. (2021). An exploratory multi-site mixed-method study with migrants at Niger transit centers: The push factors underpinning outward and return migration. *International Social Work*, *64*(4), 539–555. doi:10.1177/0020872818819736

Witte, H. D. (1999). Job insecurity and psychological well-being: Review of the literature and exploration of some unresolved issues. *European Journal of Work and Organizational Psychology*, *8*(2), 155–177. doi:10.1080/135943299398302

Yadav, R., Chaudhary, N. S., Kumar, D., & Saini, D. (2022). Mediating and moderating variables of employee relations and sustainable organizations: a systematic literature review and future research agenda. *International Journal of Organizational Analysis*. doi:10.1108/IJOA-12-2021-3091

Yeves, J., Bargsted, M., Cortes, L., Merino, C., & Cavada, G. (2019). Age and perceived employability as moderators of job insecurity and job satisfaction: A moderated moderation model. *Frontiers in Psychology*, *10*, 799. doi:10.3389/fpsyg.2019.00799 PMID:31031675

Zareen, S., & Khan, S. A. (2023). Exploring Dependence of Human Resource Management (HRM) on Internet of Things (IoT) and Digital Marketing in the Digital Era. In A. Naim & V. Devi (Eds.), *Global Applications of the Internet of Things in Digital Marketing* (pp. 51–66). IGI Global. doi:10.4018/978-1-6684-8166-0.ch004

Chapter 4
Stakeholders' Expressions of Tech Layoffs:
A Text Mining Analysis on the "Balance of Arguments"

V. Kalyani
CHRIST University, India

Babu P. Praveen
CHRIST University, India

Melvin Pradeep
KPIT Technologies GmbH, Germany

ABSTRACT

The volume and nature of work undertaken by the tech employees is humongous, tech employees are known to manage those high tides because of attractive salary packages, perks, and other incentive options, which turn out to be a catastrophic collapse when such layoffs are levied, giving little or no room for a quick transfer to another job from the viewpoint of the affected employees. User-generated unstructured data content in the forms of either tweets, reviews, or comments from around seven major social media platforms were collected to understand the various expressions and discussions linked to layoffs. The collected data is further segregated into – employee expressions, social media reviewers, news critiques views, etc., and their perspectives were further analysed. The overall analysis of sentiments on various stakeholders are formulated using Python (Juypter Notebook) package. The authors attempt to model out the viewpoints of various expressors and suggests various measures to be taken by the tech majors to better handle the phenomenon of layoffs.

DOI: 10.4018/978-1-6684-8942-0.ch004

INTRODUCTION

The phenomenon of "Layoffs" is seen as a severe threat in the recent past especially during the post-pandemic era in the Tech Industry. The average number of tech employees laid off globally between May 2022 to Dec 2022 stood at 22,785 employees per month, with a steep increase witnessed in six months - 51,160(Nov 2022), 40,486(Dec 2022), 1,08,268(Jan 2023), 50,740(Feb 2023), 61,645(Mar 2023) and 29,980(April 2023) as per the report published by trueup.io (Layoffs Tracker - TrueUp, 2023). On an average about roughly 200 companies have contributed to the above layoff data every month. In the current times, the job market and the nature of the job is greatly influenced by two large forces - automation and aggressive global competition. To adapt to these forces, companies are forced to restrategize their workforce planning through restructuring or layoffs (Sucher & Gupta, 2018). Layoffs have also infused tremendous pressure on the existing employees of tech organizations since they are burdened with humongous additional work which in the past were done by the employees who were laid-off. While the organizations have various reasons like less job orders and few clients at hand, rising salaries alongside reducing profits, unwillingness to work from office and other performance, behaviour related factors at the workplace for laying off their employees, the affected employees have often landed in a big trouble and stress in finding a new job for themselves to balance their livelihood which is trashed down due to a sudden layoff announcement. Companies are also aware of the need for good interventions in handling the layoffs smoothly and to support the employees in all possible ways. Though, layoffs carry emotional costs to an employee, they should learn to emotionally and practically process the negative aspects of it (Rathore, 2023). Many authors have explored different perspectives of employers and employees towards layoff. Layoff demands for a "balance of action" from both employees and employers. Employers need to employ fair layoff practices and interventions like organizational bad news training, concerns and query handling using open communication forums etc (Richter et al., 2016).

SIGNIFICANCE AND RELEVANCE OF THE CHAPTER

This chapter aims to deliberate on one of the most important challenges confronted by the Human Resources team in the context of the Technology Industry since the industry is partially or majorly marching towards implementing automation models using advanced technologies like Artificial Intelligence and Machine Learning. The need for physical human manpower is being questioned in many technical domains of the tech industry and this in turn is continuing to contribute to high levels of layoffs across the various job positions in the industry. While the boon in technology is attributional to the phenomenon of layoffs, the industry can utilize structured HR analytical models to diagnose the existing human resources and implement actionable processes to streamline and retain intellectual talent. HR analytical models could serve as a trade-off or a point of balance between human manpower and automation which is believed to be killing jobs. In view of the above pointers, this chapter aims at clearly representing the overall theme of the book chapter.

The major objectives of this chapter include identification of various expressions related to layoffs from both the employers and the employees who witnessed layoffs, mining various sentiments and most frequent keywords that revolve around layoffs from employees and other stakeholders perspectives using text analysis, recommending strategies for both employers and employees inorder to strike a "balance" in the tech industry by evaluating their "arguments" related to lay-offs.

RESEARCH FRAMEWORK

From a secondary data analysis perspective, about 444 mentions (between 2018 to 2023) of various stakeholders regarding tech layoffs from both within the tech industry and outside the industry were collected from across 7 social media platforms like Dailymotion, Reddit, Flickr, YouTube, VKontakte, Vimeo, and Tumblr. The social media platforms – Dailymotion, Reddit, Flickr and YouTube contributed to about 25.4%, 18.5%, 14.7% and 13.2% of the reviews respectively (Social Buzz – tech layoffs, 2023). The reviews, comments and arguments posted by various stakeholders were analysed using Python Jupyter notebook. From the analysis it was inferred that the accuracy score of the reviews is 0.704 which proves that the data congruence in this analysis is high. Further analysis on the text reviews yielded an output of the sentiments in the ratio - 124 positive, 67 negative and 253 neutral opinions which means that most reviewers and their arguments were neutral in the context of tech layoffs. While the negative opinions being very low and positive opinions being almost double that of the negative ones, it cannot be confirmed that the outlook on layoffs is positive owing to the magnitude of neutral opinions. It can be opinionated that neutral expressions are a result of the various dilemma that employees and critics are subjected to as a result of such layoffs. While it is inferred that many of the reviews and comments could be casual expressions or deliberations based on the trailing comments on social media, an in-depth analysis on specific stakeholders could be conducted via primary data collection methods to understand the exact expressions and sentiments around the tech layoffs across the globe.

TEXT ANALYSIS OF VARIOUS ARGUMENTS

The various reviews and comments of laid-off employees and other stakeholders were mined using Python Jupyter notebook codes and the following word cloud was generated based on 162 reviews which was a resultant of data cleaning and stop words removal actions.

From Fig 1 it is evident that most comments revolved around layoffs and a majority of those comments utilized the verb – stress which could be attributed to the outcome of the layoffs. Interestingly many stakeholders have commented about the layoff drive by Elon Musk globally. Many reviews centered about the major ill effect of layoffs which is seen as "salary loss". It is inferred that many of the reviewers are "unclear" about the layoffs which could be in the context of the reasons for the layoffs or the extent to which the layoffs were enforced in their organizations or the industry as a whole. Few mentions are about "work emails" being cut immediately following a layoff which could be attributed to immediate termination and blockage to the company's data which could have stranded the employee from accessing some information proving their job experience. Also, there are reviews on the sudden announcement of laying-off of large number of employees over a single video call. The various keywords briefed above are skewed mostly towards the negative outcomes or poor mental state of the employees affected by the layoffs.

Figure 1. Word cloud of laid-off employees and stakeholders comments on lay-offs

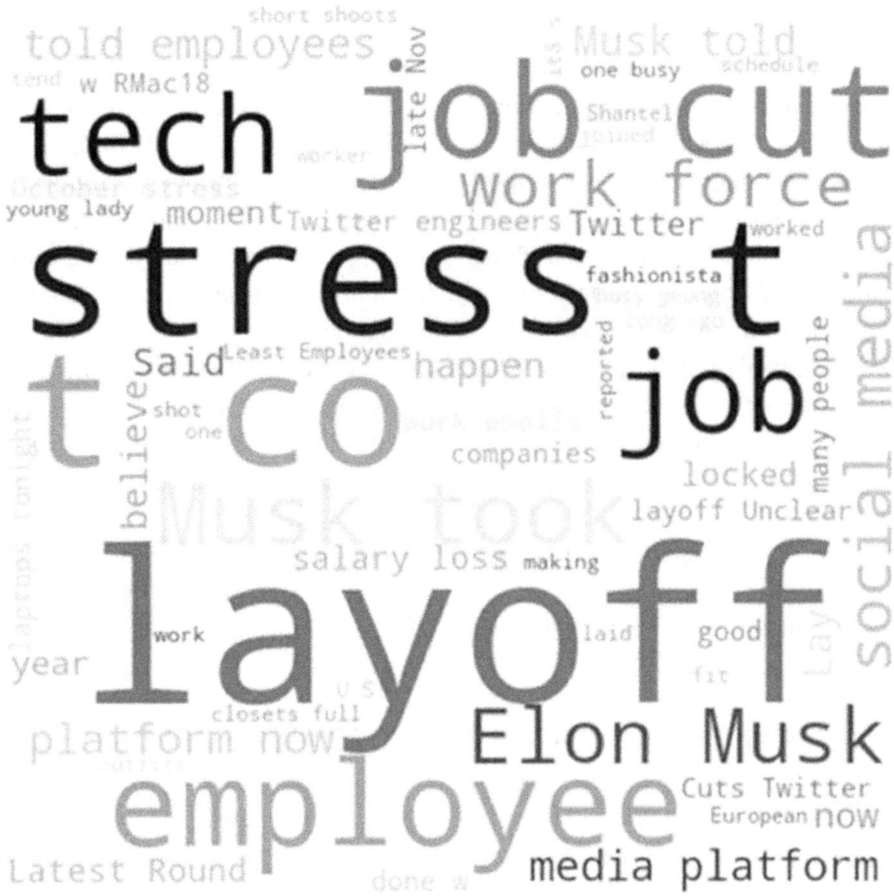

EMPLOYERS VIEWPOINTS

Tech employers across the globe are taking stringent measures to return to the pre-pandemic era which also means that they are now focussing on returning back to non-video offline ways of doing work wherever necessary. Also, careful evaluation on labour productivity and the need to look at workforce redeployment to gain competitive edge are the top priorities in the tech industry. This also is a step towards reducing the short-term additional expenses in the form of technology adaptation incurred during the pandemic which many companies view as "not a significant" growth contributor. While downsizing is seen as a very prominent measure to curb expenses in the older times (De Meuse & Marks, 2003), at present, taking minimal or no efforts on digital skilling or upskilling, simplifying processes, eliminating minor job roles across the globe etc are various tools to minimise cost by tech majors like Vimeo which is shifting its focus from online meeting tools to Artificial Intelligence tools which are believed to minimize manual work force and exponentially increase productivity at all levels. While the above could be the major reasons for layoffs, Microsoft has taken a tangent approach to reduce nearly 10000 jobs in supply chain, Artificial Intelligence and Internet of things domains. Many startup unicorns including

Unacademy are found to be quoting reduced funding and the need to constantly improve on productivity by incurring minimal costs as their reasons for layoffs.

Such tech organizations have been apologetic of the layoff exercise and have clearly articulated the reasons for such stressful decisions with some companies like IBM spinoff Kyndryl announcing a 2-month severance pay package for the laid off employees. Companies in the online technologies hardware space and related software technologies space like Logitech had mentioned about the need for adding more manpower during the pandemic due to the sudden high demand for online products as a result of the work-from-home syndrome that other industries warranted. In their opinion, the post pandemic has changed the macro-economic environment globally and brought in a sudden decrease in such online products demand which is forcing them to reduce manpower in the post pandemic era. (Times Now, 2023)

Some organizations like Accenture are still committing themselves to new hiring but contrastingly would lay off a large pool of employees in a phased manner over a longer period owing to job redundancies and desperate hiring in the past which has added more manpower than required (India Today, 2023). The largest e-commerce giant Amazon has laid off close to 27000 employees globally citing reasons like reprioritization of business avenues and careful usage of resources in order to reduce costs (India Today, 2023).

Interestingly Google had another form of layoff news to share. The company in addition to laying off 12000 employees, completely laid off its "Everyday robots" which were used for office cleaning purposes citing that those robots were not adding any productivity gains.

LAID-OFF EMPLOYEES, SURVIVORS & CRITICS VIEWPOINTS

The employees view points on layoffs and its related impact on their daily lives can be plotted on a large continuum scale with extreme diverging views. In the past, layoffs were generally applicable to senior employees because of the efforts in Change Management practices introduced by various organizations (Hallock, 2006). But at present, organizations are looking down on all levels of employees when they are pursuing layoffs.

On one side of the continuum scale are the stressed employees who are highly depressed and worried of their future and financial difficulties. A recently laid off employee from Microsoft who is on a time bound hunt for a new job being on H1B visa, had expressed her grief on LinkedIn about the layoff and how she took a few days to digest the layoff news. One of the most scary layoffs as per many employees was that of Twitter where Elon Musk had fired almost 75% of the workforce within seconds while on an online meeting. Twitter had laid off very senior employees who were entrusted with new targeted projects too. Many employees have expressed their increased levels of stress owing to the layoffs on various social media platforms (Social Buzz – tech layoffs, 2023). This has also led to a fear factor among other tech employees who are currently working in those organizations and the employment market is highly wary of the longevity of jobs in general across different industries especially after their company enters into some form of divestiture which could result in job losses if the outcomes are not favourable (Gopinath, 2003). Employees who have been laid off face discrimination at various levels owing to income losses, job loss longevity etc (Karren & Sherman, 2012).

But on the other side of the continuum scale are employees who feel that this is a new and a nice turning point in their career. A tech employee at Google articulated that his layoff was like a breakup and an opportunity to choose the next partner wisely, with a mention that he could steal "learnings" from the tech company. A senior product manager at Microsoft who faced the layoff was positive that he could now pursue things he had missed out on for a long time and improve his skills. Another opposition view to layoffs is that of the concept of "Great Resignations" which has been a very large exercise in the US and other markets which have forced organizations to rethink their workforce strategies differently Employment Screening Resources, 2023).

While the viewpoints of the directly affected employees are a testimony to the difficulties faced by them, the other side of the spectrum in terms of the life of the layoff survivors, employees who have been retained by the organizations are also largely affected by increased work overload (Virick et al., 2007). The work-family balance of such layoff survivors has largely impacted their job satisfaction levels and many such employees had very less of motivation towards their job.

Critics are often viewed as negative trendsetters and people who always paint a dark view of a trending phenomenon. But going by the reviews on various social media platforms it is observed that their replies to comments posted by tech laid off employees are highly comforting. Majority of social media critics are not in favour of the decisions taken by tech companies on mass layoffs, their viewpoints on how companies could have handled economic depression, macro environment trends in a better manner are worthy points to ponder. An extremist view to analyse, is of a woman asking suggestions on social media as to whether she should go ahead with the marriage fixed with her fiancé who was recently laid off by Microsoft India (moneycontrol, 2023). Layoffs in general impact not just the financial position of the employees but the social and personal life of such employees. Many comments and discussions on social media platforms.

BALANCE OF ARGUMENTS

The concept of layoff and reemployment occurs almost parallelly in the job market especially in the context of the tech industry. Employees who have been laid off have been able to find good job roles owing to the senior positions held by them earlier(Ali-Yrkkö et al., 2023). This strikes a "balance of arguments" between the companies that are involved in layoffs and the employees who have been able to get newer and better job opportunities in the market. Many such employees are infact thankful to their earlier employer for the layoff since they are now in a better career when compared to their previous job. Organizations have been able to strike a good deal of short-term performance gains by downsizing their workforce and this has helped them improve on their productivity and even new recruitments later (Sheaffer et al., 2009). Downsizing has also been helpful in refreshing their talent pool by building capacities of their existing teams and gave organizations the opportunity to recruit newer talent with varied skillsets. Though the laid off employees struggled for a short period, most of them were able to find enriching job opportunities in the same or different domains.

While layoffs are inevitable to most organizations, a flip-side approach is the need of the hour since it can uphold the interests of both the employers and the employees. The flip-side approach could be a result of meticulous planning and strategizing keeping in mind the most commonly used philosophy – Prevention is better than cure. Preventing layoffs could be a big saviour than laying off and finding a cure later. Preventing layoffs can strike a "balance" between employers and employees since the cloud of arguments will move away to showcase the sun of good organizational climate.

Even when layoffs turn unavoidable, researchers have recommended various strategies for employers to minimise the negative impact that layoffs cause to employees. Creating an outplacement plan covering interview coaching, resume assistance, other job assistance services, providing reference letters, eligibility or rehiring when conditions revive, job referrals with other business partners etc (He, 2023 & Rice, 2021) and few other interventions like providing transition support which includes redeploying the laid off victims to other areas of the company (Srivastava, 2022), providing separate package of financial benefits etc (Rice, 2021) are common strategies that employers can adopt instead of layoffs. Though these strategies are difficult in the real-world scenario, the percentage of layoffs could be smaller if few of these strategies are adopted.

In general, layoffs don't reflect poor skill set, but it's merely a reflection of poor planning of business strategies of companies of turbulent times (Lyons, 2022). Therefore, laid-off employees can adopt few strategies to handle life post a layoff in constructive ways which can include - holding positive mentality rather than indulging in negative self-talks which can reduce their stress levels, penning down their accomplishments by recalling their skills and capabilities, researching on new job opportunities that ensures perfect alignment with their values and hunting for the right job in various search job boards using appropriate schedule. Most often such employees would require more indulgence with friends and relatives which diverts their stress into active life. Peppercorn (2023) stated that a sense of embarrassment guilt, frustration or anger is commonly exhibited among laid off employees. Rarely, employees perceive layoff as their fault. They ruminate layoff as a result of lack of dedication and attention. Various issues hit employees by means of loss of income, social support, identity, self-esteem, career move, deterioration of physical health and mental health as well.

Some researchers recommend having positive focus and making relevant plan of action, building on one's strengths, prioritizing and strengthening career paths through profile updation with rich accomplishments, network enhancement thereby seeking necessary career support, diversifying their portfolio through project consultation or setting up a entrepreneurship venture in addition to full time job, exploring a new phase in the career or creating a new identity by reorienting oneself to a new identity (Rathore,2023; Sucher, 2018) as future avenues which re-christens the loss due to a layoff as the catalyst for one's personal growth and career fulfilment.

On the contrary, a significant percentage of laid-off employees do not end up in stressful situations, but are known to have a good relaxed break before they commit themselves to the next job.

SUGGESTIONS AND RECOMMENDATIONS

In any context, it is highly debatable that humans can be replaced by machines. Though the entire globe is utilizing different forms of machines and technologies to make work and life simple, the human workforce has capabilities that can exceed machine capabilities in various forms. In the tech industry, human workforce is still seen as an important driver of knowledge which in turn is fed into machines for smart outputs (Karimi-Majd et al., 2017). On the other hand, companies are finding it extremely challenging to hire good talent for their varied job roles (El-Deeb, 2023). Companies in the technology space need to devise strategies to reduce layoffs wherever possible and leverage the existing talent by looking at alternative HR strategies (Parzefall, 2012).

From an employers' perspective the strategy of layoffs is the most sensible and viable option to reduce costs and stay profitable in the short term, while for the employees it is a complete turn down on their career and financials. The "balance of arguments" though very obvious on both parties involved in the layoff, cannot bring peace in any organizational systems where employers and employees have equal role in the entire business ecosystem. Both the parties to the "balance of arguments" co-exist and are not independent of each other. While organizations have the potential and capabilities to chart out various measures other than layoffs in the interest and well-being of the employees it had hired with confidence in the past, it is equally important for the employees also to ensure skill enhancement alongside their regular job. This can help protect the interest of both the organizations and the employees.

All tech organizations are heavily dependent on clients coming to them for new product and services offerings from various locations across the globe and this in turn forces the organizations to always stay ahead of the competitors. This would mean that the intellectual talent pool within their organizations are also updated and upskilled with the recent and the emerging future trends in the markets. While this is not the only approach towards employee retention or layoffs, organizations are also required to invest heavily on skill enrichment amongst its employees because of the Institutional gains that it can reap in the long run. The performance of the employees also depends on how much organizations invest both in time and money for their development which is a serious vacuum in many tech organizations across the globe which expect employees to upgrade themselves on their own. The nature of divestitures, takeovers, mergers and acquisitions, multi-country/multi-culture differences are other reasons identified for mass layoffs in the tech industry. While these are seen as profitable gains in the tech industry, the employees' mindset and motivation levels during such strategic changes are also to be considered which calls for a special taskforce on change management.

FUTURE SCOPE FOR RESEARCH

This chapter is a conceptual analysis of textual expressions of employers, employees and other stakeholders in the context of layoffs. The outcomes of this chapter are purely based on secondary data in the forms of reviews, comments and opinionated sentiments which could involve certain biases owing the surge of textual content on various social media platforms from where the reviews were extracted. Hence further research can be conducted in the form of a primary data empirical analysis on the targeted respondents who are affected by layoffs which can help in deducing the actual expressions. Enough research can be done in the form of interviews with the employers who are actively laying-off employees which could bring out the various reasons associated with the decision of layoffs.

CONCLUSION

Tech Industry is one of the major recruiters of young talent from across the globe and is poised to be the most significant contributor to the global economy in the current and future times. Roughly 7 out of 10 graduating students target to join the tech industry for their jobs and life-long careers owing to advancements in technology and information. While this is being witnessed as a rapid change in urbanization and holistic development of countries and economy, the need to protect the interests of both the industry and its employees is the key to success. On one hand, organizations are eyeing on reaching higher cognitive and competitive levels by incurring the least possible cost, which could largely mean reduction in manpower cost. On the other hand, investments and working capital are becoming stringent to avoid losses. Hence, tech companies could focus on alternative productivity gains by utilizing the existing and adding new skilled manpower which could be an inherent strength to their growth. Though tech organizations have enough and more justification for layoffs, the decision to lay off employees is a very delicate and burdensome act from the employees' perspective who are the pillars of growth for all industries. Hence, tech industry should embrace the right amount of manpower with increased levels of skill sets to stay competitive and continue to finds way to upgrade skillsets of their workforce.

REFERENCES

Ali-Yrkkö, J., Kuosmanen, N., & Pajarinen, M. (2023). Structural change in the ICT sector: Where have former Nokia employees ended up? *Journal of the Finnish Economic Association*, *3*(1). doi:10.33358/jfea.112802

Amazon begins 2nd round of layoff, fires 9000 employees. (2023). *Indiatoday*. https://www.indiatoday.in/technology/news/story/amazon-starts-2nd-round-of-layoff-fires-9000-employees-2349245-2023-03-20

De Meuse, K. P., & Marks, M. L. (2003). Resizing the organization : managing layoffs, divestitures, and closings : maximizing gain while minimizing pain. *The Jossey-Bass Business & Management Series*, 91.

El-Deeb, A. (2023). The First Tech Layoff Wave After Years of Hypergrowth. *Software Engineering Notes*, *48*(1), 4–5. doi:10.1145/3573074.3573075

Timesnownews. (2023). After Google, meta, and Microsoft another company sacks employees. *Timesnownews*. https://www.timesnownews.com/business-economy/companies/after-google-meta-and-microsoft-another-company-sacks-employees-deets-inside-article-98324217

Gopinath, C. (2003). Managing the Effects of Divestiture and Layoffs on Employees. Handbook of Business Strategy, 4(1). Emerald. doi:10.1108/eb060260

"Great Resignation" Continues as 4 Million Workers Quit in February 2023 – Employment Screening Resources. (2023). *Esrcheck*. https://www.esrcheck.com/2023/04/04/great-resignation-continues-as-4-million-workers-quit-in-february-2023/

Hallock, K. F. (2006; Vol. 25). Layoffs in Large U.S. Firms from the Perspective of Senior Managers. In Research in Personnel and Human Resources Management. doi:10.1016/S0742-7301(06)25004-7

He, G. (2023). Layoff Best Practices: How to Lay Off Employees with Dignity. *Team Building*. https://teambuilding.com/blog/layoff-best-practices

Money Control. (2023). *Indian laid off after 5 years with Microsoft in US: "Since I am on H1B, clock's ticking."* Moneycontrol. https://www.moneycontrol.com/news/trends/indian-laid-off-after-5-years-with-microsoft-in-us-since-i-am-on-h1b-clocks-ticking-10173911.html

Karimi-Majd, A. M., Mahootchi, M., & Zakery, A. (2017). A reinforcement learning methodology for a human resource planning problem considering knowledge-based promotion. *Simulation Modelling Practice and Theory*, *79*, 87–99. doi:10.1016/j.simpat.2015.07.004

Karren, R., & Sherman, K. (2012). Layoffs and unemployment discrimination: A new stigma. *Journal of Managerial Psychology*, *27*(8), 848–863. Advance online publication. doi:10.1108/02683941211280193

Layoffs Tracker - All Tech and Startup Layoffs. (2023). Trueup.Io. https://www.trueup.io/layoffs#

Lyons, M. (2022).What to do after being laid off. *Harvard Business Review.*

Parzefall, M. R. (2012). A close call: Perceptions of alternative HR arrangements to layoffs. *Journal of Managerial Psychology*, *27*(8), 799–813. doi:10.1108/02683941211280166

Peppercorn,S. (2023). Managing your emotions after being laid off. *Harvard Business Review.*

Rathore, S. (2023). How to emotionally process a layoff. *Harvard Business Review.*

Rice, D. (2021). *Strategies for Dealing With Layoffs*. HREX Change Network. https://www.hrexchangenetwork.com/hr-talent-management/articles/10-strategies-for-dealing-with-layoffs

Richter, M., König, C. J., Koppermann, C., & Schilling, M. (2016). Displaying fairness while delivering bad news: Testing the effectiveness of organizational bad news training in the layoff context. *The Journal of Applied Psychology*, *101*(6), 779–792. doi:10.1037/apl0000087 PMID:26882444

Sheaffer, Z., Carmeli, A., Steiner-Revivo, M., & Zionit, S. (2009). Downsizing strategies and organizational performance: A longitudinal study. *Management Decision*, *47*(6), 950–974. doi:10.1108/00251740910966677

Social Buzz – Free Social Mentions Search and Monitoring. (2023). Social Searcher. https://www.social-searcher.com/social-buzz/?q5=%23tech+layoffs

Srivastava, S. (2022, November 22). The Big tech layoffs of 2022: A better approach to firing employees. *People Matters*. https://www.peoplematters.in/article/strategic-hr/the-big-tech-layoffs-of-2022-a-better-approach-to-firing-employees-36111

Sucher, S.J., & Gupta, S. (2018). Managing organizations-Layoffs that don't break your company. *Harvard Business Review.*

Virick, M., Lilly, J. D., & Casper, W. J. (2007). Doing more with less: An analysis of work life balance among layoff survivors. *Career Development International*, *12*(5), 463–480. doi:10.1108/13620430710773772

Woman asks internet if she should get married after fiancé gets laid off by Microsoft India. (2023). Moneycontrol. https://www.moneycontrol.com/news/trends/microsoft-layoff-woman-asks-internet-if-she-should-get-married-after-fiance-gets-fired-10015201.html

Chapter 5
Challenges Associated With HR Analytics With Special Focus on Indian Firms

Damini Saini
https://orcid.org/0000-0001-5734-5067
Indian Institute of Management, Raipur, India

Akanchha Singh
Apeejay Stya University, Gurugram, India

ABSTRACT

HR analytics is becoming increasingly important for organizations to manage their workforce effectively and make data-driven decisions. Several studies have explored the current state of HR analytics in organizations, their challenges, and the emerging trends in the field. In fact, 71% of companies see people analytics as a high priority in their organizations. In this chapter, initially, the authors will focus on the emergence of HR analytics and the current form of it. Then, the chapter will focus more on the challenges associated with the integration of analytics in the organisations This chapter can help Indian HR professionals and researchers stay up-to-date with the current state and latest trends in the field. Furthermore, this chapter can highlight the challenges associated in various forms and shapes and how they can handle these challenges. This can further improve their decision-making and drive business outcomes positively.

INTRODUCTION

In the fiercely cut-throat competitive organizational environment, human resource management (HRM) takes place effectively to attain the organizational goals and in addition to that, Strategic HRM is the implementation model used to manage human resources alongside the tasks that are intended to help the company succeed in its goals. This area includes all crucial aspects regarding HR policies, the makeup of the human capital pool, the description of essential behaviours, and the evaluation of the efficacy of

DOI: 10.4018/978-1-6684-8942-0.ch005

choices made in response to various business/competitive circumstances (Wright & McMahan, 2011). With the onset of the Great Recession in 2008, most businesses realized the importance of specific evidence-based methods for personnel management that incorporate analytics, decision-making, and problem-solving (Reddy & Lakshmikeerthi, 2017).

The makeup of the group of human capital assets is a collaborative phenomenon (Kritz, 2017). The concept of HR analytics enables us for data-driven decision-making in human resource management. Dr Jac Fitz-enz developed the concept of HR analytics in 1978 after emphasizing the need for measurements that could show how HR operations affected an organization's bottom line (Jain & Nagar, 2015). As a small administrative project at first, human resources analytics has grown from small administrative project to offer sophisticated diagnostic and predictive capabilities (Edwards & Edwards, 2016), which can be used to improve employee engagement and employee retention as well as produce benefits for entire organizations through digitally powered analytics solutions (Deloitte, 2017). Human resource Analytics reflects a pioneering shift in the ability of organizations and their leaders to comprehend, reshape, and strategically optimize their workforce (Fitz-Enz & Mattox, 2014).

HR analytics is an essential tool for advancement; it uses current data to predict future returns and is considered a source of essential advantage (BenGal, 2019; Bindu, 2016). In addition to focusing on assessing and enhancing aspects related to human capital, HR analytics also uses analytical methods in conjunction with employee data to influence organizational strategy and enhance performance. Its benefits in decision-making and management, among other things, have been supported by several types of research (Wandhe, 2020; Mohammed & Quddus, 2019).Due to the rapid growth of digitalization and automation across the globe, adopting HR analytics is highly suitable for Indian firms. Since India is a highly diverse country with a large and complex workforce, HR analytics can help the companies in India to identify patterns, and develop strategies to improve employee performance, engagement, and retention. Indian firms are excessively facing the skill gap challenge because India's education system produces many graduates (NASSCOM, 2019).

However, many of them need to gain the skills required by the industry. HR analytics can help identify skills gaps within the workforce and develop training programs to address them (Bockstael, Winne & Sels 2018). HR analytics can also help Indian firms in many other ways, like providing insights into their workforce, identifying areas of concern, helping managers make informed decisions, improving the bottom line and increasing profitability (Singh,2020). Despite the numerous proven benefits of HR Analytics, there are several challenges that Indian firms are facing in incorporating HR analytics into their operations access to poor quality data, absence of technological infrastructure, regulatory compliances and heavy initial investment. In this chapter we will try to address the challenges associated with HR analytics with special focus on Indian firms. The authors begin the chapter by briefly describing the emergence of the topic HR analytics followed by providing the detailed literature review on the benefit and impact of HR analytics on industries. Further we focused on the benefits we can achieve in Indian firms from implementing it and tried to investigate the usage and challenges of HR analytics in the Indian firm so far. Finally the authors proposed the solutions to fit in and make the most of analytics in firms of Indian origin.

HISTORY OF HR ANALYTICS

If we trace back to the HR analytics, we may refer to Jac Fitz-enz, a pioneering researcher, who introduced the first book on "How to Measure Human Resources Management" in 1984 (Fitz-enz, 1984). In the context of HR, HR Analytics is one of the most advanced technologies (Vargas et al., 2018; Marler & Bourder, 2017). The words "workforce analytics," "talent analytics," "people analytics," "human capital analytics," and "human resource analytics," having the same meaning and are used interchangeably in place of HR Analytics. Though these are the most often used phrase in the literature but still viewed as a relatively new concept (Marler & Boudreau, 2017). Due to the growing strategic importance of HR analytics for organizations and the acceptance of digital technology, its meaning and methodology have drastically changed over time. Analytics is a conceptual framework, first a logical sequence, then a set of statistical tools (Jac Fitz-Enz, 2010). HR analytics is a process that integrates and assesses employee quantitative and qualitative aspects, bringing forth significant insights to support improved decision-making in the future. It combines quantitative information with statistical techniques and modelling to analyze the data and turn it into meaningful business information for evidence-based decision-making (Momin & Mishra, 2014).

Due to the broader reach of the subject there is a lack of a single overarching definition of the field (Huselid, 2018),we may assert that the field lacks a single label or definition. When considering the development of business data analysis more broadly, three key stages may be distinguished, each of which is defined by varying degrees of complexity, worth, and intellect. First is "descriptive" analytics, which seeks to explain what occurred, why, and what is now happening. The descriptive "stage" of HR analytics involves considering ratios, metrics, HR dashboards, scorecards, and reports on human resources with a heavy historical emphasis using organizational internal and external data as well as HR administrative information. The second is "predictive analytics," which answers issues like what will occur and why it will occur.

On the other hand, predictive analytics makes judgements and predictions based on data; predictive analytics uses statistical methods, data mining, and sophisticated algorithms that can analyze procedure and workflow data. Based on the availability of extensive and diverse HR data, predictive analytics have thus given rise to the development of prescriptive analytics. Thirdly, "prescriptive" analytics, which intended to answer queries like what we should do and why we should do it (Akerkar 2013, Krumeich, Werth, & Loos 2016, Lepenioti, Bousdekis, Apostolou, & Mentzas, 2020, and Sivarajah et al. 2017).

Also, it focuses on metrics and measurements that are analytically tied to human operations, which further increases employee productivity and assures the investment made in human resources. It also verifies all decisions, from hiring to integrating new hires into the company (Alamelu. et al., 2017). This change results from using digital and data science approaches to gather, analyze, and predict complex data on specific individuals, teams, departments, and organizations, delivering helpful insight.

Benefits Associated with HR Analytics

Data-driven decision-making approach of HR analytics can increase transparency and accountability about employee performance, KSAs (Knowledge, skills & Abilities) weaknesses, and future potential that can be helpful at all stages of an employee's life cycle, be it talent acquisition, development or separation (Edwards & Edwards, 2016). Dooren (2012), as in Lochab et al. (2018), defined HR Analytics as an approach for comprehending and analyzing the causal association between HR practises and organizational performance indicators (like customer satisfaction, sales, profit, Etc.), such as well as establishing the valid and reliable basis for human capital decisions to have an impact on the business outcome with the help of statistical tools, software and experimental approaches based on metrics of efficiency, effectiveness and impact. According to Van der Togt and Rasmussen (2017), implementing HR analytics has shown to be a game-changer, allowing organizations to increase employee competence and retention and acquire an edge over their competitors.

HR analytics is not limited to metrics and scorecards (Mondore et al., 2011) but several modelling techniques, including behavioural modelling, predictive modelling, impact evaluation, cost-benefit assessment, and analysis of return on investment are associated with it(Levenson, 2011). Huselid (2018) claims that analytics is a relatively new subject that is expanding in terms of stakeholders, techniques, and influence.

HR receives choice alternatives to optimize performance and completely change the HRM decision-making process (Fitz-enz & Mattox II, 2014; Mishra et al., 2016). Technology changed with time and supported increasingly complex types of analytics, As a result, several "types" of analytics, including descriptive, predictive, and prescriptive, incorporated into more defined and integrated HR analytics efforts and processes to understand HR Analytics better. HR analytics is becoming increasingly well-established today, with a strong influence on operational and strategic decision-making, an accepted impact on business outcomes, and widespread integration with data and IT systems across organizational boundaries (van den Heuvel & Bondarouk, 2017). The importance of developing specialized human resources analytical abilities has grown due to the emergence of big data, technological advancements, and data science approaches in human resources scenarios (Angrave et al., 2016; Chitra & Srivaramangai, 2018; Edwards, 2019). The big data applies to all phases of the employment process and the complete cycle of personnel planning and management, including recruitment, acquisition, development, and retention (Isson & Harriott, 2016). Apart from this Artificial Intelligence (AI) is another field where innovation has the potential to be transformative. The influence of professional systems on job assessment (considering both job performance and psychological consequences) was the primary emphasis of the initial application of AI in HRM (Lawler & Elliot, 1996). However, the potential benefits of AI today can include workforce self-service, cv data gathering with an information extraction process, applicant search, staff rostering, and HR sentiment assessment (Strohmeier & Piazza, 2015). Advanced analytics may be supported by AI applications to uncover rich, practical insights and forecasts about human resources.

To promote HR Analytics in organizations, six below-mentioned measures are suggested (a) Preparing an analytical strategy that considers both present as well as potential needs; (b) Identifying the most important areas to concentrate on; (c) Emphasizing these questions on forward-looking issues, not previous ones; (d) Refraining from compromising on the use of the data at hand; (e) Working on data cleansing; (f) Restricting challenges to the validity of data by using established definitions of data as well as procedures in the preparation of reports and an analytics strategy that takes into account both current and future needs (McEwan,Ruohonen & Danielsson 2017). Mayo (2018) examined the possible future form of HR Analytics through a study consisting 20 HRA experts from 11 Dutch organizations and the results revealed that by 2025, HR Analytics would be an accepted discipline with a strong impact on and influence over important operational and strategic decisions that affect business outputs constructively. A McKinsey report reveals how effective HR Analytics has enhanced firms' productivity and employee engagement. One could practically halve employee attrition and lower retention expenditures by $20 million (Labbe & Schwedel 2017). It emphasizes how crucial it is to use analytics to find the best individuals to analyze data and take appropriate action, just as crucial as creating and constructing effective technology skills. That it aids and directs executives to adopt data-driven and organization-specific insights into human capital rather than serving as a replacement for personally engaging with workers.

Conclusively we can say that to overcome these challenges, Indian firms need to invest in appropriate technology infrastructure, develop skills and expertise in HR analytics, and ensure that they comply with regulatory requirements related to data privacy and security. Companies should also focus on building a culture that values data-driven decision-making and embraces change.

HR ANALYTICS IN INDIAN FIRMS

Many Indian businesses are putting more and more emphasis on HR analytics. Companies are now more aware than ever before that data-driven approaches to HR management may boost effectiveness, productivity, and overall performance. The use of HR analytics tools and software is a significant trend among Indian businesses. Many businesses are investing in cutting-edge data analysis software so they can monitor and evaluate critical indicators like employee performance and engagement. These tools enable companies to identify patterns and trends in their workforce data, which can be used to inform strategic decisions related to talent management, recruitment, retention, and more. According to Fitz-Enz and John (2014), HR analytics is a communication tool that gathers information of workers from a variety of sources, including surveys and records of their present conditions, to help them anticipate future events more accurately. The use of predictive analytics and cloud-based solutions for data have seen tremendous expansion in the retail, telecommunications, information technology, and healthcare sectors. India is now ranked among the top ten global markets for big data analytics (NASSCOM, 2016). The market demonstrates that there is enormous room for expansion. By 2025, India would have a 32 percent market share worldwide (NASSCOM, 2016). Only 7% of Indian organisations use big data analytics to locate individuals who are a good match for the position, yet 90% of those companies prefer data-based decisions to gut instincts (Times jobs, 2015).

By examining the operational information provided by data analytics, HR analytical tools may anticipate the employee turnover rate for the upcoming three months. Predictive analytical models hold the key to India's human resource development going forward. Predictive analytics has the potential to be a "Game Changer" in the dynamic path of massive amounts of big data and escalating expansion and competitiveness among organisations (Forbes, 2018). Predictive analytics involves using historical data to make predictions about future outcomes. In the context of HR, this might involve using data on employee performance, engagement, turnover, and other factors to predict which employees are most likely to leave the company, or which candidates are most likely to be successful in a given role. Many Indian firms are also focusing on building data-driven cultures within their organizations. This involves not just investing in the right tools and technologies, but also developing a mindset and approach to HR that emphasizes the importance of data and analytics. This might entail educating and training HR staff and managers, or creating procedures and rules that encourage data-driven decision making. According to a Deloitte India survey, 2018 HR analytics is rising to the top of the priority list for many Indian businesses. According to the survey, "Indian organisations are already utilising HR analytics to acquire deeper insights into their staff and make more educated decisions. The study goes on to highlight several important industry trends in India, such as the use of sophisticated data analysis tools and predictive analytics as well as the growth of data-driven organisational cultures.

Another example of an Indian company using HR analytics is Tata Consultancy Services (TCS). TCS is a multinational IT services company headquartered in Mumbai, India, and has been using HR analytics to improve its talent management processes uses HR analytics to identify patterns and trends in its workforce data, which helps the company make data-driven decisions in areas such as recruitment, retention, training, and career development. For example, TCS uses predictive analytics to identify employees who are at risk of leaving the company and take steps to retain them. The Society for Human Resource Management (SHRM), 2018 said that TCS has increased its staff retention rate by utilising HR analytics. The study also mentions how TCS was able to decrease the time and expense associated with hiring by utilising analytics to determine the most efficient recruiting channels and screening standards.

The significance of HR analytics in general for recruiting and selection strategies has been also been recognised by the Indian IT sector. According to the editorial team of People Matters (2015), more than 80% of these corporate enterprises stated that they have a full-fledged analytical methodology and framework in place. India is the world's top destination for information technology (IT) sector sourcing, accounting for 67% of the US$ 124–130 billion market and employing ten million people (IBEF, 2017). Through cloud-based HCM (Human Capital Management) software, Wipro Ltd. has begun utilising various applications for stifling talent and social media analytics for acquiring new capabilities. Labour mobility is the major element that made it necessary to implement cutting-edge technology and innovation for human resources (Wipro Annual Report, 2015). For the purpose of enhancing talent management, Wipro Ltd. switched from a cloud-based Oracle system to their proprietary Wipro HR sprinter software. This shift provides strategic support for decision-making processes. Infosys is far ahead in terms of implementing my Nest HR Analytics and dashboard software. (Infosys Consulting Blog). Understanding both the company's internal and external recruiting ratios was made possible through HR analysis. Infosys goes on to say that using analytical tools, it is possible to assess employee performance, which plays crucial role in success of the organisation. With its analytics platform, HCL Technologies is also doing great on the path of implementing HR Analytics tools. One of the technologies HCL uses to investigate its database of more than 5 million candidates and internal personnel records is semantic analysis, whereas Predictive Index helps hiring managers and recruiters choose the best candidates for the job. Additionally, talent transformational analytics are being used, and 17% of the need is being met (Singh, N., 2016).

Challenges Associated With HR Analytics

Fernandes and Gallerdo-Gallerdo (2021) identified 14 barriers to HR Analytics adoption by organizations and grouped the into four heads:

1. Data and models
2. Software and technology
3. People; and
4. Management

HR analytics can potentially offer insightful information and enhance decision-making, but there are a number of difficulties in putting it into practise. Due to difficulty in quantifying human attributes, understanding and forecasting human behaviour is one of the biggest challenges that any organisation is dealing nowadays (Momin and Mishra, 2016). The difficulty in measuring human factors presents a number of difficulties for HR managers. Though, performing HR analytics is also not simple that's why HR professionals have to face numerous challenges while executing HR Analytics. Organising and integrating data from various activities and departments inside the organisation is essential in order to deploy HR analytics. Additionally, HR professionals should carefully preserve the data they have collected for use in the future and present it in a form that allows for meaningful evaluation (Malla,2018).

Despite the fact that HR analytics has grown to be a significant driver of competitive advantage, the majority of HR professionals lack the necessary analytical skills to implement HR analytics. As a result, organisations have to spend money, time and resources on the training of managers in HR analytics. To transform data into valuable insights, training in statistical methods is crucial. Without analytical skills, HR specialists and company executives are unable to draw reliable judgements (Reddy and Lakshmi-keerthi, 2017). Data analysis and data visualisation are specialised skills that may not be available in HR executives, but are needed for HR analytics (Ulrich et al. 2015).

Apart from this HR data has to be safeguarded against unauthorised access since it contains confidential information, including personal as well as financial data (Becker et al. 2018). The privacy of employees must be taken into account by HR experts while gathering data. Carelessness in gathering employee personal information could at times put the business in legal problems (Malla,2018). Employees who view HR analytics as a threat to their privacy may be resistant to it (Bersin, 2015). To use HR analytics across the organisation successfully, top management support is also crucial. If they do consistently promote a data-driven culture within the company, it inspires other managers to use evidence-based practises and tries to make more correct judgements regarding people based on data experiments (Arora, 2020). Many times, quality of HR data can be incomplete, inaccurate, or outdated which poses difficulty in drawing meaningful insights. (Kovach et al., 2016). Sometimes ethical implications are also creating challenges on the path of adoption of HR Analytics because of data usage and the possibility of prejudice and discrimination raised by HR analytics (Raghavan et al. 2019).

Moreover, we are highly focused on the well-being and mental health of employees (Kowalski et al.,2017; Jaskeviciute et al.,2021) and several studies on HR Analytics talked about qualitative data analysysi (Marler, J. H., & Boudreau,2017; Rasmussen, T., & Ulrich, D. (2015) to assess emotions attitude and stress of employees. However, the data analysis often becomes cumbersome and difficult to assess, and organisations often lack skilled employees for that. Thematic analysis and contenet analysis can provide tremendous insights into employee behaviour, leading to employee engagement. However, there is a long way to achieve this.

Challenges Associated With HR Analytics in Indian Firms

Organisations now use HR analytics as a critical tool to make data-driven choices about hiring, retaining, and engaging employees, however Indian firms face a number of difficulties when implementing and efficiently utilising HR analytics. The quality of the data is one of the main obstacles. Poor data management practises in Indian businesses can result in fragmented, inconsistent, and erroneous HR data. This may result in flawed analysis and poor decision-making (Mahajan, 2020). according to a survey done by People Matters and Kronos it is considered one of the major issues in HR analytics by 78% of organisations in India In Indian businesses, data security and privacy are also top challenges. Personal Data Protection Bill, 2019, the country's strict data privacy legislation, makes it difficult for businesses to gather and utilise employee data. It is challenging to secure HR data due to a lack of strict data security laws, the prevalence of cybercrime, and data breaches (Kumar & Saini, 2019).

On the other hand, professionals with the necessary skills to accurately analyse and understand HR data are also in limited supply. This makes it difficult for businesses to choose the proper indicators, analyse the data, and derive valuable insights (Murali, 2019). In India, where just 1% of the workforce is qualified in data science, there is a severe lack of data science specialists, according to a Randstad survey. Wipro Ltd. described the three hurdles of HR Analytics in terms of silos, skills and smarts, suspicion and scepticism (Wipro, 2015). Resistance to change is another difficulty. It might be challenging to deploy new technology and procedures in Indian companies since they frequently have a hierarchical and conventional organisational structure (Rathi, 2019).

The use of HR analytics demands a large investment in hardware, software, and qualified personnel. The financial constraints faced by many Indian businesses, however, make it difficult to invest in HR analytics (Kumar & Saini, 2019). Investment is a big concern for HR professionals since new HR systems are needed to stay up with technological advancements. HR executives develop new KPIs, which requires more resources and time. HR analytics is now evolving in the direction of a new trend. In addition to using metrics for recruiting, attrition, and labour costs, HR leaders generally assess past accomplishments of employees and extrapolate future trends based on that data (Cindy, 2012). By reviewing the studies done in HR analytics in indian firms we have prepared a table 1 given below:

Table 1. Based on the literature available in Indian context

Authors	Year	Industry	Challenges	Solutions suggested
Deshpande & Kumar	2019	IT	Poor IT infrastructure, skill gap, privacy issues, and poor data quality	Create data governance policies, make investments in the education of HR and data teams, take data security precautions, and establishment of strong technical infrastructure.
Singh & Singh	2020	BFSI	The inability to integrate HR data with business data, lack of knowledge of HR analytics, and reluctance to change	Create an environment where decisions are made based on data, link HR metrics with business goals, include stakeholders in HR Analytics projects, provide training to the HR and business teams.
Pradhan & Mohanty	2021	Manufacturing	Lack of understanding of HR analytics, segmented data sources, and challenges quantifying ROI	Create a framework to analyse ROI, implement awareness campaigns, integrate HR data sources
Madhvapaty & Rajesh	2021	HR tech	Limited finance and a lack of investor comprehension of the Indian HR tech sector, Due to a lack of resources, knowledge, and confidence in new technology, there has only been a limited uptake of HR tech solutions. Limited HR data availability, Scaling HR IT solutions is challenging because of India's heterogeneous workforce and regulatory environment.	Educating and training users on HR tech solutions, developing user-friendly, affordable solutions, and building trust; forming strategic partnerships with HR data providers and utilising emerging technologies to generate data; developing solutions that are customizable to local workforce needs; working with industry experts to navigate regulations
Arora et al.	2022	Indian banking and financial services	Resistance to change in adopting HR analytics, lack of HR analytics knowledge and competence, lack of backing from upper management, availability of data is insufficient	Implementing change management strategies, delivering training and development programs, raising HR analytics adoption knowledge and support, developing data infrastructure, and enhancing data quality

continues on following page

Table 1. Continued

Authors	Year	Industry	Challenges	Solutions suggested
Arora, et al.	2022	Not specified	HR workers' lack of knowledge and expertise; the poor quality and availability of their data; and their resistance to change	Giving HR professionals the chance to grow professionally and in improving their understanding of HR analytics, promoting a culture of data-driven decision-making and investing in data quality, allowing access to HR data through technological means, highlighting the advantages of HR analytics to stakeholders and workers to combat change resistance
Mehrotra & Khanna	2022	IT sector	Unconscious bias, High volume of resumes, Lack of diversity, Cost of recruitment	Usage of AI-based solutions to automate the screening of resumes, using chatbots for preliminary screening, training AI models to remove bias, and using data analytics to optimise the hiring process and cut expenses.
Arora, Prakash, Mittal & Singh	2022	Construction and infrastructure industry	Slow to adapt to new technologies High employee turnover and attracting skilled workforce, which may lead to cancellation or delays of a project, inability to respond to the needs of the market and failure to innovate,	Formulate multiple strategies for the efficient implementation of various HR technologies such as automation, artificial intelligence (AI), the Internet of Things (iot), machine learning (ML), data mining and neural networks
Budhwar, Luthar & Bhatnagar	2006	BPO sector	While the number of clients satisfied with their offshoring providers has decreased from 79 percent to 62 percent. The issues related to poor infrastructure of reckless start-ups as a source of dissatisfaction in India Management of human capital, High attrition rates Problems related to stress, sexual and racial abuse, and dissatisfaction at work	A well-structured and rationalized HRM approach Accurate information system
Chaoudhary & Barman	2016	General	Lack of sophistication—fear of Numbers, poor data analysis and communications skills—among potential data users Data credibility concerns caused by limited manpower resources, privacy and security issues, legal and financial constraints, old data, employee-driven entry for some of the data, etc.	
Ekka	2021	General	Application of HR Analytics in initial phase	
Gupta	2020	Bank	Lack dedicated HR analytics team. No software is used other than MS Excel. Not measuring hiring manager satisfaction and candidate satisfaction	
Maria	2019	IT	Data overload	Rational HR professionals for strategic decision-making

Suggestion to Meet Challenges of HR Analytics in Indian Context

Data analytics are used in the rapidly expanding discipline of HR analytics to examine and enhance human resource management procedures. Some of the suggestions to meet the challenges of HR Analytics are given as follows:

Aligning HR Analytics With Organisational Plan

To make sure that HR efforts are in line with the broader objectives of the organisation, organisations should align HR Analytics with their entire business plan. As a result, HR Analytics may be utilised to pinpoint areas where HR can significantly improve the performance of the company (Boudreau & Ramstad, 2005).

Investment in Data Quality and Analytics Solutions

To guarantee that HR Analytics is founded on correct and trustworthy data, organisations should invest in data quality and analytics solutions. This may entail spending money on analytics, data cleaning, and governance technologies (Davenport, Harris, & Shapiro, 2010).

Developing HR Analytics Competency

Employing data scientists, analysts, and HR experts with strong data capabilities can help organisations develop HR Analytics competency. To help existing HR professionals strengthen their data analytics abilities, this might involve offering them training and development opportunities (Gubman, 2010).

Emphasise on Important HR Metrics

In order to make sure that HR Analytics is directed at generating business results, organisations should pay attention to important indicators only like cost per hire, training and development cost per employee, employee engagement, turnover, and productivity (Ulrich & Brockbank, 2005).

Utilising Predictive Analytics:

Organisations ought to make use of predictive analytics to find trends and patterns in HR data that can be used to forecast future results. This may entail forecasting employee churn, spotting high-potential candidates, and foreseeing future workforce requirements (Bersin, 2013).

CONCLUSION

As industries have advanced technologically, businesses have expanded the use of HR analytics to boost organisational performance. Utilising statistical models and methodologies, HR analytics quantify decisions and give data-driven decision making. All pertinent HR-related data is handled by HR analytics, which improves interpretation. This conceptual chapter draws on secondary data sources, including firm reports on HR analytics and research journals and periodicals. The development of new HR measures is necessary for Indian organisations' sound and rational decision-making. Lack of cutting-edge technology, an existing demand-supply imbalance, exorbitant costs, and inflexible cultural norms provide significant barriers for the Indian firms in developing big data analytics for the general public. As per the chapter majorly rationalised HR approach in the organisation, well trained employees in AI and chatbots, training of the users, robust data governance policies and data friendly environment can be a few areas where we need to focus a lot in relation to Indian firms. Apart from that calculating ROI per employee will make the implementation much more easier.

REFERENCES

Akerkar, R. (2013). *Advanced data analytics for business. Big Data Computing*. Chapman and Hall/CRC.

Alamelu, R., Nalini, R., Cresenta Shakila Motha, L., Amudha, R., & Bowiya, S. (2017). Adoption factors impacting human resource analytics among employees. *International Journal of Economic Research, 14*(6), 417–423.

Angrave, D., Charlwood, A., Kirkpatrick, I., Lawrence, M., & Stuart, M. (2016). HR and analytics: Why HR is set to fail the big data challenge. *Human Resource Management Journal*, *26*(1), 1–11. doi:10.1111/1748-8583.12090

Arora, A. (2020). HR Analytics in India: Opportunities and Challenges. *Analytics Insight*. https://www.analyticsinsight.net/hr-analytics-india-opportunities-challenges/

Arora, M., Prakash, A., Dixit, S., Mittal, A., & Singh, S. (2022). A critical review of HR analytics: visualization and bibliometric analysis approach. *Information Discovery and Delivery*, (ahead-of-print). doi:10.1108/IDD-07-2021-0109

Arora, M., Prakash, A., Mittal, A., & Singh, S. (2022). Examining the slow acceptance of HR analytics in the Indian engineering and construction industry: a SEM-ANN-based approach. Engineering, Construction and Architectural Management. doi:10.1108/ECAM-09-2021-0795

Arora, M., Prakash, A., Mittal, A., & Singh, S. (2022). Moderating role of resistance to change in the actual adoption of HR analytics in the Indian banking and financial services industry. *In Evidence-based HRM: a Global Forum for Empirical Scholarship*. Emerald Publishing Limited.

Becker, B. E., Huselid, M. A., & Ulrich, D. (2018). HR analytics, intellectual capital, and performance. *Human Resource Management*, *57*(1), 7–15.

Ben-Gal, H. C. (2019). An ROI-based review of HR analytics: Practical implementation tools. *Personnel Review*, *48*(6), 1429–1448. doi:10.1108/PR-11-2017-0362

Bersin, J. (2013). *The datafication of HR: Graduating from HR metrics to people analytics*. Deloitte University Press.

Bersin, J. (2015). *The growth of people analytics: Driving a new era of decision-making in HR*. Deloitte University Press.

Bindu, K. (2016). A Review of Poor HR Analytical Skills. *International Journal of Innovative Research in Technology (IJIRT)*, *3*(1), 397-4027-0362

Bockstael, A., De Winne, S., & Sels, L. (2018). HR analytics: The intersection between people and business. *Human Resource Management Review*, *28*(3), 247–263. doi:10.1016/j.hrmr.2017.07.001

Boudreau, J. W., & Ramstad, P. M. (2005). Beyond HR metrics: HR analytics. *Human Resource Management, 44*(3), 395–408.

Budhwar, P. S., Luthar, H. K., & Bhatnagar, J. (2006). The dynamics of HRM systems in Indian BPO firms. *Journal of Labor Research, 27*(3), 339–360. doi:10.100712122-006-1027-7

Chitra, S., & Srivaramangai, P. (2018). A study on analytics of human resource management in big data. *International Journal of Scientific Research in Computer Science. Engineering and Information Technology, 3*(3), 58–68.

Choudhury, H. A., & Barman, A. (2016). *Human Resource Analytics-Discovering Research Issues Posited in its Milleu in India Organization.* Discovering Research Issues in Applications of HRA in India.

Cindy, L. (2012). HR analytics: The next big thing, or a waste of time? *Strategic HR Review, 11*(4), 208–215. doi:10.1108/14754391211241116

Davenport, T. H., Harris, J. G., & Shapiro, D. (2010). Competing on talent analytics. *Harvard Business Review, 88*(10), 52–58. PMID:20929194

Deloitte. (2017). *Global Human Capital Trends 2017.* Deloitte. https://www2.deloitte.com/global/en/pages/human-capital/articles/introduction-human-capital-trends.html

Deloitte India. (2018). *Human Capital Trends Report.* Deloitte. https://www2.deloitte.com/in/en/pages/about-deloitte/articles/human-capital-trends.html

Deshpande, A., & Kumar, S. (2019). HR Analytics in India: Challenges and Solutions. *Journal of Human Resource Management, 7*(1), 1–10.

Dooren, J. V. (2012). *HR Analytics in Practice.* [Master Thesis] http://arno.uvt.nl/show.cgi?fid=127276

Edwards, J. R., & Edwards, A. L. (2016). Human resources analytics: From small data to big data. In *Big data in organizations and the role of human resource management* (pp. 145–168). Edward Elgar Publishing.

Edwards, M. R. (2019). HR metrics and analytics. In e-HRM (pp. 89-105). Routledge.

Fernandez, V., & Gallardo-Gallardo, E. (2021). Tackling the HR digitalization challenge: Key factors and barriers to HR analytics adoption. *Competitiveness Review, 31*(1), 162–187. doi:10.1108/CR-12-2019-0163

Fitz-enz, J. (1984). *How to measure human resources management.* McGraw-Hill.

Fitz-Enz, J. (2010). *The new HR analytics.* American Management Association.

Fitz-Enz, J., & John Mattox, I. I. (2014). *Predictive analytics for human resources.* John Wiley & Sons. doi:10.1002/9781118915042

Fitz-enz, J., & Mattox, J. R. (2014). *Predictive analytics for human resources.* Forbes. https://www.forbes.com/sites/sap/2018/08/17/how-predictive-analytics-is-changing-the-hr-game/?sh=2dc8d1bf2957

Gubman, E. (2010). From HR to strategic talent management. *Journal of Organizational Excellence, 29*(4), 23–33.

Gupta, P. (2015). *XISS, R*. Human Resource Analytics in Indian Banking Sector.

Huselid, M. A. (2018). The science and practice of workforce analytics: Introduction to the HRM special issue. *Human Resource Management*, *57*(3), 679–684. doi:10.1002/hrm.21916

IBEF. (2017). *Information Technology (IT) Sector in India: Market Size, Opportunities, Growth Prospects, & Investment Climate*. IBEF. https://www.ibef.org/industry/information-technology-india.aspx

SHRM India. (2018). *HR Analytics: Driving Business Results*. SHRM. https://www.shrm.org/hr-today/trends-and-forecasting/research-and-surveys/Documents/HR-Analytics-India.pdf

Infosys. (2012). *Applying HR Analytics for Competitive Advantage*. Infosys. http://www.infosysblogs.com/managementconsulting/2012/08/applying_hr_analytics_for_comp.html

Isson, J. P., & Harriott, J. S. (2016). *People analytics in the era of big data: Changing the way you attract, acquire, develop, and retain talent*. John Wiley & Sons. doi:10.1002/9781119083856

Jain, P. K., & Nagar, K. (2015). Human resource analytics: An overview. *Industrial and Commercial Training*, *47*(3), 152–158. doi:10.1108/ICT-06-2014-0044

Kovach, K. A., Hughes, A. A., Fagan, P., & Maggard, S. R. (2016). Employee job satisfaction and engagement: The doors of opportunity are open. *Journal of Business and Management*, *22*(1), 5.

Kritz, N. J. (2017). The interplay between human capital and organizational information: Implications for knowledge management. *Journal of Knowledge Management*, *21*(6), 1337–1352. doi:10.1108/JKM-06-2016-0267

Krumeich, J., Werth, D., & Loos, P. (2016). Prescriptive control of business processes: New potentials through predictive analytics of big data in the process manufacturing industry. *Business & Information Systems Engineering*, *58*(4), 261–280. doi:10.100712599-015-0412-2

Kumar, S., & Saini, S. K. (2019). Challenges in securing HR data: A study of Indian firms. *Journal of Enterprise Information Management*, *32*(4), 552–566. doi:10.1108/JEIM-05-2018-0139

Labbe, J., & Schwedel, A. (2017). *How companies are using HR analytics to drive business results*. McKinsey. https://www.mckinsey.com/business-functions/organization/our-insights/how-companies-are-using-hr-analytics-to-drive-business-results

Lawler, J. J., & Elliot, R. (1993, June). Artificial intelligence in HRM: an experimental study of an expert system. In *Proceedings of the 1993 conference on Computer personnel research* (pp. 473-480). ACM. 10.1145/158011.158264

Lepenioti, K., Bousdekis, A., Apostolou, D., & Mentzas, G. (2020). Prescriptive analytics: Literature review and research challenges. *International Journal of Information Management*, *50*, 57–70. doi:10.1016/j.ijinfomgt.2019.04.003

Levenson, A. (2011). Using targeted analytics to improve talent decisions. *People and Strategy*, *34*(2), 34.

Lochab, A., Kumar, S., & Tomar, H. (2018). Impact of human resource analytics on organizational performance: A review of literature using R-software. *International Journal of Management. Technology and Engineering*, *8*, 1252–1261.

Madhvapaty, H., & Rajesh, A. (2021). HR Tech Startups in India: Opportunities, Challenges, and the Road Ahead. *Human Resource Management Review*, *31*(1), 100811. doi:10.1016/j.hrmr.2020.100811

Mahajan, M. (2020). The Challenges of Implementing HR Analytics in India. *People Matters*. https://www.peoplematters.in/article/hr-analytics/the-challenges-of-implementing-hr-analytics-in-india-26098

Malla, J. (2018). HR Analytics Center of Excellence. *International Journal of Business, Management and Allied Sciences*, *5*, 282-284.

Marler, J. H., & Boudreau, J. W. (2017). An evidence-based review of HR Analytics. *International Journal of Human Resource Management*, *28*(1), 3–26. doi:10.1080/09585192.2016.1244699

Mayo, A. (2018). Applying HR analytics to talent management. *Strategic HR Review*, *17*(5), 247–254. doi:10.1108/SHR-08-2018-0072

McEwan, B., Ruohonen, M., & Danielsson-Ojala, R. (2017). Human resource analytics: A systematic review. *International Journal of Human Resource Management*, *28*(5), 631–664. doi:10.1080/09585192.2016.1224355

Mehrotra, S., & Khanna, A. (2022). Recruitment Through AI in Selected Indian Companies. *International Journal of Emerging Technology and Innovative Engineering*, *8*(4), 247–254. doi:10.1177/09726225211066220

Mishra, S. N., Lama, D. R., & Pal, Y. (2016). Human Resource Predictive Analytics (HRPA) for HR management in organizations. *International Journal of Scientific & Technology Research*, *5*(5), 33–35.

Mohammed, D., & Quddus, A. (2019). HR Analytics: A modern tool in hr for predictive decision making. *Journal of Management*, *6*(3). doi:10.34218/JOM.6.3.2019.007

Momin, W. Y. M., & Mishra, K. (2014). Impression of financial measures in HR analytics. *Journal of Interdisciplinary and Multidisciplinary Research*, *2*(1), 87–91.

Mondore, S., Douthitt, S., & Carson, M. (2011). Maximizing the impact and effectiveness of HR analytics to drive business outcomes. *People and Strategy*, *34*(2), 20.

Murali, D. (2019). *The challenges of implementing HR Analytics in India*. TechGig. https://content.techgig.com/The-challenges-of-implementing-HR-Analytics-in-India/articleshow/69866818.cms

NASSCOM. (2016). Big data analytics to reach $16 billion industry by 2025. *Economic Times*. https://economictimes.indiatimes.com/articleshow/52885509.cms?utm_source=contentofinterest

NASSCOM. (2019). *Future skills- The future of India's tech industry*. NASSCOM. https://www.nasscom.in/knowledge-center/publications/future-skills-future-indias-tech-industry

People Matters. (2015). HR Analytics: The Key to Unlocking the Value of HR. *People Matters*. https://www.peoplematters.in/article/hr-analytics/hr-analytics-the-key-to-unlocking-the-value-of-hr-11750

Pradhan, S., & Mohanty, S. R. (2021). HR Analytics in Indian Manufacturing Industry: Challenges and the Way Forward. *International Journal of Productivity and Performance Management*, *70*(2), 352–369.

Raghavan, R., Madhavan, R., & Phatak, A. (2019). Ethical considerations in people analytics. *Harvard Business Review*, *97*(4), 52–59.

Rasmussen, T., & Ulrich, D. (2015). Learning from practice: how HR analytics avoids being a management fad. Organizational Dynamics, 44(3), 236-242.

Rathi, A. (2019). HR analytics: Key challenges and opportunities in India. *People Matters*. https://www.peoplematters.in/article/hr-analytics/hr-analytics-key-challenges-and-opportunities-in-india-21058

Reddy, V., & Lakshmikeerthi, B. (2017). Evidence-based methods for personnel management: An overview. *International Journal of Applied and Basic Research*, *7*(1), 1–3. doi:10.4103/ijabmr.IJABMR_383_16

Singh, M., & Singh, R. (2020). Challenges and Opportunities of HR Analytics in Banking and Financial Services Industry. *International Journal of Human Resource Management*, *31*(10), 1265–1284.

Singh, N. (2016). Talent Acquisition and Management Practices in HCL Technologies. *International Journal of Scientific and Research Publications*, *6*(3), 350–356.

Singh, S. K. (2020). HR analytics: The emerging trend in HR practices. *International Journal of Business and Management Studies*, *2*(1), 1–8.

Sivarajah, U., Kamal, M. M., Irani, Z., & Weerakkody, V. (2017). Critical analysis of Big Data challenges and analytical methods. *Journal of Business Research*, *70*, 263–286. doi:10.1016/j.jbusres.2016.08.001

Strohmeier, S., & Piazza, F. (2015). Artificial intelligence techniques in human resource management—a conceptual exploration. *Intelligent Techniques in Engineering Management: Theory and Applications*, 149-172.

TimesJobs. (2015, May 4). Only 7% of Indian cos use big data for hiring decisions: Report. *TimesJobs*. https://content.timesjobs.com/only-7-of-indian-cos-use-big-data-for-hiring-decisions-report/articleshow/47192551.cms

Ulrich, D., & Brockbank, W. (2005). *The HR value proposition*. Harvard Business Press.

Ulrich, D., Younger, J., Brockbank, W., & Ulrich, M. D. (2015). *HR from the outside in: Six competencies for the future of human resources*. McGraw-Hill Education.

Ulrich, D. (2020). HR's ever-emerging contribution. *Strategic HR Review, 19*(6), 251-257.

Van den Heuvel, S., & Bondarouk, T. (2017). The rise (and fall?) of HR analytics: A study into the future application, value, structure, and system support. *Journal of Organizational Effectiveness: People and Performance*, *4*(2), 157–178. doi:10.1108/JOEPP-03-2017-0022

Van der Togt, J., & Rasmussen, T. H. (2017). Toward evidence-based HR. *Journal of Organizational Effectiveness: People and Performance*, *4*(2), 127–132. doi:10.1108/JOEPP-02-2017-0013

Vargas, R., Yurova, Y. V., Ruppel, C. P., Tworoger, L. C., & Greenwood, R. (2018). Individual adoption of HR analytics: A fine-grained view of the early stages leading to adoption. *International Journal of Human Resource Management*, *29*(22), 3046–3067. doi:10.1080/09585192.2018.1446181

Wandhe, P. (2020). HR Analytics: A Tool for Strategic Approach to HR Productivity. Available at SSRN 3700502. https://dx.doi.org/ Wiley. doi:10.2139/ssrn.3700502

Wipro Limited. (2015). *Annual Report 2015.* Wipro. https://www.wipro.com/content/dam/nexus/en/investors/reports-filings/annual-reports/2015/annual-report-2015.pdf

Wright, P. M., & Mcmahan, G. C. (2011). Exploring Human Capital: Putting "human" Back into Strategic Human Resource Management. *Human Resource Management Journal*, *21*(2), 93–104. doi:10.1111/j.1748-8583.2010.00165.x

Chapter 6
Exploring the Other Side of the Coin:
Evaluating the Dark Side of HR Analytics

Snigdha Malhotra
Fortune Institute of International Business (FIIB), New Delhi, India

Shuchi Dikshit
Fortune Institute of International Business (FIIB), New Delhi, India

Vernika Agarwal
Apeejay School of Management, New Delhi, India

ABSTRACT

Human resource analytics (HRA) has the power to revolutionize how businesses find, develop, oversee, and manage their employees. It is imperative to pay attention to the idiosyncrasies and negative implications that HRA creates leading to commotion and failing to generate value for the organizations. The chapter discusses the challenges faced in the implementation of HRA in diverse businesses. For this analysis, the authors conducted an extant literature review and later interviewed HR professionals to derive factors contributing to the dark side of HRA. The interviews were transcribed, and five themes were derived representing the experiences of the respondents with HRA implementation. This chapter gives a comprehensive understanding of the challenges faced in the implementation of HR Analytics and suggests ways to overcome these challenges as well.

1. INTRODUCTION

Modern technological developments have altered how businesses of all sizes work. The workplace, especially in human resources (HR), appears to have transformed as a result of these actions. Industry 4.0 has enabled organizations to use technology for effective and efficient management. Organizations rely on data-driven decisions rather than intuitive decision-making. Big Data in HR embraces all forms

DOI: 10.4018/978-1-6684-8942-0.ch006

of employee data from pre-hiring activities to resignation. Unstructured data is abundant, which may help firms make better data-based decisions. The employee-related big data could be utilized to make "smart" insights for decision-making in HR (Smeyers, 2015). Industry 4.0 and the rapidly advancing technology ecosystem expects HR departments to quickly adopt ad utilize people data. Transferring and applying the analytics' efficiency-driven logic to human resource management, however, comes with a number of dangers, difficulties, and moral ramifications.

HRM integration with analytics and utilization of people data is still in its nascent stage. Human resource Analytics (HRA) has progressed with the adoption of data analysis and visualization techniques to enhance strategic decisions, thus making it affluent for top decision-makers of the organization. HRA has a plethora of processes and a strong interdisciplinary nature. It is strategic in nature, exploring HR data and business data interdependence to help decision-makers (Bersin et al., 2016). HRA's strategic relevance and efficient forecasting are encouraging organizations to adopt it quickly over time. (Lepenioti et al., 2020). It is a fact-based strategy to guide decisions and activities pertaining to people. (Bassi et al., 2010). Instead of making judgments based on gut feelings, top management is being guided by factual data and logical analysis, which is supplying them with insightful data that further support their decision-making for organizational success. Thus, organizations are rigorously adopting HR analytics to optimize HR practices across their functions and become strategic partners.

Past researchers have explored the benefits of HRA adoption. We see HRA as an effective, unique, and constructive resource for enterprises based on the insights it generates (Marler and Boudreau, 2017). HRA incorporates analytical techniques together with employee data in addition to concentrating on investigating and improving human capital components to assist organizations in performing better. Analytics gives businesses the flexibility to handle a variety of additional HR issues apart from processes, such as employee engagement, diversity and inclusion, and turnover (Levenson, 2018; Simón and Ferreiro, 2018).

Need of the Study

The literature so far on HR analytics has primarily focused on a variety of concerns, such as the limitations and difficulties that currently face its development (Minbaeva, 2018; Jeske and Calvard, 2020); best practices for creating and utilizing HR analytics (Falletta and Combs, 2020); and the significance and impact of analytical skills (Mc Cartney et al., 2021). Additionally, a number of publications that provide a comprehensive overview of the state of HR analytics research have been published (Fernandez and Gallardo-Gallardo, 2020).

Research Questions

Based on these considerations, this current chapter aims to answer the following research questions (RQ):

RQ 1: How to identify the impediments to adopting HR analytics?

RQ 2: How to comprehend the negative aspects of HR analytics by identifying the impediments to their adoption and implementation pose to businesses and the workforce?

The chapter seeks to assess the difficulties that go beyond the generic adoption of any technological advancement. The authors interviewed HR heads/Analytics Heads of companies to understand if they have applied HRA in at least one HR function. Based on the participants' convenience and availability, an interview was planned and the results were analyzed. The rest of the chapter discusses the materials and methods in section 2 followed by discussion and findings in section 3. The implications and conclusion are provided in sections 4 and 5.

2. RESEARCH METHODOLOGY

2.1 Design

There are two phases to the investigation. In the first stage, a thorough literature review is done to find out what obstacles organizations face when implementing HR Analytics. This assisted us in identifying the difficulties stated in earlier studies. The qualitative technique is used to perform the study's second phase. To meet the stated objectives, the authors conducted semi-structured interviews of HR professionals of organizations who have or are in the process of HR Analytics implementation in their processes. To better understand the problems posed by the adoption challenges of HRA in firms, we sought HR experts in the sector and asked them to take part in semi-structured interviews. The HR professionals were approached via LinkedIn. The sampling technique that was utilized in the study is snowball sampling. The references shared by the professionals, helped us to reach out to other HR professionals utilizing HRA. We reached out to 20 HR professionals, but only 15 agreed to participate in the study. A briefing session was arranged to help the participants comprehend the purpose of the research. In order to better understand the alleged problem, semi-structured interviews with each participant were conducted after the session and recorded.

We utilized a qualitative technique to assist us to obtain a deeper knowledge of the phenomena from the respondents' perspective because the difficulties encountered during the implementation of HR analytics are case specific. Here, the emphasis is on learning about the difficulties respondents have had using HR analytics inside their organizations. The qualitative form of inquiry employed in the current study was semi-structured interviews. According to Myers (2019), Interviews provide a substantial methodological advantage when it comes to flexibility and immersion in the research of opaque and complex phenomena. The two-phased methodology helped us to understand the challenges at the practitioner's end and further help us to understand the real challenges faced by organizations.

2.2 Data collection

2.2.1 Phase One: Literature Review:

The literature on HRA has grown in the past few years. We searched for studies using the keyword - "HR Analytics" and "People Analytics" on the Scopus database. The search led us to 538 documents. We further restricted the search by limiting the search results to the subject area "Management". We derived 178 documents through the search. The authors went through the documents and arrived at the following key highlights from the past research on HRA.

The field of people analytics has made significant strides in recent years, promising to help organizations make more evidence-based decisions, positively impact performance, and transform HR into a strategic business partner (McCartney and Fu, 2022). HR analytics teams have been formed to identify patterns and trends in employee data related to recruitment, engagement, diversity, retention, and turnover. However, the reality of people analytics remains uncertain, with challenges and debates generating more questions than answers.

Researchers have analyzed the factors that influence why some firms use HR analytics to monitor employee performance while others do not. The analysis is multi-faceted and considers the role of organizational, market, and country factors (Bechter et al. 2022). It distinguishes between the capability, motivation, and opportunity of firms to use HR analytics to monitor employee performance. Organizational factors are considered the most important in explaining why firms make use of HR analytics to monitor employee performance, with firm size and age being decisive factors. The degree of market competitiveness is also a strong motivator for firms to use HR analytics to gain an advantage over competitors. Differences in the institutional ability and opportunity of firms to collect and store data can also explain differences in the use of HR analytics to monitor employee performance among firms in different countries.

In today's digital age, enterprises must optimize their processes for financial sustainability, especially during times of crisis and increased competition. HR-Controlling identifies and implements improvement opportunities for the HR department, ensuring consistent optimization and stability of HR processes. It is a comprehensive approach to planning, monitoring, and managing tasks in Human Resources. According to a study, HR-Analytics is the most promising digital technology for HR-Controlling (Wilfinger et al., 2022).

Prior research talked about the benefits of the application of People Analytics, but only a few studies talk about the challenges of People Analytics and further very few have mentioned adoption challenges from HR Manager's perspective which includes autonomy required as opposed to the commodification of the expertise (Jörden et al., 2022), sub- competencies to measure the analytical competencies in HR professionals (Kalvakolanu, 2022). A lot of studies have tried to explore what HRA is and how it operates in different industries. The studies which mention challenges of People Analytics adoption have mentioned challenges related to HRA alignment with business strategy (Yoon et al., 2020), technology (McCartney and Fu, 2022; Balcerak and Woźniak, 2021), workforce acceptance (Zieglmeier et al., 2022) data security challenges bring up ethical aspect associated with data bringing forward ethical concerns (Cayrat and Boxall, 2022) and data basis management challenge (Raguvir and Babu, 2020).

Many studies have specifically explored the negative side of HRA in the context of technological impediments. The drawbacks discussed speak about privacy and data protection concerns (Calvard and Jeske, 2018), and fear of loss of employee data (Belizón and Kieran, 2022). The studies also mentioned surveillance and constant tracking and algorithmic biases as common threats to HRA implementation.

The important theoretical contribution of a study that investigated employees' reactions to algorithms used in personnel decisions extends procedural justice theory by highlighting the importance of human involvement in decision-making and how it improves the use of accurate information (Newmann et al., 2020). It illuminates the fundamental psychology of algorithms and how people resist the notion that algorithms can fairly account for qualitative human attributes. Furthermore, the research shows the importance of a distinction between quantitative and qualitative factors in procedural justice. It brings out the crucial role of procedures which gives due consideration to all aspects of the individual, including those not easily quantified, such as leadership potential, intentions, and psychological commitment. This opens the prospect for research investigating the psychological and organizational determinants of organizational commitment. The mere possibility of introducing algorithms into an organization can lead to negative downstream consequences for organizational commitment. Thus, researchers should seek to better understand how to integrate analytic decision-making while minimizing damage to morale and organizational commitment. The paper highlights the importance of human involvement in decision-making and the need for procedural justice in automated algorithms and analytics.

HR Analytics legitimacy process identifies three subprocesses that are key to gaining greater legitimacy: strategic commitment, cognitive legitimacy, and socio-political legitimacy (Belizón and Kieran, 2022). The process would define institutional work activity engaged by actors in each subprocess, highlighting organizational and structural factors that may affect the HR Analytics legitimacy process. The extant literature doesn't talk about how to build acceptability from the employees and alignment with stakeholders to overcome the challenges of implementing HRA. We see a spur of HRA implementation, but if the researchers can explore the challenges and provide implications to companies, it can serve as a referral for many organizations. Thus, we found this motivation to speak to HR professionals and explore managerial and leadership-level challenges.

2.2.2 Phase Two: Qualitative Study

The selection of respondents was made via snowball sampling. We spoke with the leaders of HR Analytics at companies that were adopting or had already used HR Analytics in their business. The participants gave us the names of additional HR professionals working in related or unrelated sectors. We asked people to participate by sending them emails and messages on LinkedIn. The message discussed the objective of the study and requested participation if they have applied HR Analytics in at least one HR function. Based on the participants' convenience and availability, an interview was planned. An interview guide was prepared to understand the challenges of implementation of HR Analytics. The interview guide and participant details are mentioned in Annexure. A briefing session was arranged to help the participants comprehend the purposes of the research. In order to better understand the problem, semi-structured interviews with each participant would be conducted after the session and recorded on camera. The interviews will be conducted via Zoom, Google Meet, and Microsoft Teams as appropriate for the convenience of the participants. Themes and sub-themes will be determined when the interviews have been transcribed. A total of 15 interviews were conducted. We initially planned to interview 20 HR professionals, but the Interviews were conducted up until data saturation was noticed. According to Charmaz (2006), data collection can be terminated when categories (or themes) are saturated, which happens when adding new data no longer yields innovative insights or shows novel traits. The interviews were recorded with the respondent's permission. The interviews typically lasted 45 to 60 minutes. The recorded interview data were transcribed and analyzed using the Qualitative Data Analysis Package NVivo 12. The data were examined to discover certain themes after coding performed by authors. The themes summarize the dark side experience of HRA implementation of participants. Details of participants, industry, location and experience are mentioned in the Annexure.

3. DISCUSSION AND FINDINGS

Researchers in the past have discussed the benefits of using HR Analytics and the improvements brought about by digital transformation in HR. In the current study, the authors independently went through the transcribed conversations and derived themes. The transcribed interviews were coded and analyzed independently by two authors. The differences in the themes were clarified in order to arrive at four themes. These five themes discovered through data analysis represent respondents' experiences with HRA implementation. These themes assist us in recognizing the difficulties encountered in the implementation of HR Analytics across diverse businesses.

Theme One: Complex HR Landscape

In recent decades, HR has been driven to extend its activities as a corporate partner. HR is responsible for developing and delivering HR practices and services that complement the organization's business model while also addressing the workforce's demands in this area. HR eventually developed as a strategic partner, playing a more important role than in the past. Lawler et al. (2006) echo that HR participates actively in the organization's key business decisions, such as strategy creation, organizational design, and business model execution, as a member of the senior management team. The strategic role of HR involves coordination with all departments and functions of an organization. HR cannot work in silos and thus the landscape requires coordination with all business functions. This adds to the complexity of HRA while ensuring effective results. Implementation of HRA is a key initiative to making HR a strategic partner in any organization. Therefore, HRA must be available to business leaders to expand their impact on the organization.

Many facets of corporate operations, including human resource procedures, have benefited from technological advancements. The time has come to look more closely at the complicated HR digital world and how technology may help firms attract talent, increase applicant and employee engagement, and provide better recruiting outcomes. The complex nature of multi-faceted coordination while implementing HRA in multiple functions, comes from the complex nature of HR Landscape. The data collection process is also complex, as you are dependent on multiple departments, heads and employees for data repositories.

According to me, HR Analytics is complex because HR is a strategic role now. We are no more in an administrative era, where HR plays a non-multidisciplinary role. (Respondent 2).

When we started implementing HRA in our recruitment process, we had to continually interact with other departments for requisitions. HRA implementation and success cannot be decided by efficient HR managers only, we need to have a cross-functional understanding. (Respondent 5).

Theme Two: Limited Knowledge of How Analytics Adoption Works in Engagement and Experience

There is a fad to implement HRA in organizations across sectors. The organizations are in a rush to commence HRA implementation. There is a consistent debate about "When should we apply HRA?" Falleta (2014) performed a study of Fortune 1000 companies to identify their adoption of HRA. The research found that just 15% of respondents in a sample of 220 organizations said HRA has a critical role in executing HR strategy. Yet there is ambiguity around how to commence utilizing HRA.

Analytics adoption has become an essential aspect of engagement and experience in organizations. Analytics helps organizations to understand their customers better, and it provides them with insights that can be used to improve customer engagement and experience. However, despite its importance, there is limited knowledge of how analytics adoption works in engagement and experience. One of the challenges that organizations face when adopting analytics in engagement and experience is the lack of a clear strategy. Many organizations adopt analytics without a clear strategy, which leads to confusion and ineffective use of analytics tools. A clear strategy is essential for successful analytics adoption because it outlines the organization's goals, objectives, and the metrics that will be used to measure success. It also identifies the data sources that will be used to collect data and the tools that will be used to analyze it. Without a clear strategy, organizations are likely to waste resources and fail to achieve their goals. Another challenge that organizations face is the lack of appropriate skills and resources. Analytics requires specialized skills and resources, and many organizations do not have the required expertise (Marler and Boudreau, 2017).

Data quality is another critical challenge Organizations need to ensure that they have reliable data sources and that their data is accurate, consistent, and complete. This requires proper data governance, including data cleaning, data validation, and data integration. To properly maintain data quality, organizations should actively invest in data management solutions. (King, 2016).

....and the biggest challenge was where to start. HRA implementation was decided amongst senior management. But which process to start with was the biggest challenge (Respondent 6)

We went through case studies on how other companies started HRA implementation, and that confused us more, as some started with multiple operations at the same time, and others started with one function at a time. (Respondent 8)

The data sources, data analysts, and data management technologies were all in place, and we took our time deciding which function to begin with because we didn't want our investment to be in vain. (Respondent 15)

Theme Three: Widening Skill Gap

Another significant challenge is, "Who should or can implement HR analytics?"

Another barrier to the implementation of HRA is the continuously increasing skill gap. Data analysis, data management, and statistical modelling are specialist skills that HRA demands but are sometimes missing in standard HR jobs. Organizations may struggle to successfully gather and analyze data due to a lack of HR analytics knowledge and abilities, which might result in false conclusions and bad actions. This, in turn, can harm organizational performance and hinder the achievement of HR goals. Organizations must invest in training programs for current employees to improve their abilities in order to combat the skill gap issue (Agarwal et al., 2022). Training programs should focus on data analysis, data visualization, and statistical modelling. Additionally, organizations may need to hire external experts to assist in the implementation of HRA. The recruitment drive for new employees should include technical skills as a mandatory requirement, to bridge the gap.

Thus, the widening skill gap is a significant challenge faced in the implementation of HRA. To address the challenge, organizations need to invest in training programs to develop the skills of their employees or hire external experts to help with implementation. By overcoming this challenge, organizations can achieve effective HR Analytics implementation, leading to improved HR management and organizational performance.

...we dint realise that we would take so much time to fill these job posts, we had to increase our time to hire. (Respondent 3)

We were relying on similar resources for HR Analysts, we changed the source of recruitment and it worked for us. (Respondent 7)

Empowering and upskilling our own employees turned out to be most beneficial for us. There might be people looking forward to learning opportunities, reach out to them first. (Respondent 10)

We talk about the industry-academia gap, I think this gap has been widened by data profiles in the market. MBA Schools should focus on data skills along with soft skills, the Gen Z will make it to these profiles. (Respondent 11)

Theme Four: Job Insecurity

Building a network of helpful stakeholders throughout and up the organizational hierarchy also governs the link between the adoption of HR Analytics and organizational effect (Marler & Boudreau, 2017). An essential component of this network is the workforce. At the same time, the growing use of HRA has the potential to have a variety of effects on job security. One way is by increasing the pressure on employees to perform, as their performance can now be quantified and analyzed more accurately. This can lead to a higher level of stress and anxiety among employees, as they are constantly being evaluated and monitored.

Furthermore, HRA may also be used to find areas where a company can make savings and possibly eliminate jobs in the process. For example, if data analysis reveals that a particular department or function is not as profitable as others, the organization may decide to downsize or eliminate that function. This can result in employees losing their jobs, which can have a significant impact on their financial and psychological well-being. Two main strategies, awareness and appeal, are identified to increase employees' willingness to share their data. Managers need to increase employees' awareness about the collected data's purpose and reduce their fear of data tracking. However, awareness alone may not be enough to motivate data sharing, and appeal strategies become relevant (Zieglmeier et al., 2022).

Another way HRA can impact job security is through the potential for bias and discrimination in data analysis. HR analytics and machine-learning methods can provide a different way of understanding turnover and reveal the role of unforeseen measures in explaining the turnover phenomenon (Avrahami et. al., 2022). These techniques can be useful for predicting and preventing turnover in specific roles, particularly in the context of a globally distributed workforce and online labor markets. The potential of using machine-learning techniques to predict people-related challenges in organizations is seen as a game changer. At the same time, the data used for such techniques to evaluate performance is biased or discriminatory or inconsistent recorded (Raguvir and Babu, 2020), this can lead to unfair treatment of employees and potentially even their termination. Additionally, if HR analytics are used to identify which employees are likely to leave the company, this can result in those employees being treated differently or marginalized, leading to feelings of insecurity and potentially even their departure.

Organizations must take precautions to reduce the risks associated with the possible impact of HR analytics on job security. This means being open and honest with staff members about how their data is being used and making sure the information is reliable and impartial (Cayrat, & Boxall, 2022). Additionally, organizations can provide training and support to employees to help them understand and adapt to the changes brought about by HR analytics. By taking these steps, organizations can help ensure that HR analytics are used ethically and effectively, without compromising job security.

...when we communicated that we are going to implement performance analytics, there were resignations throughout the organization... we were taken aback, we were not expecting this....(Respondent 5)

Our HR team had lot of queries on growth opportunities for people who would not be able to do data driven job roles, we smelled some insecurity (Respondent 2)

Theme Five: Distrust Leading to Barrier in Change

Psychological barriers can arise from individual and organizational factors that limit the acceptance and adoption of HRA. One of the psychological barriers to HR Analytics implementation is resistance to change. Resistance to change is a natural human tendency that can make it challenging to adopt new practices and technologies. HR Analytics often requires a significant shift in HR management practices, and this can lead to resistance from employees who are comfortable with the status quo (Bansal et al., 2023). Another psychological barrier to HR Analytics implementation is a lack of trust in data. Data skepticism is common, and many employees may question the validity and accuracy of the data used in HR Analytics. This can lead to a lack of confidence in the insights generated by HR Analytics, making it difficult to convince employees to adopt new HR management practices based on the data.

Fear of consequences is another psychological barrier to HR Analytics implementation. HR Analytics can provide insights into employee performance, behaviour, and engagement. However, these insights may reveal issues that employees may not want to address, such as poor performance or engagement. This can lead to a fear of consequences, such as job loss or negative performance evaluations, which can hinder the adoption of HRA (Giermindl et al., 2022). There is a consistent fear of data leakage, which involves employees' critical details. There is a threat of data misuse and privacy concern. Limited access to managers as per usability has to be kept in mind to secure employee privacy and data security. Such policies would limit the perceived risks employees associate with HR analytics.

Even if the employees are ready to adapt to the technological changes, they never fully trust it, there is a fear of evaluation by machines which affects the behaviour of employees manifold. (Respondent 9)

You cannot replace the Human from the Human Resource (Respondent13)

....the rapid technological change and adoption of analytics still won't be able to replace the human touch.. But we feel insecure in this data-driven VUCA, metaverse and robot-centered world. (Respondent 14)

4. IMPLICATIONS AND FUTURE DIRECTIONS

The barriers to HRA implementation are an important topic of research that is gaining traction. Existing research has several consequences and future research areas. The study has implications for HR policymakers, top management decision-makers as well as HR professionals. The study reflects upon the importance of HRA and at the same time tries to identify key challenges faced by practitioners. The implications would help the HR managers understand key challenges faced by employees when HRA is implemented in any organization. The study would also guide the senior management to plan the HRA implementation in a way it ensures a smooth transition in change.

The study suggests future directions. Future studies should concentrate on identifying the particular obstacles to HRA adoption in various organizational environments. Depending on elements such as corporate culture, size, and sector, the obstacles to adoption may differ between firms. Organizations may create focused strategies to get over these obstacles by having a clear understanding of the unique adoption challenges that they face. Researchers ought to look into how leadership influences the uptake of HR Analytics. In creating a company culture and fostering change, leaders are essential. Organizations may create efficient change management strategies by having a thorough understanding of the leadership philosophies and techniques that encourage the implementation of HR Analytics.

5. CONCLUSION

The negative aspects of HR analytics are a real concern that must be addressed in the workplace. While data-driven insights can result in positive outcomes, they also carry significant risks. Some of the key impediments include a lack of data quality, inadequate technical expertise, and resistance to change. The study adopted qualitative techniques to derive five key themes from the interviews with 15 HR professionals from different types of industries. The professionals suggested a Complex HR Landscape, Limited knowledge of how Analytics adoption works in engagement and experience, Widening skill gap, Job Insecurity and Distrust leading to barriers in change as key themes. The article suggests that HRA is aligned with the strategic role of HR, which is complex in nature, thus leading to HRA implementation a complex process. Another discussion led to an important challenge, how to implement HRA. Organizations are ambitious to implement HRA, but there is ambiguity about how, how much, where and when to implement it. Another important issue highlighted by professionals was the widening skill gap and the need to upskill the current workforce. The last two themes that were derived were job insecurity and distrust, which talks about psychological barriers leading to resistance to change. HRA has the potential to revolutionize HR practices, but it must be used responsibly and ethically. Employers and HR professionals must be aware of the risks and take proactive steps to minimize the negative consequences of HRA.

REFERENCES

Agarwal, V., Mathiyazhagan, K., Malhotra, S., & Saikouk, T. (2022). Analysis of challenges in sustainable human resource management due to disruptions by Industry 4.0: An emerging economy perspective. *International Journal of Manpower*, *43*(2), 513–541. doi:10.1108/IJM-03-2021-0192

Avrahami, D., Pessach, D., Singer, G., & Chalutz Ben-Gal, H. (2022). A human resources analytics and machine-learning examination of turnover: Implications for theory and practice. *International Journal of Manpower*, *43*(6), 1405–1424. doi:10.1108/IJM-12-2020-0548

Balcerak, A., & Woźniak, J. (2021). Reactions to some ICT-based personnel selection tools. *Economics & Sociology (Ternopil)*, *14*(1), 214–231. doi:10.14254/2071-789X.2021/14-1/14

Bansal, A., Panchal, T., Jabeen, F., Mangla, S. K., & Singh, G. (2023). A study of human resource digital transformation (HRDT): A phenomenon of innovation capability led by digital and individual factors. *Journal of Business Research*, *157*, 113611. doi:10.1016/j.jbusres.2022.113611

Bassi, L. J., Carpenter, R., & McMurrer, D. (2012). *HR analytics handbook*. Reed Business.

Bechter, B., Brandl, B., & Lehr, A. (2022). The role of the capability, opportunity, and motivation of firms for using human resource analytics to monitor employee performance: A multi-level analysis of the organisational, market, and country context. *New Technology, Work and Employment*, *37*(3), 398–424. doi:10.1111/ntwe.12239

Belizón, M. J., & Kieran, S. (2022). Human resources analytics: A legitimacy process. *Human Resource Management Journal*, *32*(3), 603–630. doi:10.1111/1748-8583.12417

Bersin, J. (2016). The Future Of Work: It's Already Here—And Not As Scary As You Think. *Leadership*, *6*(43), 62–187.

Calvard, T. S., & Jeske, D. (2018). Developing human resource data risk management in the age of big data. *International Journal of Information Management*, *43*, 159–164. doi:10.1016/j.ijinfomgt.2018.07.011

Cayrat, C., & Boxall, P. (2022). Exploring the phenomenon of HR analytics: a study of challenges, risks and impacts in 40 large companies. *Journal of Organizational Effectiveness: People and Performance*.

Charmaz, K. (2006). *Constructing grounded theory: A practical guide through qualitative analysis*. sage.

Falletta, S. (2014). In search of HR intelligence: Evidence-based HR analytics practices in high performing companies. *People and Strategy*, *36*(4), 28.

Falletta, S. V., & Combs, W. L. (2021). The HR analytics cycle: A seven-step process for building evidence-based and ethical HR analytics capabilities. *Journal of Work-Applied Management*, *13*(1), 51–68. doi:10.1108/JWAM-03-2020-0020

Fernandez, V., & Gallardo-Gallardo, E. (2021). Tackling the HR digitalization challenge: Key factors and barriers to HR analytics adoption. *Competitiveness Review*, *31*(1), 162–187. doi:10.1108/CR-12-2019-0163

Giermindl, L. M., Strich, F., Christ, O., Leicht-Deobald, U., & Redzepi, A. (2022). The dark sides of people analytics: Reviewing the perils for organisations and employees. *European Journal of Information Systems*, *31*(3), 410–435. doi:10.1080/0960085X.2021.1927213

Jeske, D., & Calvard, T. (2020). Big data: lessons for employers and employees. *Employee Relations: The International Journal*.

Jörden, N. M., Sage, D., & Trusson, C. (2022). 'It's so fake': Identity performances and cynicism within a people analytics team. *Human Resource Management Journal*, *32*(3), 524–539. doi:10.1111/1748-8583.12412

Kalvakolanu, S. (2022). Developing a scale to assess analytical competencies of HR professionals. *International Journal of Business Information Systems*, *41*(3), 322–341. doi:10.1504/IJBIS.2022.126997

King, K. G. (2016). Data analytics in human resources: A case study and critical review. *Human Resource Development Review, 15*(4), 487–495. doi:10.1177/1534484316675818

Lawler, E. E., Boudreau, J. W., Mohrman, S. A., Mark, A. Y., & Osganian, N. (2006). *Achieving strategic excellence: An assessment of human resource organizations.* Stanford University Press.

Lepenioti, K., Bousdekis, A., Apostolou, D., & Mentzas, G. (2020). Prescriptive analytics: Literature review and research challenges. *International Journal of Information Management, 50*, 57–70. doi:10.1016/j.ijinfomgt.2019.04.003

Levenson, A. (2018). Using workforce analytics to improve strategy execution. *Human Resource Management, 57*(3), 685–700. doi:10.1002/hrm.21850

Marler, J. H., & Boudreau, J. W. (2017). An evidence-based review of HR Analytics. *International Journal of Human Resource Management, 28*(1), 3–26. doi:10.1080/09585192.2016.1244699

McCartney, S., & Fu, N. (2022). Promise versus reality: A systematic review of the ongoing debates in people analytics. *Journal of Organizational Effectiveness: People and Performance, 9*(2), 281–311. doi:10.1108/JOEPP-01-2021-0013

McCartney, S., Murphy, C., & Mccarthy, J. (2021). 21st century HR: A competency model for the emerging role of HR Analysts. *Personnel Review, 50*(6), 1495–1513. doi:10.1108/PR-12-2019-0670

Minbaeva, D. B. (2018). Building credible human capital analytics for organizational competitive advantage. *Human Resource Management, 57*(3), 701–713. doi:10.1002/hrm.21848

Newman, D. T., Fast, N. J., & Harmon, D. J. (2020). When eliminating bias isn't fair: Algorithmic reductionism and procedural justice in human resource decisions. *Organizational Behavior and Human Decision Processes, 160*, 149–167. doi:10.1016/j.obhdp.2020.03.008

Raguvir, S., & Babu, S. (2020, October). Enhance employee productivity using Talent analytics and Visualization. In *2020 International Conference on Data Analytics for Business and Industry: Way Towards a Sustainable Economy (ICDABI)* (pp. 1-5). IEEE. 10.1109/ICDABI51230.2020.9325682

Simón, C., & Ferreiro, E. (2018). Workforce analytics: A case study of scholar–practitioner collaboration. *Human Resource Management, 57*(3), 781–793. doi:10.1002/hrm.21853

Smeyers, L. (2015). What we learned about HR analytics in 2014–part 2.

Wilfinger, D., Brandstätter, C., & Mitteregger, J. (2022). Implications of the Digitalization on Human-Resource-Controlling. *Tehnički glasnik, 16*(3), 438-443.

Yoon, S. W., Chae, C., Kim, S., Lee, J., & Jo, Y. (2020). Human resource analytics in South Korea: Transforming the organization and industry. *Human Resource Development in South Korea: Theory and Cases*, 159-180.

Zieglmeier, V., Gierlich-Joas, M., & Pretschner, A. (2022, October). Increasing Employees' Willingness to Share: Introducing Appeal Strategies for People Analytics. In *Software Business: 13th International Conference, ICSOB 2022,* (pp. 213-226). Cham: Springer International Publishing.

APPENDIX

Table 1. Details of respondents

Industry	Gender	Experience (in years)	Location
Accommodation and Food Services	Male	12	Delhi - NCR
Accounting	Male	14	Mumbai
FMCG	Female	15	Mumbai
Communications	Female	13	Bangalore
Entertainment	Male	12	Mumbai
Finance, Insurance & Real Estate	Male	17	Hyderabad
Health Care	Male	13	Delhi - NCR
Manufacturing	Male	15	Delhi - NCR
Not For Profit	Female	14	Bangalore
Pharmaceuticals	Male	18	Pune
Retail	Male	12	Chennai
Consulting	Female	11	Delhi - NCR
Technology	Male	8	Bangalore

Sample Interview Questions:

Which HRA solutions are you currently employing in your organisation?
What were the key issues that employees faced when you started implementing HRA?
Was the leadership team intended to continually invest in HRA tools?
So far, what are some of the advantages of using people analytics?
Is your company struggling with digital skill gaps?
What is the most difficult difficulty you face with HR Analytics?
What is the current state of HRA in your organisation?

Chapter 7
HR Analytics in Employee Engagement and Turnover

Sunanda Vincent Jaiwant
CHRIST University, India

Kiran Vazirani
https://orcid.org/0000-0001-5591-6874
CHRIST University, India

ABSTRACT

HR Analytics has expanded increasingly in the last two decades. Nowadays, several companies use the supremacy of analytics, in gaining a competitive edge over others by recognizing all essentials of the employees. Organizations aim to optimize employee-performance, and hence are making use of HR analytics to drive strategic HR decisions. This study examines the advent of HR analytics by in measuring and improving employee engagement and turnover. Employee engagement analytics stands for exercising the use of data in decision-making process by integrating employee engagement with other HR and non-HR data. Employee engagement analytics is a subsection of workforce-analytics. It has become the standard contemporary system in advanced employee administration and retention. Employee engagement analytics benefits all stakeholders within the organization.

INTRODUCTION

Employee engagement is a constructive driver that purposes and joins employees with their organizations, either emotionally, cognitively or physically (Kahn, 1990) (Wellins & Concelman, 2005) It is essential to give prominence to employee engagement as it enhances their performances, and improves their job-satisfaction and subsequently result in controlled employee turnover. Hence, employee engagement is considered by the HR managers as an important matter that needs careful thought and insightful decisions (Seijts & Crim, 2006) since workforce stand as the central strength or asset for any business enterprise (Lockwood, 2007).

DOI: 10.4018/978-1-6684-8942-0.ch007

HR analytics is fundamentally functions on the principle of measurement-management which means that anything that we are unable to measure, it will be difficult to manage the same. HR analytics use this principle on human resources. More sophisticated analytical techniques have emerged during the past few decades, and they have the ability to produce greater understanding and more effective suggestions (Bersin, 2013).

(Kale & Anute, 2020) HR Analytic refers to the assortment and execution of talent data with the aim to sustaining vital talented employees in the industry. It is essentially employed to take more relevant and insightful decisions based on the existing data, to envisage workforce turnover and recognize good talents who perform better than others and also identify and forecast the required skills required to be upgraded. HR Analytics also called as people analytics permits your HR managers to measure the impact of HR policies on general organization performance. HR Analytics has four different categories namely, Descriptive Analytics, Diagnostic Analytics, Predictive Analytics and Prescriptive Analytics.

(Bassi & McMurrer, 2016) discussed about how analytics can be utilised to change a business enterprise beyond the generic competencies by discovering the distinctive leadership skills that influence an organization's business outcomes, including revenue, earnings, and workforce retention. (Oladipupo & Olubusayo, 2020) The extent of the relationship between staff involvement and the HR analytics factor was actually evaluated by the researchers. The results showed that HR analytics significantly contribute to the degree of employee engagement specially in case of manufacturing organizations. (Belyaeva & Kozieva, 2020) used methods of engagement research, as well as economic, statistical, sociological, psychological tools of HR analytics. The outcome of the research will technically help to understand the employee engagement estimation and research of its interrelation with indicators of economic efficiency of enterprise development.

HR analytics has its roots in the field of industrial and organisational psychology, which emerged in the early 20th century. Academics at the time were curious to understand more about the factors influencing employee performance and workplace conduct. This led to the development of numerous evaluation techniques and tools, such as personality tests, tests of cognitive ability, and job analysis techniques (Bassi & McMurrer, 2016). In the 1960s and 1970s, the field of human resources began to adopt some of these techniques and methodologies to evaluate and comprehend employee behaviour and performance. The majority of data collection and analysis tasks are still carried out manually, and the data is typically limited to the most basic demographic information, such age, gender, and level of education (Bersin, 2013).

As computer technology advanced in the 1980s and 1990s, HR began to look at the possibilities of using technology to automate and streamline data collection and analysis. HR professionals employed databases, spreadsheets, and basic statistical tools to examine data and identify trends in employee behaviour and performance (Oladipupo & Olubusayo, 2020). At the time, data analytics was still a rather specialised field, and many organisations lacked the resources or expertise necessary to get started. But a small number of early adopters—including IBM and General Electric—started to see how HR analytics could improve their HR practises and have a positive impact on their bottom lines. Generally speaking, the early history of HR analytics was characterised by a gradual acceptance of new methodologies and tools for data analysis, prompted by a growing understanding of the need of evaluating and comprehending employee performance and behaviour. Early ideas and techniques laid the groundwork for the current HR analytics industry, albeit they might need to be updated in light of today's sophisticated analytics tools (Belyaeva & Kozieva, 2020).

The practice of human resource management has seen significant development over time and is now developing quickly. HR practitioners are growing more dependent on the use of technology and information as well as to the "human" part of operating a business (Kale & Anute, 2020). The growing integration of data in HR processes leads to the emergence of human resource analytics. Making decisions based on data using HR analytics is essential to the long-term achievement of any business. Over 70% of executives place a high priority on personnel analytics. 90% more people will use HR analytics in the next three years. Analytics has revolutionised marketing and now the application of analytics is transforming HR. Insights concerning how to supervise personnel and accomplish company goals are sought for by HR analytics. Given the abundance of data available, HR teams must decide which information is most pertinent and how to use it most effectively. Analytics can be employed to help achieve this task (Bassi & McMurrer, 2016). This study intends to define HR analytics, discuss its advantages, and highlight how important it is to HR. This chapter targets to provide a comprehensive account to students, academicians, researchers and HR managers and leaders, organizations about the role and benefits of using Analytics in understanding and measuring employee engagement and turnover. The chapter intends to facilitate as a useful guide for corporate sector, education sector and the research fraternity to understand the different Analytic technologies and tools for different HR functions.

The objectives of the study are:

1. to identify the concept of HR analytics in Employee Engagement and Turnover
2. to explore the different analytics techniques which can be used for measuring employee engagement. The study will also attempt to identify the benefits and challenges in using analytics for employee engagement and turnover.

EVOLUTION OF HR ANALYTICS

The development of HR analytics refers to improvements in the application of data for assessing the employees of a business. This has included the development of novel innovations like machine learning and artificial intelligence as well as an increased focus on the importance of data security. Modern HR practises are growing increasingly dependent on HR analytics, which helps companies increase employee engagement, develop more inclusive work environments, and meet corporate goals. The development of HR analytics has been influenced by improvements in technology, data analysis methods, and a growing appreciation of the value of data-driven decision making in human resources. During the course of twenty years, HR analytics has transformed from a niche subject to a crucial component of modern HR operations. One of the main driving causes behind the growth of HR analytics has been the growing affordability and accessibility of data. As increasing amounts of information has become available, organisations are being able to use it to better understand their employees and make decisions. Big data, cloud computing, and data presentation tools have all contributed to the rapid and efficient storage, processing, and analysis of enormous volumes of data by enterprises. A significant advancement in the growth of HR analytics has been the increased application of predictive analytics (Bassi & McMurrer, 2016).

(Kalvakolanu et al., 2016) Dr. Jac Fitz-enz's groundbreaking studies as well as the preliminary comparability research he conducted by means of the Saratoga Institute are credited with the development of numerous of the HR indicators that are most often employed in organisations today. Human resources measurements and general business analysis have merged to become HR analytics. By questioning the status quo, the discipline of HR analytics was created. Despite the fact that a few companies have started using tools and metrics like score cards and human resource accounting, they were insufficient to provide businesses a competitive edge in terms of their human resources. Human resources' performance and outcomes, as well as their activities, were not being measured A 2004 article in Workforce Management (previously Personnel Journal) stated that Jac Fitz-enz put forth a bold, anti-establishment proposal in this journal in 1978. Activities involving human resources and their effects on the conclusion ought to be and might be assessed. Indifference, disagreements, and scepticism were the responses (Caudron, 2004). The American Society for Personnel Administration (ASPA), the predecessor to the present Society for Human Resource Management (SHRM), and the Saratoga Institute collaborated to establish metrics. The 30 metrics were created during the course of this project.

Organisations can predict potential employee trends by analysing past information and applying statistical models, and then take proactive steps to address these tendencies. This has enabled businesses to identify and address potential HR issues before they develop into significant issues. The growth of HR analytics has been profoundly influenced by the emergence of HR technology platforms (Lawler & Levenson, 2004). The centralization of HR data provided by such systems makes it easier to collect, analyse, and present employee information. In addition, HR technology solutions come with a wide range of advanced analytics tools and techniques, including as machine learning and artificial intelligence, which might be utilised to learn more about the workforce's productivity and behaviours. In general, improvements in technology and data analysis methodologies have prompted the growth of HR analytics, which is characterised by a tendency towards data-driven decision-making. As businesses continue to collect and analyse more data, the opportunity for HR analytics to produce commercial success will only grow (Bose & Jose, 2018).

HR ANALYTICS AND STRATEGIC DECISION MAKING

Data that has been collected in the routine manner is correlated using analytics with the HR and the objectives of the organization. This way analytics helps in understanding how the HR policies, activities, programmes are contributing to the mission and goals of the organization. The practise of employing data to decide wisely about a company's employees is known as HR analytics. It entails gathering and analysing information on a range of HR measures, including, but not limited to, employee attrition, hiring measurements, training and development initiatives, and employee engagement levels. Organisations may improve their HR strategy by utilising this data to acquire insights into their staff and make wise decisions. On the other hand, strategic decision-making entails selecting choices that support the company's objectives for the future and strategies. Making judgements that are well-informed and long-lasting for the organisation necessitates taking into account all pertinent elements, including data (Bose & Jose, 2018).

The primary use of data in HR is significantly for decision-making, which starts with clarity regarding the decisions that must be taken, followed by the collection of the appropriate data and the selection of the appropriate tools for effective decision-making. The goal of adopting HR analytics in business organizations is for innovation in order to pinpoint the factors that contribute to performance improvement and calculate a measurable return that can be shared with management. Businesses shouldn't concentrate on deploying HR analytics programmes just because it's trendy or one of their rivals is doing it (Nagpal & Mishra, 2018). HR analytics must be used because they can significantly improve a company's operations both in the present and, in the years, to come.

Organisations may make better judgements about their workforce when they employ HR analytics in strategic decision-making. HR analytics, for instance, can reveal which benefit plans work best for boosting morale and lowering attrition among employees. Organisations can use this information to make smarter choices regarding their rewards packages. Similar to this, HR analytics can assist businesses in determining which channels for hiring draw the best prospects. Organisations can increase the quality of candidates they recruit and lower the cost per hire through employing this information to modify their recruitment strategies (Lawler & Levenson, 2004).

In general, HR analytics can offer useful information that can assist businesses in making better choices regarding their staff. Organisations may enhance their HR strategies, cut expenses, and accomplish their objectives for the future by using data to guide their decisions. Data-backed insights regarding the human resources approaches and activities that are working and those that aren't are provided by HR analytics. This helps the organisation fill in the gaps in its less-than-effective strategies and procedures and introduce new, better-designed objectives and aims. As a result, HR analytics supports strategic decision-making by highlighting potential development areas and enhancing effective procedures that contribute to organisational success and expansion.

THEORETICAL BACKGROUND AND ASSOCIATE STUDIES

Technology Acceptance Model

David (1989) began his research and study on adoption models in order to understand the factors that influence the acceptance or rejection of information technology. Two crucial components were emphasised; they are described below.

According to David (1989), perceived ease of usage and effort expectation are interchangeable terms. It refers to the rate at which someone anticipates that using a specific programme would be effortless. This suggests that a person will adopt the use of an application if they believe it to be simple to use (David, 1989).

It is "the degree to which a person believes that the way they perform at work can be enhanced using a specific system," according to Davis (1989). According to Talukder et al. (2008), a person's decision on whether or not to utilise an application will be contingent upon whether or not they think doing so will improve their ability to execute their work. Although someone could think that an application could be extremely beneficial, this does not imply that it will be simple to operate. The application cannot be adopted if a person feels that the cost (learning effort and difficulty) is greater than the benefit of adoption after considering the costs and benefits of adoption (Oladipupo & Olubusayo, 2020).

(Chandra, 2023) a dataset containing employee details can provide HR managers with valuable insights into their workforce, allowing them to make data-driven decisions that promote equity, diversity, and inclusion within the organization. (Madhani, 2023) Human Resources analytics focus on various HRM activities including selection, appraisal, compensation, rewards, and development to maximize their impact on organizational performance. (Nishith Pawar, 2023) Data analytics makes it easier for companies to visualize data and act on it for better decision-making for the benefit of the organization. (Charles Cayrat, 2022) the practice of descriptive analytics is widely adopted in these companies and the majority can demonstrate improvement in the efficiency and effectiveness of HR activities through predictive analytics. (Premlal Prejith, 2022) HR analytical practices achieve a straight and positive influence on the performance of IT employees through practicing training and development skills. (Dan Avrahami, 2022) by applying machine-learning granular models, (which is based on HR analytics) one is able to show that the effects of competencies, commitment, trust and cultural values on turnover are often contingent on role, gender and cultural background. (Jawahar Supraveen, 2022) HR analytics has proven to be effective in boosting employer overall performance by lowering team of workers expenses, improving the quality of recruiting, improving expertise control and worker engagement, and generally increasing productivity. (Kamel Barbar, 2019) HR analytics allow HR professionals to assess HR practices and outcomes over time thereby facilitating the review of employees' training and development needs.

HR Analytics and Employee Engagement

(Kavyashree, 2022) HRM practices in organizations empowered employees and made them more engaged to perform better in their job roles. (Oladipupo & Olubusayo, 2020), tried to understand the dimensions of HR analytics adopted in manufacturing firms contributing to employees' engagement. The model looked at various dimensions of HR analytics such as descriptive analytics, diagnostic analytics, predictive analytics and prescriptive analytics) that could perhaps drive employees job engagement, particularly in the manufacturing firms. (Ashish Malik, 2023) tried analysing the impact of AI-assisted HRM on Employee experience and Employee Engagement levels and the results proved that the strategic focus of the firm helped elevate talent's Employee experience (Malik et al.,2021), and thus Employee Experience, leading to improved employee commitment, retention, and business level productivity outcomes. (Ridhya Goyal, 2023) proved that the variable of employee engagement has a positive and significant influence on the variable of nurse retention.

HR Analytics and Employee Turnover

(Sonal Gupta, 2022) identified that if an organization is a Cost Leadership firm, it should employ predictive or prescriptive analytics techniques for employee turnover. Also, if an organization is a Differentiator firm, it is able to employ descriptive or diagnostic analytics techniques for prediction of employee turnover. (Nitya, 2021) as the study proves significant relationship between Employee Turnover and HR analytics, the use of predictive people analytics will make it possible for practitioners to identify employee connections and use that information to analyse the risk of turnover (Kakulapati, 2023). Continuous Integration Continuous Deployment, employed for the model, can immediately learn in deployment for the wrong predictions, leading to a more accurate model to predict employee attrition. (Soumyadeb Chowdhury, 2022) offered an implementation framework that demonstrates the use of Local Interpretable Model-Agnostic Explanations (LIME) technique for explaining the exemplary case of employee turnover predictions made by AI-based Machine Learning models, thereby showing a technique to enhance AI transparency and explain-ability. (Setiawan, 2020) It was found that some variables that have a significant impact on employee attrition – 'number of companies worked,' 'total working years,' 'years with current manager.

HR Analytics and Profitability

(Bob-Manuel, 2023) HR analytics and Human resource management on organisational outcomes such as productivity and profit, and also a positive significant relationship between human resource database analytics and employee productivity which includes - Timeliness of Work, Achievement of Targets, Employee Innovativeness. (Meenal Arora, 2022) With deployment of AI and analytics in HR functions such as talent acquisition, training and development, employee retention, employee engagement and performance appraisal, organizations can enhance proficiency and productivity. (Weena Yancey M Momin, 2015) HR Analytics thus help the organization to design a strategic workforce planning by analysing every aspect of HR matrices, which includes Recruitment and selection, Succession planning, Performance management, Training & development, Turnover rate. (Navodya Gurusinghe, 2021) proposed an integrated conceptual model, based on the theoretical roots of Technological-Organisational-Environmental (TOE) framework and Resource-based view and concluded that Predictive Human Resource Analytics capability impacts the effectiveness of talent management outcomes.

PAYBACKS OF HR ANALYTICS

Because it has the potential to increase HR effectiveness and commercial results, HR departments are now required to include workforce data evaluation into their everyday operations. The following are just a few of the potential advantages of employing people analytics (Daniel, 2020):

Saves time: The process of finding, selecting, training, and developing workers can take a lot of time and isn't necessarily directly beneficial to achieving strategic goals (Levenson, 2005). The HR department can spend more time on activities that will provide greater benefits for the firm as a whole by focusing on the individuals and programmes that will be most helpful thanks to people analytics.

Increased output: People analytics can be utilised with data from employee engagement surveys to assist identify what maintains workers motivation or what gets in the way, especially as more employees work from home after the pandemic (Karmańska, 2020). The usage of HR analytics in conjunction with tracking contacts for COVID-19 is likely to increase. HR analytics may be employed as well to investigate wellness patterns, health issues and nonattendance problems.

Boost the experience of employees: The morale and productivity of an employee are frequently associated with their sense of being accepted within the organisation. People analytics may help HR and data scientists collaborating with HR identify the needs and wants of employees, improving their interpersonal and working culture (Zeidan & Itani, 2020).

Increase in retention: Retention may increase as a result of people analytics' capacity to enhance employee experience. Analytics can show recruiting team the causes of workers' unfavourable attitudes as well as the reasons why workers stick with the organisation. Such data can assist businesses in locating team member skill gaps and working to close them in an attempt to keep employees pleased and retained by the business (Zeidan & Itani, 2020).

Identify practical insights: Giving workers information they can understand is made possible by combining data visualisation with people analytics. Workers know where to adjust their efforts, and a better feeling of involvement offers a motivation for performing so, because they are able to view their achievement data inside a wider picture of company goals (Daniel, 2020).

Make better decisions: Individuals may utilise the information provided by data analytics to guide and strengthen the decisions they make. People analytics gives HR departments the ability to use worker information to make decisions that are more dependent on quantitative probability of being successful than on being more towards subjectivity and emotionally based (Angrave et al., 2016).

CHALLENGES IN IMPLEMENTING HR ANALYTICS

HR experts over the years learn about their problems and find ways in coming up with the best solutions. Although many of them have access to this plethora of HR data, they are too busy with administrative duties, performance concerns, routine hiring and workforce management, manually assessing employee satisfaction surveys, and other chores to even go deeper into the data (Fernandez & Gallardo-Gallardo, 2021). The worst aspect is that many people simply don't know what to do with their data after that. HR is traditionally thought of as being people-oriented rather than data- or number-oriented.

Data Diversity

In HR, there are several different sub-functions, and each one collects data on its own. It is a challenge to integrate all of these processes and figure out how to use them jointly to produce insightful findings. For several organisations, doing this is frequently their greatest hurdle. Nevertheless, numerous specialised technologies are currently being created to combine data.

Management attitude

Because they view the human resources division as a supplementary function, numerous companies struggle to incorporate analytics in HR (Opatha, 2020). Although this might be correct in certain situations, HR is generally what maintains the company running smoothly. This division maintains the contentment, inspiration, and productivity of the staff (Maria, 2019).

Return on Investment

Several companies struggle to create a favourable return on investment after integrating HR analytics because they cannot anticipate future events (Heuvel & Bondarouk, 2017). The majority of HR experts make sure to include information that can be used to improve the company's current or past conditions. However, they are unable to foresee what the coming years may hold or to suggest ways to lessen its harmful effects.

Data Credibility

The majority of the data gathered is unorganised and unprocessed, so companies must first clean it up before analysing it. Before gaining information, this data must be cleaned or value extracted from it. Given how challenging it is to develop a system and framework for data cleaning, this presents a significant disadvantage to many (Zeidan & Itani, 2020). Because companies have a large volume of data that is difficult to develop, gather, and maintain, HR analytics struggles with reliability challenges. Due to the absence of reliable information provided by employees, the data obtained may contain insufficient or inaccurate attributes. When moving data from one source to another, redundant information may be present or it may be impacted. The HR analytics tool produces findings on the basis of the data that is available, but if there are problems with the accuracy of the information, the outcomes could not be what was anticipated (Tomar & Gaur, 2020).

THE FOUR TYPES OF HR ANALYTICS

With personalised and pertinent solutions of their goods or services, businesses may both attract new customers and keep their current ones by using big data analytics to better comprehend what they want and what they prefer. According to the Fortune Business Insights, the global big data analytics market size was valued at $271.83 billion in 2022 & is projected to grow from $307.52 billion in 2023 to $745.15 billion by 2030. Given the numerous uses in several sectors, including smart power grid management, sentiment analysis, fraud detection, individualised services, traffic management, etc., the big data industry is exploding. The subsequent crucial stage is to begin with analytics after the organisations have gathered massive data. Numerous businesses are confused about how to start, what types of analytics might foster business expansion, and what all these Numerous businesses are unaware of where to start, which type of analytics might foster corporate success, or what each of these distinct sorts of analytics represent.

Descriptive analytics

Descriptive analytics is the first kind of HR analytics on the list. This is the most fundamental kind that examines data patterns to learn more about the past. Decision analytics is the practise of using statistical analysis methods to explain or condense a specific collection of raw, historical data. It doesn't offer forecasts for the future but instead concentrates on using historical data to explain what occurred (Ahmed et al., 2014). Combining quantitative and qualitative data is possible when using descriptive analytics. Calculations for central tendency, frequency, variation, ranking, range, deviation, etc. are performed as part of this process. This enables HR to spot trends and discrepancies to enhance planning (Williams, 2011). With descriptive analytics, one can do things like evaluating conduct, comparison of employee traits through time, finding irregularities, assessing the strengths and weaknesses, etc. The easiest type of data analysis. One only needs rudimentary mathematics abilities, and enables one to demonstrate intricate information in an understandable way.

Diagnostic analytics

Diagnostic analytics offers an explanation for the findings and elevates descriptive analytics to a higher state (Liu et al., 2020). It seeks to ascertain the fundamental causes of the revelations made by the data. It uses the same past information as descriptive analytics, but there is a significant distinction. Diagnostic analytics takes the process of analysing to another level where it summarises what transpired in plain language. It investigates the "why" underlying the patterns, correlations, and inconsistencies in the data. The subsequent actions are often taken when doing a diagnostic analysis:

- discovering trends and inconsistencies in the data presents concerns and demand additional investigation.
- identifying the pertinent data by determining what elements may be causing the trends and abnormalities.
- establishing causal relationships by applying multiple techniques of analysis to the data.

Diagnostic analytics are employed to convert data into insightful information (Balali, 2020). It recognises trends, variations, and causal connections and also taking into account potential internal and external influences. This enables HR to focus on the elements that could potentially lead to issues while also gaining a broad perspective on the situation (Williams, 2011). Then you may direct your efforts in the proper direction to reduce the issues. There are several diagnostic analytics techniques, which includes:

- *Data drilling:* It is the process of collecting details from a broader perspective and giving a more detailed analysis of the data. Data drilling is a business intelligence (BI) methodology that offers numerous perspectives of the data in visualisations, graphs, and worksheets to assist businesses in their information analysis. It's a straightforward strategy that is useful for identifying trends' root causes. Data drilling is most frequently used to investigate the detailed data that exists underlying the summarised information displayed in presentations (Ahmed et al., 2014). Organisations can frequently delve into to view information in progressively more detailed ways, allowing them to identify the specific causes of patterns or deviations. In HR analytics, the term "data drilling" denotes to the practise of thoroughly and methodically examining human resources information in order to gather knowledge and make informed choices. It entails studying staff information, employee metrics, and other pertinent data to find patterns, indications, and relationships that can guide strategic HR activities (Balali, 2020).
- *Data mining:* It is the process of finding patterns in data to aid in event prediction. Data mining in HR analytics is the practise of employing various data mining techniques to uncover useful trends and insights from HR-related data. In order to improve HR plans and practises, HR analytics entails analysing and evaluating HR data (Williams, 2011). Organisations can acquire significant understanding into their employees and use this information to inform their decisions by using data mining, which is essential in revealing inconsistencies, movements, and linkages within HR data.
- *Probability theory:* Calculating vague projections of unplanned occurrences using. Making decisions is an essential organisational task. Analysing issues or circumstances, gathering data, weighing potential remedies, and keeping an eye on the results are all part of the process (Tomar & Gaur, 2020). Probability facilitates decision-making in an organisational setting. There exists a significant relationship between probability and decision-making. To comprehend the relationship between probability and decision-making, it is crucial to define probability theory. This area of mathematics examines irrational events. According to probability theory, it is challenging to predict the result of random occurrences before they take place. Any event can have a number of possible outcomes, though. Only casual factors determine the final result (Balali, 2020).
- *Regression analysis:* (Daniel, 2020) Establishing the factors that influence a result. To comprehend the link between numerous factors and the effect they have on results associated with personnel, regression analysis is a potent statistical technique that is frequently employed in HR analytics. It enables analysts to investigate and quantify the connections between various HR elements and forecast future results. Regression analysis is frequently employed to investigate the link between employee attributes (such training, experience, and education) and performance evaluations. Organisations may choose wisely when it comes to recruitment, instruction, and performance management by recognising the elements that lead to good or bad performances. Through the use of regression analysis, it is possible to evaluate the success of training and development initiatives by looking at the correlations between factors like training duration, staff ability levels, and performance results. This analysis can help with decision-making on resource allocation and offer an understanding of the worth of training investments (Pandey, 2020).

- *Corelation analysis:* Analyses connections between factors through correlation. The statistical association among multiple factors is referred to as correlation in HR analytics. It aids analysts and HR experts in comprehending the degree to which alterations to a particular factor are connected with modifications in another one (Bob-Manuel, 2023). HR managers can learn more about many facets of their staff and arrive at informed choices by looking at correlation findings. The relationship between staff efficiency measurements (such output, revenue, or client endorsement rankings) and the quantity of instruction provided may be examined by HR experts. This kind of evaluation can show whether worker efficiency is improved by programmes of training.
- *Statistical analysis:* It is the process of gathering and analysing data to identify hidden trends. Statistical analysis is essential to HR analytics because it enables businesses to arrive at informed choices about their human resource needs. It entails using statistical methods to analyse HR data in order to get valuable insights, discover trends, and arrive at forecasts (Varma & Chavan, 2019). An overview of the HR indicators is provided by descriptive statistics, which summarise and describe data. Metrics like mean, median, mode, standard deviation, range, and percentiles are used extensively in comprehending the distribution, dispersion, and central tendency of HR data.

Predictive analytics

Predictive Analytics forecasts probable results and makes predictions of potential future occurrences. To forecast what will happen in the future, a framework is estimated after classifying previous and present data to find trends, associations, and abnormalities. The framework is then applied to fresh inputs to assess its precision (Williams, 2011).

Improved HR decision-making are supported by predictive HR analytics. Predictions regarding what to anticipate in the future are made using past data acquired from areas like job skills, staff engagement, efficiency, resumes, etc. These forecasts give the HR managers insights that will help them make better decisions on tasks like selecting qualified applicants, closing the skills disparity, and keeping top employees. It can decrease mistakes made by employees, aid in risk avoidance, enhance efficiency in operations, and improve predictions for the company.

Predictive analytics can examine data from the recruitment procedure to focus on the needed skill sets (Zeidan & Itani, 2020). The main characteristics that show that an applicant is a good fit for a long-term relationship with the company may additionally be revealed by certain components of social networking accounts and responses to computerised recruitment inquiries. After that, one can modify the hiring approach to draw in and motivate this kind of candidate. Additionally, predictive analytics can be used to predict the forthcoming requirement for particular jobs. This enables the organization to target qualified people and begin hiring at the right time.

Using predictive analytics the HR department can predict a number of talent management results, including which employees will leave the organization (Mishra & Silakari, 2013). The HR analytics can create a prediction algorithm that can determine which employees are at risk of quitting and what are the external elements responsible for such actions. Data collection and analysis for the expected chances of departure of employees can reveal which workers may quit and why. These indications highlight the areas that require evaluation. Analytics can make use of the data related to the career opportunities, compensation and rewards systems the company provides and use this insight to take decisions that will increase employee retention and decrease attrition (Shah et al., 2017).

Prescriptive analytics

(Dimitris & Nathan, 2019) The last and most difficult step in the analytics process, prescriptive analytics transforms predictive analytics into recommendations regarding what should be done subsequently. The focused advice for selecting and implementing alternatives derived from the results of predictive analytics would be a general definition of prescriptive analytics. It provides alternatives for where and how to operate in order to succeed. Big data is a key component of prescriptive analytics, which also employs a variety of technical methods, such as: Machine learning, Algorithms, Artificial intelligence, Pattern recognition (Frazzetto, 2019). Prescriptive analytics suggests actions based on regular events or an occurrence. With a more proactive outlook on the future, prescriptive analytics extends above predictive analytics. The most likely results of a decision or action are effectively predicted using predictive analytics. Prescriptive analytics allows to predict what is going to occur subsequent, why it will happen, and what can be done to prepare. It foresees the most probable results and identifies the measures with the best chance of success. It gives HR managers the tools they need to make wise decisions in the moment that will enhance performances, deal with challenging issues, and seize better prospects (Lepenioti, 2020). Prescriptive analytics is also referred to as the final threshold of analytic skills due to its complex nature. It calls for more sophisticated analytics abilities. Prescriptive analysis uses a variety of statistical tools to examine the outcomes and past information of the business. Such approaches are used to create formulas or algorithms that imitate results in order to forecast future organisational results. According to Prah (2020), prescriptive analysis in HR involves examining applications, ATS, job descriptions, and HRIS to forecast results based on talent acquisitions. A type of data analytics known as "prescriptive analytics" allows firms to integrate the strength of descriptive analytics with a forward-looking perspective.

HR ANALYTICS IN EMPLOYEE ENGAGEMENT AND TURNOVER

Analytics in HR aid in attracting, retaining, and developing employees inside the company. As a result, businesses have made significant investments in IT solutions that assist with a variety of HR tasks, including hiring, performance management, legal, engagement of staff, and talent acquisition. development. Analytics has been referred to as an essential skill for the HR occupation, a tool for unleashing the potential of employees, and a technique to increase the strategic impact of the HR department. The availability, acquisition, development, and retention of key talent was cited by almost three-quarters (72%) of CEOs in a PWC survey as the most significant business challenge their companies will face in 2016, irrespective of geography. This highlights how important it is of achieving profitable outcomes by way of skills globally and confirms the significance of HR in business operations (Varma & Chavan, 2019). In order to find the factors that influence engagement and contentment, employee engagement analytics combines employee engagement with additional HR and non-HR data sets. Employee engagement analytics is a subtype of Employee analytics, which is a widely used contemporary approach to enhanced staff administration and engagement (HCMI, 2022).

Tracking and benchmarking employee engagement score

A single data-point merely provides a momentary view of the involvement and performance of the employees. A historical pattern, on the other hand, can demonstrate how the company can be engaged and how the company can be improved across the years. Managers can assess how their organisations' performances in comparison with others using benchmarks. They provide leadership with an improved understanding of the level of employee engagement (HCMI, 2022).

Figure 1.
Source: (HCMI, 2022)

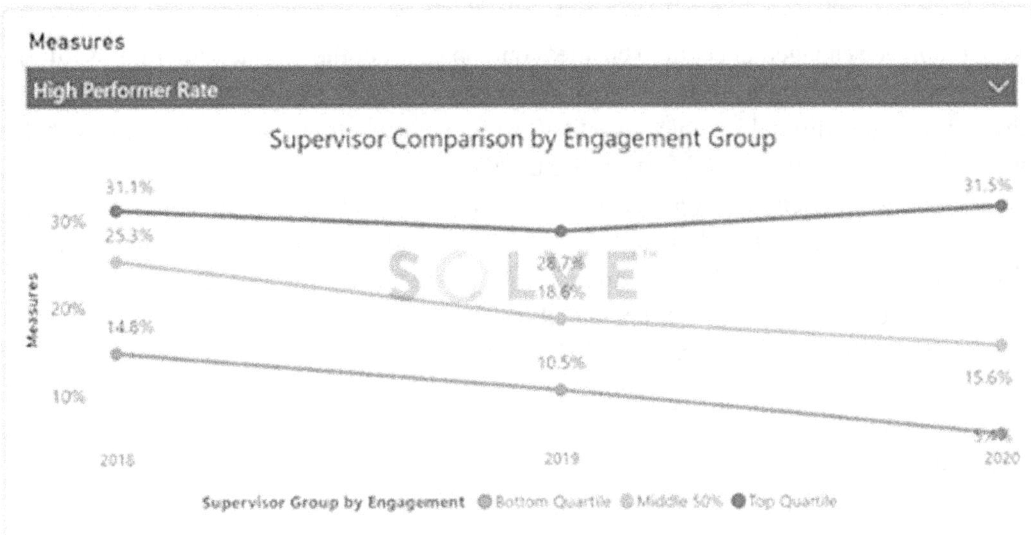

Figure 2.
Source: (HCMI, 2022)

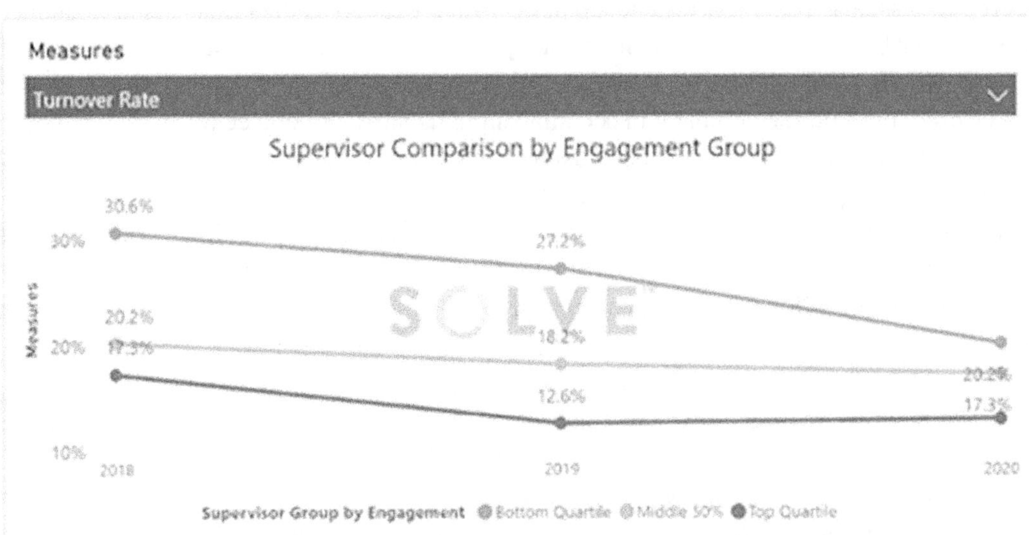

Analysing and analysing employee data to learn more about various HR-related measures including employee engagement and turnover is known as HR analytics. Turnover refers to the pace at which employees depart an organisation, whereas employee engagement measures a worker's emotional commitment to their work. Data on employee engagement and turnover can be analysed to reveal important information about how well an organisation is doing overall. HR professionals can take action to increase overall job satisfaction by monitoring employee engagement levels, identifying areas where employees may need more assistance or training, and identifying these areas. Similar to this, by monitoring turnover rates, HR experts can spot trends and patterns that might point to issues with management, pay, or other elements that might be motivating workers to quit the company (HCMI, 2022).

Measuring the impact of employee engagement on corporate outcomes

Linking employee engagement data to business outcomes is another application for this information. The majority of leaders are aware of the value of worker involvement, but they lack knowledge or data on how enhancements regarding this subject might affect monetary outcomes. Given this, it is challenging to catch the directors' and managers' focus (HCMI, 2022).

In order to draw a conclusion, satisfaction ratings are frequently given in a straightforward close comparison with other measures. Although such analysis might be adequate in certain instances, HR professionals must correctly implement employee engagement as only one aspect of the workforce strategy. HR will be able to make wiser personnel managerial choices if data on employee engagement can be examined more comprehensively (HCMI, 2022).

CONCLUSION

Effective HR planning and decision-making are driven by HR analytics. The data that analytics provide convey an increased understanding of what's actually happening in the business. This makes chances and possibilities available that the organization might not have otherwise known about. The more one comprehends the various HR metrics and analytics, the more useful details can be generated from data to support business objectives. HR leaders are in a position to support the organisation in an increased proactive manner by virtue of the skill and capacity to use analytics. or manufacturing companies to achieve a specific outcome, a variety of HR analytics parameters must be applied. When such factors are fully utilised, they aid the company in accomplishing its aims and objectives, which in turn boosts productivity and employee morale. The conclusion is that increasing employee job engagement will always result from management of manufacturing organisations paying attention to various HR analytics aspects and effectively connecting them to the business operations of the workforce. The manufacturing organisations' efficient operation may result from this. Since it is clear that there is a connection between job engagement and the HR analytics dimensions, it is advised that organisations make efficient use of the HR aspects.

The power of the huge quantity of data and the appropriate infrastructure to use that data leverages on the employee engagement analytics helping to generate reports and comprehensive analysis for all teams, geographical locations, or business lines. This enables HR functional leaders, line-managers, and heads of organizations to get discernibility and rationalized reports about the existing condition of their employees. Information like employee engagement score, engagement score of new recruits, and proportion of the employees who are engaged, etc. are like reassures in the hands of the HR. It has become the standard contemporary system in advanced employee administration and retention. Employee engagement analytics benefits all stakeholders within the organization. For executives, analytics provides them the capability and skill to quantify the impact of employee engagement on the organization and to have an improved incorporation of it into the inclusive corporate policy. These analytics offers the line-managers in-depth specifics about their team-members. Analytics also empowers the HR leaders to make use of the vast data available to them. This analytics gives a better understanding of the current trends of their personnel, identify the root cause of employee issues, and develop appropriate solutions that are more effective.

More and more organizations are employing HRIS (Human Resource Information System) and many more individuals-related instruments, making HR an incredible prospect to utilize the data sources to produce information in the form of reports, graphs, diagrams and actionable insights. This leads to making the process and end results more transparent especially with regard to the condition of the workforce. Employee engagement is one of several areas of HR management that can be analysed using data and statistical methods, which is referred to as HR analytics. HR Analytics may assist organisations in understanding and raising employee engagement levels, which is a key aspect that affects organisational success. The measurement and analysis of employee engagement can be done using a variety of HR Analytics tools and approaches. To gather information about employees' attitudes and views of their work environment, surveys and questionnaires are a typical method. To find patterns, trends, and correlations in the acquired data, statistical approaches can be used for analysis.

REFERENCES

Ahmed, A., Weifeng, L., Victor, B., Shiyu, H., & Hsinchun, C. (2014). Descriptive Analytics: Examining Expert Hackers in Web Forums. Institute of Electrical and Electronics Engineer, (pp. 56-63). The Hague, Netherlands

Angrave, D., Charlwood, A., Kirkpatrick, I., Lawrence, M., & Stuart, M. (2016). HR and analytics: why HR is set to fail the big data challenge. Human Resource Management Journal, 1-11

Ashish Malik, P. B. (2023). Employee experience–the missing link for engagingemployees: Insights from an MNE's AI-based HR ecosystem. *Human Resource Management*, 97–115. doi:10.1002/hrm.22133

Balali, F. N. (2020). Data Analytics. Data Intensive Industrial Asset Management.

Bassi, L. & McMurrer, D. (2016, October 26). Four Lessons Learned in How to Use Human Resource Analytics to Improve the Effectiveness of Leadership Development. *Journal of Leadership Studies*, *10*(2).

Bauer, V. (n.d.). *HR analytics and employee turnover*. Deloitte. https://www2.deloitte.com/cz/en/pages/deloitte-analytics/articles/hr-analytika-a-odchodovost-zamestnancu.html

Belyaeva, T., & Kozieva, I. (2020). Employee engagement in HR analytical systems. *Economic Annals-XXI*, 94-102.

Bennett, C. (2015, February 27). *HR and people analytics*. Deloitte.

Bersin. (2013). *High-impact talent analytics: Building a world-class HR*. Deloitte.

Boatman, A. (n.d.). *A Guide To The 4 Types of HR Analytics.* AIHR (Academy to Innovate HR). https://www.aihr.com/blog/types-of-hr-analytics/

Bob-Manuel, I. V. (2023). Human Resource Database Analytics and Employee Productivity in Telecommunication Companies in South Nigeria. *International Journal of Business & Entrepreneurship Research, 14.*

Bose, I. & Jose, D. (2018, February 2018). Evolution of Human Resource Analytics. *AIMA Journal of Management & Research, 12* (1/4). Retrieved from https://www.chrmp.com/the-evolution-of-hr-analytics/

Charles Cayrat, P. B. (2022). Exploring the phenomenon of HR analytics: a study of challenges, risks and impacts in 40 large companies. *Journal of Organizational Effectiveness: People and Performance*, 572-590.

Dan Avrahami, D. P.-G. (2022). A human resources analytics and machine-learning examination of turnover: Implications for theory and practice. *International Journal of Manpower*, *43*(6), 1405–1424. doi:10.1108/IJM-12-2020-0548

Daniel, D. (2020). *People Analytics (HR analytics).* Tech Target Network. https://www.techtarget.com/searchhrsoftware/definition/human-resources-analytics-talent-analytics

David, F. D. (1989). Perceived Usefulness, Perceived Ease of Use, and User Acceptance of Information Technology. MIS Quarterly, 13(3), 319-340. doi:https://doi.org/10.2307/249008

Dimitris, B., & Nathan, K. (2019). From Predictive to Prescriptive Analytics. Management Science, 1025-1044.

Fernandez, V., & Gallardo-Gallardo, E. (2021). Tackling the HR digitalization challenge: key factors and barriers to HR analytics adoption. *Competitiveness Review*, 162-187.

Frazzetto, D. N. (2019). Prescriptive analytics: a survey of emerging trends and technologies. The VLDB Journal, 575-595.

HCMI. (2022). *Employee Engagement Analytics: How to Engage and Retain Talent.* HCMI. https://www.hcmi.co/post/employee-engagement-analytics-how-to-engage-and-retain-talent

Heuvel, S. V., & Bondarouk, T. (2017). The rise (and fall?) of HR analytics: A study into the future application, value, structure, and system support. Journal of Organizational Effectiveness: People and Performance, 157-178.

Jawahar Supraveen, S. S. U. (2022). HR Analytics - The Measurement of HR Processes using a Methodical Approach. *International Conference on Computer Communication and Informatics (ICCCI)*, Coimbatore, India. 10.1109/ICCCI54379.2022.9740999

Kahn, A. (1990). Psychological conditions of personal engagement and disengagement at work. *Academy of Management Journal*, *33*(4), 692–724. doi:10.2307/256287

Kakulapati, S. S. V. (2023). Predictive Analytics of Employee Attrition using K-Fold Methodologies. *I. J. Mathematical Sciences and Computing*, 23-36.

Kale, N., & Anute, B. (2020). *HR Analytics and its Impact on Organizations Performance*. Research Gate.

Kalvakolanu, S., Madhavaiah, C., & Balaji, D. (2016, December). HR Analytics: The Emergence and Growth. *5th International Conference on Managing Human Resources at the WorkplaceAt: SDMIMD, Mysore*. IEEE. 10.6084/m9.figshare.13601357

Kamel Barbar, R. C. (2019). The Impact of HR Analytics on the Training and Development Strategy - Private Sector Case Study in Lebanon. *Journal of Management and Strategy*, 27-36.

Karmańska, A. (2020). The benefits of HR analytics. *Prace Naukowe Uniwersytetu Ekonomicznego we Wrocławiu,*, 30-39.

Kavyashree, S. K. (2022). Relationship between Human Resource Management Practices and Employee Engagement. *Brazilian Journal of Operations & Production Management*, 1331.

Lawler, E., & Levenson, A. (2004). HR Metrics and Analytics: Use and Iimpact. Human Resource Plan Journal , 27(4), 27–36. doi:https://doi.org/10.1016/j.jwb.2009.09.014

Lepenioti, K.,, Bousdekis, A., Apostolou, D., & Mentzas, G. (2020). Prescriptive analytics: Literature review and research challenges. International Journal of Information Management, 57-70.

Levenson, A. (2005, March). Harnessing the power of HR analytics. *Strategic HR Review*, 28-31.

Liu, Y., Mao, G., Leiva, V., Liu, S., & Tapia, A. (2020). Diagnostic Analytics for an Autoregressive Model under the Skew-Normal Distribution. *Mathematics 2020*, 693.

Lockwood, R. (2007). Leveraging employee engagement for competitive advantage: HR'sstrategic role. *HRMagazine*, *3*, 1–11.

Madhani, P. M. (2023). Human Resources Analytics: Leveraging Human Resources for Enhancing Business Performance. *Compensation and Benefit Review*, 31-45.

Maria, A. (2019). HR Analytics: Challenges and prospects of indian IT Sector. International Journal of Management, IT and Engineering, 404-415.

Meenal Arora, A. P. (2022). HR Analytics and Artificial Intelligence-Transforming Human Resource Management. *International Conference on Decision Aid Sciences and Application*, (pp. 288-293). ACM.

Mishra, N., & Silakari, S. (2013). Predictive Analytics: A Survey, Trends, Applications, Oppurtunities & Challenges. International Journal of Computer Science and Information Technologies, 4434-4438.

Mohammed, A. Q. (2019). HR Analytics: A Modern Tool in HR for Predictive Decision Making. *Journal of Management*, *10*(3), 51–63. doi:10.34218/JOM.6.3.2019.007

Nagpal, T., & Mishra, M. (2018, December). Decisions Making in HR: Application of HR Analytics. [IJRAR]. *International Journal of Research and Analytical Reviews*, *5*(4).

Navodya Gurusinghe, B. J. R. (2021). Predictive HR analytics and talent management: a conceptual framework. *Journal of Management Analytics*, 195.

Nishith Pawar, N. S. (January 2023). Role of analytics in HR-attrition for effective decision. *International Research Journal of Modernization in Engineering Technology and Science*, 185-188.

Nitya B, M. R. (2021). A Study On The Application Of Hr Analytics On Talent Acquisition, Compensation & Benefits And Employee Turnover In The Indian It Industry. *Sambodhi*, 66-76.

Oladipupo, O. & Olubusayo. F. H. (2020). Human Resource Analytics Dimensions and Employee Engagement in Manufacturing Industry in Nigeria a Conceptual Review. *Journal of Management Information and Decision Sciences, 23*(5), 629-637.

Opatha, H. (2020). HR Analytics: A Literature Review and New Conceptual Model. International Journal of Scientific and Research Publications, 130-141.

Pandey, S. (2020). Principles of correlation and regression analysis. Journal of the practice of cardiovascular sciences, 7.

Premlal Prejith, P. K. (2022). Influence Of HR Analytics On Training And Development Skills In IT Sector: A Case Study In Kerala. *Journal of Positive School Psychology*, 1449–1460.

Ridhya Goyal, G. K. (2023). Determining the Role of Employee Engagement in Nurse Retention along with the Mediation of Organizational Culture. *Health Care*, *2023*, 760. PMID:36900765

S.Sai Abhinav Chandra, P. M. (2023). HR Metrics and Decision Making using Tableau. *International Journal of Advances in Engineering and Management*, 1203.

Seijts, G., & Crim, D. (2006). What engages employees the most, or the ten Cs of employeeengagement. *Ivey Business Journal*, *70*(4), 1–5.

Setiawan, S. S. I. (2020). HR analytics: Employee attrition analysis using logistic regression. *IOP Conf. Series: Materials Science and Engineering.* IOP Publishing Ltd. 10.1088/1757-899X/830/3/032001

Shah, N. D., Steyerberg, E. W., & Kent, M., D. (2017). Big data and predictive analytics: recalibrating expectations. Jama 320, 27-28.

Sonal Gupta, R. S. (2022). Types of HR Analytics Used for the Prediction of Employee Turnover in Different Strategic Firms with the use of Enterprise Social Media. *5th European International Conference on Industrial Engineering and Operations Management* (pp. 1977-1994). Italy: IEOM Society International. 10.46254/EU05.20220389

Soumyadeb Chowdhury, S. J.-E. (2022). Embedding transparency in artificial intelligence machine learning models: Managerial implications on predicting and explaining employee turnover. *International Journal of Human Resource Management.*

Tomar, S. & Gaur, M. (2020). HR analytics in Business: Role, Opportunities, and Challenges of Using It. *Journal of Xi'an University of Architecture & Technology*, 1299-1306. doi:10.37896/JXAT12.07/2441

Varma, C., & Chavan, R. (2019). A Case of HR Ananlytics - To Understand Effect On EmSE of hr analytics – to understand effect on employee. *Journal of Emerging Technologies and Innovative Research*, *6*(6).

Weena Yancey, M., & Momin, K. M. (2015). HR Analytics as a Strategic Workforce Planning. *International Journal of Applied Research*, 258.

Wellins, R., & Concelman, J. (2005). Creating a culture for engagement. *WorkforcePerformance Solutions*, *4*, 1–4.

Williams, G. (2011). Descriptive and Predictive Analytics. Data Mining with Rattle and R, 171-177.

Zeidan, S., & Itani, N. (2020). HR Analytics and Organizational Effectiveness. International Journal on Emerging Technologies , 683-688.

Chapter 8
HR Analytics:
An Effective Tool for Performance Management and Business Development

Palak Gupta
https://orcid.org/0000-0001-6583-7803
Jagannath International Management School, India

ABSTRACT

HR analytics is widely recognized in organizations for measuring performance metrics, workplace and recruitment analytics, and talent retention practices. It is the collection and implementation of talent data for enhancing critical talent and business outcomes that develops HR managers for data-driven insights, talent decisions, workforce processes, and thereby promote positive employee experience. This chapter focusses on how the four types of HR analytics methods aid in effective decision making by HR Managers and boost performance of employees. An attempt is made to measure the impact of HR metrics on overall business performance and revenue model by mitigating risks and minimizing expenses. Moreover, research on the implementation and application of HR analytics is still in process. Based on a qualitative study with HR analytics experts, it is found that a shift to a more rigorous and process-oriented perspective on HR analytics is needed. A model is thus proposed for effective implementation and application of HR analytics.

1. INTRODUCTION

The field of Human Resource Management (HRM) has evolved significantly in the past few decades, and one of the most notable advancements in this area is the use of HR analytics. Organizations have shifted from focusing solely on increasing their productivity and differentiating their products and services to focusing on their human capital, considering their employees the most important asset of the organization (Elsharnouby and Elbanna, 2021, Kehinde, 2012). HR analytics refers to the application of data analysis techniques to human resource management in order to improve decision-making and overall organizational performance. HR Analytics also called as People Analytics, Talent Analytics or

DOI: 10.4018/978-1-6684-8942-0.ch008

Workforce Analytics is the collection of talent data and its application for improving organizational talent and business outcomes. HR analytics is a data-driven approach toward Human Resources Management. Managers and leaders using HR Analytics have better data-driven insights to improve workforce processes, issues, inform talent decisions and thereby promote positive business outcomes. Digitalization and technology enhancement have enabled surplus data inflow in organizations but just input and collected data is not sufficient for actionable insights. So, HR leadership is required to identify key HR metrics and drive strategic HR operations as these metrics influence budgets, hiring decisions, skill needs and shape organization-wide strategy. HR has always played a vital role in strategic business function that quantifies employee performance. "HR leaders can demonstrate their team's impact by tracking HR metrics that align with corporate strategy and inform business decisions. Using the correct metrics, HR can identify opportunities to improve workforce performance and productivity, and identify cost reduction opportunities" (Gartner, 2019).

With the advent of new technologies and Artificial Intelligence, the work pressure on HR leaders and managers has reduced as the tasks of attracting suited talent, reskilling the workforce and preparing managers to take decisions in real time has been enabled through automated HR analytic tools. These tools help in effective address of algorithmic bias, misuse of employee's personal data, changes in HR rules and regulations etc. (Gartner, 2020). Despite the growth and adoption of human resource (HR) analytics, it remains unknown whether HR analytics can impact organizational performance (McCartney, 2022). Three related, non-linear sub-processes of HR Analytics legitimation have been identified, namely, the HR data infrastructure decision, HR Analytics as a strategic commitment, and the focus of HR Analytics projects in addition to a number of delaying, enabling, and accelerating elements that influence this process (Belizón et al., 2022). Managerial decision-making determines the extent to which strategic human capital analytics, as part of a strategic performance measurement and management system, improve organisation and market performance (Samson et al., 2022).

Human Resource Analytics is the application of statistical and analytical techniques to human resource data. It enables companies to measure and analyze employee data and make informed decisions based on the insights gained from this data. HR analytics has become a vital tool for performance management and business development in organizations worldwide. Companies with higher digital maturity improve their talent management processes as Talent management benefits from Big Data, People analytics or HR Analytic systems. The organizational changes brought about by digital transformation are thus seen to influence talent management and to attract and retain talent (Guerra et al., 2023). Without the transformation of existing companies, the economic and environmental challenges that the future holds cannot be addressed in a sustainable manner (Bican and Brem, 2020). This paper will explore the use of HR analytics as an effective tool for performance management and business development.

1.1. HR Analytics as a Booster in Performance Management

Performance management is a critical component of HRM, as it involves the systematic process of identifying, evaluating, and developing employee performance to meet organizational goals (Jia et al., 2023). HR analytics can play a significant role in this process by providing valuable insights into employee performance, identifying areas for improvement, and measuring the effectiveness of performance management strategies (Hamid & Shah 2023).

One of the key benefits of HR analytics in performance management is its ability to identify high-performing employees. By analyzing data on employee performance metrics such as productivity, quality, and customer satisfaction, HR analytics can help managers identify top-performing employees and reward them accordingly. Additionally, HR analytics can also help identify areas where employees may need additional training or support, allowing managers to develop targeted performance improvement plans. Digital training effects both employee motivation and job performance, digital performance appraisal effects employee motivation and performance appraisal, and employee motivation has significant effect on job performance. Consequently, it was approved by study of Al-kharabsheh, 2023 that employee motivation partially mediated the effect of digital HRM practices on job performance. It was concluded that skilled employees who are aware of their performance level are motivated to show higher levels of job performance.

HR analytics plays a critical role in performance management by providing data-driven insights into employee performance. It enables organizations to measure employee performance against key performance indicators (KPIs) and identify areas of improvement. HR analytics can help companies create personalized development plans for employees, identify top-performing employees, and provide coaching to those who need it.

HR analytics can also be used to measure the effectiveness of performance management strategies as it can help managers identify which strategies are most effective for making data-driven decisions and thereby how to improve performance management processes. It enables suitable tracking of employee performance over time and analyzing the impact of various performance management interventions

HR analytics can also help organizations identify potential performance issues before they become problems. By analyzing employee data, organizations can identify patterns and trends that may be indicative of performance issues which can help organizations take proactive measures to address these issues and prevent them from becoming larger problems (Pichault et al., 2023). Thus, HR analytics serves as precautionary tool and measure to prevent many personnel related issues.

1.2. The Role of HR Analytics in Talent Development for Business and Overall Business Development

In addition to its role in performance management, HR analytics can also be a powerful tool for talent development for business and thereby overall business development (Kaliannan et al., 2022). By analyzing data on employee demographics, skills, and performance, HR analytics can help organizations make informed decisions about hiring, talent development, and succession planning which ultimately boosts business performance, revenue and growth.

For example, HR analytics can help organizations identify which skills are most critical to their business success and develop targeted recruitment strategies to attract candidates with those skills. HR analytics can also help identify high-potential employees and develop talent development plans to nurture their skills and prepare them for future leadership roles.

HR analytics can also be used to drive business development. By analyzing employee data, organizations can identify skills gaps and areas where additional training may be required. This can help organizations develop more effective training programs and ensure that employees have the skills they need to contribute to the company's growth. HR analytics can also help organizations identify high-potential employees and develop succession plans. By identifying employees with the potential to take on leadership roles in the future, organizations can ensure that they have a pipeline of talent to drive future growth.

Finally, HR analytics can also play a critical role in succession planning. By analyzing employee performance and potential, HR analytics can help organizations identify potential successors for key leadership roles and develop targeted development plans to prepare them for those roles.

2. LITERATURE REVIEW

Human Resource Management is to be centred around organisation as a whole; it can be understood as a domain of study that is oriented towards exploring those practices and approaches, which can be implemented in the context of employees to achieve organisational goals (Armstrong and Taylor, 2014). Human resources remain one of the primary distinguishing factors for an organisation that can be used for competitive growth in order to create necessary organisational value (Bharti, 2017). Decision-making is always one of the most critical organisational processes along with analysing and forecasting employee behaviour, levels of motivation work performance, and the amount of workplace stress (Griffin and Moorland, 2011). Human resource analytics is a relatively novel intervention in the larger domain of HRM, and it refers to the use of statistical tools, measures and procedures, which can be used in employing and masking the most effectual decisions such as HRM strategies and practices. It is often referred as people analytics or talent analytics or workforce analytics ("People Analytics", n.d.).

As per the requisite skills, knowledge dimensions and abilities, various competitive business strategies can be closely matched with organisational conditions in order to see development in critical areas, such as decision-making (Pereira, 2013). "HR Analytics" includes the use of statistical techniques, research design, and algorithms to evaluate employee data and translating results into evocative reports (Levenson, 2005). Levenson, 2011 further postulated that the use of analytics and metrics provide improvement of the decision making quality in HR issues in the firms and the metrics are important in the increasing the levels of insightful, analytically-based decision making in HR. HR Analytics act as a tool which is a combination of statistical techniques that enable collection, interpretation, measurement, and forecasting of data (Tomar, S. et al., 2020). Global HR analytics market to grow by 12% by Anushree Sharma on People Matters states the report Outlook on the World HR Analytics Market, 2019-2025 estimates around 12 percent growth at CAGR in the global HR analytics market by 2019-2025. Markets and Markets estimates growth from USD 1.9 billion in 2019 to USD 3.6 billion by 2024 at CAGR of 13.7% in the global HR analytics market size as stated in Human Resource Analytics Market Component, Application Area in Workforce Management, Recruitment, and Employee Development, Organization Size, Deployment Type, Vertical (Industry like Banking, Financial Services and Insurance, Manufacturing, and IT and Telecom), showing Region to Global Forecast from 2019-2024. Chalutz Ben-Gal, H. (2019) in his paper provided practical implementation tools for assisting decision makers concerning questions of whether and in which format to implement HR analytics by highlighting specific directions as to where the expected ROI may be found.

As per Sharma, A., 2017, the use of HR analytics will be negatively related to subjectivity bias in the Performance Appraisal system, thereby positively affecting employees' perceived accuracy and fairness. This further positively affects employees' satisfaction with the Performance Appraisal system, which subsequently increases employees' willingness to improve performance. HR Analytical practices are contributing to build a sustainable organization as these practices are balancing social, environmental and economic factors for short and long term perspectives (Kirtane, 2015). HR analytics provides a data-driven framework for solving workforce problems through analyzing data with a combination of software and methodologies that applies statistical models and derives new insights for smarter decision making that allow enterprise leaders to optimize human resource management while enhancing the strategic value of HRM (Opatha, 2020). HR analytics supports managers in making key decisions, increases the efficiency of business through better workforce planning, and budgeting. HR analytics affects efficiency through the better planning and utilizing of the workforce, and also positively impacts the company's organizational culture. Employees from large companies demonstrate knowledge of HR analytics to a greater extent than those employed in the SME sector (Karmańska, A., 2020). As per Deloitte *Global Human Capital Trends* report, 2018, "Most organizations now recognize the need to reshape rewards with a more personalized, agile, and holistic approach, matching other talent management strategies". HR analytics can help organizations and their human resources (HR) managers to predict reason behind the employee exits and reduce attrition rate and employee turnover at an early stage in the era of data science and big data analytics (Gupta, S., 2022). Now talent management strategies and personalized incentives have gained a lot popularity among HR managers and executives. (Huang, X. et al., 2023).

3. THEORETICAL BACKGROUND

Impact of HR Analytics Methods on Effective Decision Making by HR Managers and Performance Improvement of Employees

Human resource analytics (HR analytics) is the process of analyzing HR data to gain insights that can help HR managers make informed decisions. Qamar, Y. et al., 2022 in their paper did extensive study on theoretical backgrounds of HR Analytics, its concepts and recent developments in the area. They did a bibliometric analysis to identify the research trends in area. The four types of HR analytics viz. descriptive analytics, diagnostic analytics, prescriptive analytics, and predictive analytics have become increasingly popular among HR managers (Reddy, 2017) . HR analytics started as a small administrative endeavour and it has gradually evolved to provide advanced diagnostic and predictive capabilities (Edwards & Edwards, 2016). It is able to enhance employee engagement and retention, and generate benefits for whole organizations through digitally powered analytics solutions (Margherita, A., 2022). The Human Resource Information Systems (HRIS) have immensely helped decision makers in making better decisions by utilizing Human in organizations. The HRIS data has primarily been used to report simple descriptive statistics and correlations along with the use of advanced data analytics, i.e., predictive and prescriptive, has been proven in other areas such as sales, marketing and finance for better results, However, advanced data analytics are largely underutilized in Human Resources (Gupta, S., 2022). This research paper aims to study how each of these analytics methods can aid in effective decision making by HR managers and performance improvement of employees. HR Analytics has gained significant attention in recent years due to its potential to transform HR decision-making. These methods allow HR managers to make data-driven decisions, identify patterns and trends, and improve employee performance.

Descriptive Analytics

Descriptive analytics involves analyzing historical data to understand past events and identify patterns and trends. HR managers can use descriptive analytics to gain insights into the current state of their workforce. For example, they can analyze data on employee turnover rates, absenteeism, and performance to identify patterns and trends that can help them make decisions related to employee engagement and retention. It helps HR managers identify patterns in employee data and understand the current state of HR processes.

Diagnostic Analytics

Diagnostic analytics involves analyzing data to identify the cause of a problem or issue. HR managers can use diagnostic analytics to identify the root causes of employee performance issues or high turnover rates. For example, they can analyze data on employee engagement surveys to identify areas where employees are dissatisfied, and then take steps to address those issues.

Prescriptive Analytics

Prescriptive analytics involves analyzing data to determine the best course of action to take. HR managers can use prescriptive analytics to make decisions related to employee development and training. For example, they can analyze data on employee performance to identify skill gaps and then develop personalized training programs to address those gaps.

Predictive Analytics

Predictive analytics involves predictions about future activities and events. HR managers can use predictive analytics to make decisions related to workforce planning and talent management. For example, they can analyze data on employee turnover rates and use predictive modeling to identify employees who are at risk of leaving the company, and then take steps to retain them.

Figure 1. Types of HR analytics

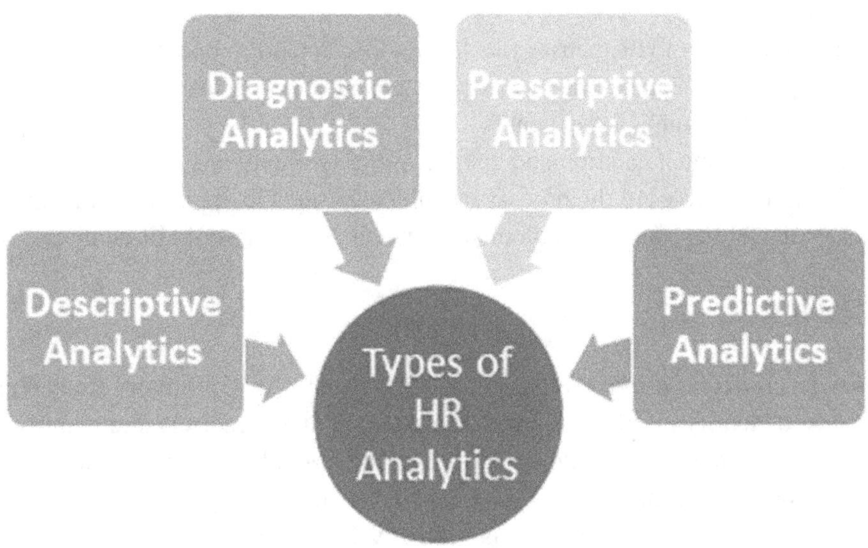

HR analytics can aid in effective decision making by HR managers and performance improvement of employees. The four types of HR analytics methods - descriptive, diagnostic, prescriptive, and predictive analytics - each have their unique benefits and can be used to address different HR challenges. By leveraging these analytics methods, HR managers can gain insights into their workforce, identify areas for improvement, and make informed decisions that can help improve employee engagement and retention, increase productivity, and drive business growth. HR Analytics is a powerful tool for HR managers looking to improve processes in HR department and entire organizational employee performance.

4. RESEARCH METHODOLOGY

Scope of the Study

In this paper a study has been done on how the four types of HR Analytics methods viz. descriptive, diagnostic, prescriptive and predictive analytics aid in effective decision making by HR Managers and performance improvement of employees. An attempt has been done to measure the impact of HR metrics like hiring time, retention rate, training efficiency, revenue per employee, offer acceptance rate etc. on overall business performance and revenue model by mitigating risks and minimizing expenses. Both internal and external data has been used for the study for proposing HR Analytics solution. A model is proposed for effective implementation and application of HR analytics.

Research Objectives

The present study has following research objectives-

1. To study how the four types of HR Analytics methods viz. descriptive, diagnostic, prescriptive and predictive analytics aid in effective decision making by HR Managers and performance improvement of employees.
2. To measure the impact of HR metrics like hiring time, retention rate, training efficiency, revenue per employee, offer acceptance rate etc. on overall business performance and revenue model by mitigating risks and minimizing expenses.
3. To research on the implementation and application of HR analytics
4. To identify the actual roles in the process of implementing and applying HR analytics
5. To propose a model for effective implementation and application of HR analytics.

Research Design

The research design used is descriptive and exploratory in nature. An exploratory study is essential when a researcher needs to identify problems, defines the problem more precisely and identifies any specific objectives or data requirements to be addressed through additional research (Kinnear & Taylor, 1996). An exploratory design is used for the purpose of research as there are hardly much literature to refer to or rely upon to predict an outcome. The aim is to finally develop a predictive model for evaluation of HR Analytics effect on performance management and business development. In a descriptive research design, the observational method is deployed. In this, the researcher can choose to be either a complete observer, an observer as a participant, a participant as an observer, or a full participant (Bhat, 2018).

Data Collection Methods

Interview and observation methods are deployed for data collection and analysis. Secondary data through journals, magazines, periodicals, books, websites, and organization records are also studied to identify research gap. Secondary data belongs to the year 2016-2023 of both national and global levels.

Sampling Design

Purposive Sampling which is a non-probability sample is selected based on characteristics of a population and the objective of the study. Since in this study only respondents using HR Analytics tools were to be administered as per the study, hence this technique was employed.

Sampling Universe-Delhi NCR

Sampling Unit-Executives & Managers working in HR domain using tools of HR Analytics and evaluating performance and business development metrics.

Sample size-65 HR Managers were interviewed and their answers were compiled and analysed further.

5. ANALYSIS AND PROPOSED MODEL FRAMEWORK

Proposed Model: The proposed model includes a framework for measuring the impact of HR metrics on mitigating risks and minimizing expenses thereby organizations can optimize HR processes and improve overall business performance. The proposed model can help organizations to develop effective strategies and make data-driven decisions for resolving HR problems, mitigating risks, and optimizing business performance. The HR Analytics involves usage of statistical models to get insights into employee data, patterns to predict employee behavioural patterns like training costs, retention, attrition rates, and employee contribution which leads to predictive analysis.

5.1 The Framework Includes the Following Steps

Step 1: Identification of possible HR Metrics such as hiring time, retention rate, training efficiency, revenue per employee, offer acceptance rate, etc. that can impact business performance and revenue model.

Step 2: Measuring the identified HR metrics using data collection and analysis tools such as surveys, performance evaluations, etc.

Step 3: Analyzing the HR metrics to identify patterns and trends and assess their impact on business performance and revenue model.

Step 4: Develop strategies to mitigate risks identified through the analysis of HR metrics. For example, if the analysis shows a high turnover rate, strategies can be developed to improve retention rates.

Step 5: Develop strategies to minimize expenses identified through the analysis of HR metrics. For example, if the analysis shows high hiring costs, develop strategies to reduce hiring costs.

Step 6: Evaluate the impact of the strategies implemented to mitigate risks and minimize expenses on overall business performance and revenue model.

Figure 2. Proposed Model for Analytics on HR Metrics

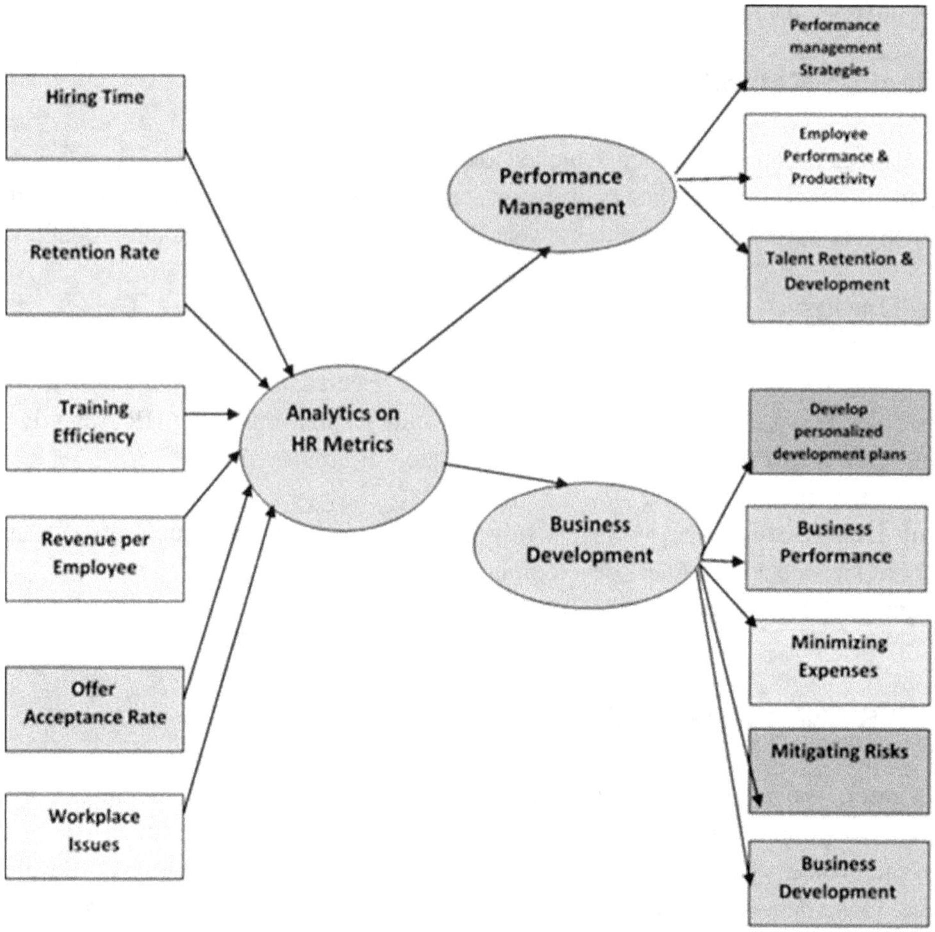

HR metrics play a critical role in optimizing business performance and revenue model by reducing expenses, increasing revenue per employee, and mitigating risks. HR metrics such as hiring time, retention rate, training efficiency, revenue per employee, offer acceptance rate, etc., provide insights into HR processes and their impact on business performance. By measuring and analyzing these metrics, organizations can make data-driven decisions and develop strategies to improve HR processes and business performance.

Based on a qualitative study with HR analytics experts, it is found that a shift to a more rigorous and process-oriented perspective on HR analytics is needed. More precisely, besides the requirements for the analysis of data, the actual roles in the process of implementing and applying HR analytics need to be defined.

5.2 Challenges for HR to Convert Their Available Data Sources Into Meaningful Strategical Value With Proposed Solutions

Human resources were undoubtedly neglected in the past as organisations focused more on solving larger issues like revenue, competitiveness, and economic instability. However, as business models and industries have evolved, HR has come to the fore as organisations now recognise how vital workforce management is to having an impact on success and growth. This has resulted in a significant increase in the duties of human resources teams, including luring top talent, creating a positive workplace culture, creating the ideal job roles and opportunities, ensuring continuous training and development, encouraging strong performance management, and providing competitive compensation. Large responsibilities come with equally large obstacles, which might hinder efficient human resource management. Digital upheavals, workplace cultural transformations, economic changes, political climate changes, etc. can all lead to several HR challenges. As an illustration, the year 2020 presented a significant challenge for HR departments to develop, manage, and lead effective remote workforces for businesses to continue operating successfully despite the epidemic.

As per discussions with HR Managers in Delhi NCR corporates, the major HR issues that organisations most frequently encounter are listed below with potential remedies:

Table 1. Challenges and issues identified in HR analytics and solutions proposed

S. No.	Challenges identified	Issues Faced	Proposed Solutions to HR Managers & Executives
1	**Talent Acquisition**	• Huge skill gap • Talent retention in the corporates • Ever increasing demand of talented workforce.	• For a company to recruit employees, having competitive pay and benefits packages is crucial. You must work more and give your people more fulfilling experiences if you want to compete. • Your employer brand, built around your most cherished and distinctive qualities, can help communicate this mission and draw in people who are driven by it. • Determine the goal, vision, and values that will serve as the cornerstones of your corporate culture in order to define your employer brand. • Increase your efforts in diversity, equity, and inclusion to provide all of your employees a stronger sense of belonging.
2	**Employee engagement**	• Since retaining employees is essential to a company's success, employee engagement is a constant worry for HR professionals. • On the other side, disengaged workers who are unhappy in their positions and feel cut off from their work can lead to serious issues at work. • They not only perform poorly, but they also cause conflict among high performers.	• Two-way dedication and communication are the foundations of employee engagement. • Employee engagement is higher when employees believe their thoughts are respected, their voices are heard, and they are an integral part of the company's expansion.
3	**Change Management**	• Organisational change might be technological, procedural, managerial, financial, geographic, or structural. • No matter the sort of change, HR teams confront significant difficulties in managing it due to low employee morale and satisfaction, self-doubt, and fatigue. • Employee resistance to change, a lack of the requisite skills and training, unexpected but draconian demands for change, etc. may all contribute to an inability to adapt to change.	• Regular and open communication before, during, and after change is an excellent place to start when trying to manage change effectively. • Provide employees ample notice and warning of impending changes • Provide them the knowledge and tools they need to adapt to and overcome their issues. • Participate with employees in decision-making and explain changes' justifications.

continues on following page

Table 1. Continued

S. No.	Challenges identified	Issues Faced	Proposed Solutions to HR Managers & Executives
4	**Managing diversity and Globalization**	• Managing varied cultures in a local team • Taking into account the needs and experience of employees of various ages, genders, nations, or ethnicities are just a few of the HR problems that come with diversity.	• To begin, assess the level of DEI (diversity, equity, and inclusion) in your workplace and establish specific objectives for diversity growth. • Assign essential outcomes, establish clear ownership, and allocate resources to each target so that their owners can provide the outcomes you require. • To promote diversity and inclusion, HR personnel should also explain to employees the significance and advantages of diversity efforts. • Activities that foster teamwork are also useful for bringing together employees from various cultural backgrounds and bringing them together to work towards shared goals.
5	**Upskilling and retraining**	• A major problem for HR is keeping up with the speed of digital change • Incorporating the newest technologies not only opens up exciting new business prospects but also puts the current workforce at a disadvantage and creates skill gaps.	• An organisation needs a workforce with the proper skills to be productive, inventive, and ultimately create more income if it wants to remain competitive. • An approach to make sure your workforce has the skills necessary to thrive and support your organization's growth is to build a learning and development plan around employee upskilling and reskilling. • Promote flexibility and provide choices that are optimal for the various learning styles and skill gaps you're seeking to fill, • Think about having a variety of staff training techniques available. • Compile a list of the talents that employees currently possess, need to develop, and need to improve upon, perform a skill gap analysis. • Delivering efficient reskilling programmes requires the use of staff training tools, such as a knowledge management system, corporate LMS, or a digital adoption platform.
6	**HR digital transformation**	• The task of developing applications on boarding, reskilling, and upskilling training content and courses for developing digital dexterity abilities rests on the HR and L&D departments • Neither digital transformation nor digital dexterity are the sole purview of a certain department.	• The organization's insurance policy for attaining ROI with digital technology is to build digital dexterity. • Investments in technology will not only fail to yield a return on investment (ROI), but will also suffer additional serious consequences like erroneous or unclean data, failure to comply with regulations, failure to accomplish objectives, etc.
7	**Employee Orientation & On boarding**	• It can take time and effort to find the perfect person to fill a vacancy in an organisation. • After spending numerous hours finding the perfect candidates, all of that effort is wasted if a new worker leaves within a few months, forcing HR to start over.	• Building an engaged staff that is committed to sticking with the company for the long term is what HR professionals must do to combat this. • Motivate and satisfy the employees so that they eventually develop the feeling of being a part of the organization and not just an employee.

6. FINDINGS

HR metrics such as hiring time, retention rate, training efficiency, revenue per employee, offer acceptance rate, etc. have a strong impact on overall business performance and revenue model by mitigating risks, increasing revenue per employee, and minimizing expenses.

The following Findings were identified from the model-

Hiring Time: Reducing hiring time can have a positive impact on overall business performance and revenue model. A shorter hiring time can help organizations fill vacant positions faster, resulting in increased productivity and revenue.

Retention Rate: Improving retention rate can have a positive impact on overall business performance and revenue model. A higher retention rate can help organizations retain valuable employees, resulting in reduced hiring and training costs, increased productivity, and revenue.

Training Efficiency: Improving training efficiency can have a positive impact on overall business performance and revenue model. Effective training programs can help employees acquire new skills, resulting in increased productivity, revenue per employee, and reduced expenses.

Revenue per Employee: Increasing revenue per employee can have a positive impact on overall business performance and revenue model. Higher revenue per employee can indicate increased productivity, which can result in increased revenue and profitability.

Offer Acceptance Rate: Improving offer acceptance rate can have a positive impact on overall business performance and revenue model. A higher offer acceptance rate can help organizations fill vacant positions faster, resulting in increased productivity and revenue.

7. CONCLUSION

HR analytics is a powerful tool for performance management and business development. By providing valuable insights into employee performance, HR analytics can help organizations identify high-performing employees, measure the effectiveness of performance management strategies, and make informed decisions about talent development and succession planning. As HR analytics continues to evolve, it is likely to become an even more important tool for HRM, helping organizations improve their overall performance and achieve their strategic goals. In conclusion, HR analytics is an effective tool for performance management and business development. It enables organizations to make data-driven decisions and gain insights into employee performance. By using HR analytics, organizations can identify areas of improvement, develop personalized development plans, and create more effective training programs. HR analytics can also help organizations identify high-potential employees and develop succession plans, ensuring that they have a pipeline of talent to drive future growth. As such, HR analytics is a critical tool for organizations looking to improve their performance and drive business development. The study concludes that HR Analytics can help HR managers make informed decisions and improve employee performance by identifying patterns and trends in employee data.

HR analytics provides ample benefits to employees and organizations but its success depends on the fairness and good intentions of HR managers. Employee privacy may be compromised due to unauthorized access to employee data. There are also security concerns about the uncontrolled use of these applications. Tracking employees without their consent increases the risk. Appropriate regulations are important for HR analytics applications along with the leadership support for the appropriate usage of HR analytics (Chatterjee, S. et al., 2022). So, the HR managers need to be loyal to the organization and never misuse the data available to them. It should be used only for the purpose of enhancing employee's performance, satisfaction, skillsets enhancement and thereby organizational objectives, mission and vision.

REFERENCES

Al-kharabsheh, S., Attiany, M., Alshawabkeh, R., Hamadneh, S., & Alshurideh, M. (2023). The impact of digital HRM on employee performance through employee motivation. *International Journal of Data and Network Science*, *7*(1), 275–282. doi:10.5267/j.ijdns.2022.10.006

Armstrong, M., & Taylor, S. (2014). *Armstrong's handbook of human resource management practice*. Kogan Page Publishers.

Belizón, M. J., & Kieran, S. (2022). Human resources analytics: A legitimacy process. *Human Resource Management Journal*, *32*(3), 603–630. doi:10.1111/1748-8583.12417

Bharti, A. (2017). Human resource analytics. *South Asian Journal of Marketing & Management Research*, *7*(5), 68–77.

Bhat, A. (2018, August 23). *Descriptive Research: Characteristics, Methods + Examples*. QuestionPro. https://www.questionpro.com/blog/descriptive- research/#:~:text=In%20a%20descriptive%20 research%20design

Bican, P., & Brem, A. (2020). Digital business model, digital transformation, digital entrepreneurship: Is there a sustainable. *Digital*, *12*, 5239–5254.

Chalutz Ben-Gal, H. (2019). An ROI-based review of HR analytics: Practical implementation tools. *Personnel Review*, *48*(6), 1429–1448. doi:10.1108/PR-11-2017-0362

Chatterjee, S., Chaudhuri, R., Vrontis, D., & Siachou, E. (2022). Examining the dark side of human resource analytics: An empirical investigation using the privacy calculus approach. *International Journal of Manpower*, *43*(1), 52–74. doi:10.1108/IJM-02-2021-0087

Deloitte. (2018). *Global Human Capital Trends report*. Deloitte. https://www2.deloitte.com/us/en/insights/focus/human-capital-trends/2018.html

Mohammed, A. (2019). HR Analytics: A Modern Tool in HR for Predictive Decision Making. *Journal ofManagement*, *6*(3), 51–63. http://www.iaeme.com/jom/issues.asp?JType=JOM&VType=6&IType=3

Edwards, M. R., & Edwards, K. (2016). *Predictive HR analytics: Mastering the HR metric*. Kogan Page.

Gartner for HR. (2020). *HR Data and AI Ethics*. Gartner. https://www.gartner.com/en/human-resources/trends/data-ai-ethics-hr

Griffin, R. W., & Moorhead, G. (2011). *Organizational behavior*. Cengage Learning.

Guerra, J. M. M., Danvila-del-Valle, I., & Méndez-Suárez, M. (2023). The impact of digital transformation on talent management. *Technological Forecasting and Social Change*, *188*, 122291. doi:10.1016/j.techfore.2022.122291

Gupta, S., & Sharma, R. R. K. (2022). *Types of HR Analytics Used for the Prediction of Employee Turnover in Different Strategic Firms with the use of Enterprise Social Media. Proceedings of the 5th European International Conference on Industrial Engineering and Operations Management Rome*, Italy. 10.46254/EU05.20220389

Hamid, Z., & Shah, S. A. (2023). Juxtaposition of Traditional and Modern Methods of Performance Appraisal in Organizations. In *Promoting Organizational Performance Through 5G and Agile Marketing* (pp. 245–266). IGI Global.

Huang, X., Yang, F., Zheng, J., Feng, C., & Zhang, L. (2023). *Personalized human resource management via HR analytics and artificial intelligence: Theory and implications*. Asia Pacific Management Review.

Jia, J., Jiao, Y., Yan, J., Wang, J., & Jia, H. (2023). Evolution path and critical influencing factors of performance management system: A longitudinal case study in China. *Asia Pacific Business Review*, *29*(1), 50–69. doi:10.1080/13602381.2022.2076449

Kaliannan, M., Darmalinggam, D., Dorasamy, M., & Abraham, M. (2022). Inclusive talent development as a key talent management approach: A systematic literature review. *Human Resource Management Review*, 100926.

Karmańska, A. (2020). The benefits of HR analytics. *Prace Naukowe Uniwersytetu Ekonomicznego we Wrocławiu, 64*(8), 30-39.

Kirtane, A. (2015). corporate sustainable HR Analytical practices. *Journal of Management & Administration Tomorrow*, *4*(1), 33–40.

Levenson, A. (2011). Using targeted analytics to improve talent decisions. *People and Strategy*, *34*(2), 34.

Margherita, A. (2022). Human resources analytics: A systematization of research topics and directions for future research. *Human Resource Management Review*, *32*(2), 100795. doi:10.1016/j.hrmr.2020.100795

McCartney, S., & Fu, N. (2022). Bridging the gap: Why, how and when HR analytics can impact organizational performance. *Management Decision*, *60*(13), 25–47. doi:10.1108/MD-12-2020-1581

Opatha, H. H. D. P. J. (2020). HR analytics: A literature review and new conceptual model. *International Journal of Scientific and Research Publications*, *10*(6), 130–141. doi:10.29322/IJSRP.10.06.2020.p10217

Pereira, V. E. (2013). *A Longitudinal Case-Study Examination of HRM Practices in HighPerforming Work Organisations in the Indian HRO/BPO Industry* [Unpublished master's thesis, University of Portsmouth]. https://researchportal.port.ac.uk/portal/files/6033330/Vijay_Phd_Oct_2013_Revised.pdf

Pichault, F., & Naedenoen, F. (2023). The challenges of total talent management in the gig economy. In *The Routledge Handbook of the Gig Economy* (pp. 74–92). Routledge.

Qamar, Y., & Samad, T. A. (2022). Human resource analytics: A review and bibliometric analysis. *Personnel Review*, *51*(1), 251–283. doi:10.1108/PR-04-2020-0247

Reddy, P. (2017). HR analytics – an effective evidence based HRM tool. *International Journal of Business and Management Invention*, *6*(7), 23–34.

Sharma, A., & Sharma, T. (2017). HR analytics and performance appraisal system: A conceptual framework for employee performance improvement. *Management Research Review*, *40*(6), 684–697. doi:10.1108/MRR-04-2016-0084

Tamer, H. & Elsharnouby, S. (2021). Change or perish: Examining the role of human capital and dynamic marketing capabilities in the hospitality sector. *Tourism Management*, *82*. doi:10.1016/j.tourman.2020.104184

Tomar, S., & Gaur, M. (2020). HR analytics in Business: Role, Opportunities, and Challenges of Using It. *Journal of Xi'an University of Architecture & Technology*, *12*(7), 1299–1306.

Chapter 9
Are Employees Disposable?
A Review on Data Driven Layoffs

Sheetal Sharma
IILM Academy of Higher Learning, Lucknow, India

Neha Tiwari
IILM Academy of Higher Learning, Lucknow, India

Vibhuti Gupta
IILM Academy of Higher Learning, Lucknow, India

ABSTRACT

People being laid off in big numbers by companies has become a trend. The economic slowdown globally and the severe financial impact due to the recent COVID-19 pandemic have compelled organizations to mass layoffs. Analyzing the transient and long-term impact of layoffs on organizations and the affected employees is a matter of utmost concern. This chapter aims to provide insights into data-driven layoff decisions, which must be the best basis for layoffs. This chapter focuses on how random layoffs affect current and laid-off workers' levels of trust. It talks about the financial implications vis-a-vis the cost of recruiting and training new employees. Additionally, it sheds some insight on intangible elements like the loss of knowledge that the laid-off worker accrued over the years as well as the erosion of trust experienced by both current and laid-off workers.

"People don't mind change; but they mind being changed."

INTRODUCTION

Layoffs are the buzzword in today's business world. The unbridled wave of layoffs across technology conglomerates, Fintech and startups till the month of April has resulted in 168,243 employees being laid off. The cumulative layoff during the first four months of 2023 exceeds the data for the previous

DOI: 10.4018/978-1-6684-8942-0.ch009

year. Macroeconomic factors have been cited as the reason for the companies that resorted to layoffs (Mascarenhas & Stringer 2023). A layoff, also known as an employee reduction, is the procedure by which a business suspends or permanently terminates a worker or group of workers in order to reduce the workforce size and improve productivity (Muhammed, 2023).

Innumerable employees have been fired by conglomerates and tech giants such as Google, Twitter, Meta, and Microsoft to name a few. Not only tech giants, but even Indian startups like Dunzo, Unacademy, Vedantu, and Go Mechanic have also undergone massive layoffs during the past six months as they are striving to generate funds in a turbulent business environment (Kashyap 2023, Dasgupta, 2023).

In the wake of the looming recession and geopolitical global tensions, startups are following a conservative hiring strategy. With the rise in chatbots like ChatGPT, the need for human resources may further go down (Jaiswar, 2023). Layoffs should not be perceived as a measure of cost-cutting, but organizations need to visualize the long-term impact of layoffs on individual and corporate performance (Cascio et al., 2021).

The word "layoff" is closely related to the concepts such as downsizing, reduction-in-force (RIF), rightsizing, firing, voluntary separation options (VSO), and restructuring when employment for some comes to an end with an organization. Generally, layoffs in organizations are designed to enhance overall productivity and competitiveness, during difficult times or when organizations are on the verge of bankruptcy. According to Sucher & Westner, (2022), organizations that resorted to layoffs proved to be underperformers as compared to those who did not opt for layoffs ().

Layoffs, being a strategic decision, must be dealt with empathy, and compassion and must be backed by relevant facts and figures. Sustainable organizations are driven by employer branding and -an employee-centric approach in which a data-driven layoff will augment the organization's image.

Planning for layoffs requires a thorough analysis of who should be laid off based on their performance and contribution to the organization. This should be preceded by an analysis as to whether layoff is the only solution. Data must also analyze the cost implications of layoffs. Will the cost of recruiting, inducting, and training be more or less than laying off must be analyzed with precision. HR analytics can pave the way for more effective and strategic laying-off decisions.

Conceptual Understanding of Layoff

Layoff has been defined in the Industrial Dispute Act, 1947 and over the years with the changes in Labour Legislations the word "layoff" has evolved. According to the Section 2(kkk) "Layoff'' is defined as the inability, failure, or refusal of the employer to employ a workman whose name is mentioned in the muster roll of his industrial establishment and who is not retrenched due to the lack of power, coal, raw materials, accumulation of stocks, breakdown of machinery or natural calamity for any other relevant reason. The same definition is also mentioned in Section (t) of The Industrial Relation Code (2020).

It is therefore not illegal to lay off any employee based on the factors that impair the capacity of the employers to provide employment. The applicability of the layoff rules and regulations is defined under Section 65 of Chapter IX under The Industrial Relations Code, 2020. None of the rules mentioned in the code apply to establishments that employ less than 50 people or are intermittent or seasonal in nature. However as per Chapter IX, if the establishment is not of seasonal nature and employs more than 50 to 300 people, no clearance from competent authorities is required before laying off employees. But if the number of persons employed exceeds 300, prior approvals from the competent authorities are required before laying off.

A layoff can be understood as a planned and intentional move aimed at reducing cost, bringing in efficiency and better profits in the wake of an economic downturn faced by an organization. The rationale is to improve the firm's performance through the reduction of employees (Datta et al., 2010).

Layoff decisions are primarily decided based on various measures of monetary and non-monetary performance indicators. At the business level declining profits, dwindling market share, and shutdown of operations may trigger the management to contemplate layoff. At the department/ unit level, a non-performing unit that may have a comparatively large slack may result in downsizing. At the individual level, a poorly performing employee based on Bell curve analysis can be considered for laying off. Automation coupled with ever-increasing competition is driving corporations to rethink their workforce planning. However, layoff can also be triggered by technological advancement and innovations. Budros (1999) perceived reduction in force as a kind of organizational innovation leading to the restructuring of systems, policies, and programs. According to Appelbaum et al, (1999), decades ago technological advancements led to more hiring of competent professionals, but now it leads to the laying of employees.

Sahdev (2004) proposed a reorientation and convergence approach to downsizing. The reorientation approach is construed as a reaction to past misalignment (Freeman, 1994). The process and systems are radically redesigned to align their internal capabilities for gaining competitive edge in the market (Appelbaum et al, 1999). This approach is aimed at improving efficiency and improving the firm's strategic position; hence the layoffs are not done randomly. The organization conducts a thorough analysis of the cost centers and based on decision criteria decides who should be laid off (Freeman, 1994). Convergence approach is aimed at continuous improvements through improving quality and operational efficiency. All tasks and units can be susceptible to downsizing to achieve operational efficiency and simplification of operational activities. (Thornhill and Saunders, 1998, Appelbaum et al.1999, Freeman, 1994).

At the micro level of organizations, the negative impact on employees cannot be negated. There is a negative effect of layoff on employee satisfaction, work climate, trust, labour unrest, union grievances, and an increase in absenteeism and fear (Brockner, et al, 1987; Brockner, 1988; Buch & Aldridge, 1991; Wagar, 2001). Layoff can even impair the health and well-being of the employees (Kivimaki et al, 2000). The employees who survive layoff are often demotivated (Wayhan & Werner, 2000). Employee commitment towards work and organizations also take a downslide (Brockner et al, 1987). The layoff decisions can also lead to resignations by high performers in the organizations (Bedeian & Armenakis, 1998; Brockner & Lee, 1995). Therefore, as per the empirical findings it can be construed that the overall impact of layoff is negative on employees. However, the employees who survive layoff exhibit different emotions and behaviour based on the perception of fairness and justice in layoff decisions. When surviving employees perceive that layoff was not legitimate, ethical, and transparent, they exhibit a loss of morale, commitment, and affiliation with the organization (Beylerian and Kleiner, 2003). If the survivors feel that their performance was not the criteria in lay-off decisions, they will feel sympathetic towards those laid off and at the same time will underperform (Appelbaum et. al., 1997). Hence there is a compelling imperative to ensure that the lay-off decisions are made based on transparent criteria. Such criteria must be openly communicated to all the employees to establish trust and perception of fairness among those laid off and among the surviving employees.

However, from the competitive advantage perspective at the macro level of the organizations, it is intended that layoffs can reduce costs and enhance a firm's performance according to the (Cascio et al., 1997). Therefore, the layoffs can produce short-term results in containing the costs (Kets de Vries & Balazs, 1997). However, the Resource Based View perceives layoff in a strategic context rather than a myopic view propounded by a competitive advantage perspective. Human Resources are the most important resource and can create strategic advantages for firms through tacit knowledge skills and attitudes (Lado & Wilson, 1994; Wright et al, 2001; Hitt, et al, 2001). Human resources are the most complex and inimitable resource because they cannot be copied (Barney, 1991). Human Resources are most vulnerable to the negative impact of layoffs. Layoff may hamper the build-up of social capital in the organizations (Leana and Buren, 1999).

It is therefore important to design layoff procedure to identify the employees that can create a competitive advantage for the firms. Layoff is a crucial decision and must be taken with due diligence rather than exercising a random and intuitive approach. Based on the empirical evidence, it can be deduced that layoffs in the short-term may yield competitive benefits to the firm whereas in the long-term it may lead to resource-based loss. A study on America's most admired company proved that layoff is detrimental to the corporate reputation (Flanagan, & O'Shaughnessy, 2005).

REVIEW OF LITERATURE

People analytics is gaining momentum, however still there is a long way to go in terms of people analytics as basis of key HR decisions. To avoid the harm that layoff causes, companies must devise a clear methodology including the relevant metrics to assess the effectiveness of restructuring (Sucher & Gupta, 2018). The mass layoffs by Google were blamed to be unplanned and devoid of any decision criteria. Employee who received performance bonus and outstanding achiever award a few months back were also laid off (Sahu,2023). According to a study titled "The State of HR Analytics- Increase HR's effectiveness by mastering people analytics," sponsored by Oracle, people analytics is still at its nascent stage. The study was conducted during the period June to August 2021. The study found that 36 percent of the organizations agree that people analytics deliver actionable insights. According to the survey findings only about one-third of organizations (34%) make at least moderate use of predictive analytics and 43% make at least moderate use of prescriptive analytics. The survey also revealed that only 38 percent and 37 percent use people analytics for performance management and retention decisions respectively. Only 26 percent of organizations surveyed were using people analytics for workforce planning. Hence the report indicates the use of analytics is severely limited specifically in retention, performance, and workforce planning. A recent article published in the Economic Times HR World South East Asia (2022) quoted the survey conducted by SkyQuest in July 2022 comprising of 1734 organizations across the globe regarding the use of workforce analytics. According to the article only 20 percent of the surveyed organizations use workforce analytics extensively. Most of the organizations (54%) were employing workforce analytics only for talent management. For succession planning only 37% of the organizations surveyed use workforce analytics while for performance management only 36% organizations. (ETHRSEA, 2022). It is therefore evident that the role of analytics in taking decisions such as layoff is still very limited.

HR Analytics is not only a critical enabler of different HR functions including Talent Acquisition, Performance Appraisal but it can also aid in workforce restructuring and ensuring cost optimization. Data can help identify underperforming business units so that resources can be redeployed or reskilled. Comparative analysis can help identify internal hires who may result in less cost to the company. HR analytics can also prescribe functions in which technology can replace human resources.

Work quality employee performance metrics, work efficiency employee performance metrics and organizational-level employee performance metrics must be analyzed to track employee performance.

Generally, those who perform are retained while the underperformers are considered for workforce reduction (Vulpen, AIHR).

Poor financial performance is an antecedent of a reduction in workforce decisions. Profitability, Return on Assets, Return on Equity, and Asset Turnover Metrics are financial metrics that are analyzed before arriving at downsizing decisions. Employee productivity and operating income per employee are analyzed as HR metrics for arriving at the right decisions (N & Currie, 2014).

Recruiting Analytics is important since it will decide whether the cost of hiring will surpass the costs associated with layoffs. Cost of Hire, New Offer Acceptance Rate, New Hire Retention Ratio, Time to Fill, and Time to Start must be analyzed to arrive at all the tangible and intangible costs associated with recruitment. Training costs per employee should not be ignored to arrive at the right decision. A comparative analysis of recruitment costs (including training costs) and cost of employee turnover helps an organization to decide if the objective of cost-cutting is achieved through a reduction in workforce.

It is a known fact that highly engaged employees are an asset to the organization, hence employee net promoter scores should also be analyzed to identify employees that should be retained while taking layoff decisions. (Brown, 2020).

Research Methodology

This chapter used a literature review approach to gather relevant information and insights on Layoff and its analytics. The literature review involved analyzing and synthesizing existing studies, theories, and empirical evidence to develop a comprehensive understanding of the subject matter. An extensive literature review was conducted using popular databases such as EBSCO host, DelNet, NDL and Google Scholar where research papers from reputed journals were reviewed from the year 2010 -2023(till date) In addition some seminal works have also been referenced and cited in the chapter. Several blogs, articles, survey reports from authentic sources were also reviewed to strengthen the discussion. A total of 300 papers were found. However, out of these only 55 papers were considered for review for this chapter. The keywords used for the search included- People Analytics, HR Metrics, Layoff, Performance metrics, Layoff analytics, Tech Giants.

HR Metrics to Aid Layoff Decisions

If an organization finds itself in an untenable position, the instinct of company leaders is to cut costs. Payroll, being the largest fixed cost of a company, is considered the first resort in reducing the cost by laying off employees. It is a challenging situation for all those involved in layoffs. Management must let go of some of its key people, and the employees also are worried about what lies ahead in their careers. It is therefore advisable that the layoffs strategy should be thoughtfully crafted.

Since cost-cutting is the prime agenda during layoffs, the management decisions are also based on the cost-benefit analysis involved in the layoff. Turnover costs are one of the human resource measures used by businesses to analyze their financial status and business plans. Turnover cost refers to what it costs to replace an employee. Firms that analyze cost of turnover typically also monitor expenditure related to layoffs. Layoff costs might seem to be considerable; yet they are only a minor component of the cost of maintaining salaries of employees when the firm cannot afford to retain existing levels of employment. Companies like Google, Oracle, HCL, Microsoft use such metrics.

Calculating Turnover Costs due to layoff involves both direct as well as indirect costs. Direct cost includes hiring costs in terms of advertisement fees, recruitment expenses, outplacement services, on-boarding costs, etc. Other forms of direct cost are unemployment benefits for involuntary leaves, severance pay, potential legal dispute, the cost for training and development, etc. On the other hand, indirect cost includes decreased productivity and morale of the employees, loss of the company's financial credibility in the markets, and much more.

Though it is not easy to estimate the total cost of layoff but is definite that the financial impact on both the affected employee and the firm is significant. Layoff decisions involve answers to two major questions:

1) How much does it cost to be reduced through layoff?
2) Who is to be laid off?

The answer to the first question can be reached with the help of the stepwise scientific calculation given below:

Let us understand how companies calculate the amount of cost to be reduced with the help of an example:

Case 1: For planning the layoff strategy in ABC Corporation, the management wants to understand how must cost has to be reduced. The following steps are followed for calculating the amount of cost it needs to reduce:

Step 1) Calculating Cost Overrun: Cost overrun simply means that expenses or cost goes beyond the revenue. It is also termed a Revenue Shortfall. So, we start by calculating the cost overrun first for the last 6 months.

For example:

Revenue (last 6 months) = Rs 10,00000
Cost (last 6 months) = Rs12,00000
Excess of Cost over Revenue for the last 6 months = **Rs.2,00000**

This is the excess of cost over revenue for the last 6 months. To calculate the excess of cost over revenue for the next year (12 months), we need to simply double this number which is **Rs 4,00000**.

Step 2) Calculating the rate of growth in cost overruns:

The second step involves calculating the rate at which this cost overrun is moving. This could probably increase or decrease based on how the company is performing.

To calculate the rate of growth in cost overruns, we split the last 6 months into two periods of 3 months and then calculate the growth in the first 3 months and then the second 3 months and compare the average percentage to monitor the percentage change/rate of growth.

For example, Revenue Vs Cost for the last 6 months:

July – Revenue: Rs. 18,000 / Cost: Rs. 20,000
August – Revenue: Rs. 15,000 / Cost: Rs. 20,000
September – Revenue: Rs. 20,000 / Cost: Rs. 30,000
October – Revenue: Rs. 20,000 / Cost: Rs. 30,000
November – Revenue: Rs. 30,000/ Cost: Rs. 40,000

December – Revenue: Rs. 40,000/ Cost: Rs. 60,000

Calculation of Loss Percentage for each month:

July = Rs. 18000 – Rs. 20,000 / Rs. 20,000 x 100 = **-10%**
August = Rs. 15,000 - Rs 20,000 / Rs. 20,000 x 100 = **-25%**
September = Rs. 20,000 – Rs. 30,000 / Rs. 30,000 x 100 = **-33%**
October = Rs. 20,000 – Rs. 30,000 / Rs. 30,000 x 100 = **-33%**
November = Rs. 30,000 – Rs. 40,000 x 100 = **-25%**
December = Rs. 40,000 – Rs. 60,000 / Rs. 60,000 x 100 = **-33%**

Calculate the Average Rate of Growth overrun for the First 3 months (July + August + September)

=> 10% + 25% + 33% / 3 = **22.66%**

Calculate the Average Rate of Growth overrun for the Second 3 months (September + October + December)

=> 33% + 25% + 33% / 3 = **30.33%**

Growth Rate = Second 3 months growth rate – First 3 months growth rate

=> 30.33% - 22.66% = **7.67%**

With this current growth rate of increasing loss, the total amount to be deducted for the next year is calculated as.

=> Cost overrun x 7.67%

=> Rs. 4,00000 x 7.67%

Thus, cost that needs to be reduced for the next year based on the growth overrun rate => Rs. 30,68000.

Step 3) Forecast changes in the rate of growth in cost revenues for the next year: Looking at the trend in the last 6 months it is assumed that the rate of loss may further increase in the next year, and it is significant to forecast this increase in loss growth rate. The finance department must be contacted for gaining information on the revenue forecast which is usually compiled by them. In the absence of any such data with the finance department on the next year's forecast, it is suggested to take an assumption of a 12% loss growth rate, assuming 1% for each month. The amount that needs to be cut based on forecast loss of growth rate.

Forecast loss of growth of next year – Actual loss of growth of this year x TWO

=> 12% - 7.67% x Rs. 30,68000

Therefore, the amount that needs to be cut based on forecast loss growth rate => Rs. 1,32,84440.

Step 4) Calculate the final and Total amount that should be cut for the next year

=> Rs. 40,0000 + Rs. 306,8000 + Rs. 13,28,4440

Thus, total amount that needs to be cut for next year => Rs. 1,67,52,440.

Thus, this gives us the scientific calculation about the amount of cost to be reduced from the next year's budget. The company starts planning its layoff strategy in accordance with the amount of cost to be reduced.

To take the data driven informed decision organizations perform layoff analytics with the help of variety of HR metrics to estimate the layoff cost.

Cost of Turnover = (Separation Costs + Replacement Costs + Training Costs + Productivity Costs) / Total Number of Employees

For example, if the total cost of employee turnover was Rs. 500,000 and there were 50 employees in the company, the cost of turnover would be Rs. 10,000 per employee.

Let us understand how the various costs mentioned in the formula are calculated using HR metrics:

1. Metrics for Separation Cost

Separation cost includes- Exit Interview (S1), administrative function related to termination (S2), Separation Pay (S3), and unemployment tax (if any) (S4).

- **Cost Elements Formula for Exit Interview (S1)**

Cost of Interviewer and Terminating Employees Time= Time required prior and for the interview (X) interviewers pay rate (X) number of turnovers during periods

It is to be noted that time for exit interviews may be estimated in one of two ways:

a) Taking a random sample of the exit interview and calculate the average time.
b) Interview a representative sample of managers who conduct exit interviews regularly and average their estimated time.

- **Administrative functions related to Termination (S2)**

Time required by the HR department for administrative functions related to termination= Average HR Dept employee pay rate(X) number of turnovers during the period

The organisation itself should identify which administrative activities are associated with the termination and how much time is required for them. The cost incurred for these activities should be documented and factored into the separation cost.

- **Separation Pay (S3)**

Separation cost includes the separation pay. Separation pay is usually in the form of severance pay. Severance pay is a type of compensation given to employees who have been laid off by their employers. In other terms, it is money or benefits paid to a person who loses their employment without any fault of their own. The amount of severance pay is calculated based on the employee's retirement account benefits, employee's length of service in the organization, payment for holiday pay or sick leave which have not been used etc. Severance pay is aimed at providing financial protection for the newly unemployed.

The formula used to calculate the Separation Pay

Amount of separation pay per employee terminated (X) number of turnovers during the period.

- Unemployment tax (If Any) (S4).

Therefore, **Total Separation Cost ST = S1 + S2 + S3 + S4**

2. Replacement Cost

The overall value of the acquisition of a new employee is considered for the cost of replacement. HR metrics preferably used for calculating the replacement cost are:

- **Cost per hire**- Cost per hire is a recruitment metric that measures the cost incurred in hiring a new employee.
- **Cost per hire formula**

Cost per hire= (Internal cost of recruitment + External cost of recruitment) /Total no. of hires

External costs variable covers all sources of expenses done on recruiting efforts outside the organization during the period considered for the calculation. Various forms of external costs include advertising costs, fees given to third-party agency, cost of organizing job fair, and any form of costs incurred during travel for the purpose of recruitment.

For calculating the internal costs, the variables included are the cost incurred on salary and benefits offered to the recruitment team, fixed cost in terms of talent acquisition cost, physical infrastructure which is component of fixed cost etc.

To calculate the total number of hires, we consider the total number of hires made in the given period considered for evaluation. The type of hires includes all types of hires including (regular full-time, regular part-time, etc.). It is assumed that irrespective of the overall number of hires, all other type of expenses for the efforts made to fill the included positions have been taken into account while calculating the external and internal costs.

For example, if a firm hires 100 people each year, and Rs. 100,000 is annually spent on the hiring process, that would imply that the cost per hire is Rs 1,000. Cost per hire is a useful measure for optimization process as per the organizational need. (SHRM, 2012).

Monitoring the cost-per-hire data enables a company to determine how much money it'll need to hire in the coming months. It aids in cost forecasting and provides a lucid contribution of recruitment's contribution to the company's bottom line.

Other metrics used for the calculation of replacement cost are:

- ***Recruiting cost rate (RCR)***

This is another recruitment metric that also takes into account external factors including market conditions and various other external factors that can impact the compensation levels .

The RCR formula is:

RCR=Total internal and external cost of recruitment/Total annual compensation of new hires in their firm

For example: Based on the amount agreed upon through the employee's employment contract the firm calculates total annual compensation.

Let us assume that a company spends Rs. 10, 000 in the recruitment process for a given position. If the new hire's annual compensation is Rs 80,000 then RCR = (10,000/80,000) *100%=12.5%. This means that for every rupee the new hire makes, the company spent 12.5 paisa to secure them.

It is better is for the company to have a lower RCR. Hiring higher-paid, senior-level employees with lower costs of recruitment is always preferred by HR teams.

3. Metrics for Calculating Training Cost per Employee

- **Training cost per employee=Total cost of training /Total no. of participants in training**

Total cost for training includes the cost of the trainer, training material, cost of the venue used for the training, cost of the choice of training method (Offline /Online), cost of employee time, and any form of administrative cost incurred during training.

- **Cost per Training Hour-**This formula can help to calculate the cost per training hour for employees.

Cost per Training Hour = Total Cost of Training / Total Number of Training Hours

For example, if the total cost of training in a year was Rs. 80,000 and the total number of training hours was 200, the cost per training hour would be Rs 400.

4._Productivity Cost

Another dimension of turnover cost is the productivity cost. Productivity is a metric that provides a fair understanding of when and how your business is required to adjust in order to attain the desired outcome.

Formula to calculate Productivity is as under:

- ***Productivity = Output / Input***
- For example, if units produced by an employee is 200 units per day and he works for 8 hours, the employee's productivity would be 25 units per hour.

Other HR metrics which are considered for layoff analytics.

- *Revenue per Employee = Total Revenue / Total Number of Employees*

Return on Investment (ROI)

ROI is calculated for the cost-benefit analysis of any HR initiative.

For example, if the firm's annual total revenue was Rs.10, 000,000 and the total number of employees was 200, the revenue per employee would be Rs. 50, 000.

- *ROI = (Gain from Investment – Cost of Investment) / Cost of Investment x 100%*

For example, if a people analytics project costs Rs. 100,000 and results in a gain of Rs. 200, 000, the ROI would be 100%.

These are the few key HR metrics that are commonly used for layoff decisions. In addition to this various financial metrics like profitability, profit margins, earnings per share, return on assets, market capitalization and revenue growth, and are also taken into consideration (De Meuse et al., 2013).

To answer the second question as to who should be laid off, companies also take into consideration multiple criteria which are both objective as well as subjective. These criteria are in addition to the various HR Metrics discussed above used for layoff analytics. Since most of the HR metrics are mostly cost-centric, therefore, to be more precise in their decision to layoff companies consider the following criteria as discussed below:

- The employee's abilities, knowledge, and adaptability.
- The employee's level of education and experience.
- Long-term potential and attitude of the employee.
- The quantity and quality of work performed by the employee.
- The employee's attendance record.
- The employee's years of service with the company.

The choice of criteria for consideration may vary from organization to organization. The potential and performance matrix of the individual employee is reviewed. Performance both in terms of quality as well as quantity of work and potential to grow and add value to the organization is also what is considered. Seniority, length of service, commitment, and engagement level are some of the important criteria which are evaluated to determine whom to layoff. The choice of the criteria may depend upon the needs of the organization.

Practitioner's Point of View

The human resources department is responsible for effectively managing the downsizing process by mitigating the ethical, social, and legal, risks that may arise as a result of layoffs. There is a lot of debate as to what will be the implications of the downsizing decision for the company. In this section we present the practitioner's point of view. According to the Vice President of Global Strategy for Phenom, an HR software company, he states that its technology "does not have any layoff button" for taking makes downsizing decisions but emphasize the importance of manager's wisdom to take such an important decision.

On the contrary, Jonathan Reynolds, CEO of Titus Talent Strategies, which is a recruiting firm using layoff analytics to make their layoff decisions stress the use of data-driven layoff decisions with a belief that it will minimize the bias and is also favourable for the health of the company in the long run.

In addition to what Mr Jonathan said, Ms. Anita Grantham, head of HR at BambooHR, a software company states that an organization having data across the entire employee experience can help companies to take more justifiable, equitable, and informed decisions. (Davidson,2023)

Challenges and Limitations of Analytics

Layoffs have become a trend these days. Sometimes it may be random layoff decisions as well like Elon Musk did at Twitter after taking it over. However, the one good thing to come out of Twitter's mass firings is that Elon Musk has brought attention to what should and shouldn't be done when organizing a staff. Recently, many other digital businesses and other industries are going through a process like the one that has Twitter in the spotlight with widespread layoffs. In these situations, with properly trained HR staff, HR analytics can come handy ensuring that decisions are based on evidence rather than the gut feelings of leaders.

HR analytics specialists can expand their sphere of impact in such circumstances by using data to drive business decisions and have an impact on the income statement as well. When we step back and review, we see that a company's financial health may be improved by concentrating not only on the bottom line, which can be achieved by reducing personnel expenses but also on concentrating on a few important questions like what are the best methods for hiring or reasons for layoffs? In the case of career opportunities, what is the average waiting time for promotions, or what is the promotion rate? Sales data, core HR data, and recruitment data may be included in the analytics system to make sound data-based decisions. HR may use HR analytics to respond to inquiries like: What are the costs of a hiring freeze? Where in the organization is the breadth of control too low if we need to cut back on the number of managers. The results of these assessments may sometimes even result in forced layoffs, but at least the analytics make sure that there is a sound business case for it rather than relying solely on the intuition of a leader or the like. These are just a few of the data-driven questions that can be used to boost a company's top and bottom lines and show how HR analytics can help a business's income statement even in the most difficult of economic circumstances.

Dr. C. Jayakumar, Executive Vice President & Head – Corporate Human Resources (CHRO) at L&T (Larsen & Toubro Limited), an Indian Multi-national Conglomerate highlights the importance of analytics when he says that amongst many important tasks he has set as CHRO is the digitalization and automation of the HR function and leveraging analytics for effective decision-making. According to him to keep pace with digitalization and automation, skilling, multiskilling, upskilling, and reskilling the existing talent are one of the biggest challenges today.

Although using HR analytics can assist in unbiased and logical decisions related to the reduction in workforce, there are some inherent challenges and limitations. The availability of an authentic database is still a challenge in most small and mid-sized organizations. The availability of quality data is a prerequisite to effective HR analytics, which is still a challenge even in large corporations. The teams responsible for HR analytics need to transform. More than ever, the HR analytics teams must convert data and results into business language. Data, as discussed, is a major obstacle for HR analytics in terms of capabilities as well. For effective HR decision making access to relevant and complete people related data would be a priority. HR must direct their efforts in updating their talent inventory. Keeping the data current is one of the major issues in this area of HR analytics because the employees will continue to develop and pick up new abilities. To obtain excellent results, effective interventions are typically required to encourage change. But the next step should be to incorporate HR analytics into selecting the fact-based KPIs that will help the company and demonstrate that it is fulfilling its objectives.

Sometimes outdated technology may also pose a challenge to database maintenance in organizations. Even if the organization ensures that the technology infrastructure is available, very limited professionals are competent in the analysis and deciphering of HR metrics. HR analytics is still at its nascent stage and hence HR personnel need extensive training to become competent enough to make logical data-based decisions. Using HR Analytics could be perceived as a beginner's challenge irrespective of the size and scale of operations of the business organizations. It is imperative to have a competent HR team as most of the HR analytics reports have their way to the boardrooms which can conveniently help make wise decisions with the help of results from analytics.

Although using HR analytics can assist in unbiased and logical decisions related to a reduction in the workforce, there are some inherent challenges and limitations. The availability of an authentic database is still a challenge in most small and mid-sized organizations. The availability of quality data is a prerequisite to effective HR analytics, which is still a challenge even in large corporations. Sometimes outdated technology may also pose a challenge to database maintenance in organizations.

CONCLUSION AND DISCUSSION

Layoffs provide human resources professionals and management with the option of restructuring and improving the company's competitive position in the industry during times of crisis. Layoff analytics provides a base for evidence-based and informed decisions related to downsizing for a fairer, justifiable, and transparent perspective. HR experts are expected to play a vital leadership role in the design and implementation of an organization's layoff and downsizing policies. As previously stated, it is sometimes necessary for managers to make required cuts in the workplace while keeping the needs of the company in mind to survive in the competitive market. The role of HR managers is very crucial in preserving the motivation and morale of the employees who continue to be with the organization. It is suggested that HR and organizational managers should frequently meet and talk with remaining employees and provide them with necessary counselling and support to make them feel secure. The biggest challenge of layoffs is that it is a unilateral decision as employees are not really involved in the decision about layoffs. Therefore, it is suggested that to make the transition seamless in the organizations, management should involve and engage both managers as well as employees in the layoff process.

The advantages of layoffs are not cutting down the cost, but sometimes it allows the company to restructure itself to bring fresh and innovative ideas. The organization also gets rid of disengaged, non-performers, excessive, and redundant employees also and establishes more control and stability moving ahead. Altogether, through well-planned layoffs and downsizing decisions, organizations can showcase a strategic move for gaining competitive advantage.

It is suggested that layoff analytics must be used with caution as they consider the cost implications only but layoff being a sensitive issue must also consider various other dimensions in cognition to take informed and thoughtful decisions to achieve the desired results.

Theoretical Contribution

The chapter attempts to educate academics as well as organisations about random layoff decisions. Companies that are thinking about or have already implemented mass layoffs should concentrate on renegotiating the psychological contract with the remaining workers by providing them with real job security, initiatives to improve employability and resources for rethinking career options for both laid-off and surviving workers. Additionally, businesses should reevaluate the necessity of mass layoffs and ponder substitute cost-cutting strategies, such as temporarily lowering pay expenses throughout the company or opting for furlough.

Future Implications

The chapter emphasises the significance of making informed decisions on layoffs. Even if layoffs are becoming more common, it's crucial to realise that if they are solely motivated by cost-cutting and not because of low competence or other problems, it could eventually hurt the employer brand. Future organisations and managers may benefit from understanding that layoffs, if necessary, must be based on informed decisions, based on metrics that take performance into account, rather than arbitrary decisions like those made recently by the tech giants like Google, Oracle, to name a few.

Limitations and Future Research

This investigation is based on secondary data. This means that the data collected may have some biases. In the future, an empirical study that takes into account a few organisations may be done to evaluate the use of HR Analytics in layoff decisions. Future studies could look at how these layoffs would affect employee morale, productivity, and company branding in the future. The future studies may also be conducted to find the impact of mass layoffs on employee work behaviours.

REFERENCES

Appelbaum, S. H., Delage, C., Labib, N., & Gault, G. (1997). The survivor syndrome: Aftermath of downsizing. *Career Development International*, *2*(6), 278–286. doi:10.1108/13620439710178639

Appelbaum, S. H., Everard, A., & Hung, L. T. (1999). Strategic downsizing: Critical success factors. *Management Decision*, *37*(7), 535–552. doi:10.1108/00251749910285674

Barney, J. (1991). Firm resources and sustained competitive advantage. *Journal of Management*, *17*(1), 99–121. doi:10.1177/014920639101700108

Bedeian, A. G., & Armenakis, A. A. (1998). The cesspool syndrome: How dreck floats to the top of declining organizations. *The Academy of Management Perspectives*, *12*(1), 58–63. doi:10.5465/ame.1998.254978

Beylerian, M., & Kleiner, B. H. (2003). The downsized workplace. *Management Research News*, *26*(2/3/4), 97-108.

Brockner, J. (1988). The effects of work layoffs on survivors: Research, theory, and practice. *Research in Organizational Behavior, 10*, 213–255.

Brockner, J., Grover, S., Reed, T., DeWitt, R., & O'Malley, M. (1987). Survivors' reactions to layoffs: We get by with a little help for our friends. *Administrative Science Quarterly, 32*(4), 526–541. doi:10.2307/2392882

Brockner, J., & Lee, R. J. (1995). Career development in downsizing organizations: A self-affirmation analysis. In M. London (Ed.), *Employees, careers, and job creation: Developing growth-oriented human resource strategies and programs* (p. 51). Jossey-Bass.

Brown, M. I. (2020). Comparing the validity of net promoter and benchmark scoring to other commonly used employee engagement metrics. *Human Resource Development Quarterly, 31*(4), 355–370. doi:10.1002/hrdq.21392

Buch, K., & Aldridge, J. (1991). O.D. under conditions of organization decline. *Organization Development Journal, 9*(1), 1–5. PMID:1996536

Budros, A. (1999). A conceptual framework for analyzing why organizations downsize. *Organization Science, 10*(1), 69–82. doi:10.1287/orsc.10.1.69

Cascio, W. F., Chatrath, A., & Christie-David, R. A. (2021). Antecedents and consequences of employee and asset restructuring. *Academy of Management Journal, 64*(2), 587–613. doi:10.5465/amj.2018.1013

Cascio, W. F., Young, C. E., & Morris, J. R. (1997). Financial consequences of employment-change decisions in major US corporations. *Academy of Management Journal, 40*(5), 1175–1189. doi:10.2307/256931

Chhinzer, N., N., & Currie, E. (2014). Assessing longitudinal relationships between financial performance and downsizing. *Management Decision, 52*(8), 1474–1490. doi:10.1108/MD-05-2014-0280

Dasgupta, G. (2023), Layoffs in 2023: Dunzo, Unacademy among Indian startups & tech companies that have cut jobs. *Economic Tours.* https://economictimes.indiatimes.com/tech/technology/layoffs-in-2023-a-list-of-indian-startups-tech-companies-that-have-cut-jobs/articleshow/97601464.cms?utm_source=contentofinterest&utm_medium=text&utm_campaign=cppst

Datta, D. K., Guthrie, J. P., Basuil, D., & Pandey, A. (2010). Causes and effects of employee downsizing: A review and synthesis. *Journal of Management, 36*(1), 281–348. doi:10.1177/0149206309346735

Davidson, P. (2023, January 23), Layoffs in a likely recession this year could be determined by software programs. *USA Today*. https://www.usatoday.com/story/money/2023/01/23/layoffs-2023-recession-software-programs/11086842002/

De Meuse, K. P., & Dai, G. (2013). Organizational downsizing: Its effect on financial performance over time. *Journal of Managerial Issues*, 324–344.

Enderle, R. (2016, September 02). *How analytics could end layoffs* CIO. https://www.cio.com/article/239041/how-analytics-could-end-layoffs.html

ETHRSEA. (2022). More than 70% organisations are using workforce analytics for cost-saving and improved decision-making: Survey. HRSEA. https://hrsea.economictimes.indiatimes.com/news/industry/more-than-70-organisations-are-using-workforce-analytics-for-cost-saving-and-improved-decision-making-survey/95282155

Flanagan, D. J., & O'Shaughnessy, K. C. (2005). The effect of layoffs on firm reputation. *Journal of Management*, *31*(3), 445–463. doi:10.1177/0149206304272186

Freeman, S. J. (1994). Organizational downsizing as convergence or reorientation: Implications for human resource management. *Human Resource Management*, *33*(2), 213–238. doi:10.1002/hrm.3930330205

Gray, R. (2022). The 3 Human Capital Metrics Your Small Business Needs to Track Patriot Software. *Patriots of Software*. https://www.patriotsoftware.com/blog/accounting/human-capital-metrics-roi-measurement/

Hitt, M. A., Bierman, L., Shimizu, K., & Kochhar, R. (2001). Direct and moderating effects of human capital on strategy and performance in professional service firms: A resource-based perspective. *Academy of Management Journal*, *44*(1), 13–28. doi:10.2307/3069334

Jaiswar, S. (2023). Tech Layoffs: Over 2700 people lost their jobs per day so far in 2023.When will lay off winter end?" *Livemint*. https://www.livemint.com/companies/news/tech-layoffs-over-2-700-people-lost-their-jobs-per-day-so-far-in-2023-when-will-layoff-winter-end-11677339547907.html>

Kashyap, H. (2023, April 25). Indian Startup Layoff Tracker: 25,370+ Employees Laid Off Since 2022 Amid Funding Winter. *Inc42*. https://inc42.com/features/indian-startup-layoffs-tracker/

Kets de Vries, M., & Balazs, K. (1997). The downside of downsizing. *Human Relations*, *50*(1), 11–51. doi:10.1177/001872679705000102

Kivimäki, M., Vahtera, J., Pentti, J., & Ferrie, J. E. (2000). Factors underlying the effect of organisational downsizing on health of employees: Longitudinal cohort study. *BMJ (Clinical Research Ed.)*, *320*(7240), 971–975. doi:10.1136/bmj.320.7240.971 PMID:10753148

Lado, A. A., & Wilson, M. C. (1994). Human resource systems and sustained competitive advantage: A competency-based perspective. *Academy of Management Review*, *19*(4), 699–727. doi:10.2307/258742

Leana, C. R., & Van Buren, H. J. III. (1999). Organizational social capital and employment practices. *Academy of Management Review*, *24*(3), 538–555. doi:10.2307/259141

Levenson, A. (2018). Using workforce analytics to improve strategy execution. *Human Resource Management*, *57*(3), 685–700. doi:10.1002/hrm.21850

Mac Keown, T. (2023, April 27), How people analytics can help organizations thrive. *Forbes*. https://www.forbes.com/sites/forbestechcouncil/2020/08/27/how-people-analytics-can-help-organizations-thrive-in-a-downturn/?sh=52b30a3740fd

Mascarenhas, N., & Stringer, A. (2023, May 04). *A comprehensive list of 2023 tech layoffs*. Techcrunch. https://techcrunch.com/2023/05/04/tech-industry-layoffs/#:~:text=The%20running%20total%20of%20layoffs,the%20data%20in%20the%20tracker

Mayhew, R. C. (2020). *Calculate Costs.* Chron. https://smallbusiness.chron.com/calculate-costs-turnover-due-lay-off-10336.html

Mohammed, D. & Abdul, O. (2019). HR Analytics: A Modern Tool in HR for Predictive Decision Making (2019). *Journal of Management, 6*(3), 51-63. https://ssrn.com/abstract=3525328

Muhammed, A. (2023). *TechLayoff.* ClearIAS. https://www.clearias.com/tech-layoff/#what-one-means-by-tech-lay-off

Mujtaba, B., & Senathip, T. (2020). Layoffs and Downsizing Implications for the Leadership Role of Human Resources. *Journal of Service Science and Management, 13*(2), 209–228. doi:10.4236/jssm.2020.132014

Sahdev, K. (2004). Revisiting the survivor syndrome: The role of leadership in implementing downsizing. *European Journal of Work and Organizational Psychology, 13*(2), 165–196. doi:10.1080/13594320444000056

Sahu, S. (2023). Google layoffs not on performance basis and systems locked mins after firing, says YouTube India employee. *India Today.* https://www.indiatoday.in/technology/news/story/google-layoffs-not-on-performance-basis-and-systems-locked-mins-after-firing-says-youtube-india-employee-2351002-2023-03-24\

SHRM. (2012). *Cost Per Hire Standard: American National Standard for Human Resource Management.* American National Standards Institute Inc. https://www.shrm.org/resourcesandtools/business-solutions/documents/shrm_ansi_cph_standard.pdf

Sucher, S. J., & Westner, M. M. (2022, December 8). What Companies Still Get Wrong about Layoffs. [website]. *Harvard Business Review.*

The State of HR Analytics- Increase HR's effectiveness by mastering people analytics. (2021). HR. https://www.oracle.com/a/ocom/docs/applications/human-capital-management/hrt-talent-analytics-hrdotcom.pdf

Thornhill, A., & Saunders, M. N. (1998). The meanings, consequences and implications of the management of downsizing and redundancy: A review. *Personnel Review, 27*(4), 271–295. doi:10.1108/00483489810213874

Van Vulpen, E. (2023). 21 Employee Performance Metrics, Academy to Innovate HR. Vulpen, E. https://www.aihr.com/blog/employee-performance-metrics/>

Wagar, T. H. (2001). Consequences of work force reduction: Some employer and union evidence. *Journal of Labor Research, 22*(4), 851–862. doi:10.100712122-001-1056-1

Wayhan, V. B., & Werner, S. (2000). The impact of workforce reductions on financial performance: A longitudinal perspective. *Journal of Management, 26*(2), 341–363. doi:10.1177/014920630002600208

Wright, P., Dunford, B., & Snell, S. (2001). Contributions of the resource-based view of the firm to the field of strategic HRM: Convergence of two fields. *Journal of Management, 27*, 701–721. doi:10.1177/014920630102700607

Chapter 10
Identifying the Antecedents and Outcomes of Happiness at Work:
A Review

Shiwani Singh
Babasaheb Bhimrao Ambedkar University, Lucknow, India

Taruna Taruna
Babasaheb Bhimrao Ambedkar University, Lucknow, India

Dinesh K. Sharma
https://orcid.org/0000-0002-8739-6516
University of Maryland, Eastern Shore, USA

ABSTRACT

Happiness or well-being has received lots of popularity due to its significant impact on the long-term profitability and sustainability of organizations. Due to the growing importance of workplace happiness, this study aims to explore the relevant factors that support happiness at work. Based on the extensive literature, it was found that mindfulness, ethical leadership, psychological capital, workplace spirituality, and thriving at work are crucial for increasing happiness at work. Happiness at work fosters job satisfaction, work engagement, and organizational citizenship behavior. It reduces deleterious repercussions like turnover intention, stress, absenteeism, counterproductive work behaviors, etc., which further enhances smooth business processes. Hence, organizations must implement appropriate measurements and practices to ensure workers' well-being and happiness at work for better outcomes and a promising future for organizations.

DOI: 10.4018/978-1-6684-8942-0.ch010

1.0 INTRODUCTION

"Happiness can be defined as subjective well-being or positive evaluation of people's lives"(Akgunduz et al., 2022). Employee happiness at work refers to the degree to which employees experience positive emotions, such as joy, contentment, and satisfaction in their work environment (Fisher, 2010).Happiness at work is a key success factor for organizations looking to grow and thrive in a stressful and competitive environment(Thompson & Bruk-Lee, 2021). Organizations that prioritize building a work environment that values employee well-being and happiness will likely see numerous benefits in employee engagement, productivity, and resilience. Employees who feel happy at work tend to have a positive attitude toward their work and the organization. They are more likely to feel a sense of pride in their work and are more motivated to perform their tasks to the best of their abilities. This translates into higher levels of engagement in their work(Fisher, 2010). Happier workers often enjoy better physical and mental health. When workers are healthy, they are less likely to experience fatigue, burnout, or illness that can negatively affect their productivity. Hence, happiness at work boosts employees' productivity (DiMaria et al., 2020). Furthermore, the Broaden-and-Build theory put forth by Fredrickson (2001) suggests that positive emotions such as happiness can have a transformative impact on an individual's cognitive and behavioral abilities. Specifically, happiness may widen the scope of an individual's thought-action repertoire, enabling them to consider a more extensive array of possibilities and solutions. This increased flexibility in thinking and behavior can lead to greater creativity and problem-solving abilities. (Bani-Melhem et al., 2020).In addition, a positive and supportive work environment that ensures employee well-being and happiness can help to build a more resilient workforce. Organizations can help employees bounce back from setbacks and persevere in the present status quo by providing the necessary resources and support to manage stress and other challenges.In essence, fostering happiness in the workplace can have a profound impact on organizations functioning as it can facilitate the retention of employees, amplify employee engagement & productivity, and build a more resilient workforce that is better equipped to face challenges and drive business success. Taking into account the significance of happiness at work, the present study seeks to explore the factors that contribute to raising employee happiness in the workplace and the potential outcomes of such happiness.

2.0 THEORETICAL FRAMEWORK

2.1 Self-Determination Theory (SDT)

SDT has gained popularity in organizational psychology as it provides a useful framework for understanding how fulfilling basic psychological needs can influence employee happiness at work (Salas-Vallina et al., 2018).SDT emphasizes the importance of nurturing autonomy, competence, and relatedness needs to promote intrinsic motivation and well-being, and foster personal growth (Deci & Ryan, 2008). In the workplace, the application of SDT can be instrumental in promoting employee happiness. There is a propensity for employees to feel a heightened level of job satisfaction, well-being,and engagement when certain factors, such as autonomy and control over their work and decision-making authority, are present at work (Gagne & Deci, 2005). Providing opportunities for employees to enhance their skills and competencies can trigger a feeling of competence and mastery, leading to increased motivation and well-being (Ryan et al., 2010).

Furthermore, a study by Van Den Broeck et al. (2008) found that fulfilling the relatedness need by providing a sense of community and supportive interpersonal relationships at work led to higher levels of job satisfaction and overall well-being for employees. Hence, SDT can play a crucial role in influencing employee well-being or happiness by promoting a work environment that supports employees' autonomy, competence, and relatedness needs. By understanding and applying SDT principles, organizations can create a more innovative work environment that fosters greater employee engagement, motivation, and well-being.

3.0 ANTECEDENTS OF HAPPINESS AT WORK

3.1 Mindfulness

A growing body of research supports the benefits of mindfulness practices for employee well-being (Klussman et al., 2022; Sulosaari et al., 2022).According to Kabat-Zinn (2003), mindfulness is "the awareness that emerges through paying attention on purpose, in the present moment, and non-judgmentally to the unfolding of experience moment by moment". Mindfulness has become increasingly popular as a tool for reducing stress and improving performance in the workplace. Organizations are focusing on mindfulness-based interventions in the present era as they lead to improved well-being or happiness,which has a ripple effect on the workplace and business operations.Mindfulness-based stress reduction (MBSR) has been shown to improve employee health and well-being, which can lead to reduced healthcare costs for organizations (Hülsheger et al., 2015). Moreover, mindfulness training can help employees to develop better coping mechanisms for dealing with work-related stress, improve their ability to focus on tasks, and to improve communication and collaboration between team members, leading to better outcomes and increased organizational success(Good et al., 2016).

3.2 Psychological Capital

Organizations recognize that psychological capital (PsyCap) is an essential resource that contributes to their competitiveness and development, along side traditional forms of capital such as financial, human, and social capital(Li, 2018). The positive psychological resources that form PsyCap, such as resilience, optimism, hope, and self-efficacy, can significantly impact employee performance, and well-being(Donaldson et al., 2022). Further, Rabenu et al.(2017) indicated that PsyCap plays a crucial role in improving the well-being of employees by acting as a buffer against stress and job demands. Employees with higher levels of PsyCap are more likely to experience positive emotions, lower levels of stress and burnout, and higher levels of life satisfaction which further improves their overall performance at the workplace.As such, investing in building and enhancing PsyCap among employees is becoming increasingly important for organizations that strive to create a sustainable, high-performing, and happy workforce.

3.3 Workplace Spirituality

Spirituality in the workplace has emerged as an important topic of interest for management researchers and academicians (Hassan et al., 2022).Workplace spirituality refers to integrating spiritual values, beliefs, and practices into the workplace to improve employees' subjective well-being, satisfaction, and retention while fostering a positive organizational culture. According to Ashar & Lane-Maher (2004), workplace spirituality "involves the desire to do purposeful work that serves others, to be part of a principled community, a yearning for connectedness and wholeness that can only be manifested when one is allowed to integrate one's inner life with one's professional role in the service of the greater good". Workplace spirituality can help organizations meet the evolving needs of their employees and create a more constructive, fulfilling, and contented work environment.The study (Mahipalan & Sheena, 2019) examined the relationship between workplace spirituality and employee subjective happiness. The study's findings revealed a significant positive relationship between workplace spirituality and employee subjective happiness. The results showed that employees who perceived their workplace as more spiritual reported higher levels of subjective happiness than those who perceived it as less spiritual.Moreover, workplace spirituality can promote employee well-being by cultivating intrinsic motivation, self-management, and a sense of community and connectedness, resulting in a more meaningful and empowered work environment (Srivastava & Gupta, 2022).Hence, promoting workplace spirituality can play a vital role in enhancing the happiness or well-being of employees.

3.4 Ethical Leadership

The well-being of employees is significantly influenced by the leadership style employed within an organization (Jia et al., 2022). Ethical leadership at work is a leadership style that follows ethical and moral principles in decision-making and behavior. Ethical leaders set a positive example for their followers by demonstrating integrity, honesty, fairness, and accountability.Llyas et al. (2022) conducted a study to investigate how ethical leadership affects the well-being of healthcare workers. The study proposed a model in which the relationship between ethical leadership and well-being is mediated by perceived organizational support and perceived ethical-philanthropic corporate social responsibility (CSR).The study's findings supported the proposed model, indicating that ethical leadership positively influenced subjective well-being through the mediating effects of perceived organizational support and ethical-philanthropic CSR. The study suggests that healthcare organizations should promote ethical leadership and demonstrate concern for the well-being of healthcare workers and society. Moreover, ethical leaders are committed to their values and principles in their decisions, behavior, and actions. They are also responsible for making impartial decisions that benefit the organization and its employees. Ethical leaders foster a culture of trust within the organization, promote workplace happiness, encourage creativity and innovation, and increase organizational commitment and identification among followers (Sharma et al., 2019).

3.5 Thriving at Work (THW)

THW is a holistic concept that encompasses personal and professional growth, essential for achieving long-term career satisfaction and success.Thriving can serve as a motivating factor for employees, as it inspires them to develop their knowledge and skills continuously. This continuous learning can promote positive well-being, as employees who excel in work often report improved intellectual and physical health (Qaiser et al., 2020). Further, (Shahid et al., 2020) study indicated that when individuals are THW, it results in various benefits. These include performing tasks effectively, feeling content with their job, exhibiting citizenship behavior, experiencing subjective well-being, demonstrating creativity, and taking initiatives for career development.Thriving employees perform better, are more committed, and have higher motivation, resulting in reduced absenteeism and improved well-being (Moloney et al., 2020). Thriving and flourishing are positive states of mind that can enhance an individual's engagement and involvement in their work (Imran et al., 2020).

4.0 OUTCOMES OF HAPPINESS AT WORK

4.1 Organizational Citizenship Behavior (OCB)

OCB refers to discretionary actions that an individual takes in the workplace which go beyond their formal job responsibilities and are aimed at improving organizational performance (Organ, 1988). Examples of OCB include helping colleagues with their work, participating in extra-curricular activities, and volunteering for tasks that are not part of one's job description. Organizations are recognizing the significance of employees' proactive and voluntary actions and attitudes to enhance corporate profitability, increase job efficacy, and maintain a competitive edge in the market. OCB serves as a catalyst for continued performance improvement within the organization (Yu et al., 2021).Happiness or positive mental states are essential for employees to engage in OCB. Individuals with a positive affect, such as feeling happy or contented, are more likely to engage in OCB than those with a negative affect, such as feeling anxious or unhappy. Mousa et al. (2020)investigated the extent to which a positive emotional state or happiness in the workplace could lead to increased voluntary contributions to the organization's overall success. This study suggests that happy employees are more inclined to display OCB within their workplace.The study by Singh & Banerji (2022) revealed that happiness at work is a critical element in driving extra-role behavior or OCB among banking employees in India. The findings suggest that promoting happiness in the workplace can significantly impact an employee's willingness to take on additional responsibilities and actively participate in the bank's success. This highlights the importance of creating strategies that promote happiness and a sense of belonging among employees to encourage them to go beyond their assigned roles.

4.2 Work Engagement

(Fisher, 2010) the study argued that happy employees are more likely to feel valued, supported, and motivated by their work environment, which can lead to greater engagement and commitment to their job and the organization. Additionally, happy employees may experience less stress and burnout, allowing them to focus their energy and attention on their work and perform at a higher level.Employees are more likely to interact with co-workers and form enduring social bonds when they are happy and satisfied. Furthermore, positive emotions can also help employees find flow in their work, which refers to a state of deep concentration and immersion in tasks, where individuals experience a sense of accomplishment and fulfillment (Thompson & Bruk-Lee, 2021). This state is similar to the concept of work engagement, which involves feeling fully absorbed and invested in one's work, resulting in improved task performance. Therefore, cultivating happiness in the workplace can lead to a range of positive outcomes, including increased social bonds, meaningful work experiences, and greater work engagement (S. Singh et al., 2018).Similarly, Tesi et al. (2019) study looked into the interactions between work engagement, psychological well-being, and job demands. The findings showed that work engagement was positively linked to psychological well-being. Additionally, moderation analyses revealed that the positive relationship between job demands and work engagement was strengthened when social workers had high levels of psychological well-being, indicating a protective effect of psychological well-being against the negative impact of job demands on work engagement.

4.3 Job Satisfaction

Several studies have shown that happier employees are satisfied with their jobs more than the their unhappy counterparts. For instance, a study conducted by the University of Warwick demonstrated that employees who are content and joyful are 12% more productive than those who are not, highlighting a robust association between happiness and job satisfaction (Oswald et al., 2015). Lyubomirsky et al. (2005) outlined that happiness leads to job satisfaction and happy individuals are more likely to experience higher levels of job satisfaction.(Salas-Vallina et al., 2018) also observed that employees who experience higher levels of happiness at work report higher levels of job satisfaction. This suggests that happiness can be an important precursor of job satisfaction.

4.4 Turnover Intention

High employee turnover can have a considerable financial impact on organizations, as it can lead to increased costs for hiring, recruiting, and training new employees, as well as decreased productivity and lower morale among remaining employees (Choi & Dickson, 2010). Research suggests that a positive work environment that fosters employee happiness can significantly reduce the likelihood of employee turnover. Employees those are contented and satisfied with their roles are more likely to be committed to the organization and less likely to seek employment elsewhere. Therefore, organizations that focus on employees' well-being or happiness and create a supportive workplace culture can expect to see a more stable and loyal workforce with reduced turnover rates. (Romão et al., 2022) investigated how engagement affected burnout & turnover intention among workers employed in manufacturing companies and explored the moderating role of happiness in this relationship. The results indicated that employees who are not engaged in their work are more susceptible to experience burnout and have the intention to leave the organization.Happiness is identified as a significant moderating factor in the relationship. The presence of happiness in the workplace has been found to reduce employees' intentions to leave their current organization, thus indicating the positive impact of happiness on employee retention.

4.5 Stress, Absenteeism, and Counterproductive Work Behavior

Job stress is the tension and pressure experienced by employees due to the demands and expectations of their job. Stress can harm employee well-being, job satisfaction, and performance, which in turn can harm the organization's overall health. The study conducted by Akgunduz et al. (2022) suggests that job stress and happiness have an inverse relationship, meaning that happiness decreases as job stress increases. The study's findings indicate that job stress causes various physical, emotional, and psychological strains on employees, reducing happiness levels. This reduction in happiness can lead to a decrease in job satisfaction and performance, which can eventually affect the overall well-being and productivity of the organization. Lyubomirsky et al.(2005) also revealed that individuals who experience positive emotions like happiness have better-coping abilities and manage stressful situations effectively.Although work-related stress can increase employee absenteeism, research suggests that happy employees are less likely to experience stress-related illnesses and take fewer sick days.Shi et al.(2013) study suggested that when employees experience a higher level of well-being, which encompasses better mental and physical health, they are more likely to attend work regularly, resulting in reduced absenteeism. Previous research findings also establish a negative relationship between employees' well-being and absenteeism (Medina-Garrido et al., 2020; Montani et al., 2020; Soane et al., 2013).

"Counterproductive work behaviour (CWB) is behavior intended to hurt the organization or other members of the organization. This includes acts with the potential for harm, such as avoiding work, doing tasks incorrectly, physical aggression, verbal hostility (insults), sabotage, and theft"(Spector & Fox, 2002). A recent study conducted by (Choi et al., 2023) aims to explore the mediating role of affective well-being in the association between relationship conflict and CWB, as well as the moderating effect of emotional intelligence. The study results showed that affective well-being acts as a mediator between relationship conflict and counterproductive work behavior. Furthermore, the mediating effect was found to be significant at a high level of emotional intelligence. Based on the study's findings, organizations can lower the chances of CWB by enhancing the well-being of their workforce.

5.0 IMPLICATIONS

On the basis of comprehensive review of the literature on happiness in the workplace, it is suggested that organizations should encourage mindfulness practices such as meditation, deep breathing, yoga, etc., to help employees reduce stress and increase concentration on their work. Mindfulness practices can also improve emotional intelligence and enhance self-awareness, leading to better decision-making and improved colleague relationships. Next, an ethical leadership style should be promoted in the workplace. Leaders who demonstrate ethical leadership by modeling honesty, integrity, and accountability can foster a culture of trust and fairness. Employees who feel they are being treated with respect and dignity are more likely to feel satisfied and happy in their work.

Furthermore,creating a workplace that acknowledges the spiritual dimension of employees' lives can contribute to a sense of purpose and meaning at work. Managers who provide opportunities for employees to express their values, beliefs, and ethics can create a sense of community and connectedness. Despite this, investing in employee development through training and coaching can help build their psychological capital. Last but not least, managers can foster thriving at work by providing opportunities for learning & growth, recognition, feedback, autonomy, and flexibility.

6.0 CONCLUSION

Studying antecedents and outcomes of happiness at work has become increasingly relevant in today's dynamic and competitive workplace. Various research has shown that creating a work environment that promotes happiness at work can lead to a range of benefits for both employees and organizations. Employees who are happy at work tend to be more efficient, committed, and dedicated to their job. This can translate into improved productivity, higher quality work, and better customer service, all of which can contribute to the organization's sustainable growth. Moreover, contented employees typically enjoy better physical & mental health;exhibit reduced absenteeism, and are less prone to engage in behaviors that impede the progress and productivity of organizations. This can lead to a more positive work culture, with higher levels of employee engagement, satisfaction, and motivation. Research has also shown that happy employees are more likely to stay with their organization, reducing employee turnover rate and associated costs. This benefits the organization by reducing recruitment and training costs and contributes to the employee's career development and overall life satisfaction.

REFERENCES

Akgunduz, Y., Bardakoglu, O., & Kizilcalioglu, G. (2022). Happiness, job stress, job dedication and perceived organizational support: A mediating model. *Journal of Hospitality and Tourism Insights*. doi:10.1108/JHTI-07-2021-0189

Ashar, H., & Lane-Maher, M. (2004). Success and spirituality in the new business paradigm. *Journal of Management Inquiry*, *13*(3), 249–260. doi:10.1177/1056492604268218

Bani-Melhem, S., Al-Hawari, M. A., & Quratulain, S. (2020). Leader-member exchange and frontline employees' innovative behaviors: The roles of employee happiness and service climate. *International Journal of Productivity and Performance Management*, *71*(2), 540–557. doi:10.1108/IJPPM-03-2020-0092

Choi, Y., & Dickson, D. R. (2010). A case study into the benefits of management training programs: Impacts on hotel employee turnover and satisfaction level. *Journal of Human Resources in Hospitality & Tourism*, *9*(1), 103–116. doi:10.1080/15332840903336499

Choi, Y., Yoon, D. J., Lee, J. D., & Lee, J. Y. E. (2023). Relationship confict and counterproductive work behavior: The roles of affective well-being and emotional intelligence. *Review of Managerial Science*, 1–20. doi:10.100711846-023-00642-z

Deci, E. L., & Ryan, R. M. (2008). Self-determination theory: A macrotheory of human motivation, development, and health. *Canadian Psychology*, *49*(3), 182–185. doi:10.1037/a0012801

DiMaria, C. H., Peroni, C., & Sarracino, F. (2020). Happiness matters: Productivity gains from subjective well-being. *Journal of Happiness Studies*, *21*(1), 139–160. doi:10.100710902-019-00074-1

Donaldson, S. I., Donaldson, S. I., Chan, L., & Kang, K. W. (2022). Positive psychological capital (PsyCap) meets multitrait-multimethod Analysis: Is PsyCap a robust predictor of well-being and performance controlling for self-report bias? *International Journal of Applied Positive Psychology*, *7*(2), 191–205. doi:10.100741042-021-00060-0

Fisher, C. D. (2010). Happiness at Work. *International Journal of Management Reviews*, *12*(4), 384–412. doi:10.1111/j.1468-2370.2009.00270.x

Fredrickson, B. L. (2001). The role of positive emotions in positive psychology: The broaden-and- build theory of positive emotions. *The American Psychologist*, *56*(3), 218–226. doi:10.1037/0003-066X.56.3.218 PMID:11315248

Gagne, M., & Deci, E. L. (2005). Self-determination theory and work motivation. *Journal of Organizational Behavior*, *26*(4), 331–362. doi:10.1002/job.322

Good, D. J., Lyddy, C. J., Glomb, T. M., Bono, J. E., Brown, K. W., Duffy, M. K., Baer, R. A., Brewer, J. A., & Lazar, S. W. (2016). Contemplating mindfulness at work: An integrative review. *Journal of Management, 42*(1), 114–142. doi:10.1177/0149206315617003

Hassan, S., Ansari, N., & Rehman, A. (2022). An exploratory study of workplace spirituality and employee well-being affecting public service motivation: An institutional perspective. *Qualitative Research Journal, 22*(2), 209–235. doi:10.1108/QRJ-07-2021-0078

Hülsheger, U. R., Feinholdt, A., & Nübold, A. (2015). A low-dose mindfulness intervention and recovery from work: Effects on psychological detachment, sleep quality, and sleep duration. *Journal of Occupational and Organizational Psychology, 88*(3), 464–489. doi:10.1111/joop.12115

Imran, M. Y., Elahi, N. S., Abid, G., Ashfaq, F., & Ilyas, S. (2020). Impact of perceived organizational support on work engagement: Mediating mechanism of thriving and flourishing. *Journal of Open Innovation, 6*(3), 82. Advance online publication. doi:10.3390/joitmc6030082

Jia, K., Zhu, T., Zhang, W., Rasool, S. F., Asghar, A., & Chin, T. (2022). The linkage between ethical leadership, well-Being, work engagement, and innovative work behavior: The empirical evidence from the higher education sector of China. *International Journal of Environmental Research and Public Health, 19*(9), 1–15. doi:10.3390/ijerph19095414 PMID:35564809

Kabat-Zinn, J. (2003). Mindfulness-based interventions in context: Past, present, and future. *Clinical Psychology: Science and Practice, 10*(2), 144–156. doi:10.1093/clipsy.bpg016

Klussman, K., Nichols, A. L., Langer, J., Curtin, N., & Lindeman, M. I. H. (2022). The relationship between mindfulness and subjective well-being: Examining the indirect effects of self-connection and meaning in life. *Applied Research in Quality of Life, 17*(4), 2423–2443. doi:10.100711482-021-10025-9

Li, Y. (2018). Building well-being among university teachers: The roles of psychological capital and meaning in life. *European Journal of Work and Organizational Psychology, 27*(5), 594–602. doi:10.1080/1359432X.2018.1496909

Llyas, S., Abid, G., & Ashfaq, F. (2022). Enhancing the perceived organizational support, perceived ethical philanthropic CSR and subjective well-being : The role of ethical leadership. *International Journal of Ethics and Systems.*

Lyubomirsky, S., King, L., & Diener, E. (2005). The benefits of frequent positive affect: Does happiness lead to success? *Psychological Bulletin, 131*(6), 803–855. doi:10.1037/0033-2909.131.6.803 PMID:16351326

Mahipalan, M., & S, S. (2019). Workplace spirituality and subjective happiness among high school teachers: Gratitude as a moderator. *Explore (New York, N.Y.), 15*(2), 107–114. doi:10.1016/j.explore.2018.07.002 PMID:30150147

Medina-Garrido, J. A., Biedma-Ferrer, J. M., & Sánchez-Ortiz, J. (2020). I can ' t go to work tomorrow! Work-family policies, well-being and absenteeism. *Sustainability (Basel), 12*(14), 5519. Advance online publication. doi:10.3390u12145519

Moloney, W., Fieldes, J., & Jacobs, S. (2020). An integrative review of how healthcare organizations can support hospital nurses to thrive at work. *International Journal of Environmental Research and Public Health, 17*(23), 1–21. doi:10.3390/ijerph17238757 PMID:33255725

Montani, F., Leon-Perez, J. M., Giorgi, G., & Shoss, M. K. (2020). Appraisal of economic crisis, psychological distress, and work-unit absenteeism: A 1-1-2 model. *Journal of Business and Psychology, 35*(5), 609–620. doi:10.100710869-019-09643-w

Mousa, M., Massoud, H. K., & Ayoubi, R. M. (2020). Gender, diversity management perceptions, workplace happiness and organisational citizenship behaviour. *Employee Relations, 42*(6), 1249–1269. doi:10.1108/ER-10-2019-0385

Organ, D. W. (1988). *Organizational citizenship behavior: The good soldier syndrome.* APA.

Oswald, A. J., Proto, E., & Sgroi, D. (2015). Happiness and Productivity. *Journal of Labor Economics, 33*(4), 789–822. doi:10.1086/681096

Qaiser, S., Abid, G., Arya, B., & Farooqi, S. (2020). Nourishing the bliss: Antecedents and mechanism of happiness at work. *Total Quality Management & Business Excellence, 31*(15–16), 1669–1683. doi: 10.1080/14783363.2018.1493919

Rabenu, E., Yaniv, E., & Elizur, D. (2017). The relationship between psychological capital, coping with Stress, well-being, and performance. *Current Psychology (New Brunswick, N.J.), 36*(4), 875–887. doi:10.100712144-016-9477-4

Romão, S., Ribeiro, N., Gomes, D. R., & Singh, S. (2022). The impact of leaders' coaching skills on employees' happiness and turnover intention. *Administrative Sciences, 12*(3), 84. Advance online publication. doi:10.3390/admsci12030084

Ryan, R. M., Bernstein, J. H., & Brown, K. W. (2010). Weekends, work, and well-being: Psychological need satisfactions and day of the week effects on mood, vitality, and physical symptoms. *Journal of Social and Clinical Psychology, 29*(1), 95–122. doi:10.1521/jscp.2010.29.1.95

Salas-Vallina, A., Alegre, J., & Fernández Guerrero, R. (2018). Happiness at work in knowledge-intensive contexts: Opening the research agenda. *European Research on Management and Business Economics, 24*(3), 149–159. doi:10.1016/j.iedeen.2018.05.003

Santhanam, N., & Srinivas, S. (2020). Modeling the impact of employee engagement and happiness on burnout and turnover intention among blue-collar workers at a manufacturing company. *Benchmarking, 27*(2), 499–516. doi:10.1108/BIJ-01-2019-0007

Shahid, S., Muchiri, M. K., & Walumbwa, F. O. (2020). Mapping the antecedents and consequences of thriving at work: A review and proposed research agenda. *The International Journal of Organizational Analysis, 29*(1), 78–103. doi:10.1108/IJOA-09-2019-1881

Sharma, A., Agrawal, R., & Khandelwal, U. (2019). Developing ethical leadership for business organizations: A conceptual model of its antecedents and consequences. *Leadership and Organization Development Journal, 40*(6), 712–734. doi:10.1108/LODJ-10-2018-0367

Shi, Y., Sears, L. E., Coberley, C. R., & Pope, J. E. (2013). The association between modifiable well-being risks and productivity: A longitudinal study in pooled employer sample. *Journal of Occupational and Environmental Medicine*, *55*(4), 353–364. doi:10.1097/JOM.0b013e3182851923 PMID:23567993

Singh, A., & Banerji, R. (2022). Happiness at work, organization citizenship behaviour and workplace diversity: A study on Indian private sector bank employees. *Industrial and Commercial Training*, *54*(3), 460–475. doi:10.1108/ICT-05-2021-0037

Singh, S., David, R., & Mikkilineni, S. (2018). Organizational virtuousness and work engagement: Mediating role of happiness in India. *Advances in Developing Human Resources*, *20*(1), 88–102. doi:10.1177/1523422317741885

Soane, E., Shantz, A., Alfes, K., Truss, C., Rees, C., & Gatenby, M. (2013). The association of meaningfulness, well-being and engagement with absenteeism: A moderated mediation model. *Human Resource Management*, *52*(3), 441–456. doi:10.1002/hrm.21534

Spector, P. E., & Fox, S. (2002). An emotion-centered model of voluntary work behavior:Some parallels between counterproductive work behavior and organizational citizenship behavior. *Human Resource Management Review*, *12*(2), 263–292. doi:10.1016/S1053-4822(02)00049-9

Srivastava, S., & Gupta, P. (2022). Workplace spirituality as panacea for waning well-being during the pandemic crisis: A SDT perspective. *Journal of Hospitality and Tourism Management*, *50*, 375–388. doi:10.1016/j.jhtm.2021.11.014

Sulosaari, V., Unal, E., & Cinar, F. I. (2022). The effectiveness of mindfulness-based interventions on the psychological well-being of nurses: A systematic review. *Applied Nursing Research*, *64*, 151565. doi:10.1016/j.apnr.2022.151565 PMID:35307128

Tesi, A., Aiello, A., & Giannetti, E. (2019). The work-related well-being of social workers: Framing job demands, psychological well-being, and work engagement. *Journal of Social Work*, *19*(1), 121–141. doi:10.1177/1468017318757397

Thompson, A., & Bruk-Lee, V. (2021). Employee happiness: Why we should care. *Applied Research in Quality of Life*, *16*(4), 1419–1437. doi:10.100711482-019-09807-z

Van Den Broeck, A., Vansteenkiste, M., De Witte, H., & Lens, W. (2008). Explaining the relationships between job characteristics, burnout, and engagement: The role of basic psychological need satisfaction. *Work and Stress*, *22*(3), 277–294. doi:10.1080/02678370802393672

Yu, J., Park, J., & Hyun, S. S. (2021). Impacts of the COVID-19 pandemic on employees' work stress, well-being, mental health, organizational citizenship behavior, and employee-customer identification. *Journal of Hospitality Marketing & Management*, *30*(5), 529–548. doi:10.1080/19368623.2021.1867283

Chapter 11
Employee Attrition and Absenteeism Analysis Using Machine Learning Methods:
Application in the Manufacturing Industry

A. Mansurali
https://orcid.org/0000-0002-4326-8360
Central University of Tamil Nadu, India

Manikandan Rajagopal
https://orcid.org/0000-0001-7915-0180
CHRIST University (Deemed), India

Rajan Subbaiah
Jazan University, India

ABSTRACT

HR analytics has been envisaged as recent research trend for providing a comprehensive decision support system to the top level management in terms of employee's performance, recruitment and behaviour analysis. Globally, organizations are using technology to support and ease HR processes. Every organization should give maximum value to every available human resource, and they should minimize the attrition and absenteeism rate and ensure what are the factors that contribute towards employee attrition as well as the causes for workmen absenteeism. The ultimate objective is to correctly identify attrition and absenteeism in order to assist the company to improve retention tactics for key personnel and increase employee satisfaction. Through this chapter, a machine learning-based model is proposed to get quick results for such employee attrition and workmen absenteeism. The model is trained and tested for its accuracy. The result shows that the proposed model has high sensitivity. The managerial implications are also discussed for taking informed decisions.

DOI: 10.4018/978-1-6684-8942-0.ch011

1. INTRODUCTION

Absenteeism within the workplace is a prevalent problem, that causes problems for business and costs money. Absenteeism can be broadly described as the inability to run the scheduled work as per the result of bad health or other circumstances. It has been estimated that the annual cost of worker absenteeism in the countries that are members of the Organization for Economic Co-operation and Development (OECD) is between 1.2 and 2% of their total GDP, which in terms of current values translates to between 0.6 and 1 trillion dollars in the United States. Therefore, it is completely reasonable to expect employers to look for answers to this issue. The request made by a company located in Kottayam, Kerala, that specialises in the production of tyres for automobiles, for developing solutions to manage work men absenteeism using data science served as the impetus for this body of work. The realisation that as much as twenty percent of the nation's population of working age suffers from specfic illnesses such as depression disorders and anxiety and that the timely application of preventative measures is essential in order to avoid transitioning into a state of long-term illness and disability led as a pathway for finding a possible solution to the problem.

Absenteeism can be caused by a wide variety of other elements, including physical distance from the place of residence, the availability of leave policies, the presence of personal issues, the degree to which one is satisfied with their salary, the presence of other sources of income, and so on. Bringing a tool that can monitor and predict worker absenteeism can help the organization to reduce lags in manufacturing. The objective of this study is to develop a model that predicts whether a worker will be taking leaves. The ultimate goal of this machine learning-based model is to accurately detect absenteeism to help the company to minimize quiet quitting and the factors leading to absenteeism.. A massive amount of employee-related information is kept up to date, which is useful for anticipating future.

1.1 Problem

One of the most critical problems that companies face nowadays is employee turnover. Employees are organization's most precious assets. They contribute to the organization's worth in terms of both number and quality. As employees are the intangible assets of an organization. The growth and downfall of an organization is dependent on the performance of its employees. When lost productivity, and temporary labour costs are factored in, the high cost of absenteeism has a greater impact on organizations. Furthermore, employers frequently fail to carefully track absenteeism rates and patterns which vary significantly across various departments. Currently, manufacturing firms face an issue of worker absenteeism and it has been conducted on white-collar employees in manufacturing firms traditionally. But blue–collar employees' absenteeism impact the production which ultimately leads to bottlenecks and increases the lead time. As a result, the easiest solution, which is to implement them for all employees at a given business, is not necessarily the one that results in the lowest total cost. Instead, it is necessary to design a decision support system that is capable of identifying the workers who are at risk of absence, which is typically only a small portion of the workforce. These workers should then be targeted with a preventive action in order to reduce the likelihood of an absence occurring.

1.2 Proposed Solution

A random forest is a collection of predictor trees constructed so that the predictions of any given tree in the forest are contingent on the values of a random vector drawn at random from the trees in the forest but following the same distribution in each case. The generalization error tends to decrease monotonically as the number of trees in forest increases, until it reaches a maximum. The error in a forest of tree classifiers' ability to generalize is proportional to the robustness of the individual trees with-in the forest and the correlations between them. The capacity of a model to properly predict the true labels is represented by its sensitivity, which is often referred to as recall. Sensitivity is essentially the same thing as the true positive rate of a model. For instance, the capacity to accurately forecast the Hours, Days, and Weeks classes contained within our dataset. For the purpose of determining the sensitivity score, the following equation has been utilized.

$$\text{Sensitivity} = \text{TP}/(\text{TP}+\text{FN}) \quad (1)$$

The accuracy score of a model represents how much more accurate the model is over-all and serves as a predictor of that accuracy. The model that has a greater accuracy score is the more successful one. It is the final statistic that will be used to select the best classifier as the one that will deliver the most number of accurate predictions in our experiment.

In order to determine the precision, we need to take into consideration the follow-ing equation

$$\text{Accuracy} = (\text{TP}/\text{TN})/(\text{TP}+\text{TN}+\text{FP}+\text{FN}) \quad (2)$$

2. LITERATURE REVIEW

Ferreira et al (2022) have devised a forecasting system employing an artificial neural network (ANN) to anticipate employee absenteeism at the workplace. The dataset utilized in this study consists of 2,243 data records encompassing thirty-eight distinct characteristics, gathered between 2008 and 2016. To streamline the model, they applied Rough Sets to reduce the features to a set of seventeen attributes. The results obtained from their approach proved to be highly satisfactory (Akgeyik, 2014).

Another study conducted by Harshit Trivedi et al (2022) aimed to predict workplace absenteeism using an ANN approach. Trivedi employed a feed-forward network design trained with the backpropagation algorithm. The dataset utilized in this study originated from a courier company and spanned the years 2007 to 2010. Additionally, he incorporated a rule-based filter to detect underperforming neurons, thereby enhancing the network's accuracy, which reached an impressive 58%. Studies on employee behaviour, including withdrawal behaviour, have been reviewed in three studies conducted by Brayfield & Crockett (1955), Herzberg (1957), and Vroom (1964). Porter and Steers (1973) conducted a more recent analysis that focused solely on absenteeism and turnover rates in the workforce. The study concluded that a significant amount of attention has been given to absenteeism compared to turnover and primarily looked at the correlations between withdrawal behaviour and other variables. Schuh (1967) provided a comprehensive examination of the factors that could be used to predict employee turnover.

Jensen (2006) differentiated between three types of absenteeism at the workplace, namely optimum, voluntary, and obligatory, and attempted to reduce absenteeism in the workplace by finding a suitable model. Zia-ud-Din (2017) examined the effects of absenteeism at the workplace and the significant variables within healthcare organizations. Naik (2016) used a liver patent data set from India and applied various classification techniques, including DecisionTree, Naive Bayes, and K-Nearest Neighbour, and K Means to determine the effective accuracy and error rate of the algorithms. Halbesleben (2014) argued that absenteeism and presenteeism are both a result of an individual's choice and reflect the decision between working and not working. Vardhan developed a model that enables people to work on various clustering techniques such as K-Means, Affinity Propagation, Hierarchical Clustering, and DBSCAN, to measure absenteeism at the workplace. Perveen (2016) applied various classification algorithms to a data set of diabetic patients to predict diabetes. Evans-Lacko (2016) investigated the decline in workplace productivity in various countries and provided information on the annual mean value for absenteeism and the maximum and minimum values for Southern India and Japan. Kocakulah (2016) discussed the issues, causes, and consequences of absenteeism. Vignoli (2015) brought attention to the role of spiritual elevation in absenteeism and evaluated the job request and the context of higher levels of absenteeism. Xu, D & Tian, Y. (2015) Data analysis is widely used in modern scientific research, with clustering being a significant component. Many tools for cluster analysis have been developed in response to the increasing amount of information and the interdisciplinary nature of the subject. However, each clustering algorithm has its own strengths and weaknesses due to the complexity of information. This literature review defines clustering and examines traditional and modern clustering algorithms, considering factors such as distance or similarity measurement and evaluation indicators. Gagolewski, Bartoszuk, and Cena (2016) The time required to apply a hierarchical clustering algorithm is often limited by the number of computations of a pairwise dissimilarity measure, making it difficult to use classical linkage criteria for larger data sets. The single linkage clustering algorithm is sensitive to outliers and does not reflect the true data structure. The proposed Genie algorithm solves these limitations by linking clusters in such a way that a chosen economic inequity measure does not increase significantly above a threshold, resulting in improved clustering quality compared to Ward or average linkage while retaining the speed of a single linkage. Pichler & Ziebarth (2017) This paper presents an analytical framework and empirical evidence of contagious presenteeism and negative externalities in sick leave insurance. Using data from the U.S. and Germany, the paper uses a reduced-form framework to show that population-level influenza-like disease rates decrease after employees gain access to paid sick leave. A theoretical framework is provided to decompose overall labor supply adjustments into contagious presenteeism and noncontagious absenteeism behavior. The empirical test using a German sick pay reform and administrative industry-level data finds that the labor supply elasticity for contagious diseases is significantly smaller than for noncontagious diseases, providing indirect evidence for the existence of contagious presenteeism.

3. METHODOLOGY AND DATA

3.1 Methodology

The process of data mining, also known as knowledge discovery, is extremely important for estimating data from a variety of sources and perspectives in order to con-solidate it into information that is of use. It is helpful in producing accurate solutions based on the results that are perceived. Absenteeism is the repeated nonattendance of a worker at their place of employment. Using classification algorithms, the purpose of this research is to identify the relevant characteristics that, when present, will result in absenteeism at the place of employment. Worker Absenteeism has significant impact not only on the organisation but also on its moral, financial, and other difficulties. It can be attributed to a wide range of factors, including health concerns, pressure related to the job, harassment, illness, and a great number of others. Loss of cost productivity is another consequence of this issue. In the system that is now in place, we have used random forest algorithms to analyse a dataset consisting of absenteeism from the job in the tyre manufacturing industry.

The data on workmen absenteeism consists of 22 columns and 101 rows including category and numeric variables, including the desired variable duration of absence.

CRISP DM Framework was used for the data mining process - There are a total of six stages involved

- Business understanding: This phase mainly focuses on understanding the objectives and requirements of the study and includes determining the business objectives, assessing the situation, determining the data mining goals and producing the project plan.
- Data understanding: This phase drives the focus to identify, collect, and analyze the data sets that can help accomplish the project goals. It includes collecting the data, describing the data, exploring the data and verifying data quality
- Data preparation: This phase aims at selecting the data, cleaning data, constructing and integrating data and also format data in the required format (if necessary).
- Modelling: This phase comprises of selecting the modelling techniques, generating the test design, building the model and assessing the model. In this stage, the dataset is split into training, testing and validation data
- Evaluation: This phase focuses at determining which model best meets the business requirements. The results of the models are evaluated and are reviewed to determine the next steps of action
- Deployment: This phase comprises of planning the deployment, planning the monitoring and maintenance, and reviewing the project

The machine learning models was constructed in the Jupyter notebook were put through their paces with test data, and the findings revealed that the model is producing positive outcomes.

3.2 Data and Methods

The data set contains 101 shop floor workers data from the tyre manufacturing plant in Kottayam. 21 features were extracted from the shop floor employees at the plant and significant features were filtered out by feature selection. These features were then used for making prediction models using Random Forest (RF) algorithms. The model was then tuned to provide better results with higher accuracy by changing various parameters in each model. The comparison between accuracy and other performance parameters of various machine learning models are carried out to come out with the best performing model. The machine learning model build will predict the chances of employee to leave the company and also it will predict the chances of workmen to take leave. The comparative analysis of different classifier's accuracy will help assess and summarize the overall predictive ability of ML algorithms in employee attrition and absenteeism.

4. PROPOSED FRAMEWORK

In this study, a random forest classification was utilized to identify the absenteeism factor that was considered to be the most significant. The system that has been pro-posed has a total of six stages, which are as follows: identifying the problem, gathering the data, performing the pre-processing steps, putting the classification algorithm into action, and analysing the results.

Figure 1. Architecture of the proposed method

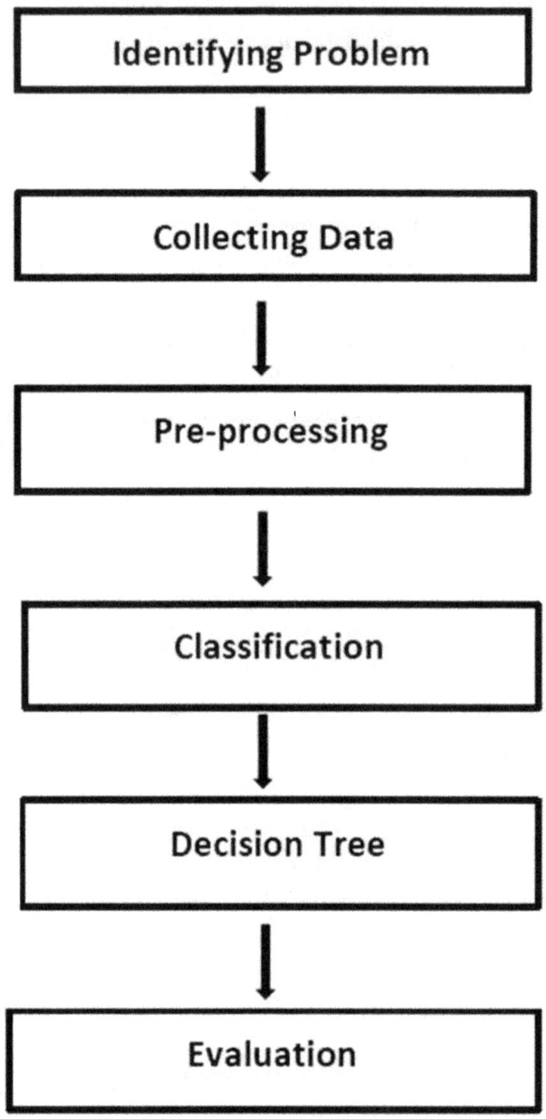

4.1 Data Description

Figure 2. Data set snapshot

```
Data columns (total 22 columns):
 #   Column                                           Non-Null Count  Dtype
---  ------                                           --------------  -----
 0   Employee ID                                      101 non-null    int64
 1   Age                                              101 non-null    int64
 2   Marital Status                                   101 non-null    int64
 3   Department                                       101 non-null    int64
 4   No. of Leaves                                    101 non-null    int64
 5   Distance from place of stay                      101 non-null    int64
 6   Experience                                       101 non-null    int64
 7   Other Source of Income                           101 non-null    int64
 8   Awareness of the leave facilities and leave rules 101 non-null   int64
 9   Leave Facilities                                 101 non-null    int64
 10  Reasons for Absenteeism                          101 non-null    int64
 11  Nature of  Job                                   101 non-null    int64
 12  Personal Problems for Absenteeism                101 non-null    int64
 13  Satisfaction on Wages                            101 non-null    int64
 14  Rewards based on performance                     101 non-null    int64
 15  Awareness on Schemes to Reduce Absenteeism       101 non-null    int64
 16  Ratings on Schemes Introduced                    101 non-null    int64
 17  Relationship with Superiors                      101 non-null    int64
 18  Satisfaction on Relationship with Co-Workers     101 non-null    int64
 19  Satisfaction on Rest Intervals                   101 non-null    int64
 20  Measure to Reduce Absenteeism                    101 non-null    int64
 21  Service Time                                     101 non-null    int64
dtypes: int64(22)
```

4.2 Analysis

Exploratory data analysis was performed on the workmen absenteeism data that was being considered for the profiling of absence through random forest algorithms. The goal of this journey was to gain a solid understanding of the data as well as validate it further for further transformation and pre-processing. The dataset has 101 rows, which stand for the total number of observations, and 22 dimensions, which are all of the variables that will be included in the study.

The analysis implicate that Most of the leaves are taken from the age group 41 to 42 followed by 48 to 50 and 36 as shown in Figure 3

It is seen that most of the leaves are taken by worker who stay nearby to the company, followed by workers who stay more than 12 km away from the company as it is seen in Figure 4

Figure 3. No. of leaves of workmen with respect to age

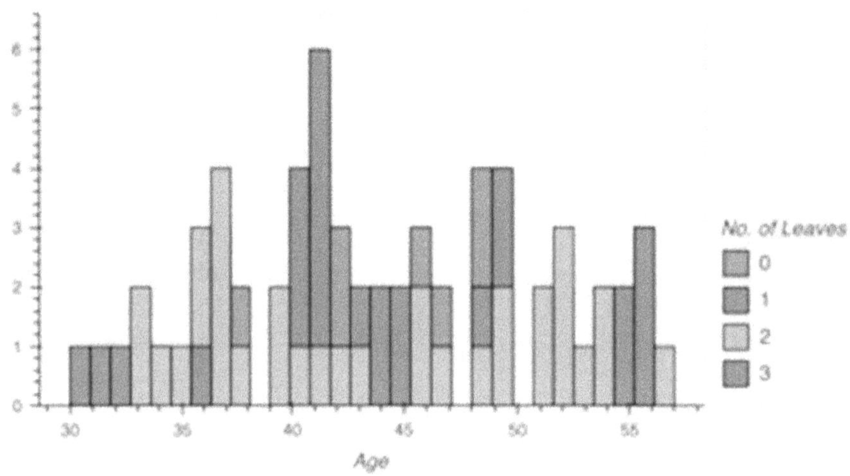

Figure 4. No. of leaves of workmen with respect to distance from place of stay

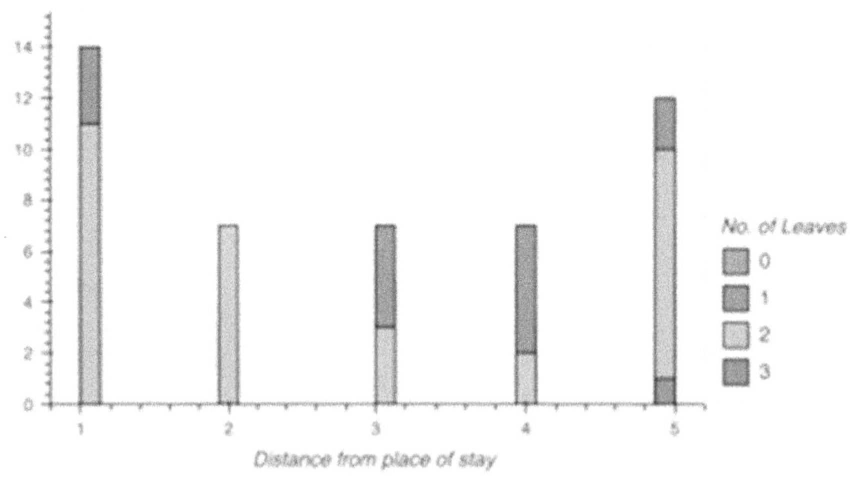

Figure 5 depict the result from the simulation of random forest of the test data. The evaluation is based on the parameters such as precision, recall, F1-score and support which are Key indicators for measuring accuracy. It is implicated that Random forest classifier has obtained 100% accuracy for the train data and 48% for the test data from figure 5.

4.3 Metrics

Precision is theoretically defined as the percentage of the total predicted relevant results/had been correctly classified, i.e., True Positive/ (True Positive + False Positive). This is also known as the sensitivity parameter of the model. The recall is interpreted as the percentage of actual results that the model has correctly classified, i.e., True Positive/ (True Positive + False Negative). F-1 score is a harmonic mean of precision and recall. It is used to identify the weighted mean of the classification model, with 1.0 being the best fit and 0.0 being the worst fit.Support is defined as the number of actual occurrences in the dataset. This value doesn't change between models but changes with the changes in test data. The confusion matrix is a performance measure of the classification model that calculates actual versus predicted data on a given dataset. The False Negative value of the confusion matrix is significant in the case of workmen absenteeism prediction. Table 1 describes the results of the Random Forest Classifier

It is observed from the Random Forest model we can see that it performs very well. However, it performs better in true positive. The Table 1 shows the results from the random forest classifier algorithms which reflects to objectives of the study

Figure 5. Machine learning model summary output

```
=========RANDOM FOREST============
Fitting 3 folds for each of 360 candidates, totalling 1080 fits
Best parameters: {'bootstrap': False, 'max_depth': 5, 'min_samples_leaf': 1, 'min_samples_split': 2, 'n_estimators': 500}
TRAINIG RESULTS:
===============================
CONFUSION MATRIX:
[[47  0]
 [ 3 20]]
ACCURACY SCORE:
0.9571
CLASSIFICATION REPORT:
                   0          1  accuracy  macro avg  weighted avg
precision   0.940000   1.000000  0.957143   0.970000      0.959714
recall      1.000000   0.869565  0.957143   0.934783      0.957143
f1-score    0.969072   0.930233  0.957143   0.949652      0.956311
support    47.000000  23.000000  0.957143  70.000000     70.000000
TESTING RESULTS:
===============================
CONFUSION MATRIX:
[[13  7]
 [ 9  2]]
ACCURACY SCORE:
0.4839
CLASSIFICATION REPORT:
                   0          1  accuracy  macro avg  weighted avg
precision   0.590909   0.222222  0.483871   0.406566      0.460085
recall      0.650000   0.181818  0.483871   0.415909      0.483871
f1-score    0.619048   0.200000  0.483871   0.409524      0.470353
support    20.000000  11.000000  0.483871  31.000000     31.000000
```

Table 1. Evaluation metric for random forest classifier

	Predicted 0	Predicted 1	Sensitivity	Accuracy
Actual 0	47	0	0.869	0.9571
Actual 1	3	20		

5. DISCUSSIONS MANAGERIAL IMPLICATIONS

Random forest analysis is a versatile and widely applicable tool that finds its usefulness across various domains, especially in situations where decision-makers must make choices from a pool of available alternatives. One such area where random forests prove invaluable is in the business landscape. By leveraging this powerful technique, companies can gain valuable insights to develop their operations and make informed investment decisions regarding new projects.

An essential application of random forest analysis in the context of business is the identification of potential workmen who may take leaves. Employee absenteeism can have significant implications for a company's productivity and operational efficiency. By employing a random forest approach, organizations can predict which workers are more likely to take leaves, allowing them to plan for contingencies and allocate resources efficiently. Another critical use of random forests is the identification of factors that significantly influence workmen absenteeism. Through the analysis of various attributes and their impact on absenteeism, businesses can gain a deeper understanding of the underlying reasons behind employee leaves. This knowledge empowers management to address specific issues and implement targeted strategies to reduce absenteeism and improve overall workforce performance. Moreover, random forest analysis plays a crucial role in streamlining workforce management. By accurately pinpointing potential workmen who frequently take unnecessary leaves, organizations can make informed decisions about retaining or replacing such employees. This process ensures that the workforce remains productive and committed to their roles, contributing positively to the company's bottom line.

Additionally, through the application of random forest analysis, businesses can attain a comprehensive understanding of the root causes of workmen absenteeism. By examining various contributing factors simultaneously, such as employee demographics, work environment, and job satisfaction levels, a clear picture emerges regarding the drivers behind absenteeism patterns. Armed with this knowledge, organizations can devise effective policies and initiatives to address these issues proactively. Hence, random forest analysis holds immense promise as a powerful tool in the realm of decision-making. In the business sphere, it provides valuable assistance in strategizing and charting a course for growth and development. By accurately identifying potential workmen who may take leaves, isolating influential factors impacting absenteeism, and optimizing workforce management, organizations can enhance productivity and create a more efficient and engaged workforce. With the ability to discern the underlying causes of workmen absenteeism, businesses can adopt targeted measures to foster a healthier work environment and ultimately achieve sustainable success. Embracing the potential of random forest analysis empowers businesses to make data-driven decisions and stay ahead in an increasingly competitive landscape.

6. METHODOLOGICAL LIMITATIONS

- A huge number of trees in random forest may cause the technique to become unusable for real-time prediction due to its excessive slowness.
- Random Forest have a propensity to quickly become crowded near the base. It's possible to make a terrible decision if you only have a few observations in the last node. In a scenario like this one, you might want to think about pruning your tree or cutting down on the amount of levels it has.
- Trees are susceptible to instability due to the fact that even minute changes in the dataset have great result in the generation of an entirely different tree.

- When it comes to classification, having some classes more prevalent than others might lead to the formation of biased trees. Therefore, prior to fitting, it is recommended to ensure that the dataset is balanced.

7. CONCLUSION

The rate of absenteeism at work is an important indicator of the overall health of the organization. Employers from all over the world are of the opinion that the absence of employees can have a significant impact on the company's finances, employee morale, and other aspects of the business. This is a widely held belief among employers. They do not hold those employees accountable who have a pattern of excessive absenteeism at work, which leads to a decrease in production and additional expenses for the organization. As a result, they have a pattern of excessive absenteeism at work. This study's objective is to gain a better understanding of the factors that contribute to absenteeism among workers by gathering relevant information. It is absolutely necessary for all different kinds of companies to implement cutting-edge technological solutions in order for them to be able to make educated decisions and progress in the cutthroat competition that exists in the market. One of the most important requirements in every industry is the ability to accurately forecast the absenteeism of workers. This can be achieved by developing projections that will assist a company in remaining an additional step ahead of its competitors in the industry. This can be done through the use of projections. It is possible that the company will decide to concentrate its efforts on the plans that are not gaining traction in the market and to formulate strategies in accordance with the conclusions that are drawn from this assessment. If this decision is made, then the company will formulate strategies in accordance with the findings. Higher absentee rates can be attributed to a wide variety of significant factors, including personal problems, the relationship with one's superiors, the distance from one's place of residence, the level of satisfaction with one's wage, the reasons for absenteeism, and other sources of money. Absenteeism may be caused, in part or in whole, by any or all of the aforementioned factors. The model that was developed can be implemented in organizations to assist with the prediction of absenteeism among their workforce.

REFERENCES

Akgeyik, T. (2014, October 1). Factors Affecting Employee Absenteeism (A Study on a Sample of Textile Workers). *European Journal of Management*, *14*(3), 69–76. doi:10.18374/EJM-14-3.7

Amit, Y., & Geman, D. (1997, October 1). Shape Quantization and Recognition with Randomized Trees. *Neural Computation*, *9*(7), 1545–1588. doi:10.1162/neco.1997.9.7.1545

Cucchiella, F., Gastaldi, M., & Ranieri, L. (2014, September). Managing Absenteeism in the Workplace: The Case of an Italian Multiutility Company. *Procedia: Social and Behavioral Sciences*, *150*, 1157–1166. doi:10.1016/j.sbspro.2014.09.131

Evans-Lacko, S., & Knapp, M. (2016, September 26). Global patterns of workplace productivity for people with depression: Absenteeism and presenteeism costs across eight diverse countries. *Social Psychiatry and Psychiatric Epidemiology*, *51*(11), 1525–1537. doi:10.100700127-016-1278-4 PMID:27667656

Halbesleben, J. R., Whitman, M. V., & Crawford, W. S. (2014, June). A dialectical theory of the decision to go to work: Bringing together absenteeism and presenteeism. *Human Resource Management Review, 24*(2), 177–192. doi:10.1016/j.hrmr.2013.09.001

Hartog, D. N., & Verburg, R. M. (2004, January). High performance work systems, organisational culture and firm effectiveness. *Human Resource Management Journal, 14*(1), 55–78. doi:10.1111/j.1748-8583.2004.tb00112.x

Jensen, S., & McIntosh, J. (2006, July 4). Absenteeism in the workplace: Results from Danish sample survey data. *Empirical Economics, 32*(1), 125–139. doi:10.100700181-006-0075-4

Jurado-Gámez, B., Guglielmi, O., Gude, F., & Buela-Casal, G. (2015, May). Workplace Accidents, Absenteeism and Productivity in Patients With Sleep Apnea. *Archivos de Bronconeumología (English Ed.), 51*(5), 213–218. doi:10.1016/j.arbr.2014.12.002 PMID:25129165

Kam, H.Tin Kam Ho. (1998). The random subspace method for constructing decision forests. *IEEE Transactions on Pattern Analysis and Machine Intelligence, 20*(8), 832–844. doi:10.1109/34.709601

Kamiński, B., Jakubczyk, M., & Szufel, P. (2017, May 24). A framework for sensitivity analysis of decision trees. *Central European Journal of Operations Research, 26*(1), 135–159. doi:10.100710100-017-0479-6 PMID:29375266

Kocakulah, M. C., Kelley, A. G., Mitchell, K. M., & Ruggieri, M. P. (2016, May 2). Absenteeism Problems And Costs: Causes, Effects And Cures. [IBER]. *The International Business & Economics Research Journal, 15*(3), 89–96. doi:10.19030/iber.v15i3.9673

Loerbroks, A., Weigl, M., Li, J., Glaser, J., Degen, C., & Angerer, P. (2015, February). Workplace bullying and depressive symptoms: A prospective study among junior physicians in Germany. *Journal of Psychosomatic Research, 78*(2), 168–172. doi:10.1016/j.jpsychores.2014.10.008 PMID:25454681

Mikami, D. J., Melvin, W. S., Murayama, M. J., & Murayama, K. M. (2017, March 31). Impact of minimally invasive surgery on healthcare utilization, cost, and workplace absenteeism in patients with Incisional/Ventral Hernia (IVH). *Surgical Endoscopy, 31*(11), 4412–4418. doi:10.100700464-017-5488-y PMID:28364155

Naik, A., & Samant, L. (2016). Correlation Review of Classification Algorithm Using Data Mining Tool: WEKA, Rapidminer, Tanagra, Orange and Knime. *Procedia Computer Science, 85*, 662–668. doi:10.1016/j.procs.2016.05.251

Nayak, J., Balas, V. E., Favorskaya, M. N., Choudhury, B. B., Rao, S. K. M., & Naik, B. (Eds.). (2020). *Applications of Robotics in Industry Using Advanced Mechanisms*. Learning and Analytics in Intelligent Systems., doi:10.1007/978-3-030-30271-9

Onoh, C., & Nwaogazie, I. (2016, January 10). Workplace Assessment of Hypertension: Prevalence and Awareness in a Food Processing Industry in Owerri Nigeria. *International Journal of Tropical Disease & Health, 16*(4), 1–11. doi:10.9734/IJTDH/2016/25873

Perveen, S., Shahbaz, M., Guergachi, A., & Keshavjee, K. (2016). Performance Analysis of Data Mining Classification Techniques to Predict Diabetes. *Procedia Computer Science*, *82*, 115–121. doi:10.1016/j.procs.2016.04.016

Pichler, S., & Ziebarth, N. R. (2017, December). The pros and cons of sick pay schemes: Testing for contagious presenteeism and noncontagious absenteeism behavior. *Journal of Public Economics*, *156*, 14–33. doi:10.1016/j.jpubeco.2017.07.003

Porter, L. W., & Steers, R. M. (1973). Organizational, work, and personal factors in employee turnover and absenteeism. *Psychological Bulletin*, *80*(2), 151–176. doi:10.1037/h0034829

Prasetya, F., Saifuddin, D. T., & Ansir, N. Y. (2020, April 25). https://www.ijser.org/research-paper-publishing-april-2020.aspx. *International Journal of Scientific and Engineering Research*, *11*(04), 1801–1806. https://www.ijser.org/research-paper-publishing-april-2020.aspx. doi:10.14299/ijser.2020.04.06

Priyanka, D., Nayak, J.: Empirical Analysis of Absenteeism at Work Place Using Machine Learning. Learning and Analytics in Intelligent Systems. 150–160 (2019). doi:10.1007/978-3-030-30271-9_15

Saidane, O., Mahmoud, I., Gafsi, L., Houda, A., Tekaya, R., & Abdelmoula, L. (2018, July). Factors leading to work absenteeism in Tunisian ankylosing spondylitis patients. *The Egyptian Rheumatologist*, *40*(3), 183–185. doi:10.1016/j.ejr.2017.06.009

Schuh, A. J. (1967). The Predictability of Employee Tenure: A Review Of The Literature. *Personnel Psychology*, *20*(2), 133–152. doi:10.1111/j.1744-6570.1967.tb02275.x

Singh, A., & Gupta, B. (2015, August 3). Job involvement, organizational commitment, professional commitment, and team commitment. *Benchmarking*, *22*(6), 1192–1211. doi:10.1108/BIJ-01-2014-0007

Verstappen, S. M. (2015, June). Rheumatoid arthritis and work: The impact of rheumatoid arthritis on absenteeism and presenteeism. *Best Practice & Research. Clinical Rheumatology*, *29*(3), 495–511. doi:10.1016/j.berh.2015.06.001 PMID:26612244

Vignoli, M., Guglielmi, D., Bonfiglioli, R., & Violante, F. S. (2015, March 27). How job demands affect absenteeism? The mediating role of work–family conflict and exhaustion. *International Archives of Occupational and Environmental Health*, *89*(1), 23–31. doi:10.100700420-015-1048-8 PMID:25808748

Zia-ud-Din, M., Arif, A., & Shabbir, M. A. (2017, May 28). The Impact of Workplace Incivility on Employee Absenteeism and Organization Commitment. *International Journal of Academic Research in Business & Social Sciences*, *7*(5). doi:10.6007/IJARBSS/v7-i5/2893

Chapter 12
Identifying the Effect of Motivation on Employee Job Performance in People Analytics:
A Review of the Retail Sector

Amandeep Kaur
https://orcid.org/0009-0004-5716-7298
Lovely Professional University, India

Veer P. Gangwar
Lovely Professional University, India

ABSTRACT

The main emphasis of this chapter is to identify the effect of motivation on variables of employee job performance in people analytics, which is seen as one of the major initiatives in human resources. The secondary sources have been utilised to identify the sources of the thematic approach. Considering this, the study explains how to determine the moderating factors in people analytics. The chapter offers an introduction to problem identification and focuses on detailed literature that helps in finding factors relevant according to the theme that has been elaborated in a thematic approach. A part of the Prisma model has been used to explain the four stages of literature identification. The moderating factors have been better explained through the case studies, and one case study has been explained in the context of an Indian scenario. While explaining the moderating factors, thematic methods have been used using manual screening. The major highlights have been reviewed, discussed, and summarised.

DOI: 10.4018/978-1-6684-8942-0.ch012

1. INTRODUCTION

The retail division has a huge influence on the global economy and employs a significant number of people worldwide. Interest in using data to enhance employees' job performance in retail establishments has increased with the emergence of people analytics (Larsson&Edwards,2021; Harter et. Al,2002; Armstrong& Taylor, 2020). Moderating factors' effects on this association, meanwhile, have not yet been completely investigated. The connection between people analytics and work performance can be influenced by moderating factors like job happiness, motivation, and organisational culture(Pawirosumarto et. Al, 2017; Garnett et. Al, 2008; yiing&ahmad, 2009). It is essential to understand how these moderating factors affect the connection among people analytics and job performance in retail sector as a whole(Marler&Boudreau,2017; Harter et. Al,2002) . In order to effectively employ people analytics in the retail industry, this research intends to investigate this relationship and offer insights into how to do so.

In the overall context of people analytics and performance while working in the retail industry, moderating influences may include components like job satisfaction, motivation, and organisational culture(Belwalker et. Al, 2018; Purnama,2013). An employee who is highly motivated, for instance, could be able to work well even in a job that is poorly planned, whereas an employee who is demotivated might find it difficult to perform effectively in a position that is perfectly created.

In the context of people analytics, moderating factors can influence how effective the use of data is in improving job performance(Sharma&Sharma,2017; Larsson&Edwards, 2022). For instance, an organization may collect data on employee performance, but if the organizational culture is not open to change or is resistant to the use of data, then this data may not be used effectively to improve job performance. Similarly, the adoption of people analytics might not have a major impact on employees' job performance if they are not motivated or dissatisfied with their jobs(Raziq & Maulabaksh, 2015; Sahinidis & Bouris, 2008; West, 2019).

It is crucial to comprehend the moderating aspects that may have an effect on the connection between people analytics and work performance in the retailer sector(Marler&Boudreau,2017; Tan&Waheed,2011). By doing so, organizations can take steps to address these factors and ensure that the use of people analytics is effective in improving employee job performance. Departmental stores, convenience stores, specialty shops, and internet retailers are just a little instance of the many categories of businesses that make up the retail subdivision, which is a sizable and varied industry. It contributes significantly to the global GDP and employs millions of people all over the world, playing a critical role in the economy.

In recent years, the retail sector has undergone significant changes due to technological advancements, changing consumer preferences, and shifts in the global economy. E-commerce has emerged as a major force in the retail sector, challenging traditional brick-and-mortar stores and changing the way that consumers shop. In order to stay competitive, merchants have had to adopt new technologies and approaches. Despite these difficulties, the retail industry carry on participating a significant role in the global economy plus employment. As such, improving job performance and employee satisfaction in the retail sector is an important goal for both retailers and policymakers(Ranjit,2022).

Employee motivation is seen as a crucial workplace factor, primarily because it has an impact on the efficiency of the business(Dartey-Baah&Amoako,2011; Gilmeanu,2015) . According to Morley (1998), motivation is a collection of mechanisms that encourage, direct, and maintain human action in the direction of a goal. Any advancement at work is thought to be the result of desired motivation. If employers can give their workers what they genuinely want, they may expect more from them. Giving people what they actually need from their work is at the core of motivation, according to Dell (1988), who wrote about it in her book "An Honest Day's Work."

Since staff members are receiving better offers elsewhere, attrition is a problem for startups that are having trouble raising capital. Employers use employee retention as a technique to keep talented workers from leaving their positions (Fox, 2012). At any stage, a startup risks suffering a significant loss if it doesn't implement effective retention and motivating techniques.

2. LITERATURE REVIEW

There are several theories related to job performance and moderating factors that are relevant to this topic. Job Satisfaction Theory: According to this hypothesis, one of the major factors influencing work performance is job happiness. Employee satisfaction increases the likelihood that they will be inspired to work hard and show dedication to their positions. As a result, job satisfaction might be able to moderate the relationship between people analytics and work performance(Patricia&Asoba, 2021; Khan et, al, 2021). Expectancy Theory: According to this theory, employees' motivation levels which are based on their expectations for the results of their performance have an impact on their performance. Therefore, the level of motivation can moderate the association between people's analytics and performance(Lawler&Suttle,1973). Social Exchange Theory: According to this theory, how employees perceive the switch association amongst themselves, and the administration affects how well they perform at work. As a result, the standard of the exchange link might moderate the connections between people's analytics and work performance(Cropanzano et.al, 2017). Goal-Setting Theory: According to this belief, giving employees clear, tough goals might inspire them to work harder. The connection between people analytics and job performance can therefore be moderated by the formulation of goals(Locke & Latham, 2012; Locke,1996).

According to these theories, moderating factors like job satisfaction, motivation, interpersonal interactions, and goal setting can have a significant impact on the association between people analytics and employment outcomes in retail businesses. The prior research investigations can be used to generalise the relevance of these hypotheses.

According to a research study conducted by Kumar and Mathimaran (2017), In order to keep their workforce, businesses must foster an environment that encourages people to stay on the job. Good management, competitive remuneration, and appreciation for the work are the three most crucial elements in employee retention (Fox, 2012). This understanding offers a strong base for solving issues that occurred with employee retention. The wide range of genres of literature were researched in order to discover more about the elements that impact employees' decisions to stay at the firm or leave it. The experiments conducted by Alias, Noor, and Hassan (2014) additionally proved the intermediary impact of worker engagement on talent administration strategies and employee retention. People are inclined to remain with a company longer when they have an interest in their work (Mttoi, 2013). Methods for retaining employees are thus preferable and should be promoted as opposed to other tactics and policies (Twum, 2015; KM & Christopher, 2015).

According to Sengupta & Gupta (2012), a worker is extra possible to remain with a company for a prolonged period if he or she has an innate desire to work, and the company encourages a sense of belonging and participation in his or her work. This discovery is in line with past studies. It was suggested that occupations be assigned based on employee interest and specialization because it was believed that interesting work was the least important motivator. Employers must provide employees with opportunities for higher education as well as both short- and long-term training related to work in order to improve performance.

People analytics have been characterised as HR analytics and talent analytics in the context of several research studies. It is crucial to emphasise organisational structure and cultural fusion inside the partnership for a superior primary risk mitigation strategy in mergers and acquisitions. For which future total quality, operational and risk management relies upon future analytics tools (Ghatak, 2022).Talking about people analytics for employees and operational connection it is relevant to handle the data more prominently and improve the quality of data. Many organizations have been able to move forward with strong connection of data showing employees attitude, loyalty of a customer, financial operations, and satisfaction (Jamison, 2020). With data advancement it is necessary to highlight the importance of the digital workplaces which enabled the advance people analytics. Talking about benefits there are some disadvantages to it too. With evolvement of data there are higher chances of implication of privacy risk which concerns employees. Voluntarily sharing of data highly depends on employees. The relevant studies make progress to identify the strategies one of them is to increase the awareness and another is to apply appealing strategies. Both will lead to conservative handling of data and data sharing. To identify dimension of strategies the expert's interview has been used to reach the initial taxonomy of strategies. These dimensions are Incentives, benefits, and values (Zieglmeier, Gierlich-Joas, & Pretschner, 2022).

To understand the relation of dimension in context to people analytics it is necessary to identify the moderating impact on people analytics. The effective understanding moderating variables can be understood through various alternatives, explanations, and case studies. In some studies, the age factor has been described as moderating factor which highly influenced the youngsters to get intimated with the online websites, platforms where they voluntarily express their emotional intelligence in regard to purchasing intention and again revisiting the sites. This explanation shows the moderating impact of age on website designs which enables the website builders to make their websites more imitating and influence the youngsters to visit the website again and again (Pelet, JE. et al., 2017). For both organisation and individuals face certain challenges in aspect of cultural diversity. This indirectly influence the employee's communication with other employees both at individual and organizational aspect. Communication mostly impacted by work experience in aspect of individual approach.

Another interesting factor which has been long ignored is expatriates. The term expatriates have been derived from Latin language the words 'ex' means outside and patria means owns country. At globalisation level this factor has been not much explored. Performance of these employees may be influenced by following factors such as cultural differences, personal safety, and healthcare, etc (Bader and Berg, 2013; Chen, Lin, and Hsu, 2014; Lee and Sukoco, 2010). By studying the factors, it become essential to manage the employees how efficiently. There are several reasons to electronically monitor personnel. Ball (2010) lists three alternative justifications, including preserving an organisation's efficiency and resources, safeguarding business interests and trade secrets, and avoiding legal obligations. Researchers (Ravid et al., 2019; Sewell & Barker, 2006) have added monitoring strategies that focus on the security and development of employees to this list of objectives. For instance, a location-sensing gadget can be used to monitor personnel while they are at work or just to find them after an accident. The majority of monitoring implementations ensure that target employee behaviour should ensure productivity and business interests. Also, employee interests might not always coincide with organizational benefits (Frey, 1993). In this approach, automated checking may have an impact on workers' performance as well as their perceptions of stress and job happiness.

Studies show a poor association between employee job happiness and technological surveillance. It makes sense to assume that technological surveillance has a detrimental impact on individuals' stress levels, just as it does on their job happiness. According to Karasek (1979), expectations from both the personal and professional spheres cause feelings of stress to be more intense. If there is a lack of independence, this energy cannot circulate, manifesting as stress and finally injuring the person. Again, limiting employee freedom and focusing on performance metrics through monitoring is likely to make individuals feel more stressed.

2.1 Performance, Stress, And Coping

Retailers are increasingly utilising people analytics as they realise the value of data-driven decision-making for growing their businesses. However, using people analytics may cause employees to feel more stressed and under pressure, particularly if performance indicators are connected to their pay or job security. In order to examining the connection amongst stress and employee performance in the retail industry, this literature study will also look at coping strategies that may be applied to lessen the harmful impacts of stress.

Employee Performance and People Analytics: Studies have demonstrated that implementing people analytics can improve employee performance in retail settings. For example, a study found that the use of people analytics improved sales performance in a Korean retail company. The link between people analytics and worker performance, however, is not always clear-cut. As highlighted in an analysis by Rasmussen and Ulrich (2015), variables like job satisfaction and motivation, including organisational culture, can attenuate this link.

Impact of Stress on Employee Performance: Stress is a common experience among employees in the retail sector, and the use of people analytics can exacerbate this stress. For example, if performance metrics are tied to job security or compensation, employees may feel increased pressure to perform well. Increased stress brought on by this strain may have a detrimental effect on workers' productivity. Multiple investigations in the retail industry have discovered a link between job stress and poor sales performance.

Employee Stress Coping Strategies: Implementing coping mechanisms is crucial to reducing the detrimental impact that stress has on employee performance. One effective coping mechanism is social support, which can come from colleagues, supervisors, or family and friends outside of work. Numerous studies have revealed that social support improves sales performance in retail businesses. Mindfulness is a method of coping those entails being in the present and objectively monitoring one's emotions and thoughts.

2.2 The Moderating Role of Work Pressure

When workplace stress is mild (as opposed to high), it is especially likely to be profitable and connected with job performance. Workers must employ all of their active capabilities to manage job pressure on days when it is already high (Bakker & Demerouti, 2017); looking for more difficulties in these circumstances is counterproductive (Petrou et al., 2012). Additionally, incorporating additional duties during these days could make the workload so heavy that it exhausts workers, raising the chance of mistakes and dropping performance (Bakker, 2015). On occasions when the number of tasks is relatively low, workers could decide to take responsibility and look for additional challenges. By doing this, they might give their work more meaning, which would increase their engagement and effectiveness.

Reducing job demands, the third job design method, seems especially crucial on days when work pressure is high. Workers are given all the time necessary to appropriately handle difficult job issues or time-consuming client demands on days when there is less work pressure. Employees must be choosy about the jobs they accept on days when the workload is heavy (Hockey, 1993). For instance, individuals will be incentivized to avoid onerous duties and paperwork on busy workdays. Additionally, due to the high level of effort required by the work, employees may prefer to lower their psychological, sentimental, and cognitive demands on these days.

Finally, we suggest that when work pressure is minimal, a humorous work environment is probably the best way to promote job performance. Employee boredom can lower productivity and work engagement when there isn't much for them to do (Harju et al., 2016). On different days when they have to finish tedious or routine tasks, people may also find it difficult to focus, and their efficiency might drop as the quantity of time they devote to the task boosts (Hopstaken et al., 2015). Similar to this, those who use humour in their daily work could develop relationships with others, foster a positive work environment, and be more satisfied with their careers (Robert, 2017).Employees do not require creative design of work to make their job more entertaining or difficult on days where the workload is already high. To properly handle the job demand, students will need to select and employ all of their energetic resources (Hockey, 1993).

3. THEORETICAL CONTRIBUTIONS

This study introduces four new concepts to the subject of study. In our first contributions, we combined the theories of JD-R (Bakker & Demerouti, 2017) and courageous conduct at work (Parker et al., 2010) to argue and show that when staff members use job crafting throughout the day, they enhance the inside of the organisational surroundings, which has a beneficial impact on daily job performance. According to additional studies (Rudolph et al., 2017; Tims et al., 2016), people who actively redesign their occupations by changing the tasks assigned to them and the resources they have access to do so because it makes their work more meaningful, engages them more, and improves their performance. Employees encounter and acquire completely new things as a consequence of their daily labour, which involves making minor but significant modifications to the subject matter of their work. People can continuously alter their careers by piloting novel employment opportunities on a small scale. In the context of fun work design, the results of three alternative job-creating strategies for performance improvement could also be contrasted. The results showed a positive association between career growth focused on expansion and other performance evaluations, including rising job demands and looking for employment resources.

When it comes to enlargement-oriented making, it implies that the principle of isomorphic job crafting means that increasing work resources and challenges have effects that are similar for all people. Because daily stress is positively correlated with additional measures of job accomplishment (see also Petrou et al., 2012), it may be possible that job crafting, an approach that involves lowering demands on employees (for instance, reducing tasks and client interactions to lower work pressure), additionally minimises challenges at work. Demerouti et al. (2017) found that decreasing job requirements could protect workers' wellbeing; however, a more recent study reveals that this approach also reduces productivity. Employees run the risk of disobeying instructions and performing below expectations if they consciously alter the terms of their employment possibilities. As a result, there may be conflict between employees who are proactive and less proactive staff (Bolino et al., 2010). According to this hypothetical stance, Tims et al.'s (2015) research demonstrated that decreasing job expectations promotes disengagement and leads to conflicts with co-workers. Future studies should look at other situations and diverse mediators of the relationship between decreased expectations and success on the job, such as routine performance. In accordance with Bakker and Oerlemans (2019), long-term studies can establish if proactive work strategies like job crafting, which entails lowering job demands, reject suggested role expectations or not.

Setting up competition may also help with concentration and goal setting. Such humorous job design strategies facilitate efficient performance every day. In conclusion, proactive behaviour that develops both professional and personal assets, supports motivation, and fosters performance can be positioned within fun work design and JD-R principles. It's comparable to job crafting. Future research should go deeper into the active processes involved in designing enjoyable work. We also looked into the circumstances in which proactive work is most beneficial.

To keep active and productive and prevent boredom, workers should employ entertaining job planning techniques. Employees can set goals and communicate with co-workers using these proactive, self-initiated tactics (Harju et al., 2016; Sonnentag, 2017)

Table 1. The following construct highlights the moderating effects as per literature

Role	Purpose	Author
Job Satisfaction	Understanding the complex mechanics and constraints of how performance-based compensation impacts performance provides organizations with insights to maximize the positive impact.	Chen, 2022
Big Data Analytics	The study places special emphasis on the relationship between big data analytics and company success in the supply chain.	Del Giudice et al, 2021
Organisation citizenship	It is also statistically significant that perceptions of organisational fairness and big data analytical skills have a moderating effect on the association between cooperative relationships between buyers and suppliers and supplier social sustainability.	Casu, 2021
Job demand	The study found that job autonomy had a contrary moderating impact, strengthening the correlations between emotional weariness and work disengagement behaviours. The study used the ideas of resource conservation and the job requirements resource model.	Hou, Wei and Zhang, 2022
Quality of Work	The study demonstrates that work quality has a considerable impact on organisational commitment, psychological empowerment, and job happiness while having a little impact on job performance.	Diana,2021
Organization programs	The study investigates the association among job fulfilment and the standard of living at work.	Rostami, 2021
Job Satisfaction	It was acknowledged in the study as a significant element affecting individuals' output as well as the quality of their work.	Halawani, 2021
Digitalization	The following hypotheses were examined in the study: for comprehensively perceived occupational stress, increasing levels of digitization would generally result in higher levels of overall job satisfaction for employees.	Kortmann, Simonson, Vogel and Huxhold, 2021
Internal service quality	Internal service quality and its impact on commitment among staff members, satisfaction with work, and wellness in the healthcare industry were examined in this study.	Abdullah et.al., 2021
Leader mentoring	The study looked at how the effectiveness of leaders' mentoring affects mentees' job happiness, which in turn affects how well they perform at work.	Kumari, et.al., 2022

continues on following page

Table 1. Continued

Role	Purpose	Author
Gender influence	In this study, we examined how certain traits and general job satisfaction varied between men and women.	Akbari, et.al., 2020
Work Stress	The study has shown how couriers' job satisfaction and workplace stress are related. In addition, psychological capital influences the link between poor sleep and occupational stress among couriers.	Xie, et.al, 2021
Time	The study explores the connections between job satisfaction and stress, as well as the connections between these variables and both work-related and recreational physical activity.	Jiménez, et.al, 2021
Managerial role	The study emphasises how the link between stress at work and managerial duties varied depending on the type of employment.	Kim and Cho, (2020)
Education	The study looks at the relationship between scholastic success and occupational satisfaction. The study found that while people with higher levels of education are more inclined to work jobs with greater advantages (like pay, independence, and variety), they are also more likely to work jobs with greater expectations (like demanding schedules, hard work, and deadlines).	Solomon, Nikolaev, & Shepherd,(2022)
Job satisfaction	The study's topics include employee job satisfaction, supervisor support, workplace autonomy, productivity, and performance.	Alfaleh, et.al., 2021
Internet usage	According to the survey, people who live in metropolitan areas, earn more money, and have more education benefit more from the Internet.	Zhou, Yang and Li, 2022
Work environment	Fit and job suitability affect employees' creative thinking abilities and willingness to leave their jobs.	Tang, et.al., 2021
Job Involvement	The study shows how other variables, like organisational dedication and work pleasure, function as mediators or moderators and influence the connection amid employment contribution and other variables.	Salessi and Omar, 2019

Figure 1. Table of global cited authors
Source: *Scopus database*

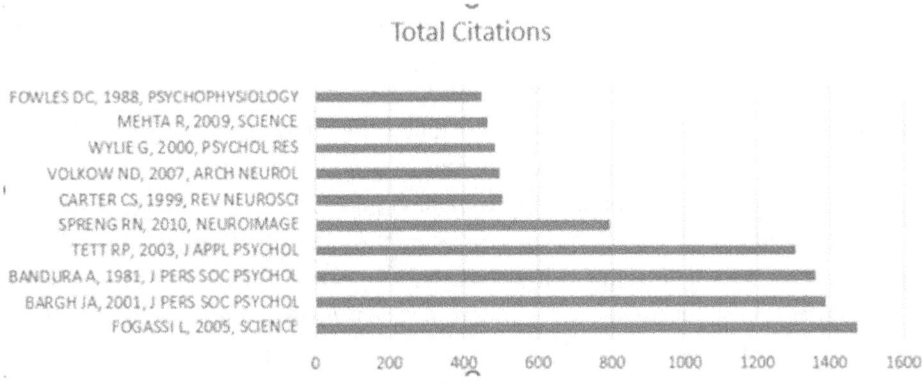

Fogassi (2005), Bargh(2001), Bandura(1981) and Tett (2003) all are having above thousand cited documents as explained in the above-mentioned figure 3.1. According to figure 3.2 three field plot has been generated using Abstracts as first field plot, Authors as the second field plot and Keywords as third field plot. The field plot has been generated using keywords "Attrition" OR "Attraction" OR "Activation" AND "Motivation" AND "Performance". Total documents has been generated was 1674 through Scopus database. The domains which are excluded from the database were Engineering, Medical, Architecture etc. Only relevant domains has been selected after screening of abstracts including Management, Social Science, and some health sector whose studies are focused on above mentioned keywords. The total of 1260 documents has been identified through final criteria of selecting appropriate Articles, Research Papers, and Chapters. Further process of screening of documents has been explained through Prisma model in the methodology section.

Figure 2. Three field plot
Source: *Three field plot using Biblioshiny with the help of Scopus database*

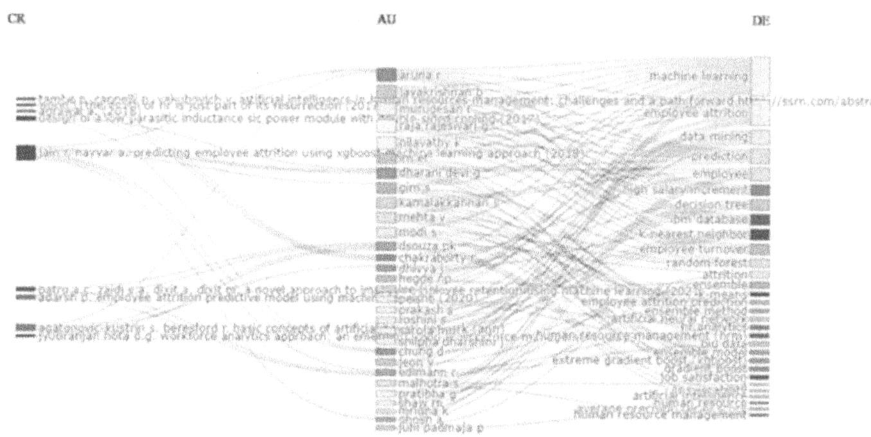

High pressure at work may make it more difficult to properly deploy workplace resources while also encouraging employees to be proactive and look for resources (Parker et al., 2010). Therefore, people who are under pressure at work might be inclined towards but also less skilled in crafting their jobs. Such competing pressures could conceal potential interactions. Similar to this, people may have quick reasons to lessen their job demands on days when they are under a lot of strain at work, but they may not be as well-prepared to rethink their position. Such circumstances may reduce the likelihood of discovering a correlation between job crafting and a decrease in workload and job demands.

A potential issue with proactively job theories of behaviour (Parker et al., 2010) specifically, the issue of competing forces should be addressed by further research, according to the observed results. Finally, depending on the precise type of need that is lowered, the connection between reducing job requirements as well as job performance can change. According to a recent investigation by the research carried out by and Peeters (2018), staff should try to raise expectations rather than reduce them (i.e., make a job less difficult). Work procedures must be made more efficient as a result. Indeed, their diary study found that, as opposed to setting low expectations, optimising demands was positively associated with work engagement. Future research that aims to broaden our current research and confirm the present results may test the hypothesis that job demand management frees up invigorating resources to focus activities and is particularly crucial for daily job productivity when the work requirement is high.

4. PROPOSED CONCEPTUAL FRAMEWORK FOR PEOPLE ANALYTICS IN RETAIL SECTOR

Figure 3. Conceptual framework
Source: *Mike west(2019); Na-nan, et al. (2018)*

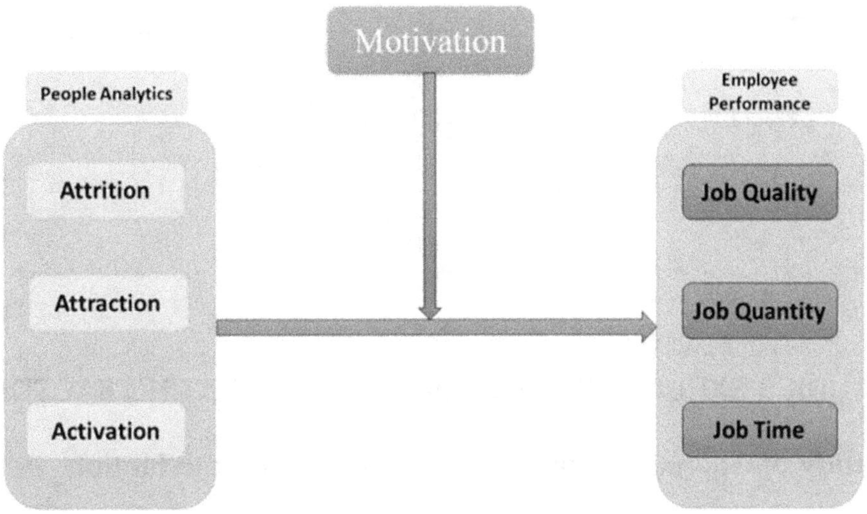

5. METHODOLOGY

The thematic analysis of paper involves the collection of 1260 total identified research articles and review paper from the Scopus, dimension.ai and Springer link. The procedure of thematic analysis involves the first step was to identify the paper more relevant for the study which includes of total of 1260 papers in addition to which 12 more papers were included. After removal of the duplication of same related articles 876 were left. The second phase of thematic selection includes of screening of the articles from which again total of 574 were selected and 302 were excluded. The third phase, include the eligibility of articles which were nearest to the domain of study were included of 270 again out of which 270 were excluded which not met the eligibility criteria of the main themes. The last phase includes of 35 most relevant articles included of both research articles and the review articles on which basis the Table 2.1 and table 3.1 were prepared. The total of 20 articles were used to prepare to highlight the major moderating factors association in the employee job performance with the similar scenario relatable to the identical criteria, these papers were highly importance as 5 major factors has been utilised to draft the questionnaire for the pilot study and has been explained as analysis in the form of case study.

Prisma model highlights that there are fewer papers available on people analytics hence through data threshold only 31 papers have been selected for drafting the literature structure the structure of chapter concept. To case studies has been utilised to explain the moderating role of various factors identified through the thematic analysis.

Figure 4. Process of identifying relevant literature

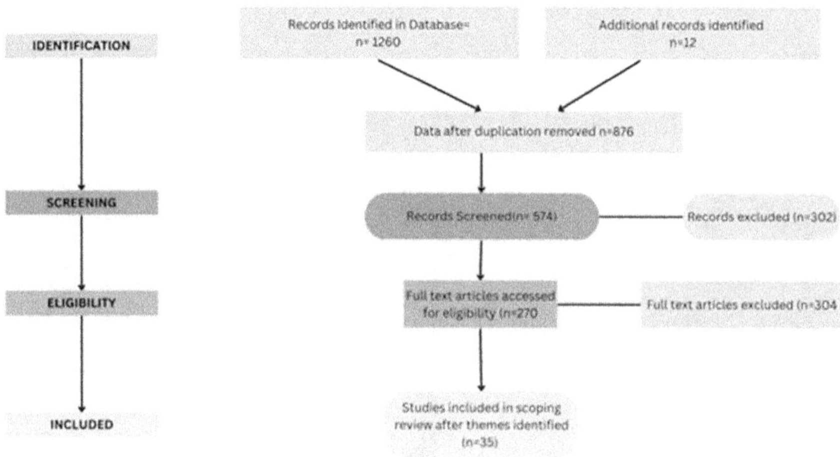

6. CASE STUDIES EXPLAINING THE ROLE OF MODERATING FACTORS

6.1 Case Study of Guanxi Explaining the Role of Job Satisfaction

A case study on how people analytics affected employee job performance in a significant retail organisation was done by Guanxi et al. in 2019. The goal of the study was to investigate the moderating role of job satisfaction in the association between people analytics and job performance. Data from 258 employees was gathered for the study through a survey at a sizable retail establishment in China. Questions in the study asked about employees' opinions of people analytics, work happiness, and job performance. According to the study's findings, work satisfaction mitigated the association between people analytics and employee job performance. People analytics specifically had a bigger beneficial impact on job performance for workers who reported greater degrees of job satisfaction.

This case study emphasises the significance of taking moderating factors like job satisfaction into account when applying people analytics in the retail sector. Organisations can create more effective strategies to enhance employee job performance and general organisational success by knowing these aspects (Guanxi, Xiaoming, and Shuling, 2019). In support of the aforementioned case study, there are numerous moderating effects of workload in organisations that impact the interaction between supervisors and subordinates. The workload, as defined by the study, is the total number of tasks and obligations that employees must manage every day. The workload symbolises the adverse working conditions that cause exhaustion of resources and emotional tiredness according to the COR theory (Conservation of Resources) (Hobfoll, 2011). The COR hypothesis states that role demands, which are expressed in high workloads, offer dangers to resource loss (Hobfoll, 1989). Stress can readily result from a person's depletion of resources when they are under a lot of pressure (Charoensukmongkol & Puyod, 2020).

However, the job demands-resources (JD-R) hypothesis must be added to the COR theory in order to completely explain how workload could diminish the positive effects of superintendent-subordinate Guanxi on emotional exhaustion. The JD-R hypothesis (Bakker & Demerouti, 2014) considers the importance of job demands and employment opportunities as key indicators of emotional tiredness, much like the COR theory does. However, according to the JD-R theory, emotional weariness can be effectively managed when employees receive more job resources than they encounter in terms of job demands (Bakker & Demerouti, 2014; Charoensukmongkol & Suthatorn, 2018). Case study analysis is required to better understand all theories and consider the moderating effect of different circumstances on employee work performance. To further understand the moderating impacts, the subsequent examples have been elaborated upon.

6.2 Case Study of KPMG Explaining the Role of Employee Engagement

The goal of the study was to comprehend how sales performance, customer happiness, and employee engagement are related in the retail industry. Over a three-year period, the study examined sales data, customer satisfaction questionnaires, and employee engagement survey data. Advanced statistical methods, including the use of regression analysis and the modelling of structural equations, were used to analyse the data. In other words, customer satisfaction and revenue growth were higher in stores with higher employee engagement levels. The study also discovered that variables including store location, size, and competition had a moderating effect on the association between staff engagement and sales performance. For instance, at smaller stores as opposed to larger stores, there was a stronger correlation between employee engagement and sales performance.

The significance of employee involvement in the retail industry and how it may affect client happiness and sales results are highlighted in this case study. It also exemplifies the importance of employing people analytics to comprehend these interactions and find moderating factors that may have an impact on them.

6.3 Case Example of National Retail Federation Explaining the Role of Work Force

A study conducted by the National Retail Federation (NRF) in 2019 analysed the use of people analytics in the retail industry. The study surveyed retail companies with at least 1,000 employees and found that 87% of respondents used people analytics to some degree. The study also found that companies that used people analytics reported higher rates of employee engagement, productivity, and retention. However, the study also identified several moderating factors that can influence the effectiveness of people analytics. For example, companies with a strong organizational culture were found to be more successful in using people analytics to improve job performance. Additionally, companies that provided regular feedback and training to employees on how to use people analytics were more likely to see positive results (NRF, 2019).

One study conducted by Wirtz, and colleagues (2016) examined the impact of people analytics on employee turnover in a large retail company. The study found that the use of people analytics helped to identify factors that were contributing to high levels of turnover, such as lack of training and development opportunities. By addressing these factors, the company was able to reduce turnover rates by 5% over a one-year period.

6.4 Case Study of Cisco

In their case study, Cisco was able to use people analytics to identify factors that were influencing employee turnover, including job satisfaction, manager effectiveness, and employee engagement. They were also able to use analytics to identify key predictors of employee performance, such as job tenure, previous job performance, and relevant skills and education.

By using people analytics, Cisco was able to develop data-driven strategies to improve employee retention and performance. For example, they implemented a program to improve manager effectiveness through training and support, which led to a 10% improvement in employee engagement and a 6% reduction in turnover. While this case study is not specifically related to the retail industry, it does demonstrate the potential benefits of using people analytics to improve employee performance and retention in any industry.

6.5. The Case Study of Punjab Explaining the Effect of Motivation as Moderating Factor Influencing the Employee Job Performance in People Analytics in Retails Industries

Following case study has been developed after pilot survey after which summary shows that total 49 respondents that has been considered for the validity of demographical variables includes of both control and uncontrollable variables have effect in employee job performance. A holistic approach has been applied to test out the reliability of these variables. The produced results have been generated using total of 139 respondents in Jalandhar and Phagwara region belongs to retail sector in marketing (includes of managers, sales executives, sales representatives, healthcare representatives, etc.) with educational qualification of technical and non-technical backgrounds.

Table 2. Internal Reliability Test

<table>
<tr><th>Variables</th><th>Cronbach alpha</th><th>Acceptable/ Not Acceptable</th><th>Dependent variable</th><th>Relationship</th></tr>
<tr><td>ATTR1</td><td>.936</td><td>Acceptable</td><td rowspan="11">Motivation</td><td rowspan="11">R square value is .416</td></tr>
<tr><td>ATTR2</td><td></td><td></td></tr>
<tr><td>ATTR3</td><td></td><td></td></tr>
<tr><td>ATTR4</td><td></td><td></td></tr>
<tr><td>ATRN1</td><td>.940</td><td>Acceptable</td></tr>
<tr><td>ATRN2</td><td></td><td></td></tr>
<tr><td>ATRN3</td><td></td><td></td></tr>
<tr><td>ATRN4</td><td></td><td></td></tr>
<tr><td>ACT1</td><td>.914</td><td>Acceptable</td></tr>
<tr><td>ACT2</td><td></td><td></td></tr>
<tr><td>ACT3</td><td></td><td></td></tr>
</table>

Source : Authors calculation through SPSS

As per the results, the Cronbach alpha of attraction, attrition, and activation is above .9, which is significant, and the dependent variable has been taken as motivation to check the relationship. To check the relationship, linear regression has been utilised to check the motivation effect on all three independent variables. The r2 value is.416, indicating a weak relationship. But in general interpretation, according to a rule of thumb, the value of r2 should be considered between 0 and 1. Hence, it can be generalised that motivation can be taken as a moderating variable to check the effect on employee job performance for future studies in people analytics.

The interpretation from the above table it has been clearly indicated that attrition, attraction, activation can be taken as independent variable and motivation as dependent variable for moderating purpose to study the employee performance *i.e.,* job quality, job time and job quantity. The data collected based on 7 Likert scale for simple interpretation.

7. LIMITATIONS AND CONCLUSION

The following limitations should be considered by viewers of the current study: First, we looked simply at the four dependent variables. Job satisfaction, however, can be used as a stand-in for other attitudinal factors like dedication and motivation at the workplace. Stress could serve as a stand-in for other factors that indicate how well-off employees are. For better identification of thematic identification of relevant literature PRISMA model has been utilised for identification of variables for questionnaire drafting. There are various and similar studies which produce associated implication of same construct to reach the conclusion. During the selection of various paper for the thematic identification of themes are closely relate to chapter title manual screening has been utilised no help of any scientific software has been considered.

Four dependent factors that are essential to understanding the impact of various moderating variables were examined in the current study. Additionally, it is also feasible to concentrate more intently on the validation of particular theories. Using case studies from KPMG, NRF, Cisco, and other companies, it was helpful to investigate whether the impacts of performance at work on the dependent variables are modified by numerous factors that affect people analytics. Theoretically, a mediation model like this one propose that monitoring influences the needs and resources of the task, which in turn influences the dependent variables.

To create the questionnaire for the pilot survey in the Punjab retail industry, numerous variables from case studies were analysed thematically. Only the motivation factor shows effectiveness in the results, including their suitability for future research, has been considered in relation to the research goal. Because numerous respondents were constrained by the company policies, the outcomes of the subsequent inquiry by means of a pilot survey demonstrated that the correct process must be followed, but another finding of the study showed that the questions that were prepared were well received. However, the three main dimensions of employee performance job quality, job time, and job quantity as well as attrition, attraction, incentive, and training have each demonstrated their respective responsiveness. For further research, it is essential to examine people analytics in retail sector with regard to startups and small businesses.

In future research psychophysiological measures directly affects motivation which must be focused on feedback given on performance indicating monetary penalties and incentives(Clement,1995). In physical activation fatigue and adaptation of a worker can considered as a factor which delimit performance and other conditions (Noakes,2000). According to Zalla et. Al, 2000 human subjects provides feedback on performance whose results may lead to activation of psychological mindset. The gap that can be taken into consideration is Quality activation through the process of identifying limitations in order to increase staff motivation in an organization (Coris, 2001). One another gap has been identified as self-regulation in participants with no awareness can perform intellectual tasks through guiding actions. Future study can directly be focused on stereotype situations that has direct impact on task performance (Smith & White, 2002). In addition to this perception directly affect motivation through cognitive processes (Erez & Isen, 2002) which can be analysed in context of people analytics in future research focusing on intangible characteristics of applicants having direct access to behaviour and motivation (Bell et. Al, 2011). References need to be included.

8. REFERENCES

Abdullah, M. I., Huang, D., Sarfraz, M., Ivascu, L., & Riaz, A. (2021). Effects of internal service quality on nurses' job satisfaction, commitment, and performance: Mediating role of employee well-being. *Nursing Open*, *8*(2), 607–619. doi:10.1002/nop2.665 PMID:33570299

Akbari, M., Bagheri, A., Fathollahi, A., & Darvish, M. (2020). Job satisfaction among nurses in Iran: Does gender matter? *Journal of Multidisciplinary Healthcare*, *13*, 71–78. doi:10.2147/JMDH.S215288 PMID:32021236

Alfaleh, A., Alkattan, A., Alageel, A., Salah, M., Almutairi, M., Sagor, K., & Alabdulkareem, K. (2021). Onsite versus remote working: The impact on satisfaction, productivity, and performance of medical call centre workers. *INQUIRY: The Journal of Health Care Organization, Provision, and Financing*, *58*, 00469580211056041. PMID:34825844

Alias, N. E., Noor, N., & Hassan, R. (2014). Examining the mediating effect of employee engagement on the relationship between talent management practices and employee retention in the Information and Technology (IT) organizations in Malaysia. *Journal of Human Resources Management and Labor Studies*, *2*(2), 227–242.

Armstrong, M., & Taylor, S. (2020). *Armstrong's handbook of human resource management practice*. Kogan Page Publishers.

Bader, B., & Berg, N. (2013). An empirical investigation of terrorism-induced stress on expatriate attitudes and performance. *Journal of International Management*, *19*(2), 163–175. doi:10.1016/j.intman.2013.01.003

Bakker, A. B., & Demerouti, E. (2014). *Job demands–resources theory. Wellbeing: A complete reference guide*. Wiley Blackwell., doi:10.1002/9781118539415.wbwell019

Bakker, A. B., & Demerouti, E. (2017). Job demands–resources theory: Taking stock and looking forward. *Journal of Occupational Health Psychology*, *22*(3), 273–285. doi:10.1037/ocp0000056 PMID:27732008

Bakker, A. B., & Oerlemans, W. G. (2019). Daily job crafting and momentary work engagement: A self-determination and self-regulation perspective. *Journal of Vocational Behavior*, *112*, 417–430. doi:10.1016/j.jvb.2018.12.005

Ball, K. (2010). Workplace surveillance: An overview. *Labor History*, *51*(1), 87–106. doi:10.1080/00236561003654776

Bell, R. M., Fann, S. A., Morrison, J. E., & Lisk, J. R. (2011). Determining personal talents and behavioral styles of applicants to surgical training: A new look at an old problem, part I. *Journal of Surgical Education*, *68*(6), 534–541. doi:10.1016/j.jsurg.2011.05.016 PMID:22000541

Belwalkar, S., Vohra, V., & Pandey, A. (2018). The relationship between workplace spirituality, job satisfaction and organizational citizenship behaviors–an empirical study. *Social Responsibility Journal*, *14*(2), 410–430. doi:10.1108/SRJ-05-2016-0096

Bolino, M., Valcea, S., & Harvey, J. (2010). Employee, manage thyself: The potentially negative implications of expecting employees to behave proactively. *Journal of Occupational and Organizational Psychology*, *83*(2), 325–345. doi:10.1348/096317910X493134

Casu, G., Mariani, M. G., Chiesa, R., Guglielmi, D., & Gremigni, P. (2021). The role of organizational citizenship behaviour and gender between job satisfaction and task performance. *International Journal of Environmental Research and Public Health*, *18*(18), 9499. doi:10.3390/ijerph18189499 PMID:34574423

Charoensukmongkol, P., & Puyod, J. V. (2022). Mindfulness and emotional exhaustion in call centre agents in the Philippines: Moderating roles of work and personal characteristics. *The Journal of General Psychology*, *149*(1), 72–96. doi:10.1080/00221309.2020.1800582 PMID:32748707

Charoensukmongkol, P., & Suthatorn, P. (2018). Salespeople's trait mindfulness and emotional exhaustion: The mediating roles of optimism, resilience, and self-efficacy. International Journal of Services. *Economics and Management*, *9*(2), 125–142. doi:10.1504/IJSEM.2018.096075

Chen, J. H., Lin, J. Z., & Hsu, S. C. (2014). Determining and classifying factors of employees' expatriation willingness using rough set theory. *Journal of Management Engineering*, *30*(5), 04014021. doi:10.1061/(ASCE)ME.1943-5479.0000206

Chen, Y., Zhang, Z., Zhou, J., Liu, C., Zhang, X., & Yu, T. (2022). A cognitive evaluation and equity-based perspective of pay for performance on job performance: A meta-analysis and path model. *Frontiers in Psychology*, 13. PMID:36743591

Clements, K., & Turpin, G. (1995). Effects of feedback and task difficulty on electrodermal activity and heart rate: An examination of Fowles' three arousal model. *Journal of Psychophysiology*.

Coris, G., & Zucchi, S. (2002). Qualità percepita in quattro servizi sanitari: Poliambulatorio di Orbassano, ASL 5-Collegno (TO). *Psicologia della Salute*, (2001/2).

Cropanzano, R., Anthony, E. L., Daniels, S. R., & Hall, A. V. (2017). Social exchange theory: A critical review with theoretical remedies. *The Academy of Management Annals*, *11*(1), 479–516. doi:10.5465/annals.2015.0099

Dartey-Baah, K., & Amoako, G. K. (2011). Application of Frederick Herzberg's Two-Factor theory in assessing and understanding employee motivation at work: A Ghanaian Perspective. *European Journal of Business and Management*, *3*(9), 1–8.

Del Giudice, M., Chierici, R., Mazzucchelli, A., & Fiano, F. (2021). Supply chain management in the era of circular economy: The moderating effect of big data. *International Journal of Logistics Management*, *32*(2), 337–356. doi:10.1108/IJLM-03-2020-0119

Erez, A., & Isen, A. M. (2002). The influence of positive affect on the components of expectancy motivation. *The Journal of Applied Psychology, 87*(6), 1055–1067. doi:10.1037/0021-9010.87.6.1055 PMID:12558213

Fox, R. J. (2012). *A Study of Employee Retention Issues in the Hospitality Industry* [Doctoral dissertation, University of Wisconsin Stout].

Frey, B. S. (1993). Does monitoring increase work effort? The rivalry with trust and loyalty. *Economic Inquiry, 31*(4), 663–670. doi:10.1111/j.1465-7295.1993.tb00897.x

Garnett, J. L., Marlowe, J., & Pandey, S. K. (2008). Penetrating the performance predicament: Communication as a mediator or moderator of organizational culture's impact on public organizational performance. *Public Administration Review, 68*(2), 266–281. doi:10.1111/j.1540-6210.2007.00861.x

Ghatak, R. (2022). People Analytics in Mergers and Acquisitions. In People Analytics: Data to Decisions (pp. 135-141). Singapore: Springer Nature Singapore. doi:10.1007/978-981-19-3873-3_8

Gîlmeanu, R. (2015). Theoretical considerations on motivation at the workplace, job satisfaction and individual performance. *Valahian. Journal of Economic Studies (Glasgow, Scotland), 6*(3), 69.

Guanxi, L., Xiaoming, Z., & Shuling, Z. (2019). The impact of people analytics on job performance: The moderating role of job satisfaction. *Journal of Retailing and Consumer Services, 50*, 369–376.

Halawani, L. A., Halawani, M. A., & Beyari, G. M. (2021). Job satisfaction among Saudi healthcare workers and its impact on the quality of health services. *Journal of Family Medicine and Primary Care, 10*(5), 1873. doi:10.4103/jfmpc.jfmpc_2236_20 PMID:34195119

Harter, J. K., Schmidt, F. L., & Hayes, T. L. (2002). Business-unit-level relationship between employee satisfaction, employee engagement, and business outcomes: A meta-analysis. *The Journal of Applied Psychology, 87*(2), 268–279. doi:10.1037/0021-9010.87.2.268 PMID:12002955

Hobfoll, S. E. (1989). Conservation of resources: A new attempt at conceptualizing stress. *The American Psychologist, 44*(3), 513–524. doi:10.1037/0003-066X.44.3.513 PMID:2648906

Hobfoll, S. E. (2011). Conservation of resource caravans and engaged settings. *Journal of Occupational and Organizational Psychology, 84*(1), 116–122. doi:10.1111/j.2044-8325.2010.02016.x

Hou, J. DA, S., Wei, Y., & Zhang, X. (2022). Work-family conflict and withdrawal behaviour among mainland China's IT employees: the mediating role of emotional exhaustion and moderating role of job autonomy. Industrial Health, (pp. 2021-0136).

Huey Yiing, L., & Zaman Bin Ahmad, K. (2009). The moderating effects of organizational culture on the relationships between leadership behaviour and organizational commitment and between organizational commitment and job satisfaction and performance. *Leadership and Organization Development Journal, 30*(1), 53–86. doi:10.1108/01437730910927106

Jamison, F. (2020). People analytics in practice: connecting employee, customer, and operational data to create evidence-based decision making. In *Smart Service Systems, Operations Management, and Analytics: Proceedings of the 2019 INFORMS International Conference on Service Science* (pp. 223-228). Springer International Publishing. 10.1007/978-3-030-30967-1_20

Khan, A. J., Bhatti, M. A., Hussain, A., Ahmad, R., & Iqbal, J. (2021). Employee Job Satisfaction in Higher Educational Institutes: A Review of Theories. *Journal of Southeast Asian Studies*, *9*(3), 257–266. doi:10.33687/jsas.009.03.3940

Kim, K. W., & Cho, Y. H. (2020). The moderating effect of managerial roles on job stress and satisfaction by employees' employment type. *International Journal of Environmental Research and Public Health*, *17*(21), 8259. doi:10.3390/ijerph17218259 PMID:33182275

KM, N. D., & Christopher, S. E. (2015). Employee Attrition of It Industry In India- Externally Volatile Internally Dark Times: A Focused Study. *International Journal of Business and Administration Research Review*, *1*(9), 8–12.

Kortmann, L. K., Simonson, J., Vogel, C., & Huxhold, O. (2021). Digitalisation and employees' subjective job quality in the second half of working life in Germany. *Social Indicators Research*, •••, 1–21. PMID:34873360

KPMG. (2015). *The link between employee engagement, customer satisfaction and business outcomes in the retail sector*. KPMG. https://assets.kpmg/content/dam/kpmg/uk/pdf/2016/07/link-between-employee-engagement-customer-satisfaction-and-business-outcomes-retail-sector.pdf

Kumar, A. A., & Mathimaran, K. B. (2017). Employee Retention Strategies in Empirical Research. *Global Journal of Management and Business Research*, *17*(1).

Kumari, K., Ali, S. B., Batool, M., Cioca, L. I., & Abbas, J. (2022). The interplay between leaders' personality traits and mentoring quality and their impact on mentees' job satisfaction and job performance. *Frontiers in Psychology*, *13*, 13. doi:10.3389/fpsyg.2022.937470 PMID:36467147

Larsson, A. S., & Edwards, M. R. (2022). Insider econometrics meets people analytics and strategic human resource management. *International Journal of Human Resource Management*, *33*(12), 2373–2419. doi:10.1080/09585192.2020.1847166

Lawler III, E. E., & Suttle, J. L. (1973). Expectancy theory and job behavior. *Organizational behavior and huma performance, 9*(3), 482-503. *n performance, 9*(3), 482.

Lee, L. Y., & Sukoco, B. M. (2010). The effects of cultural intelligence on expatriate performance: The moderating effects of international experience. *The international journal of human resource.*

Locke, E. A. (1996). Motivation through conscious goal setting. *Applied & Preventive Psychology*, *5*(2), 117–124. doi:10.1016/S0962-1849(96)80005-9

Locke, E. A., & Latham, G. P. (2012). Goal setting theory. In *Motivation: Theory and research* (pp. 23–40). Routledge.

Marler, J. H., & Boudreau, J. W. (2017). An evidence-based review of HR Analytics. *International Journal of Human Resource Management*, *28*(1), 3–26. doi:10.1080/09585192.2016.1244699

Morley, M. (1998). *Principles of organisational behaviour: An Irish text.* Gill & MacMillan.

Mttoi, D. A. (2013). *Influence of Motivation on employee's retention in Public Organizations; A case study of Tanzania Ports Authority* [Doctoral dissertation, The Open University of Tanzania]

Na-Nan, K., Chaiprasit, K., & Pukkeeree, P. (2018). Factor analysis-validated comprehensive employee job performance scale. *International Journal of Quality & Reliability Management, 35*(10), 2436–2449. doi:10.1108/IJQRM-06-2017-0117

National Retail Federation. (2019). *People Metrics in Retail: How Retailers are Using Data to Drive Human Capital Decisions*. NRF. https://nrf.com/research/people-metrics-retail-how-retailers-are-using-data-drive-human-capital-decisions

Noakes, T. D. (2000). Physiological models to understand exercise fatigue and the adaptations that predict or enhance athletic performance. *Scandinavian Journal of Medicine & Science in Sports, 10*(3), 123–145. doi:10.1034/j.1600-0838.2000.010003123.x PMID:10843507

Patricia, N. M., & Asoba, S. N. (2021). Theories of job satisfaction in the higher education context. *Academy of Entrepreneurship Journal, 27*(2), 1–16.

Pawirosumarto, S., Sarjana, P. K., & Gunawan, R. (2017). The effect of work environment, leadership style, and organizational culture towards job satisfaction and its implication towards employee performance in Parador Hotels and Resorts, Indonesia. *International journal of law and management*.

Pelet, J. E., Taieb, B., Massarini, M., Mouelhi, N. B. D., Mishra, P., Obeidat, Z. M., & Zukowska, J. (2017). Impact of M-commerce website design on consumers' behavioural intentions: an empirical study of age as a moderating influence. In *Marketing at the Confluence between Entertainment and Analytics: Proceedings of the 2016 Academy of Marketing Science (AMS) World Marketing Congress* (pp. 111-124). Springer International Publishing. 10.1007/978-3-319-47331-4_21

Purnama, C. (2013). Influence analysis of organizational culture organizational commitment job and satisfaction organizational citizenship behavior (OCB) toward improved organizational performance. *International journal of business, humanities and technology, 3*(5), 86-100.

Ranjit, G. (2022). Explicating intrinsic motivation's impact on job performance: Employee creativity as a mediator. *Journal of Strategy and Management, 15*(4), 647–664. doi:10.1108/JSMA-04-2021-0091

Rasmussen, T., & Ulrich, D. (2015). Learning from practice: How HR analytics avoids being a management fad. *Organizational Dynamics, 44*(3), 236–242. doi:10.1016/j.orgdyn.2015.05.008

Raziq, A., & Maulabakhsh, R. (2015). Impact of working environment on job satisfaction. *Procedia Economics and Finance, 23*, 717–725. doi:10.1016/S2212-5671(15)00524-9

Rostami, H. R., Akbarfahimi, M., Ghaffari, A., Kamali, M., & Rassafiani, M. (2021). Relationship between work-related quality of life and job satisfaction in Iranian occupational therapists. *Occupational Therapy International, 2021*, 1–6. doi:10.1155/2021/6692752 PMID:34629996

Rudolph, C. W., Katz, I. M., Lavigne, K. N., & Zacher, H. (2017). Job crafting: A meta-analysis of relationships with individual differences, job characteristics, and work outcomes. *Journal of Vocational Behavior, 102*, 112–138. doi:10.1016/j.jvb.2017.05.008

Sahinidis, A. G., & Bouris, J. (2008). Employee perceived training effectiveness relationship to employee attitudes. *Journal of European Industrial Training, 32*(1), 63–76. doi:10.1108/03090590810846575

Salessi, S. M., & Omar, A. G. (2019). *Job involvement in current research: Update and state of the art.*

Sengupta, S., & Gupta, A. (2012). Employee Attrition and Retention: Exploring the Dimensions in the urban centric BPO Industry. *International Journal of Human Resource Management*, *6*(23), 1259–1288. doi:10.1080/09585192.2011.561211

Sewell, G., & Barker, J. R. (2006). Coercion versus care: Using irony to make sense of organizational surveillance. *Academy of Management Review*, *31*(4), 934–961. doi:10.5465/amr.2006.22527466

Sharma, A., & Sharma, T. (2017). HR analytics and performance appraisal system: A conceptual framework for employee performance improvement. *Management Research Review*, *40*(6), 684–697. doi:10.1108/MRR-04-2016-0084

Smith, J. L., & White, P. H. (2002). An examination of implicitly activated explicitly activated, and nullified stereotypes on mathematical performance: It's not just a women's issue. *Sex Roles*, *47*(3/4), 179–191. doi:10.1023/A:1021051223441

Solomon, B. C., Nikolaev, B. N., & Shepherd, D. A. (2022). Does educational attainment promote job satisfaction? The bittersweet trade-offs between job resources, demands, and stress. *The Journal of Applied Psychology*, *107*(7), 1227–1241. doi:10.1037/apl0000904 PMID:35737558

Tan, T. H., & Waheed, A. (2011). *Herzberg's motivation-hygiene theory and job satisfaction in the Malaysian retail sector: The mediating effect of love of money*. Research Gate.

Tang, Y., Shao, Y. F., Chen, Y. J., & Ma, Y. (2021). How to keep sustainable development between enterprises and employees? Evaluating the impact of person–organization fit and person–job fit on innovative behaviour. *Frontiers in Psychology*, *12*, 653534. doi:10.3389/fpsyg.2021.653534 PMID:33995213

Tims, M., Derks, D., & Bakker, A. B. (2016). Job crafting and its relationships with person–job fit and meaningfulness: A three-wave study. *Journal of Vocational Behavior*, *92*, 44–53. doi:10.1016/j.jvb.2015.11.007

Twum, S. A. (2015). What Diversity Management Practices Do Hotel Managers and Employees View as Important for Retaining Employees? [Master's Thesis, University of Stavanger, Norway].

West, M. (2019). *People analytics for dummies*. John Wiley & Sons.

Wirtz, B. W., Schilke, O., & Ullrich, S. (2010). Strategic development of business models: Implications of the Web 2.0 for creating value on the internet. *Long Range Planning*, *43*(2-3), 272–290. doi:10.1016/j.lrp.2010.01.005

Xie, Y., Tian, J., Jiao, Y., Liu, Y., Yu, H., & Shi, L. (2021). The impact of work stress on job satisfaction and sleep quality for couriers in China: The role of psychological capital. *Frontiers in Psychology*, *12*, 730147. doi:10.3389/fpsyg.2021.730147 PMID:34970180

Zalla, T., Koechlin, E., Pietrini, P., Basso, G., Aquino, P., Sirigu, A., & Grafman, J. (2000). Differential amygdala responses to winning and losing: A functional magnetic resonance imaging study in humans. *The European Journal of Neuroscience*, *12*(5), 1764–1770. doi:10.1046/j.1460-9568.2000.00064.x PMID:10792453

Zhou, D., Yang, S., & Li, X. (2022). Internet Use and Job Satisfaction: Evidence from China. *International Journal of Environmental Research and Public Health, 19*(19), 12157. doi:10.3390/ijerph191912157 PMID:36231458

Zieglmeier, V., Gierlich-Joas, M., & Pretschner, A. (2022, October). Increasing Employees' Willingness to Share: Introducing Appeal Strategies for People Analytics. In *Software Business: 13th International Conference, ICSOB 2022,* (pp. 213-226). Cham: Springer International Publishing. 10.1007/978-3-031-20706-8_15

Chapter 13
Investigating the Cause and Effect of Employee Engagement Through the Lens of HR Analytics

Puneet Kumar
School of Management Studies, Indira Ghandi National Open University, India

ABSTRACT

This study synthesizes the various studies on the construct of employee engagement and HR analytics. This is a theoretical and methodological study substantiating the factors identified from the literature causing employee engagement and its effect on organizational performance indicators. This chapter is descriptive at first as it defines the employee engagement and HR analytics construct. Secondly, this study has the feature of being diagnostic to identify the cause and effect of employee engagement. Lastly, the study has the characteristic of being a prescriptive study to suggest solutions based on data derived through HR analytics to enhance the engagement level of employees. Thus, this three-fold study (descriptive, diagnostic, and prescriptive) is a readymade solution kit for management to investigate the low level of employee engagement through the lens of HR Analytics.

INTRODUCTION

Human resource management originated in recent times as the concept is being accepted by all organizations across the globe. This concept of humanization of work (Bhattacharyya, 2015) was developed to develop competitive advantages, strategic relevance, and sustainability. The normative perspective of HRM defines this function of management as a "process of shaping employment relationships to achieve individual, organizational and societal goals" (Boselie, Paauwe, & Jansen, 2000; p. 20). Schermerhorn (2001) defines the concept as "a process of attracting, developing, and maintaining a talented and energetic workforce to support organizational mission, objectives, and strategies" (p. 2400). The normative

DOI: 10.4018/978-1-6684-8942-0.ch013

approach of HRM incorporates a bunch of crucial HR functions such as human resource planning, recruitment and selection, compensation management, training and development, motivation, organizational culture, change and team development, work-life-balancing, employee engagement, talent management, and turnover.

Over the years the concept of HRM has become significantly complex and comprehensive. The recent development of a data-driven society has led HRM to be defined in terms of "Descriptive" and "Conceptual" perspectives. The fact-based HRM practices give rise to the descriptive concept of HRM whereas conceptual perspective relates these facts to each other. These two perspectives develop the foundation for an emerging concept of HR Analytics (HRA) and predictive decision-making process. The authenticity and validity of data have provided ample reasons for organizations to shift their focus to evidence-based (based on data) management practices for their conscientious decision-making. The concept of evidence-based management was pioneered by Pfeffer and Sutton (2006) and Briner et al. (2009). HR Analytics provides more evidence-based results which help in making better decisions to develop the capabilities of employees of an organization. Such HR analytics-based decisions are more value-adding, futuristic, and sustainable (Bhattacharyya, 2017)

Business organizations in the recent decade are taking a new turn towards a highly competitive yet sustainable business environment. In a competitive environment where every venture comes with a great opportunity to grow possesses an even greater threat of extinction. To survive in such an environment, an organization needs a skilled, experienced, and most importantly engaged workforce. The engagement of employees has been a cause of concern for many organizations witnessing setbacks in their growth. This new yet complex organizational issue has been addressed and defined by many authors and researchers like Kahn (1990); Maslach, Schaufeli, and Leiter (2001); Maslach, Schaufeli, and Leiter (2002) Hallberg and Schaufeli (2006); Schaufeli et al. (2002) and Rothbard (2001) have defined employee engagement in terms of psychological state. One of the pioneers in defining this construct was Kahn. Kahn (1990) defined employee engagement as *"the harnessing of organization members' selves to their work roles; in engagement, people employ and express themselves physically, cognitively, and emotionally during role performances*" (p.694). Authors like Macey and Schneider (2008a) described this construct as a combination of the "*psychological state*", "*behavioral aspect*" and "*Traits*" of employees. Maslach et al. (2001) referred to engagement as a *"persistent, positive affective motivational state of fulfillment"* (p.417).

In the State of global workplace study 2022 by Gallup, only 20% of the workforce is highly engaged in their work globally. A similar study in 2021 reveals the poor rank of India amongst South Asian countries in terms of employee engagement. Where Bangladesh stood first amongst five South Asian countries with a 37% engaged workforce, India has only 25% of an engaged workforce. This decreasing number of employee engagement pose a question to define the concept in quantitative terms to make better HR decision that can be absolute, reliable, and can be validated.

Research Questions and Objectives

The initial objective of this study is to extensively investigate the literature available in the field of employee engagement and HR Analysis to address the following questions concerning Employee Engagement and HR Analytics:

RQ1: What are the factors or drivers causing the engagement level of employees of the organizations?

RQ2: How does employee engagement driven by identified factors affect various organizational performance indicators?
RQ3: How HR Analytics can investigate and measure the metrics of cause and effects of employee engagement?

METHODOLOGY

This study synthesizes the various studies on the construct of employee engagement and HR analytics. This is a theoretical and methodological study substantiating the factors identified from the literature causing employee engagement and its effect on organizational performance indicators. This study is descriptive at first as it defines the employee engagement and HR analytics construct. Secondly, this study has the feature of being diagnostic to identify the cause and effect of employee engagement. Lastly, the study has the characteristic of being a prescriptive study to suggest solutions based on data derived through HR analytics to enhance the engagement level of employees. Thus this three-fold study (descriptive, diagnostic and prescriptive) is a readymade solution kit for management to investigate the low level of employee engagement through the lens of HR Analytics.

LITERATURE REVIEW

Defining and Conceptualizing HR Analytics

The novel concept of HR analytics (Marler and Boudreau, 2017) has been gaining popularity and relevance in today's data-driven business decision-making for the last recent decades. This concept is closely associated with "HR metrics". However, the two have key distinct differences in terms of HRM outcomes (efficiency, effectiveness, and impact) measured through HR metrics (Boselie, 2014). However, the concept of analytics concerning human resources is a comprehensive statistical technique to measure the impact of HR activities (Lawler et al., 2004). A constant debate has been part of HR literature concerning the distinction between HR Metrics and HRA (Marler and Boudreau, 2017). Many of the researchers found it just a "craze" or "fad" (Rasmussen and Ulrich, 2015; Angrave et al., 2016), Marler and Boudreau (2017) found many grounds for divergence in various definitions of HRA and HR Metrics. The first divergence is the "intensity of measurement". HRA is a more sophisticated analysis of HR data, unlike HR Metrics. Secondly, "The scope". The scope of HRA is more broad as it extracts data from internal and external sources. Thirdly, "purpose-oriented". HRA uses information technology for data collection, analysis, interpretation, and reporting for decision-making related to human capital. Marler and Boudreau's (2017, p. 15) defined HRA as "*an HR practice enabled by information technology that uses descriptive, visual, and statistical analyses of data related to HR processes, human capital, organizational performance, and external economic benchmarks to establish business impact and enable data-driven decision-making*".

This definition stresses the utilization of information technology and sophisticated statistical techniques and procedure to represent the outcome in an actionable report. This was also asserted by various authors (such as Levenson, 2005; Koo, and Fallon, 2017; Garcia-Sanchez et al., 2020) who assume that it involves "the proper utilization of statistical techniques, algorithms, and research designs for evaluating data of employees and transmitting the outcomes into actionable reports" (Chatterjee et. al., 2022, p.54). The author like Marler et al. (2017) referred to it as a predictive analysis as it extracts significant data on behaviour patterns, turnover rates, training costs of employees, and their contribution to an organization. The concept of HR Analytics was found to be conceptualized in three phases namely, Descriptive, Prescriptive, and Optimization (Watson, 2010; Laitinen and Sivunen, 2020). The initial and basic level of HR analytics i.e. descriptive one based on the behaviour and past data and outcomes (Fitz-enz and Mattox, 2014; Koo and Fallon, 2017). The next level as the name suggests predicts and forecasts the pattern of behaviour in the future based on previous data and patterns (Fernandez and Gallardo-Gallardo, 2020). Optimization analytics moves a step ahead by optimizing and making the best use of available information to derive the best outcomes using linear programming (Narula and Vassilev, 1994; Chalutz Ben-Gal, 2019; Makarius et al., 2020). These level significantly contributes to improving the decision-making of an organization related to HR issues (Levenson, 2011; Lopez-Arceiz et al., 2019)

The debate has been going on the conceptualization of HR analytics as the available literature in the field of HR analytics represents various concepts and dimensions of this construct. While few scholars like Marler and Boudreau (2017) see HR analytics as HR practice others (such as Huselid, 2018; McIver et al., 2018) see it as a process. For instance, as suggested by McIver et al. (2018), "Workforce Analytics is a process - one that is continuously advanced by improving problem-solving through sound measurement, appropriate research models, systematic data analysis, and technology to support organizational decision making" (p.2). Regardless of whether it is a practice or a process, HR analytics is a highly complex and comprehensive set of skills that incorporates technical, analytical, and data-centric skills which require special sets of KSAOs and competencies (Andersen, 2017; Green, 2017; van den Heuvel and Bondarouk, 2017; van der Togt and Rasmussen, 2017; Minbaeva, 2018). Though these special KSAOs are still not clear as these are based merely on observations and narratives and not empirically researched yet they are highly desirable in any organization for data-driven HR decision-making. As highlighted in De Mauro et al. (2018), the skills and responsibilities required for this analytical function are very vague and inaccurate as organizations stress only subjective interpretation but not objective evaluations of their needs. Still, the debate is ongoing on KSAOs required for HR analysts (Andersen, 2017; van der Togt and Rasmussen, 2017; McIver et al., 2018; Minbaeva, 2018).

Literature available investigating skills and knowledge required for HR analysts highlights the following sets of KSAOs (in Table 1 below):

Not only scholars in the field of behavioural sciences but HR associations and consultancies like CIPD and the Society for Human Resource Management (SHRM) are also engaged in this debate. According to SHRM (2016), HR analysts must be equipped with skills to predict, plan, correlate, and develop models based on data of workforce performance, and business outcomes.

Other consultancies like Bassi, Carpenter, and McMurrer (2010) attempted to define the term "HR Analytics" as "systematically reporting on an array of HR metrics". They advocated that the term is based on the "predictive models", and "evidence-based approach" of HR decision-making. Kapoor and Kabra (2014) defined the term as the "integration of relevant HR data from different sources, the performing of organizational and workforce analysis on this captured data and ultimately the gleaning of insights from the findings to shape decisions for better organizational performance" (p.1). Based on the definitions and concepts of HR Analytics as devised and derived by various scholar HR Analytics can be seen as EIUC (Extension, Integration, Utilisation, and Correlation). It is the Extension of HR Metrics, Integration of internal and external data of the firm, Utilisation of IT, and correlation of decisions with performance.

Table 1. KSAOs for HR analysts

Skills Required	Authors
1. Statistical and Numerical ability	Andersen (2017); Togt and Rasmussen (2017); Deloitte, 2017
2. Data Management Skills and Data Mining	Andersen (2017); Liu et al., (2020); Deloitte, 2017
3. Data Visualization	Andersen (2017); Deloitte, 2017
4. Storytelling	Andersen (2017); Togt and Rasmussen (2017); Deloitte, 2017
5. Business focus	van der Togt and Rasmussen, 2017
6. Understanding of Behavioural science	
7. Problem-solving capabilities	(Duraiet al., 2019),
8. Analytical and IT Skills	Mishra et al., (2016); McIver et al., 2018; Tonidandel et al., 2018; Falletta and Combs, 2020; Pessach et al., 2020; Deloitte, 2017
9. Ability to build and test conceptual and predictive models	Mishra et al., 2016; Minbaeva, 2018

Figure 1.
Source: Author's Creation

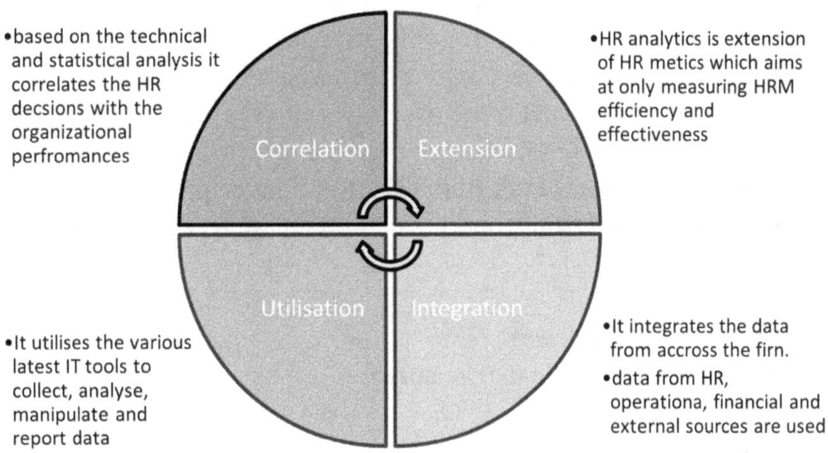

Defining and Conceptualising Employee Engagement

The ever-increasing demand for goods and services and stiff competition in the business environment have led to an entirely kind of organizational structure where "employee engagement" is flourishes and looked for. Thinking beyond psychological factors such as motivation, and work or job satisfaction, organizations are increasingly investigating this new construct of employee engagement owing to its direct association with the company's bottom-line profit. In recent decades this construct is highly researched by academics and practised amongst companies. Bibliometric studies show that there is a significant increase in the number of studies conducted in the field of employee or work engagement in recent decades where the USA, UK, and Canada are the leading contributors with the highest citation. Though the concept is highly researched and desired by any organization yet its clear definition and distinction from other similar constructs have not been made yet.

Wide literature in this field by academicians and consulting professionals inspect and examine this concept with the help of various theories and aspects of engagement making it a positive organizational matter with different meanings and interpretations. Gallups is considered to be the biggest organization that researched to define and measure the construct for almost 30 years in various organizations. According to Gallup (2006), it is a human resource management too. Their conceptualization lacks unanimity over how and why it leads to organizational effectiveness yet the concept is highly appreciated. CIPD attempts to define this concept using similar constructs like "Organizational Citizenship" and "Commitment"(Charted Institute of Personnel and Development, 2007). Similarly, IDeA(2008) assumes it to be baffling as it closely associates with similar constructs like "job satisfaction, employee commitment, internal communication or employee happiness". Taking it further from just performing jobs, CIPD (2007) defines employee engagement to be more than the concept of motivation and job satisfaction. The collaborative work of Kingston Engagement Consortium and CIPD employee engagement may refer to a "positive presence at work during the performance by contributing intellectual efforts and expressing meaning connections and positive emotions to others" (CIPD, 2003).

According to Suff (2008) of Vodaphone, employee engagement is something that employees contribute to a business that has a measurable outcome. Macey and Schneider (2008) assume this concept of employee engagement as a combination of "psychological state", "behavioral aspect" and "Traits". Work Kahn(1990)defines employee engagement as "the harnessing of organization members' selves to their work roles; in engagement, people employ and express themselves physically, cognitively, and emotionally during role performances" (p.694). Maslach et al. (2001) referred to engagement as a "persistent, positive affective motivational state of fulfillment" (p. 417). The comprehensive definition of Catteeuw et al., (2007) incorporates the following aspect to define employee engagement.

- Job satisfaction
- The feeling of being valued at work
- Trust and collaborative culture in the organization
- Retention
- Efficiency and effectiveness of employees

Researchers like Macey & Schneider (2008); Saks (2006); Zigarmi et al. (2009) define employee engagement in terms of commitment which encompasses behavioural outcomes which are demonstrated as an extra effort by an individual at work. Employee engagement is also found to be connected psychology of the employee to retain in an organization (Allen & Meyer, 1990). Other researchers like

Not only commitment but an attempt has also been made to define employee engagement concerning job involvement or just involvement. Lawler and Hall (1970) defined involvement as stressing the individual's identity that is being defined by the influence of the job. They stated that involvement is Lawler & Hall (1970) felt that employee engagement is "the psychological identification with one's work" (p. 310). Kanungo (1982) found the concept of involvement to be based on motivation which is a psychological and cognitive assertion that an individual experiences at his workplace. Saks (2006) sees the concept of employee engagement as behavioural, emotional, and cognitive immersion in the job.

A wide range of theoretical frameworks have been used to define the construct of employee engagement. The pioneer studies such as Kahn (1990); Bakker et al. (2003); Levinson (1965); Maslach et al.'s (2001); Saks (2006); defines the concept as Need-Satisfaction Approach, Job demand resource model, Burnout antithesis approach, and Social exchange theory Approach (In Table 2 below):

Table 2. Theories defining employee engagement

Theory	Authors	Employee Engagement Explanation
Need Satisfaction Approach	Kahn (1990)	"the simultaneous employment and expression of a person's 'preferred self' in task behaviors that promote connections to work and to others, personal presence, and active full role performances" (p. 700).
	Shuck (2010)	He found that employee engagement is expressed as a factor of affective commitment, psychological climate, and job fit.
	May et al. (2004)	Employee engagement can be measured using psychological dimensions such as meaningfulness and availability at work.
Burnout- Anthithesis Approach	Maslach et al., (2001)	They assume employee engagement as a positive antithesis of burnout and define it as "a persistent positive affective state . . . characterized by high levels of activation and pleasure" (p. 417).
	Salanova et al. (2005)	engagement is a "positive, fulfilling, work-related state of mind characterized by vigor, dedication, and absorption" (p. 74).
	Schaufeli, Bakker, and Salanova (2006)	Based on the MBI-GS, the widely used Utrecht Work Engagement Scale (UWES) was developed to measure engagement in terms of vigor, dedication, and absorption.
Job Demands-Resources Model	Bakker et al. (2003)	Explained the concept of employee engagement as a two-factor model of job resources and job demands. Job resources incorporate the physical, psychological, social, and organizational factors at work that may help or hamper the physical or psychological efforts (job demands) required at work.
Social Exchange Theory	Levinson (1965)	According to him, employee engagement is a transaction between employer and employee measured through labor, loyalty, interest, and rewards.
	Masterson et al. (2000)	It is a reciprocal and mutual relationship where one party expects something from the other by providing services to the other party. Moreover, it creates a sense of responsibility for the other party to return the good performance in terms of rewards.
	Saks (2006)	Employee engagement is "a distinct and unique construct consisting of cognitive, emotional, and behavioral components . . . associated with individual role performance" (p. 602).

The exhaustive literature and comprehensive conceptualization of employee engagement make the concept wide-ranging, and overarching. Thus require an attempt to define and measure the concept quantitatively using HR Analytics.

RESULTS AND FINDINGS

Causes of Employee Engagement and HR Analytics

Employee engagement is considered to be a highly comprehensive construct within the management literature as its definition and conceptualization have been conceived with different meanings and interpretations by various academicians, consultants, and practitioners. Due to its enigmatic nature identification of its causes or drivers becomes a tedious task to be performed by HR professionals of an organization. Robinson et al., (2004) found that there are considerable variations and differences concerning causes or factors of employee engagement. Thus they commented that "there is no easy answer as far as engagement is concerned- no simple pulling of one or two levers to raise engagement levels" (Robinson et al., 2004, p. 26). Robinson (2007) identified that the factors of this construct vary considerably among the "employee" who is doing the job, the "type of job" they are doing, and "the organization" they are working in. Charted Institute of personnel development also asserted the same that there are no exhaustive factors identified as the cause of employee engagement (CIPD, 2007). Thus it can be assumed that employee engagement is a multifactor construct (Kumar and Padhi, 2022). However, the Conference Board (2006) attempted to list 26 key drivers of employee engagement from 12 large-scale consultancy studies on employee engagement. A few of the identified drivers in the study were the nature of the job; career growth opportunity; a personal relationship with the manager; relationship with workers/ team members; pride in the company; trust and integrity; the line of sight between individual and company performance (The Conference Board, 2006, p. 6).

Investing various studies conducted in the field of employee engagement and similar constructs like work engagement, commitment, job satisfaction, motivation, and organizational citizenship behaviour it was found that Role Clarity; job Creativity; Supervisor's Support, Relationship with colleagues, Compensation Management System; and Recognition are considered to be a significant cause of employee engagement. The following studies dive deep into these factors.

a. **Role Clarity, Job Creativity**: While assigning any job to an individual it becomes very crucial to define the role clearly to perform the role efficiently and effectively. According to De Villiers & Stander, (2011), role clarity is about defining duties and tasks and expected behaviour without any ambiguity. Here supervisor may play a crucial role to define and let employees understand their fitness for the role or not. Twenge (2010) found that role clarity is considered to be considerably valued among millennials and baby boomers. Another author Mendes & Stander (2011) associating this concept with motivation commented that with autonomy, and infusing confidence, the employee may perceive the role differently and may get motivated. A role performed by an individual without clarity may significantly hamper his performance, productivity, and engagement level as more time will be wasted on finding how to do a task rather than doing it (Alarcon et al., 2010). In a comprehensive and confusing work situation, an organization may strengthen the performance and capabilities of employees by infusing confidence and reducing uncertainty (Panaccio &Vandenberghe, 2011). The Role Clarity Index of Lyons (1971) found a positive correlation between role clarity, work satisfaction, and work engagement and a negative correlation with voluntary turnover. Studies identify the relevance of role clarity for enhanced employee engagement. Thus employees without clear instruction and role clarity tend to be more stressed and burnt out with workload which ultimately leads to disengagement (Nansubuga & Munene, 2013). Role clarity comes at a later stage.

What is crucial for effective job performance and a higher degree of engagement is the design of the job. A considerable amount of research has been going around and earlier had also been conducted on designing a job of day-to-day nature that impacts the engagement level of employees and their personal effects (Morgeson, Dierdorff, and Hmurovic, 2010; Shantz et al., 2013). "Job design is the process of putting together a range of tasks, duties, and responsibilities to create a composite for individuals to undertake in their work and to regard as their own. It is crucial: not only is it the basis of individual satisfaction and achievement at work, but it is also necessary to get the job done efficiently, economically, reliably, and safely" (Torrington et al., 2011, p.84). Though little concern has been seen from the side of policymakers (Truss, 2012), academics and practitioner has been advocating the importance of work design to engage people at work (Humphrey, Nahrgang, and Morgeson, 2007). The work of Christian et al (2011) and studies of Fried and Ferris, (1987); Hackman and Oldham, (1980) assert that job features in terms of autonomy, variety, and feedback significance is relevant for engagement. Even the seminal work of Kahn (1990) advocates this idea. Job demands exerts greater emphasis on the engagement level of employees. Monotonous jobs, not so demands develop a feeling of stress and a certain level of disengagement from work (Morgeson and Humphrey, 2006; Work Foundation, 2009). Thus innovative and challenging jobs that require creativity bring a sense of motivation to employees to their energy in the challenging job (Crawford et al., 2013).

HR Analytics Lens: In an organization implementing and practising HR Metrics and analytics tend to be incurring more benefits than using traditional methods. With the help of HR metrics and Analytics, an organization can effectively assess the various aspects of the job and HR-related activities (Adler, 2016; Maurer, 2016; Sullivan, 2003). The engagement of employees is greatly influenced by role clarity and job creativity. Using HR metrics in terms of instructions involved in the task, the number of times mistakes are made, and job enlargement can measure the role clarity and creativity required. Moreover, the number of times task meetings are held shows what all new projects organization work time to time. All new skills and knowledge required to perform the task show the degree of job creation.

b. **Supervisor's Support and Colleagues Cooperation:** Investigating the available recent literature in the field of employee engagement, it has been found that support from supervisors and the co-operation of colleagues appears to be the significant factor of the construct. To have a supportive supervisor there should be a trust factor between employees and the supervisor. Trust is a psychological factor that shows willingness and positive expectations in a vulnerable situation (Rousseau et al., 1998). It is an "expectancy held by an individual or a group that the word, promise, verbal or written statement of another individual or group can be relied upon" (Rotter, 1967, p. 651). Alper Ertürk (2007) feels that is the sentiments held by the employees towards their supervisor for the support they receive and the commitment they offer in return. Trust in a supervisor lets an employee feel a positive attitude, respectful treatment, and an amicable relationship. Studies by HRMA (2013) and Gallup (2013) have also asserted the fact that those who are not satisfied with their immediate supervisor tend to be more disengaged in their work. Cognitive-based trust in the supervisor brings psychological security to employees as then they can predict and become more clear about work situations (Kahn, 1990; Schaubroeck et al., 2011). This reduces the fear of negative outcomes (Skinner & Searle, 2011) and develops an optimistic outlook as employees are no more scared of taking instructions from supervisors (Hon & Lu, 2010). Supportive supervisor means supportive organizations for employees which relates to job involvement (Rhoades & Eisenberger, 2002). Hirschman (1970) is considered to be the first who brought the role of "voice" in eliminating dissatisfaction at work (Kok, Sarikaya, & Coban, 2016). Employees who are free to raise their voices and concern when they are dissatisfied tend to be more loyal and stay longer in the organization (Brinsfield, Edwards, & Greenberg, 2009). "Engagement is an act of expressing views to support and enhance the working environment (Goldberg, Clark, & Henley, 2011). Another significant factor after a supportive supervisor in whom employees have trust and allow his team to raise their voice is "colleague cooperation". A colleague is the first person nearest to him whom he can seek help from. Such cooperative colleagues significantly influence the engagement level of employees. The coworker relationship creates a need for interpersonal relationships (Locke and Taylor, 1990). Such relationship makes them kind, helpful, trustworthy, and supportive which enhances their overall engagement level (Kahn, 1990). An organization where employees feel free with their colleagues, and find them friendly and supportive is considered to be a safe and secure workplace for employees where their engagement level flourishes. Janssen et al., (2016) comment that relationships at the workplace affect group functioning, performance, and climate of the workplace. Similarly, Avci (2017) feels that the effect of team and co-workers support the well-being of employees.

HR Analytics Lens: HR analytics along with HR Metrics brings out be a great tool to bring out the transformation in an organization with a data-driven and evidence-based approach to decision-making. HR Analytics along with HR Metrics provide a checklist for an organization to obtain valuable and relevant data on employee relations. Looking at the trends and various software dashboards of HRIS it was found to derive data on employee relations, an organization needs to develop metrics that must be based on a relationship system called "Relationship metrics". Under such metrics, an organization can collect all the relevant decision where employer-employee and peer relationship plays a significant role. Metrics such as Grievance Handling, Task Completion", "New Idea promotion, Team meetings, Social Gatherings at work, Workplace Bullying, Sexual Harassments cases, etc. are a few critical yet relevant data points for major HR-related decision-making.

c. **Rewards and Recognition System:** The literature on drivers of employee engagement is flooded with rewards and recognition as one of the crucial factors of employee engagement. The reward system of an organization is such an important management technique that initiates in development of a highly engaging work environment. According to Kerr, & Slocum (2005), the reward system is an exchange agreement between the employer and an employee. Thus with the help of the right reward and compensation system for the right type of individual, an organization can create engaged employees. Similar thoughts resonate in the study of Le Pine (2002) as well that an effective reward and compensation management system creates a highly engaged workforce that brings a competitive advantage to the organization. Authors (such as Thomas, 2009; Gorgievski, Antonio & Bakker, 2014) suggested the benefits of a rewards system that has benefits such extrinsic rewards in terms of medical benefits to make employees more motivated. Apart from monetary components in the reward system, non-monetary components such as training and development are found to be critical factors in determining the engagement level of employees. Dobbs (2000) states that employees may develop soft and technical skills if they are provided with required training and development opportunities. Such training and development opportunities significantly reduce the attrition rate and thereby increase the satisfaction level of employees (Wagner, 2000). Satterfield & Hughes (2007); Lee, Lee, & Wu (2010), and Manuel (2014) asserted assent on the same thought that training and development change the behaviour as well as working skills of workers which helps in upliftment of the performance and increased engagement level. An organization must have a judicious mix of extrinsic and intrinsic reward systems for increased organizational outcomes (Mahaney & Lederer, 2006). The intrinsic reward system of promotion, appreciation, and transfer is at a good location where there are more opportunities to grow and develop a sense of satisfaction, self-esteem, acknowledgement, challenge, autonomy, and responsibility (Mahaney & Lederer, 2006).

HR Analytics lens: An organization must keep a record of its reward and recognition system as it is one of the crucial factors affecting employee engagement. The HR Metrics of the organization should incorporate components like salary constituents, types, and numbers of incentives and bonuses. Several financial bonuses and eligibility to avail of such benefits. Amount of investment made in training and development programs every year, who all are getting benefitted of that. The number of times promotion, demotion, and transfer are made during a period can be used to measure the effectiveness of the reward and recognition system of the organization.

Table 3. Investigation of causes of employee engagement through HR analytics using metrics

Causes (Factors) of Employee Engagement	HR Metrics	Description
Role Clarity and Job Creativity	**Role Description metrics** • Instructions for a task • Mistake due to ambiguity • Number of tasks involved in a role • Task meetings held within a week • Skills and Knowledge Required • Type of Skills Required • Nature of Job	• The engagement of employees is greatly influenced by role clarity and job creativity. • Using HR metrics in terms of instructions involved in the task, the number of times mistakes are made, and job enlargement can measure the role clarity and creativity required. • Moreover, the number of times task meetings are held shows what all new projects organization work time to time. • All new skills and knowledge required to perform the task show degree of job creation.
Supervisor's Support and Colleagues Cooperation	**Relationship Metrics** • Grievance Handling • Task Completion • New Idea promotion • Team meetings • Social Gatherings at Work • Workplace Bullying • Sexual Harassments • Team issues	• The relationship metrics can be used to capture data on employer-employee relationships. • Grievance handling mechanism, task completion by the team, and idea promotion depict the supportive quality of a supervisor. • The number of times team meetings are held, and whether employees get the opportunity to raise their voice shows the quality of a good superior • The evidence of sexual harassment among employees, workplace bullying, and team issues shows what type of cooperative culture prevails amongst colleagues.
Rewards and Recognition System	**Rewards and Recognition Metrics** • Components of a Salary • Incentives and Bonuses • Financial Rewards • Investment by the organization in training and development • Promotion during a period • Demotion or transfer during a period	• An organization must keep a record of its reward and recognition system as it is one of the crucial factors affecting employee engagement. • The HR Metrics of the organization should incorporate components like salary constituents, types, and numbers of incentives and bonuses. • Several financial bonuses and eligibility to avail of such benefits. • Amount of investment made in training and development programs every year, who all are getting benefitted of that. • The number of times promotion, demotion, and transfer are made during a period can be used to measure the effectiveness of the reward and recognition system of the organization.

Source: Author's Creation

HR analysis is a method that provides useful data as a checkpoint list with the help of which an organization can identify the problematic drivers empirically with the help of HR Metrics. These key data points provide a track system for the human resource of an organization and evaluate the effectiveness of HR initiatives. The following Table 3 can help to identify how these causes of employee engagement can be measured using HR Metrics.

2. Effects of Employee Engagement and HR Analytics

Employee engagement is influenced by many critical factors that prevail within an organization. HR Analytics is found to be a great tool to identify and measure the impact of such factors to derive and define the employee engagement level within an organization. Employee Engagement literature and research advocate the relevance of this construct as it not only adds to the bottom line of an organization but also nurtures a creative, healthy, and competitive work environment. The effect of employee engagement can be seen in retention and turnover rate, grievances of employees, customer loyalty, employee advocacy, democratic decision-making, and the health and well-being of employees. HR Analytics with the help of relevant HR metrics can identify and measure these impacts effectively.

A. **Retention and Turnover:** Employee retention is found to be the greatest impact on employee engagement in almost all research in this field. In the words of Ologbo and Saudah (2012), "Employee engagement could be a strong factor for organizational performance and success, as it seems to have a significant potential to affect employee retention, their loyalty and productivity, and also with some link to customer satisfaction, organizational reputation and the overall stakeholder value" (p.506). studies like Towers Perrin (2007); Harvard Business School Press (2006); Levinson (2007) ; (Demourouti et al. (2001); BlessingWhite (2008); advocate that where employee engagement is practised and proposed, employees tend to be more loyal and stay in the organization. Towers Perrin (2007) states that higher employee engagement is depicted in higher performance and less number of employees quitting the organization. Harvard Business School Press (2006) found employee engagement to be the major component of retention. Salahuddin, Abdullah, & M Abdul Rani (2018) in their work cited that when employees are not managed effectively they tend to leave the organization leaving the organization with a higher turnover rate. Disengaged employees tend to be less committed and evaluate the cost of leaving the job and searching for other employment opportunities (Mobley, 1982).

HR Analytics Lens: HR analytics with metrics can develop effective formulas and rates to measure the impact of employee engagement on retention. Organizations such as Deloitte, SHRM, and AIHR, present various metrics to identify the same. Metrics such as turnover rate within a year, or after a particular HR policy, number of requests of transfers, Cost of turnover, cost per turnover, cost per hire, time spent on recruitment and selection etc. can be used to investigate the effect.

B. **Customer Loyalty:** Research suggests that satisfied and happy employees of an organization help greatly in making customers happy and thus loyal (Levinson, 2007). Such happy employees effectively identify the needs and demands of the customers (Right Management, 2006). Therefore they strive towards making more loyal and happy customers (Pont, 2004). This "Customer Engagement" (as stated by Bates, 2004) is an emotional and cognitive connection between an organization and its customers. Other authors like Salanova, Agut, & Peiro (2005) associate this with the service climate of an organization. Their study found that the relationship between customer loyalty and employee engagement is mediated by the service climate and performance of the hotel industry. Gracia, Bakker, & Grau (2011) also feel the same in the hotel industry, guests tend to be more loyal if they positively evaluate the quality of the service of hotel and restaurant. Thus with the help of engaged and happy employees, an organization can ensure repetitive sales and customer loyalty as these engaged employees are more involved and enthusiastic in their job (Harter et al., 2002; Ram, Bhargavi, & Prabhakar, 2011).

HR Analytics Lens: as loyal customers are the main constituents of sales of an organization their data is significant is relevant for HR professionals for decision making. Using relevant HR Metrics an organization can keep track of real-time sales and repetitive sales. Metrics such as number and percentage of the repetitive sale in a week/month/ quarterly/ yearly, Number of after-sale complaints received duration of the resolution, average sales cycle, etc.

C. **Employee Advocacy:** in the context of employee advocacy, the literature available states that "engaged employees are more likely to advocate the organization as a place to work and actively promote its products and services" (Scottish Executive Social Research, 2007 p. 23). Contrary to this, Penna (2006) talks about disengaged employees whom he termed "Corporate Terrorists" as they are the ones who discourage others from joining the organization. The promotion of the organization, its product, and its services as a great place to work is the result of employee engagement. Researchers (such as McLeod & Clarke 2009; Miles & Mangold 2014; Gupta & Sharma 2016) assert that employee engagement and employee advocacy are associated terms. In a study by McLeod & Clarke (2009) around 67% of engaged employees advocate their organization unlike disengaged 3% of employees who advocates. In terms of products and services, 78% of engaged employees recommend products and services of their organization. Thus it is a link between employer and employee. Schweitzer and Lyons (2008); Kim & Rhee (2014) and Men (2014) advocate that an organization must strive towards developing employee engagement policies as these employees spread positive words about the organization that helps an organization to grow. Kim and Rhee (2014) perceive this phenomenon as megaphoning effect i.e. "the likelihood of employees' voluntary information forwarding or information sharing about organizational strengths (accomplishments) or weaknesses (problems)" (p. 246).

HR Analytics Lens: through the lens of HR analytics an organization can keep track of employee advocacy. HR metrics used may incorporate metrics like reference recruitment, employee advocacy survey, perception towards product and service, number of employees using products and services of the organization, number of relatives or friends of the employees in the organization, etc. Using such critical points an organization may capture relevant HR data for better HR decision making. The following Table 4 can help to identify how these effects of employee engagement can be measured using HR Metrics.

Table 4. Investigation of effects of employee engagement through HR analytics using metrics

Effects of Employee Engagement	HR Metrics	Description
Retention and Turnover	**Retention and Turnover metrics** • turnover rate within a year, or after a particular HR policy, • number of requests for transfers, • Cost of turnover, • cost per turnover, • cost per hire, • time spent on recruitment and selection etc.	• With the help of the turnover rate, an organization may get to know about the trend of exit in an organization. • What HR policies are leading to the exodus of employees? • The requests received for transfer show whether the employee is not happy in this branch or office either due to work culture or due to commuting problems. • The cost of turnover and cost per turnover may help an organization that whether hiring a new employee and letting an existing employee leave the organization is a better deal or not. • Time spent on the recruitment process can be one of the factors to be considered.
Customer Loyalty	**Customer Loyalty Metrics** • number and percentage of repetitive sales in a week/month/ quarterly/ yearly, • Number of after-sale complaints received, • duration of the resolution, • Average sales cycle etc.	• The data on repetitive sales provide information about satisfied customers that are efforts of engaged employees. • An organization can keep of record of weekly/monthly/ quarterly/ yearly records of their loyal customers. • Several after-sale complaints provide useful information. • Adequate complaints show that customers are trying products again and again and thus making complaints if arise against those who do not make complaints and switch to other products and services. • The duration of complaint resolution may also show that employees are engaged in providing the best solution to the customers in no time.
Employee Advocacy	**Advocacy Metrics** • reference recruitment, • several relatives or friends of the employees in the organization etc. • employee advocacy survey, • perception towards products and services, • number of employees using products and services of the organization,	• The effect of good HR practices is shown in engaged employees advocating for their organization. Recruitment of the references of existing employees shows that existing employees feel their organization is the best place to work. • Several relatives or school/college friends of existing employees can be used for this. • An employee advocacy survey can be used to measure the perception of employees towards the organization as a place to work and the quality of products and services of the organization. • Moreover, employees themselves using the products and services of employees show that they like the products and services they are selling.

Source: Author's Creation

CONCLUSION

The concept of HR Analytics and Employee Engagement is in a very nascent stage to comprehend the complete meaning and concept of the construct. Available literature in these fields provides quite significant information in this regard. Where employee engagement is a complete psychological construct of complete immersion, absorption and one's commitment to one's job and organization HR Analytics is a systematic, scientific and data-driven management concept that identify and measure all the quantitative construct of management with an evidence-based approach for effective and efficient decision making. Investing various studies conducted in the field of employee engagement and similar constructs like work engagement, commitment, job satisfaction, motivation, and organizational citizenship behaviour it was found that Role Clarity; job Creativity; Supervisor's Support, Relationship with colleagues, Compensation Management System; and Recognition are considered to be a significant cause of employee engagement. Using HR metrics in terms of instructions involved in the task, the number of times mistakes are made, and job enlargement can measure the role clarity and creativity required. Using "Relationship metrics" an organization can collect all the relevant decision where employer-employee and peer relationship plays a significant role. For relevant data collection, the HR Metrics of the organization should incorporate components like salary constituents, types, and numbers of incentives and bonuses. Data on several financial bonuses and eligibility to avail of such benefits, the amount of investment made in training and development programs every year, and who all are getting benefitted from that may provide relevant information. Employee Engagement literature and research advocate the relevance of this construct as it not only adds to the bottom line of an organization but also nurtures a creative, healthy, and competitive work environment. The effect of employee engagement can be seen in retention and turnover rate, grievances of employees, customer loyalty, employee advocacy, democratic decision-making, and the health and well-being of employees. HR Analytics with the help of relevant HR metrics can identify and measure these impacts effectively.

Future Scope of the Study

Employee Engagement has been the trending issue in the organization for many years owing to its direct association with the company's bottom line profits. According to Gallup's study, employee engagement has been experiencing a downward trend though not so plunging in the last two years. A downfall of 2% has been noticed in employee engagement in the last two years. This trend will become more severe with new norms like working from home or remote working. In such a gruesome environment there is a need to identify and measure this construct with data-driven evidence with HR Analytics using HR Metrics. Thus, this study may become crucial to address the issues of employee engagement effectively.

REFERENCES

Adler, L. (2016). Metrics for better hires. *HRMagazine*, *60*(2), 60–61.

Alarcon, G., Lyons, J. B., & Tartaglia, F. (2010). Understanding predictors of engagement within the military. *Military Psychology*, *22*(3), 301–310. doi:10.1080/08995605.2010.492695

Allen, N. J., & Meyer, J. P. (1990). The measurement and antecedents of affective, continuance, and normative commitment to the organization. *Journal of Occupational Psychology*, *63*(1), 1–18. doi:10.1111/j.2044-8325.1990.tb00506.x

Andersen, M. K. (2017). Human capital analytics: The winding road. *Journal of Organizational Effectiveness*, *4*(2), 133–136. doi:10.1108/JOEPP-03-2017-0024

Angrave, D., Charlwood, A., Kirkpatrick, I., Lawrence, M., & Stuart, M. (2016). HR and analytics: Why HR is set to fail the big data challenge. *Human Resource Management Journal*, *26*(1), 1–11. doi:10.1111/1748-8583.12090

Avci, N. (2017). The relationship between coworker supports, quality of work life and wellbeing: an empirical study of hotel employees. *International Journal of Management Economics and Business, 13*(3), 577-589. doi:10.17130/ijmeb.2017331328

Bakker, A. B., Demerouti, E., Boer, E., & Schaufelia, W. B. (2003). Job demands and job resources as predictors of absence duration and frequency. *Journal of Vocational Behavior*, *62*(2), 341–356. doi:10.1016/S0001-8791(02)00030-1

Bates, S. (2004). Getting engaged. *HRMagazine*, *49*(2), 44–51.

Boselie, P. (2014). *Strategic Human Resource Management: A Balanced Approach* (2nd ed.). McGraw-Hill Education.

Boselie, P., Paauwe, J., & Jansen, P. (2000). *Human Resource Management and Performance*.

Brinsfield, C. T., Edwards, M. S., & Greenberg, J. (2009). Voice and silence in organisations: Historical review and current conceptualizations. *Voice and silence in organisations*.

Catteeuw, F., Flynn, E., & Vonderhorst, J. (2007). Employee engagement: Boosting productivity in turbulent times. *Organization Development Journal*, *25*(2), 151–157.

Chalutz Ben-Gal, H. (2019). An ROI-based review of HR analytics: Practical implementation tools. *Personnel Review*, *48*(6), 1429–1448. doi:10.1108/PR-11-2017-0362

Chartered institute of personnel and development. (2003). *Understanding the people and performance link: unlocking the black box*. London: CIPD.

Chatterjee, S., Chaudhuri, R., Vrontis, D., & Siachou, E. (2022). Examining the dark side of human resource analytics: An empirical investigation using the privacy calculus approach. *International Journal of Manpower*, *43*(1), 52–74. doi:10.1108/IJM-02-2021-0087

Christian, M. S., Garza, A. S., & Slaughter, J. E. (2011). Work engagement: A quantitative review and test of its relations with task and contextual performance. *Personnel Psychology*, *64*(1), 89–136. doi:10.1111/j.1744-6570.2010.01203.x

CIPD. (2007). Employee Engagement. CIPD. www.cipd.co.uk/subjects/empreltns/general/empengmt.htm?IsSrchRes=1

Conference Board (2006). Employee Engagement: A review of current research and its implications. *The Conference Board*.

Crawford, E., Rich, B., Buckman, B., & Bergeron, J. (2013). The Antecedents and Drivers of Employee Engagement. In C. Truss, K. Alfes, R. Delbridge, A. Shantz, & E. Soane (Eds.), *Employee Engagement in Theory and Practice*. Routledge.

De Mauro, A., Greco, M., Grimaldi, M., & Ritala, P. (2018). Human resources for Big Data professions: A systematic classification of job roles and required skill sets. *Information Processing & Management*, *54*(5), 807–817. doi:10.1016/j.ipm.2017.05.004

De Villiers, J. R., & Stander, M. W. (2011). Psychological Empowerment, Work Engagement and Turnover Intention: The Role of Leader Relations and Role Clarity in a Financial Institution. *Journal of Psychology in Africa*, *21*(3), 405–412. doi:10.1080/14330237.2011.10820474

Deloitte. (2017). *Redesigning performance management*. Deloitte insights. https://www2. deloitte.com/insights/us/en/focus/human-capital-trends/2017/redesigning-performancemanagement.html

Demerouti, E., Bakker, A. B., Nachreiner, F., & Schaufeli, W. B. (2001). The Job Demands–Resources Model of Burnout. *The Journal of Applied Psychology*, *86*(3), 499–512. doi:10.1037/0021-9010.86.3.499 PMID:11419809

Dobbs, K. (2000). Tires Plus takes the training high road. *Training (New York, N.Y.)*, *37*(4), 56–63.

Durai, S., Rudhramoorthy, K., & Sarkar, S. (2019). HR metrics and workforce analytics: It is a journey, not a destination. *Human Resource Management International Digest*, *27*(1), 4–6. doi:10.1108/HRMID-08-2018-0167

Ertürk, A. (2007). Layoff Survivors' Perceptions Of Fairness As Determinant Of Affective Commitment Following Downsizing, *Bogazici Journal, Review of Social. Economic and Administrative Studies*, *21*(1+2), 37–58.

Falletta, S. V., & Combs, W. L. (2020). The HR analytics cycle: A seven-step process for building evidence-based and ethical HR analytics capabilities. *Journal of Work-Applied Management*. doi:10.1108/JWAM-03-2020-0020

Fernandez, V., & Gallardo-Gallardo, E. (2020). Tackling the HR digitalization challenge: Key factors and barriers to HR analytics adoption, In Press. *Competitiveness Review*, *31*(1), 162–187. doi:10.1108/CR-12-2019-0163

Fitz-enz, J., & Mattox, J. R. (2014). *Predictive Analytics for Human Resources*. Wiley. doi:10.1002/9781118915042

Fried, Y., & Ferris, G. R. (1987). The Validity of the Job Characteristics Model:A Review and Meta--Analysis. *Personnel Psychology*, *40*(2), 287–322. doi:10.1111/j.1744-6570.1987.tb00605.x

Gallup, I. (2013). *State of the Global Workplace 2013*. Gallup. https://www.gallup.com/topic/STATE_OF_THE_GLOBAL_WORKPLACE_2013.aspx

Gallup. (2006). Gallup study: engaged employees inspire company innovation: national survey finds that passionate workers are most likely to drive organisations forward, *The Gallup Management Journal*, http://gmj.gallup.com/content/24880/Gallup-Study- Engaged-Employees-Inspire-Company.aspx

Garcia-Sanchez, I.-M., Raimo, N., & Vitolla, F. (2020). CEO power and integrated reporting, In Press, *Meditari. Accountability in Research*. doi:10.1108/MEDAR-11-2019-0604

Goldberg, C. B., Clark, M. A., & Henley, A. B. (2011). Speaking up: A conceptual model of voice responses following the unfair treatment of others in non-union settings. *Human Resource Management*, *50*(1), 75–94. doi:10.1002/hrm.20402

Gorgievski, M., & Moriano, J. (2014). (forthcoming). Relating Work Engagement and Workaholism to Entrepreneurial Performance. *Journal of Managerial Psychology*, *29*. doi:10.1108/JMP-06-2012-0169

Gracia, E., Bakker, A. B., & Grau, R. M. (2011). Positive emotions: The connection between customer quality evaluations and loyalty. *Cornell Hospitality Quarterly*, *52*(4), 458–465. doi:10.1177/1938965510395379

Green, D. (2017). The best practices to excel at people analytics. *Journal of Organizational Effectiveness: People and Performance*, *4*(2), 137–144. doi:10.1108/JOEPP-03-2017-0027

Gupta, N., & Sharma, V. (2016). Exploring Employee Engagement – A Way to Better Business Performance. *Global Business Review*, *17*(3), 45–63. doi:10.1177/0972150916631082

Hackman, J. R., & Oldham, G. R. (1980). *Work redesign*. AddisonWesley.

Harter, J. K., Schmidt, F. L., & Hayes, T. L. (2002). Business-unit-level relationship between employee satisfaction, employee engagement, and business outcomes: A meta-analysis. *The Journal of Applied Psychology*, *87*(2), 268–279. doi:10.1037/0021-9010.87.2.268 PMID:12002955

Harvard Business School Press. (2006). *Retaining Your Best People*. Harvard Business School Publishing Corporation.

Hirschman, A. O. (1970). *Exit, voice, and loyalty: Responses to decline in firms, organisations, and states* (Vol. 25). Harvard university press.

Hon, A. H., & Lu, L. (2010). The mediating role of trust between expatriate procedural justice and employee outcomes in Chinese hotel industry. *International Journal of Hospitality Management*, *29*(4), 669–676. doi:10.1016/j.ijhm.2010.01.002

HRMA. (2013) *Human Resources Management Association (HRMA)*. HRMA. http://www.hrvoice.org

Humphrey, S. E., Nahrgang, J. D., & Morgeson, F. P. (2007). Integrating motivational, social, and contextual work design features: A meta-analytic summary and theoretical extension of the work design literature. *The Journal of Applied Psychology*, *92*(5), 1332–1356. doi:10.1037/0021-9010.92.5.1332 PMID:17845089

Huselid, M. A. (2018). The science and practice of workforce analytics: Introduction to the HRM special issue. *Human Resource Management*, *57*(3), 679–684. doi:10.1002/hrm.21916

IDeA. (2008). *What is Employee Engagement?* IDeA. www.idea.gov.uk/idk/core/page.do?pageId=8407178

Janssen, S., Tahitu, J., van Vuuren, M., & de Jong, M. (2016). Coworkers' Perspectives on Mentoring Relationships. *Group & Organization Management*, *43*(2), 245–272. doi:10.1177/1059601116669641 PMID:29568215

Kahn, W. A. (1990). Psychological conditions of personal engagement and disengagement at work. *Academy of Management Journal*, *33*(4), 692–724. doi:10.2307/256287

Kanungo, R. N. (1982). Measurement of job and work involvement. *The Journal of Applied Psychology*, *67*(3), 341–349. doi:10.1037/0021-9010.67.3.341

Kerr, J., & Slocum, J. Jr. (2005). Managing corporate culture through reward systems. *The Academy of Management Perspectives*, *19*(4), 130–138. doi:10.5465/ame.2005.19417915

Kim, J., & Rhee, Y. (2011). Strategic Thinking about Employee Communication Behavior (ECB) in Public Relations: Testing the Models of Megaphoning and Scouting Effects in Korea. *Journal of Public Relations Research*, *23*(3), 243–268. doi:10.1080/1062726X.2011.582204

Kok, S. B., Sarikaya, M., & Coban, H. (2016). Organisational Voice Behaviour and its Investigation in Terms of Organisational Variables. *European Scientific Journal*, *12*(35), 16–33. doi:10.19044/esj.2016.v12n35p16

Koo, H. S., & Fallon, K. (2017). Preferences in tracking dimensions for wearable technology. *International Journal of Clothing Science and Technology*, *29*(2), 180–199. doi:10.1108/IJCST-03-2016-0021

Kumar, P., & Padhi, N. (2022). Development and validation of multi-factor employee engagement measuring instrument: A formative measurement model. *Personnel Review*, *51*(9), 2261–2276. doi:10.1108/PR-01-2021-0014

Laitinen, K., & Sivunen, A. (2020). Enablers of and constraints on employees' information sharing on enterprise social media, In Press. *Information Technology & People*, *34*(2), 642–665. doi:10.1108/ITP-04-2019-0186

Lawler, E., Levenson, A., & Boudreau, J. W. (2004). HR metrics and analytics: Use and impact. *Human Resource Planning*, *27*(4), 7–35.

Lawler, E. E., & Hall, D. T. (1970). Relationship of job characteristics to job involvement, satisfaction, and intrinsic motivation. *The Journal of Applied Psychology*, *54*(4), 305–312. doi:10.1037/h0029692

Lee, F., Lee, T., & Wu, W. (2010). The relationship between human resources management practices, business strategy and firm performance: Evidence from Steel Industry in Taiwan. *International Journal of Human Resource Management*, *21*(9), 1351–1372. doi:10.1080/09585192.2010.488428

LePine, J. A., Erez, A., & Johnson, D. E. (2002). The nature and dimensionality of organizational citizenship behavior: A critical review and metaanalysis. *The Journal of Applied Psychology*, *87*(1), 52–66. doi:10.1037/0021-9010.87.1.52 PMID:11916216

Levenson, A. (2005). Harnessing the power of HR analytics. [http://dx.doi.org/10.1108/14754390580000607]. *Strategic HR Review*, *4*(3), 28–31. doi:10.1108/14754390580000607

Levenson, A. (2011). Using targeted analytics to improve talent decisions. *People and Strategy*, *34*(2), 34–54.

Levinson, E. (2007). *Developing High Employee Engagement Makes Good Business Sense*. Interaction Associates. www.interactionassociates.com/ideas/2007/05/developing_high_employee_eng agement_makes_good_business_sense.php

Levinson, H. (1965). Reciprocation: The relationship between man and organization. *Administrative Science Quarterly*, *9*(4), 370–390. doi:10.2307/2391032

Liu, L., Akkineni, S., Story, P., & Davis, C. (2020). *Using HR analytics to support managerial decisions: a case study*. ACMSE 2020 - Proceedings of the 2020 ACM Southeast Conference, (pp. 168-175). ACM. 10.1145/3374135.3385281

Locke, E. A., & Taylor, M. S. (1990). Stress, coping, and the meaning of work', in Brief, A. and W.R. Nord (Eds) Meanings of Occupational Work, (pp 135-170). Lexington, Lexington Books.

Lopez-Arceiz, F. J., Torres, L., & Bellostas, A. J. B. (2019). Is online disclosure the key to corporate governance? *Online Information Review*, *43*(5), 893–921. doi:10.1108/OIR-06-2018-0191

Lyons, T. (1971). Role clarity, need for clarity, satisfaction, tension, and withdrawal. *Organizational Behavior and Human Performance*, *6*(1), 999–110. doi:10.1016/0030-5073(71)90007-9

Macey, W. H., & Schneider, B. (2008). The meaning of employee engagement. *Industrial and Organizational Psychology: Perspectives on Science and Practice, 1*(1), 3–30. doi:10.1111/j.1754-9434.2007.0002.x

Mahaney, R. C., & Lederer, A. L. (2006). The effect of intrinsic and extrinsic rewards for developers on information systems project success. *Project Management Journal, 37*(4), 42–54. doi:10.1177/875697280603700405

Makarius, E. E., Mukherjee, D., Fox, J. D., & Fox, A. K. (2020). Rising with the machines: A sociotechnical framework for bringing artificial intelligence into the organization. *Journal of Business Research, 120*, 262–273. doi:10.1016/j.jbusres.2020.07.045

Management, R. (2006). *Measuring True Employee Engagement.* Right Management.

Manuel, F. D. (2014). The Effect of Training and Development on Perceived Business Performance, *Research project for Gordon Institute of Business Science*, University of Pretoria. http://hdl.handle.net/2263/44214

Marler, J. H., & Boudreau, J. W. (2017). An evidence-based review of HR analytics. *International Journal of Human Resource Management, 28*(1), 3–26. doi:10.1080/09585192.2016.1244699

Marler, J. H., Cronemberger, F., & Tao, C. (2017). HR analytics: here to stay or short-lived management fashion? in Bondarouk, T., Ru€el, H.J.M. and Parry, E. (Eds), Electronic HRM in the Smart Era (The Changing Context of Managing People). Emerald Publishing, Bingley.

Maslach, C., Schaufeli, W. B., & Leiter, M. P. (2001). Job burnout. *Annual Review of Psychology, 52*(1), 397–422. doi:10.1146/annurev.psych.52.1.397 PMID:11148311

Maurer, R. (2016). 5 big recruiting trends. *HRMagazine, 61*(3), 7–9.

May, D. R., Gilson, R. L., & Harter, L. M. (2004). The psychological conditions of meaningfulness, safety, and availability and the engagement of the human spirit at work. *Journal of Occupational and Organizational Psychology, 77*(1), 11–37. doi:10.1348/096317904322915892

McIver, D., Lengnick-Hall, M.L. & Lengnick-Hall, C.A. (2018). A strategic approach to workforce analytics: integrating science and agility, *Business Horizons, 61(3)*, 397-407. Kelley School of Business, Indiana University. . doi:10.1016/j.bushor.2018.01.005

McLeod, D., & Clarke, N. (2009). Engaging for Success: enhancing performance through employee engagement. *A report to Government*. Engage for Success. https://engageforsuccess.org/wpcontent/uploads/2015/08/file52215.pd

Men, L. (2014). Why Leadership Matters to Internal Communication: Linking Transformational Leadership, Symmetrical Communication, and Employee Outcomes. *Journal of Public Relations Research, 26*(3), 256–279. doi:10.1080/1062726X.2014.908719

Mendes, F., & Stander, M. (2011). Positive organisation: The role of leader behaviour in work engagement and retention. *SA Journal of Industrial Psychology, 37*(1). doi:10.4102ajip.v37i1.900

Miles, S., & Mangold, G. (2014). Employee voice: Untapped resource or social media time bomb? *Business Horizons, 57*(3), 401–411. doi:10.1016/j.bushor.2013.12.011

Minbaeva, D. (2018). Building credible human capital analytics for organizational competitive advantage. *Human Resource Management*, *57*(3), 701–713. doi:10.1002/hrm.21848

Mishra, S. N., Lama, D. R., & Pal, Y. (2016). Human resource predictive analytics (HRPA) for HR management in organizations. *International Journal of Scientific and Technology Research*, *5*(5), 33–35.

Mobley, W. H. (1982). Some unanswered questions in turnover and withdrawal research. *Academy of Management Review*, *7*(1), 111–116. doi:10.2307/257255

Morgeson, F. P., Dierdorff, E. C., & Hmurovic, J. L. (2010). Work design *in situ*: Understanding the role of occupational and organizational context. *Journal of Organizational Behavior*, *31*(2-3), 351–360. doi:10.1002/job.642

Morgeson, F. P., & Humphrey, S. E. (2006). The Work Design Questionnaire (WDQ): Developing and validating a comprehensive measure for assessing job design and the nature of work. *The Journal of Applied Psychology*, *91*(6), 1321–1339. doi:10.1037/0021-9010.91.6.1321 PMID:17100487

Nansubuga, F., & Munene, J. C. (2013). Reflecting on competences to increase role clarity during service delivery in a third world setting. *Journal of Workplace Learning*, *25*(4), 231–246. doi:10.1108/13665621311316429

Narula, S. C., & Vassilev, V. (1994). An interactive algorithm for solving multiple objective integer linear programming problems. *European Journal of Operational Research*, *79*(3), 443–450. doi:10.1016/0377-2217(94)90058-2

Ologbo, A., & Saudah, S. (2012). Individual Factors Work Outcomes of Employee Engagement. *Elsevier Ltd*. https://www.sciencedirect.com/science/article/pii/S1877042812006891

Panaccio, A., & Vandenberghe, C. (2011). The Relationships of Role Clarity and Organization Based Self-Esteem to Commitment to Supervisors and Organizations and Turnover Intentions. *Journal of Applied Social Psychology*, *41*(6), 1455–1485. doi:10.1111/j.1559-1816.2011.00764.x

Penna. (2006). *Meaning at Work Research Report*. Penna. www.e- penna.com/newsopinion/research.aspx

Perrin, T. (2007). *Largest Ever Study of Global Workforce Finds Senior Management Holds Trigger to Unleash Talent Potential*. Tower Sperrin. www.towersperrin.com/tp/showdctmdoc.jsp?url=HR_Services/Canada/English/ Press_Releases/2007/20071022/2007_10_22.htm&country=global

Pessach, D., Singer, G., Avrahami, D., Chalutz Ben-Gal, H., Shmueli, E., & Ben-Gal, I. (2020). Employees recruitment: A prescriptive analytics approach via machine learning and mathematical programming. *Decision Support Systems*, *134*, 113290. doi:10.1016/j.dss.2020.113290 PMID:32501316

Pont, J. (2004). Are they really 'On the Job'? *Potentials*, *37*, 32.

Ram, P., Bhargavi, G., & Prabhakar, G. V. (2011). Work environment, service climate, and customer satisfaction: Examining theoretical and empirical connections. *International Journal of Business and Social Science*, *2*(20), 121–132.

Rasmussen, T., & Ulrich, D. (2015). Learning from practice: How HR analytics avoids being a management fad. *Organizational Dynamics*, *44*(3), 236–242. doi:10.1016/j.orgdyn.2015.05.008

Rhoades, L., & Eisenberger, R. (2002). Perceived organizational support: A review of the literature. *The Journal of Applied Psychology, 87*(4), 698–714. doi:10.1037/0021-9010.87.4.698 PMID:12184574

Robinson, D. (2007). *Engagement is marriage of various factors at work.* Thought Leaders.

Robinson, D., Perryman, S., & Hayday, S. (2004). *The drivers of employee engagement.* Employment Studies. www.employment-studies.co.uk

Rotter, J. B. (1967). A new scale for the measurement of interpersonal trust. *Journal of Personality, 35*(4), 651–665. doi:10.1111/j.1467-6494.1967.tb01454.x PMID:4865583

Rousseau, D. M., Sitkin, S. B., Burt, R. S., & Camerer, C. (1998). Not so different after all: A cross-discipline view of trust. *Academy of Management Review, 23*(3), 393–404. doi:10.5465/amr.1998.926617

Saks, A. M. (2006). Antecedents and consequences of employee engagement. *Journal of Managerial Psychology, 21*(7), 600–619. doi:10.1108/02683940610690169

Salahudin, S., N., A., M., A. R., & N., A. (2018). Management of Human Resource Policies and Its Relationship with Employee Engagement and Turnover Intention In Brunei"s Islamic Banks. *European Journal of Human Resource Management Studies, 1*(2), 78–92.

Salanova, M., Agut, S., & Peiro, J. M. (2005). Linking organizational resources and work engagement to employee performance and customer loyalty: The mediation of service climate. *The Journal of Applied Psychology, 90*(6), 1217–1227. doi:10.1037/0021-9010.90.6.1217 PMID:16316275

Satterfield, J., & Hughes, E. (2007). Emotion skills training for medical students: A systematic [review]. *Medical Education, 41*(10), 935–941. doi:10.1111/j.1365-2923.2007.02835.x PMID:17822414

Schaubroeck, J. M., Lam, S. S. K., & Peng, A. C. (2011). Cognition-based and affectbased trust as mediators of leader behavior influences on team performance. *The Journal of Applied Psychology, 96*(4), 863–871. doi:10.1037/a0022625 PMID:21299271

Schaufeli, W. B., Bakker, A. B., & Salanova, M. (2006). The Measurement of Work Engagement With a Short Questionnaire: A Cross-National Study. *Educational and Psychological Measurement, 66*(4), 701–716. doi:10.1177/0013164405282471

Schermerhorn, J. R. (2001). *Management Update 2001* (6th ed.). John Wiley and Sons.

Schweitzer, L., & Lyons, S. (2008). The market within: A marketing approach to creating and developing high-value employment relationships. *Business Horizons, 51*(6), 555–565. doi:10.1016/j.bushor.2008.03.004

Scottish Executive Social Research. (2007). *Employee engagement in the Public Sector: a review of literature.* SESR. www.scotland.gov.uk/Publications/2007/05/09111348/3

Shantz, A., Alfes, K., Truss, C., & Soane, E. (2013).The role of employee engagement in the relationship between job design and task performance, citizenship and deviant behaviours. *The International Journal of Human Resource Management, 24 (13)*, 2608- 2627. http://eprints.lse.ac.uk/48156/

Shuck, M. B. (2010). *Employee engagement: An examination of antecedent and outcome variables* [Doctoral dissertation]. FIU Electronic Theses and Dissertations. https://digitalcommons.fiu.edu/etd/235

Suff, R. (2008). Vodaphone's entertaining employee-engagement strategy', *IRS Employment Review*, 896. IRS.

Sullivan, J. (2003). *HR metrics: The world class way*. Kennedy Information.

Thomas, K. (2009). The Four Intrinsic Rewards that Drive Employee Engagement. *Ivey Business Journal*. https://iveybusinessjournal.com/publication/the-four-intrinsic-rewards-thatdrive-employee-engagement/

Tonidandel, S., King, E. B., & Cortina, J. M. (2018). Big data methods: Leveraging modern data analytic techniques to build organizational science. *Organizational Research Methods*, *21*(3), 525–547. doi:10.1177/1094428116677299

Torrington, D., Hall, L., Taylor, S., & Atkinson, C. (2011). Human Resource Management. 8thEdition. Harlow: Pearson.

Truss,C.(2012). Spinning Plates and Juggling Hats: Employee Engagement in an Era of Austerity. *Wimbledon: CIPD.*

Twenge, J. M. (2010). A review of the empirical evidence on generational differences in work attitudes. *Journal of Business and Psychology*, *25*(10), 201–210. doi:10.100710869-010-9165-6

Van den Heuvel, S., & Bondarouk, T. (2017). The rise (and fall?) of HR analytics. *Journal of Organizational Effectiveness: People and Performance*, *4*(2), 157–178. doi:10.1108/JOEPP-03-2017-0022

Van der Togt, J., & Rasmussen, T. H. (2017). Toward evidence-based HR. *Journal of Organizational Effectiveness*, *4*(2), 127–132. doi:10.1108/JOEPP-02-2017-0013

Wagner, S. (2000). Retention: Finders, keepers. *Training & Development*, *54*(8), 64.

Watson, H. (2010). All about analytics. *International Journal of Business Intelligence Research*, *4*(1), 13–28. doi:10.4018/jbir.2013010102

White, B. (2008). *The State of Employee Engagement*. Blessing White.

Work Foundation. (2009). *Knowledge Workers and Knowledge Work. A Knowledge Economy Programme Report*. Work Foundation.

Zigarmi, D., Nimon, K., Houson, D., Witt, D., & Diehl, J. (2009). Beyond engagement: Toward a framework and operational definition for employee work passion. *Human Resource Development Review*, *8*(3), 300–326. doi:10.1177/1534484309338171

Chapter 14
Talent Retention:
Factors Influencing Employee Turnover in the IT Industry

Soumya Mukherjee
Techno India, Hooghly, India

Mrinal Kanti Das
Kanchrapara College, India

ABSTRACT

The biggest challenge nowadays is finding and keeping quality employees in order to meet organizational needs and business demands. According to this perspective, talent emerges as the keystone of organizational strategy. The authors made the modest effort to identify the factors that significantly contribute in luring prospective and resourceful employees more to their employer. Sample size for this study was 440 employees currently working in IT sector in Kolkata. The authors found this research study to be a noble contribution since talent retention practice will serve as a base for employer branding and will play the influencing role for the IT companies to reach the pinnacle of success. In addition to providing a competitive edge, these factors would also allow for the establishing the employer branding concept, which would later pay off handsomely.

1. INTRODUCTION

In the VUCA world, companies are becoming increasingly aware of the importance of key personnel, or individuals with exceptional abilities (Thunnissen, 2016). These highly skilled employees are extremely valuable to enterprises, making them a scarce resource that must be attracted and retained (Jain & Bhatt, 2015; Rodríguez-Sánchez et al., 2019). In fact, Juarez-Tarraga, Santandreu-Mascarell, and Marin-Garcia's (2019) research reveals that talent management, employee engagement, and retention of the best people are among the most difficult issues for HR professionals. Additionally, CEOs are also becoming more skeptical about talent management.

DOI: 10.4018/978-1-6684-8942-0.ch014

For employee satisfaction and retention, adequate pay and benefits are crucial. According to recent studies, providing competitive pay, bonuses, and benefits has a beneficial impact on employee retention (Gupta & Sharma, 2022). For employee engagement and retention, opportunities for professional development are essential. Recent studies have shown that career development opportunities have a favourable impact on employee retention, and that this link is moderated by perceptions of organisational support (Su & Chen, 2021). For employee well-being and retention, a healthy work-life balance must be maintained. Recent studies have demonstrated that work-life balance positively affects employee retention, with organisational commitment and job satisfaction serving as the mediators of this link (Bao, Qu, & Liu, 2021). Transformational leadership has a beneficial impact on employee retention, according to recent research (Yang & Mossholder, 2020). In order to retain employees, a company needs to have a good culture. According to recent studies, a supportive workplace environment that values employee input, respect, and collaboration can increase employee engagement and retention. Lam et al. (2015) define talent retention, also known as employee retention, as the length of time an employee stays with a company. Employee retention, they argue, not only reflects a company's consistency in hiring new employees but also indicates an employee's willingness to stay for a significant period of time. This longevity of employment is influenced by factors such as job satisfaction, opportunities for growth and development, a fair appraisal system, a supportive work environment, and a competitive compensation package (Eyster, Johnson, & Toder, 2008; Kossivi, Xu, & Kalgora, 2016; Loan-Clarke et al., 2010; Mabuza & Proches, 2014; Naeem & Saif, 2010; Nyanjom, 2013; Sinha & Sinha, 2012). To retain their valuable human resources, many companies implement various strategies and tactics.

Employees are a valuable resource because they contribute the effort and knowledge necessary to achieve the goals, objectives, and missions of the organization. To accomplish their goals and acquire a competitive edge over their rivals, businesses must retain skilled personnel, especially in the age of globalization. One of the biggest problems that businesses now confront is staff retention, which is widely acknowledged. Retaining great personnel enables organizations to grow and accomplish their objectives, which contributes to their success in a global market that is continually changing. As a result, it is crucial for businesses to understand the significance of talent retention as a key component of their overall strategy. Though talent retention is acknowledged to be important, many firms still struggle with it. Due to the competitive nature of the job market, finding and keeping competent workers is becoming more difficult, so it is crucial for organisations to adopt efficient talent retention strategies. Businesses must put their employees' needs first and make investments in their growth and wellbeing if they are to successfully address these issues. By doing this, they may foster a productive workplace that encourages employee loyalty and happiness, resulting in increased levels of employee retention and, eventually, corporate success (Nyanjom, 2013).

There is a substantial favourable association between total compensation and employee retention was discovered by Gupta and Sharma's meta-analysis in 2022. Su and Chen (2021) discovered that professional development possibilities have a beneficial impact on employee retention, with perceived organizational support serving to moderate this connection. According to Bao, Qu, and Liu (2021), job satisfaction and organizational commitment serve as a mediator between work-life balance and employee retention.

2. RESEARCH PROBLEM

This study is also aligned with the framework of strategic human resource management, which recognizes the significance of employee commitment, skills, and expertise for achieving organizational success (Barney et al., 2001) and the resource-based view of the firm. While many profit-making organizations have placed great emphasis on employee retention, the IT industry has given it comparatively less attention. This study focuses on the IT sector for its comparative research on employee retention, as it is one of the most lucrative and operationally significant industries.

3. OBJECTIVE OF THE STUDY

The main objective of this investigation is to analyze the factors that affect employee retention in the IT sector. This industry often faces challenges in retaining highly skilled workers, leading to negative impacts on organizational growth and high employee turnover rates. The purpose of the study is to investigate how employees view their jobs and to uncover the major variables that affect their decision to leave an organisation. The study will shed light on the numerous facets of employee experience that affect how engaged they are at work overall and how satisfied they are with their jobs.

The study will use descriptive research design to obtain information directly from employees. We will be able to find common themes and patterns that underpin employees' decisions to stay or quit an organization thanks to this method's capacity to provide in-depth insights into their experiences and perspectives. By addressing the root causes of employee attrition, the study's conclusions will be helpful to businesses looking to increase staff retention rates. Organizations may create targeted initiatives to improve employee engagement and happiness, reduce turnover, and retain key talent by identifying the factors that contribute to employee churn. By doing so, the research aims to highlight the importance of employee retention and identify the factors that influence it, as well as the specific ways in which these factors impact staff retention.

4. THEORETICAL FRAMEWORK

Retaining talented employees has become a crucial issue for organizations in today's competitive job market. Talent retention refers to an organization's ability to keep its star performers and high-potential individuals. According to a recent study by Gupta and Sharma (2022), offering market-competitive pay and benefits is significantly associated with employee retention. The introduction of globalization has made the job market even more volatile, adding to the challenges of talent retention. Many young HR experts from diverse countries are contributing to the development efforts of emerging markets, as noted by Klun (2008). This has resulted in increased economic interconnectedness and globalization of the labor market, as highlighted by Cruzado (2004). Therefore, organizations need to be mindful of this global environment to maintain a competitive advantage over the long term. Finding and retaining the best employees is a difficult and expensive endeavor for businesses, irrespective of the individual's nationality or cultural background (Schlechter et al., 2015).

4.1 Importance of Talent Retention

Talent retention continues to be a major problem for organisations, particularly in the fast-paced and cutthroat corporate world of today. According to research (Deery et al., 2020; Mathews & Han, 2021) losing top talent can have significant adverse impacts on organizational performance, including increased expenses, decreased productivity, and worse morale among surviving staff. Organizations are putting more of an emphasis on retention tactics as a way to deal with this difficulty. This involves developing a culture of appreciation and recognition, providing chances for growth and development, delivering competitive pay and benefits, and fostering a happy work environment (Deery et al., 2020; Mathews & Han, 2021). Organizational culture is a major element that has come to be important for talent retention. According to studies (Wang et al., 2019; Zhu et al., 2021) positive organizational cultures are linked to better levels of job satisfaction and reduced rates of turnover. These cultures are characterized by high levels of employee involvement, empowerment, and collaboration. Additionally, it has been discovered that having good feedback and communication channels is crucial for keeping top talent, as employees who feel heard and appreciated are more likely to stick with a company (Deery et al., 2020). Recent studies have also emphasized the significance of employee well-being and work-life balance in terms of talent retention. Organizations that prioritize employee well-being through flexible work arrangements, encouraging leadership, and wellness programmes are more likely to keep their best employees as mental health and wellness become more widely recognized (Mathews & Han, 2021; Zhu et al., 2021). Digitalization and technology have grown to be significant determinants in talent retention. Organisations must provide the resources and technologies required for their employees to perform productively in a virtual environment in light of the expanding trend of remote work and virtual teams (Deery et al., 2020). Through platforms like social media, gamification, and online learning, technology can also be used to improve employee engagement and communication (Wang et al., 2019).

Effective employee retention strategies are critical for organizations to remain productive and profitable, particularly during this period. Employee turnover is a costly concern for employers and has been extensively studied. According to Nyanjom (2013), the departure of a professional or managerial staff member costs businesses an average of $100,000 (Torrington & Taylor, 2009). HR managers are tasked with attracting and retaining skilled workers, who prioritize building their professional networks over company loyalty, as noted by De Vos and Meganck (2008). Retention not only benefits individuals, but it also has long-term positive effects on organizations, such as increased profitability and market standing. Therefore, implementing successful employee retention strategies is essential for the success of a business.

4.2 Factors affecting Talent Retention

Recent years have seen a rise in the importance of employee retention for businesses, as losing top talent may be expensive in terms of recruitment, training, and productivity (Chen & Tjosvold, 2018). While there are many factors that can affect employee retention, research has pinpointed seven crucial elements that influence talent retention. Leadership, and more specifically the nature of the connection between workers and their immediate managers, is a crucial component. According to research, employees are more likely to stick with a company when they have a good working connection with their supervisor that is characterized by trust, communication, and support (Chen & Tjosvold, 2018; Sun et al., 2019). Additionally, strong leadership that acknowledges employee contributions and offers clear direction might improve retention (Raza et al., 2020). Benefits and remuneration are significant factors that influence talent retention. Competitive salary and benefits packages are frequently cited as an important factor in luring and keeping top people (Yusoff et al., 2018). However, studies have also shown that non-cash incentives, such praise, chances for career advancement, and work-life balance, can have a big impact on retention (Chen & Tjosvold, 2018; Raza et al., 2020). The retention of talent has been shown to be significantly impacted by organizational culture. According to Yusoff et al. (2018), retention can be improved by an environment that values open communication, teamwork, and employee wellbeing. Negative cultures, on the other hand, can result in high turnover rates due to low employee engagement, a lack of trust, and high levels of stress (Sun et al., 2019). The availability of growth and development opportunities has also become seen as a crucial component in talent retention. Employee retention rates are higher when they believe they have opportunity to enhance their careers and develop their talents inside the company (Raza et al., 2020). Additionally, offering chances for learning and development can raise employee happiness and engagement, which in turn can increase retention (Chen & Tjosvold, 2018). Work-life balance can also significantly affect talent retention, according to study. Workers are more likely to stick with a company if they believe they have the freedom to balance their personal and professional life (Sun et al., 2019). Additionally, retention can be improved by policies and practises that promote work-life balance, such as flexible work schedules and wellness initiatives (Yusoff et al., 2018). The Social Exchange Theory explains the relationship between career advancement and employee commitment and retention intention. Employees become more committed to the company as they receive benefits and services over time (Blau, 1964). Thus, businesses should design career advancement opportunities to offer a competitive edge and support upward mobility. Social exchange theorists explain how a company's commitment to an employee is linked to that employee's commitment to the company, according to Nyanjom (2013). Employee attitudes, behaviors, and performance reflect their beliefs and expectations of the company. High-involvement work practices can also enhance employee retention, according to Nyanjom (2013)

To retain employees, promotions and pay raises alone are not enough. Training and development opportunities are crucial for growth and employee loyalty. Weng and McElroy (2012) differentiate between career advancement within the current organization and career growth over the employee's lifetime. Professional goal achievement, skill development, promotion opportunities, and compensation are the four components of career advancement (Weng, 2010). Ownership and autonomy also improve job satisfaction and performance. Leadership style and management greatly impact employee retention, with poor support and job dissatisfaction leading to turnover. Management support and leadership style are key factors in retaining employees (Naeem & Saif, 2010; Hong et al., 2012; Kossivi et al. 2016).

Creating a conducive work environment is a crucial factor in retaining employees (Kossivi et al., 2016). A favourable workplace should have sufficient, flexible, and enjoyable resources. Numerous studies have highlighted the significant impact of the work environment on employee retention rates. Employers should address unfavorable working conditions that can cause employees to quit their jobs, as it enhances employee satisfaction and reduces the likelihood of quitting (Nyanjom, 2013).

Designing a remuneration system that supports employee development initiatives is a unique challenge for businesses. Some employers claim that pay increases are based on performance, but this may not always be the case. Some businesses prioritize teamwork, but they continue to reward individuals for their individual achievements, creating inconsistencies that can frustrate and upset workers (Sinha and Sinha, 2012). Remuneration satisfaction significantly impacts employee retention, and employees are more likely to remain with a company if they are content with its operations and compensation plan (Nyanjom, 2013).

Flexibility in working hours is a crucial factor in retaining employees of all ages (Luo, 2006). Employees value a healthy balance between their personal and professional lives, and workplace flexibility can take many forms, such as work from home options, flexible hours, and shift work. Optimizing the compensation system is also essential to retain the best employees without increasing payroll (Parakandi & Behery, 2016). Work-life balance techniques, such as flexible work schedules, dependent care, and job sharing, demonstrate corporate support for family and personal leave, and can improve attitudes and behaviors within the organization (Mescher, 2010; Cruzado, 2004). Finally, offering development and learning opportunities is crucial to retaining talented employees (Sinha & Sinha, 2012; Eyster et al., 2008).

4.3 Hypothesis Development

Retaining talent has become a challenging task for many firms in the era of globalization and labor mobility. In particular, talented employees have more opportunities than ever to explore the world beyond their current organization (Ott et al., 2018). Simply hiring and placing qualified workers is no longer sufficient for companies. Due to a skill shortage, it has become increasingly difficult to find and retain highly skilled employees (Festing & Schäfer, 2014). As a result, having employees with the right knowledge, skills, and abilities (KSAs) is crucial for maintaining a competitive advantage (Ali et al., 2020; Matongolo et al., 2018; Zhang et al., 2015). Talented personnel can promote organizational sustainability and economic growth if they are retained properly (Ali et al., 2020). Additionally, investments in talent development pay off if talented employees are retained (Tlaiss et al., 2017). The assumptions underlying our investigation are as follows:

H1: In the IT sector, a positive work environment significantly affects employee retention.
H2: Work-life balance significantly affects employee retention in the IT sector.
H3: In the IT sector, possibilities for career advancement have a big impact on employee retention.

Figure 1. Theoretical framework

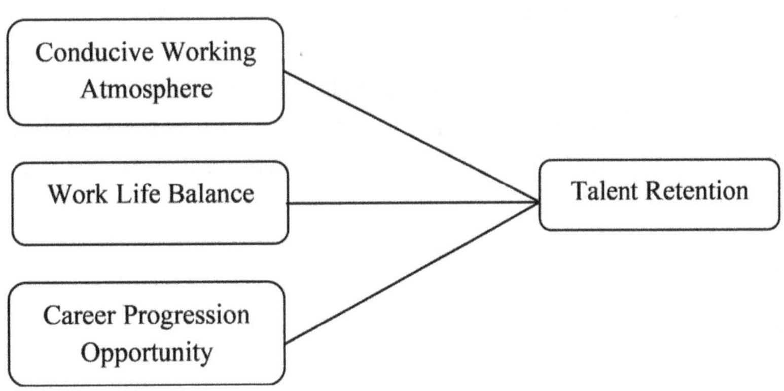

5. METHODOLOGY

All organizations must prioritize talent retention as talent is essential from every angle and is frequently viewed as a fundamental strategy for gaining a competitive advantage. It is essential for a company to achieve success, efficiency, and consistency. Therefore, we have made a modest effort to identify the key factors that play a pivotal role in talent retention.

5.1 Sample Dimensions and Sampling Procedure

This study is both cross-sectional and empirical in nature, with a strong emphasis on primary data. In order to gather the necessary information for analysis and arrive at sound conclusions, we utilized judgmental sampling. This sampling strategy allowed us to quickly access the desired population (Reddy & Ramasamy, 2016). For this study, we collected data from a sample size of 440 IT professionals in Kolkata.

5.2 Tools for Data Analysis

Factor analysis is a valuable tool in obtaining insights into the research problem. The underlying principle of factor analysis is that variables are inter-correlated to some extent. It is necessary to have at least ordinal level of measurement for the variables being analyzed (Pituch et al. 2016). The two main methods used in factor analysis are exploratory factor analysis (EFA) and confirmatory factor analysis (CFA). EFA is often used in the early stages of research to gain insight into the relationships among a group of variables and is used to test for dimensionality. On the other hand, CFA employs a more sophisticated set of techniques to test specific theories or hypotheses about the organization of a set of variables (Hair et al. 2006 & Pallant, 2010).

6. RESULTS ANALYSIS

6.1 Exploratory Factor Analysis

The KMO test is a method for determining whether data are suitable for factor analysis. It appraises whether the sample size is sufficient for our study. The test evaluates the sampling efficiency of the model as a whole and for each variable separately. The KMO measure of sampling adequacy is calculated according to the formula given by

$$KMO_j = \frac{\sum_{i-j} R_{ij}^2}{\sum_{i-j} R_{ij}^2 + \sum_{i-j} U_{ij}^2}$$

The partial covariance matrix (Uij) and the correlation matrix (Rij) are both used in the formula above. The KMO value ranges from 0 to 1. If the KMO values fall between 0.8 and 1.0, then sampling is adequate. KMO readings fall into two categories: poor between 0.6 and 0.69 and average between 0.7 and 0.79. The sampling was insufficient if the KMO value is less than 0.6, and corrective action must be taken. If the value is less than 0.5, the factor analysis results will not be suitable for the data analysis.If the sample size is less than 300, it is necessary to check the average communality of the retained items. For sample sizes between 100 and 200, an average value between 0.5 and 0.6 is acceptable (Tabachnick & Fidell, 2013, Guttman, 1954, Kaiser, 1970, Tucker, 1997). An average value of > 0.6 is appropriate for sample sizes under 100. Our study's Kaiser-Meyer-Olkin Measure of Sampling Adequacy was 0.897, indicating that the sample was adequate to carry out the study.

Table 1. Kaiser-Meyer-Olkin test

	MSA
Overall MSA	0.897
Statement1	0.904
Statement2	0.920
Statement3	0.933
Stastement4	0.934
Statement5	0.863
statement6	0.886
Statement7	0.885
Statement8	0.910
statement9	0.927
statement10	0.933
statement11	0.916
Statement12	0.887
Statement13	0.903
Statement14	0.833
statement15	0.845

The Bartlett's Test of Sphericity is a statistical method used to assess whether a set of variables is suitable for structure discovery. It compares the initial correlation matrix, which assumes that the variables are unrelated, against an alternative hypothesis that states the variables are not orthogonal. If the p-value is less than 0.05, it indicates that the null hypothesis should be rejected, and the alternative hypothesis is more likely to be true. In this case, a factor analysis could be useful to explore the relationship between the variables. To determine the overall correlation between the variables, the correlation matrix's determinant |R| is calculated. If the value is close to 1, it means there is little correlation between the variables, whereas if it is closer to 0, it indicates a high correlation.

$$\chi^2 = -\left(n - 1 - \frac{2p+5}{6}\right) \times \ln\left|R\right|$$

In this context, p represents the number of variables, n represents the total sample size, and R represents the correlation matrix (Guttman, 1954; Tucker, 1997). The Bartlett's Test of Sphericity in this study resulted in a p-value of less than 0.001, which provides strong evidence to support the research.

Table 2. Bartlett's test

X^2	df	p
1733.678	105.000	< .001

The eigenvalues of each factor indicate the amount of variance accounted for by those specific linear components. Loadings with values below 0.4 were omitted since they are considered negligible, as per Kaiser's recommendation (1970). The model's $\chi 2$ was 1733.678 with 105 degrees of freedom. Table 3 displays the factor loadings, with all loadings falling in the high range from 0.517 to 0.859, as indicated by Fabrigar et al. (1999), Williams et al. (1996), and Gie Yong & Pearce (2013). We employed promax rotation during the EFA procedure.

Table 3. Factor loadings

	Factor 1	Factor 2	Factor 3	Uniqueness
Statement14	0.849			0.409
Statement1	0.815			0.438
Statement2	0.785			0.447
Statement3	0.646			0.555
statement15	0.535			0.530
statement9	0.522			0.494
Stastement4	0.517			0.630
Statement12		0.859		0.361
Statement13		0.699		0.543
statement11		0.650		0.469
statement10		0.624		0.527
statement6			0.706	0.519
Statement5			0.611	0.574
Statement7			0.560	0.694
Statement8			0.523	0.746

Note. Applied rotation method is promax.

In summary, the EFA successfully identified three factors that align closely with the given statements. Table 3 displays the items associated with each factor, where "Conducive Working Atmosphere" comprises seven items (14, 1, 2, 3, 15, 9, 4), "Career Progression Opportunity" consists of four items (12, 13, 11, 10), and "Work Life Balance" includes four items (6, 5, 7, 8).

6.2 Confirmatory Factor Analysis

Confirmatory factor analysis has become an essential analytical method in numerous fields of the social and behavioral sciences. As a member of the structural equation modeling family, it allows for the examination of causal relationships between latent and observable variables in pre-specified, theory-based models. The primary advantage of CFA is its ability to help Researchers bridge the gap that is often present between theory and observation (Mueller & Hancock, 2001).

Each time a path diagram is employed, a model is established, and the relationships between variables are revealed. Additionally, it provides an opportunity to visually compare and contrast an alternate or competing model. The theoretical relationships between variables can be effectively represented in a path diagram, and the statistical results can be presented concisely through its use.

Figure 2. Path diagram

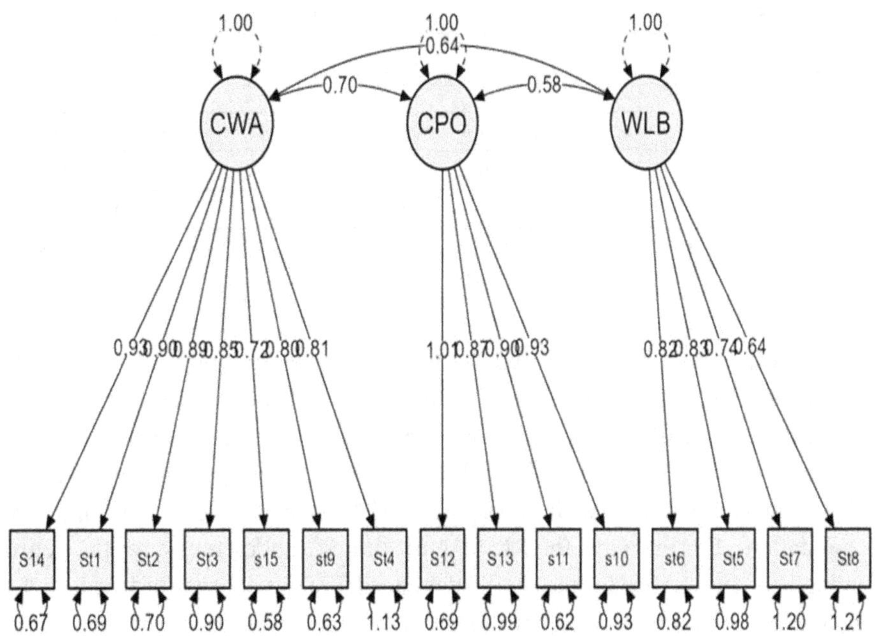

Table 4 presents the coefficients of the hypothesized relationships along with their corresponding z-values, standard errors, 95% confidence intervals, and p-values for the models tested in the study. This table provides a comprehensive summary of the statistical results obtained from the analysis of the data. By examining the coefficients and their associated p-values, researchers can determine which relationships between the variables are statistically significant and which ones are not. The inclusion of confidence intervals helps to provide a sense of the precision of the estimated coefficients, while the z-values and standard errors can be used to assess the overall goodness-of-fit of the model. Overall, Table 4 serves as a valuable tool for researchers seeking to understand the relationships between variables in their data set

Table 4. Factor loadings

							95% Confidence Interval	
Factor	**Indicator**	**Symbol**	**Estimate**	**Std. Error**	**z-value**	**p**	**Lower**	**Upper**
Conducive Working Atmosphere	Statement14	λ11	0.927	0.065	14.364	**< .001**	0.800	1.053
	Statement1	λ12	0.897	0.064	13.962	**< .001**	0.771	1.023
	Statement2	λ13	0.895	0.065	13.842	**< .001**	0.768	1.021
	Statement3	λ14	0.846	0.069	12.259	**< .001**	0.711	0.981
	statement15	λ15	0.722	0.056	12.813	**< .001**	0.612	0.833
	statement9	λ16	0.802	0.060	13.361	**< .001**	0.684	0.920
	Stastement4	λ17	0.809	0.075	10.857	**< .001**	0.663	0.956
Career Progression Opportunity	Statement12	λ21	1.014	0.070	14.476	**< .001**	0.877	1.152
	Statement13	λ22	0.874	0.074	11.752	**< .001**	0.729	1.020
	statement11	λ23	0.897	0.064	13.920	**< .001**	0.771	1.023
	statement10	λ24	0.927	0.074	12.527	**< .001**	0.782	1.072
Work Life Balance	statement6	λ31	0.824	0.075	11.011	**< .001**	0.677	0.971
	Statement5	λ32	0.826	0.079	10.404	**< .001**	0.670	0.982
	Statement7	λ33	0.739	0.083	8.910	**< .001**	0.577	0.902
	Statement8	λ34	0.638	0.081	7.899	**< .001**	0.480	0.797

In recent years, researchers have explored the use of various model fit indices that are commonly employed in CFA to determine the number of components to retain in EFA (Clark & Bowles, 2018; Garrido, Abad, & Ponsoda, 2016; Preacher, Zhang, Kim, & Mels, 2013). The efficacy of common fit indices, such as the CFI, TLI, SRMR, and RMSEA, has been extensively studied in the context of selecting appropriate CFA models. Each of these indices places slightly varying levels of importance on different aspects of model data fit. For instance, the RMSEA absolute fit index measures the degree to which the chi-square goodness-of-fit statistic for the model deviates from the degrees of freedom. Larger values of RMSEA indicate poorer fit, while values of 0.05 or less are commonly accepted as indicative of good fit. The CFI and TLI are global model fit indices that compare the fit of the target model to that of a baseline model lacking an underlying factor structure. Values of 0.9 or higher are commonly employed to identify well-fitting models, with larger CFI values indicating better fit relative to the baseline. The TLI, which is similar to the CFI, rewards more parsimonious models by incorporating the degrees of freedom from the baseline model into its calculation. Thus, TLI is more likely to prefer factor models with lower loading. Similarly to CFI, TLI values over 0.9 are frequently regarded as indicators of good model fit. The square root of the sum of squared correlation residuals for the indicator variables is known as SRMR. Higher SRMR values indicate greater divergence between model predictions and actual data or higher residual correlations, thus suggesting poorer model fit. A SRMR value in this case is greater than 0.1 are typically considered indicative of good model fit.

It should be noted that these fit indices are sensitive to a wide range of parameters, including sample size, number of indicators, factor loading values, number of factors in the model, and type of indicators

(Beauducel & Wittmann, 2005; F. Chen et al., 2008; Kenny, Kaniskan, & McCoach, 2015; Marsh, Hau, & Wen, 2004). Additionally, the thresholds that are commonly used with these indices were originally developed in the context of continuously distributed normally distributed indicators, and their performance in the context of factor analysis with categorical indicator variables has been inconsistent. Clark and Bowles (2018) extended prior work to demonstrate that thresholds commonly used with continuous indicator variable models may not be applicable when indicators are categorical. Despite these limitations, these indices are still widely used by researchers to assess how well a given factor model fits a data sample, as evidenced by their prevalence in the applied factor analysis literature. It is important to note that the obtained goodness-of-fit statistics should be interpreted while considering these factors. Models are first estimated and then evaluated using these indices.

Table 5. Fit indices

Index	Value
Comparative Fit Index (CFI)	0.918
Tucker-Lewis Index (TLI)	0.901
Bentler-Bonett Non-normed Fit Index (NNFI)	0.901
Bentler-Bonett Normed Fit Index (NFI)	0.874
Parsimony Normed Fit Index (PNFI)	0.724
Bollen's Relative Fit Index (RFI)	0.848
Bollen's Incremental Fit Index (IFI)	0.919
Relative Noncentrality Index (RNI)	0.918

Table 6. Other fit measures

Metric	Value
Root mean square error of approximation (RMSEA)	0.073
RMSEA 90% CI lower bound	0.062
RMSEA 90% CI upper bound	0.085
RMSEA p-value	7.571e-4
Standardized root mean square residual (SRMR)	0.047
Hoelter's critical N (α = .05)	144.128
Hoelter's critical N (α = .01)	158.232
Goodness of fit index (GFI)	0.910
McDonald fit index (MFI)	0.791
Expected cross validation index (ECVI)	0.993

7. DISCUSSIONS AND MANAGERIAL IMPLICATION

Talent retention is an important practice for businesses to keep their top-performing employees for a longer duration. It is an essential part of human resource management as it helps companies maintain their competitive edge in the market and avoid significant expenses related to employee turnover. The study findings indicate that a conducive work environment has a significant impact on employee retention in the IT sector. This is demonstrated by the large regression coefficients and high factor loadings for statements related to a supportive work environment. IT professionals usually prefer a workplace culture that fosters collaboration, open communication, and recognition of their efforts. Therefore, businesses in the IT industry should invest in developing a positive workplace culture to retain their employees. The study also reveals that career advancement opportunity have a substantial impact on employee retention in the IT sector. IT workers typically seek opportunities for growth and professional advancement, and companies that provide these chances through career development programmes, training opportunities, and a defined career path usually have better retention rates. Furthermore, the study suggests that Work-Life Balance significantly influences the retention of workers in the IT sector. IT workers often value work-life balance highly, and firms that offer benefits like flexible working schedules, remote work, and other work-life perks tend to retain their employees longer.

At the end, companies in the IT sector need to consider several essential factors to retain their employees, including a supportive work environment, opportunities for career advancement and development, and work-life balance benefits. By prioritizing talent retention, companies can maintain their competitive edge, enhance their organizational sustainability and economic progress, and improve their employees' satisfaction and productivity.

8. CONCLUSION

In summary, this research has highlighted the significant impact of work-life balance, professional growth opportunities, and a positive work environment on employee retention in the IT industry. The study's findings indicate that a positive work environment and opportunities for professional advancement have a more significant impact on retention than work-life balance, although it is still an important factor. The results emphasize the importance of creating a supportive and encouraging work environment, promoting work-life balance, and providing opportunities for career development and progression to retain top talent in the IT sector.

Furthermore, this study demonstrates the value of factor analysis in identifying the critical factors that influence employee retention and examining their interactions. The findings offer valuable insights for HR managers and decision-makers in the IT industry to develop effective staff retention strategies.

In a nutshell, this study contributes to the existing knowledge on employee retention in the IT industry and underscores the need for organizations to address the major causes of employee turnover. By understanding and addressing employee concerns and needs, organizations can increase their ability to attract and retain top talent in a fiercely competitive employment market.

REFERENCES

Ali, M., Khan, M. S., Khan, S., & Iqbal, S. (2020). The mediating role of employee turnover intentions in the relationship between psychological contract breach and employee performance: Evidence from Pakistan. *Journal of Human Resource Management*, *8*(2), 27–34. doi:10.12691/jhrm-8-2-1

Amundson, N. E. (2007). The influence of workplace attraction on recruitment and retention. *Journal of Employment Counseling*, *44*(4), 154–162. doi:10.1002/j.2161-1920.2007.tb00034.x

Bao, X., Qu, H., & Liu, Y. (2021). Work-life balance and employee retention: The role of job satisfaction and organizational commitment. *International Journal of Contemporary Hospitality Management*, *33*(9), 2961–2979.

Barney, J., Wright, M., & Ketchen, D. J. Jr. (2001). The resource-based view of the firm: Ten years after 1991. *Journal of Management*, *27*(6), 625–641. doi:10.1177/014920630102700601

Beauducel, A., & Wittmann, W. W. (2005). Simulation study on fit indexes in CFA based on data with slightly distorted simple structure. *Structural Equation Modeling*, *12*(1), 41–75. doi:10.120715328007sem1201_3

Blau, P. M. (1964). *Exchange and power in social life*. Wiley.

Cascio, W. F. (2006). The costly business of employee turnover. *The Academy of Management Perspectives*, *20*(3), 36–37. doi:10.5465/amp.2006.21318917

Chen, F., Curran, P. J., Bollen, K. A., Kirby, J., & Paxton, P. (2008). An empirical evaluation of the use of fixed cutoff points in RMSEA test statistic in structural equation models. *Sociological Methods & Research*, *36*(4), 462–494. doi:10.1177/0049124108314720 PMID:19756246

Chen, Y., & Tjosvold, D. (2018). Knowledge sharing, trust and employee retention: An exploratory study of a Chinese IT company. *International Journal of Human Resource Management*, *29*(1), 141–159.

Clark, L. A., & Bowles, M. A. (2018). The Personality Disorders An Integrated Approach. *Journal of Psychiatric Practice*, *24*(6), 386–394. doi:10.1097/PRA.0000000000000339

Clark, L. A., & Bowles, R. P. (2018). Methodological issues in assessing differential item functioning in psychological tests. *Journal of Personality Assessment*, *100*(4), 347–357.

Cruzado, I. (2004). Employee turnover intentions: A test of a cognitive model. *International Journal of Selection and Assessment*, *12*(1), 27–35. doi:10.1111/j.0965-075X.2004.00253.x

Cruzado, I. (2004). Organizational retention: the role of human resources management. *Journal of European Industrial Training*, *28*(2/3/4), 124-142. doi: . doi:10.1108/03090590410519568

De Vos, A., & Meganck, A. (2008). Human resource management and performance in a globalizing business environment: A Belgian perspective. *International Journal of Human Resource Management*, *19*(9), 1636–1650. doi:10.1080/09585190802290289

Deery, S. J., Iverson, R. D., Walsh, J. T., & Jacobsen, D. I. (2020). Talent retention in the face of technological change: The role of psychological contract breach and innovation. *Journal of Business Research*, *117*, 689–699.

Estes, Z., & Michael, J. (2005). The impact of compensation structure on employee turnover: A case study analysis. *Journal of Applied Business Research, 21*(3), 95–102.

Eyster, L., Johnson, R. C., & Toder, E. (2008). Retirement income for those with nontraditional careers. *Tax Notes, 119*(8), 727–736.

Eyster, L. A., Johnson, R. W., & Toder, E. J. (2008). The cost of employee turnover to employers. *Employee Benefits Research Institute Issue Brief*, (313), 1–23.

Fabrigar, L. R., Wegener, D. T., MacCallum, R. C., & Strahan, E. J. (1999). Evaluating the use of exploratory factor analysis in psychological research. *Psychological Methods, 4*(3), 272–299. doi:10.1037/1082-989X.4.3.272

Festing, M., & Schäfer, L. (2014). Generational challenges to talent management: A framework for talent retention based on the psychological-contract perspective. *Journal of World Business, 49*(2), 262–271. doi:10.1016/j.jwb.2013.11.010

Garrido, L. E., Abad, F. J., & Ponsoda, V. (2016). A new look at Horn's parallel analysis with ordinal variables. *Psychological Methods, 21*(3), 362–384. doi:10.1037/met0000076 PMID:23046000

Gie Yong, A. G., & Pearce, S. (2013). A Beginner's Guide to Factor Analysis: Focusing on Exploratory Factor Analysis. *Tutorials in Quantitative Methods for Psychology, 9*(2), 79–94. doi:10.20982/tqmp.09.2.p079

Gupta, A., & Sharma, N. (2022). The impact of total rewards on employee retention: A meta-analysis. *Journal of Business Research, 143*, 565–576.

Guttman, L. (1954). A new approach to factor analysis: The radex. In P. F. Lazarsfeld (Ed.), *Mathematical thinking in the social sciences* (pp. 258–348). Free Press.

Guttman, L. (1954). Some necessary conditions for common-factor analysis. *Psychometrika, 19*(2), 149–161. doi:10.1007/BF02289162

Hair, J. F., Black, W. C., Babin, B. J., Anderson, R. E., & Tatham, R. L. (2006). *Multivariate data analysis* (Vol. 6). Pearson Prentice Hall.

Hong, J., Hao, Y., Kumar, V., Ramendran, C., & Kadiresan, V. (2012). An empirical analysis of the factors affecting employee retention in Chinese state-owned enterprises. *Journal of Chinese Human Resource Management, 3*(2), 102–123. doi:10.1108/20408021211252555

Hu, L. T., & Bentler, P. M. (1999). Cutoff criteria for fit indexes in covariance structure analysis: Conventional criteria versus new alternatives. *Structural Equation Modeling, 6*(1), 1–55. doi:10.1080/10705519909540118

Jain, P., & Bhatt, R. (2015). Talent management: A strategic approach towards growth in IT sector. *Procedia: Social and Behavioral Sciences, 189*, 381–389. doi:10.1016/j.sbspro.2015.03.327

Juárez-Tarraga, A., Santandreu-Mascarell, C., & Marín-García, J. A. (2019). HRM practices and talent retention: The mediating role of organizational identification. *Journal of Business Research, 99*, 473–481. doi:10.1016/j.jbusres.2019.01.050

Kaiser, H. F. (1970). A second generation little jiffy. *Psychometrika*, *35*(4), 401–415. doi:10.1007/BF02291817

Kenny, D. A., Kaniskan, B., & McCoach, D. B. (2015). The performance of RMSEA in models with small degrees of freedom. *Sociological Methods & Research*, *44*(3), 486–507. doi:10.1177/0049124114543236

Klun, M. (2008). Corporate alumni programs: An emerging trend in talent management. *Journal of Management Policy and Practice*, *9*(3), 1–10.

Kossivi, B., Xu, M., & Kalgora, B. (2016). Investigating the relationship between human resource management practices and retention of employees in the banking industry. *Journal of Human Resources Management and Labor Studies*, *4*(1), 13–24.

Lam, W., Chen, Z., & Takeuchi, R. (2015). Perceived human resource management practices and intention to leave of employees: Evidence from five professional service firms in China. *International Journal of Human Resource Management*, *26*(19), 2429–2449. doi:10.1080/09585192.2015.1079867

Loan-Clarke, J., Arnold, J., Coombs, C., Hartley, J., & Bosley, S. (2010). *Managing talent: A literature review*. Institute for Employment Studies. https://www.employment-studies.co.uk/system/files/resources/files/399.pdf

Luo, Y. (2006). Building trust in cross-cultural collaborations: Toward a contingency perspective. *Journal of Management*, *32*(2), 219–237. doi:10.1177/0149206305280472

Mabuza, M. L., & Proches, C. N. (2014). Talent management and employee retention: Exploring the perceptions of South African human resource practitioners. *SA Journal of Human Resource Management*, *12*(1), 1–12. doi:10.4102ajhrm.v12i1.571

Marsh, H. W., Hau, K.-T., & Wen, Z. (2004). In search of golden rules: Comment on hypothesis-testing approaches to setting cutoff values for fit indexes and dangers in overgeneralizing Hu and Bentler's (1999) findings. *Structural Equation Modeling*, *11*(3), 320–341. doi:10.120715328007sem1103_2

Mathews, S., & Han, K. (2021). An examination of the relationship between work-life balance and employee retention in the hospitality industry. *International Journal of Hospitality Management*, *95*, 102886.

Matongolo, S., Chinomona, R., & Mpinganjira, M. (2018). An empirical investigation into the impact of talent management on employees' intention to stay. *South African Journal of Business Management*, *49*(1), 1–11. doi:10.4102ajbm.v49i1.27

Mescher, S., Benschop, Y., & Doorewaard, H. (2010). Representations of work-Life balance support. *Human Relations*, *63*(1), 21–39. doi:10.1177/0018726709349197

Mueller, R. O., & Hancock, G. R. (2001). Factor analysis and scale revision. *Psychological Assessment*, *13*(3), 347–357. PMID:11556271

Naeem, B., & Saif, M. I. (2010). Impact of training and development on employee retention in Pakistani context. *Interdisciplinary Journal of Contemporary Research in Business*, *2*(10), 452–462.

Nyanjom, P. O. (2013). The influence of talent management on job satisfaction and organizational commitment among employees in Kenyan universities. *International Journal of Academic Research in Business & Social Sciences*, *3*(9), 93–104. doi:10.6007/IJARBSS/v3-i9/239

Ott, H., Kaiser, S., Probst, T., & Konegen-Grenier, C. (2018). Perceived fairness of pay: A systematic review and meta-analysis of the literature. *Journal of Economic Psychology*, *68*, 21–40. doi:10.1016/j.joep.2018.06.003

Pallant, J. (2010). *SPSS survival manual: A step by step guide to data analysis using SPSS*. McGraw Hill International.

Parakandi, M., & Behery, M. (2016). The impact of employee engagement on employee retention: Exploring the moderating role of job burnout. *Journal of Applied Business Research*, *32*(6), 1685–1698. doi:10.19030/jabr.v32i6.9801

Pituch, K. A., Lee, Y. K., & Yoon, T. (2016). Testing the factorial validity and factorial invariance across gender of a brief form of the School Anxiety Inventory-Short Version. *Journal of Psychoeducational Assessment*, *34*(2), 157–169.

Preacher, K. J., Zhang, G., Kim, C., & Mels, G. (2013). Choosing the optimal number of factors in exploratory factor analysis: A model selection perspective. *Multivariate Behavioral Research*, *48*(1), 28–56. doi:10.1080/00273171.2012.710386 PMID:26789208

Raza, M., Khan, M. A., Ali, M., & Khan, A. (2020). Employee retention: A review of literature. *Journal of Human Resource Management*, *8*(2), 31–38.

Reddy, K. B., & Ramasamy, R. (2016). Psychological contract violation and turnover intention: Examining the mediating role of burnout and the moderating role of emotional intelligence. *South African Journal of Business Management*, *47*(1), 33–43.

Rodríguez-Sánchez, A. M., Dolores López-Guzmán, T., & Rodríguez-García, M. (2019). The relationship between talent management and organizational performance: A meta-analysis. *Journal of Business Research*, *98*, 413–424. doi:10.1016/j.jbusres.2019.01.023

Schlechter, A. F., Watt, H. M. G., & Cilliers, F. V. N. (2015). Retaining talent: Replacing misconceptions with evidence-based strategies. *SA Journal of Human Resource Management*, *13*(1), 1–11. doi:10.4102ajhrm.v13i1.712

Sinha, C., & Sinha, A. (2012). Employee retention: A review of literature. *Journal of Business and Management*, *3*(5), 41–47.

Su, Q., & Chen, X. (2021). Career development opportunities and employee retention: The moderating role of perceived organizational support. *Journal of Business Research*, *130*, 284–296.

Sun, L. Y., Aryee, S., & Law, K. S. (2019). High-performance human resource practices, employee well-being, and job involvement: An empirical study. *International Journal of Human Resource Management*, *30*(3), 483–503.

Tabachnick, B. G., & Fidell, L. S. (2013). *Using multivariate statistics* (6th ed.). Pearson.

Thunnissen, M. (2016). The relationship between HRM practices and employee retention in public organisations: An exploratory study. *Review of Public Personnel Administration, 36*(4), 381–401. doi:10.1177/0734371X16671184

Tlaiss, H. A., Hallak, R., & Aboushaar, W. (2017). The role of intrinsic and extrinsic motivation on the relationship between perceived organisational support and knowledge sharing behaviour. *Journal of Knowledge Management, 21*(2), 351–365. doi:10.1108/JKM-03-2016-0099

Torrington, D., & Taylor, S. (2009). *Human resource management* (7th ed.). Pearson Education.

Tucker, L. R. (1997). The case for confirmatory factor analysis. In *Structural equation modeling: Concepts, issues, and applications* (pp. 1–26). Sage Publications, Inc.

Wang, D., Wang, J., & Wang, Y. (2019). Workplace learning, employee engagement, and talent retention: A study of the Chinese insurance industry. *Human Resource Development International, 22*(5), 427–445.

Weng, R. H. (2010). Exploring the antecedents of employee turnover intention. *Journal of Business and Psychology, 25*(4), 585–601. doi:10.100710869-010-9189-9

Weng, R. H., & McElroy, J. C. (2012). Exploring the impact of corporate culture on employee retention. *Journal of Business and Psychology, 27*(4), 389–400. doi:10.100710869-012-9257-x

Williams, L. J., Cote, J. A., & Buckley, M. R. (1996). Lack of method variance in self-reported affect and perceptions at work: Reality or artifact? *The Journal of Applied Psychology, 81*(6), 669–681.

Yang, J. T., & Mossholder, K. W. (2020). *Transformational leadership and employee retention: A meta-analytic review.*

Yazinski, M. (2009). The influence of an online virtual environment on subjective well-being. *Cyberpsychology (Brno), 3*(2), 4.

Yusoff, Y. M., Jusoff, K., & Aziz, A. A. (2018). Factors influencing employee retention: A conceptual framework. *Journal of Administrative and Business Studies, 4*(1), 1–7.

Zhang, M., Yang, L., & Wang, L. (2015). How transformational leadership fosters employee proactive customer service behavior: The mediating role of self-efficacy and the moderating role of internal locus of control. *Journal of Business Research, 68*(4), 911–918. doi:10.1016/j.jbusres.2014.10.004

Zhu, J., Xu, D., Guo, H., & Zhang, X. (2021). Why do engaged employees stay? The role of work-life balance and job embeddedness. *Journal of Business Research, 123*, 662–671.

Chapter 15
Use of Artificial Intelligence in the Employee Selection Process

Filiz Mızrak
Istanbul Medipol University, Turkey

ABSTRACT

To remain successful and competitive, organizations must have the ability to change, grow, and evolve to meet the new challenges and realities they face. The field of human resources management has changed significantly over time and continues to develop rapidly day by day. While organizations still primarily focus on the "people" aspects of running an organization, they have also become increasingly dependent on technology and data that weren't available just a decade ago. In this respect, the role of technology in the efficient and effective maintenance of human resource management practices in businesses is an undeniable fact. In this study, artificial intelligence technology, which is one of the most advanced technologies today and has a symbiotic relationship with human resources management, and the effect of this technology on human resources management practices are examined benefiting from the recent literature.

INTRODUCTION

Technological developments that emerged with the fourth industrial revolution had a significant impact on the business world, and the role of technology in the business world began to increase gradually. Today, machines can communicate with each other, robots play an active role in production, and at the same time, a technology called artificial intelligence is trying to replace the human brain. In this way, the way of doing business is changing radically, both businesses and employees are trying to keep up with this change, and those who can't keep up with the change face the danger of extinction. At this point, the human resources department is the unit that takes the necessary steps for both businesses and employees to adapt to this change, calculates the necessary scenarios, organizes the necessary trainings, and undertakes many other vital tasks. Thanks to the HRM activities carried out by this department, businesses and employees quickly acquire the knowledge, skills and equipment required by the age and keep up with the change. Success of human resources management is closely related to the fact that the human resources department follows technology closely, acquires the necessary equipment and methods

DOI: 10.4018/978-1-6684-8942-0.ch015

in a timely manner, and leads change. At this point, all HRM activities, from employee selection to employee training and development, should be carried out with the most advanced and efficient equipment and methods (Turk, Vardarlier, & Hazar, 2020).

Today, there are many technologies that concern HRM. These technologies play an active role especially in the process of finding, evaluating, and recruiting workforce, providing assistance and mentoring services to the employees, and are frequently used in the training and development activities of the employees. To increase their qualifications, the human resources units of the enterprises follow the latest technologies brought by the day and seek ways to benefit from these technologies in the most effective way. Among these technologies, one of the most popular and useful today is artificial intelligence. Human resources managers of enterprises use artificial intelligence technologies to facilitate difficult functions in collecting accurate data about personnel and work process, in training and hiring employees, in the orientation process and in evaluating the performance of employees (Silahtaroglu & Vardarlier, 2016).

Artificial intelligence algorithms first select the candidates that they think are the most suitable for the determined job from certain candidate pools in line with the criteria specified by the business, and present a list to the recruiter, as well as presenting to the recruiter what he considered while making this choice, with short and summary notes. In this process, artificial intelligence can be commanded to act objectively or to give priority to a certain race, gender, age group. In addition, artificial intelligence can manage and report the entire interview with the job applicant or enter the interview together with the recruiter and instantly report the results of voice, mimic and body language analyzes made during the interview. Ultimately, the recruiter who comes to a report that has been evaluated, screened, and has many analyzes performed by artificial intelligence can focus more heavily on his experience, abilities, and skills in recruiting because he does not have to do many jobs that require time, energy, and effort (Budhwar et al., 2022).

One of the most important purposes of the cooperation between human and artificial intelligence or smart machines is to transfer the tasks that the workforce frequently encounters in daily life, which require operations, which are constantly repetitive, which are not difficult to do but take a long time to be done, to artificial intelligence or smart machines. In addition, artificial intelligence, or smart machines act as an excellent assistant for the workforce. Thanks to their superior features, these technologies can perform operations at an incredible speed, do not forget anything, never get tired, and can correlate data at a perfect level. In general terms, artificial intelligence technologies are like a toolbox for HRM applications (Pan, et al., 2022). Therefore, the use of these technologies by the workforce allows to increase the quality of the work done and the workforce doing the work. In this respect, attitudes towards artificial intelligence are very important in terms of HRM practices.

The purpose of this study is to examine artificial intelligence technology, which is one of the most advanced technologies today and has a symbiotic relationship with human resources management, and the effect of this technology on human resources management practices benefiting from the recent literature. In the first part of the study, general information is given about the scope and functions of human resources management and business analysis & design. Furthermore, Artificial intelligence and its relationship with human resource management is examined and some recruitment algorithms supported by artificial Intelligence is exemplified. In the conclusion part, suggestions for the businesses to apply artificial intelligence in HRM processes is provided. It is thought that the study will contribute to the literature in terms of analyzing current approaches in the literature. It will also serve as a guide for future studies on the subject.

BACKGROUND

Concept of Human Resource Management

Human resource management is a management discipline developed for the management of people in businesses. Human resources management, which entered the literature in the 1980s, has been accepted and applied on a large scale by businesses to achieve sustainable competitive advantage. When human resources management is viewed from a strategic point of view, it is seen that it plays an important role in the realization of organizational strategic goals with its many applications. The reason for this is that human resources management considers people as a primary resource rather than a cost element and tries to create a high-quality human resource profile with employee selection, training and development, performance evaluation and many other applications (Baykal, 2020).

The quality of an enterprise is directly related to the quality of the workforce it employs. The success of businesses is possible if the business has a workforce that has the competence to perform the tasks necessary to achieve its strategic goals. In this respect, the success of the decisions and methods taken within the scope of human resources management is directly related to the business's hiring and keeping the right qualified workforce (Dinçer & Yüksel). Human resource management is a sub-system that plays a very important role in the business system. Decisions made within the scope of human resources in the enterprise affect all other functions of the enterprise (Gong et al., 2022).

Human resource management practices cover a wide range of applications. Although human resources management practices differ based on their qualifications, all these practices establish a dynamic and holistic system thanks to the interaction and harmony between them. The efficient and effective maintenance of this dynamic and holistic system depends on the pre-planning and management of the relationship and interaction between the systems. The most important and essential duties and responsibilities of human resources managers are to ensure that the functions of human resources management are carried out effectively (Strohmeier, S., & Piazza, F. (2015). When the literature is examined as incoming, it is seen that the functions of human resources management are classified as planning, staffing, performance evaluation, rewarding, training and development, industrial relations and protection and development (Kaushal et al., 2021).

Business Analysis and Design

It is essential to use accurate information as input for the effective performance of human resource management activities. The most important information that human resources specialists need is information about all jobs in the business. Information such as the structure of the job, its elements, responsibilities, and job requirements are obtained as a result of job analysis studies (Nawaz, 2020). In addition, the ability of enterprises to achieve maximum performance is directly related to the correct understanding of the requirements of the business and compliance with these requirements. To achieve this, job analysis, which is the process of obtaining detailed information about jobs, is needed. Understanding what is needed to analyze the job and perform a job makes the information needed for many human resources functions accessible, from recruiting employees to evaluating their performance (Gong et al., 2022).

Job analysis is a technique that examines the quality, quantity, requirements, responsibilities and working conditions of each job in the enterprise with scientific methods and collects information to evaluate the jobs in a correct, effective and healthy way (Silahtaroglu & Vardarlier, 2016). In addition, job analysis is expressed as a comprehensive examination of all existing jobs in the enterprise. As a result of this examination, information is obtained about the work done in the enterprise and the knowledge, skills and abilities that the employees should have in order to do this job. Job analysis is the analytical and systematic examination of all the factors involved in a job (Arora et al., 2021). Job analysis activities in businesses consist of efforts to determine the duties, responsibilities, and ways of doing business. In addition, the business analysis process starts with recognizing the business where the analysis will be carried out and the purpose of the analysis, then continues with the preparation of the business for analysis studies, identifying the employees who will do the analysis, giving them the necessary training, deciding on the methods to collect the information, and the data obtained as a result of the application. It is the whole of activities that continue to be used for the realization of long, tiring, and intensive efforts (Budhwar et al., 2022).

Job analysis is a method that defines the skills and obligations required by the job, as well as the characteristics of the employee who must be hired to fulfill these skills and obligations (Hmoud & Laszlo, 2019). The purpose of job analysis is to collect and analyze information about how the job is done and the job content for the successful realization of various human resources activities. In addition, the purposes of job analysis include job evaluation studies, personnel selection, determination of training and development needs, performance evaluation, occupational safety and resolution of some conflicts between management and union, providing introductory information about working processes, professions and jobs (Malik, Budhwar & Kazmi, 2022).

It is possible to summarize the expected objectives of job analysis as follows (Caruth et al., 1988):

- Contributing to human resources planning by determining the number of employees that may be needed in the future and the characteristics that these employees should have, considering the objectives of the business,
- Creating work groups and contributing to the design of performance evaluation and related remuneration processes,
- To improve the conditions of the work environment, to eliminate the factors affecting the work performance of the employees,
- Identifying the mutual importance of jobs in the enterprise and revealing the information needed especially in terms of wage and salary system,
- To determine the recruitment criteria for the recruitment of employees and to ensure that these criteria are applied,
- To identify the trainings needed for employees to demonstrate their performance in a more qualified and effective manner,
- To clearly determine the information about all the jobs in the company to realize the career plans of the employees in a healthy way,
- To establish an environment for the determination of the mutual relations of the works and the stable progress of the workload balance between them,
- To determine the information needed for the legal regulations concerning the work and employees to become operational,
- To implement occupational safety practices to ensure employee health.

Job analysis determines what the elements of a job are, while job design identifies which elements can be brought together and how these elements should be classified. Job design is the process of determining the specific tasks to be performed, the method used to perform these tasks, and the relationship of the job with other jobs in the organization (Nawaz, 2020).

The ordinary, simple, and monotonous work carried out in the establishments causes problems for employees to be dissatisfied with the work done, physical and mental fatigue, stress, alienation from work and the environment. As a result of this, in the employees, situations such as absenteeism, excessive staff turnover, poor quality and low production, and deterioration of workplace friendship may occur. For this reason, the structural feature of the job and the change of the employee are positioned as the main purpose of the job design. Besides, there are various methods of job design carried out to increase the productivity and motivation of the employees. The main ones are; job simplification, job rotation, job enlargement and job enrichment (Kaushal et al., 2021).

Job Simplification; It is the process of dividing the work into the smallest parts and providing training to the employees and using the unqualified workforce in the most efficient way in order to reach the same output related to a job with less cost, less effort, less fatigue and in a shorter time (Garg, Gaur & Sharma, 2021).

Job Rotation; It is the periodic assignment of employees to jobs involving different tasks or directing them from one job to another. In job rotation, different jobs that require similar qualifications within a specific program are employed for specified periods. The purpose of job rotation is to ensure that the employees working in simple and repetitive jobs are not bored and to eliminate the monotony caused by excessive specialization (Yawalkar, 2019). According to another definition, job rotation is defined as the transition of employees from a job or task to other job duties, depending on a predetermined schedule and duration, and their realization within a predetermined program (Hemalatha et al., 2021).

Business Expansion; It is based on the understanding that an employee learns all or part of the job rather than specializing in only one job. The reason for this is that if the volume of work to be done is small, it requires a lot of specialization, and this can negatively affect employee motivation. In other words, job enlargement means increasing the number of different duties and responsibilities required for the realization of a job and expanding the scope of the job. Job enlargement brings about a quantitative change in the general structure of the job (Yawalkar, 2019).

Job Enrichment; It is the realization of vertical fundamental changes in the content and level of responsibility of the work done. In job enrichment, the authority and responsibility of the employee is increased, and the job is made more meaningful in behavioral terms. Job enrichment includes the whole process of increasing the depth of the work, determining the personal working speed of the employees, being responsible for the care and quality of the work done by the employees, correcting the mistakes made by the employees, and offering the opportunity to the employees to choose the working methods, equipment and forms (Hemalatha et al., 2021).

ARTIFICIAL INTELLIGENCE

Artificial intelligence is systems or machines that imitate human intelligence to perform desired tasks and can continuously improve themselves in the light of the information they collect (Ore & Sposato, 2022). In other words, artificial intelligence is a technology that makes it possible for machines to learn through experience, adapt to new inputs, and perform given tasks by imitating humans (Albert, 2019). According to IBM, artificial intelligence is the whole of algorithms developed to mimic the problem-solving and decision-making abilities of the human mind and that uses computers or machines to do this (IBM, 2021). Artificial intelligence algorithms mainly focus on three cognitive skills. These are processes of learning, reasoning, and self-correction (Jha, Jha & Gupta, 2020). In the learning process, artificial intelligence focuses on collecting data and creating rules on how to transform that data into actionable information. It focuses on choosing the right methods to achieve the desired result in the reasoning process (Son, Lee & Chang, 2019).

Artificial Intelligence Supported Recruitment Process

Having a qualified workforce is one of the most important factors for businesses. In general, the job of a recruitment specialist working in the human resources department is to examine candidates' resumes, interview them face-to-face or online (such as a video meeting or phone call), and finally, as a result of his observations, to predict the performance and behavior of the applicant at the workplace and to make his hiring decision. The recruiter must consider a lot of variables when making predictions. As the number of variables evaluated and the amount of data increase, the quality, accuracy, and difficulty of the acquisition also increase (Jha, Jha & Gupta, 2020). To make the recruitment process more efficient and effective, many different equipments have been used until today. One of them is technology. With the rapid advancement in technology, recruiters can do their jobs more effectively and efficiently, find more time to develop their own skills and broaden their perspectives.

The traditional recruitment process is one that requires end-to-end human action, which includes sourcing candidates, scanning resumes, conducting interviews, and making hiring decisions (Geetha & Bhanu, 2018). In addition, in the traditional recruitment process, as the number of CVs evaluated increases, the difficulty of scanning the CV increases and limited human resources have difficulty in scanning the best candidate-job match in a limited time. Today, recruitment activities are carried out with traditional methods. In addition, many businesses currently receive support from artificial intelligence tools and applications. The use of artificial intelligence in the recruitment process is very important because of the many advantages it provides compared to the traditional recruitment process. Good automation and unbiased decision making have a significant impact on the hiring process, thanks to increased hiring quality, faster screening of candidates, better integration, and analytics. In addition, artificial intelligence offers a more effective way than traditional methods in terms of predicting the potential future success of a candidate who is currently working in the business or will be newly recruited (Gupta & Mishra, 2023).

At this point, the human resources department cooperates with artificial intelligence to increase the quality and efficiency of recruitment. Today, thanks to artificial intelligence algorithms, the entire recruitment process can be managed effectively and efficiently. Recruiters can identify talented candidates by applying artificial intelligence in their business strategies, and they can effortlessly obtain data from artificial intelligence about whether the applicants are suitable for the job applied for (FraiJ & Lászl6, 2021). However, artificial intelligence algorithms can support businesses in many activities from finding candidates to selecting candidates, from preparing reports about candidates to conducting live interviews, from analyzing the candidate's mood to building a three-dimensional workplace simulation (Cavaliere et al., 2021).

Artificial intelligence can make accurate predictions about human behavior and can report the information it obtains. In addition, artificial intelligence does not directly perform human resource management activities such as recruitment, but instead increases the quality and efficiency of the process by presenting very valuable arguments to the relevant personnel. In addition, the cooperation of human and artificial intelligence creates a successful synergy. In this direction, while artificial intelligence analyzes and reports the data in the fastest way, the recruiter can both make decisions based on stronger data and find more time to decide. In this way, possible errors due to the fact that the recruiter is human will be minimized. The reason for this is that artificial intelligence can evaluate, analyze, and report many variables that are routine and time-consuming, as well as requiring attention, in a very short time and with high accuracy (FraiJ & László, 2021).

The ability of artificial intelligence to support the recruiter in a healthy way depends on several factors. One of the most important of these is data. Artificial intelligence algorithms cannot generate data from scratch. For this reason, for artificial intelligence algorithms to perform the desired tasks in the most accurate and efficient way, relevant data should be presented to them. Although it was a mystery before where to get this data, question marks on this subject are decreasing day by day. Initially, these algorithms were tried to provide library full of book data or loosely connect them to the internet, but eventually it was realized that the data presented for the purpose led to the most accurate result. In addition, it has been seen that the content of the presented data directly affects the output offered by artificial intelligence or smart machines. When it comes to hiring artificial intelligence within the scope of human resources management, general information (such as books, leathers, articles, blogs) was presented to these algorithms as data, but later, it was seen that artificial intelligence sometimes exhibited biased, prejudiced and even racist attitudes in line with the information presented (Cavaliere et al., 2021).

Businesses have been using enterprise resource planning (ERP-Enterprise Resource Planning), customer relationship management (CRM-Customer Relationship Management) and many similar software for many years within the scope of human resources management. Although it was thought that artificial intelligence would replace this software, an unexpected detail has come to light. As a result of the trials, it has been determined that artificial intelligence needs quality data, and that the data in which these softwares, which have been used for many years, are suitable for this job. Subsequently, artificial intelligence algorithms have been integrated into these existing software and very successful outputs have been achieved. In addition, the social media accounts of the candidates applying for the job and all information in the virtual world are examined by artificial intelligence and a near-perfect evaluation profile can be drawn about the candidate (Jha, Jha & Gupta, 2020).

Virtual Reality Supported Training and Development

For businesses to keep up with the developing technology and survive, they need employees with sufficient technical knowledge and social skills such as communication, empathy, flexibility, emotional intelligence, teamwork, and leadership. Nowadays, it is very difficult to find employees with these skills and abilities. Therefore, businesses train their employees to gain the necessary skills. These trainings usually take place face-to-face or via computers. Due to today's technological development and the emerging epidemic, the remote working system has become quite widespread and alternative ways have begun to be used in the education of individuals (Soleimani et al., 2021).

Among these alternative education ways, the most widely used one today is distance education, which reduces time and place constraints and facilitates the access of trainers and trainees to many digital resources at home and abroad. Distance education usually takes place in the form of video conferences. In addition, the verbal and visual expression that takes place in video conferences can sometimes be insufficient. This is because individuals who have had face-to-face training for most of their lives may find video conferencing boring and artificial. Today, many businesses use virtual reality platforms to prevent such negativities and to ensure that their employees can make the most of the training provided.

Virtual reality platforms differ from face-to-face training or video conferences in that they blend the physical and virtual world. The purpose in virtual reality is to make the user feel as if they are really in a virtual world by using all five senses. Some tools are used to achieve this. The most well-known of these are virtual reality glasses (Aldulaimi et al., 2021).

Virtual reality platforms are used to train employees through a situation simulation. Employees can gain an immersive sense of experience on these platforms, as well as increase the effectiveness and applicability of training through these platforms. In addition, thanks to the virtual reality glasses and control devices used during the training, a trainee's gaze, body movements and facial expressions can be easily followed on the virtual reality platform during the session. Virtual reality platforms are fun for the employees because they are a new experience, the trainees do not feel boring during the training, so they are more willing to devote themselves to the training and get the maximum result (Yang et al., 2022).

Thanks to virtual reality platforms, businesses can show and even feel a subject instead of telling it to their employees. Virtual reality platforms, which can be used in attracting potential candidates to the business, orientation training of new employees, in-house trainings, and meetings, simulate a physical environment in all its aspects and move it to the virtual environment. In this way, wherever the relevant employee is, they can participate in this designed virtual reality platform and benefit from all the opportunities as if they were in a physical environment (Yang et al., 2022).

Mursion, one of the pioneers of the industry in virtual reality supported education, is an artificial intelligence supported virtual reality platform. The purpose of this platform is to bring the physical and virtual worlds together. There is a business center simulation designed close to reality on this platform. Aim is to give the participant who is included in the system the feeling of being in a real workplace. The participant first logs into the system as an avatar using virtual reality glasses and comes together with the autonomous avatars in the system. The avatars in the system are guided by the artificial intelligence algorithm and the gender, age, skin color and clothes of the avatars can be customized. In addition, the body languages, facial expressions, and lip synchronizations of the avatars are also instantly regulated by artificial intelligence. In addition, according to the scenario, all the details, from the background noise to the background noise, are finely adjusted by artificial intelligence. The functioning of the system is as follows: First, businesses determine a scenario about the subject they want to train their employees or the situation they want to test. Afterwards, avatars suitable for this scenario are designed by artificial intelligence according to the determined physical and emotional characteristics. The purpose of these avatars, designed and driven by artificial intelligence, is to act like a human in every aspect. Each of the avatars has different facial expressions and body language. To increase realism, avatars are voiced by theater-trained voice actors in real time. The voiceover text is also prepared by artificial intelligence in real time. At the end of the training or evaluation, the artificial intelligence algorithm analyzes and reports all the activities that took place during the training. While performing this analysis, the artificial intelligence algorithm can detect all the activities of the participant, from tone of voice to gestures and mimics, down to the finest detail (Mursion, 2021).

Businesses generally use this platform for recruitment interviews, training of new employees, meetings and determining the performance of their employees. With the help of various scenarios created, especially new employees get to know different personality types and see how they react to these personality types, what behaviors they can exhibit in a crisis, how they can develop solutions to a problem in an event, and they try to improve themselves by taking lessons from their mistakes. In addition, the artificial intelligence algorithm records and analyzes everything that happens during the training, creates a report and makes a score for all employees who enter the platform. In this way, the performance evaluation of the employees can be done simultaneously easily. The advantage of experiencing all these on a virtual reality platform is the freedom to make mistakes over and over again without any hesitation, the absence of any sanction as a result of an unsuccessful experience, the ability to develop one's point of view by experiencing the same scenarios over and over and to express ideas without fear. In addition, thanks to this platform, many social skills such as communication, emotional intelligence, teamwork and leadership are not only explained but also applied in practice, so the efficiency and quality of the acquired skill can increase (Mursion, 2021).

Although businesses have mainly used face-to-face education methods in the process until now, the need for remote working and therefore distance education has increased significantly due to the developing technology, the change in the way of doing business and especially the increasing epidemic diseases. In the face of this change, the human resources units of the enterprises have conducted new searches because training and development activities are at the center of human resources management. In this context, one of the most important activities to be done is to keep up with the developing technology. Today, artificial intelligence and virtual reality platforms are used for education and development. As explained above, artificial intelligence supported virtual reality platforms are one of the new equipment of human resources management, but they have a functional quality (Votto et al., 2021).

Recruitment Algorithms Supported by Artificial Intelligence

Artificial intelligence assisted recruitment algorithms significantly increase the efficiency of the recruitment process within the scope of human resources management (FraiJ & László, 2021) Today, many businesses rely on AI-assisted recruitment algorithms to select the best possible candidates. The reason for this is that businesses are aware that the use of artificial intelligence in the recruitment process will provide a fair evaluation environment and time savings, allow being objective and positively affect the candidate evaluation process The use of artificial intelligence-assisted recruitment algorithms in recruitment helps the recruitment team to analyze repetitive findings and compare them with an existing employee in the same job, and as a result, the most ideal candidate can be selected, thus accelerating the recruitment process (Cavaliere et al., 2021).There are many artificial intelligence supported recruitment algorithms used in recruitment (Köchling, Wehner & Warkocz, 2022). In this section, some artificial intelligence-assisted recruitment algorithms that are popular today and have great importance within the scope of human resources management are examined.

Pymetrics

Artificial intelligence offers very effective solutions in the process of finding, evaluating, and recruiting employees with the right qualifications and abilities. It requires a great deal of attention, sensitivity, and judgment to attract candidates with the right talents for the business, to sift through thousands of applications, and not to miss the candidates with the right skills in this process. Although various artificial intelligence algorithms are used in this process, their approach and methods may differ. One of the most striking examples in this field is Pymetrics, an ethical and human-centered artificial intelligence platform. The mission of this algorithm is to make hiring fairer and avoid bias. Artificial intelligence is currently under development (Raub, 2018).

Pymetrics claims that there are talent losses due to various prejudices in the selections made by recruiters, and that artificial intelligence can make choices free from prejudice and proves this claim with its applications. In the first stage of the recruitment process, Pymetrics determines the candidate's characteristics such as attention, effort, fairness, decision making, emotion, focus, generosity, learning, quantitative reasoning, numerical agility, and risk tolerance, with the help of a game it has developed. In this way, it creates a very detailed profile for the candidate. The AI is then presented with a video interview to process. The video in question includes footage of the candidate answering various questions for about thirty minutes. Pymetrics analyzes these images through a mix of natural language processing and body language analysis algorithms and adds them to the personal data pool. Afterwards, it is time to eliminate the candidates one by one. As a result of all the data that Pymetrics collects, it matches the profiles it personalizes for each candidate in accordance with the candidate profile desired by the businesses. Finally, it categorizes the candidates and automatically passes the candidates, which it separates as "recommended" and "highly recommended", to the next stage. It also provides feedback to all applicants at the end of the process, including those who have been unsuccessful. In addition, it presents candidates' performance data, satisfaction rate and interview completion time in the form of a report to the recruiting team at the end of each recruitment cycle. In this way, human resources recruiters do not spend time and effort to screen out hundreds or perhaps thousands of applications one by one but concentrate only on the most suitable candidates selected by artificial intelligence and make more consistent choices. Ultimately, humans make the final choice, and artificial intelligence provides data to help humans in the decision-making process (Pymetrics AI, 2021).

Wade and Wendy

Another relevant example, Wade and Wendy, is a two-way artificial intelligence algorithm that uses machine learning. This algorithm, whose mission is to automate the recruitment process, aims to save time for human resources employees so that they can better use their skills. This recruitment algorithm, which has gained popularity with the widespread use of the remote working method, selects the most suitable candidate from a pool of approximately 150 million candidate profiles created by itself for open positions in the enterprise and recommends it to the relevant human resources specialist. With the help of a speech-based artificial intelligence algorithm, Wade and Wendy conduct written interviews with all candidates registered in the system, 24 hours a day, 7 days a week, in the form of questions and answers. These interviews can usually be completed in less than 30 minutes. The algorithm chats with the candidates in these interviews and gives the candidate information on organizational culture, recruitment process and similar issues. The algorithm, which identifies the goals, skills, experiences, and many other features of the candidate interviewed, reports these features, and presents them to the relevant human resources specialist. The algorithm, which can offer career suggestions about employees, creates special profiles by analyzing each employee one by one, compares the vacant positions and candidate profiles within the enterprise, and determines which candidate is the most suitable for the vacant position and presents them to the relevant human resources specialist. Wade and Wendy are already actively used by many businesses. In addition, the time to fill open positions and recruitment costs are significantly reduced in businesses using the algorithm (Wade and Wendy AI, 2021).

Oracle Cloud

Oracle Cloud operating under Oracle, one of the largest software companies in the world, serving 430,000 customers in 175 countries, with 138,000 employees and a company value of 40 billion dollars, is another artificial intelligence algorithm that supports the human resources department in the recruitment process. Oracle Cloud, a configurable cloud project that can work in integration with all artificial intelligence algorithms operating within Oracle, makes significant breakthroughs in human resources management. Oracle Cloud, the artificial intelligence supported cloud technology that supports almost all human resources management activities from recruitment to retirement, cooperates with many businesses in this field (Sun, Gregor & Fielt, 2021).

Mursion

Mursion, an artificial intelligence supported virtual reality platform, is building a virtual business environment for businesses. On this platform, which looks just like a real business, meeting rooms, activity areas, areas where field work is simulated, common work areas, in short, almost everything in a physical business environment has been moved to the virtual environment. Human resources officers in human resources units can conduct recruitment interviews in this virtual environment. Thus, even if the recruitment interview takes place remotely in a virtual environment, recruiters can observe the candidate's reaction and behavior in certain situations through this virtual platform. In the recruitment interviews that take place in this way, a virtual avatar is first created for the candidate. Afterwards, the candidate puts on the glasses designed for the virtual reality platform and enters the pre-designed virtual workplace. Then, by assigning certain tasks to the candidate, the candidate's behavior and reactions to different scenarios are observed and scored by the recruiter. Meanwhile, the artificial intelligence algorithm, which monitors all activities on the platform full-time, makes certain inferences and reports it to the relevant recruiter. This technology is used in remote recruitment interviews in both physical and virtual environments. The reason why this virtual platform is also used in physical interviews is to increase the quality and efficiency of the interview by bringing a different perspective to candidate evaluation (Mursion, 2021).

As a result, it has satisfactorily proven to be useful in the pre-screening process when it comes to pre-screening applicants, even if human resource management is not yet ready to delegate the entire recruitment process to AI. In addition, artificial intelligence or smart machines do what they do best, process huge amounts of data and report this data to recruiters in a meaningful way, and then recruiters use their decision-making abilities by doing what they do best. Therefore, very productive results are obtained from this symbiotic cooperation. Artificial intelligence or smart machine alleviates the burden of the human, allowing the recruiter to use and develop his decision-making skills effectively (Ferguson & Sutphin, 2022).

Cogito

Another example is Cogito, designed and managed by a team of experts in behavioral science and enterprise technology. Cogito is a mentoring algorithm with artificial intelligence. This algorithm can perform live in-call voice analysis during the call and can detect more than two hundred voice signals. Cogito, which can give intuitive warnings to the recruiter working in the human resources department or the manager responsible for any department, and instantly analyze the speech behavior and perception of the person, offers tips that will increase the empathy and performance of the relevant employee on issues such as etiquette, trust, and professionalism. It provides guidance on how to speak more efficiently. In this way, both the training activities of the relevant human resources personnel are carried out and proactive measures such as making attractive offers or ending the interview can be taken by detecting details that are not easily noticed under normal conditions such as the potential candidate's intention to enter the job, tendencies, weaknesses, and frustration level. In addition, real-time dashboards, the interview experience of the candidate participating in the interview, the behavior pattern and approach of the interviewer can be presented to the human resources manager, so that the manager can easily make an assessment. Therefore, the decision-making process becomes more efficient with the help of artificial intelligence. In addition, the AI algorithm automatically warns the human resources manager about bad interviews (Cogito Corporation, 2021).

Cogito, an artificial intelligence algorithm that is human-centered, capable of imitating and mentoring humans, has listened to millions of phone calls over a period of more than ten years to achieve a successful performance at this level. Thanks to its machine learning and natural language processing algorithm, Cogito updates its system after each analysis and continues to develop. Developing a unique style thanks to its natural language processing algorithm, Cogito uses data from people to coach people. The goal of thousands of artificial intelligence algorithms currently operating is to be like humans üto be able to think like humans, to solve the thinking system of the human mind, and thus to help humans. The achievement of this short-term goal of artificial intelligence will be thanks to machine learning. The long-term development of a continuously learning machine is not yet foreseen. Cogito is one of the best examples of human and artificial intelligence or smart machine collaboration. Creating a synergy by using the best features of artificial intelligence and human, Cogito uniquely combines rich human behavior insights with real-time natural language processing algorithm during the recruitment interview or any meeting, by combining the mood, reaction level, sensitivity of all parties participating in the meeting or the interview. It can instantly analyze dozens of facts. In addition, one of the most important features that distinguishes humans from artificial intelligence or smart machines is emotional intelligence. Cogito provides significant support to people to develop their emotional intelligence (Cogito Corporation, 2021).

The Impact of Artificial Intelligence on HRM and Its Applications

Artificial intelligence has important implications for human resource management applications. There are many advantages of using artificial intelligence within the scope of human resources management. However, the use of artificial intelligence in businesses to help human resources functions and increase the productivity of the business and employees is becoming more common day by day. Artificial intelligence, within the scope of human resources management, produces various solutions, including basic recruitment tools, intermediate applications, and advanced artificial intelligence solutions, and increases the efficiency of the enterprise by offering rewards and incentives suitable for each employee's profile. At the same time, artificial intelligence plays an active role in many human resources management, from recruitment to performance evaluation. In addition, artificial intelligence reduces the administrative burden on human resources professionals and allows them to help them make decisions based on proven data patterns, instead of making decisions based only on instinct, and increases the efficiency of the decisions taken, as well as providing significant advantages in terms of time and cost (FraiJ & Lászl6, 2021).

When evaluated in general, one of the most important functions of artificial intelligence is to lighten the burden of HRM employees, to enable them to concentrate on more value-added works and thus to use their talents more efficiently. There are many studies in the literature with similar ideas. For example, according to Cavaliere et al. (2021), artificial intelligence enables human resources specialists to focus on higher-level tasks instead of routine and time-consuming inquiries and to provide more added value

Table 1. Comparison of the impact of artificial intelligence on various HR functions

HR POLICY	Before Artificial Intelligence	After Artificial Intelligence
Recruitment	• It requires a lot of time.• Sometimes, biased decisions can be made.• It is a manual and long process.	• Recruitment quality increases.• Automation saves time.• Decisions are taken impartially.
Training and Development	• Through experienced trainersmanual learning takes place.• Programs are long and time consuming.• Feedback is slow.• The cost of education is high.	• Customized learning programs are realized through artificial intelligence and machine learning.• Learning programs are short and fast.• Real-time feedback is available.• Training cost is low.
Performance Management	• The amount of information collected is less.• In measuring performancesdelays may occur.• There is a possibility of bias.• There may be gender inequality.	• Collects data from multiple sources.• Real-time measurement is available.• All psychological prejudices are eliminated.• Less gender equality
Pricing	• Wages may be unfair.• There is group rewarding• There may be delays in rewards.• High cost to business	• There is a fair payment.• There is customized rewarding.• There is fast and flexible rewarding.• Cost reduction is possible by using artificial intelligence technology.
Retention	• It may be the case that the needs of the employees cannot be met.• Fee gaps exist.• Response time may be insufficient to retain employees and ensure their participation.	• Artificial intelligence uses wage analysis to meet employee needs.• By using rules on education, experience, certificates and more, wage gaps are reduced.• A rapid response mechanism is in place to retain and engage employees.

Source: Zahidi, F., Imam, Y., Hashmi, A. U., & Baig, M. M. (2020). Impact of artificial intelligence on HR management–A.

not only to human resources management processes, but also to the business world. According to FraiJ & Lászl6 (2021), artificial intelligence helps human resources focus more on strategic work rather than repetitive low value-added tasks. According to Soleimani et al. (2021), because artificial intelligence is responsible for dealing with monotonous and repetitive tasks efficiently, human resources personnel can focus more on innovative and strategic issues. According to Albert (2019), artificial intelligence can significantly reduce the time human resources personnel spend on candidate screening, therefore, these personnel can use their energy more efficiently and focus more on their work.

The use of artificial intelligence within the scope of human resources management in businesses has many important contributions to human resources practice. In this scope, comparison of the effect of artificial intelligence on various HR functions is shown in Table 1.

The Effect of Artificial Intelligence on Employee Selection

Today, artificial intelligence is strongly associated with recruitment practices Albert (2019). The use of artificial intelligence to recruit new candidates is spreading rapidly in every industry. The main reason for this is artificial intelligence's effort to eliminate the burden of manually scanning candidates' resumes. Screening potential candidates for a given job has been one of the biggest challenges for HR managers over the past decade, as it takes too much time and undermines managers' effective enough work. This challenging process has become very fast with the use of artificial intelligence. Artificial intelligence helps automatically match candidates to required jobs without using human intelligence. If recruitment is done manually to pre-select an interested candidate, it takes approximately twenty-three hours for the candidate to pre-select. In addition, with the use of artificial intelligence, heaps of resumes can be scanned within an hour. AI-powered recruitment software can filter relevant skills, experience, educational background, and more, thus eliminating the use of human intelligence and saving several productive hours. Artificial intelligence supported recruitment software can also send a business promotion message to thousands of job seekers at the same time (Raub, 2018).

In businesses, the duties of the HR department include screening ideal candidates and managing the selection process. With the application of artificial intelligence in the HR department, screening of applicants and their resumes, etc. the average time spent on jobs is shortened. This allows the HR department to have more time to focus on other functions that require personal effort or a human touch Therefore, AI-based HRM tools are highly efficient in terms of several objectives such as shortening a candidate's recruitment time, costs, and use of other resources. Similarly, artificial intelligence tools provide inputs to businesses such as time saving and cost reduction in the recruitment and selection process, as well as showing a good performance in terms of output efficiency by reducing the abandonment rates in the application process thanks to its efficiency (Johansson & Herranen, 2019).

There are a variety of AI-powered tools that help HR professionals evaluate potential candidates for a particular job. These AI-supported tools can support many activities, from screening candidates' applications to post-placement evaluation. These tools also help analyze candidates' profiles to check if they have the necessary skills. These tools, which communicate with candidates by sending automated e-mails or messages to candidates during the recruitment process, prepare many tasks and rewards for employees who are hired to be a part of the organization. As a result of all these, candidates applying for a job can be selected much faster by using artificial intelligence supported tools in the recruitment process (Berhil, Benlahmar & Labani, 2020).

In large businesses, recruitment interviews take place on a large scale and these businesses often have a hard time evaluating their applications and resumes. Artificial intelligence is used in businesses to facilitate the interview and recruitment process. In addition, many businesses use artificial intelligence to examine the facial expressions and body language of the candidate to evaluate whether the personality of the candidate is suitable for the job during the recruitment interview. When the recruitment interview process carried out by HR in enterprises is carried out entirely by a human, various unconscious or conscious prejudices such as gender biases against potential employees may arise. Artificial intelligence tries to eliminate these biases and provide a fair evaluation process to all candidates who are suitable for various roles determined by the business (Yawalkar, 2019). In addition, artificial intelligence is used for recruitment, reducing nepotism, and retaining the best talent (Wheeler & Buckley, 2021).

Artificial intelligence algorithms help HR teams during the hiring period to analyze the resumes received, compare them with the resumes of current employees in the same job role, and then select the best candidate. Many businesses use artificial intelligence to reduce their costs (Köchling, Wehner & Warkocz, 2022). The successful integration of artificial intelligence and HR in the recruitment process helps businesses recruit the right talent (Son, Lee & Chang, 2019). In addition, the number and variety of metrics used in recruitment can be increased by using artificial intelligence. Artificial intelligence uses sophisticated algorithms to monitor candidates' skill sets while providing recruitment solutions to businesses. However, HR leaders make use of personalized AI tools to recruit the best talent (Berhil, Benlahmar & Labani, 2020).

CONCLUSION

Although the history of artificial intelligence dates to the middle of the twentieth century, it is living its golden age today. Artificial intelligence, which initially consisted of Alan Turing's (1950) dream of producing thinking machines or scenes in science fiction movies, has reached a very important level thanks to the developing technology, and has begun to imitate the human mind to a large extent. Artificial intelligence technology is directly related to HRM. From chatbots that save employees from the stereotypical questions frequently asked by customers and spend more time on value-added work, from conversation-based artificial intelligence that can guide and mentor employees to metaverse areas with virtual and augmented reality that create an environment for providing better quality and efficient training to employees. Many algorithms have started to play vital roles in HRM, from cutting-edge artificial intelligence to the cutting-edge artificial intelligence that enables recruitment professionals to use their talents and skills to the fullest by playing an active role in the entire recruitment process (FraiJ & László, 2021).

The goal of artificial intelligence today is to achieve the ability to perfectly imitate the human mind. For an algorithm whose purpose is to imitate the human mind and contribute to humanity in this way, HRM will provide an ideal working environment because human resources are the unit in which people are at the forefront and almost all activities are related to people. Therefore, if a business wants to cooperate with artificial intelligence or machines and create a synergy, the most ideal unit that can provide this communication is human resources.

The use of artificial intelligence tools in performance evaluation applications within the scope of HRM is very important in businesses. Artificial intelligence tools have brought a new perspective to performance evaluation applications. These tools, which can process and interpret data, can report many findings to managers through their high-level relationship building skills. Therefore, managers, who can access a lot of data with the support of these tools, can evaluate the performance of their employees according to many criteria, and they can make performance evaluations from a wider perspective with the help of the findings reported by artificial intelligence. At this point, it is very important for managers to perceive artificial intelligence applications. In order to use artificial intelligence effectively in performance evaluation applications in enterprises, it is necessary to determine the perceptions of the managers on this issue and to eliminate the lack of information, if any. In addition, training should be given to managers on how to use artificial intelligence technology in performance evaluation applications, and the consequences of the cooperation of these two variables should be explained, and an environment should be prepared for them to be experienced if possible.

Artificial intelligence technology is very important for countries in terms of using the available resources and therefore human resources efficiently. At this point, policy makers need to consider some important issues. The most important of these issues is education. Policies to be decided on education have the power to control all positive and negative developments that may be encountered in the future. At this point, first of all, the technology infrastructure in the country should be brought to a level that can keep up with the times. In case of insufficient technological infrastructure, it is very difficult to carry the trainings into practice. Before providing training to individuals, the necessary infrastructure must be established. After the necessary infrastructure has been established, the next step is to decide on the human resources to be trained. At this point, the most erroneous policy to be developed is to concentrate training activities on certain areas and to carry out training activities only for areas where artificial intelligence is used. Although this policy seems to yield positive results in the short run, it is very difficult to achieve success in the long run. The success of this technology in terms of countries is possible with the creation of an educational culture to be built for this technology.

Educational policies related to artificial intelligence should be developed to cover all segments of society, especially school-age youth. The reason for this is that the way artificial intelligence is used and the maximum benefit to be obtained from this technology depends on the perspective and ability. Therefore, since it is not possible to predict which segment can develop a better perspective on this technology, educational activities related to this technology should be designed in such a way that all segments of the society can be reached. The delivery of this technology to the workforce that is working and has the potential to work may be the pioneer of an unpredictable development. Obtaining the highest efficiency from human resources will be possible by providing the necessary environment for people to reveal their potential. The development of policies with this perspective will affect the course of the future of technology.

Suggestions for future studies on the use of artificial intelligence (AI) in the employee selection process include investigating the ethical considerations surrounding AI algorithms and their potential biases, developing and validating specialized AI algorithms for employee selection, exploring the integration of AI with human decision-making to optimize selection outcomes, assessing the candidate experience and perception of AI-based selection processes, examining the long-term performance and retention of employees selected through AI, exploring user interface and interaction design for AI-based selection systems, studying the challenges and opportunities of change management and adoption of AI technologies in organizations, considering the legal and regulatory implications of AI in employee selection, examining cross-cultural and international perspectives on AI-based selection, and conducting longitudinal studies to evaluate the long-term impact and scalability of AI-driven selection systems. These future studies can provide valuable insights for organizations to optimize their employee selection processes and ensure the ethical and effective use of AI technologies.

REFERENCES

Albert, E. T. (2019). AI in talent acquisition: A review of AI-applications used in recruitment and selection. *Strategic HR Review*, *18*(5), 215–221. doi:10.1108/SHR-04-2019-0024

Aldulaimi, S. H., Abdeldayem, M. M., Mowafak, B. M., & Abdulaziz, M. M. (2021). Experimental Perspective of Artificial Intelligence Technology in Human Resources Management. *Applications of Artificial Intelligence in Business, Education and Healthcare*, 487-511.

Arora, M., Prakash, A., Mittal, A., & Singh, S. (2021, December). HR analytics and artificial intelligence-transforming human resource management. In *2021 International Conference on Decision Aid Sciences and Application (DASA)* (pp. 288-293). IEEE. 10.1109/DASA53625.2021.9682325

Baykal, E. (2020). Digital era and new methods for employee recruitment. In *Handbook of Research on Strategic Fit and Design in Business Ecosystems* (pp. 412–430). IGI Global. doi:10.4018/978-1-7998-1125-1.ch018

Berhil, S., Benlahmar, H., & Labani, N. (2020). A review paper on artificial intelligence at the service of human resources management. *Indonesian Journal of Electrical Engineering and Computer Science*, *18*(1), 32–40. doi:10.11591/ijeecs.v18.i1.pp32-40

Budhwar, P., Malik, A., De Silva, M. T., & Thevisuthan, P. (2022). Artificial intelligence–challenges and opportunities for international HRM: A review and research agenda. *International Journal of Human Resource Management*, *33*(6), 1065–1097. doi:10.1080/09585192.2022.2035161

Cavaliere, L. P. L., Nath, K., Wisetsri, W., Villalba-Condori, K. O., Arias-Chavez, D., Setiawan, R., & Regin, R. (2021). *The impact of E-recruitment and artificial intelligence (AI) tools on HR effectiveness: the case of high schools* [Doctoral dissertation, Petra Christian University].

Dinçer, H., & Yüksel, S. (Eds.). (2018). *Handbook of research on managerial thinking in global business economics*. IGI Global.

Ferguson, S., & Sutphin, L. (2022). Analyzing the impact on teacher preparedness as a result of using Mursion as a risk-free microteaching experience for pre-service teachers. *Journal of Educational Technology Systems*, *50*(4), 432–447. doi:10.1177/00472395211067731

Frai, J. J., & Lászl6, V. (2021). A literature review: Artificial intelligence impact on the recruitment process. *International Journal of Engineering and Management Sciences*, *6*(1), 108–119. doi:10.21791/IJEMS.2021.1.10.

Garg, A., Gaur, S., & Sharma, P. (2021). A Review Paper: Role of Artificial Intelligence in Recruitment Process. *Anwesh*, *6*(1), 33.

Geetha, R., & Bhanu, S. R. D. (2018). Recruitment through artificial intelligence: A conceptual study. *International Journal of Mechanical Engineering and Technology*, *9*(7), 63–70.

Gong, Y., Zhao, M., Wang, Q., & Lv, Z. (2022). Design and interactive performance of human resource management system based on artificial intelligence. *PLoS One*, *17*(1), e0262398. doi:10.1371/journal.pone.0262398 PMID:35089946

Gupta, A., & Mishra, M. (2023). Artificial Intelligence for Recruitment and Selection. In The Adoption and Effect of Artificial Intelligence on Human Resources Management, Part B(pp. 1-11). Emerald Publishing Limited. doi:10.1108/978-1-80455-662-720230001

Hemalatha, A., Kumari, P. B., Nawaz, N., & Gajenderan, V. (2021, March). Impact of artificial intelligence on recruitment and selection of information technology companies. In *2021 International Conference on Artificial Intelligence and Smart Systems (ICAIS)* (pp. 60-66). IEEE. 10.1109/ICAIS50930.2021.9396036

Hmoud, B., & Laszlo, V. (2019). Will artificial intelligence take over human resources recruitment and selection. *Network Intelligence Studies, 7*(13), 21-30. https://www.pymetrics.ai/case-studies/significant-efficiency-gains

IBM. (n.d.). *Big data analytics*. IBM. https://www.ibm.com/analytics/hadoop/big-data-analytics

Jha, S. K., Jha, S., & Gupta, M. K. (2020). Leveraging artificial intelligence for effective recruitment and selection processes. In *International Conference on Communication, Computing and Electronics Systems* [Springer Singapore.]. *Proceedings of ICCCES, 2019*, 287–293.

Johansson, J., & Herranen, S. (2019). *The application of artificial intelligence (AI) in human resource management: Current state of AI and its impact on the traditional recruitment process.*

Kaushal, N., Kaurav, R. P. S., Sivathanu, B., & Kaushik, N. (2021). Artificial intelligence and HRM: identifying future research Agenda using systematic literature review and bibliometric analysis. *Management Review Quarterly*, 1-39.

Köchling, A., Wehner, M. C., & Warkocz, J. (2022). Can I show my skills? Affective responses to artificial intelligence in the recruitment process. *Review of Managerial Science*, 1–30.

Malik, A., Budhwar, P., & Kazmi, B. A. (2022). Artificial intelligence (AI)-assisted HRM: Towards an extended strategic framework. *Human Resource Management Review*, 100940.

Nawaz, N. (2020). Exploring artificial intelligence applications in human resource management. *Journal of Management Information and Decision Sciences*, *23*(5), 552–563.

Ore, O., & Sposato, M. (2022). Opportunities and risks of artificial intelligence in recruitment and selection. *The International Journal of Organizational Analysis*, *30*(6), 1771–1782. doi:10.1108/IJOA-07-2020-2291

Pan, Y., Froese, F., Liu, N., Hu, Y., & Ye, M. (2022). The adoption of artificial intelligence in employee recruitment: The influence of contextual factors. *International Journal of Human Resource Management*, *33*(6), 1125–1147. doi:10.1080/09585192.2021.1879206

Pymetrics. (2018). Leading american fast-food chain. In Raub, M. (ed). *Bots, bias and big data: artificial intelligence, algorithmic bias and disparate impact liability in hiring practices*. Ark. L. Rev.

Raub, M. (2018). Bots, bias and big data: Artificial intelligence, algorithmic bias and disparate impact liability in hiring practices. *Arkansas Law Review*, *71*, 529.

Silahtaroglu, G., & Vardarlier, P. (2016). A novel data mining study to spot anomalies in organizations: A human resources management case. *International Journal of Business and Administrative Studies*, *2*(4), 89.

Soleimani, M., Intezari, A., Taskin, N., & Pauleen, D. (2021). *Cognitive biases in developing biased Artificial Intelligence recruitment system*. Research Gate.

Strohmeier, S., & Piazza, F. (2015). Artificial intelligence techniques in human resource management—a conceptual exploration. *Intelligent Techniques in Engineering Management: Theory and Applications*, 149-172. Research Gate.

Sun, R., Gregor, S., & Fielt, E. (2021). Generativity and the paradox of stability and flexibility in a platform architecture: A case of the Oracle Cloud Platform. *Information & Management*, *58*(8), 103548. doi:10.1016/j.im.2021.103548

Turk, A., Vardarlier, P., & Hazar, M. A. (2020). The role of employer brand practices in human resources management in job applications on company preference. *International Journal of Business Ecosystem & Strategy (2687-2293)*, *2*(4), 1-9.

Votto, A. M., Valecha, R., Najafirad, P., & Rao, H. R. (2021). Artificial intelligence in tactical human resource management: A systematic literature review. *International Journal of Information Management Data Insights*, *1*(2), 100047. doi:10.1016/j.jjimei.2021.100047

Wheeler, A. R., & Buckley, M. R. (2021). The Current State of HRM with Automation, Artificial Intelligence, and Machine Learning. In *HR without People?* (pp. 45–67). Emerald Publishing Limited. doi:10.1108/978-1-80117-037-620211004

Yang, Y., Siau, K., Xie, W., & Sun, Y. (2022). Smart Health: Intelligent Healthcare Systems in the Metaverse, Artificial Intelligence, and Data Science Era. [JOEUC]. *Journal of Organizational and End User Computing*, *34*(1), 1–14. doi:10.4018/JOEUC.308814

Yawalkar, M. V. V. (2019). a Study of Artificial Intelligence and its role in Human Resource Management. [IJRAR]. *International Journal of Research and Analytical Reviews*, *6*(1), 20–24.

Chapter 16
Talent Retention Practices:
Concepts and Analytical Perspectives

Princy Thomas
https://orcid.org/0000-0001-7625-0215
CHRIST University, India

Bharathi Venkatesh
https://orcid.org/0000-0001-5598-3057
CHRIST University, India

Susan George
CHRIST University, India

ABSTRACT

Employee retention is a huge challenge for many companies because of the difficulty of getting the right talent at the right place for the right job with the required potential to cope with the new changing environment. A Gartner survey revealed that 91% of HR leaders expect employee turnover in the immediate future. Even more so if employees have more job offers while joining a company, and if they find discrepancies from their expectations, they are ready to leave the job. In this scenario, it is the need for organizations to identify the best strategies to retain talented employees. This chapter explains the concepts of talent retention, its relevance, practices, factors, and analytics contributing in retaining employees. This chapter will be helpful for organizations to devise new strategies for retaining the employees. This will also be useful for academicians and students to apply analytics in retaining employees.

INTRODUCTION

Employee retention, also known as talent retention, refers to an organization's ability to retain its employees for a long period of time. It is an essential part of an organization's talent management strategy, and its importance cannot be overstated. Employee retention is all about creating an environment that is conducive to retaining employees and keeping them motivated to work for the company. Human resource

DOI: 10.4018/978-1-6684-8942-0.ch016

departments play an active role in developing and implementing these strategies. Organizations that adopt and implement effective employee retention strategies can expect their employees to remain committed and motivated to work towards achieving the organization's goals (Taplin et al., 2003; Gberevbie, 2008; Das, 2013), else it will end up in high employee turnover.

Employee turnover, or the rate at which employees leave a company and are replaced by new hires, can have several negative impacts on organizations. When experienced employees leave a company, their knowledge and expertise are lost. This can negatively impact the organization's productivity and ability to deliver quality work. Employee turnover can be expensive for companies, the reason being the additional costs of recruitment and training new employees, and the time and resources spent on these activities can take away from other important business initiatives. High employee turnover can create a sense of instability and uncertainty among remaining employees, leading to decreased morale, motivation, and productivity. When an employee leaves, it can disrupt the team dynamics and create a gap in communication and workflow which delays project deadlines and decreases the overall efficiency of the team. A high turnover rate can damage a company's culture and reputation. It can create a sense of instability and indicate to potential new hires that the company is not a stable or attractive place to work (Ongori, 2007; Sutherland, 2000; Matriano, 2018; Negative effects of employee turnover, 2022). According to a survey conducted by the Society for Human Resource Management (SHRM), the average cost of replacing an employee can be three to four times the position's salary (Navarra, 2022). Thus, employee turnover can be a significant challenge for organizations and it is crucial for companies to implement effective employee retention strategies to retain their top talent. The existing research on employee turnover has largely neglected the factors that contribute to an employee's decision to stay with an organization and the underlying reasons for their attachment (Maertz, 1998).

Organizations that are well-managed create their own talent retention strategies and implement them starting from an employee's first day of employment (Bhattacharyya, 2015). One of the primary reasons employees leave their jobs is due to low compensation or lack of benefits. Compensation and benefits are crucial elements in talent retention strategies as they play a significant role in attracting and retaining employees. A well-designed compensation and benefits package can motivate employees, boost their morale, and reduce turnover rates.

Organizations use competitive salaries and bonuses to attract top talent, while providing comprehensive benefits such as healthcare, retirement plans, and paid time off can improve job satisfaction and employee loyalty. Additionally, offering flexible working arrangements such as telecommuting, flexible work hours can enhance work-life balance and reduce employee stress. Employees who feel valued and appreciated are more likely to remain committed to an organization, and an effective compensation and benefits package can help to demonstrate this appreciation. In contrast, employees who feel undervalued or underpaid may become disengaged and seek employment elsewhere (How does compensation affect employee retention, 2022; Bryant & Allen, 2013).

Recognizing and rewarding employees for their hard work and contributions can increase employee satisfaction and loyalty. Companies can use different recognition and reward programs such as employee of the month, peer recognition, and spot bonuses to acknowledge and appreciate employees' efforts. A positive work environment is essential for employee retention. Employers can create a positive work environment by fostering a culture of respect, transparency, and open communication. Furthermore, providing a safe and healthy workplace can also contribute to a positive work environment and increase employee satisfaction (Mngomezulu et al., 2015; James & Mathew, 2012).

Another crucial element is the work-life balance. Employers can provide work-life balance by offering flexible work arrangements, providing time off for personal reasons, and promoting a culture that values employees' personal lives. Providing resources for stress management and mental health support can also contribute to work-life balance (Shockley et al., 2017). Employers can also provide opportunities for employee engagement by organizing team-building activities, volunteering events, or company-sponsored social events. These activities can help to foster a sense of community among employees and increase their commitment to the organization.

Employee retention is a crucial aspect for organizations, as they strive to retain their key performers. It can be measured as a percentage indicating the proportion of employees retained over a specified period, such as 87% retention rate over a year. Alternatively, employee retention can be seen as a strategic effort by organizations to retain their employees. This involves implementing measures to encourage employees to stay for longer durations. In today's globalized business world, retention management has become a significant source of competitive advantage. Employee turnover not only affects the organization but also has implications for families and society. It brings stress to families due to possible relocations and financial concerns. Organizations may face service disruptions and employee dissatisfaction due to increased workloads. Moreover, when employees with critical skills leave, it negatively impacts society. Understanding the factors that drive commitment and loyalty among employees is vital for managing turnover risk.

Workforce Planning

Workforce planning is a systematic method of analyzing the existing employees, future workforce needs, and planning workforce supply and demand, assessing gaps, and determining target talent management interventions to ensure that an organization has the right people with the right skills in the right places at the right time to accomplish the mission, goals, and objectives of the organization (National Institute of health, n.d; IPMA Workforce Planning Resource Guide, 2002). A proper workforce planning can retain employees.

Organizations face the challenge of employee turnover caused by excessive workload and role mismatch. To address this issue, organizations can adopt effective strategic workforce planning to improve employee retention. By gaining a comprehensive understanding of their talent requirements and aligning hiring and talent development initiatives with their business goals, organizations can achieve better outcomes and alleviate the burden on employees. This entails forecasting workforce needs, identifying skill gaps, and implementing plans to bridge those gaps. By implementing robust workforce planning practices, organizations can accurately identify suitable employees for specific positions also minimizing the occurrence of role mismatch and promoting long-term employee tenure.

Through the effective implementation of workforce planning, organizations can gain valuable insights into their employees' skills and identify the areas where they can contribute most effectively to the business. Instead of resorting to employee termination, organizations can leverage this understanding to retain their valuable staff through well-planned redeployment strategies. This involves identifying alternative roles or projects within the organization where employees can thrive and make significant contributions. By strategically redeploying employees based on their skills and strengths, organizations can retain talented individuals and maximize their potential within the company (Workforce planning: Model, process, steps, 2022).

Thus effective workforce planning leads to enhanced employee retention rates. Businesses that adopt this practice benefit from having a well-defined roadmap, transparent standards, and suitable staffing levels. This ensures that employees are neither overwhelmed with excessive work nor underutilized, resulting in a balanced workload. Moreover, by investing in talent development and providing growth opportunities, businesses foster an environment where employees feel valued and motivated.

When a workforce planning program aligns with strategic planning, it creates a sense of unity among employees who share a common goal. This alignment enables the workforce to work cohesively towards the organization's objectives, enhancing collaboration and overall productivity (Organ, 2023).

Workforce planning analytics helps an organization to identify the right talent for achieving the business goals and reduce retention expenses (Isson &Harriott, 2016). It helps organizations to understand the suitability of the candidate for the position, number of employees leave the organization due to involuntary and voluntary retirement, the number of employees who may leave in the next 3, 5, or 10 years (Voluntary and Involuntary), the number of employees need to replace due to the attrition and helps the organizations to identify the target segment of employees who can achieve the business goals (Isson &Harriott, 2016).

In summary, effective workforce planning promotes improved employee retention rates by maintaining a conducive work environment, fostering talent development, and establishing a shared vision among the workforce.

Career Growth Opportunities

Career Growth Opportunities is another important talent retention strategy. Employees want to feel like they are growing in their careers and developing new skills. Providing career growth opportunities like training programs, mentorship, and leadership development can motivate employees to stay with the organization long-term. It also helps to create a positive work environment where employees feel valued and supported (Ott et al., 2018).

According to Das (1996), Indian companies often lack a well-defined career development plan, which significantly reduces the chances of an individual who joins as a management trainee eventually becoming the CEO. This situation can be seen as a trap for loyal employees who aspire to grow within the company. In contrast, studies conducted by Mehta et.al, (2014), Singh (2019), and Coker (2016) indicates that when there are ample career opportunities available within a company, employees are more likely to stay for a longer duration and exhibit higher levels of loyalty towards the organization.

Career growth is a top priority for employees, as highlighted by recent findings (How to encourage career growth for employee retention & success, n.d). The significance of "opportunities to learn and grow" has surged to become the leading factor in creating a positive work culture, rising from ninth place in 2019. A concerning statistic emerges, indicating that only one in five employees believe they can achieve their career aspirations within their current organization. This belief is further compounded by the perception that their manager and the organization as a whole lack the necessary support to help them pursue their goals, even if it means transitioning to a different department or role.

The importance of career advancement opportunities becomes evident when considering the reasons behind employee resignations. A majority of U.S. employees, constituting over 60%, who left their jobs in the past year cited a lack of avenues for professional growth as a contributing factor. Even a considerable 80 percent of job seekers express concerns about their future career progression, highlighting the widespread desire for opportunities to develop and advance professionally (How to encourage career growth for employee retention & success, n.d.).

There are several types of career development opportunities that can be made available for the employees namely Experiential and skills-based training, Mentoring & reverse mentoring, Coaching, Job shadowing and Cross-functional collaboration. Tailoring learning and development opportunities to individual employees' potential and skills, rather than their job roles, directly impacts engagement, productivity, and retention. Strategic and intentional internal matching between mentors and mentees greatly contributes to personal development. Coaching builds stronger relationships and provides additional support for team members' growth.Job shadowing offers on-the-job learning opportunities, not limited to vertical moves. Observing others' work, understanding decision-making processes, and learning why things are done a certain way can benefit those seeking lateral career moves. Cross-departmental collaboration encourages employees to quickly move across teams and departments to contribute to projects that advance the company's mission (Career development: The key to improve employee retention, 2023).

The pursuit of career growth holds immense importance for employees, driving their satisfaction, engagement, and commitment to their organizations. Recognizing and addressing the need for professional development and advancement can lead to a more motivated and fulfilled workforce.

Training and Development

An effective business understands the significance of training during the initial onboarding of employees. However, a business focused on retaining its workforce also acknowledges the value of ongoing investment in training and upskilling. By dedicating time, resources, and providing access to additional education and training opportunities within employees' respective fields, businesses not only enhance employee satisfaction and retention but also strengthen the company as a whole.

Continuously upskilling employees has several benefits. Firstly, it demonstrates a commitment to employee growth and development, fostering a sense of value and loyalty among the workforce. When employees perceive that their employers are invested in their professional advancement, they are more inclined to stay with the company long-term. Moreover, upskilling employees equips them with new knowledge, skills, and expertise, making them more proficient and adaptable in their roles. This, in turn, enhances overall company performance and competitiveness. By promoting a learning culture within the organization, businesses can create an environment that encourages innovation and keeps up with industry advancements.

Investing in ongoing training and upskilling also demonstrates an employer's dedication to employee career progression. It provides opportunities for employees to expand their capabilities, take on new challenges, and contribute to the company's success. This sense of personal and professional growth further strengthens employee satisfaction and retention (Crail, 2022).

Training plays a vital role in improving employees' knowledge, skills, and abilities to perform specific tasks, leading to enhanced employee retention (Latham, 1988; Das & Baruah, 2013). Many organizations prioritize training and development opportunities for their employees. These initiatives encompass various aspects such as cross-training in different roles, job rotation, job enrichment, soft skills development, leadership development programs, internal mobility opportunities, and promotion within the organization. Some companies adopt the Personal Advancement and Career Enhancement (PACE) model to foster employee growth.

HR analytics provides data-driven insights for training and development. It helps identify skill gaps, assess training needs, and prioritize learning initiatives. By analyzing performance data, competency assessments, and employee feedback, organizations can design targeted training programs, measure their effectiveness, and make data-informed decisions to optimize employee development. This leads to more efficient and impactful training initiatives that enhance employee skills, improve performance, and drive organizational success (The Human Capital Hub, 2020).

By investing in comprehensive training and development initiatives, organizations demonstrate their commitment to employee growth, which in turn contributes to a motivated and loyal workforce.

Employee Engagement Activities

Employee engagement activities is one of the major strategies companies focus on retaining employees because many researchers found that employee engagement is positively associated with their intent to stay with the organization (Harter et al., 2002; Schaufeli & Bakker, 2004). Effective talent management practices aim to achieve employee engagement as a primary outcome, which leads to lower turnover rates, easier talent attraction, knowledge building, and a competitive advantage. Employee engagement encompasses meaningfulness of work, social and organizational security etc.

Engaged employees are more committed to the organization and its goals, resulting in improved performance, focused efforts, and better outcomes. They bring innovation, enthusiasm, productivity, and exhibit citizenship behavior. Engaged employees also demonstrate lower attrition and absenteeism rates, as they find their work meaningful and believe it influences the organization's performance. Disengaged employees, on the other hand, merely fulfill their job requirements without enthusiasm or innovation, negatively impacting the morale of engaged employees around them. Highly engaged organizations have the potential to significantly reduce staff turnover, while disengaged employees are four times more likely to leave (Balakrishnan et.al, 2013).

Engaged employees not only contribute to productivity and profitability but also form lasting relationships with customers, actively promote the company's products or services, and act as brand ambassadors. Retention efforts should focus on keeping engaged employees involved and providing them with the necessary support, tools, and a healthy workplace environment that meets their physical, social, and emotional well-being. Line managers also have a significant role to play in fostering engagement and retention by establishing meaningful relationships with their direct reports, creating a climate of learning and positive interactions, and acting as mentors or coaches. Development plans tailored to employees' needs and potential contribute to their engagement and long-term retention (Pandita & Ray, 2018; Radley, 2022).

An example of fostering employee engagement can be seen in Bosch India, where they implement various initiatives to promote engagement. These include establishing open communication channels, feedback mechanisms, employee recognition programs, and employee wellness programs. The company also prioritizes diversity and inclusion by offering equal opportunities and celebrating the diversity within their workforce (Bosch limited steps into 2021 as a great place to work - Certified™, n.d.). Some organizations utilize engagement programs to raise awareness about environmental sustainability. They conduct workshops, training sessions, and awareness campaigns to educate employees about environmentally friendly practices both at work and in their personal lives.

Employee clubs provide a platform for monthly get-togethers, typically held on a designated day each month, such as the last Friday. These gatherings serve multiple purposes, including celebrating the birthdays of employees born in that month and recognizing their achievements. This recognition serves as motivation for employees, making them feel valued and validated by the organization. The informal nature of these occasions allows employees to unwind, engage in games, and foster stronger bonds with their colleagues. The organization often hosts these events, providing free food and drinks.

Some organizations celebrate Annual Day to commemorate achievements and conduct cultural programs where employees can interact with management and receive recognition for their awards and accomplishments. In some cases, organizations extend the invitation to family members, further boosting employee morale. Team outings are another practice employed by companies to provide employees with opportunities to spend time together outside the office, fostering stronger bonds based on personal connections rather than work-related tasks. Annual trips offer employees a chance to enjoy their time outside of work with colleagues from different functions. These trips provide an opportunity for team members who don't usually interact much to get to know each other, bond, and develop a sense of belonging. These practices reinforce team spirit and create a sense of unity.

Companies also engage employees through activities such as film screenings, fun at work initiatives, workshops and discounted sales, festival parties, birthday celebrations, annual sports celebrations, and picnics (Employee engagement: Strategies, models and best practices, 2020; Forseth, 2023).

Organizations use HR analytics to measure employee engagement. They collect data through surveys, focus groups, and feedback sessions to understand employees' motivations and engagement levels. They use this data to identify the level of engagement, areas of improvement and take action to address the concerns raised by their employees. Based on the results, the company has to identify the key drivers of employee engagement, strategize employee engagement activities according to the demographic profile and later check the changes occurred in the level of employee engagement.

Communication

Effective retention strategies require ongoing efforts and communication plays a critical role in their implementation. Research has shown that sharing important information with employees builds trust and addresses their need for information. When communication from management is lacking, employees resort to seeking information through indirect means. To address this, organizations should proactively develop communication strategies that incorporate best practices. This includes explaining the reasons behind organizational changes, using multiple communication channels, prioritizing face-to-face communication, ensuring message comprehension, and recognizing the negative impact of not communicating.

Supervisors also play a key role in employee retention. Conversations between supervisors and employees regarding organizational support have been found to be strongly correlated with positive employee perceptions. To improve retention, supervisors should employ four strategies: regularly meeting with employees, providing feedback on performance management, supporting ongoing learning and professional development, and conducting periodic stay interviews (Erickson, 2015).

Research has consistently shown that effective communication within organizations fosters employee identification and contributes to a culture of openness and trust. Organizations are increasingly recognizing the importance of providing employees with information about their mission, values, performance, strategies, and relevant changes. This is often achieved through improved communication channels that prioritize timely and consistent delivery of information from credible sources, such as CEOs and top management. By meeting the information needs of employees and ensuring transparency, organizations can enhance employee engagement and satisfaction (Dutta & Banerjee, 2014; Cloutier et.al, 2015).

Grievance Redressal System

A company or employer is expected to provide an employee with a safe working environment, clear knowledge of job responsibilities, adequate compensation, respect etc. However, employee grievance is caused when there is a gap between what the employee expects and what he receives from the employer. Employee grievances may or may not be justified, but need to be tackled adequately because they not only lower the motivation and performance of the employee but also affects the work environment. Employee grievances if left unchecked can lead to large disputes within the company. It can also drop the motivation levels of other employees.

A well-functioning grievance redressal system is an essential component of employee retention strategies within organizations. It provides a mechanism for employees to voice their concerns, address issues, and seek resolution, ultimately contributing to their overall job satisfaction and commitment to the organization.

A grievance redressal system ensures that employees have a platform to express their grievances, whether they are related to work conditions, interpersonal conflicts, unfair treatment, or any other aspect of their employment. Any complaints raised by the employees are to be immediately and thoroughly investigated and solved as quickly as possible. One of the key ways a grievance redressal system contributes to employee retention is by providing a fair and transparent process for resolving conflicts. When employees have a clear understanding of how their grievances will be handled, they are more likely to trust the organization's commitment to addressing their concerns. This, in turn, increases their confidence in the organization and reduces the likelihood of them seeking external avenues or leaving the organization altogether.

An effective grievance redressal system also provides an opportunity for organizations to identify systemic issues or recurring problems. By analyzing the nature of grievances and their root causes, organizations can implement appropriate corrective measures to prevent similar issues from arising in the future. This proactive approach not only contributes to employee retention but also enhances overall organizational effectiveness and employee satisfaction (Employee Grievance and Redressal: Ensuring a Fair and Harmonious Workplace, 2023; Rao, 2020)

Professionally managed organizations always encourage and promote employees to voice their grievances through confidential surveys, satisfaction surveys to understand employee pulse and design required measures for smooth functionality or process and organization. Employees feel more comfortable if the grievance system is appropriate. Companies constitute grievance committees and helpline numbers for faster and easy communication. The various committees include:

- Internal committee
- Canteen committee
- Sexual Harassment committee
- Works committee
- Environment, Health and safety committee

Conducting frequent surveys helps companies improve the current employee-employer relations, rewards etc (Keerthi, 2020).

In summary, a well-designed and properly implemented grievance redressal system plays a crucial role in employee retention. It provides employees with a fair and transparent process to address their concerns, fosters a culture of trust and open communication, and demonstrates the organization's commitment to resolving conflicts. By promoting job satisfaction and resolving issues in a timely manner, the grievance redressal system contributes to employee engagement, loyalty, and long-term retention within the organization.

Organizational Culture

A crucial aspect of retaining employees is fostering an organizational culture that employees genuinely desire to be a part of. According to a 2019 study conducted by Glassdoor, a company's culture significantly influences both potential job candidates (77% consider a company's culture) and current employees who choose to stay in their positions. In fact, nearly two-thirds of employees stated that a positive company culture is one of the primary reasons they decide to remain with their employer.

Developing an exceptional company culture often involves implementing various strategies. These efforts may include recognizing and rewarding employees not only for their achievements but also for their dedication and effort. Creating a meaningful mission for the company and involving employees in the decision-making process regarding the organization's present and future can also contribute to a strong culture.

Additionally, it is crucial to ensure that the workplace promotes diversity and inclusion, particularly for individuals from BIPOC (Black, Indigenous, and People of Color) and LGBTQ communities, who may face challenges in finding safe and welcoming work environments. By establishing a workplace that respects individuals of all races, backgrounds, genders, and sexual orientations, organizations can attract and retain a diverse and talented workforce.

Another important aspect of having a good organizational culture is work flexibility. With the advancements in modern technology, various industries now have the potential to enable employees to work remotely, either partially or entirely. While further research is required to fully understand the long-term effects of remote work, Upwork's report highlights several positive impacts. These include a decrease in nonessential meetings, enhanced flexibility in scheduling, elimination of commuting time, fewer distractions, and increased autonomy. By eliminating the need for employees to endure traffic, worry about childcare, or face productivity disruptions caused by scheduling conflicts or lengthy meetings, remote work fosters a more productive and content workforce.

Even before the pandemic, a 2019 study indicated that nearly two-thirds of workers found themselves more productive outside of a traditional office environment due to fewer interruptions, distractions, and commuting time. Offering flexible work-from-home options can serve as an attractive incentive to retain top talent in the long run.

Moreover, reducing the number of hours in a workday or workweek can actually boost employee productivity and foster better retention. A study conducted by Stanford University in 2014 revealed that productivity sharply declines after an employee surpasses 50 hours of work per week. Contrary to the belief that workaholics who spend excessive hours at work are more dedicated and productive, much of the productivity in those extended hours is lost to burnout and exhaustion. Therefore, providing a healthy work-life balance can contribute to increased productivity and employee satisfaction (Crail, 2022).

Kerr and Slocum (1987) proposed that the influence of organizational culture on employee retention rates can be moderated by the values upheld within the culture. They observed that certain organizations have cultures that prioritize values such as teamwork, security, and respect for individual members. These values contribute to fostering loyalty and long-term commitment among all employees, irrespective of their performance levels. On the other hand, some organizations have cultures that emphasize personal initiative and individual rewards for achieving specific work objectives. In such cultures, there is a norm of entrepreneurship where long-term job security is not provided, and employees do not necessarily promise loyalty.

Developing and nurturing an organizational culture of positive relationships with peers plays a crucial role in boosting individual morale and fostering a respectful and effective team dynamic. The overall work environment significantly impacts team relationships and well-being. In a study, a significant number of respondents (around one-third) highlighted that their interactions with colleagues and peers directly influence their ongoing engagement and commitment to the organization (Rana & Gandotra, 2023).

According to Kerr and Slocum (1987), weaker performers are likely to leave organizations with an entrepreneurial culture relatively quickly, as they seek better opportunities elsewhere. Stronger performers, however, may choose to remain in such organizations in order to maximize their gains from the current situation before moving on to more rewarding prospects. As a result, in certain organizational cultures, employee retention rates might be consistently high for both strong and weak performers. In contrast, in other cultures, retention rates may vary significantly depending on employees' job performance (Sheridan, 1992; Iqbal et al., 2017; Madueke & Emerole, 2017).

Motivation: Intrinsic and Extrinsic

Employee motivation is a critical factor that significantly contributes to improving both employee and organizational performance. It enables employers to enhance employees' skills and boost their morale, thereby encouraging them to perform better. Motivators such as incentives, perks, and cash prizes can effectively inspire and motivate employees. Performance appraisals also serve as important motivators by providing feedback and recognizing employees' efforts. Ultimately, when employee motivation is high, it leads to increased performance, productivity and high retention within the organization.

Numerous psychologists have extensively studied motivation, resulting in the development of various motivational theories. These theories assist employers in understanding and addressing employees' day-to-day concerns and grievances, thereby improving motivation levels.

Maslow's Hierarchy of Needs, proposed by Abraham Maslow in 1943, is a theory that explains how motivation helps individuals satisfy their basic needs. The theory is represented as a pyramid with five levels. Fulfilling the various levels of needs within Maslow's Hierarchy is essential. When employees' physiological, safety, social, esteem, and growth needs are met, they are more likely to feel satisfied and motivated in their work, increasing their likelihood of staying with the organization.

Frederick Herzberg, who had close relations with Maslow, developed a two-factor theory of motivation. According to Herzberg, there are certain factors that directly motivate employees to work harder, known as motivators. The most important motivators are referred to as hygiene factors, which are related to the job itself. These factors include the level of interest in the work, opportunities for extra responsibility, recognition, and promotion.

Interestingly, Herzberg viewed pay as a hygiene factor, which contrasts with Taylor's perspective that pay, particularly piece-rate, is a motivator. According to Herzberg, the pay-to-work performed is a significant motivator that contributes to employee retention. In other words, when employees feel adequately compensated for their work, they are more likely to stay in a particular workplace for a longer period of time.

In terms of employee retention, understanding and addressing both motivators and hygiene factors are crucial. Providing opportunities for growth, recognition, and advancement can motivate employees to remain engaged and committed to their work. Additionally, ensuring fair and competitive compensation and creating a positive and supportive work environment are essential for retaining employees and fostering their long-term loyalty (Sandhya & Kumar, 2011; Ramlall, 2004; Lee et al., 2022)

Organizations that primarily rely on money as an extrinsic motivator often experience a decrease in intrinsic motivation. In contrast, organizations that utilize verbal praise and constructive feedback tend to see an increase in intrinsic motivation. Factors such as job security, task significance, feedback, task variety, autonomy, and authority have been found to be significantly and positively related to better employee retention (Shah & Asad, 2018).

While financial motivation, such as salary, bonuses, and insurance, is important, non-financial motivation plays a role in increasing employee morale. Organizations employ various strategies, including financial rewards, job characteristics, training, career development, recognition, employee management, and work-life balance, to enhance employee retention.

Both intrinsic and extrinsic motivation are equally important for employee retention, as they have a significant positive effect on retaining employees. Motivated employees tend to have a more positive perception of the organization and are more likely to stay with it for a longer duration. Intrinsic and extrinsic rewards play a crucial role in employee motivation and satisfaction. When employees are satisfied with their jobs, they tend to exhibit higher levels of loyalty and commitment to the organization. Employee retention can vary based on how employees perceive the level of support provided by the organization (Shah & Asad, 2018).

Work-Life Balance Initiatives

Providing work-life balance initiatives can help retain top talent. It can be telecommuting, compressed work weeks, job sharing, etc. They prioritize employee happiness at work by allowing them to take breaks in between work if they need it. They allow flexible work schedules, flexi timings, hybrid work modes, surprise work offs, and work from home for the employees to manage personal as well as professional life.

Organizations now recognize the importance of attending to employees' work-life concerns. Doing so not only improves employee well-being but also has links to the organization's bottom line in terms of attracting and retaining top talent. Empirical evidence supports the theoretical association between work-life conflict and withdrawal-related attitudes (Shockley et al., 2017).

Globalization and competitiveness are critical issues making it more difficult for firms to recruit and retain the best talent. Moreover, social changes such as the aging of the population, the decrease in birth rates, or the new generation's demands also affect talent policies. The effects of the previous elements make it necessary for firms to develop and apply talent management practices focused on the systematic attraction, identification, development, engagement, retention, and deployment of talent. These practices will have a positive impact on human resource outcomes, such as job satisfaction, motivation, and commitment, and also on the firm performance. In this context, work–life balance is gaining relevance in the current business context, as companies are facing greater management difficulties, which in many situations entail the loss of valuable HR. There is frequently a gap between the factors demanded by HR in order to satisfy their needs and motivations and the measures implemented by the organizations (Rodríguez-Sánchez et al., 2020).

Companies have to conduct a work-life balance survey among employees once a year and try to understand the work-life balance. This data will help them to develop strategies.Work life conflict increases employee turnover. According to Maxwell (2005), organizations can create a work-life policy to retain employees, especially flexible work hours and arrangements, better training, breaks from work, and better work support. Deery (2008) suggested a few areas where organizations can improve the work life balance of employees, which includes flexible working hours, flexible work arrangements (job sharing and working at home), adequate breaks during working hours, sufficient resources for staff, the required number of staff, provision for leave for personal needs and professional development, opportunities for health and wellbeing and involving family members in few events. These practices can reduce the turnover intention of employees.

Compensation and Benefits

Competitive pay and incentive mechanisms are the key measures companies use for attracting and retaining employees. Companies conduct market surveys and research to match the skill matrix and fix the pay/incentives so that employees are motivated. Extra pay to the employees for the extra man-hours contributed by them motivate people to stay with the organization. Certain companies follow fixed pay practices and other companies use fixed and incentive pay based on the performance of employees. High performing employees prefer to have performance-based pay which helps to retain the best employees.

Reward bonuses are most popularly used to attract and retain employees. Companies give reward bonuses mostly in the form of cash, sometimes it can be a stock option, gift cards, time off, or in the form of a holiday trip with family. Bonus rewards will be given to employees based on their attendance, tenure in the organization, and for their contributions.

Employee inclusion and rewards are highly encouraged in the industry which would serve greater retention and a high level of employee satisfaction in any organization. Such rewards or bonuses include Employee Referral awards for referring the suitable employee to the organization. Business Referral awards are offered for referring to the right source which could contribute to the growth and success of the organization.

Financial assistance: Organizations also offer a helping hand to their employees to keep them happy by assisting them during their financial difficulties and needs. Offering Salary advance and Compensation loans to manage their unplanned financial needs come handy in retaining the employees in a long way.

Salary Loan/Assistance-Organizations also provide financial assistance by applying for salary loans and it will be based on the tenure in the organization. . These loans are given on the basis of their gross salary and a fixed amount is deducted as EMI or any other scheme which is already existing.

Marriage gift policy- This policy applies to employees who are permanently employed. The employees can claim the amount designated by the company by producing their invitation cards as proof. Few organizations provide cash advances or cash gifts to employees.

Studies reveal that employees regard the organization culture followed by work-life balance and compensation as the most prominent organizational determinants that they consider while planning a job change (Kumar & Arora, 2012).

Retention is enhanced when organizations embrace certain proactive talent management practices, including competitive compensation and benefits. Retention prospects are also enhanced when employers maintain a positive brand or reputation in the labor market. Talent retention strategies help organizations sustain and grow, avoiding wasteful expenses triggered by the loss of talent (Bhattacharyya, 2015).

Rewards and Recognition

Rewards and Recognitions play a very vital and crucial role in employee retention. Timely reward and recognition are the key for any employee growth and up-bringing in an organization. Awards can be simple but spotting the talent and acknowledging them on time is the most meaningful exercise that organizations must have in place. Awards such as Spot awards, best buddy, best mentor, daily performer, best learner, game changer for the team are few awards to name.

Birthday gift- Celebrations of birthdays by the team create a feeling of belongingness to the employees. On birthdays all the permanent employees are given a cake as a gift from the management side to add more sweetness on their special day.

Reward and recognition have significant positive effects on job satisfaction and have indirect significant positive effects on employee retention (Tirta & Enrika, 2020). A properly structured compensation package, together with an effective reward strategy, needs to be linked to the talent management system, in order to facilitate talent retention processes (Smit et al., 2015)

Performance Management Program

Organizations should have a clear and transparent performance management system in place to provide employees with regular feedback and opportunities for growth and development. This includes setting clear performance goals, providing ongoing feedback, and conducting regular performance evaluations. Some organizations carry out MBO as a performance management tool as the managers and employees have a discussion on their objectives and see if they are being carried out.

Performance Appraisals and Incentives

The employees are evaluated and their performance is reviewed annually. If their performance meets the company's standards and expectations, the employees are rewarded in the form of incentives or salary hikes. These incentives can be monthly, quarterly or half yearly distributed. In performance Management it is very important to put the criteria based on the Key result areas. Companies which set and assess the right key performance indicators help to motivate employees to perform better.

HR analytics will use the data related to employee performance and potential, including their skills, experience, and past performance to identify high, average and poor performing employees. Companies provide better career opportunities and additional incentives and targeted development programs for the high performing employees. This also helps to retain high performing employees.

Internal Growth/Promotion Programs

Organizations offer internal job post programs to promote internal talent to higher posts. Internal growth or promotion programs are great example setters to any newcomer to visualize how they can perform and grow with-in organization. It boosts employee morale and helps great in retention.

A fair appraisal system not only increases employee's motivation and commitment level but also provides them opportunities for improving their performance. Performance appraisal has a strong effect on employee retention provided it is fair and transparent (Mehta et al., 2014). Performance appraisal has a significant impact on employee retention especially if it is communicated and shared with the employee (Saeed et al., 2013).

The performance appraisal along with career development will have positive impacts on employee's retention if practiced regularly and adequately (Gulzar et al., 2017).

Health and Wellbeing

Organizations offer different health and wellbeing measures to motivate and retain employees. An excellent benefits package that includes health coverage is extremely important for employee retention because it shows employees that their work is invested in their overall health and future. Organizations also offer volunteer Life coverage policy, Accident Insurance policy, subsidized annual health check-ups, special child care programs to uplift the morale of the working force.

Medical Leave and Emergency leave – Apart from mandatory maternity and paternity leaves, organizations also offer special medical leaves, Covid quarantine leaves, and menstrual leave to ensure employee wellbeing.

Post pandemic, many companies started offering yoga and fitness camps, 24/7 physician consultation, psychiatric consultation to ensure employee wellbeing. This is one of the retention strategies followed by companies._

Powerful retention involves mastery of physical, mental, emotional, spiritual, and organizational employee well-being. Employees need to both engage in and experience healthy well-being (Kaur, 2017). The role of psychological well-being in job performance, employee retention and cardiovascular health is very crucial (Wright, 2010).

Figure 1. Model for Retention

HR Analytics: A Conceptual Understanding

Analytics is the scientific process of turning raw data insights which are useful for decision making and performance improvement with the application of statistics, information technology and operations research. HR analytics focuses on the Analytics part of managing human resources and enable managers to take decisions based on data analysis, prediction, and experimental research. HR analytics, also called people analytics, is the systematic process of identifying and quantifying people drivers on business outcomes or analyse how people create value for the organization (Madhani, 2023). Lalwani (2021) quoted Mick Collins (Global Vice President, Workforce Analytics & Planning Solution Strategy and Chief Expert at SAP SuccessFactors) definition of HR Analytics. According to Collins, "HR analytics is a methodology for creating insights on how investments in human capital assets contribute to the success of four principal outcomes: (a) generating revenue, (b) minimizing expenses, (c) mitigating risks, and (d) executing strategic plans. This is done by applying statistical methods to integrated HR, talent management, financial, and operational data,". It is also identified that top performing organization use analytics more than low performing organizations (Lavalle, 2011). This reveals the importance of analytics.

HR analytics can be used for identify the reasons for attrition and subsequently various strategies can be framed for retaining the talented employees. The areas where HR managers has to look for improving the retention includes analyzing the age category of people leaving the organization, number of voluntary turnover rate, number of people in senior level (average seniority), involuntary turnover rate, turnover rate of talented employees, managerial staff turnover ratio, overall turnover rate, average days of absence per Average Employee, and turnover rate per manager/department. All these information will help HR to understand the sitCompensation Ratio.

APPROACHES FOLLOWED IN HR ANALYTICS

Model 1: Transformation of Opinion Into Insights

One of the characteristics of Analytics is the development of insights from opinions (Vulpen, n.d). People arrive at an opinion based on their previous experience or intuition. For example. An HR manager observed that many resignations happened after the performance appraisal and he mentioned that "*I feel many employees are leaving after the appraisal*" ***(Opinion).*** For validating the data, he checked

Figure 2. From Opinion to Insights
Source: Vulpen (n.d)

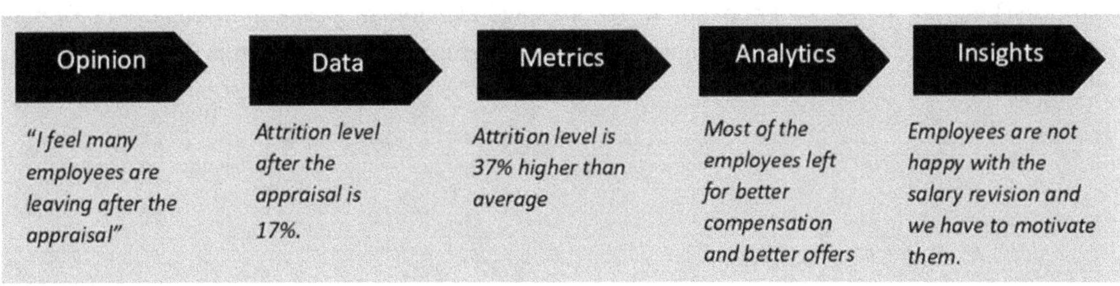

the records and found that *Attrition level after the appraisal is 17%* ***(Data).*** He also looked at the demographic details of employees especially the age, experience, marital status etc. Then he started looking at the trends happening in attrition and found that, *Attrition level is 37% higher than average* ***(Metric).*** Once he understood the variation, he started analyzing various factors. He looked at the exit interview and found that *most of the employees left for better compensation and better offers* ***(Analysis).*** This analysis forced him to check the pay satisfaction survey he has conducted before and checked the details. The pay satisfaction score was less for the employees who left the organization. The correlation results shows that there is a negative correlation between pay satisfaction and attrition level. He also noticed the attrition is high among employees who were having an experience of 3 to 4 years. This analysis gave the **insights** *that employees are not be happy with the salary revision and we have to motivate the employees.* Based on this the company can look at the average market salary range and also look at the performance appraisal system and modify accordingly.

Model 2: Descriptive, Diagnostic, Predictive, and Prescriptive Analytics

Descriptive analytics is a process of collecting and interpreting the data and explaining what happened in the past. We can use descriptive analytics for understanding what has happened in the past (High attrition -37%).

Diagnostic analysis can be used for understanding why is it happened, especially the root-cause of issues (People left after the performance appraisal, Less salary increment, not happy etc.).

Predictive analytics helps to understand what will happen in the future based on the analysis of information over a time period and identify the trends and patterns for predicting outcomes (If people leave the organization, it will have an impact on business outcomes, customer satisfaction, loss of clients). Statistical tools and techniques help to understand the relationships, impact and demographic wise analysis to understand the trend.

Prescriptive analytics uses combination of data, mathematical models, and various business rules to infer actions to influence future desired outcome explain the ways to address the issues and provides reliable solutions for organization needs and for better decision making on alternatives problems solving (Guenole et al., 2017). It explains what are the changes we have to make in future to address similar issues?

Model 3: Lagging and Leading Indicators

For making better decisions analyst use leading and lagging indicators of each situation. Lagging and leading indicators helps us to get a clarity of the situation and we can take decisions accordingly.

For example, Employee attrition is a lagging indicator (outcome measure) for the company's actions. Company assesses the leading indicators (process measures) for assessing the process that leads to attrition (Lagging Indicator). For example, the leading indicators may be employee absenteeism, low employee satisfaction surveys or low engagement level of employees (Vulpen, n.d.).

Table 1. Check sheet for reasons for attrition

Sl No	Reasons for Attrition	April-May	June-July	Aug-Sept	Oct-Nov	Dec-Jan	Feb-March	Total
1	Work place Bulling	2	0	5	0	5	3	15
2	Work Load	1	3	0	4	2	2	12
3	Lack of Growth Opportunities	1	3	0	0	2	3	9
4	Voluntary Resignation	1	2	0	0	0	0	3
5	Compensation	25	10	7	2	4	12	60
6	Lack of Recognition	1	2	1	1	1	2	8
7	Dissatisfaction	10	7	9	9	12	11	58
8	Supervisory relationship	5	5	3	4	7	8	32

Model 4: Pareto Chart

Pareto Chart: An Analytical Method for Finding the Major Reason for Attrition

Attrition is a challenge for many organizations because it causes brain drain from the organization, along with the hiring cost, the delay in work due to absence of the employee, and loosing of clients. In such cases retaining employees is one of the best medicines for organization to continue its process. A Pareto chart can help to solve the issues. Pareto chart is a chart that contains both bars and line graphs which help to identify the most prevalent issues. Pareto Analysis is a statistical technique in decision-making used for the selection of a limited number of tasks that produce significant overall effect. The Pareto principle (also known as the 80/20 rule, the law of the vital few, or the principle of factor sparsity) states that, for many events, roughly 80% of the effects come from 20% of the causes. That means doing 20% of the work can generate 80% of the benefit of doing the entire job.

Example: Softtech company found that their attrition increases 20% this year compared to the previous year. The senior management asked the HR manager to analyse the reason for attrition and the areas where they need to improve in order to reduce the attrition. HR manager used to conduct exit interviews and reported it in a check sheet. The check sheet is given in Table 1 which shows the reason for attrition.

Use a pareto chart to find out the areas where the company has to focus more on reducing the attrition.

Solution:

Step 1: Identify the reasons for employee attrition (Use data from the check box for identifying the details) and the total frequency (Table 2).

Step II: Organize the data in descending order (highest to lowest) and represent it in a bar chart (Table 3).

Step III: Identify the cumulative frequency and Cumulative frequency percentage and represent the percentage in a curved line (Table 3).

Step IV: Draw a straight line in the pareto chart at 80% place till it meets the curved line (Figure 1).

Step V: Identify the major reasons comes under the line and address the same.

Table 2. Step 1: Data emerged from the annual report

Sl No	Reasons for Attrition	Total
1	Work place Bulling	15
2	Work Load	12
3	Lack of Growth Opportunities	9
4	Voluntary Resignation	3
5	Compensation	60
6	Lack of Recognition	8
7	Job Dissatisfaction	58
8	Supervisory relationship	32

Table 3. Step 2 and Step 3: Sorted data with cumulative frequency and cumulative frequency %

Sl No	Reasons for Attrition	Total	Cumulative Frequency	Cumulative Frequency %
1	Compensation	60	60	30%
2	Dissatisfaction	58	118	60%
3	Supervisory relationship	32	150	76%
4	Work place Bulling	15	165	84%
5	Work Load	12	177	90%
6	Lack of Growth Opportunities	9	186	94%
7	Lack of Recognition	8	194	98%
8	Voluntary Resignation	3	197	100%

Figure 3. Pareto chart

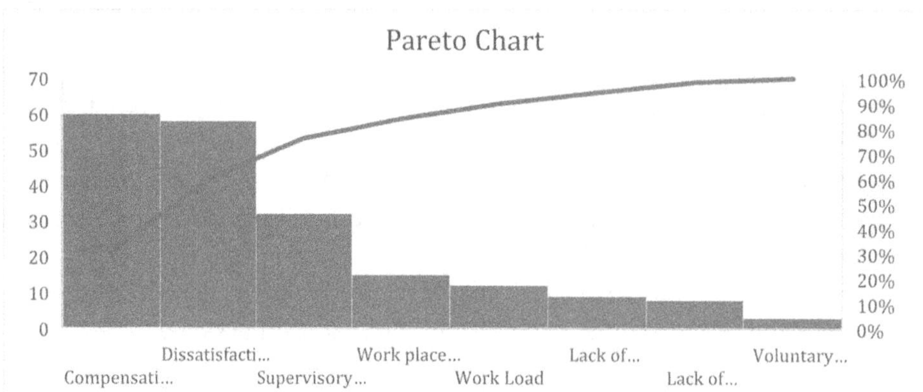

Note: (We can give step II in excel and can generating the Pareto Chart. For Example: Select Reasons for attrition and their total frequency, after that use insert function and select recommended charts and select pareto chart).

- 80% of the attrition is due to compensation, dissatisfaction and supervisory relationship. Its top two issues already contribute more than sixty percent of the problem of attrition. These two could effectively represent the "vital few" and the rest of the failures correspond the "trivial many".
- Based on this findings company can take a decision to conduct a market survey to understand the prevailing trends in the market and can take a decision to revise the salary accordingly. Similarly, company can conduct a satisfaction survey about various factors which are affecting the satisfaction of employees and improve the Factors which are leading to the dissatisfaction of employees.
- Instead of wasting money for different reasons it is important to identify the major two or three reasons for attrition and address it. A pareto chart helps managers to find the same.

Model 5. Attrition Rate Calculation

The attrition rate is the percentage of employees who leave the organization voluntarily or involuntarily over a specific period. It explains the employee resignations and terminations by the company.

Attrition rate % = (Number of employees that left during the Period)÷(Average number of employees for the period)*100

Average number of employees for the period=(Employees at the beginning of the assessment year+ Employees at the end of the assessment year)/2

Model 6: Find the Relationship/Effect of Different Variables on Turnover Intention

Organization has to conduct survey on employee satisfaction, employee engagement, job satisfaction, employee commitment, work life balance, organizational justice and its impact on turnover intention.

In this example employee satisfaction, employee engagement, job satisfaction, employee commitment, work life balance, organizational justice is independent variable. Turnover intention or attrition can be a dependent variable. For finding the relationship we can use correlation. For understanding the effect of one variable on another we can use regression analysis. Regression analysis can also be used for finding the future trends.

HOW TO REDUCE EMPLOYEE TURNOVER WITH HR ANALYTICS

After Attrition

1. Identify the Attrition Rate
2. Look for causes / drivers of employee turnover
3. Identify the demographic profile of employees who are leaving.
4. Take corrective actions based on the findings

Before Attrition: How to Improve Retention

1. Identify the employees who are likely to leave (Turnover intention)
2. Identify the employees whose attrition will impact the organization most
3. Calculate the cost of turnover
4. Identify the reason employees may likely to leave
5. Identify the motivation factors of staying back.
6. Try to reduce the turnover through a tailored employee retention program.

CONCLUSION

In conclusion, the aforementioned talent retention strategies are crucial for any organization to retain its talented employees. First of all, hire the right people who fit to the company, understand their needs, being considerate and provide suitable work environment for them to work better. Organizations also have to look at workforce planning, training and development, employee engagement activities, work-life balance initiatives, compensation and benefits, rewards and recognition, performance appraisals and incentives, internal growth/promotion programs, health and wellbeing, CSR activities, flexi work hours and leave policies, organization branding, social security and welfare programs, and a good grievance redressal system are all essential components of a comprehensive talent retention strategy. By implementing these strategies, organizations can create a positive work environment that fosters employee growth, development, and satisfaction. This leads to improved job performance, higher productivity, and reduced employee turnover, which benefits the organization in the long run. Furthermore, employees who feel valued and supported by their organization are more likely to remain loyal, motivated, and engaged, which translates to better outcomes for both the employee and the organization. In conclusion, understanding the importance of talent retention and implementing these strategies is critical for the success and growth of any organization. It requires a long-term commitment from the organization, but the benefits in terms of employee satisfaction, organizational performance, and cost savings are well worth the investment.

REFERENCES

Balakrishnan, C., Masthan, D., & Chandra, V. (2013). Employee retention through employee engagement-A study at an Indian international airport. *International Journal of Business and Management Invention*, *2*(8), 9–16.

Bhattacharyya, D. K. (2015). Compensation and benefits program a mediating variable for talent retention: A study of two Century-Old Indian organizations. *Compensation and Benefits Review*, *47*(2), 75–80. doi:10.1177/0886368715584481

Bosch limited steps into 2021 as a great place to work – Certified™. (n.d.). Bosch Media Service. https://www.bosch-press.in/pressportal/in/en/press-release-3968.html.

Cloutier, O., Felusiak, L., Hill, C., & Pemberton-Jones, E. J. (2015). The importance of developing strategies for employee retention. *Journal of Leadership, Accountability and Ethics*, *12*(2).

Coker, D. (2016, May 12). Career development has the highest impact on employee retention. *The HR digest*. https://thehrdigest.com/career-development-highest-impact-employee-retention/

Crail, C. (2022). 15 effective employee retention strategies in 2022. *Forbes Advisor*. https://www.forbes.com/advisor/business/employee-retention-strategies/

Das, B. L., & Baruah, M. (2013). Employee retention: A review of literature. *IOSR Journal of Business and Management*, *14*(2), 8–16. doi:10.9790/487X-1420816

Das, H. (1996). Retention policy: Whom to retain anyway? *Indian Journal of Industrial Relations*, *32*(2), 223–232.

Deery, M. (2008). Talent management, work-life balance and retention strategies. International journal of contemporary hospitality management, 20(7), 792-806.

Dutta, A. B., & Banerjee, S. (2014). Study of employee retention. *International Journal of Business Management & Research*, *4*(1), 83–88.

Employee engagement: Strategies, models and best practices. (2020). Valamis. https://www.valamis.com/hub/employee-engagement#employee-engagement-activities

Employee grievance and Redressal: Ensuring a fair and harmonious workplace. (2023). HR Informative. https://hrinformative.com/employee-grievance-and-redressal/

Erickson, R. A. (2015). Communication and employee retention. *The international encyclopedia of interpersonal communication*, 1–10.

Forseth, N. (2023). 19 employee engagement activities that keep employees happy. *When I work*. https://wheniwork.com/blog/employee-engagement-activities

Gulzar, S., Advani, A., & Jalees, T. (2017). Impact of Performance Appraisal on Employee Retention: A study on Banking Sector of Pakistan. *JISR Management and Social Sciences & Economics*, *15*(1), 85–101. doi:10.31384/jisrmsse/2017.15.1.6

How to encourage career growth for employee retention and success. (n.d.). LinkedIn Learning. https://learning.linkedin.com/resources/learner-engagement/encourage-career-growth-employee-retention

Iqbal, S., Guohao, L., & Akhtar, S. (2017). Effects of job organizational culture, benefits, salary on job satisfaction ultimately affecting employee retention. *Review of Public Administration and Management*, *05*(3), 1–7. doi:10.4172/2315-7844.1000229

Isson, J. P., & Harriott, J. S. (2016). *People analytics in the era of big data: Changing the way you attract, acquire, develop, and retain talent*. John Wiley & Sons. doi:10.1002/9781119083856

Kaur, R. (2017). Employee retention models and factors affecting employees retention in IT companies. *International Journal of Business Administration and Management*, *7*(1), 161–174.

Keerthi, D. (2020, May 19). Grievance: Meaning, definitions, procedure, types, model, features. *Economics discussion*. https://www.economicsdiscussion.net/human-resource-management/grievance/grievance/32442

Kumar, R., & Arora, R. (2012). Determinants of talent retention in BPO industry. *Indian Journal of Industrial Relations*, *48*(2), 259–273. https://www.jstor.org/stable/23509837

Lalwani. (2021). What is HR analytics? Definition, importance, key metrics, data requirements, and implementation. *Spiceworks*. https://www.spiceworks.com/hr/hr-analytics/articles/what-is-hr-analytics/ on Retrieved 20/6/2023

LaValle, S., Lesser, E., Shockley, R., Hopkins, M. S., & Kruschwitz, N. (2011). Big data, analytics and the path from insights to value. *MIT Sloan Management Review*, *52*(2), 21–32.

Lee, C. C., Lim, H. S., Seo, D. J., & Kwak, D. H. A. (2022, April). Examining employee retention and motivation: The moderating effect of employee generation. In *Evidence-based HRM: A global forum for empirical scholarship (No. ahead-of-print)*. Emerald Publishing Limited. doi:10.1108/EBHRM-05-2021-0101

Madhani, P. M. (2023). Human resources analytics: Leveraging human resources for enhancing business performance. *Compensation and Benefits Review*, *55*(1), 31–45. doi:10.1177/08863687221131730

Madueke, C. V., & Emerole, I. C. (2017). Organizational culture and employee retention of selected commercial banks in Anambra State. *Saudi Journal of Business and Management Studies*, *2*(3), 244–252.

Maxwell, G. A. (2005). Checks and balances: the role of managers in work–life balance policies and practices. Journal of Retailing and Consumer services, 12(3), 179-189.

Mehta, M., Kurbetti, A., & Dhankhar, R. (2014). Review paper study on employee retention and commitment. *International Journal of Advance Research in Computer Science and Management Studies*, *2*, 154–164.

Mehta, M., Kurbetti, A., & Dhankhar, R. (2014). Review paper–study on employee retention and commitment. *International Journal (Toronto, Ont.)*, *2*(2), 33–49.

Nestor. (2023, May 29). *Career development: The key to improve employee retention*. Nestor. https://nestorup.com/blog/career-development-the-key-to-improve-employee-retention/

Organ, C. (2023). Workforce planning: Definition and best practices. *Forbes Advisor*. https://www.forbes.com/advisor/business/workforce-planning/

Ott, D. L., Tolentino, J. L., & Michailova, S. (2018). Effective talent retention approaches. Mentioned regarding culture. *Human Resource Management International Digest*, *26*(7), 16–19. doi:10.1108/HRMID-07-2018-0152

Pandita, D., & Ray, S. (2018). Talent management and employee engagement–a meta-analysis of their impact on talent retention. *Industrial and Commercial Training*, *50*(4), 185–199. doi:10.1108/ICT-09-2017-0073

Radley, B. (2022). The secret to employee retention is employee engagement. *Workday blog*. https://blog.workday.com/en-us/2022/secret-employee-retention-employee-engagement.html

Ramlall, S. (2004). A review of employee motivation theories and their implications for employee retention within organizations. *The Journal of American Academy of Business, Cambridge*, *5*(1/2), 52–63.

Rana, S., & Gandotra, S. (2023). How does organisational culture affect talent retention? *India development review.* https://idronline.org/article/leadership-talent/how-does-organisational-culture-affect-talent-retention/

Rao, V. (2020). *Human resource management role in grievance handling and Redressal.* Linkedin. https://www.linkedin.com/pulse/human-resource-management-role-grievance-handling-redressal-rao/

Rodríguez-Sánchez, J. L., González-Torres, T., Montero-Navarro, A., & Gallego-Losada, R. (2020). Investing time and resources for work–life balance: The effect on talent retention. International Journal of Environmental Research and Public Health. *International Journal of Environmental Research and Public Health, 17*(6), 1920. doi:10.3390/ijerph17061920 PMID:32187973

Saeed, R., & Lodhi. (2013). The Organizational Role in CareerDevelopment of Employees. *Management and Administrative Sciences.* http://reviewwww.absronline.org/masrISSN.

Sandhya, K., & Kumar, D. P. (2011). Employee retention by motivation. *Indian Journal of Science and Technology, 4*(12), 1778–1782. doi:10.17485/ijst/2011/v4i12.34

Shah, M., & Asad, M. (2018). Effect of motivation on employee retention: Mediating role of perceived organizational support. *European online journal of natural and social sciences, 7*(2), 511.

Sheridan, J. E. (1992). Organizational culture and employee retention. *Academy of Management Journal, 35*(5), 1036–1056. doi:10.2307/256539

Shockley, K. M., Smith, C. R., & Knudsen, E. A. (2017). The impact of work–life balance on employee retention. In *The Wiley Blackwell handbook of the psychology of recruitment, selection and employee retention* (pp. 513–543). John Wiley & Sons, Ltd. doi:10.1002/9781118972472.ch24

Singh, D. (2019). A literature review on employee retention with focus on recent trends. *International Journal of Scientific Research in Science, Engineering and Technology, 6*(1), 425–431. doi:10.32628/IJSRST195463

Smit, W., Stanz, K., & Bussin, M. (2015). Retention preferences and the relationship between total rewards, perceived organisational support and perceived supervisor support. *SA Journal of Human Resource Management/SA Tydskrif vir Menslikehulpbronbestuur, 13*(1). doi:10.4102/sajhrm.v13i1.665

The human capital hub. (2020, December 18). *Use of analytics to create a learning and development program.* Human capital hub. https://www.thehumancapitalhub.com/articles/Use-Of-Analytics-To-Create-A-Learning-And-Development-Program

Tirta, A. H., & Enrika, A. (2020). Understanding the impact of reward and recognition, work life balance, on employee retention with job satisfaction as mediating variable on millennials in Indonesia. *The Journal of Business and Retail Management Research, 14*(3). doi:10.24052/JBRMR/V14IS03/ART-09

Vulpen, E. V. (2023). *HR metrics and Analytics: How both can add value.* AIHR. https://www.aihr.com/blog/hr-metrics-and-analytics-how-both-can-add-value/on. (21/06/2023).

Workforce planning: Model, process, steps [Guide 2023]. (2022, January 17). Valamis. https://www.valamis.com/hub/workforce-planning

Wright, T. A. (2010). Much more than meets the eye. *Organizational Dynamics, 39*(1), 13–23. doi:10.1016/j.orgdyn.2009.10.009

Chapter 17
Measuring Employee Happiness Index in the Modern Workplace

Surjit Singha
Kristu Jayanti College (Autonomous), India

ABSTRACT

In today's modern workplace, measuring the employee happiness index is crucial for organizations to understand and improve employee satisfaction and well-being. This abstract provides an overview of the employee happiness index, exploring the various methods used for measurement, including surveys, interviews, and data analysis. It probes into factors contributing to employee happiness, such as company culture, job satisfaction, and mental health. Additionally, it highlights the significance of artificial intelligence and machine learning in collecting and analyzing employee feedback. These technologies offer valuable tools to enhance the measurement and understanding of employee happiness. It concludes by discussing the future implications of the employee happiness index in creating a positive and inclusive workplace culture that caters to the diverse needs and preferences of all employees.

1. INTRODUCTION

In today's fast-paced and competitive business environment, employee happiness and satisfaction are crucial factors that directly impact a company's success. Measuring and improving the employee happiness index has become a priority for organizations seeking to create a positive and engaging work environment that promotes employee health, productivity, and performance. The Employee Happiness Index measures employee happiness. It can be measured through several methods, including surveys, interviews, and data analysis (Cameron & Spreitzer, 2012).

This chapter discusses the various methods used to measure the Employee Happiness Index, the factors contributing to employee happiness, and the role technology could play in measuring and enhancing the Employee Happiness Index. The chapter will also examine companies that have successfully measured and increased their Employee Happiness Index and Google's strategies and practises for achieving this objective.

DOI: 10.4018/978-1-6684-8942-0.ch017

The employee happiness index measures how happy and interested employees are. It includes work-life balance, recognition, and chances to grow and learn. Studies have shown that companies with more satisfied employees have fewer people leaving, more work getting done, and better financial results. Companies can use the index to find out where they need to improve to make their employees happier and create a better workplace (McKee, 2014). Organizations must prioritize the Employee Happiness Index because it benefits the employees and contributes to overall success.

Artificial intelligence (AI) and machine learning (ML) in collecting and analyzing employee feedback holds immense importance and has significant implications for organizations. These technologies provide powerful tools to revolutionize employee feedback gathered, processed, and utilized. Organizations can unlock several benefits by explicitly highlighting the significance of AI and ML in the context of employee feedback.

AI and ML enable organizations to collect feedback from various sources, including surveys, social media platforms, emails, and internal communication channels. These technologies can automate the data collection, saving time and resources while ensuring a more comprehensive and accurate dataset. It can analyze employee feedback at scale and extract sentiment and emotions expressed in text or voice data. This analysis helps organizations understand the overall feeling of their workforce, identify patterns, and detect potential issues or areas of improvement.

With AI and ML, organizations can gain deeper insights from employee feedback. These technologies can identify correlations, trends, and patterns within the feedback data, enabling organizations to make data-driven decisions. Such insights help identify critical areas for intervention, develop targeted strategies, and improve employee satisfaction and engagement. It can facilitate real-time monitoring of employee feedback, providing organizations with immediate visibility into employee sentiments. Organizations can promptly address concerns, mitigate risks, and create a more responsive and supportive work environment by monitoring input continuously. Can provide personalized recommendations based on employee feedback. By analyzing individual preferences and sentiments, these technologies can offer tailored suggestions for improving specific aspects of the employee experience, fostering a sense of individualized support and development.

By explicitly highlighting the significance of AI and ML in collecting and analyzing employee feedback, organizations can harness the power of these technologies to improve employee satisfaction, engagement, and overall organizational performance. Organizations must recognize the transformative potential of AI and ML in employee feedback management and adopt these tools strategically to drive positive outcomes.

The importance of AI and ML in collecting and analyzing employee feedback lies in their ability to enhance data collection, enable advanced sentiment analysis, provide actionable insights, facilitate real-time monitoring, and offer personalized recommendations. By embracing these technologies, organizations can create a more inclusive, engaging, and supportive work environment, ultimately improving employee happiness and organizational success.

A study by Sinha et al. (2023) sheds light on the observable determinants of e-working effectiveness in the education sector. It emphasizes the importance of considering work-life balance, job effectiveness, flexibility, and employee relationship and trust. Its findings contribute to understanding remote work dynamics in academia and guide educational institutions in creating supportive and productive e-working environments. The article focuses on exploring the benefits of e-working for academicians. It examines four core constructs: work-life balance, job effectiveness or performance, flexibility, and employee relationship and trusts with the organization. It sheds light on the four constructs that can lead to employee happiness and moral.

The study's findings by Saini & Yadav (2023) indicate that gratitude significantly impacts the life satisfaction of future managers. This study emphasizes the importance of meaningfulness for attaining life satisfaction among young managers. By highlighting the role of gratitude and materialism in this context, the study contributes to promoting a more humane and responsible workplace environment. The study highlights the importance of the practice of gratitude in one's life and the workplace, which can bring happiness in one's life and the workplace; the study supports Google's HR practise of a peer recognition programme called "gThanks", where employees can express appreciation for the contributions of their peers.

The chapter by Chith et al. (2022) identifies several factors contributing to psychological barriers. These include burnout, family-work conflict, work-family conflict, career-marriage conflict, implicit bias, workplace violence, imposter syndrome, mental load, and compassion fatigue. These factors significantly impact young married women's well-being and overall workplace wellness in the Indian higher education setting. By shedding light on these psychological barriers, the chapter aims to raise awareness and understanding of the challenges young married women face concerning workplace wellness. It emphasizes the need for organizations to address these barriers and create supportive environments that promote the well-being of female employees. Additionally, it highlights the importance of interventions and strategies that can help mitigate these psychological barriers and enhance workplace wellness for young married women in the Indian higher education sector.

The researcher by Benuyenah & Pandya (2020) developed a multi-dimensional scale to assess employee happiness, incorporating factors such as job satisfaction, work-life balance, organizational support, and career growth opportunities; the findings of the study highlighted significant correlations between employee happiness and both individual-level and macro-level indicators. The results of the study by Gorovei (2020) revealed a positive correlation between job satisfaction and happiness, indicating that individuals who reported higher levels of job satisfaction also experienced higher levels of happiness in their lives. The study also identified specific factors within the work context that influenced job satisfaction and subsequently impacted overall happiness, such as job security, work-life balance, career advancement opportunities, and supportive work relationships. It emphasize the significance of creating positive work environments that foster job satisfaction, as it has implications not only for individuals' happiness but also for organizational productivity and employee retention. It has a practical impact on employers and policymakers in designing interventions and policies that enhance job satisfaction and contribute to employees' happiness and well-being. The study also opens avenues for further research into the underlying mechanisms and dynamics that link job satisfaction and happiness in the modern world.

1.1 Definition of Employee Happiness Index

The Employee Happiness Index is a popular measure of employee happiness and job satisfaction. This metric typically examines factors that affect employee satisfaction, such as the work environment, the balance between work and personal life, pay, benefits, opportunities for growth, and relationships with co-workers and management. The Employee Happiness Index measures employee satisfaction, which can affect how well they perform their jobs, how productive they are, and how likely they are to remain with the organization. Organizations use this metric to evaluate the effectiveness of their HR policies and practices, identify improvement areas, and develop strategies to increase employee satisfaction and engagement.

1.2 Importance of Measuring Employee Happiness Index in the Workplace

Organizations must measure the Employee Happiness Index to maintain a healthy workplace and ensure employee satisfaction. Consider the following justifications for measuring employee satisfaction:

- **Improves Employee Retention:** Measuring the Employee Happiness Index facilitates the identification of factors that influence employee retention and satisfaction. Employees who are satisfied with their job and work environment are likelier to remain with the organization, thereby decreasing turnover rates and associated costs. One helpful tool for lowering turnover is the Employee Happiness Index. Regular surveys of workers' happiness and satisfaction demonstrate that many factors than salary level contribute to job satisfaction. Organizations may focus on increasing employee engagement and happiness by identifying upgrade areas, such as career development and workplace culture. This preventative measure improves morale, increases productivity, and lowers hiring and replacing staff costs. Companies that use the Employee Happiness Index to gauge their success might make changes to increase job satisfaction, retention, and productivity.
- **Increases Productivity:** Content employees are more productive and committed. Measuring the Employee Happiness Index facilitates the identification of areas for improvement to increase employee productivity, resulting in enhanced business outcomes. Organizations may benefit from measuring the Employee Happiness Index in several ways, including pinpointing growth areas, meeting workers' needs, increasing productivity, raising morale, and keeping the best employees. Workers are likelier to put up their best effort when they are happy. By creating a supportive workplace and listening to employees' feedback, businesses may foster a culture of productivity and boost their bottom line.
- **Attracts Top Talent:** A positive Employee Happiness Index can assist a company in attracting top-tier talent. Prospective employees are likelier to want to work for a company that prioritizes employee satisfaction. A positive Employee Happiness Index plays an essential role in attracting top talent by enhancing employer branding, encouraging word-of-mouth recommendations, acting as a talent magnet, leveraging employee testimonials and success stories, providing a competitive advantage in recruitment, and aligning with the values of prospective employees. This potent instrument creates a desirable work environment that attracts individuals of high calibre, setting the company apart from competitors and demonstrating its dedication to employee well-being. Businesses can effectively attract and retain top-tier talent by prioritizing employee happiness and fostering a positive work environment.
- **Improves Customer Satisfaction:** Happier workers are more likely to provide superior customer service, which increases customer loyalty and satisfaction. Measuring the Employee Happiness Index ensures that employees are satisfied and committed to their work, which can positively impact customer satisfaction.

  Measuring the Employee Happiness Index increases customer satisfaction by encouraging employee engagement, nurturing positive work culture, improving communication and collaboration, empowering employees, and embracing continuous improvement. Happier and more satisfied employees are more likely to provide superior customer service, resulting in greater customer loyalty and satisfaction. This leads to commercial success and expansion.
- **Enhances Reputation:** A high Employee Happiness Index can improve a company's reputation as an employer. It can result in improved stakeholder relationships and increased brand loyalty.

Organizations must measure the Employee Happiness Index to maintain a healthy work environment, increase employee satisfaction, and enhance business outcomes. Organizations can develop strategies to increase employee satisfaction and ensure long-term success by identifying areas for improvement. A high Employee Happiness Index improves a company's employer brand, attracting top talent and encouraging employee advocacy. It enhances stakeholder relations, increases brand loyalty, and generates a favourable public perception. The index promotes employee retention and productivity. By measuring employee satisfaction regularly and taking proactive measures to improve it, organizations demonstrate their dedication to a positive work culture and employee well-being. It boosts their reputation, resulting in long-term success and expansion.

2. THEORETICAL FRAMEWORK

The Employee Happiness Index can be measured in the modern workplace using a variety of theoretical frameworks. Below are three examples:

Self-Determination Theory (SDT): SDT is a psychological theory focusing on the motivations and needs driving human behaviour. According to this theory, humans have three fundamental psychological needs: autonomy, competence, and relatedness. The requirement for social connections and relationships is referred to as relatedness. Using SDT, it is possible to calculate the Employee Happiness Index by examining how employees believe their basic psychological needs are being met at work. For instance, a survey could measure employee perceptions of autonomy, competence, and relatedness in the workplace.

According to the Self-Determination Theory (SDT), individuals have three fundamental psychological requirements: autonomy, competence, and relatedness. These requirements motivate human behaviour and are essential for employee contentment and fulfilment. Through surveys assessing employees' perceptions of autonomy, competence, and relatedness, organizations can determine the Employee Happiness Index. This index provides valuable insight into the extent to which employees' psychological requirements are being met and assists in identifying improvement opportunities. Organizations can increase employee satisfaction and create a thriving work environment by fostering autonomy, providing opportunities for growth, and cultivating positive social connections.

Job Characteristics Model (JCM): JCM is a job design theory that identifies five key job characteristics contributing to job satisfaction and motivation: skill variety, task identity, task significance, autonomy, and feedback. According to this theory, jobs with high levels of these characteristics are more likely to produce positive employee outcomes, including job satisfaction, motivation, and performance. JCM can be used to calculate the Employee Happiness Index by evaluating the extent to which employees perceive their jobs possess these five essential characteristics. For example, a survey could measure employee perceptions of skill diversity, task identity, task significance, autonomy, and feedback.

The JCM identifies important employment characteristics that influence job satisfaction and motivation. These include skill variety, task identity, task significance, autonomy, and feedback. Organizations can calculate the Employee Happiness Index by measuring employees' perceptions of these characteristics. The JCM emphasizes the importance of devising positions that provide employees with meaningful work experiences, increase employee satisfaction, and boost motivation. Incorporating the JCM's principles into job design allows organizations to create environments that foster job satisfaction, inspiration, and overall success.

Positive Organizational Scholarship (POS): Positive Organizational Scholarship studies the positive aspects of organizational behaviour, such as employee well-being, positive relationships, and meaningful work. The importance of fostering employee happiness and success through the creation of positive work environments is emphasized by POS. POS can be utilized to calculate the Employee Happiness Index by analyzing how employees view their work environment as positive and supportive. For instance, a survey could assess employee perceptions of positive relationships, meaningful work, and employee well-being. Multiple theoretical frameworks, such as Self-Determination Theory, the Job Characteristics Model, and Positive Organizational Scholarship, can be used to measure the Employee Happiness Index in the modern workplace. These frameworks provide a theoretical basis for comprehending the factors contributing to employee happiness and well-being. They can be used to design surveys and interventions to increase the Employee Happiness Index.

2.1 The Concept of Employee Happiness Index in Organizational Psychology

The Employee Happiness Index is a crucial metric in organizational psychology, as it is used to assess and improve employee happiness and job satisfaction. Organizational psychology seeks to comprehend the behaviour of individuals and groups within organizations and their interactions with their work environment (Robbins & Judge, 2015). By measuring the Employee Happiness Index, organizational psychologists gain insight into the factors influencing employee satisfaction and can identify improvement opportunities.

Organizational psychologists use various techniques, including surveys, focus groups, and interviews, to measure the Employee Happiness Index and collect data on job security, work-life balance, compensation, and growth opportunities (Robbins & Judge, 2015). This data analysis enables the identification of patterns and trends in employee satisfaction and the development of strategies to enhance employee happiness and engagement.

Employee Happiness Index is closely related to employee engagement and organizational culture, two essential organizational psychology concepts (Shuck & Reio Jr, 2013). Employee engagement is the degree to which employees are emotionally invested in their work and the organization. In contrast, organizational culture refers to the shared values, beliefs, and practices that shape the behaviour of individuals and groups within an organization (Shuck & Reio Jr, 2013). The Employee Happiness Index provides insight into both of these concepts and assists businesses in fostering a positive organizational culture and boosting employee engagement.

The Employee Happiness Index is an essential component of organizational psychology, aiding in improving employee satisfaction and engagement, which can lead to improved business results and a positive work environment. Organizational psychologists use the Employee Happiness Index to identify areas for improvement and develop strategies to increase employee happiness and engagement.

The findings of the study by Albano Jr (2009) revealed that happiness at work is a multi-dimensional construct encompassing aspects of job satisfaction, engagement, positive emotions, and a sense of purpose.

2.2 The Impact of the Employee Happiness Index on Organizational Outcomes

The Employee Happiness Index has a substantial effect on business outcomes. When employees are content with their job and work environment, the following positive business outcomes can occur:

- **Increased Productivity:** Employees satisfied with their jobs are more productive and invested in their work, leading to enhanced productivity and quality. It can lead to improved business outcomes, including increased revenue and profits. Companies with high employee happiness and satisfaction levels are more likely to retain employees. It reduces costs associated with employee turnovers, such as recruitment and training, and helps maintain a stable and experienced workforce.
  Increased employee contentment and job satisfaction result in increased productivity, employee retention rates, and business outcomes. Satisfied employees are more engaged, motivated, and likely to go above and beyond, resulting in enhanced productivity and quality. Retaining experienced employees reduces attrition costs and preserves workforce stability. In addition, contented employees provide superior customer service, increasing customer retention and revenue. A positive work environment attracts top talent, enhancing productivity and creativity. Investing in the satisfaction of employees generates a highly engaged workforce, which drives improved business outcomes and competitive advantage.
- **Improved Customer Loyalty and Satisfaction:** Happier workers are more likely to provide superior customer service, which increases customer satisfaction and loyalty. It could lead to increased revenues and profits.
  Happy and content employees contribute to enhanced customer experiences by displaying a positive attitude, providing personalized service, and proactively resolving problems. Their improved product knowledge, capacity for establishing emotional connections, and dedication to continuous improvement increase customer satisfaction even further. Consequently, businesses gain increased consumer loyalty, positive word-of-mouth referrals, and higher revenues and profits.
- **Greater Innovation and Creativity:** Happier employees are more likely to be innovative and creative at work, which can lead to new concepts and improvements to products and services. It can give companies a competitive advantage and contribute to their long-term success. A positive Employee Happiness Index can contribute to an organization's appreciation, respect, and support culture. It can enhance teamwork, collaboration, and communication, enhancing business outcomes. The Employee Happiness Index has a substantial influence on organizational outcomes. When employees are satisfied with their job and work environment, it can lead to increased productivity, improved employee retention, higher customer satisfaction, more innovation and creativity, and a positive organizational culture. Organizations prioritizing employee happiness are likelier to achieve their business goals and enjoy long-term success. Through psychological safety, increased engagement, freedom to experiment, collaboration, a supportive feedback culture, and learning opportunities, happier employees foster innovation and creativity. It creates an environment in which employees feel empowered to share ideas and take risks, resulting in the development of novel solutions. Such businesses acquire a competitive advantage, adapt to market shifts effectively, and achieve long-term success.

3. MEASURING EMPLOYEE HAPPINESS INDEX

3.1 Tools and Techniques Used to Measure Employee Happiness Index

The Employee Happiness Index is computed using a variety of instruments and methods. Among the most common strategies are: Conducting a survey is a standard method for measuring employee satisfaction. These surveys may be administered online or offline and may be anonymous or confidential. The survey can include questions regarding job satisfaction, work environment, relationships with co-workers and supervisors, work-life balance, etc.

- **The Net Promoter Score (NPS)** is a straightforward and reliable method for gauging employee satisfaction. The score is based on a single question: "On a scale of 0 to 10, how likely are you to recommend this company as a workplace?" Employees with a score between 9 and 10 are considered "promoters," while those between 0 and 6 are considered "detractors."
  Based on their responses, personnel are divided into three categories. Those with a score between 9 and 10 are highly likely to recommend the company and are regarded as loyal and content. They tend to speak favourably about the company, refer prospective employees, and contribute to a positive work environment. Passives with a score of 7-8 are impartial. They are less likely to actively promote the company or go above and beyond their job responsibilities despite their level of satisfaction. Detractors with a score of 0 to 6 are unlikely to recommend the company and frequently hold negative perceptions or discontent. They may communicate dissatisfaction and criticism, discouraging others from joining the organization.
  The NPS is determined by subtracting the percentage of detractors from the percentage of promoters, yielding a score between -100 and +100. A positive Net Promoter Score (NPS) indicates more promoters than detractors, showing higher employee satisfaction and loyalty. In contrast, a negative NPS shows problem areas within the organization.
  The NPS is a valuable instrument for organizations, providing a straightforward and quantifiable measurement of employee satisfaction. It enables monitoring of changes over time and comparison to industry benchmarks. By monitoring NPS scores, organizations can identify areas for improvement and implement initiatives designed to enhance employee experiences, increase engagement, and boost overall satisfaction.
  Prioritizing Net Promoter Score (NPS) measurement and enhancement can substantially benefit organizations. It enhances employee loyalty and attracts top talent. By addressing the concerns raised by detractors and capitalizing on the positive sentiments of promoters, organizations can make well-informed decisions regarding the creation of a workplace that employees are proud to recommend.
  Ultimately, a high NPS contributes to a positive employer identity, which can enhance the reputation and competitiveness of the organization. It helps develop employee confidence and positions the organization as an employer. Organizations can cultivate a culture of employee satisfaction, engagement, and advocacy, leading to long-term business success, by perpetually monitoring and acting on NPS feedback.
- **Employee Engagement Surveys:** Employee engagement surveys aim to assess how connected employees feel to their organization. These surveys evaluate the level of employee motivation, commitment, and enthusiasm. Employee engagement surveys provide organizations with a quan-

titative measurement of employee engagement levels and aid in identifying engagement's main determinants. They allow employees to provide feedback, participate in decision-making processes, and cultivate an environment of trust and inclusion. These surveys enable organizations to develop action plans, prioritize initiatives, and allocate resources to resolve areas for improvement. Organizations can improve communication, build trust, and create a positive work environment that promotes employee satisfaction, retention, and performance by actively listening to employees and acting on survey feedback. Conducting employee engagement surveys regularly demonstrates a dedication to continuous improvement and can contribute to long-term success.

- **Pulse Surveys:** Pulse surveys are brief, frequent questionnaires administered to track employee satisfaction over time. Typically distributed weekly or monthly, these surveys assist organizations in identifying trends and improvement opportunities. Pulse surveys provide a continuous feedback cycle that provides real-time insight into employee satisfaction and engagement. They are effective, fast to complete, and aid in identifying improvement trends. Businesses can proactively address issues, monitor progress, and improve the employee experience by utilizing benchmarking and making agile, data-driven decisions.
- **Focus Groups:** Focus groups are small employee groups assembled to discuss their experiences and emotions at work. Facilitated by a facilitator, these groups provide valuable insight into employee satisfaction. Focus groups offer in-depth qualitative insights into employee satisfaction in organizations. By investigating emotions, uncovering latent issues, and leveraging group dynamics, focus groups provide organizations with valuable insights that can be used to create a positive work environment and increase employee satisfaction.
- **Exit Interviews:** Exit interviews are conducted with departing company employees. These interviews can provide valuable insight into why employees leave and how to improve employee retention. There is no standardized approach to measuring employee satisfaction. By combining these tools and techniques, organizations can comprehensively understand employee satisfaction and make corresponding improvements. Organizations must conduct exit interviews to determine why employees depart and enhance retention. They uncover reasons for employee departure, recognize patterns, and assist in refining retention strategies. Exit interviews offer finality to departing employees, disclose organizational strengths and deficiencies, and motivate actionable changes. Organizations can increase employee satisfaction, decrease attrition, and foster a positive work environment by analyzing feedback and implementing changes. Combining exit interviews with other instruments for measuring employee satisfaction provides a comprehensive understanding for implementing corresponding changes.

In addition, measuring employee happiness or satisfaction is essential for determining employee engagement and the overall health of an organization. Although there is no one-size-fits-all method for measuring employee satisfaction, the following metrics are commonly used to do so:

- **Employee surveys:** Regular surveys, such as annual or quarterly employee satisfaction surveys, can provide insightful data on various employee satisfaction factors. There may be questions regarding job satisfaction, work-life balance, career advancement opportunities, communication, collaboration, and management effectiveness.

  Regular annual or quarterly employee surveys collect information on job satisfaction, work-life balance, career opportunities, communication, collaboration, and management effectiveness. These surveys assess employee perceptions and experiences using standard queries. The collected data enables organizations to monitor trends, identify areas for development, and make informed decisions to improve employee engagement and satisfaction. Organizations can foster a positive work environment and promote organizational success by placing a premium on confidentiality and anonymity, analyzing survey results, and translating them into actionable insights.

- **Employee Net Promoter Score:** eNPS is a modified version of the customer-focused Net Promoter Score that measures the likelihood of employees recommending their employer. Typically, employees are asked to rate their likelihood of recommending the company to their colleagues or co-workers on a scale from 0 to 10. This metric provides an all-encompassing overview of employee satisfaction, including employee satisfaction, loyalty, and engagement. Organizations can evaluate employee sentiment by calculating the difference between Promoters and Detractors. eNPS is a quantitative benchmarking instrument that provides actionable insights for enhancing the employee experience. Regular measurement permits organizations to monitor trends and evaluate the efficacy of initiatives. Higher eNPS scores indicate greater engagement and brand loyalty, whereas lesser scores indicate development opportunities. eNPS assists organizations in boosting satisfaction, productivity, and retention.
- **Employee turnover rate:** High turnover rates may indicate dissatisfied employees. Keeping note of the number of employees who depart a company within a given time can help identify future problems and areas for improvement. The employee attrition rate is the proportion of workers who leave an organization within a given time frame. High turnover rates signify possible dissatisfaction and can have financial consequences. Analyzing attrition data enables the identification of problem areas, developing retention strategies, benchmarking against industry standards, and tracking long-term trends. Organizations can cultivate a positive work environment and boost their long-term success by addressing employee concerns and increasing employee satisfaction.
- **Absenteeism and sick leave:** Monitoring the frequency and duration of employee absences and sick days can shed light on employee health and job satisfaction. Increased absenteeism may indicate a decline in employee satisfaction.

  Monitoring employee absenteeism and medical leave reveals employee satisfaction, health, and productivity information. Increased absenteeism may indicate a decline in employee satisfaction, while high rates of medical leave may indicate health and work-life balance issues. Pattern analysis aids in identifying underlying issues such as work overburden or poor management. It informs the creation of support programmes and proactive measures to enhance health and prevent excessive absences. Legal compliance is ensured, and productivity is maximized. Organizations increase employee contentment and productivity by addressing concerns and fostering a positive work environment.
- **Employee performance metrics:** Performance monitoring can provide indirect insight into employee satisfaction, though it is not the only indicator. Generally, content employees are more productive and deliver superior results, whereas dissatisfied employees may experience a decline in performance.

  Monitoring employee performance metrics provides insight into employee satisfaction, as content employees are typically more productive and produce higher-quality work. Job satisfaction impacts employee engagement, motivation, and retention, enhancing performance outcomes. Content employees promote positive team dynamics, encourage collaboration, and are more receptive to development opportunities. While performance metrics are beneficial, they should be supplemented with additional feedback mechanisms to comprehend employee satisfaction completely. Regular feedback, surveys, and open communication channels are essential for addressing concerns and gaining direct insights. Overall, contented workers are more engaged and fruitful, and they contribute to an improvement in organizational performance.

- **Peer recognition and awards:** Employee satisfaction may be indicated by the frequency of peer recognition and employee awards. Recognizing and appreciating employees' achievements and contributions promotes a positive work environment.
  Peer recognition and awards increase employee satisfaction by providing appreciation, encouraging employees, and fostering a positive work environment. Recognizing employees' accomplishments increases their motivation, collaboration, and output. It also promotes a positive organizational culture, enhances employee health, and increases employee retention rates. Organizations should implement formal recognition programmes and foster a culture of appreciation to maximize these benefits.
- **Employee feedback and suggestions:** Encouragement of employee feedback and suggestions through regular channels, such as suggestion boxes or online platforms, can provide insight into their engagement and level of satisfaction. Respect for employee opinions is demonstrated by actively pursuing and implementing employee feedback.
  Employee satisfaction measurement should be an ongoing process, not a one-time event. Regularly monitoring these metrics and acting on the findings can help create a positive work environment and increase overall employee satisfaction. It is crucial to encourage employee feedback and suggestions to assess employee engagement and satisfaction. It enables employees, identifies areas for development, and assists with overcoming obstacles. Contributions from employees improve decision-making and cultivate a culture of continuous improvement. It encourages responsibility, frank communication, and trust. Implementing employee suggestions demonstrates the value and increases employee satisfaction. Essential are transparent feedback channels, evaluation procedures, and communication of results. Positive work environments and substantive adjustments are prompted by employee feedback. In conclusion, employee feedback is crucial for assessing engagement and job satisfaction, fostering improvement, and strengthening the relationship between employees and organizations.

3.2 Factors Leading to High Employee Happiness Index

- **Positive work culture:** Employee satisfaction is increased by a supportive and inclusive work environment that values collaboration, open communication, and mutual respect.
- **Fair compensation and benefits:** Employee satisfaction can be increased by providing competitive salaries, performance-based incentives, comprehensive benefit packages, and opportunities for growth and development.
- **Work-life balance:** Promoting work-life balance through flexible work arrangements, sufficient vacation time, and supportive policies can positively affect employee satisfaction.
- **Recognition and appreciation:** Recognizing and appreciating employee contributions and accomplishments regularly fosters a sense of worth and job satisfaction.
- **Growth opportunities:** Career advancement, professional development, and skill-building opportunities can increase employee engagement and satisfaction.
- **Supportive leadership:** Employee satisfaction is increased by effective and empathic leadership that provides clear direction, support, and opportunities for employee input and growth.

- **Workload management:** Employee satisfaction can be increased by ensuring manageable and reasonable workloads, providing the necessary resources and tools, and promoting a healthy work-life balance.

3.3 Benefits Derived by the Organization

- **Increased productivity:** Happier workers are frequently more engaged, motivated, and productive, resulting in more excellent organizational performance overall.
- **Reduced turnover:** High levels of employee satisfaction can result in reduced attrition rates, thereby reducing an organization's recruitment and training expenses.
- **Improved employee retention:** Satisfied Employees are more likely to remain with the company, reducing the need for continuous hiring and preserving institutional knowledge.
- **Enhanced company reputation:** Organizations prioritizing employee satisfaction frequently attract top talent and cultivate a favourable reputation as an employer of choice.
- **Better customer satisfaction:** Content employees typically provide superior customer service, increasing customer satisfaction and loyalty.

3.4 Tools for Measuring Employee Happiness

- **Employee engagement surveys:** These surveys ask about job satisfaction, the work environment, communication, and other factors that affect employee contentment. These surveys can be conducted using Gallup Q12, Culture Amp, or SurveyMonkey.
- **Pulse surveys:** These are brief, more frequent surveys that capture real-time employee sentiment. Businesses can regularly monitor their employees ' pulse using applications such as TINY pulse or Officevibe.
- **Net Promoter Score (NPS) for employees:** Organizations can ask employees if they would recommend the company as an employer using a similar methodology as consumer NPS. Tools such as Delighted or Qualtrics can assist with eNPS measurement.

3.5 Existing Scales to Measure Happiness Index

- **Subjective Happiness Scale (SHS):** A widely used scale that assesses the subjective contentment of an individual based on their comprehensive self-evaluation.
- **Satisfaction with Life Scale (SWLS):** This scale measures an individual's overall life satisfaction and is frequently used to gauge contentment and well-being.
- **Oxford Happiness Questionnaire (OHQ):** A comprehensive questionnaire that measures numerous aspects of happiness, such as positive emotions, life satisfaction, and overall happiness.
- **Job Satisfaction Survey (JSS):** A scale designed to measure a person's employment satisfaction, including aspects such as the work itself, compensation, supervision, and opportunities for advancement.

These metrics can be incorporated into employee surveys or used independently to measure employee satisfaction in specific domains.

In all these, Artificial intelligence (AI) and machine learning (ML) play a crucial role in accumulating and analyzing employee feedback in various ways, providing organizations with valuable insights and improving the efficacy of feedback processes. AI and ML have the following significance in this context:

- **Efficient data collection:** By outsourcing surveys, sentiment analysis, and data extraction, AI-enabled tools can expedite the collection of employee feedback. This reduces the manual effort and time necessary to collect employee feedback.
- **Natural language processing (NLP):** NLP algorithms allow AI systems to comprehend and interpret unstructured data, such as surveys or feedback from text comments. ML models can analyze employee feedback's sentiment, tone, and context, allowing for a more comprehensive comprehension of employee attitudes and emotions.
- **Sentiment analysis:** ML algorithms can classify employee feedback into positive, negative, and neutral sentiments, enabling businesses to identify patterns and trends in employee perceptions. This analysis serves to identify areas of organizational satisfaction or concern.
- **Real-time feedback analysis:** AI-powered systems can process and analyze feedback in real time, allowing businesses to identify and address employee concerns quickly. This allows for quicker response times and the ability to take proactive steps to increase employee satisfaction.
- **Actionable insights:** AI and ML techniques can provide organizations with actionable insights by distinguishing the most central feedback themes and highlighting attention-demanding areas. This helps organizations prioritize initiatives and make data-based decisions to improve employee satisfaction.
- **Personalization and individual feedback:** AI-based systems can personalize feedback collection and analysis by tailoring queries and suggestions to the preferences and history of each employee. This individualized approach enables a more targeted and meaningful experience with feedback.
- **Predictive analytics:** Organizations can use machine learning algorithms to anticipate future employment trends and behaviours based on past feedback data. This allows for proactive intervention and preventative measures against future problems before they escalate.
- **Continuous improvement:** AI and ML facilitate successive feedback cycles by monitoring employee sentiment and providing ongoing insights. This enables organizations to monitor progress, evaluate the impact of initiatives, and iterate employee satisfaction strategies.

AI and ML technologies improve employee feedback analysis's productivity, precision, and breadth. By utilizing these capabilities, organizations can better understand their workforce, identify enhancement areas, and cultivate a more engaged and satisfied workforce.

3.6 The Pros and Cons of Different Methods of Measuring the Employee Happiness Index

Different methods of measuring the Employee Happiness Index have their pros and cons. Here are some of them:

Surveys:

Pros:

- Surveys are simple to administer and quick to complete.
- They can be distributed to numerous employees simultaneously.
- Surveys can be tailored to measure particular aspects of employee satisfaction.
- Quantitative analysis of responses can reveal patterns and trends.

Cons:

- If employees feel uncomfortable expressing their true feelings, their survey responses may not be accurate or honest.
- Employees who are asked to complete too many surveys may experience survey fatigue.
- It is possible that surveys do not capture the entire range of feelings and experiences that contribute to employee satisfaction.

Net Promoter Score (NPS):

Pros:

- NPS is a straightforward metric.
- It can be used to compare businesses within the same industry.
- The Net Promoter Score (NPS) accurately indicates employee loyalty and propensity to recommend the company to others.

Cons:

- There is no specific information provided by NPS regarding the factors that contribute to employee satisfaction.
- Scores may be affected by external factors, such as economic or industry trends, that are beyond the organization's control.
- NPS may not apply to all industries or businesses.

Employee Engagement Surveys:

Pros:

- Engagement surveys measure how connected employees feel to their organization and work and provide valuable insight into employee motivation and commitment.
- The results can be used to identify improvement areas and develop action plans to increase employee engagement.

- Employee engagement surveys can be administered to the entire workforce or to specific groups to identify differences in engagement levels.

Cons:

- It is possible that employee satisfaction surveys do not capture the complete spectrum of feelings and experiences that contribute to employee satisfaction.
- Responses may be influenced by social desirability bias and other factors that affect survey results.
- Participation surveys can be costly and time-consuming to administer.

Pulse Surveys:

Pros:

- To monitor changes in employee satisfaction over time, frequent pulse surveys can be administered.
- Responses can be analyzed in real-time to identify trends and take prompt action.
- Traditional surveys are more time-consuming and lengthier than pulse surveys.

Cons:

- It is possible that pulse surveys do not capture the entire range of feelings and experiences that contribute to employee satisfaction.
- Recent occurrences or other mood-influencing factors may influence responses.
- Pulse surveys may not provide sufficient detail to identify specific areas for improvement.

Focus Groups:

Pros:

- Focus groups allow employees to discuss their experiences and feelings in a group setting.
- They can provide an abundance of qualitative data that can be used to comprehend the reasons behind quantitative survey results.
- Focus groups can assist employees in fostering a sense of community and belonging.

Cons:

- Focus groups are time-consuming and expensive to conduct.
- Responses may be affected by group dynamics and the desire to conform to social norms.
- Focus groups may not accurately represent the entire workforce.

Exit Interviews:

Pros:

- Exit interviews are conducted to determine why employees leave and identify improvement areas.
- Employees may feel more at ease expressing their genuine opinions during an exit interview than in other surveys.
- Exit interviews can yield valuable information for retaining other employees.

Cons:

- Employees can refuse to participate in exit interviews or provide dishonest feedback.
- It is possible that exit interviews capture only the experiences of departing employees and do not provide a comprehensive picture of employee satisfaction.
- It may not be possible to conduct exit interviews consistently or methodically, making it challenging to compare results over time.

Each technique for measuring the Employee Happiness Index has advantages and disadvantages. Organizations should employ a combination of techniques to understand employee satisfaction thoroughly.

4. FACTORS CONTRIBUTING TO EMPLOYEE HAPPINESS

4.1 Organizational Factors (e.g., Company Culture, Leadership Style, Work-Life Balance)

Organizational factors such as company culture, leadership style, and work-life balance can significantly impact employee satisfaction. Listed below are some of how these variables can influence employee satisfaction:

Company culture:

A positive company culture can help employees feel connected and belong at work, increasing their happiness. A robust company culture may include openness, respect, and collaboration as core values. On the other hand, a harmful or toxic culture may cause employees to feel unsupported or undervalued, resulting in low morale and happiness levels.

The company's culture has a substantial effect on employee satisfaction and contentment. A positive culture promotes a sense of belonging, open communication, respect, collaboration, work-life balance, and learning opportunities. It fosters an environment in which employees feel supported and valued. An unhealthy culture, on the other hand, can result in low morale and dissatisfaction. Organizations should prioritise cultivating a positive culture by delineating fundamental values, encouraging communication and collaboration, recognizing employee contributions, and promoting work-life balance. A positive company culture increases employee happiness, resulting in a more engaged and productive workforce.

Leadership style:

The managerial and executive leadership style has a significant impact on employee satisfaction. Supportive, communicative, and empathetic leaders can contribute to developing a collaborative and trustworthy workplace. On the other hand, overbearing managers disregarding their employees' input or monitoring their work excessively can make the workplace unpleasant and anxiety-inducing.

The managerial and executive leadership style significantly impacts employee satisfaction and the overall work environment. Positive work environments are created by supportive, communicative, and empathetic leaders who prioritize effective communication, collaborative decision-making, autonomy, recognition, and employee development. On the other hand, leaders who are overbearing or micromanagers can negatively impact employee satisfaction. Organizations should invest in leadership development programmes and foster a culture that values supportive and empowering leadership to increase employee contentment, engagement, and organisational success.

Work-life balance:

Achieving a balance between work and personal life is essential for employee satisfaction. Employees who believe they have enough time for their personal lives and hobbies are likelier to feel fulfilled and content at work. Organizations can promote work-life balance by offering flexible work options like telecommuting, job sharing, and reduced hours.

Achieving work-life balance is essential for employee happiness and health. It enhances employee well-being, productivity, retention and recruitment, engagement and morale, and promotes a positive organizational culture. The key to promoting work-life balance is providing flexible work arrangements and establishing supportive policies and practises. By prioritizing work-life balance, organizations foster an environment where employees can flourish on both a personal and professional level, leading to greater employee satisfaction and organizational success.

Recognition and rewards:

Organizations that frequently recognize and reward their employees can contribute to a rise in employee satisfaction and motivation. Recognition includes verbal praise, bonuses, promotions, and professional development opportunities.

Reward and recognition are essential for increasing employee satisfaction, motivation, and engagement. They reinforce positive behaviours, boost job satisfaction, and encourage loyalty. By recognizing and rewarding employees, organizations foster a positive work environment, enhance team dynamics, attract top talent, and promote employee growth. Implementing a transparent and equitable rewards and recognition programme is essential for guaranteeing equal opportunities for all employees. Recognition and rewards contribute to an appreciative culture, resulting in greater employee satisfaction and organizational success.

Communication:

Employee satisfaction is dependent on effective communication. Employees are more likely to feel engaged and motivated if they believe their opinions are valued and they are informed of company decisions and news. Organizations can foster effective communication by providing regular feedback, hosting town hall meetings, and encouraging open dialogue between employees and managers. In conclusion, organizational factors play an indispensable role in determining employee satisfaction. By fostering a supportive leadership style, promoting work-life balance, providing recognition and rewards, and facilitating effective communication, organizations can increase the happiness and satisfaction of their employees.

4.2 Personal Factors (e.g., Job Satisfaction, Mental Health, Personal Life Circumstances)

Additionally, personal factors can have a significant impact on employee satisfaction. Personal factors can influence employee satisfaction in the following ways:

Job Satisfaction:

Job satisfaction is the level of contentment an employee has with their job and position within the organization. Employees are more likely to report higher levels of job satisfaction when they find their work enjoyable, feel a sense of accomplishment, and believe their work has meaning. In contrast, employees who are dissatisfied with their job, find them monotonous, or believe it conflicts with their values are more likely to report low levels of job satisfaction (Spector, 1997).

Mental health:

Mental health is an essential factor that can influence employee satisfaction. Even if they otherwise enjoy their job, employees with mental health issues such as anxiety or depression may find it challenging to be happy at work. Employers can provide employee assistance programmes and counselling services to support the mental health of their employees. These initiatives can provide the necessary support for employees to manage their mental health and enhance their job satisfaction.

Personal life circumstances:

Personal circumstances, such as family responsibilities, financial strain, and health issues, can impact employee satisfaction. Employees dealing with difficult personal circumstances may find it challenging to focus on their work and consequently be unhappy. Employers can assist workers in balancing their personal and professional obligations by providing flexible work arrangements, such as remote work or flexible hours.

Work-life balance:

As stated, achieving a healthy work-life balance is crucial to employee satisfaction. Personal factors such as family responsibilities and extracurricular activities can influence employees' work-life balance perceptions. Employers can support their employees' work-life balance by providing flexible work arrangements, such as telecommuting or flexible schedules, along with stress management and time management resources.

Career development:

It has been discovered that personal factors such as career aspirations positively affect employee satisfaction. Employers can support the career development of their employees by providing training and development programmes, internal advancement opportunities, and mentoring or coaching programmes. In addition, by supporting employees' mental health and well-being, promoting work-life balance, and providing resources for managing personal life circumstances, employers can contribute to developing a work environment that supports the happiness and fulfilment of their employees.

5. CASE STUDIES

5.1 Examples of Organizations That Have Successfully Measured and Improved the Employee Happiness Index

Numerous businesses have successfully measured and improved Employee Happiness Index. Here are some notable examples:

Zappos:

Online shoe and clothing retailer Zappos is renowned for its dedication to employee satisfaction. The company employs various methods to measure employee satisfaction, including periodic surveys and manager check-ins. Moreover, Zappos provides its employees benefits and perks, including free food, fitness classes, and a comprehensive wellness programme. As a result, Zappos has been recognized as one of the best workplaces in the United States on numerous occasions.

Google:

Google is an organization that places a premium on employee satisfaction. The company employs various techniques to measure employee satisfaction, including surveys and regular feedback sessions (Aamodt, 2019). In addition, Google provides its employees with multiple benefits and perks, such as free meals, on-site fitness facilities, and personal and professional development opportunities. Therefore, Google has attracted and retained industry-leading talent (Secrets of Google's Talent Retention Success, 2015).

Airbnb:

Airbnb, the popular online marketplace for holiday rentals, is committed to employee happiness. The organization utilizes multiple methods, such as surveys and regular manager check-ins, to gauge employee satisfaction. In addition, Airbnb offers its employees a variety of benefits and perks, including generous holiday time, paid parental leave, and a programme that allows employees to travel and stay for free in Airbnb properties. As a result, Airbnb has been consistently recognized as one of the best workplaces in America.

Buffer:

Buffer, a social media management company, has prioritized employee satisfaction and transparency. Employees have access to the company's financial information and decision-making process, and the company measures employee satisfaction in various ways, including surveys and regular feedback sessions. Additionally, Buffer offers a variety of perks and benefits, including flexible work hours, unlimited holiday time, and a strong emphasis on work-life balance. Consequently, Buffer has been recognized as one of the top workplaces in the technology industry (Inc., 2020).

These companies demonstrate that prioritizing and improving the Employee Happiness Index can result in a more engaged, productive, and devoted workforce. These businesses have created a work environment that promotes employee happiness and satisfaction by providing various benefits and perks, promoting work-life balance, and fostering a culture of openness and communication.

5.2 Analysis of the Strategies and Practices Used by These Organizations

Google is known for its strong focus on employee happiness and has implemented several procedures and practices to measure and improve Employee Happiness Index. Here are some key strategies and methods used by Google:

Measuring employee happiness:

Google utilizes various methods to gauge employee satisfaction, including periodic surveys, feedback sessions, and pulse surveys. The company values open communication and encourages employees to offer suggestions for enhancing the work environment (Noe et al., 2020). These practices contribute to developing a culture of openness and trust, which can increase job satisfaction and employee engagement.

Promoting work-life balance:

Google promotes a healthy work-life balance by offering flexible work arrangements, such as telecommuting and flexible work hours. To promote the health and well-being of its employees, the company also provides various wellness programmes, including on-site gyms, fitness classes, and nutritious meals.

Fostering a Culture of Transparency and Communication:

Google places a premium on transparency and communication. The organization encourages open communication between employees and management and informs employees about its decision-making process and financial performance. This transparency develops employee confidence and fosters community and shared purpose.

Offering opportunities for personal and professional development:

Google provides its employees numerous personal and professional growth opportunities, such as mentorship programmes, leadership training, and skill-building and career advancement opportunities. These initiatives foster employee growth and development, resulting in increased job satisfaction.

Providing competitive compensation and Benefits:

Google has been recognized for effectively implementing strategies and practices to improve employee happiness and satisfaction. This includes competitive compensation packages and various benefits, including health insurance, retirement plans, and ample holiday time. These benefits contribute to the financial security and well-being of employees, as well as the attraction and retention of top talent. Furthermore, Google's strategies for measuring and improving the Employee Happiness Index demonstrate the importance of promoting work-life balance, fostering a culture of transparency and communication, offering opportunities for personal and professional development, and providing competitive compensation and benefits. Google has been able to create a work environment that promotes employee happiness and satisfaction, resulting in a more engaged and productive workforce by implementing these strategies and practices.

Case Study: Google's HR Practices

Background:

Google is renowned for its innovative and employee-focused approach to human resources. The company strongly emphasizes fostering a creative, innovative, and healthy work environment for its employees.

Hiring and Selection:

The recruiting process at Google is centred on identifying candidates with exceptional skills and cultural compatibility. The organization evaluates candidates using a combination of behavioural interviews, technical assessments, and problem-solving exercises. Google values characteristics such as intellectual inquiry, passion, and collaboration skills.

Employee Empowerment:

Google promotes a culture of independence and autonomy. Employees are encouraged to devote 20% of their work time to personal endeavours, referred to as "20% time." This initiative has led to innovative products like Gmail and Google News.

Performance Management:

"Objectives and Key Results" (OKRs) is the name of Google's performance management system. OKRs enable employees to establish distinct objectives and critical results, fostering transparency, alignment, and responsibility. Regular progress tracking and feedback discussions are conducted to provide support.

Employee Development:

Google invests significantly in employee development initiatives. "Googler-to-Googler" (g2g) is a comprehensive learning platform that enables employees to exchange their expertise. Additionally, the company offers internal training programmes, seminars, and conferences to enhance skills and knowledge.

Rewards and Recognition:

Google recognizes and rewards employees in a variety of methods. The company offers competitive compensation packages, which include stock options, as well as extensive benefits. In addition, Google has a peer recognition programme called "gThanks", where employees can express appreciation for the contributions of their peers.

Diversity and Inclusion:

Google places a high priority on cultivating an inclusive and diverse workplace. The company strives to increase underrepresented groups' representation and inclusion. Initiatives include training on implicit bias, recruitment efforts centred on diversity, and employee resource groups (ERGs) that support various communities.

Work-Life Balance:

Google promotes a healthy work-life equilibrium for the benefit of its employees. The company provides wellness and fitness centres, complimentary meals, and flexible work hours. Google also emphasizes the significance of mental health and provides resources to support the mental health of its employees.

Results:

Human resources practice at Google has contributed to the company's reputation as an employer of choice and nurtured a highly engaged and productive workforce. Consistently ranked among the top employers worldwide, the company attracts and retains top talent. Its innovative HR strategies have contributed to Google's success and influenced HR practises at other companies.

6. FUTURE DIRECTIONS

6.1 The Potential of Technology in Measuring Employee Happiness Index

Technology can potentially revolutionize the Employee Happiness Index's measurement and analysis. Here are some potential benefits of using technology to measure the Employee Happiness Index:

Real-time data collection:

Real-time data collection can be facilitated by technology, allowing businesses to identify trends and address issues promptly and quickly. Addressing problems before they become significant can increase employee happiness and satisfaction.

Anonymous feedback:

A platform for anonymous feedback technology can encourage employees to communicate more honestly and openly. This can help organizations identify issues that may not be raised through conventional feedback channels.

Data analysis and visualization:

Technology enables data analysis and visualization, enabling businesses to identify trends and patterns in employee feedback quickly. This can help identify areas of strength and areas needing improvement and guide decisions regarding employee happiness and satisfaction.

Personalized Insights:

Technology can provide customized insights based on employee feedback, allowing businesses to better understand each employee's needs and preferences. This can facilitate the development of tailored programmes and initiatives intended to increase employee happiness and satisfaction.

Scalability:

Technology can play a significant role in measuring employee satisfaction in large and complex organizations. By leveraging technology, businesses can ensure that all employees are included in the measurement and analysis process and that their feedback is considered when decisions about employee happiness and satisfaction are made. For example, employee engagement software such as SurveyMonkey, Qualtrics, and Glint can be used to create and administer employee surveys and collect real-time data on employee satisfaction and engagement levels. This technology can also be used to analyze and interpret data, identify trends and patterns, and generate reports to aid decision-making and increase employee satisfaction.

Technology can potentially significantly improve the Employee Happiness Index's measurement and analysis. By enabling real-time data collection, anonymous feedback, data analysis and visualization, personalized insights, and scalability, technology can help businesses develop a more engaged and satisfied workforce. Nonetheless, ensuring that technology is utilized ethically and responsibly and that employee privacy is protected throughout the process is crucial.

6.2 The Role of the Employee Happiness Index in the Future of Work

The Employee Happiness Index will likely play a more significant role in the future of work. Here are some justifications:

Attracting and retaining talent:

Organizations prioritizing employee happiness and job satisfaction are more likely to attract and retain top talent in today's highly competitive job market. By measuring and improving the Employee Happiness Index (EHI), organizations can create a positive and alluring work environment that attracts prospective employees (Schooley, 2023). Moreover, job satisfaction has been linked to greater employee engagement and commitment, which can lead to improved performance and lower turnover rates.

Improving Productivity and Performance:

Studies show happier employees are more productive and perform better than their less content counterparts. By measuring and improving the Employee Happiness Index (EHI), companies can cultivate a more productive workforce better equipped to achieve business objectives (Lyubomirsky et al., 2005). Moreover, organizations can reduce absenteeism and turnover rates by prioritizing employee well-being and job satisfaction, thereby reducing recruitment and training expenses.

Enhancing employee well-being:

The importance of employee well-being to workplace culture is now widely acknowledged. Organizations can foster a more wholesome and supportive work environment by measuring and improving the Employee Happiness Index (EHI). By prioritizing employee well-being, organizations can enhance their employees' physical and mental health, engagement, job satisfaction, and productivity.

Supporting Diversity, equity, and Inclusion:

Diversity, equity, and inclusion (DEI) can be promoted in the workplace with the help of the Employee Happiness Index. By measuring and addressing employee happiness and satisfaction, businesses can develop a more inclusive and equitable workplace culture that meets the needs of all employees. This strategy can help attract and retain diverse talent, increase employee engagement and productivity, and foster a sense of belonging among employees from diverse backgrounds. Moreover, businesses prioritizing DEI and employee happiness can enjoy improved business outcomes, such as increased innovation, improved decision-making, and enhanced financial performance.

Adapting to changing work environments:

Flexibility and remote work options are anticipated to increase in the future of work. By measuring and improving the Employee Happiness Index, organizations can foster a supportive and engaging work environment responsive to employees' changing needs and preferences. This strategy can enable organizations to attract and retain top talent, increase productivity and performance, promote diversity, equity, and inclusion, and adapt to changing work environments.

DISCUSSION

Measuring and enhancing employee satisfaction or contentment is essential for fostering a positive work environment that promotes employee health, productivity, and engagement. Organizations can obtain valuable insights into employee satisfaction and take steps to improve it by utilizing various metrics and tools.

Employee surveys are a prevalent method for measuring employee satisfaction. These surveys collect quantitative data on various facets of the workplace, including job satisfaction, work-life equilibrium, opportunities for career advancement, and communication effectiveness. By analyzing survey responses, organizations can identify areas for improvement and develop strategies to boost employee satisfaction.

In addition to surveys, eNPS can provide a comprehensive view of employee satisfaction. Organizations can determine employee engagement and job satisfaction by asking employees to rate their likelihood of recommending the company as an employer.

Important indicators of employee satisfaction include metrics relating to employee turnover and absenteeism. High churn rates and increased absenteeism may indicate underlying issues impacting employee satisfaction. Monitoring these metrics can aid organizations in identifying problems and implementing proactive solutions.

Indirectly, performance metrics can reflect employee contentment. Typically, satisfied employees are more motivated and productive, resulting in improved performance outcomes. On the other hand, a decline in performance may indicate low employee satisfaction.

Programmes for recognition and rewards are additional factors to consider. Employees are more likely to feel valued and content when acknowledged for their contributions and accomplishments. These programmes can contribute to a positive work environment and increase employee satisfaction.

It is essential to encourage employee feedback and suggestions. Providing employees with avenues to convey their thoughts and ideas demonstrates that their contributions are valued. Actively soliciting and implementing employee feedback promotes a sense of ownership and employee satisfaction.

Significant benefits result from measuring and enhancing the Employee Happiness Index. Employees who are more engaged, motivated, contented, and contented typically exhibit higher productivity. This, in turn, leads to enhanced organizational performance and success.

Reduced attrition is an additional benefit. Satisfied employees are less likely to quit an organization, which reduces recruitment and training expenses. Retaining experienced employees helps sustain a consistent workforce and preserve institutional knowledge.

Organizations that prioritize employee satisfaction frequently earn a favourable reputation as desirable employers. This reputation attracts top talent, giving the company an edge in the job market.

Moreover, employee satisfaction directly influences customer satisfaction. Satisfied employees are more likely to provide superior customer service, increasing customer loyalty and a favourable brand image.

There are numerous methods for measuring employee satisfaction available. Utilization of employee engagement surveys conducted through platforms such as Gallup Q12, Culture Amp, and SurveyMonkey is widespread. These surveys provide valuable data for analysis and encompass numerous aspects of employee satisfaction.

Pulse surveys are an additional helpful method for measuring employee satisfaction. They are brief, more frequent surveys that assess employee sentiment in real-time. Tools such as TINYpulse or Officevibe enable organizations to monitor the pulse of their employees regularly and quickly identify areas for improvement.

The Employee Happiness Index can also be determined by the Net Promoter Score (NPS). Using instruments such as Delighted or Qualtrics, organizations can ask employees if they would recommend the company as an employer, providing a quantitative measurement of employee satisfaction.

The Employee Happiness Index may be measured using several established scales. The Subjective Happiness Scale (SHS), the Satisfaction with Life Scale (SWLS), the Oxford Happiness Questionnaire

(OHQ), and the Job Satisfaction Survey (JSS) are widely recognized scales that measure various facets of happiness and contentment.

It is essential to utilize artificial intelligence (AI) and machine learning (ML) when gathering and analyzing employee feedback. AI-powered tools can efficiently collect and process large quantities of data. Natural language processing (NLP) algorithms facilitate the analysis of unstructured data, such as free-form survey responses and feedback comments, allowing businesses to extract insights and comprehend the sentiment underlying the feedback.

Techniques for sentiment analysis powered by AI and ML can classify employee feedback as positive, negative, or neutral, enabling organizations to identify patterns and trends. AI-facilitated real-time feedback analysis enables organizations to resolve employee concerns and provide prompt responses.

AI and ML enable personalized feedback analysis, tailoring the feedback collection and analysis process to the preferences and history of each employee. This individualized strategy improves the employee experience and makes feedback more pertinent and significant.

Based on past feedback data, ML algorithms' predictive analytics enable organizations to anticipate future trends and behaviours. This allows for proactive intervention and preventative measures to resolve prospective issues before they affect employee satisfaction.

Continuous feedback cycles facilitated by AI and ML technologies enable organizations to monitor employee sentiment over time and make data-based decisions to enhance satisfaction. These technologies provide a deeper comprehension of the workforce and contribute to developing a more engaged and content workforce.

Measuring and enhancing employee happiness and satisfaction is crucial for nurturing a positive work environment and attaining organizational success. Employing a variety of metrics, tools, and AI-powered technologies, organizations can gain valuable insights into employee satisfaction levels, identify areas for improvement, and take targeted steps to increase employee contentment. Prioritizing employee satisfaction results in increased productivity, decreased turnover, enhanced customer satisfaction, a positive employer brand image, and employee benefits.

CONCLUSION

Measuring and enhancing the Employee Happiness Index is crucial for creating a positive and engaging work environment that promotes employee health, productivity, and performance. By combining methods such as surveys, interviews, and data analysis, organizations can gain a more in-depth understanding of employee satisfaction and take steps to increase it. Furthermore, with the potential for technology to revolutionize the measurement and analysis of the Employee Happiness Index, businesses have even more opportunities to foster a positive and inclusive workplace culture that supports the needs and preferences of all employees. As the future of work continues to evolve, businesses prioritizing employee happiness and satisfaction will be better positioned to attract and retain top talent and achieve their business objectives.

REFERENCES

Aamodt, M. G. (2019). Industrial/organizational psychology: An applied approach. *Wadsworth Cengage Learning*. https://library.wbi.ac.id/repository/143.pdf

Albano, J. F., Jr. (2009). *Developing a measure and an understanding of the individual experience of happiness at work.* Saybrook University. https://www.proquest.com/openview/3ee650ef9eb71b611ee856480decc638/

Benuyenah, V., & Pandya, B. (2020). Measuring employee happiness in the UAE–integrating organizational data into the national statistics. *International Review of Management and Marketing, 10*(3), 83–92. doi:10.32479/irmm.9698

Cameron, K. S., & Spreitzer, G. M. (2012). *The Oxford handbook of positive organizational scholarship.* Oxford University Press., https://psycnet.apa.org/record/2011-19765-000

Chith, E. N., Vaishnavi, J., Yusaira, F., & Kureethara, J. V. (2022). Psychological Barriers to Workplace Wellness in Young Married Women in Indian Higher Education. In IGI Global eBooks (pp. 43–60). doi:10.4018/978-1-7998-7693-9.ch003

Gorovei, A. A. (2020). Does work make you happy? Job satisfaction and happiness in the modern world. *Revista Economica, 72*(1). http://economice.ulbsibiu.ro/revista.economica/archive/72108gorovei.pdf

Inc. (2020). *Best workplaces 2020.* Inc. https://www.inc.com/best-workplaces/2020.html

Lyubomirsky, S., King, L., & Diener, E. (2005). The benefits of frequent positive affect: Does happiness lead to success? *Psychological Bulletin, 131*(6), 803–855. doi:10.1037/0033-2909.131.6.803 PMID:16351326

McKee, A. (2014). Being happy at work matters. *Harvard Business Review.* https://hbr.org/2014/11/being-happy-at-work-matters

Noe, R. A., Hollenbeck, J. R., Gerhart, B., & Wright, P. M. (2020). *Human resource management: Gaining a competitive advantage.* McGraw-Hill Education.

Robbins, S. P., & Judge, T. A. (2015). Organizational Behaviour. *Pearson.* https://www.pearson.com/us/higher-education/product/Robbins-Organizational-Behavior-16th-Edition/9780133507645.html

Saini, D., & Yadav, R. (2023). *Assessing the role of materialism and gratitude in life satisfaction through IPMA: the mediating role of meaningfulness in life.* Society and Business Review., doi:10.1108/SBR-03-2022-0066

Schooley, S. (2023). 10 Ways to Attract and Retain the Best Employees. *Business News Daily.* https://www.businessnewsdaily.com/5189-attract-skilled-workers.html

Secrets of Google's talent retention success. (2015). European CEO. https://www.europeanceo.com/business-and-management/secrets-of-googles-talent-retention-success

Shuck, B., & Reio, T. G. Jr. (2013). Employee Engagement and Well-being: A Moderation Model and Implications for Practice. *Journal of Leadership & Organizational Studies, 20*(1), 43–58. doi:10.1177/1548051813494240

Sinha, M., Yadav, R., & Kishore, M. (2023). How E-Working Is Effective in Education. In *Advances in human resources management and organizational development book series* (pp. 214–233). IGI Global. doi:10.4018/978-1-6684-6745-9.ch013

Spector, P. E. (1997). *Job satisfaction: Application, assessment, causes, and consequences* (Vol. 3). Sage publications. doi:10.4135/9781452231549

Compilation of References

Aamodt, M. G. (2019). Industrial/organizational psychology: An applied approach. *Wadsworth Cengage Learning*. https://library.wbi.ac.id/repository/143.pdf

Abdullah, M. I., Huang, D., Sarfraz, M., Ivascu, L., & Riaz, A. (2021). Effects of internal service quality on nurses' job satisfaction, commitment, and performance: Mediating role of employee well-being. *Nursing Open*, *8*(2), 607–619. doi:10.1002/nop2.665 PMID:33570299

Abdullayev, M. M., & Aldulaimi, S. H. (2020). Trends and opportunities of artificial intelligence in human resource management: Aspirations for public sector in Bahrain. *International Journal of Scientific and Technology Research*, *9*(1), 3867–3871.

Adler, L. (2016). Metrics for better hires. *HRMagazine*, *60*(2), 60–61.

Agarwal, V., Mathiyazhagan, K., Malhotra, S., & Saikouk, T. (2022). Analysis of challenges in sustainable human resource management due to disruptions by Industry 4.0: An emerging economy perspective. *International Journal of Manpower*, *43*(2), 513–541. doi:10.1108/IJM-03-2021-0192

Aguirre, D., Pinder, J., & Roebuck, D. (2020). Talent Analytics for D&I: Moving Beyond Diversity Metrics. *People + Strategy, 43*(3), 20-29.

Ahmed, A., Weifeng, L., Victor, B., Shiyu, H., & Hsinchun, C. (2014). Descriptive Analytics: Examining Expert Hackers in Web Forums. Institute of Electrical and Electronics Engineer, (pp. 56-63). The Hague, Netherlands

Ahmed, S. H., & Baskaran, K. (2020). Blue-collar Workers behind the Success Story of UAE. *International Journal of Scientific & Technology Research*, *9*(2), 5221–5224.

Akbari, M., Bagheri, A., Fathollahi, A., & Darvish, M. (2020). Job satisfaction among nurses in Iran: Does gender matter? *Journal of Multidisciplinary Healthcare*, *13*, 71–78. doi:10.2147/JMDH.S215288 PMID:32021236

Akerkar, R. (2013). *Advanced data analytics for business. Big Data Computing*. Chapman and Hall/CRC.

Akgeyik, T. (2014, October 1). Factors Affecting Employee Absenteeism (A Study on a Sample of Textile Workers). *European Journal of Management*, *14*(3), 69–76. doi:10.18374/EJM-14-3.7

Akgunduz, Y., Bardakoglu, O., & Kizilcalioglu, G. (2022). Happiness, job stress, job dedication and perceived organizational support: A mediating model. *Journal of Hospitality and Tourism Insights*. doi:10.1108/JHTI-07-2021-0189

Akhtar, N., Francis, L. J., Sailer, A. B., Hasan, S. S., & McKenna, U. (2023). Introducing the Psychological Wellbeing Scale for Muslim Societies (PWS-MS): A study among young adults in Pakistan. *Mental Health, Religion & Culture*, 1–12. doi:10.1080/13674676.2022.2139364

Akin, A. (2008). The scales of psychological well-being: A study of validity and reliability. *Educational Sciences: Theory & Practice*, *8*(3), 741–750.

Alamelu, R., Nalini, R., Cresenta Shakila Motha, L., Amudha, R., & Bowiya, S. (2017). Adoption factors impacting human resource analytics among employees. *International Journal of Economic Research*, *14*(6), 417–423.

Alarcon, G., Lyons, J. B., & Tartaglia, F. (2010). Understanding predictors of engagement within the military. *Military Psychology*, *22*(3), 301–310. doi:10.1080/08995605.2010.492695

Albano, J. F., Jr. (2009). *Developing a measure and an understanding of the individual experience of happiness at work.* Saybrook University. https://www.proquest.com/openview/3ee650ef9eb71b611ee856480decc638/

Albert, E. T. (2019). AI in talent acquisition: A review of AI-applications used in recruitment and selection. *Strategic HR Review*, *18*(5), 215–221. doi:10.1108/SHR-04-2019-0024

Alcover, C. M., Salgado, S., Nazar, G., Ramírez-Vielma, R., & González-Suhr, C. (2020). Job insecurity, financial threat and mental health in the COVID-19 context: The buffer role of perceived social support. MedRxiv, 2020-07. doi:10.1101/2020.07.31.20165910

Aldulaimi, S. H., Abdeldayem, M. M., Mowafak, B. M., & Abdulaziz, M. M. (2021). Experimental Perspective of Artificial Intelligence Technology in Human Resources Management. *Applications of Artificial Intelligence in Business, Education and Healthcare*, 487-511.

Alfaleh, A., Alkattan, A., Alageel, A., Salah, M., Almutairi, M., Sagor, K., & Alabdulkareem, K. (2021). Onsite versus remote working: The impact on satisfaction, productivity, and performance of medical call centre workers. *INQUIRY: The Journal of Health Care Organization, Provision, and Financing*, *58*, 00469580211056041. PMID:34825844

Alias, N. E., Noor, N., & Hassan, R. (2014). Examining the mediating effect of employee engagement on the relationship between talent management practices and employee retention in the Information and Technology (IT) organizations in Malaysia. *Journal of Human Resources Management and Labor Studies*, *2*(2), 227–242.

Ali, M., Khan, M. S., Khan, S., & Iqbal, S. (2020). The mediating role of employee turnover intentions in the relationship between psychological contract breach and employee performance: Evidence from Pakistan. *Journal of Human Resource Management*, *8*(2), 27–34. doi:10.12691/jhrm-8-2-1

Ali-Yrkkö, J., Kuosmanen, N., & Pajarinen, M. (2023). Structural change in the ICT sector: Where have former Nokia employees ended up? *Journal of the Finnish Economic Association*, *3*(1). doi:10.33358/jfea.112802

Al-kharabsheh, S., Attiany, M., Alshawabkeh, R., Hamadneh, S., & Alshurideh, M. (2023). The impact of digital HRM on employee performance through employee motivation. *International Journal of Data and Network Science*, *7*(1), 275–282. doi:10.5267/j.ijdns.2022.10.006

Allen, N. J., & Meyer, J. P. (1990). The measurement and antecedents of affective, continuance, and normative commitment to the organization. *Journal of Occupational Psychology*, *63*(1), 1–18. doi:10.1111/j.2044-8325.1990.tb00506.x

Amazon begins 2nd round of layoff, fires 9000 employees. (2023). *Indiatoday*. https://www.indiatoday.in/technology/news/story/amazon-starts-2nd-round-of-layoff-fires-9000-employees-2349245-2023-03-20

Amit, Y., & Geman, D. (1997, October 1). Shape Quantization and Recognition with Randomized Trees. *Neural Computation*, *9*(7), 1545–1588. doi:10.1162/neco.1997.9.7.1545

Amundson, N. E. (2007). The influence of workplace attraction on recruitment and retention. *Journal of Employment Counseling*, *44*(4), 154–162. doi:10.1002/j.2161-1920.2007.tb00034.x

Andersen, M. K. (2017). Human capital analytics: The winding road. *Journal of Organizational Effectiveness*, *4*(2), 133–136. doi:10.1108/JOEPP-03-2017-0024

Angel, R. J., & Angel, J. L. (2014). *Latinos in an aging world: Social, psychological, and economic perspectives*. Routledge. doi:10.4324/9781315814582

Angrave, D., Charlwood, A., Kirkpatrick, I., Lawrence, M., & Stuart, M. (2016). HR and analytics: why HR is set to fail the big data challenge. Human Resource Management Journal, 1-11

Angrave, D., Charlwood, A., Kirkpatrick, I., Lawrence, M., & Stuart, M. (2016). HR and analytics: Why HR is set to fail the big data challenge. *Human Resource Management Journal*, *26*(1), 1–11. doi:10.1111/1748-8583.12090

Ansari, A. H., & Talan, A. (2017). Antecedents and Organizational Commitment Related Consequences of Job Insecurity among Teachers. *International Journal of Applied Business and Economic Research*, *15*(18), 321–333.

Ansari, M. S. A., & Khan, S. A. (2023). FDI, disinvestment and growth: An appraisal of Bhutanese economy. *Journal of Chinese Economic and Foreign Trade Studies*, *16*(1), 64–82. doi:10.1108/JCEFTS-05-2022-0031

Appelbaum, S. H., Delage, C., Labib, N., & Gault, G. (1997). The survivor syndrome: Aftermath of downsizing. *Career Development International*, *2*(6), 278–286. doi:10.1108/13620439710178639

Appelbaum, S. H., Everard, A., & Hung, L. T. (1999). Strategic downsizing: Critical success factors. *Management Decision*, *37*(7), 535–552. doi:10.1108/00251749910285674

Armstrong, M., & Taylor, S. (2014). *Armstrong's handbook of human resource management practice*. Kogan Page Publishers.

Arora, A. (2020). HR Analytics in India: Opportunities and Challenges. *Analytics Insight*. https://www.analyticsinsight.net/hr-analytics-india-opportunities-challenges/

Arora, M., Prakash, A., Dixit, S., Mittal, A., & Singh, S. (2022). A critical review of HR analytics: visualization and bibliometric analysis approach. *Information Discovery and Delivery*, (ahead-of-print). doi:10.1108/IDD-07-2021-0109

Arora, M., Prakash, A., Mittal, A., & Singh, S. (2022). Examining the slow acceptance of HR analytics in the Indian engineering and construction industry: a SEM-ANN-based approach. Engineering, Construction and Architectural Management. doi:10.1108/ECAM-09-2021-0795

Arora, M., Prakash, A., Mittal, A., & Singh, S. (2022). Moderating role of resistance to change in the actual adoption of HR analytics in the Indian banking and financial services industry. *In Evidence-based HRM: a Global Forum for Empirical Scholarship*. Emerald Publishing Limited.

Arora, M., Prakash, A., Mittal, A., & Singh, S. (2021, December). HR analytics and artificial intelligence-transforming human resource management. In *2021 International Conference on Decision Aid Sciences and Application (DASA)* (pp. 288-293). IEEE. 10.1109/DASA53625.2021.9682325

Ashar, H., & Lane-Maher, M. (2004). Success and spirituality in the new business paradigm. *Journal of Management Inquiry*, *13*(3), 249–260. doi:10.1177/1056492604268218

Ashish Malik, P. B. (2023). Employee experience–the missing link for engagingemployees: Insights from an MNE's AI-based HR ecosystem. *Human Resource Management*, 97–115. doi:10.1002/hrm.22133

Ashok, S., & Baskaran, K. (2019). Audit and Accounting Procedures in Organizations (with reference to Petty Cash). *Audit and Accounting Procedures in Organizations.*, *8*(4), 8759–8768. doi:10.35940/ijrte.D9165.118419

Ashok, S., & Baskaran, K. (2022). The Prominence of Corporate Governance in Banking Sector with Reference to UAE. In *Pervasive Computing and Social Networking. Lecture Notes in Networks and Systems* (Vol. 317). Springer. doi:10.1007/978-981-16-5640-8_33

Avci, N. (2017). The relationship between coworker supports, quality of work life and wellbeing: an empirical study of hotel employees. *International Journal of Management Economics and Business, 13*(3), 577-589. doi:10.17130/ijmeb.2017331328

Avery, D. R., Ruggs, E. N., Garcia, L. R., Traylor, H. D., & London, N. (2022). Improve Your Diversity Measurement for Better Outcomes. *MIT Sloan Management Review*, *64*(1), 1–6.

Avrahami, D., Pessach, D., Singer, G., & Chalutz Ben-Gal, H. (2022). A human resources analytics and machine-learning examination of turnover: Implications for theory and practice. *International Journal of Manpower*, *43*(6), 1405–1424. doi:10.1108/IJM-12-2020-0548

Bader, B., & Berg, N. (2013). An empirical investigation of terrorism-induced stress on expatriate attitudes and performance. *Journal of International Management*, *19*(2), 163–175. doi:10.1016/j.intman.2013.01.003

Baillien, E., & De Witte, H. (2009). Why is organizational change related to workplace bullying? Role conflict and job insecurity as mediators. *Economic and Industrial Democracy*, *30*(3), 348–371. doi:10.1177/0143831X09336557

Bakker, A. B., & Demerouti, E. (2014). *Job demands–resources theory. Wellbeing: A complete reference guide*. Wiley Blackwell., doi:10.1002/9781118539415.wbwell019

Bakker, A. B., & Demerouti, E. (2017). Job demands–resources theory: Taking stock and looking forward. *Journal of Occupational Health Psychology*, *22*(3), 273–285. doi:10.1037/ocp0000056 PMID:27732008

Bakker, A. B., Demerouti, E., Boer, E., & Schaufelia, W. B. (2003). Job demands and job resources as predictors of absence duration and frequency. *Journal of Vocational Behavior*, *62*(2), 341–356. doi:10.1016/S0001-8791(02)00030-1

Bakker, A. B., & Oerlemans, W. G. (2019). Daily job crafting and momentary work engagement: A self-determination and self-regulation perspective. *Journal of Vocational Behavior*, *112*, 417–430. doi:10.1016/j.jvb.2018.12.005

Balakrishnan, C., Masthan, D., & Chandra, V. (2013). Employee retention through employee engagement-A study at an Indian international airport. *International Journal of Business and Management Invention*, *2*(8), 9–16.

Balali, F. N. (2020). Data Analytics. Data Intensive Industrial Asset Management.

Balcerak, A., & Woźniak, J. (2021). Reactions to some ICT-based personnel selection tools. *Economics & Sociology (Ternopil)*, *14*(1), 214–231. doi:10.14254/2071-789X.2021/14-1/14

Ball, K. (2010). Workplace surveillance: An overview. *Labor History*, *51*(1), 87–106. doi:10.1080/00236561003654776

Bandari, V. (2019). Exploring the Transformational Potential of Emerging Technologies in Human Resource Analytics: A Comparative Study of the Applications of IoT, AI, and Cloud Computing. *Journal of Humanities and Applied Science Research*, *2*(1), 15–27.

Bani-Melhem, S., Al-Hawari, M. A., & Quratulain, S. (2020). Leader-member exchange and frontline employees' innovative behaviors: The roles of employee happiness and service climate. *International Journal of Productivity and Performance Management*, *71*(2), 540–557. doi:10.1108/IJPPM-03-2020-0092

Bansal, A., Panchal, T., Jabeen, F., Mangla, S. K., & Singh, G. (2023). A study of human resource digital transformation (HRDT): A phenomenon of innovation capability led by digital and individual factors. *Journal of Business Research*, *157*, 113611. doi:10.1016/j.jbusres.2022.113611

Bao, X., Qu, H., & Liu, Y. (2021). Work-life balance and employee retention: The role of job satisfaction and organizational commitment. *International Journal of Contemporary Hospitality Management, 33*(9), 2961–2979.

Bapna, S., & Funk, R. (2021). Interventions for Improving Professional Networking for Women: Experimental Evidence from the IT Sector. *Management Information Systems Quarterly, 45*(2), 593–636. doi:10.25300/MISQ/2021/15620

Barney, J. (1991). Firm resources and sustained competitive advantage. *Journal of Management, 17*(1), 99–121. doi:10.1177/014920639101700108

Barney, J., Wright, M., & Ketchen, D. J. Jr. (2001). The resource-based view of the firm: Ten years after 1991. *Journal of Management, 27*(6), 625–641. doi:10.1177/014920630102700601

Baskaran, K. (2019). An Interpretive Study of Customer Experience Management towards Online Shopping in UAE. *International Journal of Mechanical Engineering and Technology, 10*(2), 1071–1077.

Baskaran, K. (2019). The Impact of Digital Transformation in Singapore e-Tail Market. *International Journal of Innovative Technology and Exploring Engineering, 8*(11), 2320–2324. doi:10.35940/ijitee.I8046.0981119

Baskaran, K. (2020). *Journey of Education Technology towards Innovation. Innovations in Engineering Education Conference - Advances in Science and Engineering Technology Conferences.* ASET. doi:10.1109/ASET48392.2020.9118334

Baskaran, K. (2022). E-Consumer Behavioral Analytics: Paradigm Shift in Online Purchase Decision Making. In *Handbook of Research on Consumer Behavior Change and Data Analytics in the Socio-Digital Era* (pp. 192–209). IGI Global. doi:10.4018/978-1-6684-4168-8.ch009

Baskaran, K. (2023). Customer Experience in E-Commerce Market through virtual world of Metaverse. In *Consumer Behavioral Analytics in Metaverse and the Adoption of a Virtual World.* IGI Global. doi:10.4018/978-1-6684-7029-9.ch008

Baskaran, K., & Rajavelu, S. (2020). Digital Innovation in Industry 4.0 Era – Rebooting UAE's Retail. *International Conference on Communication and Signal Processing.* IEEE. 10.1109/ICCSP48568.2020.9182301

Bassett-Jones, N. (2005). The paradox of diversity management, creativity and innovation. *Creativity and Innovation Management, 14*(2), 169–175. doi:10.1111/j.1467-8691.00337.x

Bassi, L. & McMurrer, D. (2016, October 26). Four Lessons Learned in How to Use Human Resource Analytics to Improve the Effectiveness of Leadership Development. *Journal of Leadership Studies, 10*(2).

Bassi, L. J., Carpenter, R., & McMurrer, D. (2012). *HR analytics handbook.* Reed Business.

Bates, S. (2004). Getting engaged. *HRMagazine, 49*(2), 44–51.

Bauer, V. (n.d.). *HR analytics and employee turnover.* Deloitte. https://www2.deloitte.com/cz/en/pages/deloitte-analytics/articles/hr-analytika-a-odchodovost-zamestnancu.html

Baykal, E. (2020). Digital era and new methods for employee recruitment. In *Handbook of Research on Strategic Fit and Design in Business Ecosystems* (pp. 412–430). IGI Global. doi:10.4018/978-1-7998-1125-1.ch018

Beauducel, A., & Wittmann, W. W. (2005). Simulation study on fit indexes in CFA based on data with slightly distorted simple structure. *Structural Equation Modeling, 12*(1), 41–75. doi:10.120715328007sem1201_3

Bechter, B., Brandl, B., & Lehr, A. (2022). The role of the capability, opportunity, and motivation of firms for using human resource analytics to monitor employee performance: A multi-level analysis of the organisational, market, and country context. *New Technology, Work and Employment, 37*(3), 398–424. doi:10.1111/ntwe.12239

Becker, B. E., Huselid, M. A., & Ulrich, D. (2018). HR analytics, intellectual capital, and performance. *Human Resource Management, 57*(1), 7–15.

Bedeian, A. G., & Armenakis, A. A. (1998). The cesspool syndrome: How dreck floats to the top of declining organizations. *The Academy of Management Perspectives, 12*(1), 58–63. doi:10.5465/ame.1998.254978

Belizón, M. J., & Kieran, S. (2022). Human resources analytics: A legitimacy process. *Human Resource Management Journal, 32*(3), 603–630. doi:10.1111/1748-8583.12417

Bell, R. M., Fann, S. A., Morrison, J. E., & Lisk, J. R. (2011). Determining personal talents and behavioral styles of applicants to surgical training: A new look at an old problem, part I. *Journal of Surgical Education, 68*(6), 534–541. doi:10.1016/j.jsurg.2011.05.016 PMID:22000541

Belwalkar, S., Vohra, V., & Pandey, A. (2018). The relationship between workplace spirituality, job satisfaction and organizational citizenship behaviors–an empirical study. *Social Responsibility Journal, 14*(2), 410–430. doi:10.1108/SRJ-05-2016-0096

Belyaeva, T., & Kozieva, I. (2020). Employee engagement in HR analytical systems. *Economic Annals-XXI*, 94-102.

Ben-Gal, H. C. (2019). An ROI-based review of HR analytics: Practical implementation tools. *Personnel Review, 48*(6), 1429–1448. doi:10.1108/PR-11-2017-0362

Bennett, C. (2015, February 27). *HR and people analytics.* Deloitte.

Benuyenah, V., & Pandya, B. (2020). Measuring employee happiness in the UAE–integrating organizational data into the national statistics. *International Review of Management and Marketing, 10*(3), 83–92. doi:10.32479/irmm.9698

Berber, N., Đorđević, B., & Milanović, S. (2018). Electronic human resource management (e-HRM): A new concept for digital age. *Strategic Management-International Journal of Strategic Management and Decision Support Systems in Strategic Management, 23*(2).

Berhil, S., Benlahmar, H., & Labani, N. (2020). A review paper on artificial intelligence at the service of human resources management. *Indonesian Journal of Electrical Engineering and Computer Science, 18*(1), 32–40. doi:10.11591/ijeecs.v18.i1.pp32-40

Bersin. (2013). *High-impact talent analytics: Building a world-class HR.* Deloitte.

Bersin, J. (2013). *The datafication of HR: Graduating from HR metrics to people analytics.* Deloitte University Press.

Bersin, J. (2015). *The growth of people analytics: Driving a new era of decision-making in HR.* Deloitte University Press.

Bersin, J. (2016). The Future Of Work: It's Already Here—And Not As Scary As You Think. *Leadership, 6*(43), 62–187.

Beylerian, M., & Kleiner, B. H. (2003). The downsized workplace. *Management Research News, 26*(2/3/4), 97-108.

Bharti, A. (2017). Human resource analytics. *South Asian Journal of Marketing & Management Research, 7*(5), 68–77.

Bhat, A. (2018, August 23). *Descriptive Research: Characteristics, Methods + Examples.* QuestionPro. https://www.questionpro.com/blog/descriptive- research/#:~:text=In%20a%20descriptive%20research%20design

Bhattacharyya, D. K. (2015). Compensation and benefits program a mediating variable for talent retention: A study of two Century-Old Indian organizations. *Compensation and Benefits Review, 47*(2), 75–80. doi:10.1177/0886368715584481

Bican, P., & Brem, A. (2020). Digital business model, digital transformation, digital entrepreneurship: Is there a sustainable. *Digital, 12*, 5239–5254.

Bindu, K. (2016). A Review of Poor HR Analytical Skills. *International Journal of Innovative Research in Technology (IJIRT), 3*(1), 397-4027-0362

Blau, P. M. (1964). *Exchange and power in social life.* Wiley.

Blázquez, M., Budría, S., & Moro-Egido, A. I. (2021). Job insecurity, debt burdens, and individual health. *Review of Income and Wealth, 67*(4), 872–899. doi:10.1111/roiw.12506

Boatman, A. (n.d.). *A Guide To The 4 Types of HR Analytics.* AIHR (Academy to Innovate HR). https://www.aihr.com/blog/types-of-hr-analytics/

Bob-Manuel, I. V. (2023). Human Resource Database Analytics and Employee Productivity in Telecommunication Companies in South Nigeria. *International Journal of Business & Entrepreneurship Research, 14.*

Bocar, A. C., Khan, S. A., & Epoc, F. (2022). COVID-19 Work from Home Stressors and the Degree of its Impact: Employers and Employees Actions. *International Journal of Technology Transfer and Commercialisation. Inderscience, 19*(2), 270–291.

Bockstael, A., De Winne, S., & Sels, L. (2018). HR analytics: The intersection between people and business. *Human Resource Management Review, 28*(3), 247–263. doi:10.1016/j.hrmr.2017.07.001

Bogen, M., & Rieke, A. (2018). Help Wanted: An Examination of Hiring Algorithms, Equity, and Bias. *Upturn.* https://www.upturn.org/reports/2018/hiring-algorithms/

Bogen, M., Rieke, A., & Ahmed, S. (2020, January). Awareness in practice: tensions in access to sensitive attribute data for antidiscrimination. In *Proceedings of the 2020 conference on fairness, accountability, and transparency* (pp. 492-500). ACM.10.1145/3351095.3372877

Bolino, M., Valcea, S., & Harvey, J. (2010). Employee, manage thyself: The potentially negative implications of expecting employees to behave proactively. *Journal of Occupational and Organizational Psychology, 83*(2), 325–345. doi:10.1348/096317910X493134

Bolliger, L., Lukan, J., Luštrek, M., De Bacquer, D., & Clays, E. (2020). Protocol of the STRess At Work (STRAW) project: How to disentangle day-to-day occupational stress among academics based on EMA, physiological data, and smartphone sensor and usage data. *International Journal of Environmental Research and Public Health, 17*(23), 8835. doi:10.3390/ijerph17238835 PMID:33561061

Bosch limited steps into 2021 as a great place to work – Certified ™. (n.d.). Bosch Media Service. https://www.bosch-press.in/pressportal/in/en/press-release-3968.html.

Bose, I. & Jose, D. (2018, February 2018). Evolution of Human Resource Analytics. *AIMA Journal of Management & Research, 12* (1/4). Retrieved from https://www.chrmp.com/the-evolution-of-hr-analytics/

Boselie, P., Paauwe, J., & Jansen, P. (2000). *Human Resource Management and Performance.*

Boselie, P. (2014). *Strategic Human Resource Management: A Balanced Approach* (2nd ed.). McGraw-Hill Education.

Boudreau, J. W., & Ramstad, P. M. (2005). Beyond HR metrics: HR analytics. *Human Resource Management, 44*(3), 395–408.

Boudreau, J. W., & Ramstad, P. M. (2005). Talentship, talent segmentation, and sustainability: A new HR decision science paradigm for a new strategy definition. *Human Resource Management, 44*(2), 129–136. doi:10.1002/hrm.20054

Breaugh, J. A. (2008). Employee recruitment: Current knowledge and important areas for future research. *Human Resource Management Review, 18*(3), 103–118. doi:10.1016/j.hrmr.2008.07.003

Breevaart, K., Lopez Bohle, S., Pletzer, J. L., & Munoz Medina, F. (2020). Voice and silence as immediate consequences of job insecurity. *Career Development International*, *25*(2), 204–220. doi:10.1108/CDI-09-2018-0226

Brinsfield, C. T., Edwards, M. S., & Greenberg, J. (2009). Voice and silence in organisations: Historical review and current conceptualizations. *Voice and silence in organisations.*

Briody, J., Doyle, O., & Kelleher, C. (2020). The effect of local unemployment on health: A longitudinal study of Irish mothers 2001-2011. *Economics and Human Biology*, *37*, 100859. doi:10.1016/j.ehb.2020.100859 PMID:32114328

Brockner, J. (1988). The effects of work layoffs on survivors: Research, theory, and practice. *Research in Organizational Behavior*, *10*, 213–255.

Brockner, J., Grover, S., Reed, T., DeWitt, R., & O'Malley, M. (1987). Survivors' reactions to layoffs: We get by with a little help for our friends. *Administrative Science Quarterly*, *32*(4), 526–541. doi:10.2307/2392882

Brockner, J., & Lee, R. J. (1995). Career development in downsizing organizations: A self-affirmation analysis. In M. London (Ed.), *Employees, careers, and job creation: Developing growth-oriented human resource strategies and programs* (p. 51). Jossey-Bass.

Brouer, R., Badawy, R., & Stefanone, M. (2022). Social media and recruitment: Examining (counter) productive diversity messages. *Organizational Management Journal*, *19*(1), 34–43. doi:10.1108/OMJ-09-2020-1029

Brown, M. I. (2020). Comparing the validity of net promoter and benchmark scoring to other commonly used employee engagement metrics. *Human Resource Development Quarterly*, *31*(4), 355–370. doi:10.1002/hrdq.21392

Bruce, L., Bellesini, K., Aisbett, B., Drinkwater, E. J., & Kremer, P. (2022). A profile of the skills, attributes, development, and employment opportunities for sport scientists in Australia. *Journal of Science and Medicine in Sport*, *25*(5), 419–424. doi:10.1016/j.jsams.2021.12.009 PMID:35190264

Buch, K., & Aldridge, J. (1991). O.D. under conditions of organization decline. *Organization Development Journal*, *9*(1), 1–5. PMID:1996536

Budhwar, P. S., Luthar, H. K., & Bhatnagar, J. (2006). The dynamics of HRM systems in Indian BPO firms. *Journal of Labor Research*, *27*(3), 339–360. doi:10.100712122-006-1027-7

Budhwar, P., Malik, A., De Silva, M. T., & Thevisuthan, P. (2022). Artificial intelligence–challenges and opportunities for international HRM: A review and research agenda. *International Journal of Human Resource Management*, *33*(6), 1065–1097. doi:10.1080/09585192.2022.2035161

Budros, A. (1999). A conceptual framework for analyzing why organizations downsize. *Organization Science*, *10*(1), 69–82. doi:10.1287/orsc.10.1.69

Calvard, T. S., & Jeske, D. (2018). Developing human resource data risk management in the age of big data. *International Journal of Information Management*, *43*, 159–164. doi:10.1016/j.ijinfomgt.2018.07.011

Cameron, K. S., & Spreitzer, G. M. (2012). *The Oxford handbook of positive organizational scholarship*. Oxford University Press., https://psycnet.apa.org/record/2011-19765-000

Carada, I. G., Aliazas, J., Palacio, L., & Palacio, C. (2022). Perceived Skills and Employability of Senior High School Graduates: Basis for Youth Employment Policy. *International Journal of Social Sciences and Humanities Invention*, 6759-6766. . doi:10.18535/ijsshi/v9i01.05

Cascio, W. F., & Boudreau, J. W. (2011). Investing in people: Financial impact of human resource initiatives. Upper Saddle River, NJ: FT press.

Cascio, W. F. (2006). The costly business of employee turnover. *The Academy of Management Perspectives*, *20*(3), 36–37. doi:10.5465/amp.2006.21318917

Cascio, W. F., Chatrath, A., & Christie-David, R. A. (2021). Antecedents and consequences of employee and asset restructuring. *Academy of Management Journal*, *64*(2), 587–613. doi:10.5465/amj.2018.1013

Cascio, W. F., Young, C. E., & Morris, J. R. (1997). Financial consequences of employment-change decisions in major US corporations. *Academy of Management Journal*, *40*(5), 1175–1189. doi:10.2307/256931

Casu, G., Mariani, M. G., Chiesa, R., Guglielmi, D., & Gremigni, P. (2021). The role of organizational citizenship behaviour and gender between job satisfaction and task performance. *International Journal of Environmental Research and Public Health*, *18*(18), 9499. doi:10.3390/ijerph18189499 PMID:34574423

Catteeuw, F., Flynn, E., & Vonderhorst, J. (2007). Employee engagement: Boosting productivity in turbulent times. *Organization Development Journal*, *25*(2), 151–157.

Cavaliere, L. P. L., Nath, K., Wisetsri, W., Villalba-Condori, K. O., Arias-Chavez, D., Setiawan, R., & Regin, R. (2021). *The impact of E-recruitment and artificial intelligence (AI) tools on HR effectiveness: the case of high schools* [Doctoral dissertation, Petra Christian University].

Cayrat, C., & Boxall, P. (2022). Exploring the phenomenon of HR analytics: a study of challenges, risks and impacts in 40 large companies. *Journal of Organizational Effectiveness: People and Performance*.

Chambel, M. J., & Farina, A. (2015). HRM and temporary workers' well-being: A study in Portugal and Brazil. *Cross Cultural Management*, *22*(3), 447–463. doi:10.1108/CCM-07-2013-0105

Charles Cayrat, P. B. (2022). Exploring the phenomenon of HR analytics: a study of challenges, risks and impacts in 40 large companies. *Journal of Organizational Effectiveness: People and Performance*, 572-590.

Charmaz, K. (2006). *Constructing grounded theory: A practical guide through qualitative analysis.* sage.

Charoensukmongkol, P., & Puyod, J. V. (2022). Mindfulness and emotional exhaustion in call centre agents in the Philippines: Moderating roles of work and personal characteristics. *The Journal of General Psychology*, *149*(1), 72–96. doi:10.1080/00221309.2020.1800582 PMID:32748707

Charoensukmongkol, P., & Suthatorn, P. (2018). Salespeople's trait mindfulness and emotional exhaustion: The mediating roles of optimism, resilience, and self-efficacy. International Journal of Services. *Economics and Management*, *9*(2), 125–142. doi:10.1504/IJSEM.2018.096075

Chartered institute of personnel and development. (2003). *Understanding the people and performance link: unlocking the black box.* London: CIPD.

Chatterjee, S., Chaudhuri, R., Vrontis, D., & Siachou, E. (2022). Examining the dark side of human resource analytics: An empirical investigation using the privacy calculus approach. *International Journal of Manpower*, *43*(1), 52–74. doi:10.1108/IJM-02-2021-0087

Chen, F., Curran, P. J., Bollen, K. A., Kirby, J., & Paxton, P. (2008). An empirical evaluation of the use of fixed cutoff points in RMSEA test statistic in structural equation models. *Sociological Methods & Research*, *36*(4), 462–494. doi:10.1177/0049124108314720 PMID:19756246

Chen, J. H., Lin, J. Z., & Hsu, S. C. (2014). Determining and classifying factors of employees' expatriation willingness using rough set theory. *Journal of Management Engineering*, *30*(5), 04014021. doi:10.1061/(ASCE)ME.1943-5479.0000206

Chen, Y., & Tjosvold, D. (2018). Knowledge sharing, trust and employee retention: An exploratory study of a Chinese IT company. *International Journal of Human Resource Management, 29*(1), 141–159.

Chen, Y., Zhang, Z., Zhou, J., Liu, C., Zhang, X., & Yu, T. (2022). A cognitive evaluation and equity-based perspective of pay for performance on job performance: A meta-analysis and path model. *Frontiers in Psychology*, 13. PMID:36743591

Cheung, F. Y. L., Wu, A. M., & Ching Chi, L. (2019). Effect of job insecurity, anxiety and personal resources on job satisfaction among casino employees in macau: A moderated mediation analysis. *Journal of Hospitality Marketing & Management, 28*(3), 379–396. doi:10.1080/19368623.2019.1525332

Chhinzer, N., N., & Currie, E. (2014). Assessing longitudinal relationships between financial performance and downsizing. *Management Decision, 52*(8), 1474–1490. doi:10.1108/MD-05-2014-0280

Chith, E. N., Vaishnavi, J., Yusaira, F., & Kureethara, J. V. (2022). Psychological Barriers to Workplace Wellness in Young Married Women in Indian Higher Education. In IGI Global eBooks (pp. 43–60). doi:10.4018/978-1-7998-7693-9.ch003

Chitra, S., & Srivaramangai, P. (2018). A study on analytics of human resource management in big data. *International Journal of Scientific Research in Computer Science. Engineering and Information Technology, 3*(3), 58–68.

Choi, Y., & Dickson, D. R. (2010). A case study into the benefits of management training programs: Impacts on hotel employee turnover and satisfaction level. *Journal of Human Resources in Hospitality & Tourism, 9*(1), 103–116. doi:10.1080/15332840903336499

Choi, Y., Yoon, D. J., Lee, J. D., & Lee, J. Y. E. (2023). Relationship confict and counterproductive work behavior: The roles of affective well-being and emotional intelligence. *Review of Managerial Science*, 1–20. doi:10.100711846-023-00642-z

Choudhary, P., & Baskaran, K. (2022). The impact of Social Networking Sites among Modern Youth. *Interdisciplinary Research in Technology and Management, 2022*, 1–6. doi:10.1109/IRTM54583.2022.9791522

Choudhury, H. A., & Barman, A. (2016). *Human Resource Analytics-Discovering Research Issues Posited in its Milleu in India Organization.* Discovering Research Issues in Applications of HRA in India.

Christian, M. S., Garza, A. S., & Slaughter, J. E. (2011). Work engagement: A quantitative review and test of its relations with task and contextual performance. *Personnel Psychology, 64*(1), 89–136. doi:10.1111/j.1744-6570.2010.01203.x

Cindy, L. (2012). HR analytics: The next big thing, or a waste of time? *Strategic HR Review, 11*(4), 208–215. doi:10.1108/14754391211241116

CIPD. (2007). Employee Engagement. CIPD. www.cipd.co.uk/subjects/empreltns/general/empengmt.htm?IsSrchRes=1

Clark, L. A., & Bowles, M. A. (2018). The Personality Disorders An Integrated Approach. *Journal of Psychiatric Practice, 24*(6), 386–394. doi:10.1097/PRA.0000000000000339

Clark, L. A., & Bowles, R. P. (2018). Methodological issues in assessing differential item functioning in psychological tests. *Journal of Personality Assessment, 100*(4), 347–357.

Clements, K., & Turpin, G. (1995). Effects of feedback and task difficulty on electrodermal activity and heart rate: An examination of Fowles' three arousal model. *Journal of Psychophysiology.*

Cloutier, O., Felusiak, L., Hill, C., & Pemberton-Jones, E. J. (2015). The importance of developing strategies for employee retention. *Journal of Leadership, Accountability and Ethics, 12*(2).

Coker, D. (2016, May 12). Career development has the highest impact on employee retention. *The HR digest.* https://thehrdigest.com/career-development-highest-impact-employee-retention/

Conference Board (2006). Employee Engagement: A review of current research and its implications. *The Conference Board.*

Coris, G., & Zucchi, S. (2002). Qualità percepita in quattro servizi sanitari: Poliambulatorio di Orbassano, ASL 5-Collegno (TO). *Psicologia della Salute*, (2001/2).

Cox, T. H., & Blake, S. (1991). Managing cultural diversity: Implications for organizational competitiveness. *The Academy of Management Perspectives*, *5*(3), 45–56. doi:10.5465/ame.1991.4274465

Crail, C. (2022). 15 effective employee retention strategies in 2022. *Forbes Advisor*. https://www.forbes.com/advisor/business/employee-retention-strategies/

Crawford, E., Rich, B., Buckman, B., & Bergeron, J. (2013). The Antecedents and Drivers of Employee Engagement. In C. Truss, K. Alfes, R. Delbridge, A. Shantz, & E. Soane (Eds.), *Employee Engagement in Theory and Practice*. Routledge.

Cropanzano, R., Anthony, E. L., Daniels, S. R., & Hall, A. V. (2017). Social exchange theory: A critical review with theoretical remedies. *The Academy of Management Annals*, *11*(1), 479–516. doi:10.5465/annals.2015.0099

Crowe, L., & Butterworth, P. (2016). The role of financial hardship, mastery and social support in the association between employment status and depression: Results from an Australian longitudinal cohort study. *BMJ Open*, *6*(5), e009834. doi:10.1136/bmjopen-2015-009834 PMID:27235296

Cruzado, I. (2004). Organizational retention: the role of human resources management. *Journal of European Industrial Training*, *28*(2/3/4), 124-142. doi: . doi:10.1108/03090590410519568

Cruzado, I. (2004). Employee turnover intentions: A test of a cognitive model. *International Journal of Selection and Assessment*, *12*(1), 27–35. doi:10.1111/j.0965-075X.2004.00253.x

Cucchiella, F., Gastaldi, M., & Ranieri, L. (2014, September). Managing Absenteeism in the Workplace: The Case of an Italian Multiutility Company. *Procedia: Social and Behavioral Sciences*, *150*, 1157–1166. doi:10.1016/j.sbspro.2014.09.131

Cyriac, N. T., & Baskaran, K. (2020). A Study on the Effectiveness of Non-Monetary Retention Strategies in UAE. *International Conference on Reliability, Infocom Technologies and Optimization 2020*, IEEE. 10.1109/ICRITO48877.2020.9197867

Cyriac, N. T., & Baskaran, K. (2021). Predictive Analytics in a Post Covid-19 World: India's Travel and Tourism Industry. *International Conference on Advances in Technology, Management and Education 2021.* IEEE. 10.1109/ICATME50232.2021.9732706

Daniel, D. (2020). *People Analytics (HR analytics)*. Tech Target Network. https://www.techtarget.com/searchhrsoftware/definition/human-resources-analytics-talent-analytics

Dartey-Baah, K., & Amoako, G. K. (2011). Application of Frederick Herzberg's Two-Factor theory in assessing and understanding employee motivation at work: A Ghanaian Perspective. *European Journal of Business and Management*, *3*(9), 1–8.

Darvishmotevali, M., & Ali, F. (2020). Job insecurity, subjective well-being and job performance: The moderating role of psychological capital. *International Journal of Hospitality Management*, *87*, 102462. doi:10.1016/j.ijhm.2020.102462

Das, B. L., & Baruah, M. (2013). Employee retention: A review of literature. *IOSR Journal of Business and Management*, *14*(2), 8–16. doi:10.9790/487X-1420816

Dasgupta, G. (2023), Layoffs in 2023: Dunzo, Unacademy among Indian startups & tech companies that have cut jobs. *Economic Tours.* https://economictimes.indiatimes.com/tech/technology/layoffs-in-2023-a-list-of-indian-startups-tech-companies-that-have-cut-jobs/articleshow/97601464.cms?utm_source=contentofinterest&utm_medium=text&utm_campaign=cppst

Das, H. (1996). Retention policy: Whom to retain anyway? *Indian Journal of Industrial Relations*, *32*(2), 223–232.

Datta, D. K., Guthrie, J. P., Basuil, D., & Pandey, A. (2010). Causes and effects of employee downsizing: A review and synthesis. *Journal of Management*, *36*(1), 281–348. doi:10.1177/0149206309346735

Davenport, T. H., Harris, J., & Shapiro, J. (2010). Competing on talent analytics. *Harvard Business Review*, *88*(10), 52–58. PMID:20929194

David, F. D. (1989). Perceived Usefulness, Perceived Ease of Use, and User Acceptance of Information Technology. MIS Quarterly, 13(3), 319-340. doi:https://doi.org/10.2307/249008

Davidson, P. (2023, January 23), Layoffs in a likely recession this year could be determined by software programs. *USA Today*. https://www.usatoday.com/story/money/2023/01/23/layoffs-2023-recession-software-programs/11086842002/

De Cuyper, N., De Jong, J., De Witte, H., Isaksson, K., Rigotti, T., & Schalk, R. (2008). Literature review of theory and research on the psychological impact of temporary employment: Towards a conceptual model. *International Journal of Management Reviews*, *10*(1), 25–51. doi:10.1111/j.1468-2370.2007.00221.x

De Cuyper, N., Van Hootegem, A., Smet, K., Houben, E., & De Witte, H. (2019). All insecure, all good? Job insecurity profiles in relation to career correlates. *International Journal of Environmental Research and Public Health*, *16*(15), 2640. doi:10.3390/ijerph16152640 PMID:31344856

De Mauro, A., Greco, M., Grimaldi, M., & Ritala, P. (2018). Human resources for Big Data professions: A systematic classification of job roles and required skill sets. *Information Processing & Management*, *54*(5), 807–817. doi:10.1016/j.ipm.2017.05.004

De Meuse, K. P., & Marks, M. L. (2003). Resizing the organization : managing layoffs, divestitures, and closings : maximizing gain while minimizing pain. *The Jossey-Bass Business & Management Series*, 91.

De Meuse, K. P., & Dai, G. (2013). Organizational downsizing: Its effect on financial performance over time. *Journal of Managerial Issues*, 324–344.

De Villiers, J. R., & Stander, M. W. (2011). Psychological Empowerment, Work Engagement and Turnover Intention: The Role of Leader Relations and Role Clarity in a Financial Institution. *Journal of Psychology in Africa*, *21*(3), 405–412. doi:10.1080/14330237.2011.10820474

De Vos, A., & Meganck, A. (2008). Human resource management and performance in a globalizing business environment: A Belgian perspective. *International Journal of Human Resource Management*, *19*(9), 1636–1650. doi:10.1080/09585190802290289

De Witte, H., De Cuyper, N., Handaja, Y., Sverke, M., Näswall, K., & Hellgren, J. (2010). Associations between quantitative and qualitative job insecurity and well-being: A test in Belgian banks. *International Studies of Management & Organization*, *40*(1), 40–56. doi:10.2753/IMO0020-8825400103

Deci, E. L., & Ryan, R. M. (2008). Self-determination theory: A macrotheory of human motivation, development, and health. *Canadian Psychology*, *49*(3), 182–185. doi:10.1037/a0012801

Deery, M. (2008). Talent management, work-life balance and retention strategies. International journal of contemporary hospitality management, 20(7), 792-806.

Deery, S. J., Iverson, R. D., Walsh, J. T., & Jacobsen, D. I. (2020). Talent retention in the face of technological change: The role of psychological contract breach and innovation. *Journal of Business Research*, *117*, 689–699.

Del Giudice, M., Chierici, R., Mazzucchelli, A., & Fiano, F. (2021). Supply chain management in the era of circular economy: The moderating effect of big data. *International Journal of Logistics Management*, *32*(2), 337–356. doi:10.1108/IJLM-03-2020-0119

Deloitte India. (2018). *Human Capital Trends Report*. Deloitte. https://www2.deloitte.com/in/en/pages/about-deloitte/articles/human-capital-trends.html

Deloitte. (2017). *Global Human Capital Trends 2017*. Deloitte. https://www2.deloitte.com/global/en/pages/human-capital/articles/introduction-human-capital-trends.html

Deloitte. (2017). *Redesigning performance management*. Deloitte insights. https://www2. deloitte.com/insights/us/en/focus/human-capital-trends/2017/redesigning-performancemanagement.html

Deloitte. (2018). *Global Human Capital Trends report*. Deloitte. https://www2.deloitte.com/us/en/insights/focus/human-capital-trends/2018.html

Demerouti, E., Bakker, A. B., Nachreiner, F., & Schaufeli, W. B. (2001). The Job Demands–Resources Model of Burnout. *The Journal of Applied Psychology*, *86*(3), 499–512. doi:10.1037/0021-9010.86.3.499 PMID:11419809

Deshpande, A., & Kumar, S. (2019). HR Analytics in India: Challenges and Solutions. *Journal of Human Resource Management*, *7*(1), 1–10.

DiMaria, C. H., Peroni, C., & Sarracino, F. (2020). Happiness matters: Productivity gains from subjective well-being. *Journal of Happiness Studies*, *21*(1), 139–160. doi:10.100710902-019-00074-1

Dimitris, B., & Nathan, K. (2019). From Predictive to Prescriptive Analytics. Management Science, 1025-1044.

Dinçer, H., & Yüksel, S. (Eds.). (2018). *Handbook of research on managerial thinking in global business economics*. IGI Global.

Dixon-Fyle, S., Dolan, K., Hunt, V., & Prince, S. (2020). *How diversity, equity, and inclusion (DE&I) matter*. McKinsey. https://www.mckinsey.com/featured-insights/diversity-and-inclusion/diversity-wins-how-inclusion-matters

Dobbin, F., & Kalev, A. (2016). Why diversity programs fail. *Harvard Business Review*, *94*(7), 14.

Dobbs, K. (2000). Tires Plus takes the training high road. *Training (New York, N.Y.)*, *37*(4), 56–63.

Donaldson, S. I., Donaldson, S. I., Chan, L., & Kang, K. W. (2022). Positive psychological capital (PsyCap) meets multitrait-multimethod Analysis: Is PsyCap a robust predictor of well-being and performance controlling for self-report bias? *International Journal of Applied Positive Psychology*, *7*(2), 191–205. doi:10.100741042-021-00060-0

Dooren, J. V. (2012). *HR Analytics in Practice*. [Master Thesis] http://arno.uvt.nl/show.cgi?fid=127276

Durai, S., Rudhramoorthy, K., & Sarkar, S. (2019). HR metrics and workforce analytics: It is a journey, not a destination. *Human Resource Management International Digest*, *27*(1), 4–6. doi:10.1108/HRMID-08-2018-0167

Dutta, A. B., & Banerjee, S. (2014). Study of employee retention. *International Journal of Business Management & Research*, *4*(1), 83–88.

Edwards, M. R. (2019). HR metrics and analytics. In e-HRM (pp. 89-105). Routledge.

Edwards, J. R., & Edwards, A. L. (2016). Human resources analytics: From small data to big data. In *Big data in organizations and the role of human resource management* (pp. 145–168). Edward Elgar Publishing.

Edwards, M. R., & Edwards, K. (2016). *Predictive HR analytics: Mastering the HR metric*. Kogan Page.

El-Amin, A. (2022). Organizational climate change: diversity, equity, inclusion, and belonging. In Implementing Diversity, Equity, Inclusion, and Belonging Management in Organizational Change Initiatives (pp. 1-23). IGI Global. doi:10.4018/978-1-6684-4023-0.ch001

El-Deeb, A. (2023). The First Tech Layoff Wave After Years of Hypergrowth. *Software Engineering Notes*, *48*(1), 4–5. doi:10.1145/3573074.3573075

Employee engagement: Strategies, models and best practices. (2020). Valamis. https://www.valamis.com/hub/employee-engagement#employee-engagement-activities

Employee grievance and Redressal: Ensuring a fair and harmonious workplace. (2023). HR Informative. https://hrinformative.com/employee-grievance-and-redressal/

Enderle, R. (2016, September 02). *How analytics could end layoffs* CIO. https://www.cio.com/article/239041/how-analytics-could-end-layoffs.html

Enders, F. T., Golembiewski, E. H., Pacheco-Spann, L. M., Allyse, M., Mielke, M. M., & Balls-Berry, J. E. (2021). Building a framework for inclusion in health services research: Development of and pre-implementation faculty and staff attitudes toward the Diversity, Equity, and Inclusion (DEI) plan at Mayo Clinic. *Journal of Clinical and Translational Science*, *5*(1), e88. doi:10.1017/cts.2020.575 PMID:34007470

Erez, A., & Isen, A. M. (2002). The influence of positive affect on the components of expectancy motivation. *The Journal of Applied Psychology*, *87*(6), 1055–1067. doi:10.1037/0021-9010.87.6.1055 PMID:12558213

Erickson, R. A. (2015). Communication and employee retention. *The international encyclopedia of interpersonal communication*, 1–10.

Ertürk, A. (2007). Layoff Survivors' Perceptions Of Fairness As Determinant Of Affective Commitment Following Downsizing, *Bogazici Journal, Review of Social. Economic and Administrative Studies*, *21*(1+2), 37–58.

Estes, Z., & Michael, J. (2005). The impact of compensation structure on employee turnover: A case study analysis. *Journal of Applied Business Research*, *21*(3), 95–102.

ETHRSEA. (2022). More than 70% organisations are using workforce analytics for cost-saving and improved decision-making: Survey. HRSEA. https://hrsea.economictimes.indiatimes.com/news/industry/more-than-70-organisations-are-using-workforce-analytics-for-cost-saving-and-improved-decision-making-survey/95282155

Evans-Lacko, S., & Knapp, M. (2016, September 26). Global patterns of workplace productivity for people with depression: Absenteeism and presenteeism costs across eight diverse countries. *Social Psychiatry and Psychiatric Epidemiology*, *51*(11), 1525–1537. doi:10.100700127-016-1278-4 PMID:27667656

Eyster, L. A., Johnson, R. W., & Toder, E. J. (2008). The cost of employee turnover to employers. *Employee Benefits Research Institute Issue Brief*, (313), 1–23.

Eyster, L., Johnson, R. C., & Toder, E. (2008). Retirement income for those with nontraditional careers. *Tax Notes*, *119*(8), 727–736.

Fabrigar, L. R., Wegener, D. T., MacCallum, R. C., & Strahan, E. J. (1999). Evaluating the use of exploratory factor analysis in psychological research. *Psychological Methods*, *4*(3), 272–299. doi:10.1037/1082-989X.4.3.272

Fadhil, S. S., Ismail, R., & Alnoor, A. (2021). The influence of soft skills on employability: A Case study on technology industry sector in Malaysia. *Interdisciplinary Journal of Information, Knowledge, and Management*, *16*, 255–283. doi:10.28945/4807

Fajaryati, N., Budiyono, M. A., Akhyar, M., & Wiranto. (2020). The Employability Skills Needed To Face the Demands of Work in the Future: Systematic Literature Reviews. *Open Engineering, 10*(1), 595–603. doi:10.1515/eng-2020-0072

Falletta, S. (2014). In search of HR intelligence: Evidence-based HR analytics practices in high performing companies. *People and Strategy, 36*(4), 28.

Falletta, S. V., & Combs, W. L. (2021). The HR analytics cycle: A seven-step process for building evidence-based and ethical HR analytics capabilities. *Journal of Work-Applied Management, 13*(1), 51–68. doi:10.1108/JWAM-03-2020-0020

Fennell, A. (2022). *StandOut CV.* Standout DV. https://standout-cv.com/social-media-recruitment-statistics

Ferguson, S., & Sutphin, L. (2022). Analyzing the impact on teacher preparedness as a result of using Mursion as a risk-free microteaching experience for pre-service teachers. *Journal of Educational Technology Systems, 50*(4), 432–447. doi:10.1177/00472395211067731

Fernandez, V., & Gallardo-Gallardo, E. (2021). Tackling the HR digitalization challenge: key factors and barriers to HR analytics adoption. *Competitiveness Review*, 162-187.

Fernandez, V., & Gallardo-Gallardo, E. (2021). Tackling the HR digitalization challenge: Key factors and barriers to HR analytics adoption. *Competitiveness Review, 31*(1), 162–187. doi:10.1108/CR-12-2019-0163

Festing, M., & Schäfer, L. (2014). Generational challenges to talent management: A framework for talent retention based on the psychological-contract perspective. *Journal of World Business, 49*(2), 262–271. doi:10.1016/j.jwb.2013.11.010

Fisher, C. D. (2010). Happiness at Work. *International Journal of Management Reviews, 12*(4), 384–412. doi:10.1111/j.1468-2370.2009.00270.x

Fitz-enz, J., & Mattox, J. R. (2014). *Predictive analytics for human resources.* Forbes. https://www.forbes.com/sites/sap/2018/08/17/how-predictive-analytics-is-changing-the-hr-game/?sh=2dc8d1bf2957

Fitz-enz, J. (1984). *How to measure human resources management.* McGraw-Hill.

Fitz-Enz, J. (2010). *The new HR analytics.* American Management Association.

Fitz-Enz, J., & John Mattox, I. I. (2014). *Predictive analytics for human resources.* John Wiley & Sons. doi:10.1002/9781118915042

Flanagan, D. J., & O'Shaughnessy, K. C. (2005). The effect of layoffs on firm reputation. *Journal of Management, 31*(3), 445–463. doi:10.1177/0149206304272186

Formanek, K., & Formanek, K. (2021). Measuring and Monitoring the Vital Signs of Diversity. *Beyond D&I: Leading Diversity with Purpose and Inclusiveness*, 239-260.

Forseth, N. (2023). 19 employee engagement activities that keep employees happy. *When I work.* https://wheniwork.com/blog/employee-engagement-activities

Fox, R. J. (2012). *A Study of Employee Retention Issues in the Hospitality Industry* [Doctoral dissertation, University of Wisconsin Stout].

Frai, J. J., & László, V. (2021). A literature review: Artificial intelligence impact on the recruitment process. *International Journal of Engineering and Management Sciences, 6*(1), 108–119. doi:10.21791/IJEMS.2021.1.10.

Frazzetto, D. N. (2019). Prescriptive analytics: a survey of emerging trends and technologies. The VLDB Journal, 575-595.

Fredrickson, B. L. (2001). The role of positive emotions in positive psychology: The broaden-and- build theory of positive emotions. *The American Psychologist, 56*(3), 218–226. doi:10.1037/0003-066X.56.3.218 PMID:11315248

Freeman, S. J. (1994). Organizational downsizing as convergence or reorientation: Implications for human resource management. *Human Resource Management*, *33*(2), 213–238. doi:10.1002/hrm.3930330205

Frey, B. S. (1993). Does monitoring increase work effort? The rivalry with trust and loyalty. *Economic Inquiry*, *31*(4), 663–670. doi:10.1111/j.1465-7295.1993.tb00897.x

Fried, Y., & Ferris, G. R. (1987). The Validity of the Job Characteristics Model:A Review and Meta--Analysis. *Personnel Psychology*, *40*(2), 287–322. doi:10.1111/j.1744-6570.1987.tb00605.x

Gagne, M., & Deci, E. L. (2005). Self-determination theory and work motivation. *Journal of Organizational Behavior*, *26*(4), 331–362. doi:10.1002/job.322

Gallup, I. (2013). *State of the Global Workplace 2013*. Gallup. https://www.gallup.com/topic/STATE_OF_THE_GLOBAL_WORKPLACE_2013.aspx

Gallup. (2006). Gallup study: engaged employees inspire company innovation: national survey finds that passionate workers are most likely to drive organisations forward, *The Gallup Management Journal*, http://gmj.gallup.com/content/24880/Gallup-Study- Engaged-Employees-Inspire-Company.aspx

Garcia-Sanchez, I.-M., Raimo, N., & Vitolla, F. (2020). CEO power and integrated reporting, In Press, *Meditari. Accountability in Research*. doi:10.1108/MEDAR-11-2019-0604

Garg, A., Gaur, S., & Sharma, P. (2021). A Review Paper: Role of Artificial Intelligence in Recruitment Process. *Anwesh*, *6*(1), 33.

Garnett, J. L., Marlowe, J., & Pandey, S. K. (2008). Penetrating the performance predicament: Communication as a mediator or moderator of organizational culture's impact on public organizational performance. *Public Administration Review*, *68*(2), 266–281. doi:10.1111/j.1540-6210.2007.00861.x

Garrido, L. E., Abad, F. J., & Ponsoda, V. (2016). A new look at Horn's parallel analysis with ordinal variables. *Psychological Methods*, *21*(3), 362–384. doi:10.1037/met0000076 PMID:23046000

Gartner for HR. (2020). *HR Data and AI Ethics*. Gartner. https://www.gartner.com/en/human-resources/trends/data-ai-ethics-hr

Geetha, R., & Bhanu, S. R. D. (2018). Recruitment through artificial intelligence: A conceptual study. *International Journal of Mechanical Engineering and Technology*, *9*(7), 63–70.

Ghatak, R. (2022). People Analytics in Mergers and Acquisitions. In People Analytics: Data to Decisions (pp. 135-141). Singapore: Springer Nature Singapore. doi:10.1007/978-981-19-3873-3_8

Gie Yong, A. G., & Pearce, S. (2013). A Beginner's Guide to Factor Analysis: Focusing on Exploratory Factor Analysis. *Tutorials in Quantitative Methods for Psychology*, *9*(2), 79–94. doi:10.20982/tqmp.09.2.p079

Giermindl, L. M., Strich, F., Christ, O., Leicht-Deobald, U., & Redzepi, A. (2022). The dark sides of people analytics: Reviewing the perils for organisations and employees. *European Journal of Information Systems*, *31*(3), 410–435. doi: 10.1080/0960085X.2021.1927213

Gîlmeanu, R. (2015). Theoretical considerations on motivation at the workplace, job satisfaction and individual performance. *Valahian. Journal of Economic Studies (Glasgow, Scotland)*, *6*(3), 69.

Goldberg, C. B., Clark, M. A., & Henley, A. B. (2011). Speaking up: A conceptual model of voice responses following the unfair treatment of others in non-union settings. *Human Resource Management*, *50*(1), 75–94. doi:10.1002/hrm.20402

Gong, Y., Zhao, M., Wang, Q., & Lv, Z. (2022). Design and interactive performance of human resource management system based on artificial intelligence. *PLoS One*, *17*(1), e0262398. doi:10.1371/journal.pone.0262398 PMID:35089946

Good, D. J., Lyddy, C. J., Glomb, T. M., Bono, J. E., Brown, K. W., Duffy, M. K., Baer, R. A., Brewer, J. A., & Lazar, S. W. (2016). Contemplating mindfulness at work: An integrative review. *Journal of Management*, *42*(1), 114–142. doi:10.1177/0149206315617003

Gopinath, C. (2003). Managing the Effects of Divestiture and Layoffs on Employees. Handbook of Business Strategy, 4(1). Emerald. doi:10.1108/eb060260

Gorgievski, M., & Moriano, J. (2014). (forthcoming). Relating Work Engagement and Workaholism to Entrepreneurial Performance. *Journal of Managerial Psychology*, *29*. doi:10.1108/JMP-06-2012-0169

Gorovei, A. A. (2020). Does work make you happy? Job satisfaction and happiness in the modern world. *Revista Economica*, *72*(1). http://economice.ulbsibiu.ro/revista.economica/archive/72108gorovei.pdf

Goslinga, S. (2017). Job insecurity, union participation and the need for (new) union services. In *Job insecurity, union involvement and union activism* (pp. 81–96). Routledge. doi:10.4324/9781351154925-5

Gracia, E., Bakker, A. B., & Grau, R. M. (2011). Positive emotions: The connection between customer quality evaluations and loyalty. *Cornell Hospitality Quarterly*, *52*(4), 458–465. doi:10.1177/1938965510395379

Gray, R. (2022). The 3 Human Capital Metrics Your Small Business Needs to Track Patriot Software. *Patriots of Software.* https://www.patriotsoftware.com/blog/accounting/human-capital-metrics-roi-measurement/

Greasley, K., & Thomas, P. (2020). HR analytics: The onto-epistemology and politics of metricised HRM. *Human Resource Management Journal*, *30*(4), 494–507. doi:10.1111/1748-8583.12283

Green, D. (2017). The best practices to excel at people analytics. *Journal of Organizational Effectiveness: People and Performance*, *4*(2), 137–144. doi:10.1108/JOEPP-03-2017-0027

Griffin, R. W., & Moorhead, G. (2011). *Organizational behavior*. Cengage Learning.

Groysberg, B., Nohria, N., & Fernández-Araoz, C. (2009). The definitive guide to recruiting in good times and bad. *Harvard Business Review*, 74–84.

Guanxi, L., Xiaoming, Z., & Shuling, Z. (2019). The impact of people analytics on job performance: The moderating role of job satisfaction. *Journal of Retailing and Consumer Services*, *50*, 369–376.

Gubman, E. (2010). From HR to strategic talent management. *Journal of Organizational Excellence*, *29*(4), 23–33.

Guerra, J. M. M., Danvila-del-Valle, I., & Méndez-Suárez, M. (2023). The impact of digital transformation on talent management. *Technological Forecasting and Social Change*, *188*, 122291. doi:10.1016/j.techfore.2022.122291

Gulzar, S., Advani, A., & Jalees, T. (2017). Impact of Performance Appraisal on Employee Retention: A study on Banking Sector of Pakistan. *JISR Management and Social Sciences & Economics*, *15*(1), 85–101. doi:10.31384/jisrmsse/2017.15.1.6

Gupta, A., & Mishra, M. (2023). Artificial Intelligence for Recruitment and Selection. In The Adoption and Effect of Artificial Intelligence on Human Resources Management, Part B (pp. 1-11). Emerald Publishing Limited. doi:10.1108/978-1-80455-662-720230001

Gupta, A., & Sharma, N. (2022). The impact of total rewards on employee retention: A meta-analysis. *Journal of Business Research*, *143*, 565–576.

Gupta, N., & Sharma, V. (2016). Exploring Employee Engagement – A Way to Better Business Performance. *Global Business Review*, *17*(3), 45–63. doi:10.1177/0972150916631082

Gupta, P. (2015). *XISS, R.* Human Resource Analytics in Indian Banking Sector.

Guttman, L. (1954). A new approach to factor analysis: The radex. In P. F. Lazarsfeld (Ed.), *Mathematical thinking in the social sciences* (pp. 258–348). Free Press.

Guttman, L. (1954). Some necessary conditions for common-factor analysis. *Psychometrika*, *19*(2), 149–161. doi:10.1007/BF02289162

Haapakorpi, A. (2020). Freedom but insecurity: The business consulting profession in the post-industrial service society. *Nordic Journal of Working Life Studies*, *11*(1), 45–62. doi:10.18291/njwls.122225

Hackman, J. R., & Oldham, G. R. (1980). *Work redesign*. AddisonWesley.

Hair, J. F., Black, W. C., Babin, B. J., Anderson, R. E., & Tatham, R. L. (2006). *Multivariate data analysis* (Vol. 6). Pearson Prentice Hall.

Halawani, L. A., Halawani, M. A., & Beyari, G. M. (2021). Job satisfaction among Saudi healthcare workers and its impact on the quality of health services. *Journal of Family Medicine and Primary Care*, *10*(5), 1873. doi:10.4103/jfmpc.jfmpc_2236_20 PMID:34195119

Halbesleben, J. R., Whitman, M. V., & Crawford, W. S. (2014, June). A dialectical theory of the decision to go to work: Bringing together absenteeism and presenteeism. *Human Resource Management Review*, *24*(2), 177–192. doi:10.1016/j.hrmr.2013.09.001

Hallock, K. F. (2006; Vol. 25). Layoffs in Large U.S. Firms from the Perspective of Senior Managers. In Research in Personnel and Human Resources Management. doi:10.1016/S0742-7301(06)25004-7

Hamid, Z., & Shah, S. A. (2023). Juxtaposition of Traditional and Modern Methods of Performance Appraisal in Organizations. In *Promoting Organizational Performance Through 5G and Agile Marketing* (pp. 245–266). IGI Global.

Harter, J. K., Schmidt, F. L., & Hayes, T. L. (2002). Business-unit-level relationship between employee satisfaction, employee engagement, and business outcomes: A meta-analysis. *The Journal of Applied Psychology*, *87*(2), 268–279. doi:10.1037/0021-9010.87.2.268 PMID:12002955

Hartog, D. N., & Verburg, R. M. (2004, January). High performance work systems, organisational culture and firm effectiveness. *Human Resource Management Journal*, *14*(1), 55–78. doi:10.1111/j.1748-8583.2004.tb00112.x

Harvard Business School Press. (2006). *Retaining Your Best People*. Harvard Business School Publishing Corporation.

Hassan, S., Ansari, N., & Rehman, A. (2022). An exploratory study of workplace spirituality and employee well-being affecting public service motivation: An institutional perspective. *Qualitative Research Journal*, *22*(2), 209–235. doi:10.1108/QRJ-07-2021-0078

Hastuti, R., & Timming, A. R. (2022). Can HRM predict mental health crises? Using HR analytics to unpack the link between employment and suicidal thoughts and behaviors. *Personnel Review*.

Hausknecht, J. P., & Holwerda, J. A. (2013). When does employee turnover matter? Dynamic member configurations, productive capacity, and collective performance. *Organization Science*, *24*(1), 210–225. doi:10.1287/orsc.1110.0720

HCMI. (2022). *Employee Engagement Analytics: How to Engage and Retain Talent.* HCMI. https://www.hcmi.co/post/employee-engagement-analytics-how-to-engage-and-retain-talent

He, G. (2023). Layoff Best Practices: How to Lay Off Employees with Dignity. *Team Building.* https://teambuilding.com/blog/layoff-best-practices

Hemalatha, A., Kumari, P. B., Nawaz, N., & Gajenderan, V. (2021, March). Impact of artificial intelligence on recruitment and selection of information technology companies. In *2021 International Conference on Artificial Intelligence and Smart Systems (ICAIS)* (pp. 60-66). IEEE. 10.1109/ICAIS50930.2021.9396036

Herring, C. (2009). Does diversity pay? Race, gender, and the business case for diversity. *American Sociological Review, 74*(2), 208–224. doi:10.1177/000312240907400203

Heuvel, S. V., & Bondarouk, T. (2017). The rise (and fall?) of HR analytics: A study into the future application, value, structure, and system support. Journal of Organizational Effectiveness: People and Performance, 157-178.

Hirschman, A. O. (1970). *Exit, voice, and loyalty: Responses to decline in firms, organisations, and states* (Vol. 25). Harvard university press.

Hitt, M. A., Bierman, L., Shimizu, K., & Kochhar, R. (2001). Direct and moderating effects of human capital on strategy and performance in professional service firms: A resource-based perspective. *Academy of Management Journal, 44*(1), 13–28. doi:10.2307/3069334

Hmoud, B., & Laszlo, V. (2019). Will artificial intelligence take over human resources recruitment and selection. *Network Intelligence Studies, 7*(13), 21-30. https://www.pymetrics.ai/case-studies/significant-efficiency-gains

Hobfoll, S. E. (1989). Conservation of resources: A new attempt at conceptualizing stress. *The American Psychologist, 44*(3), 513–524. doi:10.1037/0003-066X.44.3.513 PMID:2648906

Hobfoll, S. E. (2011). Conservation of resource caravans and engaged settings. *Journal of Occupational and Organizational Psychology, 84*(1), 116–122. doi:10.1111/j.2044-8325.2010.02016.x

Hon, A. H., & Lu, L. (2010). The mediating role of trust between expatriate procedural justice and employee outcomes in Chinese hotel industry. *International Journal of Hospitality Management, 29*(4), 669–676. doi:10.1016/j.ijhm.2010.01.002

Hong, J., Hao, Y., Kumar, V., Ramendran, C., & Kadiresan, V. (2012). An empirical analysis of the factors affecting employee retention in Chinese state-owned enterprises. *Journal of Chinese Human Resource Management, 3*(2), 102–123. doi:10.1108/20408021211252555

Hou, J. DA, S., Wei, Y., & Zhang, X. (2022). Work-family conflict and withdrawal behaviour among mainland China's IT employees: the mediating role of emotional exhaustion and moderating role of job autonomy. Industrial Health, (pp. 2021-0136).

How to encourage career growth for employee retention and success. (n.d.). LinkedIn Learning. https://learning.linkedin.com/resources/learner-engagement/encourage-career-growth-employee-retention

HRMA. (2013) *Human Resources Management Association (HRMA).* HRMA. http://www.hrvoice.org

Huang, X., Yang, F., Zheng, J., Feng, C., & Zhang, L. (2023). *Personalized human resource management via HR analytics and artificial intelligence: Theory and implications.* Asia Pacific Management Review.

Huey Yiing, L., & Zaman Bin Ahmad, K. (2009). The moderating effects of organizational culture on the relationships between leadership behaviour and organizational commitment and between organizational commitment and job satisfaction and performance. *Leadership and Organization Development Journal, 30*(1), 53–86. doi:10.1108/01437730910927106

Hu, L. T., & Bentler, P. M. (1999). Cutoff criteria for fit indexes in covariance structure analysis: Conventional criteria versus new alternatives. *Structural Equation Modeling, 6*(1), 1–55. doi:10.1080/10705519909540118

Hülsheger, U. R., Feinholdt, A., & Nübold, A. (2015). A low-dose mindfulness intervention and recovery from work: Effects on psychological detachment, sleep quality, and sleep duration. *Journal of Occupational and Organizational Psychology*, *88*(3), 464–489. doi:10.1111/joop.12115

Humphrey, S. E., Nahrgang, J. D., & Morgeson, F. P. (2007). Integrating motivational, social, and contextual work design features: A meta-analytic summary and theoretical extension of the work design literature. *The Journal of Applied Psychology*, *92*(5), 1332–1356. doi:10.1037/0021-9010.92.5.1332 PMID:17845089

Hunt, V., Layton, D., & Prince, S. (2018). *Why diversity matters*. McKinsey & Company. https://www.mckinsey.com/business-functions/organization/our-insights/why-diversity-matters

Huselid, M. A. (1995). The impact of human resource management practices on turnover, productivity, and corporate financial performance. *Academy of Management Journal*, *38*(3), 635–672. doi:10.2307/256741

Huselid, M. A. (2018). The science and practice of workforce analytics: Introduction to the HRM special issue. *Human Resource Management*, *57*(3), 679–684. doi:10.1002/hrm.21916

IBEF. (2017). *Information Technology (IT) Sector in India: Market Size, Opportunities, Growth Prospects, & Investment Climate*. IBEF. https://www.ibef.org/industry/information-technology-india.aspx

IBM. (n.d.). *Big data analytics*. IBM. https://www.ibm.com/analytics/hadoop/big-data-analytics

IDeA. (2008). *What is Employee Engagement?* IDeA. www.idea.gov.uk/idk/core/page.do?pageId=8407178

Imran, M. Y., Elahi, N. S., Abid, G., Ashfaq, F., & Ilyas, S. (2020). Impact of perceived organizational support on work engagement: Mediating mechanism of thriving and flourishing. *Journal of Open Innovation*, *6*(3), 82. Advance online publication. doi:10.3390/joitmc6030082

Inanc, H. (2018). Unemployment, temporary work, and subjective well-being: The gendered effect of spousal labor market insecurity. *American Sociological Review*, *83*(3), 536–566. doi:10.1177/0003122418772061

Inc. (2020). *Best workplaces 2020*. Inc. https://www.inc.com/best-workplaces/2020.html

Indeed. (2019). The 10 Recruitment Metrics You Need to Know in 2019. *Indeed Blog*. https://www.indeed.com/hire/c/info/recruitment-metrics-you-need-to-know

Infosys. (2012). *Applying HR Analytics for Competitive Advantage*. Infosys. http://www.infosysblogs.com/management-consulting/2012/08/applying_hr_analytics_for_comp.html

Iqbal, S., Guohao, L., & Akhtar, S. (2017). Effects of job organizational culture, benefits, salary on job satisfaction ultimately affecting employee retention. *Review of Public Administration and Management*, *05*(3), 1–7. doi:10.4172/2315-7844.1000229

Isson, J. P., & Harriott, J. S. (2016). *People analytics in the era of big data: Changing the way you attract, acquire, develop, and retain talent*. John Wiley & Sons. doi:10.1002/9781119083856

Itam, U., & Bagali, M. M. (2019). Diversity and inclusion management: a focus on employee engagement. In Gender and Diversity: Concepts, Methodologies, Tools, and Applications (pp. 1771-1788). IGI Global. doi:10.4018/978-1-5225-6912-1.ch093

Jain, P. K., & Nagar, K. (2015). Human resource analytics: An overview. *Industrial and Commercial Training*, *47*(3), 152–158. doi:10.1108/ICT-06-2014-0044

Jain, P., & Bhatt, R. (2015). Talent management: A strategic approach towards growth in IT sector. *Procedia: Social and Behavioral Sciences*, *189*, 381–389. doi:10.1016/j.sbspro.2015.03.327

Jaiswar, S. (2023). Tech Layoffs: Over 2700 people lost their jobs per day so far in 2023.When will lay off winter end?" *Livemint*. https://www.livemint.com/companies/news/tech-layoffs-over-2-700-people-lost-their-jobs-per-day-so-far-in-2023-when-will-layoff-winter-end-11677339547907.html>

Jamison, F. (2020). People analytics in practice: connecting employee, customer, and operational data to create evidence-based decision making. In *Smart Service Systems, Operations Management, and Analytics: Proceedings of the 2019 INFORMS International Conference on Service Science* (pp. 223-228). Springer International Publishing. 10.1007/978-3-030-30967-1_20

Janssen, S., Tahitu, J., van Vuuren, M., & de Jong, M. (2016). Coworkers' Perspectives on Mentoring Relationships. *Group & Organization Management*, *43*(2), 245–272. doi:10.1177/1059601116669641 PMID:29568215

Jawahar Supraveen, S. S. U. (2022). HR Analytics - The Measurement of HR Processes using a Methodical Approach. *International Conference on Computer Communication and Informatics (ICCCI)*, Coimbatore, India. 10.1109/ICCCI54379.2022.9740999

Jensen, S., & McIntosh, J. (2006, July 4). Absenteeism in the workplace: Results from Danish sample survey data. *Empirical Economics*, *32*(1), 125–139. doi:10.100700181-006-0075-4

Jeske, D., & Calvard, T. (2020). Big data: lessons for employers and employees. *Employee Relations: The International Journal*.

Jha, S. K., Jha, S., & Gupta, M. K. (2020). Leveraging artificial intelligence for effective recruitment and selection processes. In *International Conference on Communication, Computing and Electronics Systems* [Springer Singapore.]. *Proceedings of ICCCES*, *2019*, 287–293.

Jia, J., Jiao, Y., Yan, J., Wang, J., & Jia, H. (2023). Evolution path and critical influencing factors of performance management system: A longitudinal case study in China. *Asia Pacific Business Review*, *29*(1), 50–69. doi:10.1080/13602381.2022.2076449

Jia, K., Zhu, T., Zhang, W., Rasool, S. F., Asghar, A., & Chin, T. (2022). The linkage between ethical leadership, well-Being, work engagement, and innovative work behavior: The empirical evidence from the higher education sector of China. *International Journal of Environmental Research and Public Health*, *19*(9), 1–15. doi:10.3390/ijerph19095414 PMID:35564809

Jiang, H., & Chen, C. (2021). Data Science Skills and Graduate Certificates: A Quantitative Text Analysis. *Journal of Computer Information Systems*, 1–17. doi:10.1080/08874417.2020.1852628

Johansson, J., & Herranen, S. (2019). *The application of artificial intelligence (AI) in human resource management: Current state of AI and its impact on the traditional recruitment process.*

Johnson, M. P., & Chichirau, G. R. (2020). Diversity, equity, and inclusion in operations research and analytics: A research agenda for scholarship, practice, and service. *Pushing the boundaries: Frontiers in impactful OR/OM research*, 1-38.

Jörden, N. M., Sage, D., & Trusson, C. (2022). 'It's so fake': Identity performances and cynicism within a people analytics team. *Human Resource Management Journal*, *32*(3), 524–539. doi:10.1111/1748-8583.12412

Juárez-Tarraga, A., Santandreu-Mascarell, C., & Marín-García, J. A. (2019). HRM practices and talent retention: The mediating role of organizational identification. *Journal of Business Research*, *99*, 473–481. doi:10.1016/j.jbusres.2019.01.050

Jurado-Gámez, B., Guglielmi, O., Gude, F., & Buela-Casal, G. (2015, May). Workplace Accidents, Absenteeism and Productivity in Patients With Sleep Apnea. *Archivos de Bronconeumología (English Ed.)*, *51*(5), 213–218. doi:10.1016/j.arbr.2014.12.002 PMID:25129165

Kabat-Zinn, J. (2003). Mindfulness-based interventions in context: Past, present, and future. *Clinical Psychology: Science and Practice*, *10*(2), 144–156. doi:10.1093/clipsy.bpg016

Kahn, A. (1990). Psychological conditions of personal engagement and disengagement at work. *Academy of Management Journal*, *33*(4), 692–724. doi:10.2307/256287

Kaiser, H. F. (1970). A second generation little jiffy. *Psychometrika*, *35*(4), 401–415. doi:10.1007/BF02291817

Kakulapati, S. S. V. (2023). Predictive Analytics of Employee Attrition using K-Fold Methodologies. *I. J. Mathematical Sciences and Computing*, 23-36.

Kale, N., & Anute, B. (2020). *HR Analytics and its Impact on Organizations Performance*. Research Gate.

Kaliannan, M., Darmalinggam, D., Dorasamy, M., & Abraham, M. (2022). Inclusive talent development as a key talent management approach: A systematic literature review. *Human Resource Management Review*, 100926.

Kalvakolanu, S., Madhavaiah, C., & Balaji, D. (2016, December). HR Analytics: The Emergence and Growth. *5th International Conference on Managing Human Resources at the WorkplaceAt: SDMIMD, Mysore*. IEEE. 10.6084/m9.figshare.13601357

Kalvakolanu, S. (2022). Developing a scale to assess analytical competencies of HR professionals. *International Journal of Business Information Systems*, *41*(3), 322–341. doi:10.1504/IJBIS.2022.126997

Kamal, S., Naim, A., Magd, H., Khan, S. A., & Khan, F. M. (2022). The Relationship Between E-Service Quality, Ease of Use, and E-CRM Performance Referred by Brand Image. In *Building a Brand Image Through Electronic Customer Relationship Management* (pp. 84–108). IGI Global. doi:10.4018/978-1-6684-5386-5.ch005

Kamel Barbar, R. C. (2019). The Impact of HR Analytics on the Training and Development Strategy - Private Sector Case Study in Lebanon. *Journal of Management and Strategy*, 27-36.

Kam, H.Tin Kam Ho. (1998). The random subspace method for constructing decision forests. *IEEE Transactions on Pattern Analysis and Machine Intelligence*, *20*(8), 832–844. doi:10.1109/34.709601

Kamiński, B., Jakubczyk, M., & Szufel, P. (2017, May 24). A framework for sensitivity analysis of decision trees. *Central European Journal of Operations Research*, *26*(1), 135–159. doi:10.100710100-017-0479-6 PMID:29375266

Kanungo, R. N. (1982). Measurement of job and work involvement. *The Journal of Applied Psychology*, *67*(3), 341–349. doi:10.1037/0021-9010.67.3.341

Karakhan, A. A., Gambatese, J. A., Simmons, D. R., & Al-Bayati, A. J. (2021). Identifying pertinent indicators for assessing and fostering diversity, equity, and inclusion of the construction workforce. *Journal of Management Engineering*, *37*(2), 04020114. doi:10.1061/(ASCE)ME.1943-5479.0000885

Karimi-Majd, A. M., Mahootchi, M., & Zakery, A. (2017). A reinforcement learning methodology for a human resource planning problem considering knowledge-based promotion. *Simulation Modelling Practice and Theory*, *79*, 87–99. doi:10.1016/j.simpat.2015.07.004

Karmańska, A. (2020). The benefits of HR analytics. *Prace Naukowe Uniwersytetu Ekonomicznego we Wrocławiu*, *64*(8), 30-39.

Karmańska, A. (2020). The benefits of HR analytics. *Prace Naukowe Uniwersytetu Ekonomicznego we Wrocławiu*,, 30-39.

Karren, R., & Sherman, K. (2012). Layoffs and unemployment discrimination: A new stigma. *Journal of Managerial Psychology*, *27*(8), 848–863. Advance online publication. doi:10.1108/02683941211280193

Kashyap, H. (2023, April 25). Indian Startup Layoff Tracker: 25,370+ Employees Laid Off Since 2022 Amid Funding Winter. *Inc42*. https://inc42.com/features/indian-startup-layoffs-tracker/

Kaur, R. (2017). Employee retention models and factors affecting employees retention in IT companies. *International Journal of Business Administration and Management*, *7*(1), 161–174.

Kaushal, N., Kaurav, R. P. S., Sivathanu, B., & Kaushik, N. (2021). Artificial intelligence and HRM: identifying future research Agenda using systematic literature review and bibliometric analysis. *Management Review Quarterly*, 1-39.

Kavyashree, S. K. (2022). Relationship between Human Resource Management Practices and Employee Engagement. *Brazilian Journal of Operations & Production Management*, 1331.

Keerthi, D. (2020, May 19). Grievance: Meaning, definitions, procedure, types, model, features. *Economics discussion*. https://www.economicsdiscussion.net/human-resource-management/grievance/grievance/32442

Kenny, D. A., Kaniskan, B., & McCoach, D. B. (2015). The performance of RMSEA in models with small degrees of freedom. *Sociological Methods & Research*, *44*(3), 486–507. doi:10.1177/0049124114543236

Kerr, J., & Slocum, J. Jr. (2005). Managing corporate culture through reward systems. *The Academy of Management Perspectives*, *19*(4), 130–138. doi:10.5465/ame.2005.19417915

Kets de Vries, M., & Balazs, K. (1997). The downside of downsizing. *Human Relations*, *50*(1), 11–51. doi:10.1177/001872679705000102

Khan, S.A, Epoc, F., Gangwar, V.P., Ligori T.A.A, & Ansari, Z.A. (2021). Will Online banking sustain in Bhutan post Covid – 19? A quantitative analysis of the customer e-satisfaction and e-loyalty in the Kingdom of Bhutan, *Transnational Marketing Journal*, *9*(3), 607-624. doi:10.33182/tmj.v9i3.1288

Khan. S.A. & Magd. H. (2021). Empirical Examination of MS Teams in Conducting Webinar: Evidence from International Online Program conducted in Oman. *Journal of Content, Community and Communication, 14*. doi:10.31620/JCCC.12.21/13

Khan, A. J., Bhatti, M. A., Hussain, A., Ahmad, R., & Iqbal, J. (2021). Employee Job Satisfaction in Higher Educational Institutes: A Review of Theories. *Journal of Southeast Asian Studies*, *9*(3), 257–266. doi:10.33687/jsas.009.03.3940

Khan, S. A. (2023). E-Marketing, E-Commerce, E-Business, and Internet of Things: An Overview of Terms in the Context of Small and Medium Enterprises (SMEs). In A. Naim & V. Devi (Eds.), *Global Applications of the Internet of Things in Digital Marketing* (pp. 332–348). IGI Global. doi:10.4018/978-1-6684-8166-0.ch017

Khan, S. A., Devi, T. P., Ligori, T. A. A., & Saleem, M. (2020). Customer Satisfaction and Customer Loyalty in Online Shopping: A Study on University Students of Bhutan. *Delhi Business Review.*, *21*(2), 11–22. doi:10.51768/dbr.v21i2.212202002

Khan, S. A., & Magd, H. (2023). New Technology Anxiety and Acceptance of Technology: An Appraisal of MS Teams. In *Advances in Distance Learning in Times of Pandemic* (pp. 105–134). CRC Press, Taylor and Francis. doi:10.1201/9781003322252-5

Khan, S. A., Magd, H., & Epoc, F. (2022). Application of Data Management System in Business to Business Electronic Commerce. In A. Naim & P. K. Malik (Eds.), *Competitive Trends and Technologies in Business Management* (pp. 109–124). Nova Science Publishers. [REMOVED HYPERLINK FIELD]

Khan, S. A., Magd, H., Khatri, B., Arora, S., & Sharma, N. (2023). Critical Success Factors of Internet of Things and Digital Marketing. In A. Naim & V. Devi (Eds.), *Global Applications of the Internet of Things in Digital Marketing* (pp. 233–253). IGI Global. doi:10.4018/978-1-6684-8166-0.ch012

Khan, S. A., & Rena, R. (2023). Emerging Green Practices, Internet of Things, and Digital Marketing: A Response to the Global Economic and Climate Crises. In A. Naim & V. Devi (Eds.), *Global Applications of the Internet of Things in Digital Marketing* (pp. 1–16). IGI Global. doi:10.4018/978-1-6684-8166-0.ch001

Kim, J., & Rhee, Y. (2011). Strategic Thinking about Employee Communication Behavior (ECB) in Public Relations: Testing the Models of Megaphoning and Scouting Effects in Korea. *Journal of Public Relations Research, 23*(3), 243–268. doi:10.1080/1062726X.2011.582204

Kim, K. W., & Cho, Y. H. (2020). The moderating effect of managerial roles on job stress and satisfaction by employees' employment type. *International Journal of Environmental Research and Public Health, 17*(21), 8259. doi:10.3390/ijerph17218259 PMID:33182275

Kim, Y. K., Kramer, A., & Pak, S. (2021). Job insecurity and subjective sleep quality: The role of spillover and gender. *Stress and Health, 37*(1), 72–92. doi:10.1002mi.2974 PMID:32790912

King, K. G. (2016). Data analytics in human resources: A case study and critical review. *Human Resource Development Review, 15*(4), 487–495. doi:10.1177/1534484316675818

Kirtane, A. (2015). corporate sustainable HR Analytical practices. *Journal of Management & Administration Tomorrow, 4*(1), 33–40.

Kivimäki, M., Vahtera, J., Pentti, J., & Ferrie, J. E. (2000). Factors underlying the effect of organisational downsizing on health of employees: Longitudinal cohort study. *BMJ (Clinical Research Ed.), 320*(7240), 971–975. doi:10.1136/bmj.320.7240.971 PMID:10753148

Klun, M. (2008). Corporate alumni programs: An emerging trend in talent management. *Journal of Management Policy and Practice, 9*(3), 1–10.

Klussman, K., Nichols, A. L., Langer, J., Curtin, N., & Lindeman, M. I. H. (2022). The relationship between mindfulness and subjective well-being: Examining the indirect effects of self-connection and meaning in life. *Applied Research in Quality of Life, 17*(4), 2423–2443. doi:10.100711482-021-10025-9

KM, N. D., & Christopher, S. E. (2015). Employee Attrition of It Industry In India- Externally Volatile Internally Dark Times: A Focused Study. *International Journal of Business and Administration Research Review, 1*(9), 8–12.

Knight, R. (2017). *7 Practical ways to reduce bias in your hiring process*. Harvard Business Review.

Kocakulah, M. C., Kelley, A. G., Mitchell, K. M., & Ruggieri, M. P. (2016, May 2). Absenteeism Problems And Costs: Causes, Effects And Cures. [IBER]. *The International Business & Economics Research Journal, 15*(3), 89–96. doi:10.19030/iber.v15i3.9673

Köchling, A., Wehner, M. C., & Warkocz, J. (2022). Can I show my skills? Affective responses to artificial intelligence in the recruitment process. *Review of Managerial Science*, 1–30.

Koen, J., Low, J. T., & Van Vianen, A. (2019). Job preservation efforts: When does job insecurity prompt performance? *Career Development International, 25*(3), 287–305. doi:10.1108/CDI-04-2018-0099

Kok, S. B., Sarikaya, M., & Coban, H. (2016). Organisational Voice Behaviour and its Investigation in Terms of Organisational Variables. *European Scientific Journal, 12*(35), 16–33. doi:10.19044/esj.2016.v12n35p16

Kollen, T. (2019). Diversity management: A comprehensive review of the field. *Journal of Business Research, 98*, 319–330.

Koo, H. S., & Fallon, K. (2017). Preferences in tracking dimensions for wearable technology. *International Journal of Clothing Science and Technology, 29*(2), 180–199. doi:10.1108/IJCST-03-2016-0021

Kortmann, L. K., Simonson, J., Vogel, C., & Huxhold, O. (2021). Digitalisation and employees' subjective job quality in the second half of working life in Germany. *Social Indicators Research*, •••, 1–21. PMID:34873360

Kossivi, B., Xu, M., & Kalgora, B. (2016). Investigating the relationship between human resource management practices and retention of employees in the banking industry. *Journal of Human Resources Management and Labor Studies*, *4*(1), 13–24.

Kovach, K. A., Hughes, A. A., Fagan, P., & Maggard, S. R. (2016). Employee job satisfaction and engagement: The doors of opportunity are open. *Journal of Business and Management*, *22*(1), 5.

KPMG. (2015). *The link between employee engagement, customer satisfaction and business outcomes in the retail sector*. KPMG. https://assets.kpmg/content/dam/kpmg/uk/pdf/2016/07/link-between-employee-engagement-customer-satisfaction-and-business-outcomes-retail-sector.pdf

Kritz, N. J. (2017). The interplay between human capital and organizational information: Implications for knowledge management. *Journal of Knowledge Management*, *21*(6), 1337–1352. doi:10.1108/JKM-06-2016-0267

Krumeich, J., Werth, D., & Loos, P. (2016). Prescriptive control of business processes: New potentials through predictive analytics of big data in the process manufacturing industry. *Business & Information Systems Engineering*, *58*(4), 261–280. doi:10.100712599-015-0412-2

Kumar, A. A., & Mathimaran, K. B. (2017). Employee Retention Strategies in Empirical Research. *Global Journal of Management and Business Research*, *17*(1).

Kumari, K., Ali, S. B., Batool, M., Cioca, L. I., & Abbas, J. (2022). The interplay between leaders' personality traits and mentoring quality and their impact on mentees' job satisfaction and job performance. *Frontiers in Psychology*, *13*, 13. doi:10.3389/fpsyg.2022.937470 PMID:36467147

Kumar, P., & Padhi, N. (2022). Development and validation of multi-factor employee engagement measuring instrument: A formative measurement model. *Personnel Review*, *51*(9), 2261–2276. doi:10.1108/PR-01-2021-0014

Kumar, R., & Arora, R. (2012). Determinants of talent retention in BPO industry. *Indian Journal of Industrial Relations*, *48*(2), 259–273. https://www.jstor.org/stable/23509837

Kumar, S., & Saini, S. K. (2019). Challenges in securing HR data: A study of Indian firms. *Journal of Enterprise Information Management*, *32*(4), 552–566. doi:10.1108/JEIM-05-2018-0139

Labbe, J., & Schwedel, A. (2017). *How companies are using HR analytics to drive business results.* McKinsey. https://www.mckinsey.com/business-functions/organization/our-insights/how-companies-are-using-hr-analytics-to-drive-business-results

Lado, A. A., & Wilson, M. C. (1994). Human resource systems and sustained competitive advantage: A competency-based perspective. *Academy of Management Review*, *19*(4), 699–727. doi:10.2307/258742

Laitinen, K., & Sivunen, A. (2020). Enablers of and constraints on employees' information sharing on enterprise social media, In Press. *Information Technology & People*, *34*(2), 642–665. doi:10.1108/ITP-04-2019-0186

Lalwani. (2021). What is HR analytics? Definition, importance, key metrics, data requirements, and implementation. *Spiceworks.* https://www.spiceworks.com/hr/hr-analytics/articles/what-is-hr-analytics/on Retrieved 20/6/2023

Lam, W., Chen, Z., & Takeuchi, R. (2015). Perceived human resource management practices and intention to leave of employees: Evidence from five professional service firms in China. *International Journal of Human Resource Management*, *26*(19), 2429–2449. doi:10.1080/09585192.2015.1079867

Larsson, A. S., & Edwards, M. R. (2022). Insider econometrics meets people analytics and strategic human resource management. *International Journal of Human Resource Management, 33*(12), 2373–2419. doi:10.1080/09585192.2020.1847166

LaValle, S., Lesser, E., Shockley, R., Hopkins, M. S., & Kruschwitz, N. (2011). Big data, analytics and the path from insights to value. *MIT Sloan Management Review, 52*(2), 21–32.

Lawler III, E. E., & Suttle, J. L. (1973). Expectancy theory and job behavior. *Organizational behavior and huma performance, 9*(3), 482-503. *n performance, 9*(3), 482.

Lawler, E. E., Boudreau, J. W., Mohrman, S. A., Mark, A. Y., & Osganian, N. (2006). *Achieving strategic excellence: An assessment of human resource organizations*. Stanford University Press.

Lawler, E. E., & Hall, D. T. (1970). Relationship of job characteristics to job involvement, satisfaction, and intrinsic motivation. *The Journal of Applied Psychology, 54*(4), 305–312. doi:10.1037/h0029692

Lawler, E., & Levenson, A. (2004). HR Metrics and Analytics: Use and Iimpact. Human Resource Plan Journal , 27(4), 27–36. doi:https://doi.org/10.1016/j.jwb.2009.09.014

Lawler, E., Levenson, A., & Boudreau, J. W. (2004). HR metrics and analytics: Use and impact. *Human Resource Planning, 27*(4), 7–35.

Lawler, J. J., & Elliot, R. (1993, June). Artificial intelligence in HRM: an experimental study of an expert system. In *Proceedings of the 1993 conference on Computer personnel research* (pp. 473-480). ACM. 10.1145/158011.158264

Lawrance, N., Petrides, G., & Guerry, M. A. (2021). Predicting employee absenteeism for cost effective interventions. *Decision Support Systems, 147*, 113539. doi:10.1016/j.dss.2021.113539

Layoffs Tracker - All Tech and Startup Layoffs. (2023). Trueup.Io. https://www.trueup.io/layoffs#

Leana, C. R., & Van Buren, H. J. III. (1999). Organizational social capital and employment practices. *Academy of Management Review, 24*(3), 538–555. doi:10.2307/259141

Lee, L. Y., & Sukoco, B. M. (2010). The effects of cultural intelligence on expatriate performance: The moderating effects of international experience. *The international journal of human resource.*

Lee, C. C., Lim, H. S., Seo, D. J., & Kwak, D. H. A. (2022, April). Examining employee retention and motivation: The moderating effect of employee generation. In *Evidence-based HRM: A global forum for empirical scholarship (No. ahead-of-print).* Emerald Publishing Limited. doi:10.1108/EBHRM-05-2021-0101

Lee, F., Lee, T., & Wu, W. (2010). The relationship between human resources management practices, business strategy and firm performance: Evidence from Steel Industry in Taiwan. *International Journal of Human Resource Management, 21*(9), 1351–1372. doi:10.1080/09585192.2010.488428

Lepenioti, K.,, Bousdekis, A., Apostolou, D., & Mentzas, G. (2020). Prescriptive analytics: Literature review and research challenges. International Journal of Information Management, 57-70.

Lepenioti, K., Bousdekis, A., Apostolou, D., & Mentzas, G. (2020). Prescriptive analytics: Literature review and research challenges. *International Journal of Information Management, 50*, 57–70. doi:10.1016/j.ijinfomgt.2019.04.003

LePine, J. A., Erez, A., & Johnson, D. E. (2002). The nature and dimensionality of organizational citizenship behavior: A critical review and metaanalysis. *The Journal of Applied Psychology, 87*(1), 52–66. doi:10.1037/0021-9010.87.1.52 PMID:11916216

Levenson, A. (2005, March). Harnessing the power of HR analytics. *Strategic HR Review*, 28-31.

Levenson, A. (2005). Harnessing the power of HR analytics. [http://dx.doi.org/10.1108/14754390580000607]. *Strategic HR Review*, *4*(3), 28–31. doi:10.1108/14754390580000607

Levenson, A. (2011). Using targeted analytics to improve talent decisions. *People and Strategy*, *34*(2), 34.

Levenson, A. (2011). Using targeted analytics to improve talent decisions. *People and Strategy*, *34*(2), 34–54.

Levenson, A. (2018). Using workforce analytics to improve strategy execution. *Human Resource Management*, *57*(3), 685–700. doi:10.1002/hrm.21850

Levinson, E. (2007). *Developing High Employee Engagement Makes Good Business Sense*. Interaction Associates. www.interactionassociates.com/ideas/2007/05/developing_high_employee_eng agement_makes_good_business_sense.php

Levinson, H. (1965). Reciprocation: The relationship between man and organization. *Administrative Science Quarterly*, *9*(4), 370–390. doi:10.2307/2391032

Ligori, T. A. A., Suresh, N., & Khan, S. A. (2019). Measuring Student Satisfaction Index using Structural Equation Modeling. [Special Issue]. *International Journal of Research in Social Sciences*, *9*(6), 15–24.

Ligori, T. A. A., Suresh, N., Khan, S. A., Rabgay, T., & Yezer, K. (2022). The mediating effect of university image on the relationship between curriculum and student satisfaction: An empirical study of the Royal University of Bhutan. *International Journal of Pluralism and Economics Education. Inderscience*, *13*(2), 192–208.

Lima, L., Wangb, Y., Hoshinoc, Y., & Islamd, M. N. (2015). Unveiling the mysteries of the "black hole" in recruiting systems: Connecting recruiters and job seekers like a jigsaw puzzle. *Procedia Manufacturing*, *3*, 3470–3477. doi:10.1016/j.promfg.2015.07.652

Liu, L., Akkineni, S., Story, P., & Davis, C. (2020). *Using HR analytics to support managerial decisions: a case study*. ACMSE 2020 - Proceedings of the 2020 ACM Southeast Conference, (pp. 168-175). ACM. 10.1145/3374135.3385281

Liu, Y., Mao, G., Leiva, V., Liu, S., & Tapia, A. (2020). Diagnostic Analytics for an Autoregressive Model under the Skew-Normal Distribution. *Mathematics 2020*, 693.

Li, Y. (2018). Building well-being among university teachers: The roles of psychological capital and meaning in life. *European Journal of Work and Organizational Psychology*, *27*(5), 594–602. doi:10.1080/1359432X.2018.1496909

Llyas, S., Abid, G., & Ashfaq, F. (2022). Enhancing the perceived organizational support, perceived ethical philanthropic CSR and subjective well-being : The role of ethical leadership. *International Journal of Ethics and Systems*.

Loan-Clarke, J., Arnold, J., Coombs, C., Hartley, J., & Bosley, S. (2010). *Managing talent: A literature review*. Institute for Employment Studies. https://www.employment-studies.co.uk/system/files/resources/files/399.pdf

Lochab, A., Kumar, S., & Tomar, H. (2018). Impact of human resource analytics on organizational performance: A review of literature using R-software. *International Journal of Management. Technology and Engineering*, *8*, 1252–1261.

Locke, E. A., & Taylor, M. S. (1990). Stress, coping, and the meaning of work', in Brief, A. and W.R. Nord (Eds) Meanings of Occupational Work, (pp 135-170). Lexington, Lexington Books.

Locke, E. A. (1996). Motivation through conscious goal setting. *Applied & Preventive Psychology*, *5*(2), 117–124. doi:10.1016/S0962-1849(96)80005-9

Locke, E. A., & Latham, G. P. (2012). Goal setting theory. In *Motivation: Theory and research* (pp. 23–40). Routledge.

Lockwood, R. (2007). Leveraging employee engagement for competitive advantage: HR'sstrategic role. *HRMagazine*, *3*, 1–11.

Loerbroks, A., Weigl, M., Li, J., Glaser, J., Degen, C., & Angerer, P. (2015, February). Workplace bullying and depressive symptoms: A prospective study among junior physicians in Germany. *Journal of Psychosomatic Research, 78*(2), 168–172. doi:10.1016/j.jpsychores.2014.10.008 PMID:25454681

Lokaj, A., Miftari, V., & Hajdari. V. (2021). Leading students toward a new soft-skills perspective: development. *Journal of Education Culture and Society,* 283-296. . doi:10.15503/jecs2021.1.283.296

Long, L. R., Tu, Y., Wang, H. J., & Jiang, L. (2021). The content of the threat matters: The differential effects of quantitative and qualitative job insecurity on different types of employee motivation. *Journal of Business and Psychology*, 1–14.

Lopez-Arceiz, F. J., Torres, L., & Bellostas, A. J. B. (2019). Is online disclosure the key to corporate governance? *Online Information Review, 43*(5), 893–921. doi:10.1108/OIR-06-2018-0191

Luo, Y. (2006). Building trust in cross-cultural collaborations: Toward a contingency perspective. *Journal of Management, 32*(2), 219–237. doi:10.1177/0149206305280472

Lyons, M. (2022).What to do after being laid off. *Harvard Business Review.*

Lyons, T. (1971). Role clarity, need for clarity, satisfaction, tension, and withdrawal. *Organizational Behavior and Human Performance, 6*(1), 999–110. doi:10.1016/0030-5073(71)90007-9

Lyubomirsky, S., King, L., & Diener, E. (2005). The benefits of frequent positive affect: Does happiness lead to success? *Psychological Bulletin, 131*(6), 803–855. doi:10.1037/0033-2909.131.6.803 PMID:16351326

Mabuza, M. L., & Proches, C. N. (2014). Talent management and employee retention: Exploring the perceptions of South African human resource practitioners. *SA Journal of Human Resource Management, 12*(1), 1–12. doi:10.4102ajhrm.v12i1.571

Mac Keown, T. (2023, April 27), How people analytics can help organizations thrive. *Forbes*. https://www.forbes.com/sites/forbestechcouncil/2020/08/27/how-people-analytics-can-help-organizations-thrive-in-a-downturn/?sh=52b30a3740fd

Macey, W. H., & Schneider, B. (2008). The meaning of employee engagement. *Industrial and Organizational Psychology: Perspectives on Science and Practice, 1*(1), 3–30. doi:10.1111/j.1754-9434.2007.0002.x

Madhani, P. M. (2023). Human Resources Analytics: Leveraging Human Resources for Enhancing Business Performance. *Compensation and Benefit Review*, 31-45.

Madhani, P. M. (2023). Human resources analytics: Leveraging human resources for enhancing business performance. *Compensation and Benefits Review, 55*(1), 31–45. doi:10.1177/08863687221131730

Madhvapaty, H., & Rajesh, A. (2021). HR Tech Startups in India: Opportunities, Challenges, and the Road Ahead. *Human Resource Management Review, 31*(1), 100811. doi:10.1016/j.hrmr.2020.100811

Madueke, C. V., & Emerole, I. C. (2017). Organizational culture and employee retention of selected commercial banks in Anambra State. *Saudi Journal of Business and Management Studies, 2*(3), 244–252.

Magd, H., & Khan, S. A. (2022). Strategic Framework for Entrepreneurship Education in Promoting Social Entrepreneurship in GCC Countries During and Post COVID-19. In Magd. H., Syed, R.T., Spicer, D. (Eds). International Perspectives on Value Creation and Sustainability Through Social Entrepreneurship (pp. 61-75). IGI Global.

Magd, H., Jonathan, H., & Khan, S. A. (2023). Education Situation in Online Education before the Pandemic and in the Time of Pandemic. In Advances in Distance Learning in Times of Pandemic, 53-72. CRC Press, Taylor and Francis. doi:10.1201/9781003322252-3

Magd. H., & Khan. S.A. (2022). Effectiveness of using online teaching platforms as communication tools in higher education institutions in Oman: Stakeholders perspectives. *Journal of Content, Community and Communication, 16*, 148- 160. Doi:10.31620/JCCC.12.22/13

Magd, H., Jonathan, H., Khan, S. A., & El Geddawy, M. (2023). *Artificial Intelligence—The Driving Force of Industry 4.0. A Roadmap for Enabling Industry 4.0 by Artificial Intelligence*. Wiley.

Mahajan, M. (2020). The Challenges of Implementing HR Analytics in India. *People Matters*. https://www.peoplematters.in/article/hr-analytics/the-challenges-of-implementing-hr-analytics-in-india-26098

Mahaney, R. C., & Lederer, A. L. (2006). The effect of intrinsic and extrinsic rewards for developers on information systems project success. *Project Management Journal, 37*(4), 42–54. doi:10.1177/875697280603700405

Mahipalan, M., & S, S. (2019). Workplace spirituality and subjective happiness among high school teachers: Gratitude as a moderator. *Explore (New York, N.Y.), 15*(2), 107–114. doi:10.1016/j.explore.2018.07.002 PMID:30150147

Mahmud, A., & Islam, M. R. (2021). Social stigma as a barrier to Covid-19 responses to community well-being in Bangladesh. *International Journal of Community Well-being, 4*(3), 315–321. doi:10.100742413-020-00071-w PMID:34723103

Majji, K. C., & Baskaran, K. (2021). Artificial Intelligence Analytics—Virtual Assistant in UAE Automotive Industry. In *Inventive Systems and Control - Lecture Notes in Networks and Systems* (Vol. 204, pp. 309–322). Springer. doi:10.1007/978-981-16-1395-1_24

Makarius, E. E., Mukherjee, D., Fox, J. D., & Fox, A. K. (2020). Rising with the machines: A sociotechnical framework for bringing artificial intelligence into the organization. *Journal of Business Research, 120*, 262–273. doi:10.1016/j.jbusres.2020.07.045

Malik, A., Budhwar, P., & Kazmi, B. A. (2022). Artificial intelligence (AI)-assisted HRM: Towards an extended strategic framework. *Human Resource Management Review*, 100940.

Malki, Z., & Atlam, E. (2021). Graduate Students and Companies Web Based E-Recruitment System. *Journal of Computer and Communications, 9*(9), 71–84. doi:10.4236/jcc.2021.99005

Malla, J. (2018). HR Analytics Center of Excellence. *International Journal of Business, Management and Allied Sciences, 5*, 282-284.

Management, R. (2006). *Measuring True Employee Engagement*. Right Management.

Manuel, F. D. (2014). The Effect of Training and Development on Perceived Business Performance, *Research project for Gordon Institute of Business Science*, University of Pretoria. http://hdl.handle.net/2263/44214

Margherita, A. (2022). Human resources analytics: A systematization of research topics and directions for future research. *Human Resource Management Review, 32*(2), 100795. doi:10.1016/j.hrmr.2020.100795

Maria, A. (2019). HR Analytics: Challenges and prospects of indian IT Sector. International Journal of Management, IT and Engineering, 404-415.

Marler, J. H., Cronemberger, F., & Tao, C. (2017). HR analytics: here to stay or short-lived management fashion? in Bondarouk, T., Ru€el, H.J.M. and Parry, E. (Eds), Electronic HRM in the Smart Era (The Changing Context of Managing People). Emerald Publishing, Bingley.

Marler, J. H., & Boudreau, J. W. (2017). An evidence-based review of HR Analytics. *International Journal of Human Resource Management, 28*(1), 3–26. doi:10.1080/09585192.2016.1244699

Marsh, H. W., Hau, K.-T., & Wen, Z. (2004). In search of golden rules: Comment on hypothesis-testing approaches to setting cutoff values for fit indexes and dangers in overgeneralizing Hu and Bentler's (1999) findings. *Structural Equation Modeling, 11*(3), 320–341. doi:10.120715328007sem1103_2

Mascarenhas, N., & Stringer, A. (2023, May 04). *A comprehensive list of 2023 tech layoffs.* Techcrunch. https://techcrunch.com/2023/05/04/tech-industry-layoffs/#:~:text=The%20running%20total%20of%20layoffs,the%20data%20in%20the%20tracker

Maslach, C., Schaufeli, W. B., & Leiter, M. P. (2001). Job burnout. *Annual Review of Psychology, 52*(1), 397–422. doi:10.1146/annurev.psych.52.1.397 PMID:11148311

Mathews, S., & Han, K. (2021). An examination of the relationship between work-life balance and employee retention in the hospitality industry. *International Journal of Hospitality Management, 95*, 102886.

Matongolo, S., Chinomona, R., & Mpinganjira, M. (2018). An empirical investigation into the impact of talent management on employees' intention to stay. *South African Journal of Business Management, 49*(1), 1–11. doi:10.4102ajbm.v49i1.27

Matuska, E., & Sałek-Iminska, A. (2014). Diversity Management as Employer Branding Strategy-Theory and Practice. *Human Resources Management & Ergonomics, 8*(2), 72–87.

Maurer, R. (2016). 5 big recruiting trends. *HRMagazine, 61*(3), 7–9.

Maxwell, G. A. (2005). Checks and balances: the role of managers in work–life balance policies and practices. Journal of Retailing and Consumer services, 12(3), 179-189.

May, D. R., Gilson, R. L., & Harter, L. M. (2004). The psychological conditions of meaningfulness, safety, and availability and the engagement of the human spirit at work. *Journal of Occupational and Organizational Psychology, 77*(1), 11–37. doi:10.1348/096317904322915892

Mayhew, R. C. (2020). *Calculate Costs.* Chron. https://smallbusiness.chron.com/calculate-costs-turnover-due-lay-off-10336.html

Mayhew, C. (2018). Exploration of the links between workplace stress and precarious employment. In *Work Stress* (pp. 203–219). Routledge. doi:10.4324/9781315223339-10

Mayo, A. (2018). Applying HR analytics to talent management. *Strategic HR Review, 17*(5), 247–254. doi:10.1108/SHR-08-2018-0072

McCartney, S., & Fu, N. (2022). Bridging the gap: Why, how and when HR analytics can impact organizational performance. *Management Decision, 60*(13), 25–47. doi:10.1108/MD-12-2020-1581

McCartney, S., & Fu, N. (2022). Promise versus reality: A systematic review of the ongoing debates in people analytics. *Journal of Organizational Effectiveness: People and Performance, 9*(2), 281–311. doi:10.1108/JOEPP-01-2021-0013

McCartney, S., Murphy, C., & Mccarthy, J. (2021). 21st century HR: A competency model for the emerging role of HR Analysts. *Personnel Review, 50*(6), 1495–1513. doi:10.1108/PR-12-2019-0670

McEwan, B., Ruohonen, M., & Danielsson-Ojala, R. (2017). Human resource analytics: A systematic review. *International Journal of Human Resource Management, 28*(5), 631–664. doi:10.1080/09585192.2016.1224355

McIver, D., Lengnick-Hall, M.L. & Lengnick-Hall, C.A. (2018). A strategic approach to workforce analytics: integrating science and agility, *Business Horizons, 61(3)*, 397-407. Kelley School of Business, Indiana University. . doi:10.1016/j.bushor.2018.01.005

McKee, A. (2014). Being happy at work matters. *Harvard Business Review*. https://hbr.org/2014/11/being-happy-at-work-matters

McKeown, T., Bryant, M., & Cochrane, R. (2011). The role of emotions in supporting independent professionals. In What Have We Learned? Ten Years On (Vol. 7, pp. 133-147). Emerald Group Publishing Limited. doi:10.1108/S1746-9791(2011)0000007010

McLeod, D., & Clarke, N. (2009). Engaging for Success: enhancing performance through employee engagement. *A report to Government*. Engage for Success. https://engageforsuccess.org/wpcontent/uploads/2015/08/file52215.pd

Medina-Garrido, J. A., Biedma-Ferrer, J. M., & Sánchez-Ortiz, J. (2020). I can ' t go to work tomorrow! Work-family policies, well-being and absenteeism. *Sustainability (Basel)*, *12*(14), 5519. Advance online publication. doi:10.3390u12145519

Meenal Arora, A. P. (2022). HR Analytics and Artificial Intelligence-Transforming Human Resource Management. *International Conference on Decision Aid Sciences and Application*, (pp. 288-293). ACM.

Mehrotra, S., & Khanna, A. (2022). Recruitment Through AI in Selected Indian Companies. *International Journal of Emerging Technology and Innovative Engineering*, *8*(4), 247–254. doi:10.1177/09726225211066220

Mehta, M., Kurbetti, A., & Dhankhar, R. (2014). Review paper study on employee retention and commitment. *International Journal of Advance Research in Computer Science and Management Studies*, *2*, 154–164.

Mehta, M., Kurbetti, A., & Dhankhar, R. (2014). Review paper–study on employee retention and commitment. *International Journal (Toronto, Ont.)*, *2*(2), 33–49.

Meisler, G., Vigoda-Gadot, E., & Drory, A. (2017). Stress, psychological strain, and reduced organizational effectiveness: the destructive consequences of the use of intimidation and pressure by supervisors. In *Power, politics, and political skill in job stress* (Vol. 15, pp. 51–80). Emerald Publishing Limited. doi:10.1108/S1479-355520170000015005

Mendes, F., & Stander, M. (2011). Positive organisation: The role of leader behaviour in work engagement and retention. *SA Journal of Industrial Psychology*, *37*(1). doi:10.4102ajip.v37i1.900

Men, L. (2014). Why Leadership Matters to Internal Communication: Linking Transformational Leadership, Symmetrical Communication, and Employee Outcomes. *Journal of Public Relations Research*, *26*(3), 256–279. doi:10.1080/1062726X.2014.908719

Mescher, S., Benschop, Y., & Doorewaard, H. (2010). Representations of work-Life balance support. *Human Relations*, *63*(1), 21–39. doi:10.1177/0018726709349197

Mikami, D. J., Melvin, W. S., Murayama, M. J., & Murayama, K. M. (2017, March 31). Impact of minimally invasive surgery on healthcare utilization, cost, and workplace absenteeism in patients with Incisional/Ventral Hernia (IVH). *Surgical Endoscopy*, *31*(11), 4412–4418. doi:10.100700464-017-5488-y PMID:28364155

Miles, S., & Mangold, G. (2014). Employee voice: Untapped resource or social media time bomb? *Business Horizons*, *57*(3), 401–411. doi:10.1016/j.bushor.2013.12.011

Minbaeva, D. B. (2018). Building credible human capital analytics for organizational competitive advantage. *Human Resource Management*, *57*(3), 701–713. doi:10.1002/hrm.21848

Mishra, N., & Silakari, S. (2013). Predictive Analytics: A Survey, Trends, Applications, Oppurtunities & Challenges. International Journal of Computer Science and Information Technologies, 4434-4438.

Mishra, S. N., Lama, D. R., & Pal, Y. (2016). Human Resource Predictive Analytics (HRPA) for HR management in organizations. *International Journal of Scientific & Technology Research*, *5*(5), 33–35.

Mishra, S. N., Lama, D. R., & Pal, Y. (2016). Human resource predictive analytics (HRPA) for HR management in organizations. *International Journal of Scientific and Technology Research*, *5*(5), 33–35.

Mobley, W. H. (1982). Some unanswered questions in turnover and withdrawal research. *Academy of Management Review*, *7*(1), 111–116. doi:10.2307/257255

Mohammed, A. (2019). HR Analytics: A Modern Tool in HR for Predictive Decision Making. *Journal of Management*, *6*(3), 51–63. http://www.iaeme.com/jom/issues.asp?JType=JOM&VType=6&IType=3

Mohammed, D. & Abdul, O. (2019). HR Analytics: A Modern Tool in HR for Predictive Decision Making (2019). *Journal of Management, 6*(3), 51-63. https://ssrn.com/abstract=3525328

Mohammed, D., & Quddus, A. (2019). HR analytics: A modern tool in HR for predictive decision making. *Journal of Management*, *6*(3). doi:10.34218/JOM.6.3.2019.007

Mohan, M., & Baskaran, K. (2021). Financial Analytics: Investment Behavior of Middle Income Group In South India. *International Conference on Cloud Computing, Data Science & Engineering*. IEEE. 10.1109/Confluence51648.2021.9377029

Moloney, W., Fieldes, J., & Jacobs, S. (2020). An integrative review of how healthcare organizations can support hospital nurses to thrive at work. *International Journal of Environmental Research and Public Health*, *17*(23), 1–21. doi:10.3390/ijerph17238757 PMID:33255725

Momin, W. Y. M., & Mishra, K. (2014). Impression of financial measures in HR analytics. *Journal of Interdisciplinary and Multidisciplinary Research*, *2*(1), 87–91.

Moncey, A. A., & Baskaran, K. (2020). Digital Marketing Analytics: Building Brand Awareness and Loyalty in UAE. *International Conference on Technology Management, Operations and Decisions*. IEEE. 10.1109/ICTMOD49425.2020.9380579

Mondore, S., Douthitt, S., & Carson, M. (2011). Maximizing the impact and effectiveness of HR analytics to drive business outcomes. *People and Strategy*, *34*(2), 20.

Money Control. (2023). *Indian laid off after 5 years with Microsoft in US: "Since I am on H1B, clock's ticking."* Moneycontrol. https://www.moneycontrol.com/news/trends/indian-laid-off-after-5-years-with-microsoft-in-us-since-i-am-on-h1b-clocks-ticking-10173911.html

Montani, F., Leon-Perez, J. M., Giorgi, G., & Shoss, M. K. (2020). Appraisal of economic crisis, psychological distress, and work-unit absenteeism: A 1-1-2 model. *Journal of Business and Psychology*, *35*(5), 609–620. doi:10.100710869-019-09643-w

Morgeson, F. P., Dierdorff, E. C., & Hmurovic, J. L. (2010). Work design *in situ*: Understanding the role of occupational and organizational context. *Journal of Organizational Behavior*, *31*(2-3), 351–360. doi:10.1002/job.642

Morgeson, F. P., & Humphrey, S. E. (2006). The Work Design Questionnaire (WDQ): Developing and validating a comprehensive measure for assessing job design and the nature of work. *The Journal of Applied Psychology*, *91*(6), 1321–1339. doi:10.1037/0021-9010.91.6.1321 PMID:17100487

Morley, M. (1998). *Principles of organisational behaviour: An Irish text*. Gill & MacMillan.

Mousa, M., Massoud, H. K., & Ayoubi, R. M. (2020). Gender, diversity management perceptions, workplace happiness and organisational citizenship behaviour. *Employee Relations*, *42*(6), 1249–1269. doi:10.1108/ER-10-2019-0385

Mttoi, D. A. (2013). *Influence of Motivation on employee's retention in Public Organizations; A case study of Tanzania Ports Authority* [Doctoral dissertation, The Open University of Tanzania]

Mueller, R. O., & Hancock, G. R. (2001). Factor analysis and scale revision. *Psychological Assessment*, *13*(3), 347–357. PMID:11556271

Muhammed, A. (2023). *TechLayoff.* ClearIAS. https://www.clearias.com/tech-layoff/#what-one-means-by-tech-lay-off

Mujtaba, B., & Senathip, T. (2020). Layoffs and Downsizing Implications for the Leadership Role of Human Resources. *Journal of Service Science and Management*, *13*(2), 209–228. doi:10.4236/jssm.2020.132014

Murali, D. (2019). *The challenges of implementing HR Analytics in India.* TechGig. https://content.techgig.com/The-challenges-of-implementing-HR-Analytics-in-India/articleshow/69866818.cms

Naeem, B., & Saif, M. I. (2010). Impact of training and development on employee retention in Pakistani context. *Interdisciplinary Journal of Contemporary Research in Business*, *2*(10), 452–462.

Nagpal, T., & Mishra, M. (2018, December). Decisions Making in HR: Application of HR Analytics. [IJRAR]. *International Journal of Research and Analytical Reviews*, *5*(4).

Naik, A., & Samant, L. (2016). Correlation Review of Classification Algorithm Using Data Mining Tool: WEKA, Rapidminer, Tanagra, Orange and Knime. *Procedia Computer Science*, *85*, 662–668. doi:10.1016/j.procs.2016.05.251

Naim, A. (2022). Application of Digital Technologies for the Students with Diverse Skills During COVID: 19. *American Journal of Research in Humanities and Social Sciences*, *1*, 46–53.

Na-Nan, K., Chaiprasit, K., & Pukkeeree, P. (2018). Factor analysis-validated comprehensive employee job performance scale. *International Journal of Quality & Reliability Management*, *35*(10), 2436–2449. doi:10.1108/IJQRM-06-2017-0117

Nansubuga, F., & Munene, J. C. (2013). Reflecting on competences to increase role clarity during service delivery in a third world setting. *Journal of Workplace Learning*, *25*(4), 231–246. doi:10.1108/13665621311316429

Narula, S. C., & Vassilev, V. (1994). An interactive algorithm for solving multiple objective integer linear programming problems. *European Journal of Operational Research*, *79*(3), 443–450. doi:10.1016/0377-2217(94)90058-2

NASSCOM. (2016). Big data analytics to reach $16 billion industry by 2025. *Economic Times.* https://economictimes.indiatimes.com/articleshow/52885509.cms?utm_source=contentofinterest

NASSCOM. (2019). *Future skills- The future of India's tech industry.* NASSCOM. https://www.nasscom.in/knowledge-center/publications/future-skills-future-indias-tech-industry

National Retail Federation. (2019). *People Metrics in Retail: How Retailers are Using Data to Drive Human Capital Decisions.* NRF. https://nrf.com/research/people-metrics-retail-how-retailers-are-using-data-drive-human-capital-decisions

Navodya Gurusinghe, B. J. R. (2021). Predictive HR analytics and talent management: a conceptual framework. *Journal of Management Analytics*, 195.

Nawaz, N. (2020). Exploring artificial intelligence applications in human resource management. *Journal of Management Information and Decision Sciences*, *23*(5), 552–563.

Nayak, J., Balas, V. E., Favorskaya, M. N., Choudhury, B. B., Rao, S. K. M., & Naik, B. (Eds.). (2020). *Applications of Robotics in Industry Using Advanced Mechanisms.* Learning and Analytics in Intelligent Systems., doi:10.1007/978-3-030-30271-9

Nestor. (2023, May 29). *Career development: The key to improve employee retention.* Nestor. https://nestorup.com/blog/career-development-the-key-to-improve-employee-retention/

Newman, D. T., Fast, N. J., & Harmon, D. J. (2020). When eliminating bias isn't fair: Algorithmic reductionism and procedural justice in human resource decisions. *Organizational Behavior and Human Decision Processes*, *160*, 149–167. doi:10.1016/j.obhdp.2020.03.008

Nishith Pawar, N. S. (January 2023). Role of analytics in HR-attrition for effective decision. *International Research Journal of Modernization in Engineering Technology and Science*, 185-188.

Nitya B, M. R. (2021). A Study On The Application Of Hr Analytics On Talent Acquisition, Compensation & Benefits And Employee Turnover In The Indian It Industry. *Sambodhi*, 66-76.

Noakes, T. D. (2000). Physiological models to understand exercise fatigue and the adaptations that predict or enhance athletic performance. *Scandinavian Journal of Medicine & Science in Sports*, *10*(3), 123–145. doi:10.1034/j.1600-0838.2000.010003123.x PMID:10843507

Noe, R. A., Hollenbeck, J. R., Gerhart, B., & Wright, P. M. (2020). *Human resource management: Gaining a competitive advantage*. McGraw-Hill Education.

Nyanjom, P. O. (2013). The influence of talent management on job satisfaction and organizational commitment among employees in Kenyan universities. *International Journal of Academic Research in Business & Social Sciences*, *3*(9), 93–104. doi:10.6007/IJARBSS/v3-i9/239

Oladipupo, O. & Olubusayo. F. H. (2020). Human Resource Analytics Dimensions and Employee Engagement in Manufacturing Industry in Nigeria a Conceptual Review. *Journal of Management Information and Decision Sciences*, *23*(5), 629-637.

Ologbo, A., & Saudah, S. (2012). Individual Factors Work Outcomes of Employee Engagement. *Elsevier Ltd*. https://www.sciencedirect.com/science/article/pii/S1877042812006891

Onoh, C., & Nwaogazie, I. (2016, January 10). Workplace Assessment of Hypertension: Prevalence and Awareness in a Food Processing Industry in Owerri Nigeria. *International Journal of Tropical Disease & Health*, *16*(4), 1–11. doi:10.9734/IJTDH/2016/25873

Ons Cappa, M., Sánchez Ollero, J. L., & García Pozo, A. (2020). Gender differences in the returns on human capital in the Spanish hospitality sector. *Investigaciones Turísticas*, (19), 28–49. doi:10.14198/INTURI2020.19.02

Opatha, H. (2020). HR Analytics: A Literature Review and New Conceptual Model. International Journal of Scientific and Research Publications, 130-141.

Opatha, H. H. D. P. J. (2020). HR analytics: A literature review and new conceptual model. *International Journal of Scientific and Research Publications*, *10*(6), 130–141. doi:10.29322/IJSRP.10.06.2020.p10217

Orben, A., & Przybylski, A. K. (2019). Screens, teens, and psychological well-being: Evidence from three time-use-diary studies. *Psychological Science*, *30*(5), 682–696. doi:10.1177/0956797619830329 PMID:30939250

Ore, O., & Sposato, M. (2022). Opportunities and risks of artificial intelligence in recruitment and selection. *The International Journal of Organizational Analysis*, *30*(6), 1771–1782. doi:10.1108/IJOA-07-2020-2291

Organ, C. (2023). Workforce planning: Definition and best practices. *Forbes Advisor*. https://www.forbes.com/advisor/business/workforce-planning/

Organ, D. W. (1988). *Organizational citizenship behavior: The good soldier syndrome*. APA.

Oswald, A. J., Proto, E., & Sgroi, D. (2015). Happiness and Productivity. *Journal of Labor Economics*, *33*(4), 789–822. doi:10.1086/681096

Ott, D. L., Tolentino, J. L., & Michailova, S. (2018). Effective talent retention approaches. Mentioned regarding culture. *Human Resource Management International Digest*, *26*(7), 16–19. doi:10.1108/HRMID-07-2018-0152

Ott, H., Kaiser, S., Probst, T., & Konegen-Grenier, C. (2018). Perceived fairness of pay: A systematic review and meta-analysis of the literature. *Journal of Economic Psychology*, *68*, 21–40. doi:10.1016/j.joep.2018.06.003

Page, S. E. (2007). *The difference: How the power of diversity creates better groups, firms, schools, and societies*. Princeton University Press.

Pallant, J. (2010). *SPSS survival manual: A step by step guide to data analysis using SPSS*. McGraw Hill International.

Panaccio, A., & Vandenberghe, C. (2011). The Relationships of Role Clarity and Organization Based Self-Esteem to Commitment to Supervisors and Organizations and Turnover Intentions. *Journal of Applied Social Psychology*, *41*(6), 1455–1485. doi:10.1111/j.1559-1816.2011.00764.x

Pandey, S. (2020). Principles of correlation and regression analysis. Journal of the practice of cardiovascular sciences, 7.

Pandita, D., & Ray, S. (2018). Talent management and employee engagement–a meta-analysis of their impact on talent retention. *Industrial and Commercial Training*, *50*(4), 185–199. doi:10.1108/ICT-09-2017-0073

Pan, Y., Froese, F., Liu, N., Hu, Y., & Ye, M. (2022). The adoption of artificial intelligence in employee recruitment: The influence of contextual factors. *International Journal of Human Resource Management*, *33*(6), 1125–1147. doi:10.1080/09585192.2021.1879206

Papacharissi, Z. (2010). *A Networked Self: Identity, Community, and Culture on Social Network Sites*. Routledge. doi:10.4324/9780203876527

Parakandi, M., & Behery, M. (2016). The impact of employee engagement on employee retention: Exploring the moderating role of job burnout. *Journal of Applied Business Research*, *32*(6), 1685–1698. doi:10.19030/jabr.v32i6.9801

Parent-Lamarche, A., Marchand, A., & Saade, S. (2021). How do work organization conditions affect job performance? The mediating role of workers' well-being. *Journal of Workplace Behavioral Health*, *36*(1), 48–76. doi:10.1080/15555240.2021.1872382

Park, J. H., & Ono, M. (2017). Effects of workplace bullying on work engagement and health: The mediating role of job insecurity. *International Journal of Human Resource Management*, *28*(22), 3202–3225. doi:10.1080/09585192.2016.1155164

Parzefall, M. R. (2012). A close call: Perceptions of alternative HR arrangements to layoffs. *Journal of Managerial Psychology*, *27*(8), 799–813. doi:10.1108/02683941211280166

Patricia, N. M., & Asoba, S. N. (2021). Theories of job satisfaction in the higher education context. *Academy of Entrepreneurship Journal*, *27*(2), 1–16.

Pawirosumarto, S., Sarjana, P. K., & Gunawan, R. (2017). The effect of work environment, leadership style, and organizational culture towards job satisfaction and its implication towards employee performance in Parador Hotels and Resorts, Indonesia. *International journal of law and management*.

Pelet, J. E., Taieb, B., Massarini, M., Mouelhi, N. B. D., Mishra, P., Obeidat, Z. M., & Zukowska, J. (2017). Impact of M-commerce website design on consumers' behavioural intentions: an empirical study of age as a moderating influence. In *Marketing at the Confluence between Entertainment and Analytics: Proceedings of the 2016 Academy of Marketing Science (AMS) World Marketing Congress* (pp. 111-124). Springer International Publishing. 10.1007/978-3-319-47331-4_21

Penna. (2006). *Meaning at Work Research Report*. Penna. www.e- penna.com/newsopinion/research.aspx

Pentón Herrera, L. J., Trinh, E. T., & Gómez Portillo, M. D. J. (2022). Cultivating calm and stillness at the doctoral level: A collaborative autoethnography. *Educational Studies (Ames)*, *58*(2), 121–140. doi:10.1080/00131946.2021.1947817

People Matters. (2015). HR Analytics: The Key to Unlocking the Value of HR. *People Matters*. https://www.peoplematters.in/article/hr-analytics/hr-analytics-the-key-to-unlocking-the-value-of-hr-11750

Peppercorn,S. (2023). Managing your emotions after being laid off. *Harvard Business Review*.

Pereira, V. E. (2013). *A Longitudinal Case-Study Examination of HRM Practices in HighPerforming Work Organisations in the Indian HRO/BPO Industry* [Unpublished master's thesis, University of Portsmouth]. https://researchportal.port.ac.uk/portal/files/6033330/Vijay_Phd_Oct_2013_Revised.pdf

Perrin, T. (2007). *Largest Ever Study of Global Workforce Finds Senior Management Holds Trigger to Unleash Talent Potential*. Tower Sperrin. www.towersperrin.com/tp/showdctmdoc.jsp?url=HR_Services/Canada/English/ Press_Releases/2007/20071022/2007_10_22.htm&country=global

Perveen, S., Shahbaz, M., Guergachi, A., & Keshavjee, K. (2016). Performance Analysis of Data Mining Classification Techniques to Predict Diabetes. *Procedia Computer Science*, *82*, 115–121. doi:10.1016/j.procs.2016.04.016

Pessach, D., Singer, G., Avrahami, D., Chalutz Ben-Gal, H., Shmueli, E., & Ben-Gal, I. (2020). Employees recruitment: A prescriptive analytics approach via machine learning and mathematical programming. *Decision Support Systems*, *134*, 113290. doi:10.1016/j.dss.2020.113290 PMID:32501316

Pichault, F., & Naedenoen, F. (2023). The challenges of total talent management in the gig economy. In *The Routledge Handbook of the Gig Economy* (pp. 74–92). Routledge.

Pichler, S., & Ziebarth, N. R. (2017, December). The pros and cons of sick pay schemes: Testing for contagious presenteeism and noncontagious absenteeism behavior. *Journal of Public Economics*, *156*, 14–33. doi:10.1016/j.jpubeco.2017.07.003

Pinkett, R. (2023). *Data-driven DEI: The Tools and Metrics You Need to Measure, Analyse, and Improve Diversity, Equity, and Inclusion*. John Wiley & Sons.

Pituch, K. A., Lee, Y. K., & Yoon, T. (2016). Testing the factorial validity and factorial invariance across gender of a brief form of the School Anxiety Inventory-Short Version. *Journal of Psychoeducational Assessment*, *34*(2), 157–169.

Ployhart, R. E., & Ryan, A. M. (1998). Toward an explanation of applicant reactions: An examination of organizational justice and attribution frameworks. *Organizational Behavior and Human Decision Processes*, *74*(3), 199–214. doi:10.1006/obhd.1998.2777 PMID:9606169

Pont, J. (2004). Are they really 'On the Job'? *Potentials*, *37*, 32.

Porter, L. W., & Steers, R. M. (1973). Organizational, work, and personal factors in employee turnover and absenteeism. *Psychological Bulletin*, *80*(2), 151–176. doi:10.1037/h0034829

Pradhan, S., & Mohanty, S. R. (2021). HR Analytics in Indian Manufacturing Industry: Challenges and the Way Forward. *International Journal of Productivity and Performance Management*, *70*(2), 352–369.

Prasad, K. D. V., Rao, M., & Vaidya, R. (2019). Recruitment metrics and accomplishments: A study with reference to information technology sector. *Journal of Management Research and Analysis*, *6*(2), 106–111. doi:10.18231/j.jmra.2019.020

Prasetya, F., Saifuddin, D. T., & Ansir, N. Y. (2020, April 25). https://www.ijser.org/research-paper-publishing-april-2020.aspx. *International Journal of Scientific and Engineering Research*, *11*(04), 1801–1806. https://www.ijser.org/research-paper-publishing-april-2020.aspx. doi:10.14299/ijser.2020.04.06

Preacher, K. J., Zhang, G., Kim, C., & Mels, G. (2013). Choosing the optimal number of factors in exploratory factor analysis: A model selection perspective. *Multivariate Behavioral Research, 48*(1), 28–56. doi:10.1080/00273171.2012.710386 PMID:26789208

Premlal Prejith, P. K. (2022). Influence Of HR Analytics On Training And Development Skills In IT Sector: A Case Study In Kerala. *Journal of Positive School Psychology*, 1449–1460.

Priyanka, D., Nayak, J.: Empirical Analysis of Absenteeism at Work Place Using Machine Learning. Learning and Analytics in Intelligent Systems. 150–160 (2019). doi:10.1007/978-3-030-30271-9_15

Probst, T. M., Sinclair, R. R., Sears, L. E., Gailey, N. J., Black, K. J., & Cheung, J. H. (2018). Economic stress and well-being: Does population health context matter? *The Journal of Applied Psychology, 103*(9), 959–979. doi:10.1037/apl0000309 PMID:29733623

Purnama, C. (2013). Influence analysis of organizational culture organizational commitment job and satisfaction organizational citizenship behavior (OCB) toward improved organizational performance. *International journal of business, humanities and technology, 3*(5), 86-100.

Pymetrics. (2018). Leading american fast-food chain. In Raub, M. (ed). *Bots, bias and big data: artificial intelligence, algorithmic bias and disparate impact liability in hiring practices*. Ark. L. Rev.

Qaiser, S., Abid, G., Arya, B., & Farooqi, S. (2020). Nourishing the bliss: Antecedents and mechanism of happiness at work. *Total Quality Management & Business Excellence, 31*(15–16), 1669–1683. doi:10.1080/14783363.2018.1493919

Qamar, Y., & Samad, T. A. (2022). Human resource analytics: A review and bibliometric analysis. *Personnel Review, 51*(1), 251–283. doi:10.1108/PR-04-2020-0247

Rabenu, E., Yaniv, E., & Elizur, D. (2017). The relationship between psychological capital, coping with Stress, well-being, and performance. *Current Psychology (New Brunswick, N.J.), 36*(4), 875–887. doi:10.100712144-016-9477-4

Radley, B. (2022). The secret to employee retention is employee engagement. *Workday blog*. https://blog.workday.com/en-us/2022/secret-employee-retention-employee-engagement.html

Raghavan, M., Barocas, S., Kleinberg, J., & Levy, K. (2020, January). Mitigating bias in algorithmic hiring: Evaluating claims and practices. In *Proceedings of the 2020 conference on fairness, accountability, and transparency* (pp. 469-481). 10.1145/3351095.3372828

Raghavan, R., Madhavan, R., & Phatak, A. (2019). Ethical considerations in people analytics. *Harvard Business Review, 97*(4), 52–59.

Raguvir, S., & Babu, S. (2020, October). Enhance employee productivity using Talent analytics and Visualization. In *2020 International Conference on Data Analytics for Business and Industry: Way Towards a Sustainable Economy (ICDABI)* (pp. 1-5). IEEE. 10.1109/ICDABI51230.2020.9325682

Ramlall, S. (2004). A review of employee motivation theories and their implications for employee retention within organizations. *The Journal of American Academy of Business, Cambridge, 5*(1/2), 52–63.

Ram, P., Bhargavi, G., & Prabhakar, G. V. (2011). Work environment, service climate, and customer satisfaction: Examining theoretical and empirical connections. *International Journal of Business and Social Science*, 2(20), 121–132.

Rana, S., & Gandotra, S. (2023). How does organisational culture affect talent retention? *India development review*. https://idronline.org/article/leadership-talent/how-does-organisational-culture-affect-talent-retention/

Ranjit, G. (2022). Explicating intrinsic motivation's impact on job performance: Employee creativity as a mediator. *Journal of Strategy and Management*, *15*(4), 647–664. doi:10.1108/JSMA-04-2021-0091

Rao, V. (2020). *Human resource management role in grievance handling and Redressal*. Linkedin. https://www.linkedin.com/pulse/human-resource-management-role-grievance-handling-redressal-rao/

Rasmussen, T., & Ulrich, D. (2015). Learning from practice: how HR analytics avoids being a management fad. Organizational Dynamics, 44(3), 236-242.

Rasmussen, T., & Ulrich, D. (2015). Learning from practice: How HR analytics avoids being a management fad. *Organizational Dynamics*, *44*(3), 236–242. doi:10.1016/j.orgdyn.2015.05.008

Rathi, A. (2019). HR analytics: Key challenges and opportunities in India. *People Matters*. https://www.peoplematters.in/article/hr-analytics/hr-analytics-key-challenges-and-opportunities-in-india-21058

Rathore, S. (2023). How to emotionally process a layoff. *Harvard Business Review*.

Raub, M. (2018). Bots, bias and big data: Artificial intelligence, algorithmic bias and disparate impact liability in hiring practices. *Arkansas Law Review*, *71*, 529.

Raza, M., Khan, M. A., Ali, M., & Khan, A. (2020). Employee retention: A review of literature. *Journal of Human Resource Management*, *8*(2), 31–38.

Raziq, A., & Maulabakhsh, R. (2015). Impact of working environment on job satisfaction. *Procedia Economics and Finance*, *23*, 717–725. doi:10.1016/S2212-5671(15)00524-9

Reddy, K. B., & Ramasamy, R. (2016). Psychological contract violation and turnover intention: Examining the mediating role of burnout and the moderating role of emotional intelligence. *South African Journal of Business Management*, *47*(1), 33–43.

Reddy, P. (2017). HR analytics – an effective evidence based HRM tool. *International Journal of Business and Management Invention*, *6*(7), 23–34.

Reddy, V., & Lakshmikeerthi, B. (2017). Evidence-based methods for personnel management: An overview. *International Journal of Applied and Basic Research*, *7*(1), 1–3. doi:10.4103/ijabmr.IJABMR_383_16

Rhoades, L., & Eisenberger, R. (2002). Perceived organizational support: A review of the literature. *The Journal of Applied Psychology*, *87*(4), 698–714. doi:10.1037/0021-9010.87.4.698 PMID:12184574

Rice, D. (2021). *Strategies for Dealing With Layoffs*. HREX Change Network. https://www.hrexchangenetwork.com/hr-talent-management/articles/10-strategies-for-dealing-with-layoffs

Richter, M., König, C. J., Koppermann, C., & Schilling, M. (2016). Displaying fairness while delivering bad news: Testing the effectiveness of organizational bad news training in the layoff context. *The Journal of Applied Psychology*, *101*(6), 779–792. doi:10.1037/apl0000087 PMID:26882444

Ridhya Goyal, G. K. (2023). Determining the Role of Employee Engagement in Nurse Retention along with the Mediation of Organizational Culture. *Health Care*, *2023*, 760. PMID:36900765

Robbins, S. P., & Judge, T. A. (2015). Organizational Behaviour. *Pearson*. https://www.pearson.com/us/higher-education/product/Robbins-Organizational-Behavior-16th-Edition/9780133507645.html

Robinson, D., Perryman, S., & Hayday, S. (2004). *The drivers of employee engagement*. Employment Studies. www.employment-studies.co.uk

Robinson, D. (2007). *Engagement is marriage of various factors at work.* Thought Leaders.

Rockwood, K. (2021). The Hard Facts About Soft Skills. *HR Magazine Summer 2021.* https://www.shrm.org/hr-today/news/hr-magazine/summer2021/pages/why-soft-skills-are-important.aspx

Rodríguez-Sánchez, A. M., Dolores López-Guzmán, T., & Rodríguez-García, M. (2019). The relationship between talent management and organizational performance: A meta-analysis. *Journal of Business Research, 98*, 413–424. doi:10.1016/j.jbusres.2019.01.023

Rodríguez-Sánchez, J. L., González-Torres, T., Montero-Navarro, A., & Gallego-Losada, R. (2020). Investing time and resources for work–life balance: The effect on talent retention. International Journal of Environmental Research and Public Health. *International Journal of Environmental Research and Public Health, 17*(6), 1920. doi:10.3390/ijerph17061920 PMID:32187973

Romansky, L., Garrod, M., Brown, K., & Deo, K. (2021). How to measure inclusion in the workplace. *Harvard Business Review*, 27.

Romão, S., Ribeiro, N., Gomes, D. R., & Singh, S. (2022). The impact of leaders' coaching skills on employees' happiness and turnover intention. *Administrative Sciences, 12*(3), 84. Advance online publication. doi:10.3390/admsci12030084

Rostami, H. R., Akbarfahimi, M., Ghaffari, A., Kamali, M., & Rassafiani, M. (2021). Relationship between work-related quality of life and job satisfaction in Iranian occupational therapists. *Occupational Therapy International, 2021*, 1–6. doi:10.1155/2021/6692752 PMID:34629996

Rotter, J. B. (1967). A new scale for the measurement of interpersonal trust. *Journal of Personality, 35*(4), 651–665. doi:10.1111/j.1467-6494.1967.tb01454.x PMID:4865583

Rousseau, D. M., Sitkin, S. B., Burt, R. S., & Camerer, C. (1998). Not so different after all: A cross-discipline view of trust. *Academy of Management Review, 23*(3), 393–404. doi:10.5465/amr.1998.926617

Rudolph, C. W., Katz, I. M., Lavigne, K. N., & Zacher, H. (2017). Job crafting: A meta-analysis of relationships with individual differences, job characteristics, and work outcomes. *Journal of Vocational Behavior, 102*, 112–138. doi:10.1016/j.jvb.2017.05.008

Ruyle, K., Peterson, S., & Rassi, R. (2021). The Business Case for Diversity, Equity, and Inclusion Metrics in Recruitment Analytics. *Journal of Corporate Recruiting Leadership, 5*(2), 31–39.

Ryan, R. M., Bernstein, J. H., & Brown, K. W. (2010). Weekends, work, and well-being: Psychological need satisfactions and day of the week effects on mood, vitality, and physical symptoms. *Journal of Social and Clinical Psychology, 29*(1), 95–122. doi:10.1521/jscp.2010.29.1.95

S.Sai Abhinav Chandra, P. M. (2023). HR Metrics and Decision Making using Tableau. *International Journal of Advances in Engineering and Management*, 1203.

Saeed, R., & Lodhi. (2013). The Organizational Role in CareerDevelopment of Employees. *Management and Administrative Sciences*. http://reviewwww.absronline.org/masrISSN.

Sahdev, K. (2004). Revisiting the survivor syndrome: The role of leadership in implementing downsizing. *European Journal of Work and Organizational Psychology, 13*(2), 165–196. doi:10.1080/13594320444000056

Sahinidis, A. G., & Bouris, J. (2008). Employee perceived training effectiveness relationship to employee attitudes. *Journal of European Industrial Training, 32*(1), 63–76. doi:10.1108/03090590810846575

Sahu, S. (2023). Google layoffs not on performance basis and systems locked mins after firing, says YouTube India employee. *India Today*. https://www.indiatoday.in/technology/news/story/google-layoffs-not-on-performance-basis-and-systems-locked-mins-after-firing-says-youtube-india-employee-2351002-2023-03-24\

Saidane, O., Mahmoud, I., Gafsi, L., Houda, A., Tekaya, R., & Abdelmoula, L. (2018, July). Factors leading to work absenteeism in Tunisian ankylosing spondylitis patients. *The Egyptian Rheumatologist*, *40*(3), 183–185. doi:10.1016/j.ejr.2017.06.009

Saini, D., & Yadav, R. (2023). *Assessing the role of materialism and gratitude in life satisfaction through IPMA: the mediating role of meaningfulness in life*. Society and Business Review., doi:10.1108/SBR-03-2022-0066

Saks, A. M. (2006). Antecedents and consequences of employee engagement. *Journal of Managerial Psychology*, *21*(7), 600–619. doi:10.1108/02683940610690169

Salahudin, S., N., A., M., A. R., & N., A. (2018). Management of Human Resource Policies and Its Relationship with Employee Engagement and Turnover Intention In Brunei"s Islamic Banks. *European Journal of Human Resource Management Studies*, *1*(2), 78–92.

Salanova, M., Agut, S., & Peiro, J. M. (2005). Linking organizational resources and work engagement to employee performance and customer loyalty: The mediation of service climate. *The Journal of Applied Psychology*, *90*(6), 1217–1227. doi:10.1037/0021-9010.90.6.1217 PMID:16316275

Salas-Vallina, A., Alegre, J., & Fernández Guerrero, R. (2018). Happiness at work in knowledge-intensive contexts: Opening the research agenda. *European Research on Management and Business Economics*, *24*(3), 149–159. doi:10.1016/j.iedeen.2018.05.003

Saleem, M., Khan, S. A., & Magd, H. (2022). Content Marketing Framework for Building Brand Image: A Case Study of Sohar International School, Oman. In Building a Brand Image Through Electronic Customer Relationship Management (pp. 64-83). IGI Global.

Saleem, M., Khan, S. A., Al Shamsi, I. R., & Magd, H. (2023). Digital Marketing Through Social Media Best Practices: A Case Study of HEIs in the GCC Region. In A. Naim & V. Devi (Eds.), *Global Applications of the Internet of Things in Digital Marketing* (pp. 17–30). IGI Global. doi:10.4018/978-1-6684-8166-0.ch002

Salessi, S. M., & Omar, A. G. (2019). *Job involvement in current research: Update and state of the art.*

Sandhya, K., & Kumar, D. P. (2011). Employee retention by motivation. *Indian Journal of Science and Technology*, *4*(12), 1778–1782. doi:10.17485/ijst/2011/v4i12.34

Santhanam, N., & Srinivas, S. (2020). Modeling the impact of employee engagement and happiness on burnout and turnover intention among blue-collar workers at a manufacturing company. *Benchmarking*, *27*(2), 499–516. doi:10.1108/BIJ-01-2019-0007

Satterfield, J., & Hughes, E. (2007). Emotion skills training for medical students: A systematic [review]. *Medical Education*, *41*(10), 935–941. doi:10.1111/j.1365-2923.2007.02835.x PMID:17822414

Schaubroeck, J. M., Lam, S. S. K., & Peng, A. C. (2011). Cognition-based and affectbased trust as mediators of leader behavior influences on team performance. *The Journal of Applied Psychology*, *96*(4), 863–871. doi:10.1037/a0022625 PMID:21299271

Schaufeli, W. B., Bakker, A. B., & Salanova, M. (2006). The Measurement of Work Engagement With a Short Questionnaire: A Cross-National Study. *Educational and Psychological Measurement*, *66*(4), 701–716. doi:10.1177/0013164405282471

Schermerhorn, J. R. (2001). *Management Update 2001* (6th ed.). John Wiley and Sons.

Schlechter, A. F., Watt, H. M. G., & Cilliers, F. V. N. (2015). Retaining talent: Replacing misconceptions with evidence-based strategies. *SA Journal of Human Resource Management, 13*(1), 1–11. doi:10.4102ajhrm.v13i1.712

Schoen, J., & Rost, K. (2020). Organizational diversity management: A systematic review integrating two decades of research. *Journal of Business Research, 117*, 182–195.

Schooley, S. (2023). 10 Ways to Attract and Retain the Best Employees. *Business News Daily*. https://www.businessnewsdaily.com/5189-attract-skilled-workers.html

Schuh, A. J. (1967). The Predictability of Employee Tenure: A Review Of The Literature. *Personnel Psychology, 20*(2), 133–152. doi:10.1111/j.1744-6570.1967.tb02275.x

Schweitzer, L., & Lyons, S. (2008). The market within: A marketing approach to creating and developing high-value employment relationships. *Business Horizons, 51*(6), 555–565. doi:10.1016/j.bushor.2008.03.004

Scottish Executive Social Research. (2007). *Employee engagement in the Public Sector: a review of literature.* SESR. www.scotland.gov.uk/Publications/2007/05/09111348/3

Secrets of Google's talent retention success. (2015). European CEO. https://www.europeanceo.com/business-and-management/secrets-of-googles-talent-retention-success

Seijts, G., & Crim, D. (2006). What engages employees the most, or the ten Cs of employeeengagement. *Ivey Business Journal, 70*(4), 1–5.

Sengupta, S., & Gupta, A. (2012). Employee Attrition and Retention: Exploring the Dimensions in the urban centric BPO Industry. *International Journal of Human Resource Management, 6*(23), 1259–1288. doi:10.1080/09585192.2011.561211

Setiawan, S. S. I. (2020). HR analytics: Employee attrition analysis using logistic regression. *IOP Conf. Series: Materials Science and Engineering.* IOP Publishing Ltd. 10.1088/1757-899X/830/3/032001

Sewell, G., & Barker, J. R. (2006). Coercion versus care: Using irony to make sense of organizational surveillance. *Academy of Management Review, 31*(4), 934–961. doi:10.5465/amr.2006.22527466

Shah, M., & Asad, M. (2018). Effect of motivation on employee retention: Mediating role of perceived organizational support. *European online journal of natural and social sciences, 7(*2), 511.

Shahid, S., Muchiri, M. K., & Walumbwa, F. O. (2020). Mapping the antecedents and consequences of thriving at work: A review and proposed research agenda. *The International Journal of Organizational Analysis, 29*(1), 78–103. doi:10.1108/IJOA-09-2019-1881

Shah, N. D., Steyerberg, E. W., & Kent, M., D. (2017). Big data and predictive analytics: recalibrating expectations. Jama 320, 27-28.

Shantz, A., Alfes, K., Truss, C., & Soane, E. (2013).The role of employee engagement in the relationship between job design and task performance, citizenship and deviant behaviours. *The International Journal of Human Resource Management, 24 (13)*, 2608- 2627. http://eprints.lse.ac.uk/48156/

Sharma, A., Agrawal, R., & Khandelwal, U. (2019). Developing ethical leadership for business organizations: A conceptual model of its antecedents and consequences. *Leadership and Organization Development Journal, 40*(6), 712–734. doi:10.1108/LODJ-10-2018-0367

Sharma, A., & Sharma, T. (2017). HR analytics and performance appraisal system: A conceptual framework for employee performance improvement. *Management Research Review, 40*(6), 684–697. doi:10.1108/MRR-04-2016-0084

Sharma, N., Khatri, B., Khan, S. A., & Shamsi, M. S. (2023). Extending the UTAUT Model to Examine the Influence of social media on Tourists' Destination Selection. *Indian Journal of Marketing, 53*(4), 47–64. doi:10.17010/ijom/2023/v53/i4/172689

Sheaffer, Z., Carmeli, A., Steiner-Revivo, M., & Zionit, S. (2009). Downsizing strategies and organizational performance: A longitudinal study. *Management Decision, 47*(6), 950–974. doi:10.1108/00251740910966677

Sheridan, J. E. (1992). Organizational culture and employee retention. *Academy of Management Journal, 35*(5), 1036–1056. doi:10.2307/256539

Shi, Y., Sears, L. E., Coberley, C. R., & Pope, J. E. (2013). The association between modifiable well-being risks and productivity: A longitudinal study in pooled employer sample. *Journal of Occupational and Environmental Medicine, 55*(4), 353–364. doi:10.1097/JOM.0b013e3182851923 PMID:23567993

Shockley, K. M., Smith, C. R., & Knudsen, E. A. (2017). The impact of work–life balance on employee retention. In *The Wiley Blackwell handbook of the psychology of recruitment, selection and employee retention* (pp. 513–543). John Wiley & Sons, Ltd. doi:10.1002/9781118972472.ch24

Shoss, M. K. (2017). Job insecurity: An integrative review and agenda for future research. *Journal of Management, 43*(6), 1911–1939. doi:10.1177/0149206317691574

SHRM India. (2018). *HR Analytics: Driving Business Results.* SHRM. https://www.shrm.org/hr-today/trends-and-forecasting/research-and-surveys/Documents/HR-Analytics-India.pdf

SHRM. (2012). *Cost Per Hire Standard: American National Standard for Human Resource Management.* American National Standards Institute Inc. https://www.shrm.org/resourcesandtools/business-solutions/documents/shrm_ansi_cph_standard.pdf

Shuck, M. B. (2010). *Employee engagement: An examination of antecedent and outcome variables* [Doctoral dissertation]. FIU Electronic Theses and Dissertations. https://digitalcommons.fiu.edu/etd/235

Shuck, B., & Reio, T. G. Jr. (2013). Employee Engagement and Well-being: A Moderation Model and Implications for Practice. *Journal of Leadership & Organizational Studies, 20*(1), 43–58. doi:10.1177/1548051813494240

Silahtaroglu, G., & Vardarlier, P. (2016). A novel data mining study to spot anomalies in organizations: A human resources management case. *International Journal of Business and Administrative Studies, 2*(4), 89.

Simón, C., & Ferreiro, E. (2018). Workforce analytics: A case study of scholar–practitioner collaboration. *Human Resource Management, 57*(3), 781–793. doi:10.1002/hrm.21853

Singh, A., & Banerji, R. (2022). Happiness at work, organization citizenship behaviour and workplace diversity: A study on Indian private sector bank employees. *Industrial and Commercial Training, 54*(3), 460–475. doi:10.1108/ICT-05-2021-0037

Singh, A., & Gupta, B. (2015, August 3). Job involvement, organizational commitment, professional commitment, and team commitment. *Benchmarking, 22*(6), 1192–1211. doi:10.1108/BIJ-01-2014-0007

Singh, D. (2019). A literature review on employee retention with focus on recent trends. *International Journal of Scientific Research in Science, Engineering and Technology, 6*(1), 425–431. doi:10.32628/IJSRST195463

Singh, M., & Singh, R. (2020). Challenges and Opportunities of HR Analytics in Banking and Financial Services Industry. *International Journal of Human Resource Management, 31*(10), 1265–1284.

Singh, N. (2016). Talent Acquisition and Management Practices in HCL Technologies. *International Journal of Scientific and Research Publications*, *6*(3), 350–356.

Singh, S. K. (2020). HR analytics: The emerging trend in HR practices. *International Journal of Business and Management Studies*, *2*(1), 1–8.

Singh, S., David, R., & Mikkilineni, S. (2018). Organizational virtuousness and work engagement: Mediating role of happiness in India. *Advances in Developing Human Resources*, *20*(1), 88–102. doi:10.1177/1523422317741885

Sinha, M., Yadav, R., & Kishore, M. (2023). How E-Working Is Effective in Education: Observable Determinants and Challenges. In Managing Technology Integration for Human Resources in Industry 5.0 (pp. 214-233). IGI Global.

Sinha, C., & Sinha, A. (2012). Employee retention: A review of literature. *Journal of Business and Management*, *3*(5), 41–47.

Sinha, M., Yadav, R., & Kishore, M. (2023). How E-Working Is Effective in Education. In *Advances in human resources management and organizational development book series* (pp. 214–233). IGI Global. doi:10.4018/978-1-6684-6745-9.ch013

Sivarajah, U., Kamal, M. M., Irani, Z., & Weerakkody, V. (2017). Critical analysis of Big Data challenges and analytical methods. *Journal of Business Research*, *70*, 263–286. doi:10.1016/j.jbusres.2016.08.001

Smeyers, L. (2015). What we learned about HR analytics in 2014–part 2.

Smit, W., Stanz, K., & Bussin, M. (2015). Retention preferences and the relationship between total rewards, perceived organisational support and perceived supervisor support. *SA Journal of Human Resource Management/SA Tydskrif vir Menslikehulpbronbestuur, 13*(1). doi:10.4102/sajhrm.v13i1.665

Smith, J. L., & White, P. H. (2002). An examination of implicitly activated explicitly activated, and nullified stereotypes on mathematical performance: It's not just a women's issue. *Sex Roles*, *47*(3/4), 179–191. doi:10.1023/A:1021051223441

Soane, E., Shantz, A., Alfes, K., Truss, C., Rees, C., & Gatenby, M. (2013). The association of meaningfulness, well-being and engagement with absenteeism: A moderated mediation model. *Human Resource Management*, *52*(3), 441–456. doi:10.1002/hrm.21534

Social Buzz – Free Social Mentions Search and Monitoring . (2023). Social Searcher. https://www.social-searcher.com/social-buzz/?q5=%23tech+layoffs

Soleimani, M., Intezari, A., Taskin, N., & Pauleen, D. (2021). *Cognitive biases in developing biased Artificial Intelligence recruitment system.* Research Gate.

Solomon, B. C., Nikolaev, B. N., & Shepherd, D. A. (2022). Does educational attainment promote job satisfaction? The bittersweet trade-offs between job resources, demands, and stress. *The Journal of Applied Psychology*, *107*(7), 1227–1241. doi:10.1037/apl0000904 PMID:35737558

Sonal Gupta, R. S. (2022). Types of HR Analytics Used for the Prediction of Employee Turnover in Different Strategic Firms with the use of Enterprise Social Media. *5th European International Conference on Industrial Engineering and Operations Management* (pp. 1977-1994). Italy: IEOM Society International. 10.46254/EU05.20220389

Soumyadeb Chowdhury, S. J.-E. (2022). Embedding transparency in artificial intelligence machine learning models: Managerial implications on predicting and explaining employee turnover. *International Journal of Human Resource Management*.

Spector, P. E. (1997). *Job satisfaction: Application, assessment, causes, and consequences* (Vol. 3). Sage publications. doi:10.4135/9781452231549

Spector, P. E., & Fox, S. (2002). An emotion-centered model of voluntary work behavior:Some parallels between counterproductive work behavior and organizational citizenship behavior. *Human Resource Management Review*, *12*(2), 263–292. doi:10.1016/S1053-4822(02)00049-9

Srivastava, S. (2022, November 22). The Big tech layoffs of 2022: A better approach to firing employees. *People Matters*. https://www.peoplematters.in/article/strategic-hr/the-big-tech-layoffs-of-2022-a-better-approach-to-firing-employees-36111

Srivastava, S., & Gupta, P. (2022). Workplace spirituality as panacea for waning well-being during the pandemic crisis: A SDT perspective. *Journal of Hospitality and Tourism Management*, *50*, 375–388. doi:10.1016/j.jhtm.2021.11.014

Strohmeier, S., & Piazza, F. (2015). Artificial intelligence techniques in human resource management—a conceptual exploration. *Intelligent Techniques in Engineering Management: Theory and Applications*, 149-172.

Strohmeier, S., & Piazza, F. (2015). Artificial intelligence techniques in human resource management—a conceptual exploration. *Intelligent Techniques in Engineering Management: Theory and Applications*, 149-172. Research Gate.

Sucher, S.J., & Gupta, S. (2018). Managing organizations-Layoffs that don't break your company. *Harvard Business Review*.

Sucher, S. J., & Westner, M. M. (2022, December 8). What Companies Still Get Wrong about Layoffs. [website]. *Harvard Business Review*.

Suff, R. (2008). Vodaphone's entertaining employee-engagement strategy', *IRS Employment Review*, 896. IRS.

Sullivan, J. (2003). *HR metrics: The world class way*. Kennedy Information.

Sullivan, J. (2004). Rethinking strategic HR: A change in approach to delivering results. *Strategic HR Review*, *3*(2), 20–23.

Sulosaari, V., Unal, E., & Cinar, F. I. (2022). The effectiveness of mindfulness-based interventions on the psychological well-being of nurses: A systematic review. *Applied Nursing Research*, *64*, 151565. doi:10.1016/j.apnr.2022.151565 PMID:35307128

Sun, L. Y., Aryee, S., & Law, K. S. (2019). High-performance human resource practices, employee well-being, and job involvement: An empirical study. *International Journal of Human Resource Management*, *30*(3), 483–503.

Sun, R., Gregor, S., & Fielt, E. (2021). Generativity and the paradox of stability and flexibility in a platform architecture: A case of the Oracle Cloud Platform. *Information & Management*, *58*(8), 103548. doi:10.1016/j.im.2021.103548

Sun, X., Chan, D. W., & Chan, L. K. (2016). Self-compassion and psychological well-being among adolescents in Hong Kong: Exploring gender differences. *Personality and Individual Differences*, *101*, 288–292. doi:10.1016/j.paid.2016.06.011

Su, Q., & Chen, X. (2021). Career development opportunities and employee retention: The moderating role of perceived organizational support. *Journal of Business Research*, *130*, 284–296.

Tabachnick, B. G., & Fidell, L. S. (2013). *Using multivariate statistics* (6th ed.). Pearson.

Tamer, H. & Elsharnouby, S. (2021). Change or perish: Examining the role of human capital and dynamic marketing capabilities in the hospitality sector. *Tourism Management*, *82*. doi:10.1016/j.tourman.2020.104184

Tan, T. H., & Waheed, A. (2011). *Herzberg's motivation-hygiene theory and job satisfaction in the Malaysian retail sector: The mediating effect of love of money*. Research Gate.

Tang, Y., Shao, Y. F., Chen, Y. J., & Ma, Y. (2021). How to keep sustainable development between enterprises and employees? Evaluating the impact of person–organization fit and person–job fit on innovative behaviour. *Frontiers in Psychology*, *12*, 653534. doi:10.3389/fpsyg.2021.653534 PMID:33995213

Tesi, A., Aiello, A., & Giannetti, E. (2019). The work-related well-being of social workers: Framing job demands, psychological well-being, and work engagement. *Journal of Social Work, 19*(1), 121–141. doi:10.1177/1468017318757397

The human capital hub. (2020, December 18). *Use of analytics to create a learning and development program.* Human capital hub. https://www.thehumancapitalhub.com/articles/Use-Of-Analytics-To-Create-A-Learning-And-Development-Program

The State of HR Analytics- Increase HR's effectiveness by mastering people analytics. (2021). HR. https://www.oracle.com/a/ocom/docs/applications/human-capital-management/hrt-talent-analytics-hrdotcom.pdf

Thomas, K. (2009). The Four Intrinsic Rewards that Drive Employee Engagement. *Ivey Business Journal.* https://iveybusinessjournal.com/publication/the-four-intrinsic-rewards-thatdrive-employee-engagement/

Thompson, A., & Bruk-Lee, V. (2021). Employee happiness: Why we should care. *Applied Research in Quality of Life, 16*(4), 1419–1437. doi:10.100711482-019-09807-z

Thornhill, A., & Saunders, M. N. (1998). The meanings, consequences and implications of the management of downsizing and redundancy: A review. *Personnel Review, 27*(4), 271–295. doi:10.1108/00483489810213874

Thunnissen, M. (2016). The relationship between HRM practices and employee retention in public organisations: An exploratory study. *Review of Public Personnel Administration, 36*(4), 381–401. doi:10.1177/0734371X16671184

TimesJobs. (2015, May 4). Only 7% of Indian cos use big data for hiring decisions: Report. *TimesJobs.* https://content.timesjobs.com/only-7-of-indian-cos-use-big-data-for-hiring-decisions-report/articleshow/47192551.cms

Timesnownews. (2023). After Google, meta, and Microsoft another company sacks employees. *Timesnownews.* https://www.timesnownews.com/business-economy/companies/after-google-meta-and-microsoft-another-company-sacks-employees-deets-inside-article-98324217

Tims, M., Derks, D., & Bakker, A. B. (2016). Job crafting and its relationships with person–job fit and meaningfulness: A three-wave study. *Journal of Vocational Behavior, 92*, 44–53. doi:10.1016/j.jvb.2015.11.007

Tirta, A. H., & Enrika, A. (2020). Understanding the impact of reward and recognition, work life balance, on employee retention with job satisfaction as mediating variable on millennials in Indonesia. *The Journal of Business and Retail Management Research, 14*(3). doi:10.24052/JBRMR/V14IS03/ART-09

Tlaiss, H. A., Hallak, R., & Aboushaar, W. (2017). The role of intrinsic and extrinsic motivation on the relationship between perceived organisational support and knowledge sharing behaviour. *Journal of Knowledge Management, 21*(2), 351–365. doi:10.1108/JKM-03-2016-0099

Tomar, S. & Gaur, M. (2020). HR analytics in Business: Role, Opportunities, and Challenges of Using It. *Journal of Xi'an University of Architecture & Technology*, 1299-1306. doi:10.37896/JXAT12.07/2441

Tomar, S., & Gaur, M. (2020). HR analytics in Business: Role, Opportunities, and Challenges of Using It. *Journal of Xi'an University of Architecture & Technology, 12*(7), 1299–1306.

Tonidandel, S., King, E. B., & Cortina, J. M. (2018). Big data methods: Leveraging modern data analytic techniques to build organizational science. *Organizational Research Methods, 21*(3), 525–547. doi:10.1177/1094428116677299

Torrington, D., Hall, L., Taylor, S., & Atkinson, C. (2011). Human Resource Management. 8thEdition. Harlow: Pearson.

Torrington, D., & Taylor, S. (2009). *Human resource management* (7th ed.). Pearson Education.

Truss,C.(2012). Spinning Plates and Juggling Hats: Employee Engagement in an Era of Austerity. *Wimbledon: CIPD.*

Tucker, L. R. (1997). The case for confirmatory factor analysis. In *Structural equation modeling: Concepts, issues, and applications* (pp. 1–26). Sage Publications, Inc.

Turk, A., Vardarlier, P., & Hazar, M. A. (2020). The role of employer brand practices in human resources management in job applications on company preference. *International Journal of Business Ecosystem & Strategy (2687-2293), 2*(4), 1-9.

Tursunbayeva, A., Pagliari, C., Di Lauro, S., & Antonelli, G. (2022). The ethics of people analytics: Risks, opportunities and recommendations. *Personnel Review, 51*(3), 900–921. doi:10.1108/PR-12-2019-0680

Twenge, J. M. (2010). A review of the empirical evidence on generational differences in work attitudes. *Journal of Business and Psychology, 25*(10), 201–210. doi:10.100710869-010-9165-6

Twum, S. A. (2015). What Diversity Management Practices Do Hotel Managers and Employees View as Important for Retaining Employees? [Master's Thesis, University of Stavanger, Norway].

Ulrich, D. (2020). HR's ever-emerging contribution. *Strategic HR Review, 19*(6), 251-257.

Ulrich, D., & Brockbank, W. (2005). *The HR value proposition*. Harvard Business Press.

Ulrich, D., Younger, J., Brockbank, W., & Ulrich, M. D. (2015). *HR from the outside in: Six competencies for the future of human resources*. McGraw-Hill Education.

Uma, V. R., Velchamy, I., & Upadhyay, D. (2023). Recruitment Analytics: Hiring in the Era of Artificial Intelligence. In The Adoption and Effect of Artificial Intelligence on Human Resources Management, Part A (pp. 155-174). Emerald Publishing Limited.

Van Den Broeck, A., Vansteenkiste, M., De Witte, H., & Lens, W. (2008). Explaining the relationships between job characteristics, burnout, and engagement: The role of basic psychological need satisfaction. *Work and Stress, 22*(3), 277–294. doi:10.1080/02678370802393672

Van den Heuvel, S., & Bondarouk, T. (2017). The rise (and fall?) of HR analytics: A study into the future application, value, structure, and system support. *Journal of Organizational Effectiveness: People and Performance, 4*(2), 157–178. doi:10.1108/JOEPP-03-2017-0022

Van der Togt, J., & Rasmussen, T. H. (2017). Toward evidence-based HR. *Journal of Organizational Effectiveness: People and Performance, 4*(2), 127–132. doi:10.1108/JOEPP-02-2017-0013

Van Vulpen, E. (2023). 21 Employee Performance Metrics, Academy to Innovate HR. Vulpen, E. https://www.aihr.com/blog/employee-performance-metrics/>

Vargas, R., Yurova, Y. V., Ruppel, C. P., Tworoger, L. C., & Greenwood, R. (2018). Individual adoption of HR analytics: A fine-grained view of the early stages leading to adoption. *International Journal of Human Resource Management, 29*(22), 3046–3067. doi:10.1080/09585192.2018.1446181

Varma, C., & Chavan, R. (2019). A Case of HR Ananlytics - To Understand Effect On EmSE of hr analytics – to understand effect on employee. *Journal of Emerging Technologies and Innovative Research, 6*(6).

Veronese, G., Pepe, A., & Vigliaroni, M. (2021). An exploratory multi-site mixed-method study with migrants at Niger transit centers: The push factors underpinning outward and return migration. *International Social Work, 64*(4), 539–555. doi:10.1177/0020872818819736

Verstappen, S. M. (2015, June). Rheumatoid arthritis and work: The impact of rheumatoid arthritis on absenteeism and presenteeism. *Best Practice & Research. Clinical Rheumatology, 29*(3), 495–511. doi:10.1016/j.berh.2015.06.001 PMID:26612244

Vignoli, M., Guglielmi, D., Bonfiglioli, R., & Violante, F. S. (2015, March 27). How job demands affect absenteeism? The mediating role of work–family conflict and exhaustion. *International Archives of Occupational and Environmental Health*, *89*(1), 23–31. doi:10.100700420-015-1048-8 PMID:25808748

Virick, M., Lilly, J. D., & Casper, W. J. (2007). Doing more with less: An analysis of work life balance among layoff survivors. *Career Development International*, *12*(5), 463–480. doi:10.1108/13620430710773772

Vlastelica, R., & Holmstrom, A. (2019). Diversity, Inclusion, and the Use of Analytics in Recruiting. *Harvard Business Review*. https://hbr.org/2019/03/diversity-inclusion-and-the-use-of-analytics-in-recruiting

Votto, A. M., Valecha, R., Najafirad, P., & Rao, H. R. (2021). Artificial intelligence in tactical human resource management: A systematic literature review. *International Journal of Information Management Data Insights*, *1*(2), 100047. doi:10.1016/j.jjimei.2021.100047

Vulpen, E. V. (2023). *HR metrics and Analytics: How both can add value*. AIHR. https://www.aihr.com/blog/hr-metrics-and-analytics-how-both-can-add-value/on. (21/06/2023).

Wade, J. T., Roth, P. L., Thatcher, J. B., & Dinger, M. (2020). Social Media and Selection: Political Issue Similarity, Liking, and the Moderating Effect of Social Media Platform. *Management Information Systems Quarterly*, *44*(3), 1301–1357. doi:10.25300/MISQ/2020/14119

Wagar, T. H. (2001). Consequences of work force reduction: Some employer and union evidence. *Journal of Labor Research*, *22*(4), 851–862. doi:10.100712122-001-1056-1

Wagner, S. (2000). Retention: Finders, keepers. *Training & Development*, *54*(8), 64.

Wandhe, P. (2020). HR Analytics: A Tool for Strategic Approach to HR Productivity. Available at SSRN 3700502. https://dx.doi.org/ Wiley. doi:10.2139/ssrn.3700502

Wang, D., Wang, J., & Wang, Y. (2019). Workplace learning, employee engagement, and talent retention: A study of the Chinese insurance industry. *Human Resource Development International*, *22*(5), 427–445.

Watson, H. (2010). All about analytics. *International Journal of Business Intelligence Research*, *4*(1), 13–28. doi:10.4018/jbir.2013010102

Wayhan, V. B., & Werner, S. (2000). The impact of workforce reductions on financial performance: A longitudinal perspective. *Journal of Management*, *26*(2), 341–363. doi:10.1177/014920630002600208

Weena Yancey, M., & Momin, K. M. (2015). HR Analytics as a Strategic Workforce Planning. *International Journal of Applied Research*, 258.

Wellins, R., & Concelman, J. (2005). Creating a culture for engagement. *WorkforcePerformance Solutions*, *4*, 1–4.

Weng, R. H. (2010). Exploring the antecedents of employee turnover intention. *Journal of Business and Psychology*, *25*(4), 585–601. doi:10.100710869-010-9189-9

Weng, R. H., & McElroy, J. C. (2012). Exploring the impact of corporate culture on employee retention. *Journal of Business and Psychology*, *27*(4), 389–400. doi:10.100710869-012-9257-x

West, M. (2019). *People analytics for dummies*. John Wiley & Sons.

Wheeler, A. R., & Buckley, M. R. (2021). The Current State of HRM with Automation, Artificial Intelligence, and Machine Learning. In *HR without People?* (pp. 45–67). Emerald Publishing Limited. doi:10.1108/978-1-80117-037-620211004

White, B. (2008). *The State of Employee Engagement*. Blessing White.

Wilfinger, D., Brandstätter, C., & Mitteregger, J. (2022). Implications of the Digitalization on Human-Resource-Controlling. *Tehnički glasnik, 16*(3), 438-443.

Williams, G. (2011). Descriptive and Predictive Analytics. Data Mining with Rattle and R, 171-177.

Williams, L. J., Cote, J. A., & Buckley, M. R. (1996). Lack of method variance in self-reported affect and perceptions at work: Reality or artifact? *The Journal of Applied Psychology, 81*(6), 669–681.

Wipro Limited. (2015). *Annual Report 2015.* Wipro. https://www.wipro.com/content/dam/nexus/en/investors/reports-filings/annual-reports/2015/annual-report-2015.pdf

Wirth, R., & Hipp, J. (2000). CRISP-DM: Towards a standard process model for data mining. *Proceedings of the 4th international conference on the practical applications of knowledge discovery and data mining*, (pp. 29-39). ACM.

Wirtz, B. W., Schilke, O., & Ullrich, S. (2010). Strategic development of business models: Implications of the Web 2.0 for creating value on the internet. *Long Range Planning, 43*(2-3), 272–290. doi:10.1016/j.lrp.2010.01.005

WISE. (2020). *Diversity management in the workplace.* WISE. https://www.wise-qatar.org/diversity-management-workplace/

Witte, H. D. (1999). Job insecurity and psychological well-being: Review of the literature and exploration of some unresolved issues. *European Journal of Work and Organizational Psychology, 8*(2), 155–177. doi:10.1080/135943299398302

Woman asks internet if she should get married after fiancé gets laid off by Microsoft India . (2023). Moneycontrol. https://www.moneycontrol.com/news/trends/microsoft-layoff-woman-asks-internet-if-she-should-get-married-after-fiance-gets-fired-10015201.html

Work Foundation. (2009). *Knowledge Workers and Knowledge Work. A Knowledge Economy Programme Report.* Work Foundation.

Workforce planning: Model, process, steps [Guide 2023] . (2022, January 17). Valamis. https://www.valamis.com/hub/workforce-planning

Wright, P. M., & Mcmahan, G. C. (2011). Exploring Human Capital: Putting "human" Back into Strategic Human Resource Management. *Human Resource Management Journal, 21*(2), 93–104. doi:10.1111/j.1748-8583.2010.00165.x

Wright, P., Dunford, B., & Snell, S. (2001). Contributions of the resource-based view of the firm to the field of strategic HRM: Convergence of two fields. *Journal of Management, 27*, 701–721. doi:10.1177/014920630102700607

Wright, T. A. (2010). Much more than meets the eye. *Organizational Dynamics, 39*(1), 13–23. doi:10.1016/j.orgdyn.2009.10.009

Xie, Y., Tian, J., Jiao, Y., Liu, Y., Yu, H., & Shi, L. (2021). The impact of work stress on job satisfaction and sleep quality for couriers in China: The role of psychological capital. *Frontiers in Psychology, 12*, 730147. doi:10.3389/fpsyg.2021.730147 PMID:34970180

Yadav, R., Chaudhary, N. S., Kumar, D., & Saini, D. (2022). Mediating and moderating variables of employee relations and sustainable organizations: a systematic literature review and future research agenda. *International Journal of Organizational Analysis.* doi:10.1108/IJOA-12-2021-3091

Yang, J. T., & Mossholder, K. W. (2020). *Transformational leadership and employee retention: A meta-analytic review.*

Yang, Y., Siau, K., Xie, W., & Sun, Y. (2022). Smart Health: Intelligent Healthcare Systems in the Metaverse, Artificial Intelligence, and Data Science Era. [JOEUC]. *Journal of Organizational and End User Computing, 34*(1), 1–14. doi:10.4018/JOEUC.308814

Yarger, L., Cobb Payton, F., & Neupane, B. (2020). Algorithmic equity in the hiring of underrepresented IT job candidates. *Online Information Review, 44*(2), 383–395. doi:10.1108/OIR-10-2018-0334

Yawalkar, M. V. V. (2019). a Study of Artificial Intelligence and its role in Human Resource Management. [IJRAR]. *International Journal of Research and Analytical Reviews, 6*(1), 20–24.

Yazinski, M. (2009). The influence of an online virtual environment on subjective well-being. *Cyberpsychology (Brno), 3*(2), 4.

Yeves, J., Bargsted, M., Cortes, L., Merino, C., & Cavada, G. (2019). Age and perceived employability as moderators of job insecurity and job satisfaction: A moderated moderation model. *Frontiers in Psychology, 10*, 799. doi:10.3389/fpsyg.2019.00799 PMID:31031675

Yoon, S. W., Chae, C., Kim, S., Lee, J., & Jo, Y. (2020). Human resource analytics in South Korea: Transforming the organization and industry. *Human Resource Development in South Korea: Theory and Cases*, 159-180.

Yu, J., Park, J., & Hyun, S. S. (2021). Impacts of the COVID-19 pandemic on employees' work stress, well-being, mental health, organizational citizenship behavior, and employee-customer identification. *Journal of Hospitality Marketing & Management, 30*(5), 529–548. doi:10.1080/19368623.2021.1867283

Yusoff, Y. M., Jusoff, K., & Aziz, A. A. (2018). Factors influencing employee retention: A conceptual framework. *Journal of Administrative and Business Studies, 4*(1), 1–7.

Zalla, T., Koechlin, E., Pietrini, P., Basso, G., Aquino, P., Sirigu, A., & Grafman, J. (2000). Differential amygdala responses to winning and losing: A functional magnetic resonance imaging study in humans. *The European Journal of Neuroscience, 12*(5), 1764–1770. doi:10.1046/j.1460-9568.2000.00064.x PMID:10792453

Zareen, S., & Khan, S. A. (2023). Exploring Dependence of Human Resource Management (HRM) on Internet of Things (IoT) and Digital Marketing in the Digital Era. In A. Naim & V. Devi (Eds.), *Global Applications of the Internet of Things in Digital Marketing* (pp. 51–66). IGI Global. doi:10.4018/978-1-6684-8166-0.ch004

Zeidan, S., & Itani, N. (2020). HR Analytics and Organizational Effectiveness. International Journal on Emerging Technologies , 683-688.

Zhang, M., Yang, L., & Wang, L. (2015). How transformational leadership fosters employee proactive customer service behavior: The mediating role of self-efficacy and the moderating role of internal locus of control. *Journal of Business Research, 68*(4), 911–918. doi:10.1016/j.jbusres.2014.10.004

Zhou, D., Yang, S., & Li, X. (2022). Internet Use and Job Satisfaction: Evidence from China. *International Journal of Environmental Research and Public Health, 19*(19), 12157. doi:10.3390/ijerph191912157 PMID:36231458

Zhu, J., Xu, D., Guo, H., & Zhang, X. (2021). Why do engaged employees stay? The role of work-life balance and job embeddedness. *Journal of Business Research, 123*, 662–671.

Zia-ud-Din, M., Arif, A., & Shabbir, M. A. (2017, May 28). The Impact of Workplace Incivility on Employee Absenteeism and Organization Commitment. *International Journal of Academic Research in Business & Social Sciences, 7*(5). doi:10.6007/IJARBSS/v7-i5/2893

Zieglmeier, V., Gierlich-Joas, M., & Pretschner, A. (2022, October). Increasing Employees' Willingness to Share: Introducing Appeal Strategies for People Analytics. In *Software Business: 13th International Conference, ICSOB 2022,* (pp. 213-226). Cham: Springer International Publishing.

Zieglmeier, V., Gierlich-Joas, M., & Pretschner, A. (2022, October). Increasing Employees' Willingness to Share: Introducing Appeal Strategies for People Analytics. In *Software Business: 13th International Conference, ICSOB 2022,* (pp. 213-226). Cham: Springer International Publishing. 10.1007/978-3-031-20706-8_15

Zigarmi, D., Nimon, K., Houson, D., Witt, D., & Diehl, J. (2009). Beyond engagement: Toward a framework and operational definition for employee work passion. *Human Resource Development Review*, *8*(3), 300–326. doi:10.1177/1534484309338171

About the Contributors

Radha Yadav is an Assistant Professor (HR/OB) at Christ University, Bangalore. Before this, She was associated with the Dayananda Sagar University, Chandigarh University, Jaipuria School of Business, and Symbiosis Centre of Management Studies. She completed her doctorate from the Indian Institute of Technology Roorkee, Uttarakhand (India). She has over eight years of experience in academics and research. Dr. Yadav has published numerous articles in reputed ABDC & ABS journals like Business Strategy and the Environment, International Journal of Hospitality Management, Society and Business Review, and many more. She is also experienced as an Editor in a special Scopus & ABDC Category Journals issue. She represents India on the International project "Climate change and well-being" with De Montfort University, Leicester, UK.

Mudita Sinha is currently associated with Christ University as an Associate Professor of Marketing. She has completed her Ph.D., Masters in Marketing Management, and MBA. Dr. Sinha is an experienced researcher, faculty, and salesperson with proven abilities. She is a competent professional with over 12 years of combined experience in Industry, Business Education, Institutional Affairs & administrative functions. Dr. Sinha has published several articles in various National and International Journals of repute in Marketing and General Management. To keep her knowledge updated and deliver the best quality she participates and presents research articles at different National and international conferences.

Joseph Varghese Kureethara is a professor of Mathematics at Christ University. He has over eighteen years of experience in teaching and research at Christ University, Bengaluru. He has published over 170 articles on Graph Theory, Number Theory, History, Religious Studies and Sports in English and Malayalam. Kureethara has co-edited five books, including Recent Trends in Signal and Image Processing, Neuro-Systemic Applications in Learning and Data Science and Security, and authored five books. His blog articles, comments, facts and poems have earned about 1.7 lakh pageviews. He has delivered invited talks at over fifty conferences and workshops. He is a member of the Editorial Board and a reviewer of several journals. He has worked as a member of several institutions' Board of Studies, Board of Examiners and Management Committees. He was the Director, Centre for Research, Christ University and was its Personnel Officer. He has supervised 8 PhDs and 12 MPhils, and is supervising 7 PhD scholars.

***

Mansurali Anifa is an Assistant professor.

Kamaladevi Baskaran has over 18 years of International work experience in Industry, Applied Research & Academics. She is currently Programme Leader for MBA in Amity Business School, Dubai, UAE. She holds an Executive Education in Business Analytics from Wharton School at the University of Pennsylvania, USA. She is a certified Trainer to teach Innovation and Entrepreneurship from Stanford University Program Ambassadors. In the past, she worked as Director at Zelus Events, Dubai, UAE. Dr. Kamaladevi has vast skill & experience in creating, producing & executing large scale corporate & academic events. She has managed more than 120 large scale International professional events including business conferences & corporate incentive programs globally. Dr. Kamaladevi completed her Ph.D in Management at Bharathiar University, India and her graduate studies M.Phil & MBA at Dravidian University and Bharathidasan University respectively from India. Dr. Kamaladevi's research interests lie in the area of Business Analytics, Entrepreneurship, Business Research Methods and ecommerce ranging from theory to design to implementation. She has collaborated actively with researchers in several other disciplines of management & engineering in the areas of search engine optimization & digital transformational technologies in addressing real world problems at the process to root cause analysis level for the success of online stores. In her areas of research, Dr. Kamaladevi has written three management books as single author. She also presented and published in more than 35 peer-reviewed International conferences and journal research articles. She has served as a Keynote Speaker at various International conferences and Forums held in France, Spain, Thailand, UAE, India & Malaysia. Dr. Kamaladevi also has substantial influence in professional, community, and outreach activities that is demonstrated by the various roles she has undertaken.

Praveen Babu P. is an Assistant Professor at the School of Business and Management, CHRIST (Deemed to be University), Bangalore

Kartikeya Bolar holds a PhD in Technology Management, MBA in Information Systems and B.E in Computer Engineering. He is working as an Associate Professor in the area of Information Systems and Analytics at T A Pai Management Institute (TAPMI), Manipal Academy of Higher Education, Manipal. His research interests are in the field of E- Commerce Diffusion, Data mining, Business Analytics and Technology Adoption.

Mrinal Kanti Das is serving as Assistant Professor in Commerce at Kanchrapara College, Kanchrapara, West Bengal, India. Before that, he was at the Centre for Management Studies, JISCE, Kalyani, West Bengal, as a faculty of Marketing Management. He has more than 16 years of experience in teaching. One scholar has already been awarded a PhD in Marketing Management under his supervision. He has authored four books and has contributed research articles in various journals and also in edited volumes to his credit. He is also one of the editors of Perspectives in Human Resources of Taylor & Francis (Routledge Publication). He is associated with different management institutions and Universities in the capacity of visiting faculty, paper setter, examiner, and moderator.

Susan George is a Research Scholar in the Department of Sociology & Social Work at Christ (Deemed to be University), Bengaluru. Her work specializes in Employee Engagement. She worked as an Assistant Professor in the Department of Epidemiology & Public Health at the Central University of Tamil Nadu, Thiruvarur. She is a post-graduate in Social Work specializedin Personnel Management & Industrial Relations.

Vibhuti Gupta is Associate Professor (HRM & OB) at IILM Academy of Higher Learning, Lucknow. She has more than 12 years of experience. Her qualifications include UGC-NET, Ph.D., MPA, MBA, PGD-HRD, MSE and Proficiency in French. Her areas of interests include Emotional Intelligence, Stress Management, Negotiation and Conflict Management, Ikigai and Mindfulness. She has presented her research work in various national and international conferences. She has published her research work in various high- quality peer reviewed national and international journals in the area Emotional Intelligence, Mindfulness, Happiness at Work, Organizational Citizenship Behavior to name just a few, amongst a varied population like students, police, health and corporate professionals.

Palak Gupta has rich academic experience of over 18 years in teaching IT and Business Analytics courses. She is UGC NET qualified in Computer Science and Applications and has done Masters in Computer Science and DOEACC "B" Level course (Master's Diploma in Computer Applications). She has done Doctorate in domain of Business Intelligence, Data Warehousing and Data Mining. She has many research publications in reputed UGC Care, IEEE Xplore and Scopus indexed International Journals and has presented papers in many National and International Conferences. She is also associated with International Conferences as PC member and reviewer. She has made projects for Indian Army and Air Force in Ambala Cantt and Uttar Pradesh State Industrial Development Corporation, a Public Sector Undertaking (PSU) of the Government of Uttar Pradesh. She specializes in areas of Database, Data Warehousing, Data Mining, Business Intelligence, Cloud computing, Big Data tools and applications, Digital Marketing, Advanced Excel and many Analytical & Statistical tools. She has the right analytical skills to use technology for better understanding, visualizations, applications and decisions.

Sunanda Vincent Jaiwant completed her M.B.A in Finance and Marketing. She has a Doctoral degree in Marketing. She is a versatile faculty in Management with excellent communication skills demonstrated by 17 years of teaching experience as well as around two years in the industry. Throughout her career, Dr Sunanda Vincent J has combined her academic interests with different marketing and entrepreneurial skills. She considers herself a marketing professional and a marketing educator, owing to a diverse background in consumer behavior, advertising, branding, digital marketing, and education. She has earned digital marketing certifications in Inbound Marketing & Marketing Software by Hubspot, a leading platform for marketing, sales, customer service, and CRM. Since 2006, Dr Sunanda has been developing and teaching a variety of marketing papers across tertiary education institutions in India. She uses her degree in commerce and business management combined with her professional experiences to create a learning environment for students grounded in real-world business contexts. She is a motivated, enthusiastic educator with a strong desire to foster a cohesive student learning atmosphere. Specialized in managing students effectively and maximizing learning opportunities through various practical oriented activities. She is motivated with a strong work ethic and a commitment to excellence in teaching and research. She specializes in using behavior economics and decision design to drive consumer decision making. Dr Sunanda's research interests cover a range of business and educational topics. Her publications include research papers and book chapters on varied topics. She has made numerous national and international conference presentations. Outside of teaching, she is a content writer. Presently she is working as Assistant Professor at the School of Business and Management Christ University.

Rajan John is an Assistant Professor of Computer Science.

Shad Ahmad Khan is serving as Assistant Professor in College of Business, University of Buraimi in Sultanate of Oman. He is an active researcher who has a professional strength in the area of Business Management and Marketing. He has a vast experience of organizing international events like conferences and seminars. His area of interest is Data Sciences, green practices, entrepreneurship, administration sciences and marketing.

Bhanupriya Khatri has worked as an Associate Professor of Management in University School of Business, Chandigarh University, Mohali. She did her doctorate in the field of Talent Management. Her area of specialization is Human Resource Management. With more than 10 years of teaching experience, she is a versatile researcher in the field of HR. She has published 20 research papers in reputed national and international peer-reviewed journals. Her area of expertise includes talent management, diversity management and entrepreneurship.

Puneet Kumar has worked with People Metrics Pvt Ltd., an Indian subsidiary of Thomas Assessment. He has experience in conducting Behavioural Assessment and Psychometric Analysis of Employees. He is a graduate in Commerce from Shri Ram College of Commerce, University of Delhi and completed his masters from Department of Commerce, Delhi School of Economics, University of Delhi. He is doctorate of Philosophy in the discipline of management from IGNOU and pursuing research in the area of 'Employee Engagement'. He specializes in the field of Employee Engagement, Ethical Climate, Emotional Intelligence, and Organizational Politics.

Arunima K V is Assistant Professor in area of HR, OB, and Communications at T A Pai Management Institute (TAPMI), Manipal Academy of Higher Education, Manipal. Her research interests are in Knowledge Management. She teaches HR metrics and dashboards, HR analytics and Digital Transformation in HR.

Filiz Mizrak is an Assistant Professor holding a Doctorate degree in Management and Strategy from Istanbul Medipol University. She was born on May 12, 1986. She completed her undergraduate studies in American Culture and Literature at Istanbul University in 2009. Later, she pursued her Master's degree in Executive MBA at Bahçeşehir University in 2015. Filiz MIZRAK's passion for research and academia led her to obtain her doctoral degree in Management and Strategy from Istanbul Medipol University in 2021. Currently, she is working as an Assistant Professor at Istanbul Medipol University. Her research interests include strategic management, organizational behavior, and business strategy.

Soumya Mukherjee is Associate Professor in Business Administration at Techno India (Hooghly Campus), Chinsurah, West Bengal, India. He is an accomplished educator with demonstrated ability and experience to teach, motivate, and direct students while maintaining high interest and achievement. He has more than 15 years of experience in academics. He has authored two books and has several research articles in journal and conference proceedings to his credit.

Arshi Naim is an Associate Professor and Quality Programme head in Business Management, KSA She has completed her PHD in business management Singhania University Rajasthan, MBA in marketing management from HNB University and economics honours from AMU, Aligarh, India. Also, she has accomplished some certificates like QM peer reviewer and E-Learning expert from quality matters,

US, ICDL from Australia and certificate on digital skills and digital marketing from UK. She is expert in curriculum and programme development, quality and accreditation process, E-learning and Quality Matters Peer Reviewer. She has research publications in Web of Sceince, IEEE, ACM, and Scopus Indexed Journals. She has also published books with Taylor and Francis, Nova Science Publications, IGI, and Springer. She is also closely associated with international and national universities for supervising PHD students.

Manikandan Rajagopal is an Associate Professor of Lean Operationsa and Systems.

Damini Saini is associated with IIM Raipur as an Assistant Professor in OB/HRM. She is also a key editorial member for the Journal of Applied Research in Higher Education. Dr Saini received her PhD from the prestigious Faculty of Management Studies, University of Delhi. Her research is in ethical leadership, the spiritual climate of business, and positive psychology. Recognition of her research comes from the best paper awards conferred to her work thrice. Apart from this, her scholarly interests are leadership, business ethics, the significance of ethical education in management, value-based management etc. She has contributed to various internationally acclaimed journals and book chapters. She has also actively taken part in various conferences and seminars.

Sheetal Sharma is a keen researcher and hard core academician. Her core area of interest are-Human Resource Management, Organizational Behaviour & Cross cultural management. She has contributed quality research papers to various reputed journals and designed study materials for country's reputed universities. Her jointly authored book titled "Personal Growth and Training & Development" by Excel Book Publishers has been released and received commendation by Former President of India, Prof A P J Abdul Kalam and has also been received Book Award Year 2009-10 by ISTD (Indian Society for Training & Development). She is on the review panel of a prestigious international journals and PhD Guide & Evaluator for leading universities of India; coached & mentored students and corporate on across different domains of business management.

Akanchha Singh is an Assistant Professor at Apeejay Stya University, Gurugram with 5 years of experience in teaching undergraduate and post graduate courses. She has completed her PhD from khwaja Moinuddin Chisti Language University, Lucknow. Her 15 papers are published in various renowned national and international journals and edited books. Recently, one of her book chapters also got featured in World Health Organization (WHO) COVID-19 research database. She has presented 15 papers in various national/international conferences and seminars. She has also won the best paper award in international conference of Thakur college of science & commerce. Her current research interest includes HR, organizational behaviour, marketing etc.

Shiwani Singh is a research scholar, currently pursuing Ph.D. from Babasaheb Bhimrao Ambedkar University, Lucknow, Uttar Pradesh, India.

Surjit Singha is a dedicated researcher actively involved in Research & Development (R&D) and publishing on a wide range of topics, including UN Sustainable Development Goals, Organizational Climate, Workforce Diversity, Organizational Culture, HRM, Marketing, Finance, IB, Global Business, Business, AI, Women Studies, Cultural Studies, and Data Science. Currently serving as a faculty member in the Department of Commerce at Kristu Jayanti College (Autonomous), Dr. Surjit holds the position of Editor, reviewer, and author for various esteemed Global Publications and Journals. With over 13 years of experience in Administration, Teaching, and Research in both Industry and Higher Education Institutions (HEIs), Dr. Surjit is committed to imparting knowledge and guiding students in their research pursuits. As a research mentor for students, Dr. Surjit plays a vital role in nurturing young minds and fostering their academic growth. Additionally, Dr. Surjit heads the website management, promotion, and social media publicity, leading a team of approximately 35 faculty members. Dr. Surjit Singha's notable affiliations include being a Member of the British Council (British Library) and an Editor and Reviewer for TNT (Publication) (TNT-UN Recognized Publisher). Furthermore, Dr. Surjit serves as a Reviewer and Author for reputed publishers like IGI Global (United States) (SCOPUS), Hershey, Pennsylvania, US. Additionally, Dr. Surjit contributes as a Reviewer for esteemed journals like Religions (SCOPUS & WoS), Q1, Switzerland, Economies (SCOPUS & WoS), Q2, Switzerland, and Sustainability (SCOPUS & WoS), Q1, Switzerland. Dr. Surjit's dedication to continuous learning is evident through certifications as a Life Skill Trainer by RGNYID (An Institution of National Importance introduced by the Act of Parliament), a Microsoft Innovative Educator by Microsoft, and a Yoga Volunteer certified by The Yoga Certification Board, Ministry of AYUSH, Gov. of India, and evaluated by Morarji Desai National Institute of Yoga. As a dedicated leader in academia, Dr. Surjit has guided and mentored 21 student projects in the academic year 2022-23, resulting in all 21 students publishing papers under Dr. Surjit's astute guidance. As NSS Faculty Mentor, Dr. Surjit has successfully mentored 65 students in the academic year 2022-23, ensuring all students achieve credits and qualifications. Dr. Surjit has an impressive track record with over 65 publications in SCOPUS-indexed articles, including chapters in books, edited books, and various textbooks. Granted 2 US Copyright and received two fully funded minor research projects (Completed and Published) from Kristu Jayanti College (Autonomous). With an unwavering commitment to excellence in education and research, Dr. Surjit Singha continues to impact various domains profoundly, elevating the institution's status and fostering an environment of knowledge dissemination and growth.

Taruna Taruna is an Assistant Professor in Babasaheb Bhimrao Ambedkar University, Lucknow, Uttar Pradesh, India.

Princy Thomas is an Associate Professor working with Christ University, Bangalore. Prior to this, she worked with the Indian Institute of Management Bangalore (IIMB), Xavier Institute of Management and Entrepreneurship (XIME), and Nitte Meenakshi Institute of Technology (NMIT), Bangalore. Princy holds Ph.D. from Visveswaraya Technological University. At the Master's level, she has specialized in Management Science, Human Resource Management, and Computer Applications. She has over 19 years of experience in teaching and research with top-rated Universities and business schools in India. She has presented papers at various national and international conferences, published articles in national and international journals, published an edited book on Entrepreneurship education with Springer Publisher, and developed case studies on related management and entrepreneurship issues, besides reviewing manuscripts for academic journals.

Neha Tiwari is Assistant Professor (HR & OB) at IILM Academy of Higher Learning, Lucknow. Her qualifications include Ph.D in the area of Women Entrepreneurship. She qualified UGC NET and Junior Research Fellowship in Management. She completed her MBA in Human Resource Management from University of Lucknow. Her areas of interest include Women entrepreneurship, Micro, small and Medium enterprises, Organizational Behavior and Design thinking. She has presented her research work in national and International conferences of repute. She has publications in the area of Entrepreneurship, Women entrepreneurship, Human Resource issues in small enterprises in C category Journals indexed in ABDC and UGC CARE.

Kalyani V. is an Assistant Professor at the School of Business and Management, CHRIST (Deemed to be University), Bangalore. She holds a Bachelor's Degree in Metallurgy Engineering, a Master's Degree in Business Administration and a PhD in Management with specialization in the field of Human Resources. Her research interests are in the fields of Human Resources and Statistics.

Bharathi Venkatesh is an Associate Professor working in CHRIST (Deemed to be University), Bangalore. She has completed Ph.D. from Bharathiar University. She is a member of different professional bodies.

Index

A

C

D

E

F

H

I

J

L

M

O

P

R

S

T

W

www.ingramcontent.com/pod-product-compliance
Lightning Source LLC
LaVergne TN
LVHW060412300926
849162LV00006B/1412
* 9 7 8 1 6 6 8 4 8 9 4 2 0 *